# *Contexts*

## *for*

# COMPOSITION

EDITED BY

## Stanley A. Clayes

AND

## David G. Spencer

LOYOLA UNIVERSITY
CHICAGO

*New York*

# APPLETON-CENTURY-CROFTS

DIVISION OF MEREDITH PUBLISHING COMPANY

*To Jeff*

Copyright © 1965, by

MEREDITH PUBLISHING COMPANY

6366

LIBRARY OF CONGRESS CARD NUMBER: 65-14617

PRINTED IN THE UNITED STATES OF AMERICA
E 19790

# PREFACE

CONTEXTS FOR COMPOSITION is designed as an anthology that requires no separate rhetoric text. Not only do the selections themselves exemplify aspects of rhetoric, but many of them also examine principles of rhetoric deliberately and in detail: for example, the essays by Hayakawa, Altick, Robert G. Davis, Orwell, Barzun, and Ciardi. Where necessary, the introductions to each section provide essential distinctions that any reader and writer should master at the very outset. Questions follow almost every selection; initially they focus on language and rhetorical principles and toward the end shift to the selection's subject matter and the student's own experience and outlook. One or more topics which suggest themes for writing from the selection's discourse and within the student's grasp conclude most reading assignments. Periodically we have refrained from punctuating a selection with questions and theme topics on the ground that individual instructors—and indeed students themselves—may occasionally wish to provide, without interference, their own editorial direction.

Most anthologies for composition include works that are, hopefully, as good for their purpose as they are new to the eyes of instructors. This collection presents models for analysis and discussion which, though excellent in our own experience for this purpose, make no large claim to novelty. In garnering the "best," we have tried to judge the quality as well as the quantity of student responses throughout our classes in recent years not only to specific selections but also to general topics. Apart from their known value in eliciting student thought and comment, these selections link at many points with one another.

At what point to begin building a text on the process of composition—and analogously at what point to begin organizing a course on it—varies, of course, with the imagination and ability of the instructor as well as his tastes and opinions. We have attempted to make our choices ample and their articulation flexible in the hope that, while Contexts for Composition retains integrity and coherence, the preferences and judgments of many colleagues can be met.

To friends and associates in various parts of the country we owe many individual debts of gratitude for repeated discussions on the teachability of the works chosen (and discarded) for this book. To Fran Spencer for her generous help with the manuscript, and to Jeff Spencer for sharing her intelligence and taste, we are both especially indebted.

S. A. C.

D. G. S.

# CONTENTS

## Part Two: Style

## IX: ILLUSTRATION AND NATURALNESS

# Part Three: Arguments

## X: LANGUAGE AND CORRECTNESS
## ISSUES, ASSUMPTIONS, AND METHODS OF
## REFUTATION

## XI: THE AMERICAN SCENE
## VALUES, ABSOLUTES, AND FOCUS FOR ARGUMENT

*Part One*

# METHODS OF EXPOSITION

# *Defining*

## ~ I ~

# TECHNIQUES FOR DEFINITION

DEFINITION IS A METHOD of analysis, as logical as possible, in which the subject is located in a general class and then distinguished from all other members of that class. If a definition is effective, the reader will understand the word *in much the same way* that the author intended.

Such an understanding is made difficult by the connotative meanings most words convey (for a definition of connotation see the second essay of this section), and it is these meanings that must be reduced and controlled in the language of reports. In the case of abstract terms, connotative meanings are especially difficult to control as well as difficult to define. Our understanding of a word is obviously limited by our experience and our opinions, and no two sets of experiences and opinions are identical. A word like "liberal" or "conservative" has widely varied meanings for different people. Hence one must try to define the sense in which he uses such terms; one must say how they are to be understood or run the risk of alienating a large portion of his audience, those who respond only emotionally to words as signs of everything they approve or disapprove.

A number of techniques or methods of definition are useful to the writer and at times indispensable. In reading the essays of this section, try to observe as many instances of their use as possible.

1. *Assigning the Term to a Genus or Class.* To say "a dog is an animal," "my Fritz is a schnauzer" is to assign a species to a genus, an individual to a class; the same is true with statements such as "a table is a piece of furniture," "that is a Louis Quinze taboret." But if we go on to say "love is an emotion," the genus is not so precise since a psychological dimension in which we all exist has not yet been neatly charted. Again, communism may be defined by classifying it, along with socialism and fascism, as a type of statist society. But now the burden becomes one of describing clearly and definitely the essential characteristics of statist society and its varied and recognizable forms.

2. *Comparing and Contrasting.* Or the term communism may be defined by pointing out its similarities to and differences from the term socialism. Or again a term may be compared and contrasted as laconically as Samuel Johnson is reported to have defined the word "surprise" in the apocryphal story. His wife, entering the room unexpectedly, found him with the maid

3

on his lap and said: "Dr. Johnson, I am surprised!" "No, madam," he replied, "I am surprised. You are astonished."

3. *Using Analogy.* The term may be defined by referring it to more easily understood concepts. An eloquent example is the definition of drama Hamlet sketches for the troupe of itinerant actors: "the purpose of playing, whose end, both at the first and now, was and is, to hold as 'twere the mirror up to nature, to show virtue her own feature, scorn her own image, and the very age and body of the time his form and pressure." An analogy, originally fresh, may become so imbedded in the language that it sinks to the class of clichés, for example, "the ship of state," "a house divided against itself must fall."

4. *Using Familiar Examples.* "Prejudice" may be defined extensively by listing examples familiar to all of us, terms that most of us accept as connoting a prejudiced point of view: "wop," "frog," "kraut," "spic."

5. *Using Historical Meanings.* It provides some insight into the present meaning of the term to know that among the earlier meanings of "technique," for example, are those of "art" and "trick."

6. *Defining Negatively.* "Courtesy" and "manners" are often considered as equivalents, yet one can define courtesy negatively by pointing out that someone may show good manners but lack entirely a sense of common courtesy.

7. *Enumerating Essential Characteristics.* Rather than define "democracy" by pointing to governments or to acts that are or are not democratic, one may list some of the attributes or essential characteristics of democracy; for example, "everyone is to count for one and no one for more than one," "freedom and justice for all," "governments derive their just powers from the consent of the governed."

8. *Isolating One Essential Characteristic.* Notice how St. Paul isolates an essential quality of the Christian. "Brethren: if I should speak with the tongues of men and of angels, but do not have charity, I have become as sounding brass or a tinkling cymbal, and if I have prophecy and know all mysteries and all knowledge, and if I have all faith so as to remove mountains, yet do not have charity, I am nothing—and if I distribute all my goods to feed the poor, and if I deliver my body to be burned, yet do not have charity, it profits me nothing."

## ·1·

## S. I. Hayakawa

# REPORTS, INFERENCES, JUDGMENTS

*To put it briefly, in human speech, different sounds have different meanings. To study this co-ordination of certain sounds with certain meanings is to study language. This co-ordination makes it possible for man to interact with great precision. When we tell someone, for instance, the address of a house he has never seen, we are doing something which no animal can do.* —LEONARD BLOOMFIELD

*Vague and insignificant forms of speech, and abuse of language, have so long passed for mysteries of science; and hard or misapplied words with little or no meaning have, by prescription, such a right to be mistaken for deep learning and height of speculation, that it will not be easy to persuade either those who speak or those who hear them, that they are but the covers of ignorance and hindrance of true knowlege.* —JOHN LOCKE

1. For the purposes of the interchange of information, the basic symbolic act is the *report* of what we have seen, heard, or felt: "There is a ditch on each side of the road." "You can get those at Smith's hardware store for $2.75." "There aren't any fish on that side of the lake, but there are on this side." Then there are reports of reports: "The longest waterfall in the world is Victoria Falls in Rhodesia." "The Battle of Hastings took place in 1066." "The papers say that there was a smash-up on Highway 41 near Evansville." Reports adhere to the following rules: first, they are *capable of verification;* second, they *exclude,* as far as possible, *inferences* and *judgments.* (These terms will be defined later.)

2. Reports are verifiable. We may not always be able to verify them ourselves, since we cannot track down the evidence for every piece of history we know, nor can we all go to Evansville to see the remains of the smash-up before they are cleared away. But if we are roughly agreed on the names of things, on what constitutes a "foot," "yard," "bushel," and so on, and on how to measure time, there is relatively little danger of our misunderstanding each other. Even in a world such as we have today, in which

everybody seems to be quarreling with everybody else, *we still to a sur-prising degree trust each other's reports.* We ask directions of total stran-gers when we are traveling. We follow directions on road signs without being suspicious of the people who put them up. We read books of in-formation about science, mathematics, automotive engineering, travel, geography, the history of costume, and other such factual matters, and we usually assume that the author is doing his best to tell us as truly as he can what he knows. And we are safe in so assuming most of the time. With the interest given today to the discussion of biased newspapers, propa-gandists, and the general untrustworthiness of many of the communica-tions we receive, we are likely to forget that we still have an enormous amount of reliable information available and that deliberate misinforma-tion, except in warfare, is still more the exception than the rule. The desire for self-preservation that compelled men to evolve means for the exchange of information also compels them to regard the giving of false information as profoundly reprehensible.

3. At its highest development, the language of reports is the language of science. By "highest development" we mean greatest general usefulness. Presbyterian and Catholic, workingman and capitalist, East German and West German, *agree* on the meanings of such symbols as $2 \times 2 = 4$, *100° C., $HNO_3$, 3:35 A.M., 1940 A.D., 1000 kilowatts, Quercus agrifolia,* and so on. But how, it may be asked, can there be agreement about even this much among people who disagree about political philosophies, ethical ideas, religious beliefs, and the survival of my business *versus* the survival of yours? The answer is that circumstances *compel men to agree,* whether they wish to or not. If, for example, there were a dozen different religious sects in the United States, each insisting on its own way of naming the time of the day and the days of the year, the mere necessity of having a dozen different calendars, a dozen different kinds of watches, and a dozen sets of schedules for business hours, trains, and television programs, to say nothing of the effort that would be required for translating terms from one nomenclature to another, would make life as we know it impossible.[1]

---

[1] According to information supplied by the Association of American Railroads, "Be-fore 1883 there were nearly 100 different time zones in the United States. It wasn't until November 18 of that year that . . . a system of standard time was adopted here and in Canada. Before then there was nothing but local or 'solar' time. . . . The Pennsylvania Railroad in the East used Philadelphia time, which was five minutes slower than New York time and five minutes faster than Baltimore time. The Balti-more & Ohio used Baltimore time for trains running out of Baltimore, Columbus time for Ohio, Vincennes (Indiana) time for those going out of Cincinnati. . . . When it was noon in Chicago, it was 12:31 in Pittsburgh; 12:24 in Cleveland; 12:17 in Toledo; 12:13 in Cincinnati; 12:09 in Louisville; 12:07 in Indianapolis; 11:50 in St. Louis; 11:48 in Dubuque; 11:39 in St. Paul, and 11:27 in Omaha. There were 27 local time zones in Michigan alone. . . . A person traveling from Eastport, Maine, to San Fran-cisco, if he wanted always to have the right railroad time and get off at the right place, had to twist the hands of his watch 20 times en route." Chicago *Daily News* (September 29, 1948).

4. The language of reports, then, including the more accurate reports of science, is "map" language, and because it gives us reasonably accurate representations of the "territory," it enables us to get work done. Such language may often be dull or uninteresting reading: one does not usually read logarithmic tables or telephone directories for entertainment. But we could not get along without it. There are numberless occasions in the talking and writing we do in everyday life that *require that we state things in such a way that everybody will be able to understand and agree with our formulation.*

## INFERENCES

5. The reader will find that practice in writing reports is a quick means of increasing his linguistic awareness. It is an exercise which will constantly provide him with his own examples of the principles of language and interpretation under discussion. The reports should be about first-hand experience—scenes the reader has witnessed himself, meetings and social events he has taken part in, people he knows well. They should be of such a nature that they can be verified and agreed upon. For the purpose of this exercise, inferences will be excluded.

6. Not that inferences are not important—we rely in everyday life and in science as much on *inferences* as on reports—in some areas of thought, for example, geology, paleontology, and nuclear physics, reports are the foundations, but inferences (and inferences upon inferences) are the main body of the science. An inference, as we shall use the term, is *a statement about the unknown made on the basis of the known.* We may *infer* from the material and cut of a woman's clothes her wealth or social position; we may *infer* from the character of the ruins the origin of the fire that destroyed the building; we may *infer* from a man's calloused hands the nature of his occupation; we may infer from a senator's vote on an armaments bill his attitude toward Russia; we may *infer* from the structure of the land the path of a prehistoric glacier; we may *infer* from a halo on an unexposed photographic plate that it has been in the vicinity of radioactive materials; we may *infer* from the sound of an engine the condition of its connecting rods. Inferences may be carelessly or carefully made. They may be made on the basis of a broad background of previous experience with the subject matter, or no experience at all. For example, the inferences a good mechanic can make about the internal condition of a motor by listening to it are often startlingly accurate, while the inferences made by an amateur (if he tries to make any) may be entirely wrong. But the common characteristic of inferences is that they are statements about matters which are not directly known, statements made on the basis of what has been observed.

7. The avoidance of inferences in our suggested practice in report-

writing requires that we make no guesses as to what is going on in other people's minds. When we say, "He was angry," we are not reporting; we are making an inference from such observable facts as the following: "He pounded his fist on the table; he swore; he threw the telephone directory at his stenographer." In this particular example, the inference appears to be fairly safe; nevertheless, it is important to remember, especially for the purposes of training oneself, that it is an inference. Such expressions as "He thought a lot of himself," "He was scared of girls," "He has an inferiority complex," made on the basis of casual social observation, and "What Russia really wants to do is to establish a world communist dictatorship," made on the basis of casual newspaper reading, are highly inferential. We should keep in mind their inferential character and, in our suggested exercises, should substitute for them such statements as "He rarely spoke to subordinates in the plant," "I saw him at a party, and he never danced except when one of the girls asked him to," "He wouldn't apply for the scholarship although I believe he could have won it easily," and "The Russian delegation to the United Nations has asked for *A*, *B*, and *C*. Last year they voted against *M* and *N*, and voted for *X* and *Y*. On the basis of facts such as these, the newspaper I read makes the inference that what Russia really wants is to establish a world communist dictatorship. I agree."

8. In spite of the exercise of every caution in avoiding inferences and reporting only what is seen and experienced, we all remain prone to error, since the making of inferences is a quick, almost automatic process. We may watch a car weaving as it goes down the road and say, "Look at that *drunken driver*," although what we *see* is only *the irregular motion of the car*. The writer once saw a man leave a one-dollar tip at a lunch counter and hurry out. Just as the writer was wondering why anyone should leave so generous a tip in so modest an establishment, the waitress came, picked up the dollar, put it in the cash register as she punched up ninety cents, and put a dime in her pocket. In other words, the writer's description to himself of the event, "a one-dollar tip," turned out to be not a report but an inference.

9. All this is not to say that we should never make inferences. The inability to make inferences is itself a sign of mental disorder. For example, the speech therapist Laura L. Lee writes, "The aphasic [brain-damaged] adult with whom I worked had great difficulty in making inferences about a picture I showed her. She could tell me what was happening at the moment in the picture, but could not tell me what might have happened just before the picture or just afterward."[2] Hence the question is not whether or not we make inferences; the question is whether or not we are aware of the inferences we make.

[2] "Brain Damage and the Process of Abstracting: A Problem in Language Learning," *ETC.: A Review of General Semantics*, XVI (1959), 154-62.

## JUDGMENTS

*10.* In our suggested writing exercise, judgments are also to be excluded. By judgments, we shall mean *all expressions of the writer's approval or disapproval of the occurrences, persons, or objects he is describing.* For example, a report cannot say, "It was a wonderful car," but must say something like this: "It has been driven 50,000 miles and has never required any repairs." Again statements such as "Jack lied to us" must be suppressed in favor of the more verifiable statement, "Jack told us he didn't have the keys to his car with him. However, when he pulled a handkerchief out of his pocket a few minutes later, a bunch of car keys fell out." Also a report may not say, "The senator was stubborn, defiant, and uncooperative," or "The senator courageously stood by his principles"; it must say instead, "The senator's vote was the only one against the bill."

*11.* Many people regard statements such as the following as statements of "fact": "Jack *lied* to us," "Jerry is a *thief*," "Tommy is *clever*." As ordinarily employed, however, the word "lied" involves first an inference (that Jack knew otherwise and deliberately misstated the facts) and second a judgment (that the speaker disapproves of what he has inferred that Jack did). In the other two instances, we may substitute such expressions as, "Jerry was convicted of theft and served two years at Waupun," and "Tommy plays the violin, leads his class in school, and is captain of the debating team." After all, to say of a man that he is a "thief" is to say in effect, "He has stolen *and will steal again*"—which is more of a prediction than a report. Even to say, "He has stolen," is to make an inference (and simultaneously to pass a judgment) on an act about which there may be difference of opinion among those who have examined the evidence upon which the conviction was obtained. But to say that he was "convicted of theft" is to make a statement capable of being agreed upon through verification in court and prison records.

*12.* Scientific verifiability rests upon the external observation of facts, not upon the heaping up of judgments. If one person says, "Peter is a deadbeat," and another says, "I think so too," the statement has not been verified. In court cases, considerable trouble is sometimes caused by witnesses who cannot distinguish their judgments from the facts upon which those judgments are based. Cross-examinations under these circumstances go something like this:

WITNESS: That dirty double-crosser Jacobs ratted on me.

DEFENSE ATTORNEY: Your honor, I object.

JUDGE: Objection sustained. (Witness's remark is stricken from the record.) Now, try to tell the court exactly what happened.

WITNESS: He double-crossed me, the dirty, lying rat!

DEFENSE ATTORNEY: Your honor, I object!

JUDGE: Objection sustained. (Witness's remark is again stricken from the record.) Will the witness try to stick to the facts.

WITNESS: But I'm telling you the facts, your honor. He did double-cross me.

This can continue indefinitely unless the cross-examiner exercises some ingenuity in order to get at the facts behind the judgment. To the witness it is a "fact" that he was "double-crossed." Often patient questioning is required before the factual bases of the judgment are revealed.

13. Many words, of course, simultaneously convey a report and a judgment on the fact reported, as will be discussed more fully in a later chapter. For the purposes of a report as here defined, these should be avoided. Instead of "sneaked in," one might say "entered quietly"; instead of "politicians," "congressmen" or "aldermen" or "candidates for office"; instead of "bureaucrat," "public official"; instead of "tramp," "homeless unemployed"; instead of "dictatorial set-up," "centralized authority"; instead of "crackpots," "holders of nonconformist views." A newspaper reporter, for example, is not permitted to write, "A crowd of suckers came to listen to Senator Smith last evening in that rickety firetrap and ex-dive that disfigures the south edge of town." Instead he says, "Between seventy-five and a hundred people heard an address last evening by Senator Smith at the Evergreen Gardens near the South Side city limits."

## SNARL-WORDS AND PURR-WORDS

14. Throughout this book, it is important to remember that we are not considering language as an isolated phenomenon. Our concern, instead, is with language in action—language in the full context of the nonlinguistic events which are its setting. The making of noises with the vocal organs is a muscular activity and, like other muscular activities, often involuntary. Our responses to powerful stimuli, such as to things that make us very angry, are a complex of muscular and physiological events: the contracting of fighting muscles, the increase of blood pressure, a change in body chemistry, clutching of our hair, *and* the making of noises, such as growls and snarls. We are a little too dignified, perhaps, to growl like dogs, but we do the next best thing and substitute series of words, such as "You dirty double-crosser!" "The filthy scum!" Similarly, if we are pleasurably agitated, we may, instead of purring or wagging the tail, say things like "She's the sweetest girl in all the world!"

15. Speeches such as these are, as direct expressions of approval or disapproval, judgments in their simplest form. They may be said to be human equivalents of snarling and purring. "She's the sweetest girl in all the world" is not a statement about the girl; it is a purr. This seems to be a fairly obvious fact; nevertheless, it is surprising how often, when such a statement is made, both the speaker and the hearer feel that something

has been said about the girl. This error is especially common in the interpretation of utterances of orators and editorialists in some of their more excited denunciations of "Reds," "greedy monopolists," "Wall Street," "radicals," "foreign ideologies," and in their more fulsome dithyrambs about "our way of life." Constantly, because of the impressive sound of the words, the elaborate structure of the sentences, and the appearance of intellectual progression, we get the feeling that something is being said about something. On closer examination, however, we discover that these utterances merely say, "What I hate ('Reds,' 'Wall Street,' or whatever) I hate very, very much," and "What I like ('our way of life') I like very, very much." We may call such utterances "snarl-words" and "purr-words." They are not reports describing conditions in the extensional world in any way.

16. To call these judgments "snarl-words" and "purr-words" does not mean that we should simply shrug them off. It means that we should be careful to *allocate the meaning correctly*—placing such a statement as "She's the sweetest girl in the world" as a revelation of the speaker's state of mind, and not as a revelation of facts about the girl. If the "snarl-words" about "Reds" or "greedy monopolists" are accompanied by verifiable reports (which would also mean that we have previously agreed as to who, specifically, is meant by the terms "Reds" or "greedy monopolists"), we might find reason to be just as disturbed as the speaker. If the "purr-words" about the sweetest girl in the world are accompanied by verifiable reports about her appearance, manners, character, and so on, we might find reason to admire her too. But "snarl-words" and "purr-words" as such, unaccompanied by reports, offer nothing further to discuss, except possibly the question, "Why do you feel as you do?"

17. It is usually fruitless to debate such questions as "Is President Kennedy a great statesman or merely a skillful politician?" "Is the music of Wagner the greatest music of all time, or is it merely hysterical screeching?" "Which is the finer sport, tennis or baseball?" "Could Joe Louis in his prime have licked Bob Fitzsimmons in his prime?" To take sides on such issues of conflicting judgments is to reduce oneself to the same level of stubborn imbecility as one's opponents. But to ask questions of the form, "Why do you like (or dislike) Kennedy (or Wagner, or tennis, or Joe Louis)?" is to learn something about one's friends and neighbors. After listening to their opinions and their reasons for them, we may leave the discussion slightly wiser, slightly better informed, and perhaps slightly less one-sided than we were before the discussion began.

## HOW JUDGMENTS STOP THOUGHT

18. A judgment ("He is a fine boy," "It was a beautiful service," "Baseball is a healthful sport," "She is an awful bore") is a conclusion, summing

up a large number of previously observed facts. The reader is probably familiar with the fact that students almost always have difficulty in writing themes of the required length because their ideas give out after a paragraph or two. The reason for this is that those early paragraphs contain so many judgments that there is little left to be said. When the conclusions are carefully excluded, however, and observed facts are given instead, there is never any trouble about the length of papers; in fact, they tend to become too long, since inexperienced writers, when told to give facts, often give far more than are necessary, because they lack discrimination between the important and the trivial.

19. Still another consequence of judgments early in the course of a written exercise—and this applies also to hasty judgments in everyday thought— is the temporary blindness they induce. When, for example, a description starts with the words, "He was a real Madison Avenue executive," or "She was a typical sorority girl," if we continue writing at all, we must make all our later statements consistent with those judgments. The result is that all the individual characteristics of this particular "executive" or this particular "sorority girl" are lost sight of; and the rest of the account is likely to deal not with observed facts but with the writer's private notion (based on previously read stories, movies, pictures, and so forth) of what "Madison Avenue executives" or "typical sorority girls" are like. The premature judgment, that is, often prevents us from seeing what is directly in front of us, so that clichés take the place of fresh description. Therefore, even if the writer feels sure at the beginning of a written account that the man he is describing is a "real leatherneck" or that the scene he is describing is a "beautiful residential suburb," he will conscientiously keep such notions out of his head, lest his vision be obstructed. He is specifically warned against describing *anybody* as a "beatnik"—a term (originally applied to literary and artistic Bohemians) which was blown up by sensational journalism and movies into an almost completely fictional and misleading stereotype. If a writer applies the term to any actual living human being, he will have to spend so much energy thereafter explaining what he does *not* mean by it that he will save himself trouble by not bringing it up at all.


SLANTING

20. In the course of writing reports of personal experiences, it will be found that in spite of all endeavors to keep judgments out, some will creep in. An account of a man, for example, may go like this: "He had apparently not shaved for several days, and his face and hands were covered with grime. His shoes were torn, and his coat, which was several sizes too small for him, was spotted with dried clay." Now, in spite of the fact that no judgment has been stated, a very obvious one is implied. Let

us contrast this with another description of the same man. "Although his face was bearded and neglected, his eyes were clear, and he looked straight ahead as he walked rapidly down the road. He seemed very tall; perhaps the fact that his coat was too small for him emphasized that impression. He was carrying a book under his left arm, and a small terrier ran at his heels." In this example, the impression about the same man is considerably changed, simply by the inclusion of new details and the subordination of unfavorable ones. Even if explicit judgments are kept out of one's writing, implied judgments will get in.

21. How, then, can we ever give an impartial report? The answer is, of course, that we cannot attain complete impartiality while we use the language of everyday life. Even with the very impersonal language of science, the task is sometimes difficult. Nevertheless, we can, by being aware of the favorable or unfavorable feelings that certain words and facts can arouse, attain enough impartiality for practical purposes. Such awareness enables us to balance the implied favorable and unfavorable judgments against each other. To learn to do this, it is a good idea to write two accounts of the same subject, both strict reports, to be read side by side: the first to contain facts and details likely to prejudice the reader in favor of the subject, the second to contain those likely to prejudice the reader against it. For example:

| FOR | AGAINST |
|---|---|
| He had white teeth. | His teeth were uneven. |
| His eyes were blue, his hair blond and abundant. | He rarely looked people straight in the eye. |
| He had on a clean white shirt. | His shirt was frayed at the cuffs. |
| His speech was courteous. | He had a high-pitched voice. |
| His employer spoke highly of him. | His landlord said he was slow in paying his rent. |
| He liked dogs. | He disliked children. |

22. This process of selecting details favorable or unfavorable to the subject being described may be termed *slanting*. Slanting gives no explicit judgments, but it differs from reporting in that it deliberately makes certain judgments inescapable. Let us assume for a moment the truth of the statement "When Clyde was in New York last November he was seen having dinner with a show girl. . . ." The inferences that can be drawn from this statement are changed considerably when the following words are added: ". . . and her husband and their two children." Yet, if Clyde is a married man, his enemies could conceivably do him a great deal of harm by talking about his "dinner-date with a New York show girl." One-sided or biased slanting of this kind, not uncommon in private gossip and backbiting, and all too common in the "interpretative reporting" of newspapers and news magazines, can be described as a technique of lying without actually telling any lies.

## DISCOVERING ONE'S BIAS

23. Here, however, a caution is necessary. When, for example, a newspaper tells a story in a way that we dislike, leaving out facts we think important and playing up important facts in ways that we think unfair, we are tempted to say, "Look how unfairly they've slanted the story!" In making such a statement we are, of course, making an inference about the newspaper's editors. We are assuming that what seems important or unimportant to us seems equally important or unimportant to them, and on the basis of that assumption we infer that the editors "deliberately" gave the story a misleading emphasis. Is this necessarily the case? Can the reader, as an outsider, say whether a story assumes a given form because the editors "deliberately slanted it that way" or because that was the way the events appeared to them?

24. The point is that, by the process of selection and abstraction imposed on us by our own interests and background, experience comes to all of us (including newspaper editors) already "slanted." If you happen to be pro-labor, pro-Catholic, and a stock-car racing fan, your ideas of what is important or unimportant will of necessity be different from those of a man who happens to be indifferent to all three of your favorite interests. If, then, some newspapers often seem to side with the big businessman on public issues, the reason is less a matter of "deliberate" slanting than the fact that publishers are often, in enterprises as large as modern urban newspapers, big businessmen themselves, accustomed both in work and in social life to associating with other big businessmen. Nevertheless, the best newspapers, whether owned by "big businessmen" or not, do try to tell us as accurately as possible what is going on in the world, because they are run by newspapermen who conceive it to be part of their professional responsibility to present fairly the conflicting points of view in controversial issues. Such newspapermen are *reporters* indeed.

25. The writer who is neither an advocate nor an opponent avoids slanting, except when he is seeking special literary effects. The avoidance of slanting is not only a matter of being fair and impartial; it is even more importantly a matter of making good maps of the territory of experience. The profoundly biased individual cannot make good maps because he can see an enemy *only* as an enemy and a friend *only* as a friend. The individual with genuine skill in writing—one who has imagination and insight—can look at the same subject from many points of view. The following examples may illustrate the fullness and solidity of descriptions thus written:

Adam turned to look at him. It was, in a way, as though this were the first time he had laid eyes on him. He saw the strong, black shoulders under the red-check calico, the long arms lying loose, forward over the knees, the strong hands, seamed and calloused, holding the reins. He looked at the face. The thrust of the jawbone was strong, but the lips were heavy and low, with a piece of chewed straw hanging out one side of the mouth. The eyelids were pendulous, slightly swollen-looking, and the eyes bloodshot. Those eyes, Adam knew, could sharpen to a quick, penetrating, assessing glance. But now, looking at that slack, somnolent face, he could scarcely believe that.

—ROBERT PENN WARREN, *Wilderness*

Soon after the little princess, there walked in a massively built, stout young man in spectacles, with a cropped head, light breeches in the mode of the day, with a high lace ruffle and a ginger-coloured coat. This stout young man [Pierre] was the illegitimate son of a celebrated dandy of the days of Catherine, Count Bezuhov, who was now dying in Moscow. He had not yet entered any branch of the service; he had only just returned from abroad, where he had been educated, and this was his first appearance in society. Anna Pavlovna greeted him with a nod reserved for persons of the very lowest hierarchy in her drawing-room. . . .

Pierre was clumsy, stout and uncommonly tall, with huge, red hands; he did not, as they say, know how to come into a drawing-room and still less how to get out of one, that is, how to say something particularly agreeable on going away. Moreover, he was dreamy. He stood up, and picking up a three-cornered hat with the plume of a general in it instead of his own, he kept hold of it, pulling the feathers until the general asked him to restore it. But all his dreaminess and his inability to enter a drawing-room or talk properly in it were atoned for by his expression of good-nature, simplicity and modesty.

—COUNT LEO TOLSTOY, *War and Peace*
(Translated by Constance Garnett)

### Applications

I. Here are a number of statements which the reader may attempt to classify as judgments, inferences, or reports. Since the distinctions are not always clear-cut, a one-word answer will not ordinarily be adequate. Note that we are concerned here with the nature of the statements, not the truth or falsity of them; for example, the statement, "Water freezes at 10° centigrade," is, although inaccurate, a report.

1. She goes to church only in order to show off her clothes.

   SAMPLE ANALYSIS: In usual circumstances under which such a statement would be made, this would be an *inference*, since people ordinarily do not admit that they go to church for that reason. A *judgment* is also strongly implied, since it is assumed that one ought to have better reasons.

2. There is something essentially unclean about eating meat and fish.

3. Cary Grant has lots of personality.

4. Rough-grained Split Leather Brief Case; artificial leather gussets. 3 position lock with key. 16 × 11 in. Color: black or brown. Shpg. wt. 2 lbs. Price, $4.86.                    —Sears, Roebuck and Company Catalog

> Commuter—one who spends his life
> In riding to and from his wife;
> A man who shaves and takes a train
> And then rides back to shave again.
>
> —E. B. WHITE

6. To commit murder is wrong under all circumstances.

7. The Russian people do not want war.

8. He is a typical bureaucrat.

9. An intelligent man makes his own opportunities.

10. The senator's support of the bill was a move to catch the veteran vote.

11.
> That time of year thou may'st in me behold
> When yellow leaves, or few, or none do hang
> Upon those boughs that shake against the cold,
> Bare ruined choirs where late the sweet birds sang.
>
> —WILLIAM SHAKESPEARE

12. And Adam lived an hundred and thirty years, and begat a son in his likeness, after his image; and called his name Seth: And the days of Adam after he had begotten Seth were eight hundred years: and he begat sons and daughters: And all the days that Adam lived were nine hundred and thirty years: and he died.      —Genesis 5:3–5

13. Crisp as Jack Frost, crunchy and crackle-happy . . . redder than a fire sale of long-handle flannels. Your big delicious beauties arrive so fresh we don't guarantee they won't talk back to folks . . . in a flavor-full language all their own. Shipping weight about 9 pounds."

> —Advertising material accompanying
> a Fruit-of-the-Month Club delivery

14. William Jameson is a skinny, crippled, tuberculosis-ridden little man, weighing only 95 pounds and standing only 5 feet tall. And every ounce and inch of him is criminal—incorrigible, remorseless and vicious.

> —New York *World-Telegram & Sun*

15. Research scientists proved that regular after-meal brushing with new Ipana reduced bacteria in the mouth—including decay and bad-breath bacteria— *by an average of 84%.*     —Advertisement for Ipana toothpaste

16. *C'est Magnifique! Une maison Ranch très originale avec 8 rooms, 2½ baths . . . 2-Cadillac garage . . . $21,990 . . . No cash for veterans.*

> —Advertisement for a Long Island development

17. Our shameful Justice of the Peace system allows many legal ignoramuses— more intent on picking our pockets than on guarding our rights—to mishandle the law in rural areas.     —*Reader's Digest*

18. But the delegates [at the U.S. Chamber of Commerce convention] remained wary. "He [President Kennedy] gave a nice speech," said one of them afterward, "but actions speak louder than words. Nothing he said here this morn

ing erased his actions taken against the steel industry." The business community had cause for concern. Kennedy is not ideologically against business; he probably thinks he is all for it. But the fact is that as a millionaire's
son with no experience in any calling but politics, the President has led an
economically sheltered life—and he does not seem to understand business
or businessmen too well.                                              —*Time*

II. In addition to trying such exercises in report-writing and the exclusion of
judgments and inferences as are suggested in this chapter, the reader might try
writing (a) reports heavily slanted *against* persons or organizations he *likes*,
and (b) reports heavily slanted *in favor of* persons or organizations he *dislikes*.
For example, imagine that your luncheon club or fraternity or lodge is a subversive organization and report the facts about its activities and members upon
which unfavorable inferences could be made; or imagine that one of your most
disagreeable neighbors has been offered a job two thousand miles away and
write a factual letter of recommendation to help him get the job.

It is also amusing and instructive to write parodies of biased writing, i.e., to
write with so strong a bias that you ridicule the bias. A strongly biased account
consists, of course, of slanted reports and unqualified judgments. The following
is a quotation from *Mad* magazine's attempt to see the Boy Scouts through
*Pravda's* eyes:

> After three years of servitude in the Cub Scouts, the boys, now hooligan
> adolescents, are forced to join the older, more corrupt Boy Scouts. Here,
> they are snatched away from their families and taken to primitive forests
> where they must live in unheated tents.
>
> The most deceitful ritual is the shameful "Court of Honor," where the
> young warmongers are decorated with so-called "Merit Badges." It is here
> that they receive awards for their work in such insidious fields as "Swim-
> ming" (Underwater Demolition and Sabotage), "Chemistry" (Germ and
> Poison Gas Warfare), "Pathfinding" (Counter-espionage), and "Pioneering"
> (Exploitation of Undeveloped Nations).

III. "A youth and a man were killed and three teenagers seriously injured
early today in two auto accidents." Write:

1. A *report* of these accidents, inventing names and places.

2. A *slanted report* for a newspaper campaigning for stricter laws against juvenile delinquency. (Be sure to use factual statements only, letting your
   reader make his own inferences and judgments.)

3. A *slanted report* for a newspaper highly critical of the local city administration. (Again, use factual statements only.)

IV. Discuss the use of inference in the following passage from Sir Arthur
Conan Doyle. Are the inferences made by Sherlock Holmes the kind that are
described in this chapter? Comment on the validity and verifiability of Holmes's
inferences.

With a resigned air and a somewhat weary smile, Holmes begged the beautiful intruder to take a seat, and to inform us what it was that was troubling her.

"At least it cannot be your health," said he, as his keen eyes darted over her; "so ardent a bicyclist must be full of energy."

She glanced down in surprise at her own feet, and I observed the slight roughening of the side of the sole caused by the friction of the edge of the pedal.

"Yes, I bicycle a good deal, Mr. Holmes. . . ."

My friend took the lady's ungloved hand, and examined it with as close an attention and as little sentiment as a scientist would show to a specimen.

"You will excuse me, I am sure. It is my business," said he, as he dropped it. "I nearly fell into the error of supposing you were typewriting. Of course, it is obvious that it is music. You observe the spatulate finger-ends, Watson, which is common to both professions? There is a spirituality about the face, however"—she gently turned it towards the light—"which the typewriter does not generate. This lady is a musician."

"Yes, Mr. Holmes, I teach music."

"In the country, I presume, from your complexion."

"Yes, sir, near Farnham, on the borders of Surrey."

V. "Harry Thompson visited Russia in 1958"; "Rex Davis is a millionaire"; "Betty Armstrong does not believe in God"; "Dr. Baxter is in disagreement with the policies of the American Medical Association." Accepting these statements as true, write several hundred words of unfounded inferences, and inferences upon inferences about these people. Of course, you don't know who they are, but don't let that stop you. Just go ahead and make inferences.

This exercise is also amusing and instructive for discussion groups, the members taking turns in adding inferences.

VI. Select a topic about which you have little information but many prejudices, such as "Whither Modern Youth?" "The Menace of Federal Encroachments on American Freedom," "The National Association of Manufacturers: A Threat to Democracy," "Big Unions: A Threat to Free Enterprise," "What's Wrong with Modern Women," "Let's Cut the Fads and Frills from Education," or "The South: Yesterday and Today," and write a one-thousand-word essay consisting solely of sweeping generalizations, broad judgments, and unfounded inferences. Use plenty of "loaded" words. Knock off five points (out of a possible 100) for each verifiable fact used. If you can consistently score 95 or better on all these and other such topics, and your grammar and spelling are plausible, leave your present job. Or quit school. Fame and fortune are within your grasp.

# Questions

1. In paragraph 1, why does Hayakawa exclude inferences and judgments in reports? Why does he qualify this statement with "as far as possible"?

2. Why, in paragraph 3, does he italicize an entire clause? Show how this clause is a key assumption.

3. If report language is "map" language, how does Hayakawa justify inferences? Would he consider news editorials largely inferential? Why?

4. Distinguish between inference and judgment.

5. Illustrate how his article on the language of reports is written in the language of reports.

6. What technique of definition is Hayakawa using in paragraph 2? Show how he develops this technique.

7. In paragraph 5, he makes a series of statements about inference. What technique does he use here consistently? Assess its effectiveness or special appropriateness to his subject?

8. In paragraphs 20 and 21, what technique does Hayakawa make use of to define "slanting"?

·2·

*Richard D. Altick*

# DENOTATION AND CONNOTATION

1. Incidents like this are happening every day. A teacher in a college English course has returned a student's theme on the subject of a poem. One sentence in the theme reads, "Like all of Keats's best work, the 'Ode to Autumn' has a sensual quality that makes it especially appealing to me." The instructor's red pencil has underscored the word *sensual*, and in the margin he has written "Accurate?" or whatever his customary comment is in such cases. The student has checked the dictionary and comes back puzzled. "I don't see what you mean," he says. "The dictionary says *sensual* means 'of or pertaining to the senses or physical sensation.' And that's what I wanted to say. Keats's poem is filled with words and images that suggest physical sensation."

2. "Yes," replies the instructor, "that's what the word *means*—according to the dictionary." And then he takes his copy of the *American College Dictionary*, which contains the definition the student quoted, and turns to the word *sensual*. "Look here," he says, pointing to a passage in small type just after the various definitions of the word:

From *A Preface to Critical Reading*, 4th Edition, by Richard D. Altick, copyright © 1960, Holt, Rinehart and Winston, Inc. Used by permission.

SENSUAL, SENSUOUS, VOLUPTUOUS refer to experience through the senses. SEN-
SUAL refers, usually unfavorably, to the enjoyments derived from the senses,
generally implying grossness or lewdness: *a sensual delight in eating, sensual
excesses.* SENSUOUS refers, favorably or literally, to what is experienced through
the senses: *sensuous impressions, sensuous poetry,* VOLUPTUOUS implies the
luxurious gratification of sensuous or sensual desires: *voluptuous joys, voluptuous beauty.*[1]

3. The student reads the passage carefully and begins to see light. The
word *sensual* carries with it a shade of meaning, an unfavorable implication, which he did not intend; the word he wanted was *sensuous.* He has
had a useful lesson in the dangers of taking dictionary definitions uncritically, as well as in the vital difference between denotation and connotation.

4. The difference between the two is succinctly phrased in another of
those small-type paragraphs of explanation, taken this time from *Webster's
New Collegiate Dictionary:* "Denote implies all that strictly belongs to the
definition of the word, *connote* all of the ideas that are suggested by the
term; thus, 'home' *denotes* the place where one lives with one's family, but it
usually *connotes* comfort, intimacy, and privacy. The same implications distinguish *denotation* and *connotation.*"[2] The denotation of a word is its dictionary definition, which is what the word "stands for." According to the
dictionary, *sensuous* and *sensual* have the same general denotation: they
agree in meaning "experience through the senses." Yet they *suggest* different things. And that difference in suggestion constitutes a difference in connotation.

5. Nothing is more essential to intelligent, profitable reading than sensitivity to connotation. Only when we possess such sensitivity can we understand both what the author *means,* which may be pretty plain, and what he
wants to *suggest,* which may actually be far more important than the superficial meaning. The difference between reading a book or story or essay
or poem for surface meaning and reading it for implication is the difference
between listening to the New York Philharmonic Symphony Orchestra on a
battered old radio and listening to it on a high-fidelity stereophonic record
player. Only the latter brings out the nuances that are often more significant
than the obvious, and therefore easily comprehended, meaning.

6. An unfailing awareness of the connotative power of words is just as
vital, of course, to the writer. His eternal task is to select the word which
will convey, not approximately but exactly, what he wants to say. He must
remember that two words may be "synonymous' in respect to denotation;
that is, they *mean* the same thing. But to the practiced writer, as to the practiced reader, few if any words are exactly synonymous in connotation; in a

---

[1] Reprinted by courtesy of the publishers from *The American College Dictionary.*
Copyright 1947 by Random House, Inc.
[2] By permission. From *Webster's New Collegiate Dictionary,* copyright, 1949, 1951,
1953, by G. & C. Merriam Co.

given context one particular word will convey the precise implication the writer desires to communicate to his reader. The inexperienced writer, forgetting this, often has recourse to Roget's *Thesaurus,* where he finds, conveniently marshaled, whole regiments of synonyms; not knowing which to choose, he either closes his eyes and picks a word at random or else chooses the one that "sounds" best. In either case he is neglecting the delicate shadings of implication which differentiate each word in a category from its neighbors. To be certain that the word he has selected conveys exactly the sense he has in mind, he should check it in those invaluable little paragraphs in the dictionary.[3] For further help, he can look up the fuller discussions in *Webster's Dictionary of Synonyms.*

### Exercise 1

*Explain why the italicized words in the following sentences reflect the writer's insensitivity to connotation, and in each case supply a more appropriate word.*

1. Although she was really twenty-one, there was a certain *childishness* in her voice and manner which set her apart from the other girls and delighted everyone who met her.
2. Handle this Ming vase with extreme care. It's very *brittle.*
3. What especially interests newcomers is the absolute *smoothness* of the countryside.
4. When she got out of the hospital she was pretty *lean,* but a good wholesome diet of home cooking soon remedied that.
5. Attractive though it was in terms of pay and prospects for advancement, Clem decided finally to *spurn* the offer and look for some other job.
6. I've been taking aspirins by the carload, but they haven't *healed* my headache.
7. I knew she had studied the lesson thoroughly, so after asking my question I waited a little. Finally the *retort* came, in her usual quiet, almost hesitant manner.
8. One of the best things the Scouts and Hi-Y did for him was to develop genuinely *mannish* qualities. He's a fine, upstanding youth.
9. I was glad to see by his *agile* gait as he strode down the street that he was fully recovered.
10. What I *pined* for above all was a thick, juicy hamburger, with plenty of relish and a side order of French fries and onions.

### Exercise 2

*Explain the differences in connotation among the members of each of the following groups of words. Make up sentences that illustrate the accurate use of as many words as your instructor directs. (It is also useful, as well as entertaining, to compose sentences in which the words are conspicuously misused, as in the preceding exercise.)*

[3] If the definition of the word in question is not followed by a paragraph discriminating between its "synonyms," there is a cross-reference to the place where this paragraph occurs.

1. dash, hurry, race, gallop, speed, hurtle, run
2. corpulent, plump, obese, heavy-set, fleshy, fat, paunchy, burly, overweight, rolypoly, bulky
3. mansion, dwelling, domicile, residence, house, home
4. racket, uproar, hubbub, clatter, noise, commotion
5. titter, giggle, chuckle, guffaw, laugh, roar
6. dress, frock, costume, outfit, gown, ensemble, get-up, apparel, clothes
7. dilapidated, ramshackle, ruined, neglected, deteriorated, tumbledown
8. shrewd, cunning, calculating, sly, adroit, knowing, clever, astute
9. cheat, phony, quack, crook, impostor, charlatan
10. admire, love, relish, like, approve, idolize, respect, revere, esteem
11. snooty, arrogant, conceited, cocky, egotistical, proud, high-and-mighty, overbearing, high-hat
12. common, ordinary, vulgar, run-of-the-mill, average, everyday
13. frighten, alarm, terrify, scare, intimidate, startle
14. impertinent, impudent, saucy, cheeky, insolent, fresh
15. confess, acknowledge, concede, grant, admit, come clean

### Exercise 3

*The difference between denotation and connotation is often illustrated by the fact that of two words which roughly "mean" the same, one has a complimentary, the other an unflattering, connotation. Thus while you may like to think of yourself as an idealist, people who do not sympathize with your attitudes might call you prudish. Taking as many of the following pairs as your instructor designates, write paragraphs explaining why you would like to be described by one of the terms but not by the other.*

a middle-of-the-roader/a fence sitter  trusting/gullible
enthusiastic/fanatical  original/screwball
cautious/cowardly  stolid/even-tempered
touchy/sensitive  thrifty/penny-pinching
fluent/gabby  practical/unimaginative
coy/modest  hypocritical/tactful

7. Not all words possess connotative powers. Articles, conjunctions, prepositions, and many common adverbs lack connotative qualities because they are words used to connect ideas and to show relationships between them; these parts of speech do not themselves stand for ideas. But most words which stand for ideas have connotations, even though they are often scarcely perceptible. That is because ideas themselves have connotations: they produce some sort of intellectual or emotional reaction inside us.

### CONNOTATIONS: PERSONAL AND GENERAL

8. There are two types of connotation: personal and general. Personal connotations are the result of the experience of the individual man or

woman. The way we react to ideas and objects, and thus to the words that stand for those "referents," is determined by the precise nature of our earlier experience with the referents. Taken all together, the connotations that surround most of the words in our vocabulary are a complex and intimate record of our life to date. Our present reaction to a word may be the cumulative result of all our experiences with the word and its referent. In the case of another word, our reaction may have been determined once and for all by an early or a particularly memorable experience with it. A student's reaction to the word *teacher*, for instance, may be determined by all his experience with teachers, which has been subtly synthesized, in the course of time, into a single image or emotional response. In it are mingled memories of Miss Smith, the first-grade teacher who dried his tears when he lost a fight in the schoolyard at recess; of Miss Jones, the sixth-grade teacher who bored her pupils with thrice-told tales of her trip to Mexico ten years earlier; of Mr. Johnson, the high-school gym teacher who merely laughed when he saw the brush burns a boy sustained when he inexpertly slid down a rope; of Mr. Miller, the college professor who somehow packed a tremendous amount of information into lectures that seemed too entertaining to be instructive. Or, on the other hand, when the student thinks of *teacher* he may think of a particular teacher who for one reason or another has made an especially deep impression upon him—the chemistry teacher in high school, for instance, who encouraged him, by example and advice, to make chemistry his life work.

9. A moment's thought will show the relationship between personal and general connotations as well as the fact that there is no line of demarcation between the two types. Since "the mass mind" is the sum total of the individual minds that comprise it, general connotations result when the reaction of the majority of people to a specific word is substantially the same. The reasons why one word should possess a certain connotation, while another word has a quite different connotation, are complex. We shall spend a little time on the subject later. Here it need only be said that differences in general connotation derive from at least two major sources. For one thing, the exact shade of meaning a word possesses in our language is often due to the use to which it was put by a writer who had especially great influence over the language because he was, and is, so widely read. The King James version of the Bible, for instance, is responsible for the crystallizing of many connotations. People came to know a given word from its occurrence in certain passages in the Bible, and thus the word came to connote to them on *all* occasions what it connoted in those familiar passages; it was permanently colored by particular associations. Such words include *trespass, money-changers, manger, Samaritan* (originally the name of a person living in a certain region of Asia Minor), *salvation, vanity, righteous, anoint,* and *charity*. The same is true of many words used in other books which, being widely read and studied, influenced the vocabularies of following

generations—Malory's *Morte d'Arthur*, for example, or Shakespeare's plays, or the essays of Addison and Steele.

*10.* But general connotation is not always a matter of literary development. It can result also from the experience that men as a social group have had with the ideas which words represent. Before 1938, the word *appease* had an inoffensive connotation. In the edition of *Webster's Collegiate Dictionary* current in that year it was defined simply as "to pacify, often by satisfying; quiet; calm; soothe; allay." But then the word became associated with the ill-fated attempts of Neville Chamberlain to stave off war with Hitler by giving in to his demands, and that association has now strongly colored its meaning. The latest edition of the same dictionary adds to the meaning quoted above this newer one: "to conciliate by political, economic, or other considerations;—now usually signifying a sacrifice of moral principle in order to avert aggression." Laden as the word is with its suggestions of the disaster of Munich, no British or American official ever uses it in referring to a conciliating move in foreign policy for which he wants to win public acceptance. On the other hand, opponents of that move use the word freely to arouse sentiment against it, even though the situation in question may have little or no resemblance to that of Munich. In other words, events have conditioned us to react in a particular way to the verb *appease* and the noun *appeasement*. If our support is desired for a policy of *give and take, live and let live,* or *peaceful coexistence* in international relations, its advocates will use the terms just italicized, as well as *negotiation* and *compromise,* which convey the idea of mutual concessions without sacrifice of principle; or *horse-trading,* which has a homely American flavor, suggesting shrewd bargaining with the additional implication that a good profit can be made on the deal.

*11.* All general connotations thus have their origin in private connotations—in personal, individual, but generally shared reactions to words and the ideas for which they stand. But later, after general connotations have been established, the process works the other way: the individual, who may have had no personal experience with the idea represented by a given word, may acquire a personal attitude toward it by observing how society in general reacts to the word. In the future, men and women who were children when Klaus Fuchs and other men stole American and British atomic secrets and relayed them to Russia may react negatively to mention of such names. If they do, it will be because they have acquired the feelings of revulsion that people associate with the names of traitors—just as Americans almost two centuries later still react to the mention of Benedict Arnold.

*12.* Every writer must cultivate his awareness of the differentiation between general connotations and personal ones. It is the general ones—those which he can be reasonably sure his readers share with him—which he must rely on to convey the accurate spirit of his message. If he uses words which have additional connotations to him alone, he runs the risk of writing in a

private shorthand to which only he holds the key. Since there is no clear
dividing line between general and personal connotations, it would, of
course, be unrealistic to require that a writer absolutely confine himself to
the former. Moreover, some of the subtle richness of poetry, and to some degree that of imaginative prose, is derived (assuming that the reader discovers the secret) from the author's use of words in private sense. But in
most forms of practical communication, the writer does well to confine
himself to words whose connotations are approximately the same to his
readers as they are to him.

## THE USES OF CONNOTATIONS

*13.* What forms do our reactions to words take? By no means all words
evoke any distinguishable emotional response; *delusion* and *illusion,* for instance, probably do not do so for most people. Here the response is largely
an intellectual one, a recognition that the two words are customarily used
in different contexts, that they "imply" slightly different things.

*14.* But for our purposes the most important words are the ones which
touch the emotions of those who hear or see them. They are words that
arouse people to a positive or negative judgment—words that often stir
them to action. *Atheist* arouses deep-seated prejudices for or against the
ideas that the word is said to represent, for or against people who are
said to be atheists. *Streamlined* connotes modern design, clean lines,
efficiency, and thus has a generally pleasant suggestion. (On the other
hand, like many words that become too fashionable and thus are overused
and even abused, *streamlined* has come to have a negative connotation to
many fastidious readers. Too often it has been loosely used as a means of
glossing over, skimping and corner-cutting—as in *streamlined* education.)
Mention of *McCarthy* evokes fervent sentiments, of very diverse quality,
from both those who admired him and those who did not. *Subdeb* eases the
selling of clothing to adolescent girls, of whom not one in a hundred thousand will ever have a debut. *Nigger* connotes very different things to a
champion of white supremacy in Mississippi and a member of the National
Association for the Advancement of Colored People. *Draft* and *selective
service* mean the same thing, but one term has a more unpleasant connotation than the other. And so on, *ad infinitum.*

*15.* Intimately associated with emotional response, and often directly
responsible for it, are the images that many words inspire in our minds.
The commonest type of image is the visual: that is, a given word habitually
calls forth a certain picture on the screen of our inner consciousness. Mention of places we have seen and people we have known produces a visual
recollection of them. Of course the precise content of these pictures is determined by the sort of experience one has had with their originals. *Mary*
may not recall the picture of one's childhood sweetheart, but it may evoke
instead a picture of a pink hair-ribbon which Mary must once have worn.

*Boston* may recall only the picture of a street accident, which was the most vivid memory one carried away from that city. And so on! It is a fascinating game to examine in this fashion the mental images thus spontaneously conjured up by words; equally rewarding is the effort to explain why many words evoke images which on first thought seem so completely irrelevant to their denotations.

*16.* It is not only words referring to concrete objects which have this power of evoking a visual response in the imagination. Our picture-making faculty also enables us to visualize abstractions in concrete terms—and, as we shall see, it gets us into a great deal of trouble on that account. *Capitalist* is an abstract noun; it denotes a person who has a certain function in a certain kind of economic system. But to many people it connotes a definite picture, obviously derived from the old-time cartoonist's stock figure, of a bloated banker in striped pants, cutaway coat, top hat, and spats; he is smoking a Corona-Corona cigar, on his fingers are rings with huge stones, and across his middle reposes a gold watch chain with links as thick as frankfurters. To many, in a similar way, the noun *radical* conjures up a picture of an intellectual-looking man with thick glasses, bushy hair, wrinkled clothes, and a wild expression on his face. Thus abstractions are made concrete, and our reactions to the words that represent those abstractions are patterned in terms of that visual image. What visual images do the words *statesman* and *politician* suggest to you?

*17.* In addition to visual responses in the imagination, words evoke responses associated with the other senses. Many words have connotations that appeal to our inward ear: *tick-tock, harmony, squeak, trumpet, dirge, shrill, thunder, croon, lisp.* Others appeal to our sense of touch—*gritty, needle, ice-cold, lather, soft, kiss, baby's cheek, woolen underwear.* Another class invites palatal responses—*buttermilk, spicy, mellow, roast beef, castor oil, menthol, bitter.* And a final group invites olfactory responses—*burning dump, incense, new-mown hay, sweaty, coffee roaster, fragrance, Diesel fumes.* Many words, like some already mentioned, appeal to two or more senses at once: for instance, *dry, bubbly, satin, wine, wrinkle, mossy, sea breeze, snowy, cigarette, sugar.*

*18.* Since our sensory experience may be either pleasant or unpleasant, the words that evoke their imaginative equivalents have the power to sway us to accept or reject an idea. "So soft, yet manageable . . . so sweetly clean! Come-hither loveliness—that's what your hair has after a luxurious Prell shampoo! It's caressably soft, yet *so obedient!* Yes, angel-soft, smooth as satin, glowing with that 'Radiantly Alive' look *he'll* love!" Thus exclaims the advertising man who wants millions of women to buy a certain solution for washing their hair. Or: "It's a foul, evil-smelling mess!" Thus speaks a minority-party congressman who is dissatisfied with something the administration has done.

*19.* In some of the pages that follow, we shall concentrate upon this persuasive power of words, especially as found in advertising and political discussion. There is perhaps no simpler or better way of showing how connotation works. But this preliminary emphasis on the ways in which language may be manipulated for selfish purposes must not lead you to assume that all, or even most, writers have wicked designs upon you. On the contrary, the greater part of what people read has the sole purpose of informing or entertaining them—of giving them new knowledge, or fresh food for the imagination and the emotions. And here language is used simply to heighten the effectiveness, the accuracy, and the vividness of the writer's communication.

*20.* Take the best of today's journalism—not run-of-the-mill newspaper reporting, but, say, feature stories and magazine articles. Really good descriptive journalism requires a high degree of skill in the use of words; and the more skillfully and attentively we read what the author has set down, the greater will be our pleasure. Examine the sure sense of connotative values employed in this description of a Pennsylvania industrial town:

Donora is twenty-eight miles south of Pittsburgh and covers the tip of a lumpy point formed by the most convulsive of the Monongahela's many horseshoe bends. Though accessible by road, rail, and river, it is an extraordinarily secluded place. The river and the bluffs that lift abruptly from the water's edge to a height of four hundred and fifty feet enclose it on the north and east and south, and just above it to the west is a range of rolling but even higher hills. On its outskirts are acres of sidings and rusting gondolas, abandoned mines, smoldering slag piles, and gulches filled with rubbish. Its limits are marked by sooty signs that read, "Donora. Next to Yours the Best Town in the U.S.A." It is a harsh, gritty town, founded in 1901 and old for its age, with a gaudy main street and a thousand identical gaunt gray houses. Some of its streets are paved with concrete and some are cobbled, but many are of dirt and crushed coal. At least half of them are as steep as roofs, and several have steps instead of sidewalks. It is treeless and all but grassless, and much of it is slowly sliding downhill. After a rain, it is a smear of mud. Its vacant lots and many of its yards are mortally gullied, and one of its three cemeteries is an eroded ruin of gravelly clay and toppled tombstones. Its population is 12,300.[4]

Here, in familiar but carefully chosen words, the reporter has produced a graphic impression of a dismal community. He was obviously depressed by what he saw—a feeling he means us to have, too. And, were we to read on past the passage quoted, we would discover that even the seemingly casual reference to the population and the cemeteries is part of his plan; for the article as a whole is about the poison-laden smog that de-

[4] Berton Roueché, "The Fog," *The New Yorker,* Sept. 30, 1950. Reprinted with the permission of *The New Yorker.*

scended on Donora some years ago and killed at least a score of its inhabitants. The whole passage, with its single-minded stress on language suggestive of griminess, ugliness, deterioration, prepares us for the disaster to come.

21. In the same way, but on a less ephemeral plane of interest, with more exalted purpose and greater intensity of feeling, poets too utilize the connotative potentialities of language. They employ words lovingly, unschemingly, wishing to delight and move the reader through an imparting of their own vivid experience:

> Season of mists and mellow fruitfulness,
>     Close bosom-friend of the maturing sun;
> Conspiring with him how to load and bless
>     With fruit the vines that round the thatch-eaves run;
> To bend with apples the mossed cottage-trees,
>     And fill all fruit with ripeness to the core;
>         To swell the gourd, and plump the hazel shells
>     With a sweet kernel; to set budding more,
> And still more, later flowers for the bees,
> Until they think warm days will never cease,
>         For Summer has o'er-brimmed their clammy cells.

Or:

> It is a beauteous evening, calm and free,
> The holy time is quiet as a Nun
> Breathless with adoration; the broad sun
> Is sinking down in its tranquillity;
> The gentleness of heaven broods o'er the Sea:
> Listen! the mighty Being is awake,
> And doth with his eternal motion make
> A sound like thunder—everlastingly.

### Exercise 4

*A scholarly study has shown that the following nouns and adjectives are among those most frequently used by English poets in the past five hundred years. They are part of the basic vocabulary of poetry. How many of them possess particularly strong emotional appeal today? Why are these so filled with suggestion?*

good, great, day, God, heart, king, life, lord, love, man, thing, time, soul, youth, long, light, spirit, cruel, dear, fair, high, old, poor, sweet, true, beauty, death, eye, fortune, gold, hand, heaven, lady, night, pain, woe, word, world, earth, bright, dark, happy, new, rich, blood, face, fire, grace, name, nature, power, sin, son, sun, tear, year, soft, air, friend, joy, divine, nature, proud, tender, vain, art, breast, fate, flower, head, hour, land, maid, sky, song, virtue, deep, dim, holy, child, dream, father, hope, mother, prayer, sea, star, white, black, green, bird, leaf, moon, nothing, stone, tree, water, wind

### Exercise 5

*What are the present connotations of the following words? To what extent do your answers agree with those of others in the class?*

Winston Churchill, sputnik, brainwashing, censorship, security, United Nations, socialized medicine, minority group, Hitler, concentration camp, thermonuclear warfare, imperialism, witch hunt, welfare state, inflation

### Exercise 6

1. *What reaction, if any, do you have when you hear the name "Gwendolyn"? Do you see any specific picture in your mind? How can you account for it? Try the same experiment with "Elmer."*
2. *What personal connotations does each of the following names have to you? Do your reactions match those of others in the class? Explain why they do—or don't.*

Bill, Will, Willy, William, Billy
Meg, Margie, Margaret, Peg, Peggy, Marge

### Exercise 7

*What do the following words or phrases connote to you personally?*

1. serenade, examination, sandpaper, romantic, wryly, skunk, Inquisition, mangled, primitive, kiss, trample, messily, slither, mother, doleful, crackle, sunrise, ostentatiously, cooperate, refresh, bleak, celestial, chocolate, orchid, gurgle, midnight oil, crimson, soggy, space man, cathedral
2. an old biddy, an old fuddy-duddy, a smooth operator, a campus queen, a junior executive
3. Madison Avenue, Wall Street, the Pentagon, Shangri-La, the Kremlin, Main Street, Bali, Sun Valley, San Francisco, Siberia, the Nile

*Devote paragraphs to several of these words, describing, as accurately and in as concrete detail as possible, the pictures and reactions that are evoked in your mind when you happen to encounter each term. Search your memory for the personal associations and experiences that have resulted in the word's present cluster of connotations.*

### Exercise 8

*According to chronological age, you probably are one of those persons who can be described as a teen-ager, an adolescent, a youth, a juvenile, a guy, or a gal. Write a short theme analyzing your personal responses to these words as they apply to you. Do you like them or dislike them? Why? What does each connote? Are there any other words that you prefer as self-description?*

### Exercise 9

*To most people the following words have more or less pronounced connotations. Select two or three words that arouse particularly strong reactions in you and devote a paragraph to each, explaining why the word affects you as it does.*

|            |                   |
|------------|-------------------|
| socialism  | working class     |
| puritanical| plagiarism        |
| liberal    | chastity          |
| Jew        | intolerance       |
| capitalism | racial integration|
| atheism    | conformity        |

*Exercise 10*

*How sensitive to connotative values are you in your own writing? Take one of the subjects listed below and write about it, at whatever length is appropriate. Your sole purpose is to portray it, as precisely and vividly as you can: to make the reader share the sensations (sight, sound, touch, odor) that you have, or had. The best way to perform this exercise is to write it as soon as you can, in as good a form as possible. Then put it out of sight for at least twenty-four hours. At the end of that time, look at it again, with fresh eyes. Test for connotation every word (noun, adjective, verb, adverb) that has descriptive force. Check the dictionary for every word about which you have the slightest doubt. Try to find better—that is, more accurate—words. Then rewrite the paper. The final test is: Have I succeeded in communicating to my reader the true nature and flavor of my observation and experience?*

The inside of a good restaurant (or of a restaurant I'd rather die than go into again )
The scene of a bad accident
A room decorated in the modern manner (or a "period" room)
A barber shop (or a beauty parlor)
An empty auditorium
The city room in a newspaper office
A small shop where a product is made by hand
One set in a television studio
A hen house (or a horse barn)
A florist's shop or greenhouse
The latest thing in motels (or a run-down tourist court)
An old-fashioned kitchen
A jet airliner (or a helicopter) takes off—with me inside
Kickoff!
Landing a big one
Stuck!
Getting awake (or coming out of anesthesia)
Sunrise (or sunset) in ———
Then the lights went out
A sudden storm
Pursuit!
The time I *knew* one's heart could be in one's mouth (or butterflies can flutter in one's stomach)
A piece of antique furniture
A modern fire truck

A prize-winning animal (dog, shoat, bull, or whatnot)
The contents of a baker's shop window
The cover of the current issue of a magazine
A coin machine in a campus hangout
A girl behind the counter in the five-and-ten
A super-sandwich (or a super-sundae)
A much-used telephone booth
A man in a white coat
An example of "calendar art"

· 3 ·

*Reinhold Niebuhr*

# LIBERALISM: ILLUSIONS AND
# REALITIES

*1.* The spate of books on conservatism and liberalism in America has resulted in debates about the respective merits of these allegedly opposing political creeds in which a great deal of semantic confusion is manifest. Mr. Clinton Rossiter in his *Conservatism in America* has accurately defined the conservative mood in our nation as a combination of nationalistic preferences and a passion for the economics of *laissez-faire,* which is to say, that our conservatism in domestic politics is the old liberalism of the Manchester School. Mr. Russell Kirk in his *Conservative Mind* seems to assume that there is some authentic conservatism in the mere desire to preserve the status quo of the American paradise; and he rather uncritically seeks to relate this American conservatism with a British conservatism which is rooted in the aristocratic tradition and has none of Kirk's prejudice against the Welfare State, and with the rather pathetic aristocratic tradition of our own Southland, as expounded by Randolph and Calhoun. This Southern tradition was pathetic because it was but a remnant of an old aristocratic society in a nation which had no conscious relations with the European feudal past, and because it was a form of aristocracy based upon chattel slavery and was naturally destroyed with the institution of slavery.

*2.* It is obviously necessary to make the most careful distinctions be-

From *The New Republic,* 133 (July 4, 1955). Reprinted by permission of the author.

tween the conservatism and liberalism which are merely moods or ideologies according to which one defends a status quo or seeks to leave it
behind, and the conservatism and liberalism which are cogent political
philosophies. We can dismiss the sort of conservatism and liberalism
which are dispositions toward some status quo very simply by giving an
*a priori* preference for liberalism over conservatism on the grounds that
it is not reasonable to defend any status quo uncritically; and that it is
certainly not reasonable to do so in the rapidly changing conditions of a
technical society in which "new conditions teach new duties and time
makes ancient truth uncouth." If being for or against change were the
only issue involved, any critical person would be bound to be a "liberal."

3. If we study the various meanings of "liberalism" and "conservatism"
in Western and particularly in American social history, it soon becomes
apparent that "liberalism" in the broadest sense is rightly identified with
the rise of a modern technical society availing itself of democratic political
forms and of capitalistic economic institutions. This "liberal society" came
to birth in Britain, France and America in opposition to the feudal aristocratic culture of the European past. "Liberalism" in the broadest sense is
therefore synonymous with "democracy." Its strategy is to free the individual from the traditional restraints of a society, to endow the "governed"
with the power of the franchise, to establish the principle of the "consent
of the governed" as the basis of political society; to challenge all hereditary privileges and traditional restraints upon human initiative, particularly in the economic sphere and to create the mobility and flexibility
which are the virtues and achievements of every "liberal society" as distinguished from feudal ones.

4. But liberalism has more distinct connotations; and upon them hang
all the issues of contemporary political controversy. One of these connotations arises out of the history of technical societies; the other arises out
of the peculiar philosophy of the French Enlightenment and the French
Revolution. In the first instance, the narrower connotation of liberalism is
identified with the peculiar and unique ethos of middle-class life. But
since the middle classes soon found the laboring classes to the Left of
them, liberalism soon ceased to be the exclusive philosophy of democracy.
Even without the rise of labor as a political power, modern democracies,
as they developed from commercialism to industrialism, found that the
freeing of economic initiative from political restraint was only one side of
the problem of justice. The other side was the placing of restraints upon
initiative in the interest of security and justice.

5. Thus in every modern industrial nation the word "liberalism"
achieved two contradictory definitions. It was on the one hand the philosophy which insisted that economic life was to be free of any restraint.
In this form it was identical with the only conservatism which nations,
such as our own, who had no feudal past, could understand. It was the

philosophy of the more successful middle classes who possessed enough personal skill, property or power to be able to prefer liberty to security. On the other hand the word was also used to describe the political strategy of those classes which preferred security to absolute liberty and which sought to bring economic enterprise under political control for the sake of establishing minimal standards of security and welfare. It has been rather confusing that both of these strategies go by the name of "liberalism."

6. The new conservatism about which one hears so much these days may claim a right to the title of "liberalism" on the ground that its promise of gaining justice through economic liberty is actually closer to the old classical economic liberalism than the new liberalism is. On the other hand if the concern for justice is the primary hallmark of liberalism, those who want to bring economic enterprise under at least minimal control have as much right to this title as those who want to preserve economic freedom. For a technical society, moving from commercial to industrial activities, was bound to find the emancipation from traditional restraints inadequate in the long run as a program for justice.

7. Thus it was significant that John Stuart Mill, who gave the liberal creed the most classic expression in the 19th Century, moved in the latter years of his life from pure libertarianism to a liberal socialism. It is even more significant that the Liberal Party in Britain took this turn at the beginning of the century before the Labour Party became a power. In Lloyd George's radical budget the taxing power of the state was used to guarantee minimal security for the workers. This development, in which incidentally Lloyd George was supported by Winston Churchill, Britain anticipated by a quarter of a century the transmutation of Jeffersonian liberalism into Roosevelt's "New Deal." American conservatives have made much of this *volte-face* of the liberal tradition; and in their "liberty leagues" tried to fill the political niche of the seemingly abandoned Jeffersonianism.

8. In European democracies the desire to establish justice by bringing economic power under political control was advanced by the Socialist parties. In Britain, the old Liberal Party slowly lost ground in the postwar years to labor and the new conservatism. At this moment, the old debate between freedom and control of economic life has narrowed to a very small difference in emphasis between the Tories and the Labour Party, a difference which has become slight in all modern nations. The debate between a responsible Right and a responsible Left is both inconclusive and insoluble because the degree of emphasis which must be put on planning or spontaneity, on control or freedom, cannot be solved in terms of fixed principles. The peculiar conditions of each nation and of each period within a nation must and will determine the degree of emphasis on the one side or the other of the equation.

9. In all stable modern nations the political situation reflects the insolubility of this problem. Responsible parties, when not corrupted by demagogy and dishonesty, know that the economic and political life of a community cannot go too far in a collectivist direction without becoming prey to bureaucratic stagnation. Nor can it go too far in the direction of an uncontrolled economy without aggravating the perils of insecurity and the evils of inequality arising from centralization of power. Both evils are inherent in the economic process itself, particularly in our era of rapid growth of techniques.

10. The semantic difficulties arising from this shift in meaning of the word liberal as a technical civilization moves farther and farther from its original contest with an organic and aristocratic society, are, however, simple compared with the confusions of definition which arise from the fact that "liberalism" is both a political philosophy, identified with the rising technical civilization, and a total philosophy of life which was elaborated in the French Enlightenment. This confusion becomes the greater because liberalism and a modern technical society had their simultaneous inception in three modern nations, Great Britain, France and America. In one of these, France, the aristocratic past, based upon an organic society, was always in the background with its reactionary illusions which in turn incited the illusions of the Enlightenment. In another, Great Britain, the old society was broken in the Cromwellian revolution. Britain finally settled down at the end of the century with a constitutional monarchy of William and Mary which fused both liberal democracy and a more creative version of the old society. This fusion has ever since characterized British life and made John Locke on the one hand, and Edmund Burke on the other, the exponents of the chief strains of British political philosophy. In America the liberal society and the new nation had a simultaneous birth on a virgin continent with only a few vestigial remnants of the old society, and these were finally eliminated in our Civil War. For these and other reasons, American liberalism drew its primary inspiration from the ideological presuppositions of the culture which gave rise to the French Revolution and excluded a part of the British inheritance.

11. The French Enlightenment was "liberal" in its social policy in the sense that it championed all the extensions of political power and freedom from political control of economic enterprise which characterized the whole middle-class movement in its struggle with the feudal past. But it also had a total philosophy of life based on confidence in the perfectibility of man and on the idea of historical progress. These two ideas were basic to all the political miscalculations of the Enlightenment and were the source of its errors. "Liberalism" acquired a special connotation as a philosophy of life which did not take the factors of interest and power seriously, which expected all parochial loyalties to be dissolved in more universal loyalties; and which was indifferent to organically or historically

established loyalties and rights under the illusion that it would be simple for rational man to devise more ideal communities and rights. The liberalism of the French Enlightenment was thus based upon illusions as to the nature of man and of history. It was quasi-anarchistic and pacifist in its attitude toward the coercions which are a necessary part of communal cohesion and toward the conflicts of interest which always take place between communities. These were the illusions which Burke challenged in *Reflections on the Revolution in France.*

12. The philosophy of the Enlightenment was not shared by such conservatives as John Adams or such Jeffersonians as James Madison. Our Constitution was, in fact, informed by a realism which contradicted all the illusions of the Enlightenment. Nevertheless it became the primary source of inspiration for the democratic movement in America. When sectarian Christian perfectionism merged with the thought of the Enlightenment on our frontier, perfectionist illusions in regard to man became the staples of the American liberal movement.

13. It must be apparent to anyone that it adds to the semantic confusion if those who do not share the illusions of Diderot and Condorcet are termed "conservatives." Such persons would be more accurately defined as "realistics," particularly since a realistic estimate of perennial factors in the historical and social situation may be put into the service of either a conservative or advancing social policy. It would certainly be wrong to define a labor leader as "conservative" merely because he knew, as every good labor leader must know, that a collective bargaining agreement is not merely a rational or moral encounter, and that its success depends upon the strength and unity of the force at his disposal. Incidentally, it must be observed that organized labor has always been "realistic" in this sense. Its realism included preference for proximate goals of justice, while the more academic liberalism was frequently beguiled by the utopian illusions of the Enlightenment.

14. In terms of international policy, confusion would be avoided if the word "conservative" were confined to the pure nationalist. It certainly does not fit the internationalist who knows about the perils and responsibilities of a nation in the potential global community, but who is not persuaded that "world government" is the answer.

15. There is, in short, no reason why the errors of the Enlightenment should continue to bedevil the "progressive" political movements, and why "liberalism" should be identified with illusions about human nature and history. Sometimes the foes of liberalism insist that the illusions are inherent in the policy. There are even some belated liberals who darkly insinuate that a realist who professes to be liberal in social policy must be a crypto-conservative who has yet to reveal his true colors. These confusions could be eliminated if the clear evidence of history were presented to prove that the "liberal" illusions are not necessary for democracy, and

might actually have a baneful influence upon its life. The best evidence for this thesis is a comparison between the course of British and French democracy. In France the enthusiasm for a liberal society soon degenerated into Jacobin fanaticism and Bonapartist absolutism.

16. In contrast, the curious blend of aristocracy and democracy in Britain slowly evolved into the world's most stable democracy, in which "liberty broadened down from precedent to precedent." The only remnant of the old feudalism is the still prevalent class snobbishness of British life. This superior achievement was due, partly to the superior wisdom of the Lockean type of liberalism and partly to the interplay between the Lockean liberalism and the Burkean type of conservatism. The aristocratic tradition at its worst tried to maintain the traditional privileges of the feudal order. At its best it appreciated the organic aspects of community better than urban-centered liberalism. One must include under the "organic" aspect of community the force of mutually and historically acknowledged rights and responsibilities, in comparison with the "inalienable" rights which are worthless if no community acknowledges them. One must also include standards of justice which have developed by slow and unconscious growth rather than by conscious political intervention. Finally, to the organic aspects one must reckon the hierarchies of authority which develop in every political and economic realm, and without which the community could not be organized.

17. It is rather ironic that the rigorous equalitarian creed of Communism should in practice generate the monstrous inequalities of power and privilege which we see in the Russian scene. The inequalities are more excessive than usual because there is nothing in the creed that would come to terms with functional hierarchies as such. We have lesser ironic realities in so-called liberal communities, whether in labor unions or in churches. In every case justified inequalities of authority develop, and usually some unjustified inequalities of privilege.

18. An academic liberalism with its abstract notions of liberty and equality has never been able to come to terms with these realities of the community. There is, therefore, some truth in the aristocratic-conservative tradition which the most democratic society must rescue from the error of aristocratic pretentions and must incorporate into the wisdom by which the life of the community is regulated and integrated. This truth may be imbedded in a conservative tradition. But it must be freed from the errors which are also transmitted in the conservative tradition. If that is done the result can only be a realistic liberalism. It will be a liberalism because only that philosophy, stripped of its utopian errors, leaves the way to the future open.

19. There is, unfortunately, no social locus in America for a valid "conservative" philosophy. The more parochial part of the business community

is bound to develop a conservatism in which a decadent *laissez-faire* liberalism in domestic politics is compounded with nationalism. It can be beguiled from these prejudices only by the prestige of an Eisenhower. The realism embodied in a valid conservatism, therefore, becomes the property of all parties and tendencies which have enough pragmatic wisdom to discern the perennial factors in the shifting historical scene.

# Questions

1. Notice that Niebuhr begins almost immediately to distinguish and to discard. He proceeds by means of negative definition, discerning first what a thing is not. In the first two paragraphs he disposes of the "status-quo" liberal-conservative distinction. What means does he use to lead us to discard what is perhaps the most common definition of liberalism? Upon what grounds does he base his argument that laissez-faire conservatism is really the old liberalism? How does he thereby shatter "illusion"?

2. In paragraphs 3 through 5 Niebuhr moves to the central issue, the contradictory definition of liberalism. In paragraph 3, when he links liberalism and democracy, what technique of definition is he using? Why does he distinguish a "liberal" society from a "feudal" one?

3. In paragraph 3 we are given a very broad definition of liberalism; what linking device does Niebuhr use in moving to the more specific definition of paragraph 4?

4. How in paragraphs 6 through 7 does Niebuhr dissociate liberalism from the "new conservatism"?

5. In paragraph 9 Niebuhr makes use of a number of "loaded" words. What are they? Why does he employ them?

6. How does Niebuhr show that the "liberalism" of the French Enlightenment was alien to the philosophy of such men as Adams and Madison? If it was alien, how then did it become the "primary source of inspiration for the democratic movement in America"? How does this shift illustrate the complex history of the word "liberalism"?

7. In the first thirteen paragraphs he employs the historical technique of definition. How does this technique prepare for paragraphs 14 through 19?

8. What final distinction does Niebuhr make between liberalism and conservatism, and what effect does this distinction have on both as viable philosophies?

# Theme Topics

1. Write an essay in which you define one of the following terms: love, honor, security, conformity, humility.
2. Write an essay establishing some stereotyped belief in which illusion should be separated from reality and establish some basis for declaring part of the stereotype to be illusion.

·4·

*C. S. Lewis*

## WHAT CHRISTIANS BELIEVE

*1.* I have been asked to tell you what Christians believe, and I am going to begin by telling you one thing that Christians don't need to believe. If you are a Christian you don't have to believe that all the other religions are simply wrong all through. If you are an atheist you do have to believe that the main point in all the religions of the whole world is simply one huge mistake. If you are a Christian, you are free to think that all these religions, even the queerest ones, contain at least some hint of the truth. When I was an atheist I had to try to persuade myself that the whole human race were pretty good fools until about one hundred years ago; when I became a Christian I was able to take a more liberal view. But, of course, being a Christian does mean thinking that where Christianity differs from other religions, Christianity is right and they are wrong. Like in arithmetic—there's only one right answer to a sum, and all other answers are wrong: but some of the wrong answers are much nearer being right than others.

2. The first big division of humanity is into the majority, who believe in some kind of God or gods, and the minority who don't. On this point, Christianity lines up with the majority—lines up with ancient Greeks and Romans, modern savages, Stoics, Platonists, Hindoos, Mohammedans, etc.,

against the modern Western European materialist. There are all sorts of different reasons for believing in God, and here I'll mention only one. It is this. Supposing there was no intelligence behind the universe, no creative mind. In that case nobody designed my brain for the purpose of thinking. It is merely that when the atoms inside my skull happen for physical or chemical reasons to arrange themselves in a certain way, this gives me, as a by-product, the sensation I call thought. But if so, how can I trust my own thinking to be true? It's like upsetting a milk-jug and hoping that the way the splash arranges itself will give you a map of London. But if I can't trust my own thinking, of course I can't trust the arguments leading to atheism, and therefore have no reason to be an atheist, or anything else. Unless I believe in God, I can't believe in thought: so I can never use thought to disbelieve in God.

3. Now I go on to the next big division. People who all believe in God can be divided according to the sort of God they believe in. There are two very different ideas on this subject. One of them is the idea that He is beyond good and evil. *We* call one thing good and another thing bad. But according to some people that's merely our human point of view. These people would say that the wiser you become the less you'd want to call anything good or bad, and the more clearly you'd see that everything is good in one way and bad in another, and that nothing could have been different. Consequently, these people think that long before you got anywhere near the divine point of view the distinction would have disappeared altogether. We call a cancer bad, they'd say, because it kills a man; but you might just as well call a successful surgeon bad because he kills a cancer. It all depends on the point of view. The other and opposite idea is that God is quite definitely "good" or "righteous," a God who takes sides, who loves love and hates hatred, who wants us to behave in one way and not in another. The first of these views—the one that thinks God beyond good and evil—is called Pantheism. It was held by the great Prussian philosopher Hegel and, as far as I can understand them, by the Hindoos. The other view is held by Jews, Mohammedans, and Christians.

4. And with this big difference between Pantheism and the Christian idea of God, there usually goes another. Pantheists usually believe that God, so to speak, animates the universe as you animate your body: that the universe almost *is* God, so that if it didn't exist He wouldn't exist either, and anything you find in the universe is a part of God. The Christian idea is quite different. They think God *made* the universe—like a man making a picture or composing a tune. A painter isn't a picture, and he doesn't die if his picture is destroyed. You may say, "He's put a lot of himself into it," but that only means that all its beauty and interest have come out of his head. His skill isn't in the picture in the same way that it's in his head, or even in his hands. I expect you see how this difference between Pantheists and Christians hangs together with the other one. If

you don't take the distinction between good and bad very seriously, then it's easy to say that anything you find in this world is a part of God. But, of course, if you think some things really bad, and God really good, then you can't talk like that. You must believe that God is separate from the world and that some of the things we see in it are contrary to His will. Confronted with a cancer or a slum the Pantheist can say, "If you could only see it from the divine point of view, you would realise that this also is God." The Christian replies, "Don't talk damned nonsense."[1] For Christianity is a fighting religion. It thinks God made the world—that space and time, heat and cold, and all the colours and tastes, and all the animals and vegetables, are things that God "made up out of His head" as a man makes up a story. But it also thinks that a great many things have gone wrong with the world that God made and that God insists, and insists very loudly, on our putting them right again.

5. And, of course, that raises a very big question. If a good God made the world why has it gone wrong? And for many years I simply wouldn't listen to the Christian answers to this question, because I kept on feeling "whatever you say, and however clever your arguments are, isn't it much simpler and easier to say that the world was *not* made by any intelligent power? Aren't all your arguments simply a complicated attempt to avoid the obvious?" But then that threw me back into those difficulties about atheism which I spoke of a moment ago. And soon I saw another difficulty.

6. My argument against God was that the universe seemed so cruel and unjust. But how had I got this idea of *just* and *unjust?* A man doesn't call a line crooked unless he has some idea of a straight line. What was I comparing this universe with when I called it unjust? If the whole show was bad and senseless from A to Z, so to speak, why did I, who was supposed to be part of the show, find myself in such violent reaction against it? A man feels wet when he falls into water, because man isn't a water animal: a fish wouldn't feel wet. Of course I could have given up my idea of justice by saying it was nothing but a private idea of my own. But if I did that then my argument against God collapsed too—for the argument depended on saying that the world was really unjust, not that it just didn't happen to please my private fancies. Thus in the very act of trying to prove that God didn't exist—in other words, that the whole of reality was senseless—I found I was forced to assume that one part of reality—namely my idea of justice—was full of sense. Consequently atheism turns out to be too simple. If the whole universe has no meaning, we should never have found out that it has no meaning: just as if there were no light in the universe and therefore no creatures with eyes we should never know it was dark. *Dark* would be a word without meaning.

[1] One listener complained of the word *damned* as frivolous swearing. But I mean exactly what I say—nonsense that is *damned* is under God's curse, and will (apart from God's grace) lead those who believe it to eternal death.

## II

7. Very well then, atheism is too simple. And I'll tell you another view that is also too simple. It's the view I call Christianity-and-water, the view that just says there's a good God in Heaven and everything is all right—leaving out all the difficult and terrible doctrines about sin and hell and the devil, and the redemption. Both these are boys' philosophies.

8. It is no good asking for a simple religion. After all, real things *aren't* simple. They *look* simple, but they're not. The table I'm sitting at looks simple: but ask a scientist to tell you what it's really made of—all about the atoms and how the light waves rebound from them and hit my eye and what they do to the optic nerve and what it does to my brain—and, of course, you find that what we call "seeing a table" lands you in mysteries and complications which you can hardly get to the end of. A child, saying a child's prayer, looks simple. And if you're content to stop here, well and good. But if you're not—and the modern world usually isn't—if you want to go on and ask what's really happening—then you must be prepared for something difficult. If we ask for something more than simplicity, it's silly then to complain that the something more isn't simple. Another thing I've noticed about reality is that, besides being difficult, it's odd: it isn't neat, it isn't what you expect. I mean, when you've grasped that the earth and the other planets all go round the sun, you'd naturally expect that all the planets were made to match—all at equal distances from each other, say, or distances that regularly increased, or all the same size, or else getting bigger or smaller as you go further from the sun. In fact, you find no rhyme or reason (that we can see) about either the sizes or the distances; and some of them have one moon, one has four, one has two, some have none, and one has a ring.

9. Reality, in fact, is always something you couldn't have guessed. That's *one* of the reasons I believe Christianity. It's a religion you couldn't have guessed. If it offered us just the kind of universe we'd always expected, I'd feel we were making it up. But, in fact, it's not the sort of thing anyone would have made up. It has just that queer twist about it that real things have. So let's leave behind all these boys' philosophies—these over-simple answers. The problem isn't simple and the answer isn't going to be simple either.

10. What is the problem? A universe that contains much that is obviously bad and apparently meaningless, but containing creatures like ourselves who know that it is bad and meaningless. There are only two views that face all the facts. One is the Christian view that this is a good world that has gone wrong, but still retains the memory of what it ought to have been. The other is the view called Dualism. Dualism means the belief that there are two equal and independent powers at the back of everything, one of them good and the other bad, and that this universe is the

battlefield in which they fight out an endless war. I personally think that next to Christianity Dualism is the manliest and most sensible creed on the market. But it has a catch in it.

*11.* The two powers, or spirits, or gods—the good one and the bad one —are supposed to be quite independent. They both existed from all eternity. Neither of them made the other, neither of them has any more right than the other to call itself God. Each presumably thinks it is good and thinks the other bad. One of them likes hatred and cruelty, the other likes love and mercy, and each backs its own view. Now what do we mean when we call one of them the Good Power and the other the Bad Power? Either we're merely saying that we happen to prefer the one to the other —like preferring beer to cider—or else we're saying that, whatever *they* say about it, and whichever *we* happen to like, one of them is actually wrong, actually mistaken, in regarding itself as good. Now if we mean merely that we happen to prefer the first, then we must give up talking about good and evil at all. For good means what you ought to prefer quite regardless of what you happen to like at any given moment. If "being good" meant simply joining the side you happened to fancy, for no real reason, then good wouldn't *be* good. So we must mean that one of the two powers is actually wrong and the other actually right.

*12.* But the moment you say that, you are putting into the universe a third thing in addition to the two Powers: some law or standard or rule of good which one of the powers conforms to and the other fails to conform to. But since the two powers are judged by this standard, then this standard, or the being who made this standard, is farther back and higher up than either of them, and He will be the real God. In fact, what we meant by calling them good and bad turns out to be that one of them is in a right relation to the real ultimate God and the other in a wrong relation to Him.

*13.* The same point can be made in a different way. If Dualism is true, then the Bad Power must be a being who likes badness for its own sake. But in reality we have no experience of anyone liking badness just because it is bad. The nearest we can get to it is in cruelty. But in real life people are cruel for one of two reasons—either because they are sadists, that is, because they have a sexual perversion which makes cruelty a cause of sensual pleasure to them, or else for the sake of something they are going to get out of it—money, or power, or safety. But pleasure, money, power, and safety are all, as far as they go, good things. The badness consists in pursuing them by the wrong method, or in the wrong way, or too much. I don't mean, of course, that the people who do this aren't desperately wicked. I do mean that wickedness, when you examine it, turns out to be the pursuit of some good in the wrong way. You can be good for the mere sake of goodness: you can't be bad for the mere sake of badness. You can do a kind action when you're not feeling kind and when it gives you no pleasure, simply because kindness is right; but no one ever did a cruel action simply because cruelty is wrong—only because cruelty was pleasant or useful to him. In other words, badness can't succeed even in being bad *in the same way* in which goodness is good. Goodness is, so to speak, itself: badness is only spoiled goodness. And there must be something good first before it can be spoiled. We called Sadism a sexual perversion; but you must first have the idea of a normal sexuality before you can talk of it being perverted; and you can see which is the perversion, because you can explain the perverted from the normal, and can't explain the normal from the perverted. It follows that the Bad Power, who is supposed to be on an equal footing with the Good Power, and to love badness in the same way as the good one loves goodness, is a mere bogey. In order to be bad he must have good things to want and then to pursue in the wrong way: he must have impulses which were originally good in order to be able to pervert them. But if he is bad he can't supply himself either with good things to desire or with good impulses to pervert. He must be getting both from the Good Power. And if so, then he is not independent. He is part of the Good Power's world: he was made either by the Good Power or by some power above them both.

14. Put it more simply still. To be bad, he must exist and have intelligence and will. But existence, intelligence, and will are in themselves good. Therefore he must be getting them from the Good Power: even to be bad he must borrow or steal from his opponent. And do you now begin to see why Christianity has always said that the devil is a fallen angel? That isn't a mere story for the children. It's a real recognition of the fact that evil is a parasite, not an original thing. The powers which enable evil to carry on are powers given it by goodness. All the things which enable a bad man to be effectively bad are in themselves good things—resolution, cleverness, good looks, existence itself. That's why Dualism, in a strict sense, won't work.

15. But I want to say that real Christianity (as distinct from Christianity-and-water) goes much nearer to Dualism than people think. One of the things that surprised me when I first read the New Testament seriously was that it was always talking about a Dark Power in the universe—a mighty evil spirit who was held to be the Power behind death and disease, and sin. The difference is that Christianity thinks this Dark Power was created by God, and was good when he was created, and went wrong. Christianity agrees with Dualism that this universe is at war. But it doesn't think this is a war between independent powers. It thinks it's a civil war, a rebellion, and that we are living in a part of the universe occupied by the rebel.

16. Enemy-occupied territory—that's what this world is. Christianity is the story of how the rightful king has landed, you might say landed in disguise, and is calling us all to take part in a great campaign of sabotage.

When you go to church you're really listening in to the secret wireless from our friends: that's why the enemy is so anxious to prevent us going. He does it by playing on our conceit and laziness and intellectual snobbery. I know someone will ask me, "Do you really mean, at this time of day, to re-introduce our old friend the devil—hoofs and horns and all?" Well, what the time of day has to do with it I don't know. And I'm not particular about the hoofs and horns. But in other respects my answer is, "Yes, I do." I don't claim to know anything about his personal appearance. If anybody really wants to know him better I'd say to that person, "Don't worry. If you really want to, you will. Whether you'll like it when you do is another question."

### III

*17.* Christians, then, believe that an evil power has made himself for the present the Prince of this World. And, of course, that raises problems. Is this state of affairs in accordance with God's will or not? If it is, He's a strange God, you'll say: and if it isn't, how *can* anything happen contrary to the will of a being with absolute power?

*18.* But anyone who has been in authority knows how a thing can be in accordance with your will in one way and not in another. It may be quite sensible for a mother to say to the children, "I'm not going to go and make you tidy the school-room every night. You've got to learn to keep it tidy on your own." Then she goes up one night and finds the Teddy bear and the ink and the French Grammar all lying in the grate. That's against her will. She would prefer the children to be tidy. But on the other hand, it is her will which has left the children free to be untidy. The same thing arises in any regiment, or trades union, or school. You make a thing voluntary and then half the people don't do it. That isn't what you willed, but your will has made it possible.

*19.* It's probably the same in the universe. God created things which had free will. That means creatures which can go wrong *or* right. Some people think they can imagine a creature which was free but had no possibility of going wrong, but I can't. If a thing is free to be good it's also free to be bad. And free will is what has made evil possible. Why, then, did God give them free will? Because free will, though it makes evil possible, is also the only thing that makes possible any love or goodness or joy worth having. A world of automata—of creatures that worked like machines—would hardly be worth creating. The happiness which God designs for His higher creatures is the happiness of being freely, voluntarily united to Him and to each other in an ecstasy of love and delight compared with which the most rapturous love between a man and a woman on this earth is *mere milk and water*. And for that they've got to be free.

*20.* Of course God knew that would happen if they used their freedom the wrong way: apparently He thought it worth the risk. Perhaps we feel inclined to disagree with Him. But there's a difficulty about disagreeing with God. He is the source from which all your reasoning power comes: you couldn't be right and He wrong any more than a stream can rise higher than its own source. When you are arguing against Him you're arguing against the very power that makes you able to argue at all: it's like cutting off the branch you're sitting on. If God thinks this state of war in the universe a price worth paying for free will—that is, for making a *real* world in which creatures can do real good or harm and something of real importance can happen, instead of a toy world which only moves when He pulls the strings—then we may take it it *is* worth paying.

21. When we've understood about free will, we shall see how silly it is to ask, as somebody once asked me: "Why did God make a creature of such rotten stuff that it went wrong?" The better stuff a creature is made of—the cleverer and stronger and freer it is—then the better it will be if it goes right, but also the worse it will be if it goes wrong. A cow can't be very good or very bad; a dog can be both better and worse; a child better and worse still; an ordinary man, still more so; a man of genius, still more so; a superhuman spirit best—or worst—of all.

22. How did the Dark Power go wrong? Well, the moment you have a self at all, there is a possibility of putting yourself first—wanting to be the centre—wanting to *be* God, in fact. That was the sin of Satan: and that was the sin he taught the human race. Some people think the fall of man had something to do with sex, but that's a mistake. What Satan put into the heads of our remote ancestors was the idea that they could "be like gods" could set up on their own as if they had created themselves—be their own masters—invent some sort of happiness for themselves outside God, apart from God. And out of that hopeless attempt has come nearly all that we call human history—money, poverty, ambition, war, prostitution, classes, empires, slavery—the long terrible story of man trying to find something other than God which will make him happy.

23. The reason why it can never succeed is this. God made us: invented us as a man invents an engine. A car is made to run on petrol, and it won't run properly on anything else. Now God designed the human machine to run on Himself. He Himself is the fuel our spirits were designed to burn, or the food our spirits were designed to feed on. There isn't any other. That's why it's just no good asking God to make us happy in our own way without bothering about religion. God can't give us a happiness and peace apart from Himself, because it isn't there. There's no such thing.

24. That is the key to history. Terrific energy is expended—civilisations are built up—excellent institutions devised; but each time something goes wrong. Some fatal flaw always brings the selfish and cruel people to the top and it all slides back into misery and ruin. In fact, the machine konks. It seems to start up all right and runs a few yards, and then it breaks

down. They're trying to run it on the wrong juice. That's what Satan has done to us humans.

25. And what did God do? First of all He left us conscience, the sense of right and wrong: and all through history there have been people trying (some of them very hard) to obey it. None of them ever quite succeeded. Secondly, He sent the human race what I call good dreams: I mean those queer stories scattered all through the heathen religions about a god who dies and comes to life again and, by his death, has somehow given new life to men. Thirdly, He selected one particular people and spent several centuries hammering into their heads the sort of God He was—that there was only one of Him and that He cared about right conduct. Those people were the Jews, and the Old Testament gives an account of the hammering process.

26. Then comes the real shock. Among these Jews there suddenly turns up a man who goes about talking as if He was God. He claims to forgive sins. He says He has always existed. He says He is coming to judge the world at the end of time. Now let us get this clear. Among Pantheists, like the Indians, anyone might say that he was a part of God, or one with God: there'd be nothing very odd about it. But this man, since He was a Jew, couldn't mean that kind of God. God, in their language, meant the Being outside the world Who had made it and was infinitely different from anything else. And when you've grasped that, you will see that what this man said was, quite simply, the most shocking thing that has ever been uttered by human lips.

27. I'm trying here to prevent anyone from saying the really silly thing that people often say about Him: "I'm ready to accept Jesus as a great moral teacher, but I don't accept His claim to be God." That's the one thing we mustn't say. A man who was merely a man and said the sort of things Jesus said wouldn't be a great moral teacher. He'd either be a lunatic—on a level with the man who says he's a poached egg—or else he'd be the Devil of Hell. You must make your choice. Either this man was, and is, the Son of God: or else a madman or something worse. You can shut Him up for a fool; you can spit at Him and kill Him as a demon; or you can fall at His feet and call Him Lord and God. But don't let us come with any patronising nonsense about His being a great human teacher. He hasn't left that open to us. He didn't intend to.

# Questions

1. Lewis' essay is a very tightly organized argument that utilizes several techniques of definition. What are these techniques?

2. Examine the first six paragraphs. Comment on Lewis' use of classification.

3. What linking devices does Lewis use and how appropriate are they to the classification technique?

4. In what sense does Lewis' definition of Christianity depend on his distinction between "the universe almost *is* God" and "God *made* the universe"?

5. After considering Lewis' initial distinctions, trace the development of his argument. Consider the last three sentences. What effect has the decreasing sentence length?

6. In Lewis' essay we have reached the opposite pole from Hayakawa's. Here we find connotation used heavily, and in such a fashion that the words seem almost paradoxical in the context in which they appear: for example, in paragraph 1 what meanings does Lewis attach to "liberal"? In what way does he use this word to point up a paradoxical difference between Christianity and atheism?

7. In paragraph 2, what justification is there for saying that "materialist" is a loaded word?

8. List the terms used by Lewis with a heavy burden of connotation and state what the connotations are in each case.

9. In paragraph 4, what functions does the word "damned" perform?

10. Although Lewis deals with very complex matters in his essay, he achieves deceptive simplicity in style and thought. Examine the entire essay in the light of this statement; point out the devices used by Lewis to produce simple assent to most complex propositions.

# Theme Topics

1. Using Lewis' techniques, write an essay in which you explain a belief or feeling of your own: for example, you might explain to those who condemn teenagers the real feelings of this group, or you might attempt to define your own religious feeling, or lack of it, or your political beliefs.

2. Write an essay on Lewis' article in which you analyze the slanting techniques, observe the lack of evidence, and attempt to justify these qualities.

# *Discriminating*

## ~ II ~

## COMPARISON, CONTRAST, AND ANALOGY

IN EVERYDAY WRITING OR CONVERSATION, nothing is more common than such statements as "How like his father Charlie is," "Utopia State Teachers is certainly no Harvard," "She's really an all-American girl." These statements exemplify the techniques of comparing and contrasting. Their purpose is to make a vivid comment or to clarify a position by drawing our attention to similarities or dissimilarities that exist between an object presently under scrutiny and others with which we are already familiar. All three of the examples here presuppose a knowledge of the referent—Charlie's father, Harvard, the all-American girl. Neither of these two comparisons nor the single contrast is fully elucidated. Indeed, a given act of comparison or contrast is seldom complete and may frequently be indirect. The writer generally presupposes some knowledge on the part of his reader. For the same reason one rarely thinks or talks in perfect syllogisms. Something is generally implied or omitted.

Comparing and contrasting are almost always concerned either with arguing or illustrating a point of view, a position, a subject. The important thing is the core of the illustration; the peripheral implications are brushed aside. Suppose we want to show the differences between two students; both are "A" caliber, but one is plodding, uninspired and methodical, while the other is brilliant and intuitive but erratic. Here our interest lies in the differences. The fact that both are "A" students, both twenty, both male, both juniors (all facts dear to the hearts of pollsters)—all this is, for the moment, irrelevant. On the other hand, suppose we should wish to compare society in the United States with that of the Roman Empire during its decline and fall. Our purpose would be to stress the supposed decadence of the United States, the point of comparison being that it too is now moving toward dissolution. For this purpose we would ignore the many differences: that our economy is not based on slavery, that our senators have not assassinated a head of state, that our agricultural problems arise not from scarcity but abundance, that a millennium and a half lies between ourselves and ancient Rome. A person searching for similarities would have either to ignore such differences or to declare them irrelevant.

48

Comparing our condition with that of the citizens of imperial Rome may lead, if one is ready to dismiss substantive differences between the two, to false analogy. A dazzling inventory of likenesses and complete silence about dissimilarities or firm declarations of their insignificance, will not alter the case. Here the differences between the two societies are so substantive that they create a difference in kind rather than in degree. And the process of comparing and contrasting, if its end is not simply that of the mind at play for its own sake, must be between entities that exhibit real kinship, between things of the same class (A:B::A':B'). Analogy emphasizes resemblances between things of different classes (A:B::C:D) and, when true, does not insist upon resemblances at the expense of dismissing or hiding unlikenesses.

Unlike the prose writer, whose aim is unequivocal meaning, the poet uses concrete terms analogically in the form of similes ("His folks/ Pursue their lives like toy trains on a track") and metaphors, explicit or implicit ("My vegetable Love should grow"). In the hands of a good poet words and their values, denotative as well as connotative, can achieve immediacy and evocation, precision and ambiguity, simultaneously. The vision of a nation and its government as "a ship of state," for example, may possess immediacy and precision in its first poetic appearance and serve as a point of departure for generations of cartoonists. To the prose writer, however, the implied identifications in this or in other poetic figures of speech may be wearisome and unfortunate, certainly in his own struggle for immediacy and precision. Who or what is the rudder? The foremast? The anchor? Or even the atomic pile?

The above considerations lead to certain conclusions about the effective use of the principle of comparison and contrast. You should:

1. Compare things of the same class.
2. Be clear and distinct in your own mind about the purpose for which the comparing is being done.
3. Deal with meaningful details of contrast, not with obvious but irrelevant ones.
4. Establish the basis upon which two things are comparable before proceeding to make your point, whether your point is that one is preferable or that what happened in one case may occur in the other.
5. Work for details that are accurate, ones that you can endow with meaning and, if possible, ones that also have a force and a color of their own.

In the essays that follow various techniques of comparison and contrast are illustrated, each conditioned by the author's purpose. Sartre uses implied contrast in distinguishing New York from European cities, and Cooke uses more direct contrast in setting forth his impression of the real

New York as opposed to Priestley's false view. Sears avowedly employs both comparison and contrast as he defines the liberal and the conservative as they have functioned in America, and attempts to refute Niebuhr's position that a viable conservatism no longer exists. His definition is achieved efficiently in contrasting it point-by-point with liberalism. Fadiman's distinctions among four words commonly confused illustrate a more complex kind of discrimination in which the distinguishing quality of each is isolated; Daiches, on the other hand, in examining English and American education, specifies the important similarities and differences with the aim of presenting information only.

## ·5·

*Jean-Paul Sartre*

# NEW YORK, THE COLONIAL CITY

*1.* I really knew I would like New York, but I thought I'd be able to like it immediately, as I had liked the red brick of Venice and London's massive, sombre houses. I didn't know that, for the newly arrived European, there was a "New York sickness," like sea-sickness, air-sickness and mountain-sickness.

*2.* At midnight, an official bus took me from La Guardia field to the Plaza Hotel. I had pressed my forehead against the window, but had been able to see only red and green lights and dark buildings. The next day, without any transition, I found myself at the corner of 58th Street and Fifth Avenue. I walked for a long time under the icy sky. It was a Sunday in January, 1945, a deserted Sunday. I was looking for New York and couldn't find it. The further I progressed along an avenue that seemed coldly mediocre and banal, the further the city seemed to retreat before me, like a ghost town. What I was looking for was probably a European city.

*3.* We Europeans live on the myth of the big city that we forged during the nineteenth century. American myths are not ours, and the American city is not our city; it has neither the same character nor the same functions. In Spain, Italy, Germany and France we find circular cities that were

originally surrounded by ramparts meant not only to protect the inhabit- *unrelenting*
ants against enemy invasion, but also to conceal the inexorable presence *cannot be*
of Nature. These cities are, moreover, divided into sections that are simi- *influenced*
larly round and closed. The piled-up tangle of houses weighs heavily on
the soil. They seem to have a natural tendency to draw together, so much
so that now and then we have to clear a way through with an axe, as in a
virgin forest. Streets run into other streets. Closed at both ends, they do
not look as though they lead outside the city. Inside them, you go around
in circles. They are more than mere arteries; each one constitutes a social
milieu. *environment*

4. You stop along these streets, meet people, drink, eat and linger. On
Sundays, you get dressed and take a stroll for the sole pleasure of greeting
friends, to see and be seen. These are the streets that inspired Jules Ro-
mains' "unanisme." They are filled with a communal spirit that changes
from hour to hour.

5. Thus, my near-sighted European eyes, slowly venturing out, on the
watch for everything, vainly tried to find something to arrest them. Anything at all—a row of houses suddenly barring the way, a street corner, or
some old, time-mellowed house. But it was no use. New York is a city
for far-sighted people, a city in which you can only "adjust" to infinity.
My glance met nothing but space. It slid over blocks of identical houses,
with nothing to arrest it; it was about to lose itself in empty space, at the
horizon.

6. Céline has remarked of New York that "it is a vertical city." This is
true, but it seemed to me, at first, like a lengthwise city. The traffic that
comes to a standstill in the side streets is all-privileged and flows tirelessly
down the avenues. How often the taxi-drivers, willing to take passengers
from north to south, flatly refuse to take any for the east and west! The
side streets have hardly any function other than to mark off the limits of
the apartment houses between the avenues. They are cut by the avenues,
spread and thrown toward the north. That was why I, a naïve tourist,
vainly tried for a long time to find *quartiers*. In France we are surrounded
and protected by urban centres; the prosperous districts protect the rich
from the poor, and the poor districts protect us from the disdain of the
rich, and similarly, the entire city protects us against Nature.

7. In New York, where the major axes are parallel avenues, I was unable to discover *quartiers* except on Lower Broadway. I could only find
filmy atmospheres, longitudinally stretched masses with nothing to mark
a beginning or end. I gradually learned to recognize the atmosphere of
Third Avenue where, under the shadow of the noisy elevated railway,
people meet, smile and chat without even knowing each other; and that
Irish bar in which a German, passing by my table, stopped for a minute
to say: "Are you French? I'm a Jerry"; the reassuring comfort of the
Lexington Avenue shops; the dreary elegance of Park Avenue; the cold

luxury and stucco impassiveness of Fifth Avenue; the gay frivolity of Sixth and Seventh Avenues; the food markets on Ninth Avenue; and the No Man's Land of Tenth Avenue. Each avenue wraps its neighbouring streets in its own atmosphere, but one street down, you're suddenly plunged into another world. Not far from the palpitating silence of Park Avenue where glide the cars of the lords and masters, I come to First Avenue where the earth is constantly trembling under the passing of trucks. How am I to feel safe on one of those endless "north-south" highways when, a few steps away to east or west, other lengthwise worlds await me? Behind the Waldorf-Astoria and the blue and white canopies of "smart" buildings, I glimpse the "Elevated," which carries with it something of the Bowery's poverty.

8. All of New York is striped this way with parallel and noncommunicating significances. These long, perfectly straight lines suddenly gave me the feeling of space. Our cities are constructed to protect us against it; the houses cluster like sheep. But space crosses through New York, quickening and expanding it. The space, the great, empty space of the steppes and pampas, flows through New York's arteries like a draught of cold air, separating one side from the other. An American friend who was showing me about the smart sections of Boston pointed to the left side of a boulevard and said, "The 'nice' people live there," And then, pointing to the right side, he added ironically, "No one has ever been able to find out who lives here." The same is true of New York; between the two sides of a given street, you have all of space.

9. New York is half-way between a pedestrian's and a driver's city. You do not go for walks in New York; you fly through it; it is a city in motion. I feel at ease if I walk quickly; if I stop, I get flustered and wonder, "Why am I in this street rather than in one of the hundreds of others like it?" Why am I standing in front of this drug-store, or this Schrafft's or Woolworth branch, rather than in front of any other of these thousands of identical ones?

10. And suddenly pure space looms into view. I imagine that if a triangle could become conscious of its position in space, it would be terrified at the realization of the rigorousness of its defining co-ordinates, but that it would also be terrified to discover that it is merely any triangle, any place. You never lose your way in New York; one glance is enough for you to get your bearings; you are on the East Side, at the corner of 52nd Street and Lexington Avenue. But this spacial precision is not accompanied by any precision of feeling. In the numerical anonymity of the streets and avenues, I am simply anybody, anywhere. No matter where I may be, my position is marked out in longitude and latitude. But no valid reason justifies my presence in this place rather than in any other, since this one is so like another. You never lose your way, and you are always lost.

11. Is it a city I am lost in, or is it Nature? New York is no protection

against Nature's violence. It is an open-skied city. Storms flood its wide streets that take so long to cross when it rains. Hurricanes shake the brick houses and rock the skyscrapers. They are announced formally over the radio, like declarations of war. In summer, the air vibrates between the houses; in winter, the city is flooded, so that you might think yourself in some Parisian suburb flooded by the Seine, but in America, it is only melting snow.

12. Nature weighs so heavily on New York that this most modern of cities is also the dirtiest. From my window I see thick, muddy papers, tossed by the wind, flitting over the pavement. When I go out, I walk in a blackish snow, a sort of puffy crust the same colour as the sidewalk, so that it looks as if the sidewalk itself is buckling. From the first of May, the heat crashes down on the city like an atomic bomb. The heat is Evil. People go up to one another and say, "It's murder!" The trains carry off millions of fleeing city-dwellers who, on descending from the train, leave damp marks on the seat, like snails. It is not the city they are fleeing, but Nature. Even in the depths of my apartment, I am open to attack from a mysterious and secretly hostile Nature. I feel as though I were camping in the heart of a jungle crawling with insects. There is the wailing of the wind, the electric shocks I get each time I touch a doorbell or shake a friend's hand, the cockroaches that scoot across my kitchen, the elevators that make me nauseous and the inextinguishable thirst that rages in me from morning till night. New York is a colonial city, an outpost. All the hostility and cruelty of Nature are present in this city, the most prodigious monument man has ever erected to himself. It is a light city; its apparent lack of weight surprises most Europeans. In this immense and malevolent space, in this rocky desert that will tolerate no vegetation of any kind, millions of brick, wooden and reinforced concrete houses, that all look as if they are about to fly away, have been constructed.

13. I like New York. I learned to like it. I become accustomed to its massive groupings and its long vistas. My eyes no longer linger over the façades in quest of a house which might, by some remote chance, not be identical with the others. My eyes immediately slip by to the horizon to look for the buildings lost in fog, mere volumes, merely the sky's austere framework. One is rewarded when one has learned how to look at the two rows of apartment houses which, like cliffs, line a great artery; their mission is completed down there, at the avenue's end, in simple, harmonious lines; a scrap of sky floats between them.

14. New York reveals itself only at a certain height, a certain distance, and a certain speed; these are not the pedestrian's height, distance or speed. This city looks amazingly like the great plains of Andalusia—monotonous when travelled over on foot, magnificent and changing when seen from a car.

15. I learned to like New York's sky. In European cities where roofs are

low, the sky crawls close to the earth and seems tamed. The New York sky
is beautiful because the skyscrapers push it back, very far over our heads.
Pure and lonely as a wild beast, it guards and watches over the city. And
it is not only a local protection; one feels that it stretches out into the distance over all America; it is the whole world's sky.

16. I learned to like Manhattan's avenues. They are not sober little
walks closed in between houses, but national highways. The moment you
set foot on one of them, you understand that it has to go on to Boston or
Chicago. It fades away outside the city and the eye can almost follow it
into the country. A wild sky over parallel rails, that, more than anything
else, is New York. When you are at the heart of this city, you are at the
heart of Nature.

17. I had to get used to it, but now that I have, there is no place in
which I feel more free than in the New York crowds. This light, ephemeral
city that looks every morning and evening, under the sun's inquisitive rays,
like a simple juxtaposition of rectangular parallelepipeds, is never oppressing or depressing. You can experience the anguish of solitude here, but
never that of oppression.

18. In Europe, we become atttached to a neighbourhood, to a cluster of
houses or a street-corner, and we are no longer free. But hardly have you
plunged into New York than your life is completely cut to New York's
size. You can gaze down in the evening from the top of the Queens-
borough Bridge, in the morning from New Jersey, at noon from the
seventy-seventh storey of Rockefeller Centre, but you will never be captivated by any of the city's streets, because none of them has a distinctive
beauty of its own. There is beauty in all of them, as all of America's nature
and sky is present in them. Nowhere will you ever have a stronger feeling
of the simultaneity of human lives.

19. New York moves Europeans in spite of its austerity. Of course, we
have learned to love our old cities, but their touching quality for us lies in
a Roman wall that forms part of an inn's façade, or a house that Cervantes
lived in, or the Place des Vosges, or the town hall at Rouen. We like
museum-cities, and all our cities are rather like museums in which we
wander about amidst ancestral homes. New York is not a museum-city,
yet, for Frenchmen of my generation, it already possesses a melancholy of
the past. When we were twenty, around 1925, we heard about the skyscrapers. For us they symbolized America's fabulous prosperity. We discovered them with amazement in the films. They were the architecture of
the future, just as the cinema was the art of the future and jazz the music
of the future. Today we know what to think about jazz. We know that it
has more of a past than a future. It is a music of popular, Negro inspiration, capable of limited development and in a process of slow decline. Jazz
is outliving its day. The talking film has not fulfilled the promise of the silent one. Hollywood is making no headway in a well-worn rut.

20. The war has certainly taught the Americans that their country was the greatest power in the world. But the period of easy living is over; many economists fear a new depression. Thus, no more skyscrapers are being built. It seems they are too hard to rent.

21. The man who walked about in New York before 1930 saw in the big buildings that dominated the city the first signs of an architecture destined to radiate over the whole country. The skyscrapers were alive then. Today, for a Frenchman arriving from Europe, they are already mere historical monuments, relics of a bygone age. They still rear up against the sky, but my mind is no longer with them, and the New Yorkers pass by at their feet without even looking. I cannot think of them without a certain sadness; they tell of an age in which we thought that the very last war had just ended and when we believed in peace. They are already a bit rundown; tomorrow, perhaps, they will be torn down. In any case, their construction required a faith we no longer have.

22. I walk between the little brick houses the colour of dried blood. They are younger than Europe's houses, but their fragility makes them look much older. Far away I see the Empire State or the Chrysler Building reaching vainly toward the sky, and suddenly I think that New York is about to acquire a History and that it already possesses its ruins.

23. That is enough to lend a bit of softness to the world's harshest city.

# Questions

1. In paragraph 1, how does Sartre introduce the contrast he will make the subject of his essay?

2. How does the last sentence of paragraph 2 serve as a transition to paragraphs 3 and 4?

3. Why, in paragraph 5, does Sartre refer to his "near-sighted European eyes"?

4. How, in paragraphs 6 through 8, does Sartre develop the contrast between European cities and New York?

5. In paragraphs 12 and 13 are two apparently conflicting points of view. How does Sartre achieve the transition from one to the other?

6. Paradox is an apparent contradiction, both parts of which are true. List as many paradoxes as you can find in Sartre's essay.

7. How does Sartre use the terms "Nature" and "History" to contrast the essential characteristics of American and of European cities?

8. Argue, on the basis of the essay itself, that a more appropriate subtitle for this selection would be "The Frontier City" rather than "The Colonial City."

9. Since Sartre claims the building of skyscrapers requires a faith we no longer possess, how would you account for the many skyscrapers erected in New

York since Sartre first published his essay? Does this change in the face of New York, an "American" city, in any way invalidate or confirm Sartre's major distinctions?

# Theme Topics

1. Since Sartre's essay is concerned partially with contrasting preconceptions and realities, write an essay in which you contrast your views of a place, perhaps your college.
2. Write an essay in which you show how the physical conditions and the history of a place have conditioned the habits and beliefs of the people living there.

## ·6·

*Alistair Cooke*

## NEW YORK, NEW YORK

*1.* An English novelist came through New York a little time ago and, as all travellers must, brooded awhile about our ways. When he got home he did a radio talk about it. Nothing more would have been heard about it if the script of this talk had not been reprinted in the *New York Times*. It was no sooner out than the ambulances were summoned to handle a rush of high-blood-pressure cases, and the mail-trucks dumped bags of protests on the *New York Times*. From these outcries you would never have guessed that Mr. Priestley had just been a delegate to the United Nations Educational, Scientific and Cultural Organization, and that he was a man chosen to spread light and understanding among us.

*2.* Too bad, said Mr. Priestley, that New York's skyscrapers are not dedicated 'to God or to some noble aspect of communal life' but only to 'buying and selling dividends.' 'Is that so?' asked one correspondent. 'Then let me tell him that the American Bible Society, the American Association of Social Workers, the American Cancer Society, the Medical Society of New York and the British Information Services, to name only a few,' don't buy or sell dividends. Mr. Rockefeller of course might plead guilty, but his conviction would carry the reminder that his skill in these things helped to cure a lot of dysentery and scurvy in tropical places and helped a lot of Englishmen to come to the United States and have the leisure, after their work with microscopes, to share some of Mr. Priestley's feelings about New York. Mr. Priestley conceded that this was 'just a passing thought.'

3. 'It hardly seems worth while holding on to,' snapped this New Yorker.

4. As for the dismal state of the drama in these parts our man referred Mr. Priestley to the theatre pages of the newspapers, 'where he will note many plays he may later see in London.'

5. New York is overcrowded, complained Mr. Priestley. Granted, said the New Yorker, but New York takes to people and likes to crowd them in.

6. I creep into the argument at this point only because I possess a rather dog-eared but still unexpired credential. It is that I have lived in New York steadily—continuously, anyway—for nearly fifteen years; that I came here first as a transatlantic visitor, on money dished out from one of Mr. Harkness's skyscrapers; and that in those days I saw New York much as Mr. Priestley sees it now. I think we were both wrong. And I hope it will throw light on more places than New York if I try to say why.

7. Neither a native nor a traveller can ever be objective about any place on the map. And all we can sensibly discuss is how true for each of them are their feelings about the place. There is a special flow of moods in a traveller. And I think Mr. Priestley now, and I nineteen years ago, were talking more about ourselves than about New York. Because travellers are never the same at home and abroad. They always think they are, but the people you travel among notice pretty soon that you have thrown off your responsibilities to your own country and don't have to take on any of theirs. This is the state of natural anarchy and for some grown-ups is the only time they know again the huge relief of kids when school's out. Travellers, however, once they are no longer young and scampy, feel embarrassed, not to say guilty, about their freedom. They can express it in one of two ways. They can be secretly frightened by the alien life around them and retreat more tenaciously than ever into habits that belong to their country and nowhere else. Hence the cricket clubs in Brazil and Hollywood, which, I have noticed, manage to recruit some Britons who would not be playing cricket at home. I have known Englishmen who in England can take their tea or leave it but who get to insist on it in the United States, precisely because afternoon tea is not a custom of the country.

8. The other reflex looks like the opposite, but deep in the springs of our childish fear it may be only another reaction to the same threat. It is to go out and do with much bravery all the things you do not do at home. Thus the Englishman who becomes a baseball fan or learns to shudder at

Brussels sprouts. This is a plucky show that he is no longer bound by nostalgia or habit to the old life he left behind him.

9. I believe there is a peculiar mythical appeal to Englishmen in the distant prospect of America. It may go as far back as the Elizabethans, the travellers' tales of fat turkeys, gigantic oysters and succulent fruits, the news of an Eldorado begging for settlement. 'Oh My America, my new founde land!' cried Donne, though at that particular moment he wasn't thinking of leaving home. This myth has been modified down the years, until there are at least two or three generations of Britons conditioned by a whole childhood literature about the West, and now by the glittering stereotypes of the movies, and more regrettably by the solid tradition of reporting back to England only what is corrupt or eccentric or scandalous. From this there emerges a modern myth about America, some of which is poetic and true, some of which is a punching-bag for stay-at-homes. The city of New York has come to crystallize the nightmare aspect of this dream country. It becomes a hard and hideous place, with frightening canyons of skyscrapers. Its life is, in Mr. Priestley's words, 'restless . . . in its nightly pursuit of diminishing pleasures. Not a flower,' he moans, 'can blossom on these concrete cliffs.' Well, I am told that in the granite veins of this city, on Manhattan alone, they have found a hundred and seventy varieties of semi-precious stones. Slit into the grey hunk of rock we inhabit there are garnets and amethysts and opals and beryls and tourmalines, and other jewels even less pronounceable. There are still about half as many trees as human beings. And the commonest backyard tree is the ailanthus, which—I hate to tell Mr. Priestley—the Chinese call the tree of heaven.

10. But this doesn't fit in with anything Europeans have been told, and the heck with it. To more Europeans than would admit it, there is always at the back of the mind this neon-lit image of New York as Babylon, where innocence is banished, where anything goes, where everything has its price, where—in the vivacious version current among my schoolmates in England—you rode a perpetual shoot-the-chutes and bounded the waves of pleasure, to the music of Duke Ellington, while at your side snuggled a beautiful girl, beautiful and up to no good.

11. If you think I am romancing about this, let me remind you that the symbol of an island of pleasure, presided over by a beckoning female, is almost a constant of the human imagination. It was Circe in Greece, Izanami in Japan, Semiramis who built Babylon. These, you may say, are only legends. But what is more real and indispensable than the ideas that burst into life from men's imaginations precisely because they do not exist? They express the permanent dissatisfactions of man with his lot, and this particular one relieves the secret fear that, like Marley's ghost, we may be wasting our days on earth weaving chains of bankbooks, files, ledgers, insurance policies.

*12.* When Mr. Priestley calls New York 'Babylon piled on Imperial Rome,' I think he is the victim of this myth. Once you stay and live in this city, you have to admit that it is nothing of the sort. The intelligentsia will claim that New York tries to be the city they would like to despise. But the intelligentsia is the same everywhere and is a poor guide to the real life of cities. And to the people who live this life, the overpowering number of middle-class New Yorkers, who have as much town pride as Leeds or Manchester, there was one sentence of old Jeremiah Priestley's that really hurt: 'The lonely heart of man cannot come home here.'

*13.* No? On Manhattan Island alone (and Mr. Priestley was talking about only one of the five boroughs) there are two million people who won't live anywhere else and wouldn't want to, even after three drinks. New York is their home town. It is not Babylon. It is the place where we rise in the mornings to the clicking of the radiator or the bawling of the downstairs brat. We take in the milk. We descend on the schools with a rush of kisses and a greeting of neighbors. We head for the subway. We hear a great bass reverberate over the island. It is not, as Mr. Priestley might suspect, the trump of doom. It is only the *basso profundo* of the *Queen Elizabeth* going downriver. We spend the day at work, restlessly perhaps to the extent of leaving home for a distant workshop and then at the end of the day reversing the process and leaving the workshop to go home again. Maybe, if it is not slushy or damp, we decide to walk home and watch a copper sun sinking into an El Greco sky over against the Jersey shore. If the skies of New York often lift us, miserable ants that we are, into delusions of grandeur, we will often spot on the corner, as we turn to go in our building, something casual or scurrilous that restores us to the affectionate human scale. On the wall of a bricked-up lot a tiny New Yorker scribbled a typical sentence. 'Nuts,' it said. 'Nuts to all the boys on Second Avenue'—a long struggling pause, then the concession, 'except between 68th and 69th Streets.'

*14.* We come in and we play with the children or bawl them out. We enjoy, if we have any sense, the variety of the people of our town, and there is often some crazy thing to tell. I have daily dealings with a score of Americans whom I shall only identify here as an Italian shoeshine man, a garrulous German elevator man, a warm, wise-cracking Jewish news-agent, and a range of shopkeepers who span the gamut of New York names from Mr. O'Byrne De Witt to Circumstance H. Smith, a Negro with fine manners.

*15.* The thermometer dips overnight and we look forward to tomorrow, when the red ball goes up over Central Park—no signal for revolution this, Mr. Priestley, or even retribution, but the City's cue to tell us there's going to be skating. Whenever we go to the Park and find, say, there's not enough sand in the sand box the children play in, we telephone the office of Mr. Moses, the Park Commissioner. Next morning two attendants come along with replenishing boxes of sand. The city works pretty hard on the organizing of the citizen's play, and in summer there are handball courts to be repaired, there are city band concerts, city outdoor opera, city fish to be fed into the surrounding streams, and swimming for thousands who leap the trains for the vast, city-sponsored lay-out of Jones Beach.

*16.* In the evening, what do we do? Well, I see from a city survey that only one in fifteen of us has ever been in a night-club. We sit and read, or have friends in, listen to the radio or go to lectures, or a movie, play pinochle or checkers or poker, putter with this and that. And ninety-two in a hundred of us begin to go to bed about ten-thirty.

*17.* Our days and months are bound by work, and fun, and quarrels, and taxes, and movies and savings, and children and death and friendship. When we are far from home we think of New York, and it is not Circe with a henna rinse bawling into a night-club microphone. We see in imagination the white steam hissing through the pavements. We smell the fishy smell of the Fulton market, or the whiff of chicory over Foley Square, or the malty brew that hangs around the East Nineties. We recall the Bronx Zoo, and Mercury standing on his muscular thighs over the traffic lights on Fifth Avenue. We see in the mind's eye the magic dioramas of Africa and Hawaii in the Museum of Natural History, or the pink front page of the morning tabloids. We hear of a girl who was loaded with furs and automobiles by a sharpie using absconded funds. Over the transatlantic wires they flash her confession: 'I never knew he was in an illegal business. He told me he was a gambler.' Glory be! We know her for our own.

*18.* Or some dank day in Britanny or Paris, we recall the one day in three or four that is blindingly clear, brilliant as a knight in armour, the sun slashing down the avenues like a sword. On such a day, my cab-driver stopped for a red light at St. Patrick's. And so did a herd of young teenagers before they turned in to say their prayers. Most of them, I should say, were in sweaters of every colour. He leered at their faces and caught their twinkling shapes in the shafts of sunlight. He hit the steering-wheel with his open hand. And said to me, or perhaps to God: 'They come in all shapes and sizes. Yes, sir. Great stuff. Whaddya say, Mac?' He laughed himself silly.

*19.* Restless we *are,* and very small, threading through our canyons. But are we, as Mr. Priestley assures us we are, 'full of unease, disquiet, bewilderment'? Last summer Dr. Gallup found that over ninety per cent of us thought we were happy. Suppose we allow ten per cent for pride or bravado and another ten per cent for Mr. Priestley's transatlantic insight. That still leaves seventy per cent who believe, maybe wrongly, that they are happy. Better let 'em wallow in their ignorance, Mr. Priestley, these placid dopes who don't even know when they're 'deeply bewildered and frustrated.' Whaddya say, Mac?

# Questions

1. What details in paragraph 1 give you the impression that Mr. Cooke does not regard Priestley's view of New York too seriously?
2. Why does Cooke quote the correspondent in paragraph 2?
3. Mr. Priestley's first name is John. Why then does Cooke refer to him in paragraph 12 as "old Jeremiah Priestley"?
4. What is the function of the "No?" at the beginning of paragraph 13 and how effective is it?
5. In view of the essay's point, what is the function of the shifts in the level of diction and the kind of detail he uses? How does his detail differ from Sartre's?
6. How in the following details has Cooke confined himself to meaningful ones —rising to the clicking of the radiator, taking in milk, skating in Central Park, coming home with some crazy story to tell, and the girl loaded with furs who thought her boy friend was just a gambler?
7. How does the last sentence of paragraph 13 restore us to the "affectionate human scale"?
8. What is the function of the contrast between two kinds of travelers in paragraphs 7 and 8? If neither is going to form an accurate picture of what he sees and one is Cooke, isn't Cooke admitting some distortion for his own view here? Why does he do this?
9. Why does Cooke conclude a literate essay with the highly colloquial "Whaddya say, Mac?"

# Theme Topics

1. Alistair Cooke's essay is an excellent refutation of the distorted view of reality that results from a moralizing mind. Write an essay refuting another distorted view, perhaps of teenagers, or drinking, or a novel, a movie or a play.
2. Write an essay with the thesis that we see everything with either the distortion of our own prejudices or the limitations of our own insights.

## ·7·

*Laurence Sears*

# LIBERALS AND CONSERVATIVES

*1.* It is one of the significant facts of our time that there is a growing
concern with the meaning of political conservatism, and a dissatisfaction
with the way that the term is popularly used. To a large degree both "liberal" and "conservative" are today little more than honorific terms used to
give a comfortable glow of satisfaction, or else epithets designed to destroy the influence of those with whom we disagree. But even though the
concepts are blurred, nonetheless one assumption is held in common, that
*either* one *or* the other is the true belief, and that, although we may tolerate the opposite and mistaken view, *we* hold the truth and must be ready
to do battle for it. It is the right versus the wrong. But there is another position which holds: (1) that it is one of the urgent tasks of our time to get
these terms sharply defined; and (2) that when we do so, we will find that
each position holds both a profound and a partial truth. That view needs
re-examination today.

*2.* One of the difficulties that lie in the path of clear definition arises
from the fact that we have largely forgotten our own political tradition.
The picture often drawn of the conservative does not correspond with the
features of men like Burke in England or James Madison or John Adams
in this country. This is not surprising in the light of the fact that there
have been so few clear-headed and consistent conservatives in this country in the last century that we have forgotten what they look like, grown
contemptuous of their contribution, and identified them with the reactionary (as fatal a blunder as to identify the liberal with the radical). We are
continually faced with this danger of identifying the conservative with
men of our own time who are striving to get back to the good old days,
who are worshiping at the shrine of the economic Gods of the things as
they were, and who would formulate a program entirely around such policies as the reduction of taxes, the removal of economic controls, and the
cessation of any attempt to break up monopolies. But this is a travesty of
our tradition and confirms Reinhold Niebuhr's contention that contemporary American conservatism is little more than a decayed form of nine-

teenth-century liberalism. It is time that we rescued this word "conservative," and gave to it something of the meaning and dignity that it once had.

3. By way of comparison and contrast, it might be well to look briefly at the tradition of liberalism, of which Jefferson is the outstanding example among the founding fathers. All political philosophies rest back ultimately upon an assumption about human nature. Madison recognized this when he wrote: "What is government itself, but the greatest of all reflections on human nature?" Jefferson was perfectly explicit at this point—he believed profoundly in the potential rationality of man. Hence the appeal to reason by facts was his answer to all political problems. "Enlighten the people generally, and tyranny and oppressions of body and mind will vanish like evil spirits at the dawn of day." Here is the faith of the liberal; men can be appealed to through their intelligence, and in the light of what is wise, they can in the long run be trusted to act not solely in terms of their narrow self-interest, but on behalf of that which is good for all.

4. It is worth noting that it is because of this belief in the reasonableness of man that liberals have to a large extent rejected the necessity of force. L. T. Hobhouse saw this when he declared that it was of the essence of liberalism to oppose the use of force since it was the basis of tyranny.

5. A second characteristic of Jefferson was his deep concern with the rights of man. It was not an accident that it was he who wrote the Declaration of Independence with its insistence upon the fact that all men are endowed by their creator with the inalienable rights of life and liberty and the pursuit of happiness. As time went on he stressed freedom of speech as the central right in any democracy. Here again was his faith that men could be trusted with such freedom and that the state would be the stronger for it. "If there be any among us who would wish to dissolve this union or to change its republican form, let them stand undisturbed as monuments of the safety with which error of opinion may be tolerated where reason is left free to combat it." Finally, there was a commitment on Jefferson's part to the belief that old ways were never good enough. He sometimes loosely phrased this attitude so as to make it seem that he was advocating revolution, when in effect he was stressing the necessity of continually altering the political and social patterns in such a way as to meet the demands of a new day. Like all liberals, he seemed continually to be saying: "Hurry; the hour is very late and our work has just begun."

6. When one turns to the tradition of political conservatism, one inevitably examines the philosophy of John Adams and James Madison, and the first discovery is that, contrary to contemporary notions, theirs is not the position of reactionaries seeking merely to cling to their privilege, property, and power. These men are concerned with the achievement of positive values.

7. As regards their view of human nature, one finds a startling contrast with that of Jefferson. John Adams gives a classic statement:

It is weakness rather than wickedness which renders men unfit to be trusted with unlimited power. The passions are all unlimited; nature has left them so; if they could be bounded, they would be extinct. . . . The love of gold grows faster than the heap of acquisition; the love of praise increases by every gratification, till it stings like an adder, and bites like a serpent; till the man is miserable every moment when he does not snuff the incense. Ambition strengthens at every advance, and at last takes possession of the whole soul so absolutely that a man sees nothing in the world of importance to others or himself but in his object.

Nor is this lack of faith in the rationality of men confined to those who are uneducated. The élite are mistrusted as much as the masses. Education is no answer to irrationality and greed. John Adams was suspicious of both groups alike—

The more knowledge is diffused, the more the passions are extended, and the more furious they grow. . . . The increase and dissemination of knowledge, instead of rendering unnecessary the checks of emulation and the balances of rivalry in the orders of society and constitution of government, augment the necessity of both. . . . Bad men increase in knowledge as fast as good men; and science, arts, taste, sense, and letters are employed for the purposes of injustice and tyranny as well as those of law and liberty; for corruption as well as virtue.

8. Because of his lack of faith in the possibility of a rational appeal to the disinterested behavior of men, his primary concern was with the fact of power. Here is the core of the conservative philosophy, as true in England and on the Continent as it has been in this country. Though it is possible to define power in terms either of coercion or of persuasion, the distinction remains. It is a matter of emphasis. Both sides would agree that the ideal situation is where power is delegated under maximum conditions of persuasion and with a minimum of pressure and force. But the liberal believes that his ends can be largely achieved through persuasion, while the conservative believes that persuasion is inadequate and coercion is inevitable. The play of contending groups seeking power for the achievement of their ends has always been the dominant concern of men like Adams, and they have sought to understand not only its source but also its effect. Adams would wholeheartedly have agreed with Lord Acton in his insistence that power always corrupts and absolute power corrupts absolutely. Because of his conviction that this was the effect of power, he was concerned to find the means of distributing and balancing it so that no group or man should hold an inordinate amount. Since we cannot depend upon rational and disinterested behavior, the balance of power is the only answer to the selfishness of men. As John Randolph phrased it, "You may

cover whole skins of parchment with limitations, but power alone can limit power."

9. It was James Madison, the man who had more influence in the drafting of our Constitution than anyone else, who formulated the patterns which have become an integral part of our political life, even though we are scarcely conscious of the philosophy which lies behind them. He started with a recognition of the existence of factions within society which he believed were based upon economic interests. The most common and durable source of factions has always been the various and unequal distribution of property. "Those who hold and those who are without property have ever formed distinct interests in society." It is startling to realize that at this point he was not far from the position of Marx as to the economic basis of politics; in his conviction that men are motivated primarily by their economic interests. But from then on he broke drastically with the Marxian philosophy. Whereas Marx believed that the history of the world lay in the struggle between classes, where one class must inevitably destroy the other, Madison did not believe that it was possible to give to all men the same economic interests, no matter what the economic structure might be, and insisted that any such attempt to remove factions would inevitably destroy liberty. And liberty was always his supreme value. Since, therefore, you cannot remove the causes, you must control the effects, and that can only be done in one of two ways.

10. In the first place, by a check upon the people's direct control over their government. It was because of this that he sought so strenuously for the system of checks and balances which lies at the heart of our Constitution. In the second place, he believed in extending the sphere of interests, of expanding the number of factions and thereby taking in a greater variety of interests, thus giving an effective voice to all.

11. In summarizing this conservative philosophy in order to see more clearly its relevance in our own time, it is redundant to do more than mention the lack of faith in man, which was at its heart. There was little faith in men, either the common people or the aristocracy. Most men are seen as selfish when their interests are involved and many are potentially corrupt. One is reminded of the closing lines of the ballad "Frankie and Johnnie":

> This story has no moral
> This story has no end
> This story only goes to show
> That there ain't no good in men.

Viereck, to whom we are indebted for reminding us of the conservative tradition, has emphasized this fact of human frailty; of the extent to which men are prone to sin and selfishness, and has recognized that this was the foundation of the conservative position.

*12.* In the second place, because of this mistrust, the conservative has been determined to distribute and balance power. John Adams said, ". . . every project has been found to be no better than committing the lamb to the custody of the wolf, except the one which is called the balance of power. . . ." Power naturally grows because human passions are insatiable, but that power alone can grow which is unchecked, which has no equal power to control it.

*13.* Contemporary psychology has made an interesting contribution to this analysis of the meaning of power and its relation to democracy. James Marshall has written recently a brilliant article[1] exploring the meaning of power for a theory of democracy. He starts with an insistence that one cannot understand democracy without reducing it to the various elements of power. He goes on to point out that to "exercise power of any nature over people is to that extent to deny or relieve them of responsibility and that such denial limits their personalities, their opportunities for growth, and is the source of immaturity." Hence for him "the measure of a people's democracy is the extent of its freedom from dependence," for dependence has as its corollaries submissiveness and apathy, which are the denial of the whole spirit of democracy. "Freedom from dependence is requisite to maturity." His test of political democracy, therefore, is the freedom from dependence of its people, and its necessary condition is the diffusion of power.

*14.* In the third place, this conservative philosophy means an acceptance in bluntest terms of pressure politics. In fact, the question is raised as to what other politics there are. The definition of politics as the art of who gets what, when and how is widely accepted. Again it is worth reminding ourselves that the differences between the conservative and the liberal are matters of emphasis; each recognizes the need for persuasion as well as the facing of power by power. Perhaps an illustration will make clearer the distinction. We have in this country many hundreds of thousands of migrant workers who are, politically speaking, the forgotten men. As we face this obvious injustice, the liberal would seem more likely to depend upon an appeal to those who do have political power to share it with those without, trusting to the reason and decency of men to see how grossly unfair this situation is. I suspect that the genuine conservative would spend little time in such an appeal—rather he would try to see the migrants organized so that they could make an effective demand upon the body politic.

*15.* Such a philosophy implies that the basic economic conflicts of society must always remain. Any political kingdom of heaven where the lions and the lambs lie down together is not likely to transpire, and the philosophy of the Marxian that it is possible to remove these tensions by the de-

[1] *Democracy in a World of Tension:* A Symposium prepared by UNESCO, pp. 214-227.

struction of one class is seen to be obvious nonsense, if, of course, one places any value whatever on liberty. This is a hard fact to face. We would like to get rid of the tensions of society. In some cases we will, but essentially any vital society is one which will contain multiple tensions, differences, and interests. As Tannenbaum has put it,[2] "Conflict, strife, divergence, difference of interest and opinion over many things for many reasons, and in varying degrees of intensity, are the conditions of social peace. The conflicting processes of democracy are consistent with and essentially a part of the stresses and strains of life itself." The emphasis lies upon the democratic *process* rather than upon any specific goals. Once again we must remind ourselves that the conservative is not uninterested in justice or in equality, but rather that every achievement is but one step in an endless process which is itself the condition of growth, vitality, and hope.

16. A fourth characteristic of the conservative faith is its emphasis upon expediency rather than upon ultimate rights or principles. An illustration might be drawn from the career of Woodrow Wilson. When he faced the close of World War I, he formulated his famous Fourteen Points, among which was the self-determination of small nations. This was an appealing principle but many came to question whether it did not do more harm than good. The conservative would have been suspicious of any such principle and would certainly have been more likely to seek for adjustments which were at least possible, even though something less than ideal. There is less of a glorious vision held out by the conservative than by the liberal, but there is a sturdy insistence that starting with where we are we may achieve something better even though it falls far short of the dreams of men. There is the belief that although we may never achieve the day when all men may have life and liberty and be free to seek their happiness, yet we will make progress toward this achievement.

17. No specific economic system is necessarily assumed but there is a general approach to our economic problems. The liberal tends to look for that system which will give a maximum of equality and justice based upon deliberate adjustment of means to ends. The conservative tends to trust much more the invisible hand operating through the play of economic forces upon each other than he does to any conscious planning or centralized control. Once again it is the process rather than the results which are important. Galbraith, in *American Capitalism*, has approached the economic problem in such a spirit. He starts with a concern about the extent of governmental power and defends, as an alternative, a system where private economic power is held in check by the countervailing power of those who are subject to it. Politically, this means that the primary role of the state is to give assistance in the development of such balances of power. Controls, in other words, would be largely automatic, the result

2 "Balance of Power in Society," in *Political Science Quarterly*, December, 1947.

of the balancing of forces rather than the deliberate and conscious control by those in power.

*18.* Finally, it needs to be said that the conservative, although he tends to move more slowly, is not committed to the preservation of a *status quo*. He is not, as was said before, a reactionary, and the distinction needs to be kept clear. He too would move ahead, though more slowly. The great English conservative, Burke, characterized the role of the statesman as "the disposition to preserve and the ability to improve," and any genuine conservative would agree.

*19.* The contribution of, and commitment to, democracy on the part of the liberal is widely recognized, but we must understand clearly what the liberal means. Henry L. Stimson, himself one of the few consistent conservatives we have had in America in modern times, defined the liberal position acutely, even though he disagreed with it. Speaking of the dominant philosophy of the early years of the twentieth century, he said:

> The theoretically easy and emotionally satisfactory solution to the failures of democracy lay in "more democracy." If government was inefficient or subservient to powerful private interests, turn it back to the people. This solution, which was in direct line with the traditions of Jeffersonian democracy, found its expression in the movement for the direct election of senators and the direct primary and more exuberantly in the campaigns for the initiative, the referendum, and the recall. . . . The people had lost control of their government because its complexities provided a smoke screen for the manipulation of bosses and private interests; then let the people themselves take charge.[3]

Give information to the people, put into their hands direct control of their government, and ultimately our problems will be solved. The liberal would define democracy, in other words, as that system of government where freely elected representatives are directly responsible to an informed and participating citizenry.

*20.* The conservative definition is different, though only in emphasis. Since the primary function of government lies in the maintenance of balance between influences, democracy will mean the distribution and therefore the minimization of power. It is not the mere tossing of direct and unlimited power into the hands of individual citizens, but a balance between competing groups which is the condition of political health, and compromise between varying interests becomes the condition of liberty. In fact a conservative might very well define democracy as that system of government where no one gets all he wants.

*21.* But if there are differences of definition, there is certainly as great a commitment to democracy on the part of the conservative as there is with the liberal. However, here again the reason differs. It is less his faith

---

[3] *On Active Service in Peace and War,* by Henry L. Stimson and McGeorge Bundy, Harper and Brothers.

in the goodness of human nature than it is his conviction of the depravity of man which lies behind his devotion to democracy. Niebuhr has said that "Man's capacity for justice makes democracy possible but man's inclination to injustice makes democracy necessary." Thus, by profoundly different roads the liberal and the conservative come to the democratic conclusion that sovereignty must be vested in all the people. In this conviction that we the people hold the ultimate authority, the two philosophies unite.

22. It is not difficult to see the strength of the liberal position. Throughout the entire tradition there has been a deep concern with human rights, with justice and equality, with a recognition of the need for change. Old ways have never been good enough. What is difficult for the liberal is to recognize that there have been weaknesses associated with his faith, that all too often people operating as groups cannot be depended upon to be disinterested, that only under specific conditions are they rational in their decisions. And most of all, the liberal has tended to forget that politics is always power politics and to ignore not merely the source of power but its effect. There were not many liberals who thought Hitler could be met with reason, but there have been many who thought that Stalin could be dealt with on a basis of reasonable compromise. They would have been wiser to have listened more carefully to the warning of Lord Acton.

23. To a liberal, the weaknesses within the conservative's position seem equally obvious. Conservatives forget that man can, under certain conditions, act rationally. There is the tendency for them to be contemptuous of what they call "the masses"; to ignore the fact that there is more than coercive power involved in politics, that men have been and will be moved by the power of ideas and ideals. In their concern with the immediate, they have tended to forget that without a vision the people perish, and all too often they have been complacent in the face of the denial of the rights of man, and smugly timid in the presence of injustice. To be sure, John Morley spoke as a liberal with little respect for the Tory position, but there was truth in his criticism of the Conservative—

. . . with his inexhaustible patience of abuses that only torment others; his apologetic words for beliefs that may not be so precisely true as one might wish, and institutions that are not altogether so useful as some might think possible; his cordiality towards progress and improvement in a general way, and his coldness or antipathy to each progressive proposal in particular; his pygmy hope that life will one day become somewhat better, punily shivering by the side of his gigantic conviction that it might well be infinitely worse.[4]

24. So much for the weakness of the conservative position, but its strength should be equally clear. Based on a recognition of the fact that men do not often act as wisely as the situations demand—that always

---

[4] Quoted by Randall in *The Making of the Modern Mind*, Chapter 7.

groups are in conflict as they strive to further separate interests, they know that any effective democracy will be based upon an adequate dividing and balancing of strength. Such a philosophy must recognize the obvious fact that, as John Adams said, "power follows property" and that therefore if power is to be distributed, property must be more equitably held. Such an honest and consistent conservatism would be far more than a façade behind which are to be protected the property, privilege and power of a minority.

25. To one who thinks of himself as a liberal, the value of such a political philosophy committed to the preservation and extension of democracy and consistently and honestly devoted to the balancing of pressures through effective organization of all interest groups would seem to be obvious. It would certainly be a profoundly constructive force in American political history.

26. The reaction from the liberalism of recent years is obvious. In part it is due to the loss of confidence in human nature that has accompanied the spectacle of the past decade. In part it is a recognition of the fact that persuasion has seemed relatively impotent during these years, and that power could only be challenged by power. Whatever the reasons, the swing of the pendulum is carrying us away from the liberal faith. The danger is that this may not bring us a genuine conservative movement. Instead we may not only destroy the profound contributions of the liberal; we may mistake a decadent reactionism for a constructive conservatism. The radical and the reactionary should have little place in our society, but the liberal *and* the conservative we desperately need.

# Questions

1. Sears proposes to define sharply the terms liberal and conservative. How does his opening paragraph indicate the method (comparison and contrast) he will use as a central technique in his essay?

2. How does Sears use the technique of comparison in paragraph 2?

3. How does Sears' use of negative definition in paragraph 2 prepare the ground for paragraphs 3 through 10?

4. Can you, by considering the techniques Sears uses, determine whether he is a "liberal" or a "conservative"?

5. Does Sears agree with Niebuhr's position or refute it?

6. In paragraphs 3 through 5 Sears sets forth the tradition of liberalism. What technique of comparison and contrast does he use to clarify this tradition?

7. In paragraphs 6 through 8 Sears turns to the conservative tradition and illumines it through the technique of contrast. What elements does he make central in his contrast?

8. What is the "profound and partial truth" held by the liberal and that held by the conservative? Consider in your answer the contrasts he establishes in the thinking of each on the following subjects: human nature; expediency; democracy; pressure groups.

9. In paragraph 22 Sears refers to Lord Acton who said that power corrupts and absolute power corrupts absolutely. What relevance has the allusion?

10. What distinctions does Sears imply between the liberal and the radical on the one hand and the conservative and the reactionary on the other?

# Theme Topics

1. Write an essay contrasting Sears and Niebuhr on the subject of conservatism.

2. Write a statement of Sears' distinctions which you then criticize, enlarge or qualify.

3. Compare and contrast two or three abstractions you know something about from politics (socialism and communism), literature (classical, romantic, realistic), music (classical and romantic) or art (abstract and representational).

· 8 ·

*Clifton Fadiman*

## EGGHEADS, INTELLECTUALS, IDEOLOGUES, HIGHBROWS

1. Several serious observers, including David Riesman and Jacques Barzun, have recently concluded that the current fashionable attack (for there *is* an attack and it *is* fashionable) on the man of ideas is a kind of inverted tribute to him. Mr. Barzun writes: "We think we are riding a wave of anti-intellectualism because certain such men are attacked; the fact is they are attacked because they have become important." Perhaps, if I may employ a nonintellectual expression, the intellectuals never had

it so good. But let us not fall into an occupational weakness of intellectuals by pushing this notion too far.

2. If the mind-man needs further consolation he can always remind himself that the "wave of anti-intellectualism" is nothing new. If it is a wave of the present, it is also a wave of the past and will doubtless be a wave, one wave, of the future. (It is part of the nature of the intellectual to think anything tolerable if he can only convince himself that it is recurrent.)

3. In 1876 Senator Simon Cameron helped to quash the nomination of Richard Henry Dana to the Court of St. James's with the comment, "One of those damn literary fellers." Long before that, in 1837, Emerson had looked forward wistfully to the time when "the study of letters shall no longer be a name for pity," thus pointing indirectly to the dismal state of affairs in his own era. Indeed the American intellectual was in the doghouse during most of the nineteenth century. As I have elsewhere suggested, it is as though we were rebelling against Papa. For the fact is that this country was set going by a bunch of calm-eyed intellectuals, otherwise known as the Founding Fathers, and we have remained a bit embarrassed ever since by the cerebral immaculacy of our birth.

4. It is also true that our nineteenth century was in no position to make good use of men of ideas. We had a continent to conquer and a bare century in which to conquer it. The nonintellectual's "Let's do it" or "Let's get it" made more apparent sense than the intellectual's "Once we've done it and got it, what have we got and what do we do with it?" That was Thoreau's question and for some time he kept on talking to himself.

5. It was only with the closing of the frontier, roughly in 1914, that the intellectual's question, even when his answers were wrong, became obviously useful. The election of Woodrow Wilson marked a hesitant return (on a lower level) to the kind of mentality of which Jefferson, Madison, and the two Presidential Adamses provide early examples. Ever since then the intellectual has played an increasingly conspicuous role in our national life. He has suffered that normal consequence of conspicuousness, abuse. He irritates us, not because we dislike him (we are merely *told* that we dislike him or should dislike him) but because we need him. It is natural enough to resent a support of which all along we had supposed ourselves independent.

6. I suggest that we can slightly decrease the sum total of bad temper in our land by separating four words. Currently these are violent words, full of unnecessary or carefully built-up heat. Let's see whether we can induce them to simmer down. The four words are intellectual, ideologue, highbrow, and egghead.

7. An intellectual is simply a man in whom is writ large what makes you and me specifically human—an interest in the rational mind and an ability to use it. As such he is nothing more nor less than the most important kind

of person the human race can produce. One early intellectual figured out the use of fire. A recent one figured out how the universe hangs together. Between Ugug and Einstein stretches a long line of intellectuals, great and small, able to supply nothing but ideas. These ideas, however, make everything else possible—including attacks on intellectuals, for these very attacks depend on a series of ideas dreamed up by such visionaries as the inventors of the alphabet or those nineteenth-century lunatics who worked out the equations that have made radio and television possible. In a way the rest of us, no matter how industrious or transiently useful, are parasites living luxuriously on the work of a handful of superior minds. In my own case Hertz and Marconi for some years paid my insurance premiums and grocery bills.

8. As I pointed out above we don't need these impractical chaps all the time. We merely need them in a general long-term way in order to keep the human race human. To attack intellectuals, as thus defined, is simply to attack what is best, after our immortal souls, in ourselves. It is a form of attempted suicide. Those in whom the death wish is unusually strong, such as Hitler, are precisely those who *really* hate intellectuals, as opposed to those who merely *think* they hate them.

9. An ideologue may be defined as a mad intellectual. He is not interested in ideas, but—almost the exact contrary—in one idea. When he erects this idea into a system and forces the system to give birth to a way of life, confusion often results, usually to his great surprise. Two examples are Robespierre and Lenin.

10. The intellectual is occasionally blamed for the work of the ideologue, which is like condemning the psychiatrist because he and the patient are both involved in the same thing, mental illness. The ideologue is often brilliant. Consequently some of us distrust brilliance when we should distrust the ideologue, a fact of which the ingenious inventors of the egghead were well aware. The ideologue is often more persuasive than the intellectual because he has a simpler line of goods to sell and never questions its value. Sometimes he achieves great success by *attacking* the real intellectual—Bryan is a good example.

11. The intellectual level of any society must be measured not merely by its ability to produce intellectuals but also by its ability to distinguish them at once from ideologues. On this double scale England ranks high, Germany low.

12. Both intellectuals and ideologues are pros. Both live by ideas, just as the farmer lives by the soil. But the highbrow is not a pro. He doesn't usually work at the job, any more than the audience works at the writing of a play. He takes in and enjoys what intellectuals, particularly artists, produce. This is his avocation. His vocation may be anything. I have known highbrow house painters, and I once taught a class of highbrows of whom few made a living with their brains.

*13.* Like the lowbrow, the highbrow is limited in his conversation. He will stick to Sartre or Stravinsky or Picasso because they are what his temperament permits him to enjoy. The lowbrow will stick to Yogi Berra or Jackie Gleason for exactly the same reason. The highbrow *may* also be an intellectual; he is more often simply an appreciator. Asked what books he would take to a desert island George Bernard Shaw replied, "Some blank notebooks." There spoke the true intellectual. Equipped only with blank notebooks the highbrow would go crazy—though less rapidly than would the nonhighbrow.

*14.* The highbrow is never an ideologue. Indeed, as with Bryan and Stalin, it is the lowbrow who is more apt to be also the ideologue.

*15.* Except in the statistical sense there is nothing queer or eccentric about the highbrow. There are fewer cassowaries than there are sparrows, but both are equally part of nature, though the cassowary seems a little queer because we don't see him around much. At the moment we have fewer highbrows than lowbrows, but it is easy enough to conceive of a society in which the reverse would be the case.

*16.* Of course there are phony highbrows but, oddly enough, rather few of them. I have, when permitted, spent a good deal of time with highbrows, and I should say that what makes them difficult at times is not insincerity but rather the contrary—the wholeheartedness of their devotion to a fairly narrow range of interests. The same is true of the lowbrow, whose avocational passion for baseball or comic strips is as purehearted as it is boring—to the nonlowbrow only, of course.

*17.* The egghead is not an intellectual, not an ideologue, not a highbrow. He is not any of these things because he doesn't exist. He is a political invention or, better, a cartoon character. The egghead, I have been informed by both Republicans and Democrats, was constructed during the 1952 presidential campaign out of imaginary yolk and albumen. Certain qualities of those very different types—the intellectual, the ideologue, the highbrow—which some average voters could be persuaded they disliked, were built up into a synthetic figure who was then christened egghead.

*18.* The whole egghead controversy, now that its political utility is decreasing, is beginning to reveal its basic absurdity. By this time it should be apparent that Dwight Eisenhower is not the folksy, cracker-barrel tintype the publicity boys projected on their magic-lantern screen. He is a man of dignity and substance, perfectly open to the impact of large ideas and capable, as he has shown, of rapid mental growth. It should also be apparent that Adlai Stevenson is no utopian visionary, but a practical, highly intelligent politician, in the British sense of the word. He is not an intellectual as, let us say, Bertrand Russell is an intellectual. He is certainly not an ideologue. And I can't perceive that he's much of a highbrow. The worst you can say of him is that he's well educated, but even that is a risky charge to make. Mr. Dulles is well educated too. It is true, however, that Mr. Stevenson's gift for language is considerable and that Mr. Eisenhower's is limited. This rather minor difference (hardly a matter on which one's vote should turn) was blown up, it would appear, by a group of able propagandists and given currency through the picturesque and meaningless term, egghead.

19. It would be a good thing to drop the word from the national vocabulary. It would be a good thing, too, to use the words intellectual, ideologue, and highbrow with some feeling for their different meanings.

20. One of the most diverting oddities about the egghead controversy is the notion, presently entertained by some bewildered elements of the electorate, that Democrats are by nature cursed with an excess of intellect and Republicans are by nature blessed with an excess of good old-fashioned American horse sense. The charge against the Democrats can be refuted easily enough by recalling that once one of their Presidential aspirants was given to such highly intellectual behavior as wearing a coonskin cap while campaigning. As for the Republicans, one hates to dig up old scandals but it is a fact that again and again they have produced leaders like John Hay and Henry Cabot Lodge, Sr., who, in addition to being able politicians, were also high-grade intellectuals. It took a good deal of probably deliberate clowning on Theodore Roosevelt's part to obscure the embarrassing fact that he was one of the best-read Americans of his day.

21. The truth is that intellectuality does not to any extent link with either party—nor indeed with any general political orientation. Liberals are not more intellectual than conservatives. As a matter of fact, at the moment more interesting political ideas are being produced by conservatives, though twenty years ago the reverse happened to be the case. In the long run intellectuals are above party. That does not mean that they are bad citizens or snobbish folk. It means only that they think most easily and fruitfully in long-haul abstractions, whereas party politicians (and the human race generally) think most easily in short-haul concretions.

22. Just as we should try to dissociate the intellectual from the political liberal, so we should try to dissociate him from the nonconformist. He *may* be a nonconformist—Bertrand Russell was one, at one stage of his great career. He may be a conforming nonconformist—Galileo was one. And he may be in many respects an outer conformist—as, to take two very different illustrations, Gladstone and Santayana were. But I should like to remark that few types are more typically *non*intellectual than the village atheist, the reefer-smoking jive musician, Norman Mailer's *Deer Park* sex lunatics, and the Union Square soap-boxer: nonconformists, every man jack of them.

23. Nor should the intellectual be confounded with the pessimist. The most genuinely cheerful and well-integrated men I know are those whose lives are concerned mainly with ideas. Equations kept Einstein equable.

Indeed this very equanimity may be one reason why some of us distrust intellectuals. Our distrust masks unconscious envy. As was pointed out in sublimer terms almost two thousand years ago, things, which you can hold in your hand, let you down, whereas ideas, which you can hold only in your head, don't. But the dismaying fact is that most of us own more things than we do ideas.

24. I am less convinced than I was some years ago that our civilization is endangered by the assault on the intellect. I do feel that at the moment the idea man is not generally admired. He is certainly not well-paid. Yet a great deal of attention is being given him, and, as we noted above, this may well be the first sign of a rise in his prestige. The next step may be a general and more thoughtful recognition of the probability that the twenty-first century is going to need him in vast quantities.

25. At the moment I am more inclined to think that the danger (probably a passing thing) lies less in a distrust of ideas by the naturally non-intellectual than in a distrust of ideas by the naturally intellectual. We are not in peril because George F. Babbitt prefers Marilyn Monroe to Dostoevski. But we are in peril when good minds, minds that might energize our educational system or raise our religious experience above decorous joinerism, bow down, in cynicism or fatigue, to lesser gods.

26. One weakness of intellectuals is that they are fascinated by any fresh idea. The current attack on them, though its roots are deep in time, does have a certain spurious novelty. Some intellectuals—and remember, we can't spare a single one—have been taken in by it. My experience has been that few Joe Doakeses talk cynically about the intellect but that a fairish number of presumptive or potential intellectuals do. It is no longer considered bright to be bright. Thus I am less disquieted by the instigated hooliganism of those whom some highbrows call primitives than I am by the occasional defection of those whom some lowbrows call sophisticates. It is when an intellectual like Donald MacLean turns into an ideologue, when a man cut out to be a brilliant economist becomes a public-relations expert—it is then that one gets a hollow feeling. For mere stupidity can never kill the man of ideas. If he should die, it will be by suicide.

# Questions

1. In paragraphs 1 through 5 what does Fadiman accomplish and by what devices?
2. In paragraph 6 Fadiman indicates that four words have been used more or less indiscriminately and that these are loaded words. Why does he wish to discriminate?

3. Why does Fadiman say that an "intellectual" is "nothing more nor less than the most important kind of person the human race can produce"? Are not intellectuals by definition somewhat unworldly? In this complex modern world, is the really important man not the man of action? Why?

4. Why does Fadiman choose "Ugug" and Einstein as the beginning and end of his line of intellectuals? Does Ugug humanize the word "intellectual" more than Einstein could?

5. Why in paragraph 7 does Fadiman call the inventor of the alphabet a visionary? Why does he refer to the inventors of radio and television as lunatics?

6. What devices of contrast and definition, in short of discrimination, can you find in the essay?

7. In discriminating among the four terms, why did Fadiman begin with the intellectual? What advantages would result from his starting with each of the others? What disadvantages?

8. In paragraph 12 Fadiman refers to the intellectual and the ideologue as pros, but he classes the highbrow as an amateur. Why?

9. Why in paragraphs 21 through 23 does Fadiman try to dissociate the intellectual from the liberal, the nonconformist, and the pessimist? Does he mean that the intellectual is conservative, conformist, and optimistic?

10. Fadiman says in paragraph 24 that the idea man is not generally admired. Does he feel that this is dangerous? Why?

11. Why does Fadiman close his essay with a paragraph on the weakness of the intellectual?

12. What does the last sentence of paragraph 25 mean?

13. Why does Fadiman say that if the intellectual should die, not stupidity but suicide will bring his death?

# Theme Topics

1. Employing the techniques that Fadiman uses distinguish the following terms: non-conformist, beatnik, juvenile delinquent, and artist.

2. Distinguish between *pride* and *vanity*, establishing where natural and healthy traits become excessive.

## ·9·

## *David Daiches*

# EDUCATION IN A DEMOCRATIC SOCIETY

1. The other day I heard a professor of education at an important Mid-western university give a talk to a group of his colleagues on his experiences in Thailand, where he had been for over a year advising on education. In shocked tones he told his audience that in Thai schools the pupils have to pass an examination before they can be moved up from one grade into the next. He added that the American team out there were trying to remove this dangerously undemocratic practice, and so enable a much higher percentage of pupils to move up each year and complete their schooling. Thus everybody would be educated, not only a tiny few, with the happy consequence that the people would be fortified against the seductions of Communism. At another point in his talk he said that Thai education was too "intellectual" and not sufficiently practical and vocational: no garage mechanic in Thailand was really competent to do automobile repairs. (Whether the kind of technical education which the professor advocated, a kind of education in which Soviet Russia, if the statistics published in the Western press are accurate, leads the world, was also a defense against Communism, he did not say.) In general, he seemed to regard education as either (a) the moving up a ladder to the top, regardless of what was done or learned in the process of moving, or (b) training to do a particular job of work, which will be the pupil's means of livelihood in afterlife.

2. Educators in Britain and America would agree that education must be democratic and it must be useful. Of course these are sensible ideals; few would claim that education ought to be undemocratic and useless. The difference between the British and the American approach lies in their respective definitions, or at least implicit definitions, of democracy and usefulness as applied to education. A democracy, in British eyes, has the duty of providing free education to every child according to his "age, ability, and aptitude" (in the words of the Education Act of 1944). The

more democratic the educational system, the more the schools will strive to give to each pupil, whatever his class or economic background, that education which encourages and makes full use of whatever abilities he possesses.

3. As for the *usefulness* of education, there is still much general feeling in England that the function of education is to teach the pupil how to spend money, not how to make it. That is one reason why the British are having such difficulty in persuading youngsters to go in for the sciences rather than the humanities; the latter are concerned with the art of living, with books and music and good conversation, with the training of "a gentleman or noble person in virtuous and gentle discipline" (as Spenser put it in explaining the object of his *Faerie Queene*). A surprising number of British middle-class parents still consider that kind of education the "best," and they want their children to have it. So if—to oversimplify—the American definition of the democratic and the useful in education leads to the contradictory ideals of equality of curriculum and of promotion on the one hand, and vocational training according to a future job on the other, the British definition of the same terms leads to the equally contradictory ideals of training according to individual abilities and aptitude on the one hand, and on the other to a general preference for the "arts side" over the "science side."

4. This, of course, applies to secondary education rather than to the colleges and universities, and each attitude is rooted in history in a complex manner. (The Harvard report on *General Education in a Free Society* discusses the historical background of the American situation with considerable insight.) I begin with a reference to secondary education deliberately, because the whole pattern of differences between the British and American academic scenes derives from basic differences in their attitudes to secondary education. The British have always put far more emphasis on secondary education; the large majority of the educational reforms of the last hundred years in England have been concerned with the elementary or secondary education, and in the last quarter-century and more all concern about the curriculum, about "general education in a free society," about distinguishing between pupils of different abilities within the same age group, about language teaching, aptitude testing, teaching methods, and so on, has been concentrated on education at the secondary level.

5. The schools, not the colleges and universities, have been the main objects of controversy between humanists and scientists and between all other opposed or professedly opposed schools of thought about education. On the whole, the universities have gone quietly on training the relatively few people sent up to them from the top forms of the secondary schools. My impression is that in America many more of these problems have been discussed with reference to the colleges (e.g., the question of "freshman English" and of basic literature courses) and there has been more excite-

ment among serious and responsible educators about the college curriculum than about earlier educational levels (e.g., the Hutchins experiment in Chicago, the Harvard report, the continuous experimentation in so many liberal arts colleges).

6. The reason for this appears to me to be that while in America the ideal is that everybody should move right up to the top of the educational ladder—that is, right up to the university—the British ideal is that it is the object of secondary education, going ideally up to the age of seventeen or eighteen, to train the complete man, or as much of him as is available in any given individual, and that education beyond that level is for a minority with special gifts or special purposes. American secondary education is in some respects committed by its interpretation of the democratic doctrine to going at the pace of the slowest, and thus the high school curriculum is watered, leaving much basic knowledge to be acquired at college. British secondary education, which has chosen the other horn of the dilemma and tends to go at the pace of the quickest, being geared really to the needs of the brightest pupils and giving them every kind of special treatment and "forcing," puts the main burden of education onto the secondary level. The British schoolboy who is at all bright will work harder between the ages of, say, thirteen and eighteen than he will ever need to work at the university.

7. I remember myself with what immense relief I left school at Edinburgh to proceed to the university. Now at last I was free to do only the subjects that really interested me, and no longer hard hours of homework every evening on a great variety of subjects. I had had five years each of mathematics, physics and chemistry, and Greek; and six years each of English, history, and Latin, together with three years of French and two of German. (In recent years there has been an increasing tendency to specialize in the last two years of school, and concentrate on two or three subjects in preparation for university scholarship examinations.) And these subjects were all learned cumulatively, building each year on what was learned the year before, not taken in isolated units as is so often done in American high schools. I am not saying that my education was ideal—it was fiercely competitive, and it did very little for the large number of pupils who could not keep up with the competitive pace set by the bright pupils at the top, and it also was sometimes too formal and mechanical—but it was *solid*. It told me nothing about how to be a good citizen, but it taught me some basic skills, including several languages and more mathematics and sciences than is generally taught in the first and sometimes the second year of American colleges. It also taught me how to write essays, one of the most stressed features of British secondary education.

8. There is a good case against this kind of secondary education. American educators would say that it penalized heavily the non-academic type of pupil, and that the whole curriculum was conceived in too narrowly

academic terms. The first charge is certainly justified; the second can be
debated. The Education Act of 1944 tried to meet the first charge by distinguishing between different types of schools, or of curricula within a
single "comprehensive" school, at which a child was entitled to a free education. There was the academic "grammar school" for those who showed
an aptitude for it, and "modern" schools or technical schools for the others. The sifting is done by the now famous—or notorious—"eleven plus" examination.[1] Thus the non-academic students are taken care of in a much
more general and flexible kind of education, but not at the expense of the
progress of the traditional "bright boy." The trouble is that the "grammar
school" (which alone leads to the university) still enjoys the highest social
prestige, and middle-class parents want to send their children there
whether they qualify for a free place or not. The Education Act promised "parity of esteem" between the different types of school and of
teacher; but it has not worked out that way. The British know very well
that the grammar school type of education is for the brightest pupils—in
the traditional sense of that term—and it is they who are being trained as
an elite to do the most responsible of the nation's jobs. And, naturally,
they want their children to be among the elite.

9. All this is by way of explanation of the often noted fact that the British student generally knows more when he comes up to the university than
the American college freshman does. If going to college is a democratic
right, then education must be spread out in order to leave something for
the college to do for those who have no aptitude for higher learning. At
Indiana University, where I am at the moment, the freshman and even
sophomore courses in language and literature represent, in both content
and level of teaching, what is taught in Britain two or even three years before the end of secondary education. And yet this is not altogether true.
For the American freshman and sophomore has often a kind of curiosity,
a provocative, uninformed but insistent "show me" attitude, an insistence
on pitting his own limited experience against his teacher's knowledge,
that makes the American college classroom at these levels very different
indeed from the classroom of either the British grammar school or the
British university.

10. "Why did Ulysses spend all that time in getting home to his wife
after he left Troy?" a freshman asked one of my colleagues here the other
day, during a lesson on the Odyssey. "If he'd really wanted to get home
quickly, he would have managed it. I think he was kidding himself when
he said he was so anxious to get back." This is naïve, but it is not stupid,
and it is not the kind of thing an English schoolboy would ask. The bright
English schoolboy would mug up the standard works on the Homeric
world and turn out a sophisticated essay on "Homer and the Heroic Age"

[1] An examination (in English and arithmetic, together with intelligence and aptitude
tests) taken as a rule when the child is eleven years old or a little over.

based on a conflation of half a dozen books he had read in the school library; but it would never occur to him to ask whether Ulysses was kidding himself when he expressed his anxiety to return home quickly. The English schoolboy tends to relate knowledge to other knowledge, in order to form an elegant pattern (the bright essay being always the standard of achievement in the humanities); the American freshman wants to relate everything he reads or is told to his own experience. The latter as a rule has no sense of history or of form or of the *otherness* of different times and places; the former often lacks a sense of personal implication in what he studies.

11. To British—and indeed European—eyes, American education seems to waste some of the best learning years, at least for the brighter pupils, and to postpone until an unnecessarily late stage the essential core of education. But there is another side to the picture. The better American students are less blasé and work harder than their British opposite numbers, and by the end of their four undergraduate years have often achieved a kind of sophistication in terms of their subject which is at the opposite pole from the attitude revealed by the freshman's question about Ulysses. That kind of sophistication, which is particularly noticeable among the brighter students of literature, is consciously won by hard effort; it is (and I am talking of the best students) often the prelude to the use of specialized techniques in graduate work. The English student, building on his school training, will develop his accustomed skill with a kind of leisurely elegance and often, by the time he gets his degree, is not fundamentally any better educated than when he left school. He is likely to be less ambitious, more skeptical, less fundamentally serious than the American.

12. In such fields as literature, philosophy, and history, at least, the bright British student will most appreciate the lecturer who plays with ideas cleverly and suggestively, but the bright American student resents that: he wants the truth, or the right methods, and no nonsense. "Do you believe in that view of literature you were developing in your lecture this morning?" a Cornell student once asked me. I said that I did not, but I thought it was interesting to play with the idea a little and see where it led us. He replied, almost angrily, that if I did not believe the theory to be true I should not waste my own and the class's time discussing it at such length; it was sheer verbal gymnastics, and the students were there to *learn,* not to be played with. "Is C. S. Lewis's book on sixteenth-century literature a book to be read?" a graduate student asked me the other day at Indiana. I replied that it was a fresh and sometimes brilliant reading of the texts of the period, and though I quarreled sharply with some of the views expressed in it, I thought it a most stimulating book, well worth reading. "But will it give me a proper view of the period?" she persisted. "I don't know," I replied. "I'm not sure what the 'proper' view of the

period is. Read it and make up your own mind about it." This answer was not regarded as satisfactory.

*13.* I often have the feeling that the American student, who works hard and learns fast, never has time to enjoy his work. I am thinking especially of those who go on to graduate study. They have learned an immense amount by the time they enter graduate school and have often surpassed in knowledge and in methodological skill their British counterparts, but they have the air of never having lived long enough with their subject. A graduate student in English literature will rush on to do research on Marvell's imagery before he is really at home in English literature and really inward with its traditions and achievements. And there will be even less likelihood of his having any true sense of European culture as a whole. The reason for this is partly, of course, that he is American and not English or European, and to this extent it is unfair to take a European literature as an example. But there is another reason, too: his whole education —his *real* education, that is, which began with college—has been too rushed. No one, I might suggest in passing, ought ever to take a course in such a subject as "Masterpieces of World Literature," for one can only become acquainted with the great tradition in world literature by leisurely reading over a long period of time. It is true, as modern educational psychologists so often point out, that adults learn faster than children and that there is no point in pushing youngsters to learn over a long period of time what concentrated effort can teach them later in life. But I think there is something to be said for spreading things out,[2] for slow and cumulative learning. The hard-working, conscientious, somewhat puritanical American graduate student often outstrips his British opposite number at surprising speed; but in the process he grows old faster, too, and he also learns to regard his subject as a field to be covered rather than as a body of knowledge to be explored and relished.

*14.* The dangers on the British side are, however, just as great, though different. They differ not only from the American dangers I have described but also among different British universities. For there are three main types of British universities, as distinct from each other in methods, organization, and traditions as British universities as a whole are from American universities. The three groups are: Oxford and Cambridge; the four Scottish universities; and the English universities other than Oxford and Cambridge—the so-called "provincial" universities. Oxford and Cambridge are unique in that the tutorial system rather than lecture courses provides the essential teaching, and although, at least in Cambridge, the complex relationship between the colleges and the university is showing signs of strain

[2] This may appear to contradict what I said earlier about the excessive spreading in American high school teaching, but that spreading is not the result of steady cumulative study but of scattered and fragmented study.

in some quarters, the main business of these universities remains the cultivation of the student's mind through regular discussion with a tutor or
supervisor. This of course leaves the student at the mercy of the particular
tutor he is landed with, and the student often has no contact at all with
the most distinguished teachers of his subject in the university. The dangers of the Oxford and Cambridge system are dilettantism, a tendency, at
least in arts subjects, to value a superficial "brilliance" above knowledge
and deep understanding, and a disparity in tutorial possibilities. But the
advantages are enormous, and my own conviction—having studied and
taught at Edinburgh and Oxford, and taught at Chicago, Cornell, and
Cambridge—is that it is still the best system that has been worked out.

15. It should be realized that the large majority of present-day students
at Oxford and Cambridge as well as at other British universities have their
fees and maintenance paid for by grants or scholarships of one kind or
another. No one who can enter a university is now prevented by lack of
means from going there. But no one who has not had the grammar school
type of education can qualify for university entrance, and a pupil who has
just missed qualifying for a free grammar school education at eleven plus,
and whose parents are too poor to send him to a fee-paying grammar
school or boarding school, may in this way be deprived of a university
education. But, apart from this problem (and it is a serious one), it is true
to say that the economic factor in sending one's children to a university is
today less of a worry to British parents than it is to Americans.

16. The shifting social patterns at Oxford and Cambridge have had
some interesting results. Before the war it was the regular thing for the
good student to do the bulk of his reading in the vacations, and to spend
his terms discussing what he had read or amusing himself. But now more
and more students take jobs during vacations (not during term time,
which would be unthinkable, for the whole concept of university education demands that during term the student remain free to respond to all
the currents flowing in a university community, of which formal teaching
is only one). This means that they have not the time to do vast amounts
of reading between terms, and this is shifting the whole pattern of teaching. The tendency to get by on a minimum of reading, often that done at
school, and to compensate by wit and elegance for lack of knowledge, presents a real danger. To avoid that, tutors and supervisors (they are "tutors"
at Oxford and "supervisors" at Cambridge) are growing more inclined to
give out weekly reading assignments in the American manner.

17. The Scottish universities are in general organized more like the
American. Teaching is done in formal lecture courses, and there is an air
of serious professionalism about it. The student who takes an honors degree in English at a Scottish university is expected to plough through the
whole of English literature. There is a great deal of reading of factual
lectures to large classes, and a general conservatism in the form and con-

tent of the teaching. A degree in English literature at Cambridge is intended to produce a cultivated young man who has read and thought enough about a selected number of literary works to have an understanding and an appreciation of the values and varieties of literature. In Edinburgh, the objective is to train a future teacher of English, and a thorough, solid training is provided. The Cambridge degree in an arts subject is not designed primarily as a professional qualification, but at a Scottish university it is so designed.

18. Too much teaching at Scottish universities is plain dull. And even if the professor himself (there is only one person with the title of professor in each subject at British universities, and in Scotland and the provincial universities he runs the department) gives the large survey course to first-year students, the advantages of contact with the great man are often nullified by the routine way in which he fulfills his task. Here the liveliness and informality of American college teaching would be a welcome innovation.

19. The English provincial universities suffer from the fact that the best students still tend to be siphoned off to Oxford or Cambridge, and also from certain confusions about the nature and function of the teaching they provide. They fall sometimes between the two stools of Scottish professionalism and Oxford amateurism. But they have some of the best men in the country—particularly the younger men—on their staffs and, in spite of the large formal lecture course which carries much of the burden of teaching, there is often liveliness and experiment as well as a very high level of academic competence, notably in certain scientific subjects. But the shadow of Oxford and Cambridge still hangs over these universities, making both staff and students uncertain of themselves and sometimes restless and discontented. Kingsley Amis's novel *Lucky Jim* is set in a provincial university, and the masochistic clowning through which Amis reveals that the graces of the older universities are not for him betrays an almost spiteful withdrawal from "culture" that is a disturbing symptom.

20. Finally, a word about administration. Britain has always resisted the notion that university administrators should form a separate class from scholars and teachers, and has almost always drawn its heads of universities from the world of scholarship. In Oxford and Cambridge, the vice-chancellor, who is the administrative head of the university, is drawn from the heads of colleges, each one serving only for a few years. The real work of administration on the academic policy level is done by committees of members of the faculty. Details of financial administration and the execution of policy as it affects the daily routine of university life are alone in the hands of permanent administrators. No single person in any British university has the power that a college dean has in America: such power is vested in the hands of faculty boards. There is no such thing as a board of trustees. Government money comes to the universities through the Uni-

versity Grants Committee, which consists of vice chancellors of the various universities, and whose function is to get government money without government control. The device works well, and the British universities, which are extremely jealous of their independence, are proud of the machinery they have set up for getting money from the Treasury without strings. No questions about universities can be asked in Parliament because no minister is responsible for them (the Minister of Education has no responsibility for or control over the universities).

21. But administration by committees has some serious drawbacks. It is a heart-breaking job to carry an organizational reform through, especially in Oxford or Cambridge, because the agreement of so many diverse persons must first be secured. A few older members of committees can successfully postpone any innovation almost indefinitely. No one in Britain could possibly do the sort of thing that, say, Hutchins did at the University of Chicago. The result is that traditions are maintained and continuity preserved, but often at the price of the indefinite postponement of needed reforms and the minimizing of profitable experimentation.

22. The American tendency to put non-academic administrators at the head of universities seems to me dangerous, though the sheer size of many of the American universities makes some aspects at least of administration a highly technical problem. And then there is the fund-raising aspect. But most of all it seems to me that the vitality and flexibility of American universities, which are their greatest assets, are seriously threatened by the I.B.M. machine. I am astonished at the degree to which procedures are *gleichgeschaltet* in a large state university and the human element ignored in order that the machines may be kept rolling.

23. The chief glory of the American university lies in the fact that it is not really a university in the British sense at all, but a vast collection of educational machinery, good and bad, elementary and advanced, in which the most exciting and fruitful educational activities can go on, as well as the silliest and most useless. To it come students of every degree of ability and with all kinds of interests, and amidst all the proliferating courses and degrees each, if he is lucky, can find something to help him in one way or another. A British university, on the other hand, is an institution of higher learning intended for the minority of citizens who are interested in and can profit by higher learning. That, at least, is the ideal. Now the American system, which results from the belief that ideally every citizen should go to a university and that the university should therefore have something to offer in every sphere and at every level, needs a rigid administrative machinery to hold it together. If in the British system the high objectives of the universities are often found to be in contradiction with professional needs on the one hand, and with ideals of urbane gentlemanly culture on the other, in the American system the freedom and variety which its very

lack of discrimination makes possible are threatened by growing administrative rigidity.

24. Underlying the many differences between the educational systems of the two countries are some significant differences in social philosophy. The British believe that the function of higher education is to train an elite who will perform the most responsible and demanding tasks of the nation. The more democratic you are the more you will strive to make sure that you will choose this elite on the basis of innate ability and aptitude alone, regardless of any other consideration, economic, social, or personal. Equalitarianism is preached by a large section of the British Labor party, and it is in fact being rapidly achieved. But it is *economic* equalitarianism: Britain today is probably the country with the most economic equality in the world. You train the best people to do the most important jobs—but you mustn't pay them any more than you pay people with a less academic education doing more routine jobs.

25. In spite of the well-meant efforts of left-wing politicians and educators, some kind of social snobbery is bound to continue in England, for it is bound up with the whole concept of different education for different abilities. But this snobbery will be a matter of kind of job, kind of accent (which in England largely depends on where you are educated), and level of intellectual interest, rather than of birth, ancestry, or income. How far an elite of this kind can maintain its dominance without economic superiority or stability of social background remains to be seen.

26. In America, where the paradox of equality and individualism has long existed (equality demands that everybody get the same education, which is anti-individualistic, but it also demands that each person get ahead in a free enterprise economy, which produces extreme economic individualism), the relation between education and prestige is much more complicated. Suspicion of the intellectual in politics, which strikes a European as such a characteristic feature of the American scene, is bound up with the traditional national refusal to regard differences in quality of education as necessary or desirable. But as America becomes more and more the leader of the democratic world, the problem of training informed and responsible citizens to fill the crucial jobs in domestic and international affairs may well force American educators into accepting in both theory and practice greater differences in education than have hitherto been regarded as desirable.

27. Suspicion of the intellectual in politics is a feature of a self-contained and more or less isolated country; it may well be that America's role in world affairs today will have a greater long-term effect on the pattern of American education than any of the democratic theorists have had. It was Britain's need for an elite to run a vast empire in the nineteenth century that produced the basic pattern of modern British education, and

America, which has taken over so many international responsibilities from the older powers, may have to modify its own educational system in order to fulfill them adequately.

# Questions

1. What use of irony does Daiches make in paragraph 1? How does this irony prepare you for his own views?
2. Does Daiches accept either the (a) or (b) in paragraph 1?
3. Daiches points out that both English and American educators would agree that education must be "democratic" and "useful." How does Daiches then contrast American and English views of "democratic" and "useful"?
4. Does Daiches appear to agree with either view of "democratic" or "useful" education?
5. What reason does Daiches give for beginning with secondary education rather than going directly to college or university education?
6. Daiches seems to say in paragraph 5 that there is a controversy between scientists and humanists. Is the controversy central to his argument? Does he adopt one or the other side?
7. In paragraph 6 Daiches contrasts the two ideals of education. What is the essential difference?
8. What function does paragraph 7 serve in relation to the distinctions made in paragraph 6?
9. Is Daiches' secondary education at Edinburgh implicitly contrasted to American high school education? On what grounds? Does Daiches believe his training was superior?
10. If he had a superior training, why in paragraph 8 does he appear to argue against it?
11. Why, in paragraph 10, does Daiches use the rather peculiar word "conflation" in speaking of the "bright English schoolboy"? Why is the American student's naive question preferable to the English schoolboy's sophisticated essay?
12. In paragraphs 13 and 14 Daiches suggests the dangers inherent in each system. What are they? Which are more acute?
13. Daiches presents details on three methods of university instruction in Great Britain in paragraphs 14 through 19. What contrasting elements does he stress? Why? Which system does he appear to favor?
14. Why in paragraph 22 does Daiches say that it is dangerous to put non-academic administrators at the head of universities? How can an I.B.M. machine threaten a university?
15. What sequence of topics relevant to education in the United States and

Great Britain does Daiches follow in his essay? How would you justify or challenge each transition in the sequence? What topics, if any, ought to have been explored but were not?

16. What is the chief glory of the American university? How does its system stem from American social philosophy? Do you agree with Daiches? Disagree? Why?

# Theme Topics

1. Compare and contrast methods of education you have observed in high school and college.
2. Write an essay in which you compare and contrast two ways of doing something, noting certain advantages of each: for example, two methods of quitting smoking, two modes of travel, two attitudes toward life, two teaching techniques, two ways of raising children.

# *Classifying*

## ~ III ~

## DIVISION AND CLASSIFICATION

WHEN WE TRY TO UNDERSTAND an idea or an event, either we think of it as it relates to other, larger ideas or events; or we try to understand it by examining its component parts. We *divide* a group of things and we *classify* a single object. For example, a student might be classified as of A, B, C, D, or F quality. A group of students might be divided into these categories.

We understand politics better by dividing problems into foreign and domestic; we classify a given problem under one or the other category. Dividing a complex operation makes it easier for us to understand. Doctors recognize and classify the symptoms of ailments under categories too complex for the layman to understand, but meaningful to them in diagnosis and treatment.

Three general rules have proved valuable in dividing and classifying.

1. The basis for the division must be clear and consistent. We might divide paintings by technique into oils, gouaches, and water colors (though this division is hardly exhaustive). It would be incorrect, however, to divide paintings into oils, gouaches, water colors, and portraits. The basis for the division would no longer be consistent.

2. The classifications must be mutually exclusive. Overlapping classifications such as cars divided into U.S., foreign, and expensive create not clarity but confusion. The category "expensive" does not exclude the other two nor do they in turn exclude it.

3. The classification must exhaust the possibilities of the principle without becoming tedious. The approximate accuracy necessary to make a point clear is all that is required. The classification, long part of our Navy's folklore, of people who whistle into two groups—boatswain's mates and damned fools—makes its point unambiguously. But division of automobiles, say, into those of American and European manufacture does not exhaust the existing universe of automobiles, even though for some purposes these two groupings might be adequate. A third category of "Other" would exhaust the possibilities; a listing of every country producing automobiles as distinguished from those that only manufacture

parts and from those that only assemble parts manufactured exclusively abroad, would be unnecessarily tedious.

The same topic can be divided and classified in any number of ways. For purposes, let us say, of understanding the problem of high school dropouts, we might divide and classify them according to their reasons for leaving school. Some leave willingly, some against their will. Each category might then be subdivided one or more times: namely, those who leave willingly (a) because of feelings of social failure, (b) because of personal distress over their academic program, (c) because of greater attractions outside, for example, marriage, a lucrative job, or both. Those who leave unwillingly do so as a result of pressures from either outside or inside the school; they are expelled, must support someone financially, or become gravely ill. But this division might seem too complex. A different division of the same subject on the same basis—reasons for leaving—is then possible. A simple three-part division might be preferable: (1) deficiency in intelligence and ability, (2) psychological pressures, (3) practical and economic pressures. Notice that these three reasons, though the categories are themselves mutually exclusive, might all apply in any particular case; a single student might drop out of high school for all three reasons, but the classification is not thereby invalidated. It still serves its function in enabling us to analyze any particular case.

The principle of simple enumeration, employed by Robert Gorham Davis to present kinds of logical fallacies, is enormously useful in organizing categories whose interrelations are not always clear. The principle it self, however, carries little logical force since a listing of categories, to say nothing of citing examples, seldom exhausts all possibilities of classes and subclasses—and certainly not of individual instances—in a given subject. On the other hand, a set of exhaustive classes, which Russell Lynes describes with some minor reservations, is well illustrated in his tripartite division of all Americans of his day on the basis of their tastes. This set also shows the complexity that occurs in assigning, perhaps quite arbitrarily, definitive characteristics to each class. Finally, repeated use of the principles of division and classification, when applied to analysis and definition with the skill of Philip Wheelwright, makes intricate subjects easier for the writer to explain and for the reader to understand.

## ·10·

*Robert Gorham Davis*

# LOGIC AND LOGICAL FALLACIES

### UNDEFINED TERMS

1. The first requirement for logical discourse is knowing what the words you use actually mean. Words are not like paper money or counters in a game. Except for technical terms in some of the sciences, they do not have a fixed face value. Their meanings are fluid and changing, influenced by many considerations of context and reference, circumstance and association. This is just as true of common words such as *fast* as it is of literary terms such as *romantic*. Moreover, if there is to be communication, words must have approximately the same meaning for the reader that they have for the writer. A speech in an unknown language means nothing to the hearer. When an adult speaks to a small child or an expert to a layman, communication may be seriously limited by lack of a mature vocabulary or ignorance of technical terms. Many arguments are meaningless because the speakers are using important words in quite different senses.

2. Because we learn most words—or guess at them—from the contexts in which we first encounter them, our sense of them is often incomplete or wrong. Readers sometimes visualize the Assyrian who comes down like the wolf on the fold as an enormous man dressed in cohorts (some kind of fancy armor, possibly) gleaming in purple and gold. "A rift in the lute" suggests vaguely a cracked mandolin. Failure to ascertain the literal meaning of figurative language is a frequent reason for mixed metaphors. We are surprised to find that the "devil" in "the devil to pay" and "the devil and the deep blue sea" is not Old Nick, but part of a ship. Unless terms mean the same thing to both writer and reader, proper understanding is impossible.

### ABSTRACTIONS

3. The most serious logical difficulties occur with abstract terms. An abstraction is a word which stands for a quality found in a number of dif-

ferent objects or events from which it has been "abstracted" or taken away. We may, for instance, talk of the "whiteness" of paper or cotton or snow without considering qualities of cold or inflammability or usefulness which these materials happen also to possess. Usually, however, our minds carry over other qualities by association. See, for instance, the chapter called "The Whiteness of the Whale" in *Moby-Dick*.

4. In much theoretic discussion the process of abstraction is carried so far that although vague associations and connotations persist, the original objects or events from which the qualities have been abstracted are lost sight of completely. Instead of thinking of words like *sincerity* and *Americanism* as symbols standing for qualities that have to be abstracted with great care from examples and test cases, we come to think of them as real things in themselves. We assume that Americanism is Americanism just as a bicycle is a bicycle, and that everyone knows what it means. We forget that before the question, "Is Arthur Godfrey sincere?" can mean anything, we have to agree on the criteria of sincerity.

5. When we try to define such words and find examples, we discover that almost no one agrees on their meaning. The word *church* may refer to anything from a building on the corner of Spring Street to the whole tradition of institutionalized Christianity. *Germany* may mean a geographical section of Europe, a people, a governing group, a cultural tradition, or a military power. Abstractions such as *freedom, courage, race, beauty, truth, justice, nature, honor, humanism, democracy,* should never be used in a theme unless their meaning is defined or indicated clearly by the context. Freedom for whom? To do what? Under what circumstances? Abstract terms have merely emotional value unless they are strictly defined by asking questions of this kind. The study of a word such as *nature* in a good unabridged dictionary will show that even the dictionary, indispensable though it is, cannot determine for us the sense in which a word is being used in any given instance. Once the student understands the importance of definition, he will no longer be betrayed into fruitless arguments over such questions as whether free verse is "poetry" or whether you can change "human nature."

## NAME-CALLING

6. It is a common unfairness in controversy to place what the writer dislikes or opposes in a generally odious category. The humanist dismisses what he dislikes by calling it *romantic;* the liberal, by calling it *fascist;* the conservative, by calling it *communistic.* These terms tell the reader nothing. What is *piety* to some will be *bigotry* to others. *Non-Catholics* would rather be called *Protestants* than *heretics.* What is *right-thinking* except a designation for those who agree with the writer? Social security measures become *creeping socialism;* industrial organizations, *forces of reaction;*

investigation into communism, *witch hunts;* prison reform, *coddling;* progressive education, *fads and frills.* Such terms are intended to block
thought by an appeal to prejudice and associative habits. Three steps are
necessary before such epithets have real meaning. First, they must be defined; second, it must be shown that the object to which they are applied
actually possesses these qualities; third, it must be shown that the possession of such qualities in this particular situation is necessarily undesirable.
Unless a person is alert and critical both in choosing and in interpreting
words, he may be alienated from ideas with which he would be in sympathy if he had not been frightened by a mere name.

### GENERALIZATION

7. Similar to the abuse of abstract terms and epithets is the habit of
presenting personal opinions in the guise of universal laws. The student
often seems to feel that the broader the terms in which he states an opinion, the more effective he will be. Ordinarily the reverse is true. An enthusiasm for Thomas Wolfe should lead to a specific critical analysis of
Wolfe's novels that will enable the writer to explain his enthusiasm to
others; it should not be turned into the argument that Wolfe is "the greatest American novelist," particularly if the writer's knowledge of American
novelists is somewhat limited. The same questions of *who* and *when* and
*why* and under what *circumstances* which are used to check abstract
terms should be applied to generalizations. Consider how contradictory
proverbial wisdom is when detached from particular circumstances. "Look
before you leap," but "he who hesitates is lost."

8. Superlatives and the words *right* and *wrong, true* and *untrue, never*
and *always* must be used with caution in matters of opinion. When a student says flatly that X is true, he often is really saying that he or his family
or the author of a book he has just been reading, persons of certain tastes
and background and experience, *think* that X is true. If his statement is
based not on logic and examination of evidence, but merely reproduces
other people's opinions, it can have little value or relevance unless these
people are identified and their reasons for thinking so explained. Because
many freshmen are taking survey courses in which they read a single work
by an author or see an historical event through the eyes of a single historian whose bias they may not be able to measure, they must guard against
this error.

### SAMPLING

9. Assertions of a general nature are frequently open to question because they are based on insufficient evidence. Some persons are quite

ready, after meeting one Armenian or reading one medieval romance, to
generalize about Armenians and medieval romances. One ought, of
course, to examine objectively as many examples as possible before making a generalization, but the number is less important than the representa-
tiveness of the example chosen. The Literary Digest Presidential Poll, sent
to hundreds of thousands of people selected from telephone directories,
was far less accurate than the Gallup Poll which questioned far fewer
voters, but selected them carefully and proportionately from all different
social groups. The "typical" college student, as portrayed by moving pictures and cartoons, is very different from the "average" college student as
determined statistically. We cannot let uncontrolled experience do our
sampling for us; instances and examples which impress themselves upon
our minds do so usually because they are exceptional. In propaganda and
arguments extreme cases are customarily treated as if they were characteristic.

10. If one is permitted arbitrarily to select some examples and ignore
others, it is possible to find convincing evidence for almost any theory, no
matter how fantastic. The fact that the mind tends naturally to remember
those instances which confirm its opinions imposes a duty upon the
writer, unless he wishes to encourage prejudice and superstition, to look
carefully for exceptions to all generalizations which he is tempted to make.
We forget the premonitions which are not followed by disaster and the
times when our hunches failed to select the winner in a race. Patent medicine advertisements print the letters of those who survived their cure, and
not of those who died during it. All Americans did not gamble on the stock
exchange in the twenties, or become Marxists in the thirties, and all Ver-
monters are not thin-lipped and shrewd. Of course the search for negative
examples can be carried too far. Outside of mathematics or the laboratory,
few generalizations can be made airtight, and most are not intended to be.
But quibbling is so easy that resort to it is very common, and the knowledge that people can and will quibble over generalizations is another
reason for making assertions as limited and explicitly conditional as possible.

## FALSE ANALOGY

11. Illustration, comparison, analogy are most valuable in making an
essay clear and interesting. It must not be supposed, however, that they
prove anything or have much argumentative weight. The rule that what
is true of one thing in one set of circumstances is not necessarily true of
another thing in another set of circumstances seems almost too obvious to
need stating. Yet constantly nations and businesses are discussed as if they
were human beings with human habits and feelings; human bodies are

discussed as if they were machines; the universe, as if it were a clock. It is assumed that what held true for seventeenth century New England or the thirteen Atlantic colonies also holds true for an industrial nation of 150,000,000 people. Carlyle dismissed the arguments for representative democracy by saying that if a captain had to take a vote among his crew every time he wanted to do something, he would never get around Cape Horn. This analogy calmly ignores the distinction between the lawmaking and the executive branches of constitutional democracies. Moreover, voters may be considered much more like the stockholders of a merchant line than its hired sailors. Such arguments introduce assumptions in a metaphorical guise in which they are not readily detected or easily criticized. In place of analysis they attempt to identify their position with some familiar symbol which will evoke a predictable, emotional response in the reader. The revival during the 1932 presidential campaign of Lincoln's remark, "Don't swap horses in the middle of the stream," was not merely a picturesque way of saying keep Hoover in the White House. It made a number of assumptions about the nature of depressions and the function of government. This propagandist technique can be seen most clearly in political cartoons.

### DEGREE

*12.* Often differences in degree are more important than differences in kind. By legal and social standards there is more difference between an habitual drunkard and a man who drinks temperately, than between a temperate drinker and a total abstainer. In fact differences of degree produce what are regarded as differences of kind. At known temperatures ice turns to water and water boils. At an indeterminate point affection becomes love and a man who needs a shave becomes a man with a beard. The fact that no men or systems are perfect makes rejoinders and counter-accusations very easy if differences in degree are ignored. Newspapers in totalitarian states, answering American accusations of brutality and suppression, refer to lynchings and gangsterism here. Before a disinterested judge could evaluate these mutual accusations, he would have to settle the question of the degree to which violent suppression and lynching are respectively prevalent in the countries under consideration. On the other hand, differences in degree may be merely apparent. Lincoln Steffens pointed out that newspapers can create a "crime wave" any time they wish, simply by emphasizing all the minor assaults and thefts commonly ignored or given an inch or two on a back page. The great reported increases in insanity may be due to the fact that in a more urban and institutionalized society cases of insanity more frequently come to the attention of authorities and hence are recorded in statistics.

CAUSATION

*13.* The most common way of deciding that one thing causes another thing is the simple principle: *post hoc, ergo propter hoc,"* "After this, therefore because of this." Rome fell after the introduction of Christianity; therefore Christianity was responsible for the fall of Rome. Such reasoning illustrates another kind of faulty generalization. But even if one could find ten cases in which a nation "fell" after the introduction of Christianity, it still would not be at all certain that Christianity caused the fall. Day, it has frequently been pointed out, follows night in every observable instance, and yet night cannot be called the cause of day. Usually a combination of causes produces a result. Sitting in a draught may cause a cold, but only given a certain physical condition in the person sitting there. In such instances one may distinguish between necessary and sufficient conditions. Air is a necessary condition for the maintenance of plant life, but air alone is not sufficient to produce plant life. And often different causes at different times may produce the same result. This relation is known as plurality of causes. If, after sitting in a stuffy theatre on Monday, and then again after eating in a stuffy restaurant on Thursday, a man suffered from headaches, he might say, generalizing, that bad air gave him headaches. But actually the headache on Monday may have been caused by eyestrain and on Thursday by indigestion. To isolate the causative factor it is necessary that all other conditions be precisely the same. Such isolation is possible, except in very simple instances, only in the laboratory or with scientific methods. If a picture falls from the wall every time a truck passes, we can quite certainly say that the truck's passing is the proximate or immediate cause. But with anything as complex and conditional as a nation's economy or human character, the determination of cause is not easy or certain. A psychiatrist often sees a patient for an hour daily for a year or more before he feels that he understands his neurosis.

*14.* Ordinarily when we speak of cause we mean the proximate or immediate cause. The plants were killed by frost; we had indigestion from eating lobster salad. But any single cause is one in an unbroken series. When a man is murdered, is his death caused by the loss of blood from the wound, or by the firing of the pistol, or by the malice aforethought of the murderer? Was the World War "caused" by the assassination at Sarajevo? Were the Navigation Acts or the ideas of John Locke more important in "causing" the American Revolution? A complete statement of cause would comprise the sum total of the conditions which preceded an event, conditions stretching back indefinitely into the past. Historical events are so interrelated that the isolation of a causative sequence is dependent chiefly on the particular preoccupations of the historian. An economic determinist can "explain" history entirely in terms of economic developments; an idealist, entirely in terms of the development of ideas.

### SYLLOGISTIC REASONING

*15.* The formal syllogism of the type,

> All men are mortal
> John is a man
> Therefore John is mortal,

is not so highly regarded today as in some earlier periods. It merely fixes an individual as a member of a class, and then assumes that the individual has the given characteristics of the class. Once we have decided who John is, and what "man" and "mortal" mean, and have canvassed all men, including John, to make sure that they are mortal, the conclusion naturally follows. It can be seen that the chief difficulties arise in trying to establish acceptable premises. Faults in the premises are known as "material" fallacies, and are usually more serious than the "formal" fallacies, which are logical defects in drawing a conclusion from the premises. But although directly syllogistic reasoning is not much practiced, buried syllogism can be found in all argument, and it is often a useful clarification to outline your own or another writer's essay in syllogistic form. The two most frequent defects in the syllogism itself are the undistributed and the ambiguous middle. The middle term is the one that appears in each of the premises and not in the conclusion. In the syllogism,

> All good citizens vote
> John votes
> Therefore John is a good citizen,

the middle term is not "good citizens," but "votes." Even though it were true that all good citizens vote, nothing prevents bad citizens from voting also, and John may be one of the bad citizens. To distribute the middle term "votes" one might say (but only if that is what one meant),

> All voters are good citizens
> John is a voter
> Therefore John is a good citizen.

*16.* The ambiguous middle term is even more common. It represents a problem in definition, while the undistributed middle is a problem in generalization. All acts which benefit others are virtuous, losing money at poker benefits others, therefore losing at poker is a virtuous act. Here the middle term "act which benefits others" is obviously used very loosely and ambiguously.

### NON-SEQUITUR

*17.* This phrase, meaning "it does not follow," is used to characterize the kind of humor found in pictures in which the Marx Brothers perform. It is an amusing illogicality because it usually expresses, beneath its apparent incongruity, an imaginative, associative, or personal truth. "My ancestors came over on the Mayflower; therefore I am naturally opposed to labor unions." It is not logically necessary that those whose ancestors came over on the Mayflower should be opposed to unions; but it may happen to be true as a personal fact in a given case. It is usually a strong personal conviction which keeps people from realizing that their arguments are non-sequiturs, that they do not follow the given premises with logical necessity. Contemporary psychologists have effectively shown us that there is often such a wide difference between the true and the purported reasons for an attitude that, in rationalizing our behavior, we are often quite unconscious of the motives that actually influence us. A fanatical antivivisectionist, for instance, may have temperamental impulses toward cruelty which he is suppressing and compensating for by a reasoned opposition to any kind of permitted suffering. We may expect, then, to come upon many conclusions which are psychologically interesting in themselves, but have nothing to do with the given premises.

### IGNORATIO ELENCHII

*18.* This means, in idiomatic English, "arguing off the point," or ignoring the question at issue. A man trying to show that monarchy is the best form of government for the British Empire may devote most of his attention to the charm of Elizabeth II and the affection her people feel for her. In ordinary conversational argument it is almost impossible for disputants to keep to the point. Constantly turning up are tempting side-issues through which one can discomfit an opponent or force him to irrelevant admissions that seem to weaken his case.

### BEGGING THE QUESTION; ARGUING IN A CIRCLE

*19.* The first of these terms means to assume in the premises what you are pretending to prove in the course of your argument. The function of logic is to demonstrate that because one thing or group of things is true, another must be true as a consequence. But in begging the question you simply say in varying language that what is assumed to be true is assumed to be true. An argument which asserts that we shall enjoy immortality because we have souls which are immaterial and indestructible establishes nothing, because the idea of immortality is already contained in the assumption about the soul. It is the premise which needs to be demonstrated, not the conclusion. Arguing in a circle is another form of this fallacy. It proves the premise by the conclusion and the conclusion by the premise. The conscience forbids an act because it is wrong; the act is wrong because the conscience forbids it.

## ARGUMENTS AD HOMINEM AND AD POPULUM

20. It is very difficult for men to be persuaded by reason when their interest or prestige is at stake. If one wishes to preach the significance of physiognomy, it is well to choose a hearer with a high forehead and a determined jaw. The arguments in favor of repealing the protective tariff on corn or wheat in England were more readily entertained by manufacturers than by landowners. The cotton manufacturers in New England who were doing a profitable trade with the South were the last to be moved by descriptions of the evils of slavery. Because interest and desire are so deeply seated in human nature, arguments are frequently mingled with attempts to appeal to emotion, arouse fear, play upon pride, attack the characters of proponents of an opposite view, show that their practice is inconsistent with their principles; all matters which have, strictly speaking, nothing to do with the truth or falsity, the general desirability or undesirability, of some particular measure. If men are desperate enough they will listen to arguments proper only to an insane asylum but which seem to promise them relief.

21. After reading these suggestions, which are largely negative, the student may feel that any original assertion he can make will probably contain one or several logical faults. This assumption is not true. Even if it were, we know from reading newspapers and magazines that worldly fame is not dimmed by the constant and, one suspects, conscious practice of illogicality. But generalizations are not made only by charlatans and sophists. Intelligent and scrupulous writers also have a great many fresh and provocative observations and conclusions to express and are expressing them influentially. What is intelligence but the ability to see the connection between things, to discern causes, to relate the particular to the general, to define and discriminate and compare? Any man who thinks and feels and observes closely will not want for something to express.

22. And in his expression a proponent will find that a due regard for logic does not limit but rather increases the force of his argument. When statements are not trite, they are usually controversial. Men arrive at truth dialectically; error is weeded out in the course of discussion, argument, attack, and counterattack. Not only can a writer who understands logic show the weaknesses of arguments he disagrees with, but also, by anticipating the kind of attack likely to be made on his own ideas, he can so

arrange them, properly modified with qualifications and exceptions, that the anticipated attack is made much less effective. Thus, fortunately, we do not have to depend on the spirit of fairness and love of truth to lead men to logic; it has the strong support of argumentative necessity and of the universal desire to make ideas prevail.

# Questions

Identify logical fallacies in the statements that follow. Some may contain more than one fallacy as described by Davis.

1. Give me liberty or give me death!
2. Either you agree with me or your position is un-American.
3. Because all urban areas in the United States have a higher incidence of violent crimes than suburban ones, people who live in U.S. cities are more criminally inclined than those who live in its suburbs.
4. No one with such unattractive features could possibly make a good district attorney.
5. Anyone who does not love animals should not be elected to the Presidency of the United States.
6. Of course he is guilty! He is on trial, isn't he?
7. Unless we have effective ordinances to control air pollution in urban areas, it will eventually be impossible for anyone to live in them.
8. A tough and unbending attitude is all we need to solve this crisis. Remember how our ancestors defied the British?
9. Man's tranquility began to be threatened seriously because illuminating gas began to give way to the electric light.
10. The latest figures show that the price of rum in Jamaica rises with the salaries of Presbyterian ministers in Vermont. The WCTU ought to investigate.
11. To the extent a culture devotes its resources to funerary processions and memorials it makes death less real.
12. Why study for my mathematics test? I studied for English and flunked it.
13. I guess my dog is a tiger. After all, he has four feet, a tail, and whiskers.
14. Cigarettes cannot be bad for you. Don't baseball players smoke them?
15. You can not vote for Adams for Senator. He never met a payroll, did he?
16. Franklin D. Roosevelt, who was President when World War II began, must have been responsible for the war.

# ·11·

*Russell Lynes*

# HIGHBROW, LOWBROW, MIDDLEBROW

*"It becomes increasingly difficult to tell who is serious and who is not."*

*1.* My wife's grandmother, the wife of a distinguished lawyer, once declined to dine with the Cartiers of jewelry fame because they were, as she put it, "in trade." Life for grandmother, who lived in a properly elegant but nondescript town house in New York, was relatively simply where social distinctions were concerned. While there are still a few people who think and act as she did, the passage of time has eliminated a great deal of that particular kind of snobbishness from American society. We are replacing it with another kind. The old structure of the upper class, the middle class, and the lower class is on the wane. It isn't wealth or family that makes prestige these days. It's taste and high thinking.

*2.* Edith Wharton's theory that if the taste of the rich could be improved the general level of public taste would benefit has turned out to be a fallacy. The consumers and makers of taste, it appears, cannot be divided according to the conventional social strata. Good taste and bad taste, adventurous and timid taste, cannot be explained by wealth or education, by breeding or background. Each of these plays a part, but there is no longer such a thing as upper-class taste and lower-class taste as there was once supposed to be. In recent years a new social structure has emerged in which taste and intellectual pretension and accomplishment plays a major role. What we see growing around us is a sort of social stratification in which the highbrows are the elite, the middlebrows are the bourgeoisie, and the lowbrows are *hoi polloi*.

*3.* For the time being this is perhaps largely an urban phenomenon, and the true middlebrow may readily be mistaken in the small community for a genuine highbrow, but the pattern is emerging with increasing clarity, and the new distinctions do not seem to be based either on money or on breeding. Some lowbrows are as rich as Billy Rose, and as flamboyant, some as poor as Rosie O'Grady and as modest. Some middlebrows run industries; some run the women's auxiliary of the Second Baptist Church.

Some highbrows eat caviar with their Proust; some eat hamburger when they can afford it. It is true that most highbrows are in the ill-paid professions, notably the academic, and that most middlebrows are at least reasonably well off. Only the lowbrows can be found in about equal percentages at all financial levels. There may be a time, of course, when the highbrows will be paid in accordance with their own estimate of their worth, but that is not likely to happen in any form of society in which creature comforts are in greater demand than intellectual uplift. Like poets they will have to be content mostly with prestige. The middlebrows are influential today, but neither the highbrows nor the lowbrows like them; and if we ever have intellectual totalitarianism, it may well be the lowbrows and the highbrows who will run things, and the middlebrows who will be exiled in boxcars to a collecting point probably in the vicinity of Independence, Missouri.

4. While this social shift, which is also a shift in the weight that we give to taste, is still in its early stages, and the dividing lines are still indistinct and the species not yet (if ever) frozen, let us examine the principal categories, with their subdivisions and splinter groups, and see where we ourselves are likely to fetch up.

5. The highbrows come first. Edgar Wallace, who was certainly not a highbrow himself, was asked by a newspaper reporter in Hollywood some years ago to define one. "What is a highbrow?" he said. "A highbrow is a man who has found something more interesting than women."

6. Presumably at some time in every man's life there are things he finds more interesting than women; alcohol, for example, or the World Series. Mr. Wallace has only partially defined the highbrow. Brander Matthews came closer when he said that "a highbrow is a person educated beyond his intelligence," and A. P. Herbert came closest of all when he wrote that "a highbrow is the kind of person who looks at a sausage and thinks of Picasso."

7. It is this association of culture with every aspect of daily life, from the design of his razor to the shape of the bottle that holds his sleeping pills, that distinguishes the highbrow from the middlebrow or the lowbrow. Spiritually and intellectually the highbrow inhabits a precinct well up the slopes of Parnassus, and his view of the cultural scene is from above. His vision pinpoints certain lakes and quarries upon which his special affections are concentrated—a perturbed lake called Rilke or a deserted quarry called Kierkegaard or a meadow of exotic flowers called Henry James—but he believes that he sees them, as he sees the functional design of his razor, always in relation to the broader cultural scene. There is a certain air of omniscience about the highbrow, though that air is in many cases the thin variety encountered on the tops of high mountains from which the view is extensive but the details are lost.

*8.* You cannot tell a man that he is a lowbrow any more than you can tell a woman that her clothes are in bad taste, but a highbrow does not mind being called a highbrow. He has worked hard, read widely, traveled far, and listened attentively in order to satisfy his curiosity and establish his squatters' rights in this little corner of intellectualism, and he does not care who knows it. And this is true of both kinds of highbrow—the militant, or crusader, type and the passive, or dilettante, type. These types in general live happily together; the militant highbrow carries the torch of culture, the passive highbrow reads by its light.

*9.* The carrier of the torch makes a profession of being a highbrow and lives by his calling. He is most frequently found in university and college towns, a member of the liberal-arts faculty, teaching languages (ancient or modern), the fine arts, or literature. His spare time is often devoted to editing a magazine which is read mainly by other highbrows, ambitious undergraduates, and the editors of middlebrow publications in search of talent. When he writes for the magazine himself (or for another "little" magazine) it is usually criticism or criticism *of* criticism. He leaves the writing of fiction and poetry to others more bent on creation than on what has been created, for the highbrow is primarily a critic and not an artist— a taster, not a cook. He is often more interested in where the arts have been, and where they are going, than in the objects themselves. He is devoted to the proposition that the arts must be pigeonholed, and that their trends should be plotted, or as W. H. Auden puts it—

> Our intellectual marines,
> Landing in Little Magazines,
> Capture a trend.

*10.* This gravitation of the highbrows to the universities is fairly recent. In the twenties, when the little magazines were devoted to publishing experimental writing rather than criticism of exhumed experimental writing, the highbrows flocked to Paris, New York, and Chicago. The *transatlantic review, transition,* and the *Little Review,* of the lower-case era of literature, were all published in Paris; BROOM was published in New York; *Poetry* was (and still is) published in Chicago. The principal little magazines now, with the exception of *Partisan Review,* a New York product but written mostly by academics, are published in the colleges—the *Kenyon Review,* the *Sewanee Review,* the *Virginia Quarterly,* and so on— and their flavor reflects this. But this does not mean that highbrows do not prefer the centers in which cultural activities are the most varied and active, and these are still London, Paris, New York, and more recently Rome. Especially in the fine arts, the highbrow has a chance to make a living in the metropolis where museums are centered and where art is bought and sold as well as created. This is also true of commercial publishing, in which many highbrows find suitable, if not entirely congenial, refuge.

*11.* But no matter where they may make their homes, all highbrows live in a world which they believe is inhabited almost entirely by Philistines— those who through viciousness or smugness or the worship of materialism gnaw away at the foundations of culture. And the highbrow sees as his real enemy the middlebrow, whom he regards as a pretentious and frivolous man or woman who uses culture to satisfy social or business ambitions, who, to quote Clement Greenberg in *Partisan Review,* is busy "devaluating the precious, infecting the healthy, corrupting the honest, and stultifying the wise."

*12.* It takes a man who feels strongly to use such harsh words, but the militant highbrow has no patience with his enemies. He is a serious man who will not tolerate frivolity where the arts are concerned. It is part of his function as a highbrow to protect the arts from the culture mongers, and he spits venom at those he suspects of selling the Muses short.

*13.* The fact that nowadays everyone has access to culture through schools and colleges, through the press, radio, and museums, disturbs him deeply; for it tends to blur the distinctions between those who are serious and those who are frivolous. "Culturally what we have," wrote William Phillips in *Horizon* several years ago, "is a democratic free-for-all in which every individual, being as good as every other one, has the right to question any form of intellectual authority." To this Mr. Greenberg adds, "It becomes increasingly difficult to tell who is serious and who not."

*14.* The highbrow does not like to be confused, nor does he like to have his authority questioned, except by other highbrows of whose seriousness he is certain. The result is precisely what you would expect: the highbrows believe in, and would establish, an intellectual elite, "a fluid body of intellectuals . . . whose accepted role in society is to perpetuate traditional ideas and values and to create new ones." Such an elite would like to see the middlebrow eliminated, for it regards him as the undesirable element in our, and anybody else's, culture.

*15.* "It must be obvious to anyone that the volume and social weight of middlebrow culture," Mr. Greenberg writes, "borne along as it has been by the great recent increase in the American middle class, have multiplied at least tenfold in the past three decades. This culture presents a more serious threat to the genuine article than the old-time pulp dime novel, Tin Pan Alley, *Schund* variety ever has or will. Unlike the latter, which has its social limits clearly marked out for it, middlebrow culture attacks distinctions as such and insinuates itself everywhere. . . . Insidiousness is of its essence, and in recent years its avenues of penetration have become infinitely more difficult to detect and block."

*16.* By no means all highbrows take such a strong position as this or are so concerned with the tastes of others. Many of them, the passive ones, are merely consumers totally indifferent to the middlebrows or supercilious about them. Some without a great deal of hope but in ardent good faith expend themselves in endeavor to widen the circle of those who can enjoy the arts in their purest forms. Many museums, colleges, and publishing houses are at least partly staffed by highbrows who exert a more than half-hearted effort to make the arts exciting and important to the public. But they are aware that most of their labors are wasted. In his heart of hearts nearly every highbrow believes with Ortega y Gasset that "the average citizen [is] a creature incapable of receiving the sacrament of art, blind and deaf to pure beauty." When, for example, the Metropolitan Museum planned to expand its facilities a few years ago, an art dealer who can clearly be classified as a highbrow remarked: "All this means is less art for more people."

*17.* There are also many highbrows who are not concerned in the least with the arts or with literature, and who do not fret themselves about the upstart state of middlebrow culture. These are the specialized highbrows who toil in the remote corners of science and history, of philology and mathematics. They are concerned with their investigations of fruit flies or Elizabethan taxation or whatever it may be, and they do not talk about them, as the dilettante always talks of the arts, to the first person they can latch onto at a cocktail party. When not in their laboratories or the library, they are often as not thoroughly middlebrow in their attitudes and tastes.

*18.* The real highbrow's way of life is as intellectualized as his way of thinking, and as carefully plotted. He is likely to be either extremely self-conscious about his physical surroundings and creature comforts or else sublimely, and rather ostentatiously, indifferent to them. If he affects the former attitude, he will within the limits of his income surround himself with works of art. If he cannot afford paintings he buys drawings. Color reproductions, except as casual reminders tucked in the frame of a mirror or thrown down on a table, are beneath him. The facsimile is no substitute in his mind for the genuine, and he would rather have a slight sketch by a master, Braque or Picasso or even Jackson Pollock, than a fully-realized canvas by an artist he considers not quite first-rate. Drawings by his friends he hangs in the bathroom. His furniture, if it is modern, consists of identifiable pieces by Aalto, or Breuer, or Mies van der Rohe, or Eames; it does not come from department stores. If he finds modern unsympathetic, he will tend to use Biedermeier or the more "entertaining" varieties of Victorian, which he collects piece by piece with an eye to the slightly eccentric. If he has antiques, you may be sure they are not maple; the cult of Early American is offensive to him.

*19.* The food that he serves will be planned with the greatest care, either very simple (a perfect French omelette made with sweet butter) or elaborate recipes from *Wine and Food* magazine published in London and edited by André Simon. If he cannot afford a pound of butter with every guinea fowl, he will in all probability resort to the casserole, and peasant cookery with the sparer parts of animals and birds seasoned me-

ticulously with herbs that he gets from a little importer in the wholesale
district. His wine is more likely to be a "perfectly adequate little red
wine" for eighty-nine cents a half gallon than an imported French vintage.
(Anybody with good advice can buy French wines, but the discovery
of a good domestic bottle shows perception and educated taste.) He
wouldn't dream of washing his salad bowl. His collection of phonograph
records is likely to bulk large at the ends and sag in the middle—a pre-
dominance of Bach-and-before at one end and Stravinsky, Schönberg, Bar-
tok, and New Orleans jazz at the other. The nineteenth century is represented, perhaps, by Beethoven quartets and late sonatas, and some French
"art songs" recorded by Maggie Teyte. His radio, if he has one, is turned
on rarely; he wouldn't have a television set in the house.

20. The highbrow who disregards his creature comforts does it with a
will. He lives with whatever furniture happens to come his way in a dis-
organized conglomeration of Victorian, department store, and Mexican
bits and pieces. He takes care of his books in that he knows where each
one is no matter in what disorder they may appear. Every other detail of
domestic life he leaves to his wife, of whose taste he is largely unaware,
and he eats what she gives him without comment. If he is a bachelor, he
eats in a cafeteria or drugstore or diner and sometimes spills soup on the
open pages of his book. He is oblivious of the man who sits down opposite
him, and if Edgar Wallace is right, to the woman who shares his table.
He is not a man without passions, but they have their place. Dress is a
matter of indifference to him.

21. The highbrows about whom I have been writing are mainly consumers and not creators—editors, critics, and dilettantes. The creative
artists who are generally considered highbrows—such men as T. S. Eliot,
E. M. Forster, Picasso, and Stravinsky—seem to me to fall in another category, that of the professional man who, while he may be concerned with
communicating with a limited (and perhaps largely highbrow) audience,
is primarily a doer and not a done-by. When Eliot or Forster or Picasso or
Stravinsky sits down at his work table, I do not know whether he says to
himself, "I am going to create Art," but I very much doubt if that is what
is in his mind. He is concerned rather with the communication of ideas
within the frame of a poem, a novel, a painting, or a ballet suite, and if it
turns out to be art (which many think it frequently does) that is to him
a by-product of creation, an extra dividend of craftsmanship, intelligence,
and sensibility. But when this happens he is taken up by the highbrow
consumer and made much of. In fact he may become, whether he likes it
or not, a vested interest, and his reputation will be every bit as carefully
guarded by the highbrows as a hundred shares of Standard Oil of New
Jersey by the middlebrows. He will be sold—at a par decided upon by the
highbrows—to the middlebrows, who are natural gamblers in the commodi-
ties of culture.

22. In a sense it is this determination of par that is the particular contribution of the highbrow. Others may quarrel with his evaluations, but the fact remains that unless there were a relatively small group of self-appointed intellectuals who took it upon themselves to ransack the studios of artists, devour the manuscripts of promising writers, and listen at the keyholes of young composers, many talented men and women might pass unnoticed and our culture be the poorer. Their noncommercial attitude toward discovery of talent is useful, though they have an obsession with the evils of the monetary temptations with which America strews the artist's path. They stand as a wavering bulwark against the enticements of Hollywood and the advertising agencies, and they are saddened by the writers and painters who have set out to be serious men, as Hemingway did, and then become popular by being taken up by the middlebrows. They even go so far as to say that a story published in *Partisan Review* is a better story than if it were published in *The New Yorker* or *Harper's Bazaar*, for the reason that "what we have is at once a general raising and lowering of the level, for which the blurring of distinctions new writing tends to become more and more serious and intellectual and less and less bold and extreme. . . ."

23. This attitude, which is the attitude of the purist, is valuable. It is the sort of statement that James Jackson Jarves might have made a century before, or James Fenimore Cooper even earlier. They were dismayed at the way every man pretended to be a connoisseur—"knowledge or no knowledge; brains or no brains; taste or no taste." The ground in which the arts grow stays fertile only when it is fought over by both artists and consumers, and the phalanx of highbrows in the field, a somewhat impenetrable square of warriors, can be counted on to keep the fray alive.

24. The highbrow's friend is the lowbrow. The highbrow enjoys and respects the lowbrow's art—jazz for instance—which he is likely to call a spontaneous expression of folk culture. The lowbrow is not interested, as the middlebrow is, in pre-empting any of the highbrow's function or in any way threatening to blur the lines between the serious and the frivolous. In fact he is almost completely oblivious of the highbrow unless he happens to be taken up by him—as many jazz musicians, primitive painters, and ballad writers have been—and then he is likely to be flattered, a little suspicious, and somewhat amused. A creative lowbrow like the jazz musician is a prominent citizen in his own world, and the fact that he is taken up by the highbrows has very little effect on his social standing therein. He is tolerant of the highbrow, whom he regards as somewhat odd and out-of-place in a world in which people do things and enjoy them without analyzing why or worrying about their cultural implications.

25. The lowbrow doesn't give a hang about art *qua* art. He knows what he likes, and he doesn't care why he likes it—which implies that all children are lowbrows. The word "beautiful," which has long since ceased

to mean anything to the highbrow, is a perfectly good word to the low-brow. Beautiful blues, beautiful sunsets, beautiful women, all things that do something to a man inside without passing through the mind, associa-tions without allusions, illusions without implications. The arts created by the lowbrow are made in the expression of immediate pleasure or grief, like most forms of jazz; or of usefulness, like the manufacturing of a tool or a piece of machinery or even a bridge across the Hudson. The form, to use a highbrow phrase, follows the function. When the lowbrow arts follow this formula (which they don't always do), then the highbrow finds much in them to admire, and he calls it the vernacular. When, how-ever, the lowbrow arts get mixed up with middlebrow ideas of culture, then the highbrow turns away in disgust. Look, for example, at what hap-pened to the circus, a traditional form of lowbrow art. They got in Nor-man Bel Geddes to fancy it up, and now its special flavor of authenticity is gone—all wrapped up in pink middlebrow sequins. This is not to say that the lowbrow doesn't like it just as much as he ever did. It is the high-brow who is pained.

26. Part of the highbrow's admiration for the lowbrow stems from the lowbrow's indifference to art. This makes it possible for the highbrow to blame whatever he doesn't like about lowbrow taste on the middlebrow. If the lowbrow reads the comics, the highbrow understands; he is fre-quently a connoisseur of the comics himself. But if he likes grade-B double features, the highbrow blames that on the corrupting influence of the middlebrow moneybags of Hollywood. If he participates in give away quiz programs, it is because the radio pollsters have decided that the average mental age of the listening audience is thirteen, and that radio and television are venal for taking advantage of the adolescent.

27. The lowbrow consumer, whether he is an engineer of bridges or a bus driver, wants to be comfortable and to enjoy himself without having to worry about whether he has good taste or not. It doesn't make any dif-ference to him that a chair is a bad Grand Rapids copy of an eighteenth-century *fauteuil* as long as he's happy when he sits down in it. He doesn't care whether the movies are art, or the television improving, so long as he has fun while he is giving them his attention and getting a fair return of pleasure from his investment. It wouldn't occur to him to tell a novelist what kind of book he should write, or a movie director what kind of a movie to make. If he doesn't like a book he ignores it; if he doesn't like a movie he says so, whether it is a Martin and Lewis show or *Henry V*. If he likes jive or square dancing, he doesn't worry about whether they are fashionable or not. If other people like the ballet, that's all right with him, so long as he doesn't have to go himself. In general the lowbrow attitude toward the arts is live and let live. Lowbrows are not Philistines. One has to know enough about the arts to argue about them with highbrows to be a Philistine.

28. The popular press, and also much of the unpopular press, is run by the middlebrows, and it is against them that the highbrow inveighs.

29. "The true battle," wrote Virginia Woolf in an essay called "Middlebrow" (she was the first, I believe, to define the species) ". . . lies not between the highbrows and the lowbrows joined together in blood brotherhood but against the bloodless and pernicious pest who comes between. . . . Highbrows and lowbrows must band together to exterminate a pest which is the bane of all thinking and living."

30. Pushing Mrs. Woolf's definition a step further, the pests divide themselves into two groups: the upper middlebrows and the lower middlebrows. It is the upper middlebrows who are the principal purveyors of highbrow ideas and the lower middlebrows who are the principal consumers of what the upper middlebrows pass along to them.

31. Many publishers, for example, are upper middlebrows—as are most educators, museum directors, movie producers, art dealers, lecturers, and the editors of most magazines which combine national circulation with an adult vocabulary. These are the men and women who devote themselves professionally to the dissemination of ideas and cultural artifacts and, not in the least incidentally, make a living along the way. They are the cultural do-gooders, and they see their mission clearly and pursue it with determination. Some of them are disappointed highbrows; some of them try to work both sides of the street; nearly all of them straddle the fence between highbrow and middlebrow and enjoy their equivocal position.

32. The conscientious publisher, for instance, believes in the importance of literature and the dignity of publishing as a profession. He spends a large part of his time on books that will not yield him a decent return on his investment. He searches out writers of promise; he pores over the "little" magazines (or pays other people to); he leafs through hundreds and hundreds of pages of manuscript. He advises writers, encourages them, coaxes them to do their best work; he even advances them money. But he is not able to be a publisher at all (unless he is willing to put his personal fortune at the disposal of financially naïve muses) if he does not publish to make money. In order to publish slender volumes of poetry he must also publish fat volumes of historical romance, and in order to encourage the first novel of a promising young writer he must sell tens of thousands of copies of a book by an old hand who grinds out one best seller a year. He must take the measure of popular taste and cater to it at the same time that he tries to create a taste for new talent. If he is a successful publisher he makes money, lives comfortably, patronizes the other arts, serves on museum boards and committees for the Prevention of This and the Preservation of That, contributes to the symphony, and occasionally buys pictures by contemporary painters.

33. The highbrow suspects that the publisher does not pace his book-lined office contriving ways to serve the muses and that these same muses

have to wait their turn in line until the balance sheet has been served. He believes that the publisher is really happy only when he can sell a couple of hundred thousand copies of a novel about a hussy with a horsewhip or a book on how to look forty when forty-five. To the highbrow he is a tool to be cultivated and used, but not to be trusted.

34. The museum director, as we have already seen, is in much the same position, caught between the muses and the masses. If he doesn't make a constant effort to swell the door count, his middlebrow trustees want to know why he isn't serving the community; if he does, the highbrows want to know why he is pandering to popular taste and not minding his main business—the service of scholarship and the support of artists currently certified to be "serious." Educators are in the same position, bound to be concerned with mass education often at the expense of the potential scholar, and editors of all magazines except those supported by private angels or cultural institutions know that they must not only enlighten but entertain if they are to have enough readers to pay the bills. To the highbrow this can lead to nothing but compromise and mediocrity.

35. The upper-middlebrow consumer takes his culture seriously, as seriously as his job allows, for he is gainfully employed. In his leisure hours he reads Toynbee or Osbert Sitwell's serialized memoirs. He goes to museum openings and to the theater and he keeps up on the foreign films. He buys pictures, sometimes old masters if he can afford them, sometimes contemporary works. He has a few etchings and lithographs, and he is not above an occasional color reproduction of a Cézanne or a Lautrec. Writers and painters are his friends and dine at his house; if, however, his own son were to express an interest in being an artist, he would be dismayed ("so few artists ever really pull it off")—though he would keep a stiff upper lip and hope the boy would learn better before it was too late. His house is tastefully decorated, sometimes in the very latest mode, a model of the modern architect's dream of functionalism, in which case he can discourse on the theory of the open plan and the derivations of the International Style with the zest and uncertain vocabulary of a convert. If his house is "traditional" in character, he will not put up with Grand Rapids copies of old pieces; he will have authentic ones, and will settle for Victorian if he cannot afford Empire. He, or his wife, will ransack second-hand shops for entertaining bibelots and lamps or a piece of Brussels carpet from Andrew Jackson Downing's day for the bedroom. He never refers to curtains as "drapes." He talks about television as potentially a new art form, and he watches the Ford Foundation's TV program Omnibus. His library contains a few of the more respectable current best sellers which he reads out of "curiosity" rather than interest. There are a few shelves of first editions, some of them autographed by friends who have dined at his house, some of them things (like a presentation copy of Jurgen) that he "just happened to pick up" and a sampling of American and British poets.

There is also a shelf of paper-bound French novels—most of them by nineteenth-century writers. The magazines on his table span the areas from *Time* and *The New Yorker* to *Harper's* and the *Atlantic*, with an occasional copy of the *Yale* and *Partisan Reviews*, and the *Art News*.

36. From this it can be seen that he supports the highbrows—buys some of the books they recommend and an occasional picture they have looked upon with favor—and contributes to organized efforts to promote the arts both by serving on boards and shelling out money. In general he is modest about expressing his opinion on cultural matters in the presence of highbrows but takes a slightly lordly tone when he is talking to other middlebrows. If he discovers a "little" painter or poet, the chances are excellent that the man has already been discovered and promoted by a highbrow or by an upper-middlebrow entrepreneur (art dealer or publisher). Once in a while he will take a flyer on an unknown artist, and hang his picture inconspicuously in the bedroom. He takes his function as a patron of the arts seriously, but he does it for the pleasure it gives him to be part of the cultural scene. If he does it for "money, fame, power, or prestige," as Virginia Woolf says he does, these motives are so obscured by a general sense of well-being and well-meaning that he would be shocked and surprised to be accused of venality.

37. If the upper middlebrow is unsure of his own tastes, but firm in his belief that taste is extremely important, the lower middlebrow is his counterpart. The lower middlebrow ardently believes that he knows what he likes, and yet his taste is constantly susceptible to the pressures that put him in knickerbockers one year and rust-colored slacks the next. Actually he is unsure about almost everything, especially about what he likes. This may explain his pronouncements on taste, which he considers an effete and questionable virtue, and his resentment of the arts; but it may also explain his strength.

38. When America and Americans are characterized by foreigners and highbrows, the middlebrows are likely to emerge as the dominant group in our society—a dreadful mass of insensible back-slappers, given to sentimentality as a prime virtue, the willing victims of slogans and the whims of the bosses, both political and economic. The picture painted by middlebrow exploiters of the middlebrow, such as the advertisers of nationally advertised brands, is strikingly similar to that painted by the highbrow; their attitudes and motives are quite different (the highbrow paints with a snarl, the advertiser with a gleam), but they both make the middlebrow out to be much the same kind of creature. The villain of the highbrow and the hero of the advertisers is envisaged as "the typical American family"— happy little women, happy little children, all spotless or sticky in the jam pot, framed against dimity curtains in the windows or decalcomania

flowers on the cupboard doors. Lower-middlebrowism is a world pictured
without tragedy, a world of new two-door sedans, and Bendix washers,
and reproductions of hunting prints over the living-room mantel. It is a
world in which the ingenuity and patience of the housewife are equaled
only by the fidelity of her husband and his love of home, pipe, and television. It is a world that smells of soap. But it is a world of ambition as
well, the constant striving for a better way of life—better furniture, bigger
refrigerators, more books in the bookcase, more evenings at the movies.
To the advertisers this is Americanism; to the highbrows this is the dead
weight around the neck of progress, the gag in the mouth of art.

39. The lower middlebrows are not like this, of course, and unlike the
highbrows and the upper middlebrows, whose numbers are tiny by comparison, they are hard to pin down. They live everywhere, rubbing elbows
with lowbrows in apartment houses like vast beehives, in row houses all
alike from the outside except for the planting, in large houses at the ends
of gravel driveways, in big cities, in medium cities and suburbs, and in
small towns, from Boston to San Francisco, from Seattle to Jacksonville.
They are the members of the book clubs who read difficult books along
with racy and innocuous ones that are sent along by Messrs. Fadiman,
Canby, Beecroft *et al.* They are the course takers who swell the enrollments of adult education classes in everything from "The Technique of the
Short Story" to "Child Care." They are the people who go to hear the lecturers that swarm out from New York lecture bureaus with tales of travel
on the Dark Continent and panaceas for saving the world from a fate
worse than capitalism. They eat in tea shoppes and hold barbecues in their
back yards. They are hell-bent on improving their minds as well as their
fortunes. They decorate their homes under the careful guidance of *Good
Housekeeping* and the *Ladies' Home Journal,* or, if they are well off, of
*House and Garden,* and are subject to fads in furniture so long as these
don't depart too radically from the traditional and the safe, from the copy
of Colonial and the reproduction of Sheraton. In matters of taste, the
lower-middlebrow world is largely dominated by women. They select the
furniture, buy the fabrics, pick out the wallpapers, the pictures, the books,
the china. Except in the selection of his personal apparel and the car, it is
almost *infra dig* for a man to have taste; it is not considered quite manly
for the male to express opinions about things which come under the category of "artistic."

40. Nonetheless, as a member of the school board or the hospital board
he decides which design shall be accepted when a new building goes up.
The lower middlebrows are the organizers of the community fund, the
members of the legislature, the park commissioners. They pay their taxes
and they demand services in return. There are millions of them, conscientious stabilizers of society, slow to change, slow to panic. But they are not

as predictable as either the highbrows or the bosses, political or economic, think they are. They can be led, they can be seduced, but they cannot be pushed around.

*41.* Highbrow, lowbrow, upper middlebrow, and lower middlebrow—the lines between them are sometimes indistinct, as the lines between upper class, lower class, and middle class have always been in our traditionally fluid society. But gradually they are finding their own levels and confining themselves more and more to the company of their own kind.

*42.* The highbrows would apparently like to eliminate the middlebrows and devise a society that would approximate an intellectual feudal system in which the lowbrows do the work and create folk arts, and the highbrows do the thinking and create fine arts. All middlebrows, presumably, would have their televisions taken away, be suspended from society until they had agreed to give up their subscriptions to the Book-of-the-Month, turned their color reproductions over to a Commission for the Dissolution of Middlebrow Taste, and renounced their affiliation with all educational and other cultural institutions whatsoever. They would be taxed for the support of all writers, artists, musicians, critics, and critics-of-criticism whose production could be certified "serious"—said writers, artists, musicians, and critics to be selected by representatives of qualified magazines with circulations of not more than five thousand copies. Middlebrows, both upper and lower, who persisted in "devaluating the precious, infecting the healthy, corrupting the honest, and stultifying the wise" would be disposed of forthwith.

*43.* If life for grandmother, who wouldn't dine with the Cartiers, was simple in its social distinctions, life is becoming equally simple for us. The rungs of the ladder may be different, it may even be a different ladder, but it's onward and upward just the same. You may not be known by which fork you use for the fish these days, but you will be known by which key you use for your *Finnegan's Wake.*

# Questions

1. Show how Lynes' story about his wife's grandmother is directly relevant to the divisions of taste he sets up in the last sentence of paragraph 2. Why does he return to her in the end?

2. Why does Lynes indicate in paragraph 3 that these categories may not be entirely clear? Are they mutually exclusive?

3. What essential quality of the highbrow does Lynes isolate in paragraph 7?

4. In paragraph 11 Lynes points out that the highbrow sees as his real enemy the middlebrow. Why not the lowbrow?

5. Lynes divides highbrows into two categories, militant and passive. What principle distinguishes the passive highbrow? *Works High Lives Low or Middle*

6. Why in paragraph 22 does Lynes say that "it is this determination of par that is the particular contribution of the highbrow"? *Someone has to set the*

7. The first sentence of paragraph 24 is transitional. How effective is it in *price value* light of what Lynes has earlier said about the highbrow and the middle- *such* brow? *as art*

8. What principles of selection guide Lynes in determining whether one is a lowbrow?

9. The transition in paragraph 28 to the discussion of the middlebrow is rather abrupt. Why? Is the abruptness effective?

10. Lynes discusses the highbrow first. Show how this discussion is a key to the discussion of the lowbrow and the middlebrow. How is the highbrow used as a linking device?

11. Why does Lynes classify the middlebrow as either upper or lower when the same categories were not used for the highbrow and the lowbrow?

12. What final relevance does the opening quotation seem to have to Lynes' classifications?

# Theme Topics

Classify one of the following into two or three types using Lynes' techniques:

1. your friends
2. colleges
3. teachers or college professors
4. clothing salespeople
5. personality types
6. parent types
7. attitudes toward life
8. high school problem students
9. taste in clothes, movies, or art
10. varieties of religious experience
11. college student snobs
12. generosity, hypocrisy, or leadership

## ·12·

*Philip Wheelwright*

# THE MEANING OF ETHICS

*For you see, Callicles, our discussion is concerned with a matter in which even a man of slight intelligence must take the profoundest interest—namely, what course of life is best.*

SOCRATES, in Plato's Gorgias

*1.* Man is the animal who can reflect. Like other animals, no doubt, he spends much of his time in merely reacting to the pressures and urgencies of his environment. But being a man he has moments also of conscious stock-taking, when he becomes aware not only of his world but of himself confronting his world, evaluating it, and making choices with regard to it. It is this ability to know himself and on the basis of self-knowledge to make evaluations and reflective choices that differentiates man from his subhuman cousins.

*2.* There are, as Aristotle has pointed out, two main ways in which man's power of reflection becomes active. They are called, in Aristotle's language, *theoretikos* and *praktikos* respectively; which is to say, thinking about what is actually the case and thinking about what had better be done. In English translation the words *contemplative* and *operative* probably come closest to Aristotle's intent. To think contemplatively is to ask oneself what *is;* to think operatively is to ask oneself what to *do.* These are the two modes of serious, one might even say of genuine thought—as distinguished from daydreams, emotional vaporizings, laryngeal chatter, and the repetition of clichés. To think seriously is to think either for the sake of knowing things as they are or for the sake of acting upon, and producing or helping to produce, things as they might be.

*3.* Although in practice the two types of thinking are much interrelated, it is operative thinking with which our present study is primarily concerned. Ethics, although it must be guided, limited, and qualified constantly by considerations of what is actually the case, is focused upon questions of what should be done. The converse, however, does not fol-

Philip Wheelwright, *A Critical Introduction to Ethics,* Third Edition (New York: Odyssey Press, 1959), pp. 3-20. Copyright © by The Odyssey Press, Inc. Reprinted by permission of the copyright holder.

low. Not all questions about what should be done are ethical questions. Much of our operative thinking is given to more immediate needs—to means whereby some given end can be achieved. A person who deliberates as to the most effective way of making money, or of passing a course, or of winning a battle, or of achieving popularity, is thinking operatively, but if that is as far as his planning goes it cannot be called ethical. Such deliberations about adapting means to an end would acquire an ethical character only if some thought were given to the nature and value of the end itself. Ethics cannot dispense with questions of means, but neither can it stop there.

4. Accordingly, ethics may be defined as that branch of philosophy which is the systematic study of reflective choice, of the standards of right and wrong by which it is to be guided, and of the goods toward which it may ultimately be directed. The relation between the parts of this definition, particularly between standards of right and wrong on the one hand and ultimately desirable goods on the other, will be an important part of the forthcoming study.

## THE NATURE OF MORAL DELIBERATION

5. The soundest approach to ethical method is through reflection on our experience of moral situations which from time to time we have had occasion to face, or through an imagined confrontation of situations which others have faced and which we can thus make sympathetically real to ourselves. For instance:

Arthur Ames is a rising young district attorney engaged on his most important case. A prominent political boss has been murdered. Suspicion points at a certain ex-convict, known to have borne the politician a grudge. Aided by the newspapers, which have reported the murder in such a way as to persuade the public of the suspect's guilt, Ames feels certain that he can secure a conviction on the circumstantial evidence in his possession. If he succeeds in sending the man to the chair he will become a strong candidate for governor at the next election.

During the course of the trial, however, he accidentally stumbles on some fresh evidence, known only to himself and capable of being destroyed if he chooses, which appears to establish the ex-convict's innocence. If this new evidence were to be introduced at the trial an acquittal would be practically certain. What ought the District Attorney to do? Surrender the evidence to the defence, in order that, as a matter of fair play, the accused might be given every legitimate chance of establishing his innocence? But to do that will mean the loss of a case that has received enormous publicity; the District Attorney will lose the backing of the press; he will appear to have failed, and his political career may be blocked. In that event not only will he himself suffer disappointment, but his ample plans for bestowing comforts on his family and for giving his children the benefits of a superior education may have to be curtailed. On the other hand, ought he to be instrumental in sending a man to the chair for a crime that in all probability he did not commit? And yet the ex-convict is a bad lot; even if innocent in the present case he has doubtless committed many other crimes in which he has escaped detection. Is a fellow like that worth the sacrifice of one's career? Still, there is no proof that he has ever committed a crime punishable by death. Until a man has been proved guilty he must be regarded, by a sound principle of American legal theory, as innocent. To conceal and destroy the new evidence, then, is not that tantamount to railroading an innocent man to the chair?

So District Attorney Ames reasons back and forth. He knows that it is a widespread custom for a district attorney to conceal evidence prejudicial to his side of a case. But is the custom, particularly when a human life is at stake, morally right? A district attorney is an agent of the government, and his chief aim in that capacity should be to present his accusations in such a way as to ensure for the accused not condemnation but justice. The question, then, cannot be answered by appealing simply to law or to legal practice. It is a moral one: *What is Arthur Ames' duty? What ought he to do?*

Benjamin Bates has a friend who lies in a hospital, slowly dying of a painful and incurable disease. Although there is no hope of recovery, the disease sometimes permits its victim to linger on for many months, in ever greater torment and with threatened loss of sanity. The dying man, apprised of the outcome and knowing that the hospital expenses are a severe drain on his family's limited financial resources, decides that death had better come at once. His physician, he knows, will not run the risk of providing him with the necessary drug. There is only his friend Bates to appeal to.

How shall Bates decide? Dare he be instrumental in hastening another's death? Has he a moral right to be accessory to the taking of a human life? Besides, suspicion would point his way, and his honorable motives would not avert a charge of murder. On the other hand, can he morally refuse to alleviate a friend's suffering and the financial distress of a family when the means of doing so are in his hands? And has he not an obligation to respect a friend's declared will in the matter? To acquiesce and to refuse seem both somehow in different ways wrong, yet one course or the other must be chosen. *What ought Bates to do? Which way does his duty lie?*

In the city occupied by Crampton College a strike is declared by the employees of all the public-transit lines. Their wages have not been increased to meet the rising cost of living, and the justice of their grievance is rather widely admitted by neutral observers. The strike ties up business and causes much general inconvenience; except for the people who have cars of their own or can afford taxi fare, there is no way of getting from one part of the city to another. Labor being at this period scarce, an appeal is made by the mayor to college students to serve the community by acting in their spare time as motormen and drivers. The appeal is backed by a promise of lucrative wages and by the college administration's agreement to coöperate by permitting necessary absences from classes.

What ought the students of Crampton College to do? If they act as strike-breakers they aid in forcing the employees back to work on the corporations' own terms. Have they any right to interfere so drastically and one-sidedly in the lives and happiness of others? On the other hand, if they turn down the mayor's request the community will continue to suffer grave inconveniences until the fight is somehow settled. *What is the students' duty in the matter? What is the right course for them to follow?*

6. These three situations, although perhaps unusual in the severity of their challenge, offer examples of problems distinctively moral. When the act of moral deliberation implicit in each of them is fully carried out, certain characteristic phases can be discerned.

7. (i) *Examination and clarification of the alternatives.* What are the relevant possibilities of action in the situation confronting me? Am I clear about the nature of each? Have I clearly distinguished them from one another? And are they mutually exhaustive, or would a more attentive search reveal others? In the case of District Attorney Ames, for example, a third alternative might have been to make a private deal with the ex-convict by which, in exchange for his acquittal, the District Attorney would receive the profits from some lucrative racket of which the ex-convict had control. No doubt to a reputable public servant this line of conduct would be too repugnant for consideration; it exemplifies, nevertheless, the ever-present logical possibility of going "between the horns"[1] of the original dilemma.

8. (ii) *Rational elaboration of consequences.* The next step is to think out the probable consequences of each of the alternatives in question. As this step involves predictions about a hypothetical future, the conclusions can have, at most, a high degree of probability, never certainty. The degree of probability is heightened according as there is found some precedent in past experience for each of the proposed choices. Even if the present situation seems wholly new, analysis will always reveal *some* particulars for which analogies in past experience can be found or to which known laws of causal sequence are applicable. Such particulars will be dealt with partly by analogy (an act similar to the one now being deliberated about had on a previous occasion such and such consequences) and partly by the inductive-deductive method: appealing to general laws (deduction) which in turn have been built up as generalizations from observed particulars (induction). Mr. Ames, we may suppose, found the materials for this step in his professional knowledge of law and legal precedent, as well as in his more general knowledge of the policies of the press, the gullibility of its readers, and the high cost of domestic luxuries.

9. (iii) *Imaginative projection of the self into the predicted situation.* It is not enough to reason out the probable consequences of a choice. In

[1] I.e., finding a third alternative.

a moral deliberation the chief interests involved are not scientific but human and practical. The only way to judge the comparative desirability of two possible futures is to live through them both in imagination. The third step, then, is to project oneself imaginatively into the future; i.e., establish a dramatic identification of the present self with that future self to which the now merely imagined experiences may become real. Few persons, unfortunately, are capable of an imaginative identification forceful enough to give the claims of the future self an even break. Present goods loom larger than future goods, and goods in the immediate future than goods that are remote. The trained ethical thinker must have a sound *temporal perspective*, the acquisition of which is to be sought by a frequent, orderly, and detailed exercise of the imagination with respect to not yet actual situations.

*10.* (iv) *Imaginative identification of the self with the points of view of those persons whom the proposed act will most seriously affect.* Whatever decision I make here and now, if of any importance, is likely to have consequences, in varying degrees, for persons other than myself. An important part of a moral inquiry is to envisage the results of a proposed act as they will appear to those other persons affected by them. I must undertake, then, a dramatic identification of my own self with the selves of other persons. The possibility of doing this is evident from a consideration of how anyone's dramatic imagination works in the reading of a novel or the witnessing of a play. If the persons in the novel or play are dramatically convincing it is not because their characters and actions have been established by logical proof, but because they are presented so as to provoke in the reader an impulse to project himself into the world of the novel or play, to identify himself with this and that character in it, to share their feelings and moods, to get their slant on things.

*11.* In most persons, even very benevolent ones, the social consciousness works by fits and starts. To examine fairly the needs and claims of other selves is no less hard and is often harder than to perform a similar task with regard to one's own future self. Accordingly the ethical thinker must develop *social perspective*—that balanced appreciation of others' needs and claims which is the basis of justice.

*12.* In this fourth, as in the third step, the imaginative projection is to be carried out for each of the alternatives, according as their consequences shall have been predicted by Step ii.

*13.* (v) *Estimation and comparison of the values involved.* Implicit in the third and fourth steps is a recognition that certain values both positive and negative are latent in each of the hypothetical situations to which moral choice may lead. The values must be made explicit in order that they may be justly compared, for it is as a result of their comparison that a choice is to be made. To make values explicit is to give them a relatively abstract formulation; they still, however, derive concrete significance from their imagined exemplifications. District Attorney Ames, for example, might have envisaged his dilemma as a choice between family happiness and worldly success on the one hand as against professional honor on the other. Each of these is undoubtedly good, that is to say a value, but the values cannot be reduced to a common denominator. Family happiness enters as a factor into Benjamin Bates' dilemma no less than into that of Arthur Ames, but it stands to be affected in a different way and therefore, in spite of the identical words by which our linguistic poverty forces us to describe it, it does not mean the same thing. Family happiness may mean any number of things; so may success, and honor—although these different meanings have, of course, an intelligible bond of unity. Arthur Ames' task is to compare not just any family happiness with any professional honor but the particular exemplifications of each that enter into his problem. The comparison is not a simple calculation but an imaginative deliberation, in which the abstract values that serve as the logical ground of the comparison are continuous with, and interactive with, the concrete particulars that serve as its starting-point.

*14.* (vi *Decision.* Comparison of the alternative future situations and the values embodied in each must terminate in a decision. Which of the possible situations do I deem it better to bring into existence? There are no rules for the making of this decision. I must simply decide as wisely and as fairly and as relevantly to the total comparison as I can. Every moral decision is a risk, for the way in which a person decides is a factor in determining the kind of self he is going to become.

*15.* (vii) *Action.* The probable means of carrying out the decision have been established by Step ii. The wished-for object or situation is an end, certain specific means toward the fulfillment of which lie here and now within my power. These conditions supply the premises for an ethical syllogism. When a certain end, $x$, is recognized as the best of the available alternatives, and when the achievement of it is seen to be possible through a set of means $a, b, c \ldots$ which lie within my power, then whichever of the means $a, b, c \ldots$ is an action that can here and now be performed becomes at just this point my duty. If the deliberative process has been carried out forcefully and wisely it will have supplied a categorical answer to the question, What ought I to do?—even though the answer in some cases may be, Do nothing.

*16.* Naturally, not all experiences of moral deliberation and choice reveal these seven phases in a distinct, clear-cut way. Nor is the order here given always the actual order. Sometimes we may begin by deliberating about the relative merits of two ends, seeking the means simultaneously with this abstract inquiry, or after its completion. The foregoing analysis does, however, throw some light on the nature of a moral problem, and may be tested by applying it to the three cases described at the beginning of the chapter.

### LOGICAL ANALYSIS OF A MORAL SITUATION

*17.* The usual sign of a moral question is the auxiliary verb, *ought.* Not every "ought," however, is a moral ought. There must be distinguished: (1) the logical "ought," as in "The balance ought to be $34 but I make it $29," "From the appearance of the sky I should say we ought to have snow tonight," "The story ought never to have had a happy ending"; (2) the prudential "ought," as in "If you want to avoid colds you ought to try Hydrolux Vapo-lite." These two uses of the word "ought" express, like the moral ought, propriety with respect to a certain end or standard. But unlike the moral ought, the ought in (1) does not refer directly to human conduct, and while the ought in (2) does have this reference, the imperative that it expresses is conditional on a wish. The imperative expressed by the moral ought is, on the contrary, unconditional: You ought to be honorable—not *if* you wish men to respect you; men's respect is a desirable adjunct of being honorable, but you ought to be honorable in any case. The moral ought is what Kant has called a categorical imperative. In being categorical it is distinguished from the prudential ought; in being an imperative, i.e., a call to action, it is distinguished also from the logical ought. It is the moral ought that is the subject-matter of ethics, and it is in this ethical sense, therefore, that the word "ought" will be used in the present volume. We may now consider the principal factors which the moral ought involves.

VALUE AND POSSIBILITY

*18.* The first factor to be noted in a moral situation is the *presence of value.* Whenever an inclination is felt, that toward which the inclination points is felt to have value. What is felt to have value need not on reflection be *judged* to have value. Judgment can correct our immediate feelings of value, just as in an act of sense-perception judgment corrects and interprets the immediate sense-data. Inclination is thus not identical with value; but it is the psycho-physical basis of its presence.

*19.* To say that a value is present in an object is to declare that the object is *in some sense* good. We may therefore restate the first requirement of a moral situation by saying that some things must be recognized as good; or, since good is a relative term, that *some things are recognized as better than others.* But if *a* is better than *b, b* is worse than *a.* It follows, then, that some things are *worse* than others, and the first requirement may therefore be restated as an ability to distinguish what is comparatively good from what is comparatively bad. What particular things are good, and what bad, is of course another question. The principle here laid down is simply that to a person who did not set a higher value on some things than on others there could be no moral problem. (Indeed, it is a little hard to see how such a person could have any *problems* at all.) A moral situation presupposes, then, as the first condition of its existence, the recognition of some values or other.

20. This primary characteristic of a moral situation defines ethics as a normative science. Ethics is not a science at all in the same way that the empirical sciences are so designated, and its methods are fundamentally distinct. It shares, nevertheless, the larger meaning of science, for its subject-matter can be arranged systematically and certain guiding principles be found. But while such sciences as physics, psychology, economics, etc. are primarily concerned with the recording, predicting, and structuralizing of facts, ethics is concerned with facts only secondarily, only so far as they are morally evaluated or judged to be in some way relevant to the application of moral values. That skies are sunny in New Mexico is a fact; that many people are without lucrative employment is also a fact. Both are equally facts, but our valuations of them differ. It is such differences in valuation, such *normative* differences, that establish the basis of a moral situation.

21. A second element in any moral situation is *the presence of possible alternatives.* To evaluate anything as good is equivalent to declaring that it ought to be, or ought to persist. Ethics does not stop with the good, with what merely ought to *be;* it accepts this as but one element in the question, What ought to *be done?* To say that a person ought to do a thing implies a power on his part *to do or refrain from doing it.* We do not say that the President of the United States ought to put an immediate stop to all human suffering, for the President, however much he might desire such a consummation, has not the power of achieving it; the most we can say is that the President ought to take such steps as may lie within his power to move toward the goal. Nor, on the other hand, do we say, speaking accurately, that a man ought to obey the law of gravitation, for this is something that he must do willy-nilly. Neither "must" nor "cannot" is in the strict sense compatible with "ought."

22. These two elements, the presence of value and the presence of possible alternatives in a moral situation, are intimately related, for in order that the alternatives may have moral significance some kind of value must be attached to each of them. In some cases the value of each alternative is assigned rationally. In other cases, the most familiar of which are those described as "battling with temptation," our rational judgment assigns value to only one of the alternatives; the other is merely *felt* to have value, as a result of our experiencing a strong inclination toward it. But in either type of situation there must be some value, whether deliberately judged or spontaneously felt, attached to both alternatives, in order that there may be a moral problem.

23. For example, there exist for me the possible alternatives of plucking a blade of grass or of not doing so, but the situation is not a moral

one, for neither alternative has (on any likely occasion) any value. Or again, it lies in my power to go without my dinner. In this instance one of the alternatives (eating dinner) has value, the other (going without it) has probably none, so that again there is no moral problem. If, however, I judged that abstention from dinner would be a stoic discipline good for my character, or if by abstaining I could afford to attend a play that I wanted to see, or could devote the dinner hour to some work that needed to be done, the situation would be to this extent a moral one, for a value would be set on each of the alternatives. Indeed, the great difficulty of moral problems and the indecisiveness of much moral deliberation are due principally to this fact, that both of the alternatives with which our deliberation is concerned are in some manner valued and their values are often incommensurate.

MORAL INSIGHT

*24.* A moral situation, furthermore, must have a consequential character. Even where value and possibility are both present a situation may still be amoral—which is to say, it may be a situation to which ethical considerations do not properly apply. Choosing between different dishes on a restaurant menu provides a familiar example. If pot roast and sweetbreads are offered as alternative choices at the same price, the only thing that a diner would ordinarily have to consider is which one of them he would prefer. If his decision is not automatic, if he spends any time in deliberating over the choice, then he must evidently have set some value upon each of the two dishes, between which he regards himself as free to choose. Thus the first two conditions of a moral situation are met: there is a conflict between values, and a choice between them is possible. Nevertheless, the situation as it stands is not a moral one. The alternatives are considered simply as ends in themselves; the values involved in the diner's choice will terminate in the enjoyment of what he has chosen, and the duration of that enjoyment will be short. Nothing of any significance will be entailed by his ordering one meat rather than the other. The situation is pretty much isolated from the main lines of his experience and his choices.

*25.* Even where no social relationships are immediately involved, a choice may have moral character, to the degree that it is significantly consequential. If a certain action promises a greater intensity of pleasure at the moment but appears likely to entail later pains or inconveniences of an important kind, moral insight into these future consequences is called for, and the situation is thus a moral one, although not in a social way. Whether consideration must be taken of the claims of other selves or only of one's own future self, in either case the choice is related to, and partly concerned with, something beyond the immediate result. Mechanical computation is not possible here as it is in the case of physical measurements, for there are no sets of physical units that can be compared. In a moral situation the difference between the competing values is at least partly one of kind, not merely of degree, and human interests and valuations are so manifold, so subject to continual growth and reconsideration, that the insights themselves have only a tenuous stability. What is required is an insight into the remoter values involved, and the probable embodiments they would take in relation to those affected. It is in the deepening and maturing of men's moral insights that the best index of human development is to be found.

26. The third requirement of a moral situation, then, has a double aspect. The choice must be consequential, and this may be seen from two sides. The alternatives are not simple ends-in-themselves terminating here and now; they involve values over and beyond the values of immediate enjoyment. And the agent by whom the choice is to be made must therefore have an imaginative grasp of the consequences, an imaginative insight into the nature of the values that are only hinted at in the immediate situation.

27. But is insight enough? Even when I fully comprehend that a certain course of action is both possible and the best one for me to undertake, is it guaranteed that I will therefore undertake it? We all know that it is not. The experience of temptation is familiar to everybody—the inward tension and struggle in which I perceive that one way of acting is the right way but am powerfully drawn towards some enticing but more limited good. Let us look at the nature of this kind of experience more closely.

## THE GOOD AND THE RIGHT

28. What I want to do is frequently opposed to what I know I ought to do; i.e., the present good is often incompatible with what seems to be right. As previously stated, there must be some inclination toward both of the alternatives with which any moral deliberation is concerned. This is the same thing as to say that both alternatives are felt or thought to be somehow good. But the qualities of the competing goods may be radically different. Say that I am tempted to sit drinking beer with friends when I know that I ought to be devoting the evening to my studies. There is an inclination to linger on; there is also an inclination, of another kind, to say good night and leave. The former inclination is strong and attractive but without rational sanction; whereas—

Quite other is the prompting of the "ought." It is not so much a drive as an inner exhortation. It is not impulsive, but imperative. And what we experience is not ourselves impelled, but ourselves impelling, ourselves impelling ourselves, indeed ourselves impelling ourselves against impulse.[2]

[2] Horace G. Wyatt, *The Art of Feeling*, pp. 169-170.

The situation is a sufficiently familiar one. The strongest actual propensity at a given moment is toward a course of action contrary to the one toward which duty beckons. An effort is required to break away from the fascination of the immediate. The sense that such an effort is required, that it *can* be made, and that it would be better to make it because the result would be an eventually greater good, are conditions of a feeling of "ought."

29. The good and the right, though often specifically opposed, are related at bottom. Their actual conflicts are explained by a distinction within the meaning of "good"—between intrinsic and extrinsic goods. A good is called *intrinsic* when it is judged worthy of being sought for its own sake, i.e., when it is an end in itself; *extrinsic* or *instrumental* when it is sought as a means to some other good. The relation is a shifting one, for it is not always possible to distinguish sharply between the end and the means: what is an end from one point of view may be regarded as a means from another. Nevertheless we can say in general that the good of a surgical operation is extrinsic: it must be referred to the greater health that is to come. The enjoyment of a glass of wine is an intrinsic good, a "good in itself": the wine is not enjoyed for the sake of anything distinct from the enjoyment. Still other goods are at once intrinsic and extrinsic; an enjoyable *and* nourishing dinner, a refreshing *and* cleansing bath, and the like. Often the right course of action will consist in choosing some extrinsic good (say, diligent study) which is the only available means to the attainment of some important intrinsic good (say, a professional career). On such occasions the rightness of the action is founded on the good to which it leads, but to the agent it may not appear to partake of any of the character of that remote good. Thus it happens that if the agent is tempted by some more immediate good (such as the pleasures of a lazy life) the conflict, which would be more rationally conceived as a conflict between two goods (present leisure vs. future career) acquires the appearance of a conflict between the present good (leisure) and the present right course of action (diligent study).

THE PARADOX OF VOLITION

30. Situations in which there is a genuine moral struggle, in which a temptation must be conquered by a putting forth of moral effort, are crucial for morality. The ultimate justification of a moral principle (and, indirectly, for any ethical theory) is the possibility that it can be made an effective force in moral struggles. William James describes the moral struggle as a situation in which "a rarer and more ideal impulse is called upon to neutralize others of a more instinctive and habitual kind"; in which "strongly explosive tendencies are checked, or strongly obstructive conditions overcome." He continues:

We *feel*, in all hard cases of volition, as if the line taken, when the rarer and more ideal motives prevail, were the line of greater resistance, as if the line of coarser motivation were the more pervious and easy one, even at the very moment when we refuse to follow it. He who under the surgeon's knife represses cries of pain, or he who exposes himself to social obloquy for duty's sake, feels as if he were following the line of greatest temporary resistance. . . .

The ideal impulse appears . . . a still small voice which must be artificially reinforced to prevail. Effort is what reinforces it, making things seem as if, while the force of propensity were essentially a fixed quantity, the ideal force might be of various amount. But what determines the amount of the effort when, by its aid, an ideal motive becomes victorious over a great sensual resistance? The very greatness of the resistance itself. If the sensual propensity is small, the effort is small. The latter is *made great* by the presence of a great antagonist to overcome. And if a brief definition of ideal or moral action were required, none could be given which would better fit the appearances than this: *It is action in the line of greatest resistance.*[3]

*31.* In order to understand James' profoundly valid paradox we must avoid the popular tendency to explain a moral situation wholly by analogies drawn from the physical world. In those aspects of nature studied by physics and chemistry it is always the line of least, never of greater resistance that is followed. The universality of the physical law of least physical resistance, however, is due to the fact that it is not directly applicable to concrete experience, for in *concrete* experience no laws are applicable with unremitting exactitude. Physicists may be allowed to formulate their own laws by the methodology which their technical interests require. But scientific laws tell us nothing directly about moral experience. In this province everyone must be, to a large extent, his own observer. And what is a more assured fact of introspective observation than that in cases of moral struggle *we often can and sometimes do follow the path of greatest resistance?*

*32.* What we ought to do, however unappealing originally, can be made, by a concentration of purpose, what we want to do. Intelligence (or, as it has previously been called, insight) is the mediator. The reason why it may be *right for my present self* to forego the pleasure of a drinking party is that the sacrifice may promote a good for my future self, time for study, or a clear head for tomorrow morning, or money saved, or all three. What I choose is distinct from the greatest immediate satisfaction but not separate from all satisfaction whatever. I have put myself imaginatively in the place of my future self and am thus able to consider the good or the pleasure or the emotional satisfaction apart from, *abstracted* from (i.e., separated by the imagination from) the present experience. This abstractive ability of man is what marks him as rational, and, so far as it becomes effective in directing his conduct, as moral.

[3] William James, *The Principles of Psychology*, Vol. II, pp. 548-549.

33. There is another way, too, in which man's abstractive ability shows itself: in the altruistic "ought." A person can recognize duties not only toward his own future self but toward other persons also.

Here again intelligence is the mediator. Man is able to consider the good or the pleasure or the emotional satisfaction apart from the individual to be satisfied, apart not only from [the particular experience] but from the experiencer. If emotional satisfaction is the thing desired, it is so for B, C, D and others as well as for A. The happiness of others is just as much an end as my happiness and just as much to be sought after. The "ought" is the peculiar emotion which now enters to convert this intellectual achievement into conduct.[4]

By this abstractive process the Golden Rule of Jesus, "Do unto others as you would have them do unto you," and the less positive form of the same command, given half a millennium earlier by Confucius, "Refrain from doing to others what you would not have them do to yourself," can be realized as expressions of a binding obligation.

34. Right and wrong, then, are not hollow sounds nor is discussion about them an idle game. If we mean what we say in designating an action right or wrong, if we are doing more than mouthing a conventional formula, our judgment will in some manner affect our subsequent conduct. Ethics is not a pastime for the understanding alone. Ethical theory calls for moral practice, and the full meaning of ethics becomes intelligible only as we translate theories into moral principles that can be made effective forces in the struggle toward ideal ends.


THE SEARCH FOR A STANDARD

35. But how, it will be asked, is the particular character of right and wrong on any given occasion to be determined? How can one be sure that the development of moral insight (even if such an accomplishment were not in any case formidably difficult) will necessarily lead to a "right" judgment of where one's duties lie? Or, to shift the perspective, how can one be sure that one's moral insight is sufficiently developed? Superior intelligence is not always enough; it may be put at the service of evil ends. Satan, whatever his delinquencies, was no fool. What clear test, then, (so the popular quandary runs) can be applied to human conduct so as to determine on each occasion whether it is right or wrong; or (from a somewhat more mature point of view) so as to distinguish the higher of two contending values from the lower? Various criteria are proposed, such as the following.

36. (i) *Natural Inclinations.* "Follow your impulses; do whatever gives you the most enjoyment": people sometimes talk as if in these trite maxims they had discovered a significant moral truth. Actually they have done the

[4] Wyatt, *op. cit.*, p. 168.

contrary: they have denied that moral truth exists. If inclinations are the only standard of conduct, then there is no standard by which to choose between one inclination and another. Whatever inclination is strongest at any moment becomes for that reason right. Temptation becomes honorable by the sheer fact of being tempting. Evidently there is no moral standard offered here; there is merely a negation of moral standard.

37. Sometimes the claims of irrational impulse are bolstered by philosophical arguments based on the alleged facts of human nature. Such arguments will be examined more fully in Chapter 3; here it need only be remarked that human nature is too complex and mysterious to be reduced to any single set or type of facts. If it is a fact that men yield to impulse it is no less a fact that they can and sometimes do rationally redirect or halt their initial impulses. To overcome and remake one's nature is itself an expression of one's nature. That a man faced with alternatives can choose the harder course as against the easier is a supremely important fact, without which moral action would be powerless and moral judgment empty. But it is just this kind of *ideal fact* which the champions of impulse, instinct, and inclination as sufficient guides of life habitually overlook.

38. (ii) *Statute law.* The law of the land is a standard of right and wrong from which no individual is wholly exempt. At the same time it is safe to say that no one obeys all the laws. In the first place, there are numerous laws on the statute books that have long ago become obsolete without ever having been annulled. To obey all the laws an individual would have to employ legal aid to find out what laws there are and exactly what they require in terms of conduct. Secondly, even among the laws that are known, some are held in higher respect than others. During the period when the eighteenth amendment to the Constitution was in force there were many so-called "law-abiding citizens" who had no scruples about buying a drink. Besides, it is a recognized right of an American citizen (by voting and in related ways) to seek to change the existing laws. There must, therefore, be some standard by which the goodness or badness of actual laws, as well as of proposed laws, can be judged.

39. (iii) *Public opinion* is in the long run more authoritative than statute law, for a law that lacks public support will not be obeyed and in the end will either be repealed or, as in the case of many "blue laws," ignored by common consent. Nevertheless, public opinion is often wrong. Its fallibility in particular cases is recognized even by those who accept it as a generally reliable guide. The vast majority of men think emotionally and gregariously. One of the chief tasks of education is admittedly to raise the standard of public opinion. There must be some higher standard, then, by which we can judge the state of public opinion at any time to be bad or good.

40. (iv) There are those who hold that the higher standard is furnished

by *religious authority*. Such a view presupposes: (1) a belief in God, (2) a belief that God communicates His will either directly or indirectly to men, and (3) more particularly, a belief that one's own Church or sect or Holy Book is the channel through which God's will is revealed, as a check on the vagaries of one's individual conscience. Even if these beliefs can all be accepted without difficulty, questions of interpretation frequently arise. The Ten Commandments, for example, forbid stealing. Does this prohibition apply to the practice of ruining your business competitor by price-cutting, and so eventually pocketing his expected receipts? Does is apply to the practice of certain oil, mining, and lumber companies of wasting the country's (i.e., the American people's) natural resources for private gain? Since no clear definition of stealing receives universal consent, the divine command, though indubitably just and important, is subject to numerous ambiguities. Again, Christ's law of love is pretty clearly the keynote of his teaching. But Christians disagree widely on the method of applying that law to such socially urgent problems as war and labor relations.

*41.* (v) *Conscience* is a part of everyone's standard. Regardless of how we may explain it the existence of a "still small voice" that sometimes on crucial occasions says "Do!" or "Refrain!" is an inescapable phenomenon. The voice of conscience often opposes itself to the inclinations of the moment, sometimes to public opinion; and in fundamental matters it may be, for the dedicated man, a higher court of appeal than any outer law, secular or religious. Still, conscience is far from infallible. It can and ought to be educated, and when a man relies on it uncritically it may turn out to be but the prompting of self-interest satanically masquerading in holy dress.

*42.* (vi) Conscience then must be controlled, and revelation must be interpreted, by *reason*. Very true. But that is not to say that reason is *the* standard. Immanuel Kant is the outstanding example of a philosopher who tried to make it so, and as might have been expected, his *applications* of his rationally established principles are quite as debatable as those of any other moralist. If generosity is better than selfishness that is not because it is more rational: some philosophers, in fact, have held it to be less so. Rationality is a necessary aspect of ethics but not its sufficient criterion. Ethics, in short, must be logical, but ethics is not logic.

*43.* Evidently no isolated standard of right and wrong is proof against attack. The function of ethics is not to provide a simple and sure rule by which moral problems can be "solved." An active intelligence revolts against whatever doctrine claims to utter the last word on any matter. Especially is this true in ethics, where the conclusions sought are of such intimate importance to each serious inquirer. Immediate decisions will often have to be reached by appealing to some convenient rule of thumb or to some already developed habit or preference. But it is an advantage of theories that they can be inquired into at leisure. The task of theoretical ethics is not to lay down static norms by which each new moral problem that arises can be decisively answered. Its task is rather to develop a method suitable for the evaluation and criticism of existing norms and for the exploration of new value possibilities, in order that when moral decisions have henceforth to be made their grounds may be more adequate and more worthy.

# Assigning Causes

## ~ IV ~

## CAUSAL RELATIONS

AS ERICH FROMM'S ESSAY ILLUSTRATES, the process of assigning causes to effects is often, as we can observe without disagreement, a matter of individual interpretation. When the existence of the effect itself may be questioned—for example, Fromm's view that we *are* a society of repressed conformists—the situation becomes even more complex. The mind of an educated man continues, though baffled, to assign causes to effects it perceives, that is, to recognize similarities and differences in the sequence of two discernible things or events. What event invariably and immediately precedes another event? What event invariably and immediately succeeds another?

While almost everyone at the scene of an accident or a fire wants to know how the catastrophe happened, many people remain without curiosity about the proximate and remote causes of political behavior, civil disobedience, or economic hardship in other societies, and even in their own. Indeed, they are equally incurious and unreflective about their own behavior in arguing, drinking, fighting, divorcing; they lead unexamined lives. The enlightened man, however, is engaged in trying to understand himself, his acquaintances, and the problems of his business or profession and those of society at large. Instead of simply accepting effects, he hypothesizes causes with a temper of mind that is always open to fresh observations and ready for new evaluations. For his reasoning mind, the perceivable world is not held together entirely by chance (or freedom) but also by causality (or necessity). If he is to avoid painful consequences and discover those that are pleasureful, he must know, from his own experiences and from scrutiny of reports by others, how events associate themselves.

Establishing probable causes for observed effects and predicting likely effects from known causes may be largely matters of opinion, but it is often in exchanging opinion that men arrive at truth. Why an automobile accident occurred is not often in dispute (though drivers may lie and spectators render various accounts), but why a national election was won or a war lost, why sales fell or a temperature rose, why love ended or death came so soon are questions men have pondered and debated as long as there have been love, death, war, and sales charts. Simple minds accept more easily acts of chance, fate, and God. Educated men attempt to understand and control effects as far as human nature, chance, and God will allow.

Developing the ability to analyze cause and effect with accuracy and insight is a matter of practice. The college freshman should not assume he knows nothing of the causes of certain phenomena in our society. He is at least informed on aspects of his own generation. He may write with the authority of an eyewitness on the causes of juvenile delinquency, the rise of high school dropouts, the causes of conformity, the popularity of teenage entertainment idols, the reasons that youth today seeks minimal success with security rather than dubious success but a venturesome life, the pressures of an organized society in a nuclear age—all subjects on which an older generation needs the opinions of a younger if it is to do more than flounder into our future.

Frequently a bewildering number of causes, which may be classified in various ways, exist in a given situation. An act by officials in our State Department may result in a foreign power's responding in a certain way. We would call this act the *immediate* cause of that government's response. The *ultimate* cause, however, must be sought in factors that shaped the differences in the political and social structures of the two nations. One may also distinguish, and most easily among repeatable and controllable events, between a *necessary* and a *sufficient* condition to cause a given effect. In saying "*x is a cause of y*" we may mean that whenever *x* exists *y* follows and that *y* will also follow when conditions other than *x* occur. For example, "The Dutch elm disease is fatal to any American elms it infects;" but other factors—the runoff of salts used to melt snow and ice, or bulldozers from the state highway department—may also be fatal to elms, especially near highways. On the other hand, we may mean when we say "*x is a cause of y*" that *y* will not follow unless *x* occurs. That is, whenever *y* occurs *x* is a necessary and prior condition; but, given *x*, we have no assurance *y* does in fact follow. For example, "Water makes plants grow," but the mere adding of water to soil surrounding plants will not guarantee their growth. A "broken home" may be an ultimate cause and sufficient condition for delinquency but not, except in certain cases, the immediate cause. It is quite unlikely to be a necessary condition since some persons who come from homes that are classifiable legally and sociologically as "broken" escape delinquency.

Events may appear to observers to be so coexistent, so numerous, or so entwined that any causal relation, whether immediate, ultimate, sufficient, or necessary, is difficult if not impossible to establish. As Orwell points out, "an effect can become a cause, reinforcing the original cause and producing the same effect in an intensified form and so on indefinitely. A man may take to drink because he feels himself to be a failure, and then fail all the more completely because he drinks." In such cases, however, one can often take practical steps that will slow, if not completely halt, such spirals even though he may not be able to reduce the complex interplay of cause-and-effect to a set of casual statements.

## · 13 ·

## *Erich Fromm*

# THE ILLUSION OF INDIVIDUALITY

*1.* It is important to consider how our culture fosters this tendency to conform, even though there is space for only a few outstanding examples. The suppression of spontaneous feelings, and thereby of the development of genuine individuality, starts very early, as a matter of fact with the earliest training of a child. This is not to say that training must inevitably lead to suppression of spontaneity if the real aim of education is to further the inner independence and individuality of the child, its growth and integrity. The restrictions which such a kind of education may have to impose upon the growing child are only transitory measures that really support the process of growth and expansion. In our culture, however, education too often results in the elimination of spontaneity and in the substitution of original psychic acts by superimposed feelings, thoughts, and wishes. (By original I do not mean, let me repeat, that an idea has not been thought before by someone else, but that it originates in the individual, that it is the result of his own activity and in this sense is *his* thought.) To choose one illustration somewhat arbitrarily, one of the earliest suppressions of *feelings* concerns hostility and dislike. To start with, most children have a certain measure of hostility and rebelliousness as a result of their conflicts with a surrounding world that tends to block their expansiveness and to which, as the weaker opponent, they usually have to yield. It is one of the essential aims of the educational process to eliminate this antagonistic reaction. The methods are different; they vary from threats and punishments, which frighten the child, to the subtler methods of bribery or "explanations," which confuse the child and make him give up his hostility. The child starts with giving up the expression of his feeling and eventually gives up the very feeling itself. Together with that, he is taught to suppress the awareness of hostility and insincerity in others; sometimes this is not entirely easy, since children have a capacity for noticing such negative qualities in others without being so easily deceived by words as adults usually are. They still dislike somebody "for no good reason"—except the very good one that they feel the hostility, or insincerity, radiating from that person. This reaction is soon discouraged; it does not take long for the child to reach the "maturity" of the average adult and to lose the sense of discrimination between a decent person and a scoundrel, as long as the latter has not committed some flagrant act.

2. On the other hand, early in his education, the child is taught to have feelings that are not at all "his"; particularly is he taught to like people, to be uncritically friendly to them, and to smile. What education may not have accomplished is usually done by social pressure in later life. If you do not smile you are judged lacking in a "pleasing personality"—and you need to have a pleasing personality if you want to sell your services, whether as a waitress, a salesman, or a physician. Only those at the bottom of the social pyramid, who sell nothing but their physical labor, and those at the very top do not need to be particularly "pleasant." Friendliness, cheerfulness, and everything that a smile is supposed to express, become automatic responses which one turns on and off like an electric switch.[1]

3. To be sure, in many instances the person is aware of merely making a gesture; in most cases, however, he loses that awareness and thereby the ability to discriminate between the pseudo feeling and spontaneous friendliness.

4. It is not only hostility that is directly suppressed and friendliness that is killed by superimposing its counterfeit. A wide range of spontaneous emotions are suppressed and replaced by pseudo feelings. Freud has taken one such suppression and put it in the center of his whole system, namely the suppression of sex. Although I believe that the discouragement of sexual joy is not the only important suppression of spontaneous reactions but one of many, certainly its importance is not to be underrated. Its results are obvious in cases of sexual inhibitions and also in those where sex assumes a compulsive quality and is consumed like liquor or a drug, which has no particular taste but makes you forget yourself. Regardless of the one or the other effect, their suppression, because of the intensity of sexual desires, not only affects the sexual sphere but also weakens the person's courage for spontaneous expression in all other spheres.

[1] As one telling illustration of the commercialization of friendliness I should like to cite *Fortune*'s report on "The Howard Johnson Restaurants." (*Fortune*, September, 1940, p. 96.) Johnson employs a force of "shoppers" who go from restaurant to restaurant to watch for lapses. "Since everything is cooked on the premises according to standard recipes and measurements issued by the home office, the inspector knows how large a portion of steak he should receive and how the vegetable should taste. He also knows how long it should take for the dinner to be served and he knows the exact degree of friendliness that should be shown by the hostess and the waitress."

5. In our society emotions in general are discouraged. While there can be no doubt that any creative thinking—as well as any other creative activity—is inseparably linked with emotion, it has become an ideal to think and to live without emotions. To be "emotional" has become synonymous with being unsound or unbalanced. By the acceptance of this standard the individual has become greatly weakened; his thinking is impoverished and flattened. On the other hand, since emotions cannot be completely killed, they must have their existence totally apart from the intellectual side of the personality; the result is the cheap and insincere sentimentality with which movies and popular songs feed millions of emotion-starved customers.

6. There is one tabooed emotion that I want to mention in particular, because its suppression touches deeply on the roots of personality: the sense of tragedy. As we saw in an earlier chapter, the awareness of death and of the tragic aspect of life, whether dim or clear, is one of the basic characteristics of man. Each culture has its own way of coping with the problem of death. For those societies in which the process of individuation has progressed but little, the end of individual existence is less of a problem since the experience of individual existence itself is less developed. Death is not yet conceived as being basically different from life. Cultures in which we find a higher development of individuation have treated death according to their social and psychological structure. The Greeks put all emphasis on life and pictured death as nothing but a shadowy and dreary continuation of life. The Egyptians based their hopes on a belief in the indestructibility of the human body, at least of those whose power during life was indestructible. The Jews admitted the fact of death realistically and were able to reconcile themselves with the idea of the destruction of individual life by the vision of a state of happiness and justice ultimately to be reached by mankind in this world. Christianity has made death unreal and tried to comfort the unhappy individual by promises of a life after death. Our own era simply denies death and with it one fundamental aspect of life. Instead of allowing the awareness of death and suffering to become one of the strongest incentives for life, the basis for human solidarity, and an experience without which joy and enthusiasm lack intensity and depth, the individual is forced to repress it. But, as is always the case with repression, by being removed from sight the repressed elements do not cease to exist. Thus the fear of death lives an illegitimate existence among us. It remains alive in spite of the attempt to deny it, but being repressed it remains sterile. It is one source of the flatness of other experiences, of the restlessness pervading life, and it explains, I would venture to say, the exorbitant amount of money this nation pays for its funerals.

7. In the process of tabooing emotions modern psychiatry plays an ambiguous role. On the one hand its greatest representative, Freud, has

broken through the fiction of the rational, purposeful character of the human mind and opened a path which allows a view into the abyss of human passions. On the other hand psychiatry, enriched by these very achievements of Freud, has made itself an instrument of the general trends in the manipulation of personality. Many psychiatrists, including psychoanalysts, have painted the picture of a "normal" personality which is never too sad, too angry, or too excited. They use words like "infantile" or "neurotic" to denounce traits or types of personalities that do not conform with the conventional pattern of a "normal" individual. This kind of influence is in a way more dangerous than the older and franker forms of name-calling. Then the individual knew at least that there was some person or some doctrine which criticized him and he could fight back. But who can fight back at "science"?

8. The same distortion happens to original *thinking* as happens to feeling and emotions. From the very start of education original thinking is discouraged and ready-made thoughts are put into people's heads. How this is done with young children is easy enough to see. They are filled with curiosity about the world, they want to grasp it physically as well as intellectually. They want to know the truth, since that is the safest way to orient themselves in a strange and powerful world. Instead, they are not taken seriously, and it does not matter whether this attitude takes the form of open disrespect or of the subtle condescension which is usual towards all who have no power (such as children, aged or sick people). Although this treatment by itself offers strong discouragement to independent thinking, there is a worse handicap: the insincerity—often unintentional—which is typical of the average adult's behavior toward a child. This insincerity consists partly in the fictitious picture of the world which the child is given. It is about as useful as instructions concerning life in the Arctic would be to someone who has asked how to prepare for an expedition to the Sahara Desert. Besides this general misrepresentation of the world there are the many specific lies that tend to conceal facts which, for various personal reasons, adults do not want children to know. From a bad temper, which is rationalized as justified dissatisfaction with the child's behavior, to concealment of the parents' sexual activities and their quarrels, the child is "not supposed to know" and his inquiries meet with hostile or polite discouragement.

9. The child thus prepared enters school and perhaps college. I want to mention briefly some of the educational methods used today which in effect further discourage original thinking. One is the emphasis on knowledge of facts, or I should rather say on information. The pathetic superstition prevails that by knowing more and more facts one arrives at knowledge of reality. Hundreds of scattered and unrelated facts are dumped into the heads of students; their time and energy are taken up by learning more and more facts so that there is little left for thinking. To be sure,

thinking without a knowledge of facts remains empty and fictitious; but "information" alone can be just as much of an obstacle to thinking as the lack of it.

10. Another closely related way of discouraging original thinking is to regard all truth as relative. Truth is made out to be a metaphysical concept, and if anyone speaks about wanting to discover the truth he is thought backward by the "progressive" thinkers of our age. Truth is declared to be an entirely subjective matter, almost a matter of taste. Scientific endeavor must be detached from subjective factors, and its aim is to look at the world without passion and interest. The scientist has to approach facts with sterilized hands as a surgeon approaches his patient. The result of this relativism, which often presents itself by the name of empiricism or positivism or which recommends itself by its concern for the correct usage of words, is that thinking loses its essential stimulus—the wishes and interests of the person who thinks; instead it becomes a machine to register "facts." Actually, just as thinking in general has developed out of the need for mastery of material life, so the quest for truth is rooted in the interests and needs of individuals and social groups. Without such interest the stimulus for seeking the truth would be lacking. There are always groups whose interest is furthered by truth, and their representatives have been the pioneers of human thought; there are other groups whose interests are furthered by concealing truth. Only in the latter case does interest prove harmful to the cause of truth. The problem, therefore, is not that there is *an* interest at stake, but *which kind* of interest is at stake. I might say that inasmuch as there is some longing for the truth in every human being, it is because every human being has some need for it.

11. This holds true in the first place with regard to a person's orientation in the outer world, and it holds especially true for the child. As a child, every human being passes through a state of powerlessness, and truth is one of the strongest weapons of those who have no power. But the truth is in the individual's interest not only with regard to his orientation in the outer world; his own strength depends to a great extent on his knowing the truth about himself. Illusions about oneself can become crutches useful to those who are not able to walk alone; but they increase a person's weakness. The individual's greatest strength is based on the maximum of integration of his personality, and that means also on the maximum of transparence to himself. "Know thyself" is one of the fundamental commands that aim at human strength and happiness.

12. In addition to the factors just mentioned there are others which actively tend to confuse whatever is left of the capacity for original thinking in the average adult. With regard to all basic questions of individual and social life, with regard to psychological, economic, political, and moral problems, a great sector of our culture has just one function—to befog the issues. One kind of smokescreen is the assertion that the problems are too

complicated for the average individual to grasp. On the contrary it would seem that many of the basic issues of individual and social life are very simple, so simple, in fact, that everyone should be expected to understand them. To let them appear to be so enormously complicated that only a "specialist" can understand them, and he only in his own limited field, actually—and often intentionally—tends to discourage people from trusting their own capacity to think about those problems that really matter. The individual feels helplessly caught in a chaotic mass of data and with pathetic patience waits until the specialists have found out what to do and where to go.

13. The result of this kind of influence is a twofold one: one is a scepticism and cynicism towards everything which is said or printed, while the other is a childish belief in anything that a person is told with authority. This combination of cynicism and naïveté is very typical of the modern individual. Its essential result is to discourage him from doing his own thinking and deciding.

# Questions

1. Fromm presents his case establishing the causes of conformity by making other generalizations about the nature of our society for which he then cites examples. List those generalizations.

2. Is training a necessary or a sufficient condition leading to supression of spontaneous feeling? See paragraph 1.

3. Would you agree with Fromm that Christianity by promising an afterlife has made death unreal? Is it not a characteristic of most religions to promise an afterlife?

4. What observations of life in America as you see it seem to support Fromm's assertion that our era simply denies death? What evidence to the contrary can you see? Do his observations have an inner consistency? Are there any which might have proved inconsistent and are glaring by the fact of their omission?

5. Would you agree that modern problems—psychological, economic, political, and moral—are so complex that they discourage individuals from attempting to understand them? Granted their complexity to the point of insolvability, does it necessarily follow that the individual, feeling helplessly caught in a chaotic mass of data and controlled by decisions of specialists, becomes increasingly conformist?

6. State Fromm's point in paragraphs 10 and 11 in your own words. Have there not always been individuals whose interests were furthered by concealing truth? Is his point in paragraph 10, therefore, merely that there are more such persons with more power in our age?

7. By what logic does Fromm move from his point in paragraph 10 to the "Know Thyself" point in paragraph 11?

8. Why is it more difficult to know oneself in our age?

9. Do you agree or disagree that there are absolute truths in economic, political, and moral realms that ought neither to be denied nor concealed, that individuals have a natural desire to know and accept them, and that denial of them will have harmful effects upon the individual and the society? Name some. (See C. S. Lewis, "The Law of Right and Wrong.")

10. Assuming Fromm's view of the causes of our conformity and insecurity to be accurate, what corrective action might we take as individuals and as a society?

# Theme Topics

1. Write your own account of the causes of conformity in your own personality.

2. Write your understanding of the causes of teen-age delinquency.

3. If we begin in America to educate in separate vocational schools students on the lower levels of intelligence and ability, describe the probable effects of this separation upon the attitudes and personalities of students in vocational as well as academic high schools.

4. After doing some reading on a current event in national or international politics, write a paper discussing its causes.

5. Discuss the reasons for the popularity with your generation of a certain book, movie, or play.

## ·14·

*Bruno Bettelheim*

# ADJUSTMENT FOR SURVIVAL

### OLD AND NEW PRISONERS

*1.* Perhaps the changes forced upon most survivors in the concentration camp may best be illustrated by comparing "new" prisoners, in whom the process of enforced self reeducation had barely started, with "old" prisoners, in whom it was nearly finished. The term "new" prisoner is used for those who had spent no more than one year in the camp; "old" prisoners are those who had been there at least three years. As far as old prisoners are concerned, I can offer only observations but no findings based on introspection.

*2.* There was, of course, considerable variation in the time it took prisoners to make their peace with the possibility of having to spend the rest of their lives in the camp. Some became part of camp life rather soon, some probably never, though they may have spent more than ten years in the camps. When a new prisoner arrived he was told, "If you survive the first three weeks, you have a good chance of surviving a year; if you survive three months you will survive the next three years.[1]

*3.* During the first month in camp (including casualties of the transport) the monthly death rate for newcomers actually was at least 10% and probably close to 15%. In the following month—if there were no special mass persecutions—this figure was usually cut in half; that is, the death rate among new prisoners during the second month might be somewhere around 7%. During the third month it might again be halved to about 3%. And from then on (again barring mass executions) the monthly death rate for the surviving 75% may have dropped to 1% or less, where it remained, by and large.

*4.* This reduction in the death rate was due largely to the fact that by

Reprinted with permission of the publisher from *The Informed Heart* by Bruno Bettelheim. Copyright © 1960 by The Free Press, a Corporation. Reprinted also by permission of Thames and Hudson, Ltd.

Bruno Bettelheim, born in Vienna in 1903, studied psychoanalysis there, and in 1938–39 was sent by the Nazis to the concentration camps at Dachau and Buchenwald.

[1] At the time this comment was made, the yearly death rate, in my estimation, was about 30%. The yearly death rate of 50% . . . pertains to a later period of the camps.

that time all those who could not survive the rigors of camp life had been weeded out. Those with physical disabilities, such as heart conditions, were already dead. So were most of those with personalities too rigid to develop the necessary defenses and adjustments; they, too, succumbed in the first few weeks. The lowered death rate was thus a measure of both the survival of the fittest, and of the heightened chances for survival as one learned to adjust. By the same token the halt in deaths was a compelling reason for prisoners to change, to do it on their own steam, and do it fast, if they meant to survive.[2]

5. The chief concerns of new prisoners were to remain physically intact and return to the outer world the same person who had left it. Therefore all efforts were directed toward these goals, and they tried to combat as much as possible any weakening of their maturity or self sufficiency. Old prisoners seemed mainly concerned with the problem of how to live as well as possible inside the camp. Therefore they tried to reorganize their personalities as well as they could to become more acceptable to the SS. Once they had embraced this attitude, everything that happened to them, even the worst atrocity, was "real." No longer was there a split between a figure to whom things happened and the prisoner who observed in detachment. The split in personality had disappeared, but at the price of the prisoner's personality no longer being integrated. It dropped to a different, lower level: one of resignation, dependency, submission, and passivity.

6. Old prisoners could accept this because they could scarcely believe they would ever return to the outer world which had grown strange to them. But once they had changed, there was every indication that they were afraid of returning. They did not admit it directly, but from their talk it was clear that in their own minds, only a cataclysmic event—a world war or world revolution—could free them. They seemed aware of what had happened to them as they aged in the camp. They realized they had adapted to camp life and that this process had brought a basic change in their personalities.

7. The realization was given dramatic expression by those few prisoners who became convinced that no one could live in the camps longer than a certain number of years without changing his attitudes so radically that

[2] What I have explained here by statistics has been described by an "old" prisoner as an inner experience.

Kupfer, after two years at Dachau, reflected on what went on in him as he adjusted to life in the camp: "Now I am a 'Dachauer,' prisoner no. 24814. I think and feel as is fitting for a prisoner at Dachau. Slowly a process of acclimatization has taken place in me. I did not realize it then, but for life in the camp this is great progress, because whoever becomes a concentration camp prisoner through and through does not perish so soon, compared to the prisoner who remains a newcomer inside, and therefore one who externally and internally tries to remain outside of it all. I began in the very center of my inner life, but also in all externals, to act and feel like a true 'Dachauer,' ["old prisoner"—B. B.] though I did not realize this at all at the time."

he could no longer be considered, or again become, the person he once was. Therefore they set a time limit for themselves beyond which, in their opinion, there was no point staying alive since from then on life would simply consist of being prisoners in a concentration camp. These were men who could not endure acquiring those attitudes and behaviors they saw developing in most old prisoners. They therefore set a fixed date for committing suicide. One of them set the sixth anniversary of his arrival in the camp because he felt that nobody there was worth saving after five years. His friends tried to watch him carefully on that day, but nevertheless he succeeded.[3]

8. One characteristic difference between old and new prisoners was that old prisoners could no longer evaluate correctly the outside, non-Gestapo controlled world. Whereas new prisoners tried to retain their attitude toward the world of the camp as being nonreal, to old prisoners it was the only reality. How long it took a prisoner to stop considering life outside the camp as real depended to a great extent on the strength of his emotional ties to his family and friends, the strength and richness of his personality and the degree to which he was able to preserve important aspects of his old interests and attitudes. The greater the area of his interests, and the more he contrived to take advantage of them in the camp situation, the better able he was to protect his personality against too early impoverishment.

9. Some indications of changes in attitude were: the tendency toward scheming to find a better place of work in the camp rather than trying to contact the outer world. New prisoners, for instance, would spend all their money on efforts to smuggle letters out of the camp or to get letters without having them censored. Old prisoners used their money to get "soft" jobs such as clerical work in the camp offices, or labor in the shops where they at least had protection from the weather. This change also found expression in their dominant thoughts and topics of conversation: new prisoners were most concerned with life outside of camp; old prisoners were interested only in camp life.

10. It so happened, for instance, that on one and the same day, news was received of a speech by President Roosevelt denouncing Hitler and Germany, and rumors spread that one SS officer was going to be replaced by another. New prisoners discussed the President's speech excitedly and paid scant attention to the rumors; old prisoners were indifferent to the speech, but devoted their conversation to the rumored change in camp officers.

11. When old prisoners were asked why they spoke so little about their futures outside the camp, they often admitted they could no longer visualize themselves living in a free world, making decisions, taking care of themselves and their families.

[3] I witnessed this suicide. A very similar suicide is described by Kautsky, p. 283.

*12.* The attitude of the old prisoner toward his family had undergone a significant change. One reason for this was the total reversal of his status within the family. In line with the paternalistic structure of most German households, the family had been wholly dependent on the man for decisions, much more so than would be true in an American family. Now he was not only unable to influence his wife's or his children's decisions, but was utterly dependent on them for taking steps to secure his release and to send him the money that was so important to him in the camp.

*13.* As a matter of fact, although many families behaved decently toward prisoners, serious problems were created. During the first months they spent a great deal of energy, time, and money in their efforts to free the prisoners, quite often more than they could afford. Later on they ran out of money, while new demands were being made on their time and energy. To have lost the wage earner meant great hardship for the family. Also, it should not be overlooked that the wife had often objected to the husband's political activities as being too dangerous or too time consuming. Now as she pleaded with the Gestapo, an unpleasant task at best, they told her repeatedly that it was the prisoner's own fault that he was imprisoned. Wives had a hard time finding employment because a family member was suspect; they were excluded from public relief; their children had difficulties at school, etc. So it was natural that many came to resent having a family member in the camp.

*14.* Their friends showed them little compassion, because the German population at large developed its own defenses against the concentration camp, most important of which was denial. As discussed in the last chapter, they refused to believe that prisoners in the camps had not committed outrageous crimes to warrant such punishment.

*15.* Another subtle, but most effective device the SS used to alienate the family from the prisoners, was to tell the wife or other relatives (usually only closest relatives were permitted to plead the prisoner's case), that not only was it the prisoner's own fault that he was in the camp, but that he would have been released long ago had he behaved there as he should. This led to recriminations in letters; relatives pleaded with the prisoner to behave better, which often outraged him, considering the conditions of his camp existence.[4] He, of course, could not answer such accusations. At the same time he was resentful because what probably enraged him most

[4] The Gestapo had numerous devices to make pleading for the prisoner seem senseless, and make it easy for the family in self-preservation to separate itself from the prisoner. They would set a date for the prisoner's release, only to inform the relatives on that date that some new misdeed made freedom impossible. Often not even that much reason was given for misinformation. My mother was several times given a date for my release, each one untrue. Once she was told I was probably home already, waiting for her, and to hurry home. Another time she was encouraged to travel from Vienna to Weimar, the town closest to Buchenwald, either to receive me on my release, or at least have a visit with me. She presented herself in Weimar, where she was given a run-around for several days until in desperation she returned to Vienna.

was the family's own ability to act and move about freely when he was so helplessly unable to act for himself. In any case it was one more experience separating the prisoner from his few remaining ties to the non-camp world.

16. These and similar attitudes were reflected in letters to and from home, but often mail for prisoners came irregularly or not at all. Naturally, letters contained hopes and promises of reunion, sometimes because the Gestapo had made promises to the family, sometimes because relatives were trying to cheer the prisoners up. But when promises did not materialize, they led to still greater disappointment, and added resentment toward home.

17. In another effort to cut prisoners off from all connection with the outer world, the SS forbade them to have pictures of their relatives; if they got hold of any pictures, they were taken away and the prisoners were punished for keeping them. So actually a slow alienation took place between the men and their families. But for the new prisoners, this process was only beginning. As recollections of the family grew dimmer, this strongest bond linking prisoners to the outside world grew weaker. The resentment of those who, rightly or wrongly, felt deserted by their families only reinforced it. The less emotional support they got from the outside, the more they were forced to adjust to life in the camp.

18. Therefore, old prisoners did not like to be reminded of their families and former friends. When they spoke about them, it was in a very detached way. They still liked to get letters, but it was not very important to them because they had lost touch with the events related in them. Also, they had come to hate all those living outside the camp, who "enjoyed life as if we were not rotting away." This outside world which continued to live as if nothing had happened was represented, in the minds of the prisoners, by those whom they used to know best, namely their relatives and friends. But even this hatred was very subdued in old prisoners. Just as they had forgotten how to love their kin, they seemed to have lost the ability to hate them. Showing little emotion either way, they seemed unable to feel strongly about anybody.

19. New prisoners, after an initial delay, were usually the ones who received most letters, money, and other signs of attention. But even newcomers consistently accused their families of not doing enough, of betraying them. At the same time they loved to speak of their families and friends even when they were complaining about them. Despite open ambivalence, they never doubted they were going to resume living with them just where they had left off.

20. Similarly they hoped to continue their professional lives just as before. Unlike old prisoners, they loved to talk about their positions in the outside world and of their hopes for the future. They spoke boastfully, and seemed to be trying to keep their pride alive by letting others know

how important they had been, the implication being that they were still important people. Old prisoners seemed to have accepted their state of dejection; to compare it with their former splendor (and anything was magnificent compared to their present existence) was probably too depressing.

21. For such reasons it made a difference to prisoners, psychologically, whether the camp was enclosed by just a wire fence (which let them see the surrounding world) or whether a solid wall blocked their view. The wire fence was usually preferred by new prisoners who tried to deny their exclusion from the world, while those who preferred the additional wall sought protection from nostalgia. On labor assignments outside the camp, prisoners were always in contact with some segments of the outside world, but were also exposed to the sometimes curious but often hostile stare of the passerby. Here again, old prisoners detested the experience while newcomers enjoyed seeing civilians, particularly women and children.

22. Probably as a result of malnutrition, mental anguish, and ambivalence toward the outside world, prisoners tended to forget names, places and events of their past lives. Often they could not recall the names of their closest relatives, even while remembering insignificant details. It was as if their emotional ties to the past were breaking, as if the ordinary order of importance, of the connections of experiences, was no longer valid. Prisoners were quite upset about this loss of memory for things past, which added to their sense of frustration and incompetence. This too was a process which had only begun for new prisoners, and was nearly completed in most old prisoners.

23. All prisoners engaged in a great deal of daydreaming. Both individual and group daydreams were wildly wishfulfilling and a favorite pastime if the general emotional climate was not too depressed. Nevertheless, there was a marked difference between the daydreams of new and old prisoners. In general, the longer the time a prisoner had spent in camp, the less specific, concrete and true to reality were his daydreams. This was in line with the expectation that only such an event as the end of the existing world order would liberate them.

24. They would vaguely daydream of some coming cataclysm. Out of this earth shaking event they felt sure of emerging as the new leaders of Germany, if not the world. This was the least to which their sufferings entitled them. Alongside of these grandiose expectations went a great vagueness about the nature of their leadership, or what ends it would serve; they were even more nebulous about how they were going to arrange their future private lives. In their daydreams they were certain to emerge as prominent leaders of the future, but they were less certain they would continue to live with their wives and children, or be able to resume their roles as husbands and fathers. Partly these fantasies were an effort to deny their utter dejection, and partly a confession of the feeling that only

high public office could help them to regain standing within their families, or win back their own good opinion of themselves.

25. In the process of forcing prisoners to relinquish maturity, the group exercised a strong influence. The group did not interfere with a prisoner's private daydreams or his ambivalence toward his family, but it asserted its power over those who objected to childlike deviations from normal adult behavior. Those who objected to an absolute obedience to the guards were accused of risking the security of the group, an accusation that was not without foundation, since the SS punished the group for the individual misdeed. Therefore, regression into childlike behavior was more inescapable than other types of behavior imposed on the individual because it was triply enforced: by the SS, by the prisoner's inner psychological defenses, and by his fellow prisoners.

26. The result was that most prisoners developed types of behavior more usually characteristic of infancy or early youth. Some of these behaviors developed slowly, others were immediately imposed on the prisoners and increased only in intensity as time went on.

27. The prisoners, like children, sought their satisfactions in empty daydreams, or worse, in contradictory ones. If real satisfactions were available, they were the most primitive kind: eating, sleeping, resting. Like children, they lived only in the immediate present; they lost their feeling for the sequence of time, they became unable to plan for the future or to give up tiny immediate satisfactions to gain greater ones in the near future. They were unable to establish durable relations. Friendships developed as quickly as they broke up. Prisoners would, like children, fight one another tooth and nail, declare they would never look at one another or speak to one another, only to become fast friends within minutes. They were boastful, telling tales of what they had achieved in their former lives, or how they had contrived to cheat foremen or guards. Like children, they felt not at all set back or ashamed when it became known that they had lied about their prowess.

## FINAL ADJUSTMENT

28. The result of all these changes, by no means fully produced in all old prisoners, was a personality structure willing and able to accept SS values and behavior as its own. Of these, German nationalism and the Nazi race ideology seemed easiest to accept. It was notable how far even well-educated political prisoners went in this identification. At one time, for instance, American and English newspapers were full of stories about cruelties committed in the camps. The SS punished prisoners for the appearance of these stories, true to its policy of group punishment—for the stories must have originated in reports by former prisoners. In discussing this event old prisoners insisted that foreign newspapers had no business

bothering with internal German institutions and expressed their hatred of the journalists who tried to help them.

29. When in 1938·I asked more than one hundred old political prisoners if they thought the story of the camp should be reported in foreign newspapers, many hesitated to agree that it was desirable. When asked if they would join a foreign power in a war to defeat National Socialism, only two made the unqualified statement that everyone escaping Germany ought to fight the Nazis to the best of his ability.

30. Nearly all non-Jewish prisoners believed in the superiority of the German race. Nearly all of them took great pride in the so-called achievements of the National Socialist state, particularly its policy of expansion through annexation. In line with their acceptance of the new ideology, most old prisoners took over Gestapo attitudes toward the so-called unfit prisoner. Even before an extermination policy went into effect, the Gestapo had been liquidating unfit persons. Prisoners, for reasons of their own, followed their example. They considered their actions justifiable; some even thought them to be correct.

31. Newcomers to the camp presented old prisoners with difficult problems. Their complaints about the misery of the camp situation added new strain to life in the barracks; so did their inability to adjust to it. Bad behavior in the labor gang or in the barrack endangered the whole group. To become conspicuous was always dangerous, and usually the group to which the conspicuous person belonged at the moment would also be singled out by the SS for special attention. So newcomers who did not stand up well under the strain tended to be a liability to others.

32. Moreover, weaklings were those most apt to turn traitor. Weaklings, it was reasoned, usually died in the first weeks anyway, so it seemed as well to get rid of them sooner. Therefore, old prisoners were sometimes instrumental in getting rid of so-called unfit new prisoners, thus patterning their own behavior after Gestapo ideology. They did it by giving newcomers dangerous assignments, or by denying them help that could have been given.

33. This was one of many situations in which old prisoners showed toughness, and modeled their way of treating fellow prisoners on examples set by the SS. That it was really a taking over of SS attitudes could be seen from their handling of traitors. Self protection asked for the elimination of traitors, but the way in which they were tortured for days and slowly killed was taken over from the Gestapo. Here the excuse was that it might deter others. Yet the rationalization did not apply when prisoners turned their hostility against one another, as they did continuously. New prisoners did it much as they would have done in the world outside the camp. But slowly most prisoners accepted terms of verbal aggression that definitely did not originate in their previous vocabulary, but were taken over from the very different vocabulary of the SS. Only attempts to emulate the SS can explain such behavior.

34. From copying SS verbal aggressions to copying their form of bodily aggression was one more step, but it took several years to reach that. It was not unusual, when prisoners were in charge of others, to find old prisoners (and not only former criminals) behaving worse than the SS. Sometimes they were trying to find favor with the guards, but more often it was because they considered it the best way to treat prisoners in the camp.

35. Old prisoners tended to identify with the SS not only in their goals and values, but even in appearance. They tried to arrogate to themselves old pieces of SS uniforms, and when that was not possible they tried to sew and mend their prison garb until it resembled the uniforms. The lengths prisoners would go to was sometimes hard to believe, particularly since they were sometimes punished for trying to look like the SS. When asked why they did it, they said it was because they wanted to look smart. To them looking smart meant to look like their enemies.

36. Old prisoners felt great satisfaction if, during the twice daily counting of prisoners, they really had stood well at attention or given a snappy salute. They prided themselves on being as tough, or tougher, than the SS. In their identification they went so far as to copy SS leisure time activities. One of the games played by the guards was to find out who could stand being hit the longest without uttering a complaint. This game was copied by old prisoners, as if they were not hit often enough without repeating the experience as a game.

37. Often an SS man would for a while enforce some nonsensical rule, originating in a whim of the moment. Usually it was quickly forgotten, but there were always some old prisoners who continued to observe it and tried to enforce it on others long after the SS had lost interest. Once, for example, an SS man was inspecting the prisoners' apparel and found that some of their shoes were dirty on the inside. He ordered all prisoners to wash their shoes inside and out with soap and water. Treated this way, the heavy shoes became hard as stone. The order was never repeated, and many prisoners did not even carry it out the first time, since the SS, as was often the case, gave the order, stood around for a few minutes, and then left. Until he was gone, every prisoner busied himself with carrying out the order, after which they promptly quit. Nevertheless there were some old prisoners who not only continued to wash the insides of their shoes every day but cursed all who failed to do so as being negligent and dirty. These prisoners believed firmly that all rules set down by the SS were desirable standards of behavior, at least in the camp.

38. Since old prisoners had accepted, or been forced to accept, a childlike dependency on the SS, many of them seemed to want to feel that at least some of the people they were accepting as all-powerful father images were just and kind. Therefore, strange as it may seem, they also had positive feelings toward the SS. They divided their positive and negative feelings in such a way that all positive emotions were concentrated on a few

officers relatively far up in the hierarchy of the camp, but hardly ever on
the commander himself. They insisted that behind a rough exterior these
officers hid feelings of justice and propriety. They were alleged to be
genuinely interested in the prisoners and even trying, in a small way, to
help them. Since not much of these assumed feelings became apparent, it
was explained that they had to be well hidden or there would be no way
for them to help.

39. The eagerness of some prisoners to find reasons for such claims was
sometimes pitiful. A whole legend was woven around the fact that of two
SS inspecting a barrack, one had cleaned the mud off his shoes before
entering. He probably did it automatically, but it was interpreted as a
rebuff to the other, and a clear demonstration of how he felt about the
concentration camp.

40. These examples, to which many could be added, suggest how, and
to what degree, old prisoners came to identify with the enemy, and tried
to justify it somehow in their own eyes. But was the SS really just an
enemy any more? If so, the identification would be hard to understand.
The SS was in fact the callous, unpredictable enemy, and remained so. But
the longer prisoners survived in the camp—that is, the more they became
old prisoners who had lost hope of any other life and tried to make a go
of the camps—the more prisoners and SS found areas in common where
cooperation was better for both of them than being at cross purposes.
Having to live together, if one can call it that, led with necessity to such
areas of common interest.

41. For example, one or several barracks were usually supervised
by a noncommissioned SS officer, called a blockleader. Each blockleader
wanted his barracks to be beyond reproach. It should not only be incon-
spicuous, but the one found in best order; this would keep him out of trouble with his superiors or even gain him a promotion. But the prisoners
who lived there had the same interest: namely, that he should find it beyond reproach, and thus avoid severe penalty for themselves. In this sense
they shared a common interest.

42. This was even more true of the workshops. The N.C.O. in charge of
a production unit was vitally interested that everything in his workshop
be in top shape when it was inspected by his superiors, that the output
should be great, etc. The prisoners, for their own reasons, had identical
interests. And the longer a prisoner had been in the camp, the more skilled
his labor, or the more a particular SS came to rely on it for making his
command show up well with his superiors, the greater the area of common
interest.[5]

43. The fate of a Jewish command of bricklayers at Buchenwald is a

[5] A parallel to this development may be found in the situation of the anti-Nazi German outside the camp. He could not help himself from taking advantage of certain
features of the Nazi regime, such as acquiring a better home or livelihood from the
expropriation of Jewish property, the exploitation of Polish slave labor, etc.

telling example. While tens of thousands of Jewish prisoners were killed
in the camp this group of some forty Jews survived with only a few losses
of life. The group, made up of Jewish political prisoners, decided at the
beginning of the war that with the shortage of steel, concrete, etc., the
camp command would soon return to using bricks for its buildings. They
managed to be assigned to the bricklayers' command, and since skilled
bricklayers were scarce, they were considered unexpendable throughout
the war. While nearly all other Jews were destroyed, most of this command was alive on the day of liberation. Had they served the SS poorly,
they would have served themselves not at all. But had they taken professional pride in their bricklaying skill, without continuing to hate having
to work for the SS, their inner resistance might have died, and they with it.

44. In closing this summary of the adjustments made by old prisoners,
I wish to emphasize again that all these changes worked only within
limitations, that there were great individual variations, that in reality the
categories of old and new prisoners were always overlapping. Despite
what I have said about the psychological reasons forcing old prisoners to
conform and identify with the SS, it must be stressed that this was only
part of the picture; there were also strong defenses within them that
worked in the opposite direction. All prisoners, including those old prisoners who identified with the SS on many levels, at other times defied its
rules. In doing so, a few occasionally showed extraordinary courage, and
many more retained some of their decency and integrity all during their
stay in the camps.


· 15 ·

*Claude Bernard*

# EXAMPLES OF EXPERIMENTAL
# PHYSIOLOGICAL INVESTIGATION

1. The ideas explained in the first two parts of this introduction will be
all the better understood if we can connect them with actual investigations
in experimental physiology and medicine. For this reason, I have put together in the following part a certain number of examples that seem to
me appropriate. As far as possible, I have quoted from myself in all these

From *Introduction à l'étude de la médicine expérimentale,* by Claude Bernard (Paris,
1865). Translated by Henry Copley Greene.

examples, for the sole reason that, in the matter of reasoning and intellectual processes, I shall be much more certain of what I describe in telling what has happened to me than in interpreting what may have taken place in the minds of others. I am not, however, so fatuous as to give these examples as models to follow; I use them only to express my ideas better and to make my thought easier to grasp.

2. In scientific investigations, various circumstances may serve as starting points for research; I will reduce all these varieties, however, to two chief types:

1. Where the starting point for experimental research is an observation;

2. Where the starting point for experimental research is an hypothesis or a theory.

## WHERE THE STARTING POINT FOR EXPERIMENTAL RESEARCH IS AN OBSERVATION

3. Experimental ideas are often born by chance, with the help of some casual observation. Nothing is more common; and this is really the simplest way of beginning a piece of scientific work. We take a walk, so to speak, in the realm of science, and we pursue what happens to present itself to our eyes. Bacon compares scientific investigation with hunting; the observations that present themselves are the game. Keeping the same simile, we may add that, if the game presents itself when we are looking for it, it may also present itself when we are not looking for it, or when we are looking for game of another kind. I shall cite an example in which these two cases presented themselves in succession. . . .

4. *First example.*—One day, rabbits from the market were brought into my laboratory. They were put on the table where they urinated, and I happened to observe that their urine was clear and acid. This fact struck me, because rabbits, which are herbivora, generally have turbid and alkaline urine; while on the other hand carnivora, as we know, have clear and acid urine. This observation of acidity in the rabbits' urine gave me an idea that these animals must be in the nutritional condition of carnivora. I assumed that they had probably not eaten for a long time, and that they had been transformed by fasting, into veritable carnivorous animals, living on their own blood. Nothing was easier than to verify this preconceived idea or hypothesis by experiment. I gave the rabbits grass to eat; and a few hours later, their urine became turbid and alkaline. I then subjected them to fasting and after twenty-four hours or thirty-six hours at most, their urine again became clear and strongly acid; then after eating grass, their urine became alkaline again, etc. I repeated this very simple experiment a great many times, and always with the same result. I then repeated it on a horse, an herbivorous animal which also has turbid and alkaline

urine. I found that fasting, as in rabbits, produced prompt acidity of the urine, with such an increase in urea, that it spontaneously crystallizes at times in the cooled urine. As a result of my experiments, I thus reached the general proposition which then was still unknown, to wit, that all fasting animals feed on meat, so that herbivora then have urine like that of carnivora.

5. We are here dealing with a very simple, particular fact which allows us easily to follow the evolution of experimental reasoning. When we see a phenomenon which we are not in the habit of seeing, we must always ask ourselves what it is connected with, or putting it differently, what is its proximate cause; the answer or the idea, which presents itself to the mind, must then be submitted to experiment. When I saw the rabbits' acid urine, I instinctively asked myself what could be its cause. The experimental idea consisted in the connection, which my mind spontaneously made, between acidity of the rabbits' urine, and the state of fasting which I considered equivalent to a true flesh-eater's diet. The inductive reasoning which I implicitly went through was the following syllogism: the urine of carnivora is acid; now the rabbits before me have acid urine, therefore they are carnivora, i.e., fasting. This remained to be established by experiment.

6. But to prove that my fasting rabbits were really carnivorous, a counterproof was required. A carnivorous rabbit had to be experimentally produced by feeding it with meat, so as to see if its urine would then be clear, as it was during fasting. So I had rabbits fed on cold boiled beef (which they eat very nicely when they are given nothing else). My expectation was again verified, and, as long as the animal diet was continued, the rabbits kept their clear and acid urine.

7. To complete my experiment, I made an autopsy on my animals, to see if meat was digested in the same way in rabbits as in carnivora. I found, in fact, all the phenomena of an excellent digestion in their intestinal reactions, and I noted that all the chyliferous vessels were gorged with very abundant white, milky chyle, just as in carnivora. But à propos of these autopsies which confirmed my ideas on meat digestion in rabbits, lo and behold a fact presented itself which I had not remotely thought of, but which became, as we shall see, my starting point in a new piece of work.

8. Second example.—(Sequel to the last)—In sacrificing the rabbits which I had fed on the meat, I happened to notice that the white and milky lymphatics were first visible in the small intestine at the lower part of the duodenum, about thirty centimeters below the pylorus. This fact caught my attention because in dogs they are first visible much higher in the duodenum just below the pylorus. On examining more closely, I noted that this peculiarity in rabbits coincided with the position of the pancreatic duct which was inserted very low and near the exact place where

the lymphatics began to contain a chyle made white and milky by emulsion of fatty nutritive materials.

9. Chance observation of this fact evoked the idea which brought to birth the thought in my mind, that pancreatic juice might well cause the emulsion of fatty materials and consequently their absorption by the lymphatic vessels. Instinctively again, I made the following syllogism: the white chyle is due to emulsion of the fat; now in rabbits white chyle is formed at the level where pancreatic juice is poured into the intestine; therefore it is pancreatic juice that makes the emulsion of fat and forms the white chyle. This had to be decided by experiment.

10. In view of this preconceived idea I imagined and at once performed a suitable experiment to verify the truth or falsity of my suppositions. The experiment consisted in trying the properties of pancreatic juice directly on neutral fats. But pancreatic juice does not spontaneously flow outside of the body, like saliva, for instance, or urine; its secretory organ is, on the contrary, lodged deep in the abdominal cavity. I was therefore forced to use the method of experimentation to secure the pancreatic fluid from living animals in suitable physiological conditions and in sufficient quantity. Only then could I carry out my experiment, that is to say, control my preconceived idea; and the experiment proved that my idea was correct. In fact pancreatic juice obtained in suitable conditions from dogs, rabbits and various other animals, and mixed with oil or melted fat, always instantly emulsified, and later split these fatty bodies into fatty acids, glycerine, etc., etc., by means of a specific ferment.

11. I shall not follow these experiments further, having explained them at length in a special work.[1] I wish here to show merely how an accidental first observation of the acidity of rabbits' urine suggested to me the idea of making experiments on them with carnivorous feeding, and how later, in continuing these experiments, I brought to light, without seeing it, another observation concerning the peculiar arrangement of the junction of the pancreatic duct in rabbits. This second observation gave me, in turn, the idea of experimenting on the behavior of pancreatic juice.

12. From the above examples we see how chance observation of a fact or phenomenon brings to birth, by anticipation, a preconceived idea or hypothesis about the probable cause of the phenomenon observed; how the preconceived idea begets reasoning which results in the experiment which verifies it; how, in one case, we had to have recourse to experimentation, i.e., to the use of more or less complicated operative processes, etc., to work out the verification. In the last example, experiment played a double rôle; it first judged and confirmed the provisions of the reasoning which it had begotten; but what is more, it produced a fresh observation. We may therefore call this observation an observation produced or begot-

---

[1] Claude Bernard, *Mémoire sur le pancréas et sur le rôle du suc pancréatique dans les phénomènes digestifs*. Paris, 1856.

ten by experiment. This proves that, as we said, all the results of an experiment must be observed, both those connected with the preconceived idea and those without any relation to it. If we saw only facts connected with our preconceived idea, we should often cut ourselves off from making discoveries. For it often happens that an unsuccessful experiment may produce an excellent observation, as the following example will prove.

*13. Third example.*—In 1857, I undertook a series of experiments on the elimination of substances in the urine, and this time the results of the experiment, unlike the previous examples, did not confirm my previsions or preconceived ideas. I had therefore made what we habitually call an unsuccessful experiment. But we have already posited the principle that there are no unsuccessful experiments; for, when they do not serve the investigation for which they were devised, we must still profit by observation to find occasion for other experiments.

*14.* In investigating how the blood, leaving the kidney, eliminated substances that I had injected, I chanced to observe that the blood in the renal vein was crimson, while the blood in the neighboring veins was dark like ordinary venous blood. This unexpected peculiarity struck me, and I thus made observation of a fresh fact begotten by the experiment, but foreign to the experimental aim pursued at the moment. I therefore gave up my unverified original idea, and directed my attention to the singular coloring of the venous renal blood; and when I had noted it well and assured myself that there was no source of error in my observation, I naturally asked myself what could be its cause. As I examined the urine flowing through the urethra and reflected about it, it occurred to me that the red coloring of the venous blood might well be connected with the secreting or active state of the kidney. On this hypothesis, if the renal secretion was stopped, the venous blood should become dark: that is what happened; when the renal secretion was reëstablished, the venous blood should become crimson again; this I also succeeded in verifying whenever I excited the secretion of urine. I thus secured experimental proof that there is a connection between the secretion of urine and the coloring of blood in the renal vein.

*15.* But that is still by no means all. In the normal state, venous blood in the kidney is almost constantly crimson, because the urinary organ secretes almost continuously, though alternately for each kidney. Now I wished to know whether the crimson color is a general fact characteristic of the other glands, and in this way to get a clear-cut counterproof demonstrating that the phenomenon of secretion itself was what led to the alteration in the color of the venous blood. I reasoned thus: if, said I, secretion, as it seems to be, causes the crimson color of glandular venous blood, then, in such glandular organs as the salivary glands which secrete intermittently, the venous blood will change color intermittently and become dark, while the gland is at rest, and red during secretion. So I uncovered a dog's submaxillary gland, its ducts, its nerves and its vessels. In its normal state, this gland supplies an intermittent secretion which we can excite or stop at pleasure. Now while the gland was at rest, and nothing flowed through the salivary duct, I clearly noted that the venous blood was, indeed, dark, while, as soon as secretion appeared, the blood became crimson, to resume its dark color when the secretion stopped; and it remained dark as long as the intermission lasted, etc.[2]

16. These last observations later became the starting point for new ideas which guided me in making investigations as to the chemical cause of the change in color of glandular blood during secretion. I shall not further describe these experiments which, moreover, I have published in detail.[3] It is enough for me to prove that scientific investigations and experimental ideas may have their birth in almost involuntary chance observations which present themselves either spontaneously or in an experiment made with a different purpose.

17. Let me cite another case,—one in which an experimenter produces an observation and voluntarily brings it to birth. This case is, so to speak, included in the preceding case; but it differs from it in this, that, instead of waiting for an observation to present itself by chance in fortuitous circumstances, we produce it by experiment. Returning to Bacon's comparison, we might say that an experimenter, in this instance, is like a hunter who, instead of waiting quietly for game, tries to make it rise, by beating up the locality where he assumes it is. We use this method whenever we have no preconceived idea in respect to a subject as to which previous observations are lacking. So we experiment to bring to birth observations which in turn may bring to birth ideas. This continually occurs in medicine when we wish to investigate the action of a poison or of some medicinal substance, on an animal's economy; we make experiments to see, and we then take our direction from what we have seen.

18. *Fourth example.*—In 1845, Monsieur Pelouze gave me a toxic substance, called *curare*, which had been brought to him from America. We then knew nothing about the physiological action of this substance. From old observations and from the interesting accounts of Alex. von Humboldt and of Roulin and Boussingault, we knew only that the preparation of this substance was complex and difficult, and that it very speedily kills an animal if introduced under the skin. But from the earlier observations, I could get no idea of the mechanism of death by curare; to get such an idea I had to make fresh observations as to the organic disturbances to which this poison might lead. I therefore made experiments *to see* things about which I had absolutely no preconceived idea. First, I put curare under the

[2] Claude Bernard, *Leçons sur les propriétés physiologiques et les altérations pathologiques des liquides de l'organisme.* Paris, 1859. Vol. II.

[3] Claude Bernard, *Sur la quantité d'oxygène que contient le sang veineux des organes glandulaires.* (*Compt. rend. de l'Acad. des sciences.* Vol. XLVII, Sept. 6, 1858.)

skin of a frog: it died after a few minutes; I opened it at once, and in this physiological autopsy I studied in succession what had become of the known physiological properties of its various tissues. I say physiological autopsy purposely, because no others are really instructive. The disappearance of physiological properties is what explains death, and not anatomical changes. Indeed, in the present state of science, we see physiological properties disappear in any number of cases without being able to show, by our present means of observation, any corresponding anatomical change; such, for example, is the case with curare. Meantime, we shall find examples, on the contrary, in which physiological properties persist, in spite of very marked anatomical changes with which the functions are by no means incompatible. Now in my frog poisoned with curare, the heart maintained its movements, the blood was apparently no more changed in physiological properties than the muscles, which kept their normal contractility. But while the nervous system had kept its normal anatomical appearance, the properties of the nerves had nevertheless completely disappeared. There were no movements, either voluntary or reflex, and when the motor nerves were stimulated directly, they no longer caused any contraction in the muscles. To learn whether there was anything accidental or mistaken in this first observation, I repeated it several times and verified it in various ways; for when we wish to reason experimentally, the first thing necessary is to be a good observer and to make quite certain that the starting point of our reasoning is not a mistake in observation. In mammals and in birds, I found the same phenomena as in frogs, and disappearance of the physiological properties of the motor nervous system became my constant fact. Starting from this well established fact, I could then carry analysis of the phenomena further and determine the mechanism of death from curare. I still proceeded by reasonings analogous to those quoted in the above example, and, from idea to idea and experiment to experiment, I progressed to more and more definite facts. I finally reached this general proposition, that *curare causes death by destroying all the motor nerves, without affecting the sensory nerves.*[4]

19. In cases where we make an experiment in which both preconceived idea and reasoning seem completely lacking, we yet necessarily reason by syllogism without knowing it. In the case of curare, I instinctively reasoned in the following way: no phenomenon is without a cause, and consequently no poisoning without a physiological lesion peculiar or proper to the poison used; now, thought I, curare must cause death by an activity special to itself and by acting on certain definite organic parts. So by poisoning an animal with curare and by examining the properties of its various tissues immediately after death, I can perhaps find and study the lesions peculiar to it.

[4] Cf. Claude Bernard, *Leçons sur les effets des substances toxiques;* Paris, 1857; *Du curare.* (*Revue des Deux Mondes,* Sept. 1, 1864.)

20. The mind, then, is still active here, and an experiment in order to see is included, nevertheless, in our general definition of an experiment. In every enterprise, in fact, the mind is always reasoning, and, even when we seem to act without a motive, an instinctive logic still directs the mind. Only we are not aware of it, because we begin by reasoning before we know or say that we are reasoning, just as we begin by speaking before we observe that we are speaking, and just as we begin by seeing and hearing before we know what we see or what we hear.

21. *Fifth example.*—About 1846, I wished to make experiments on the cause of poisoning with carbon monoxide. I knew that this gas had been described as toxic, but I knew literally nothing about the mechanism of its poisoning; I therefore could not have a preconceived opinion. What, then, was to be done? I must bring to birth an idea by making a fact appear, i.e., make another experiment to see. In fact I poisoned a dog by making him breathe carbon monoxide and after death I at once opened his body. I looked at the state of the organs and fluids. What caught my attention at once was that its blood was scarlet in all the vessels, in the veins as well as the arteries, in the right heart as well as in the left. I repeated the experiment on rabbits, birds and frogs, and everywhere I found the same scarlet coloring of the blood. But I was diverted from continuing this investigation, and I kept this observation a long time unused except for quoting it in my course *à propos* of the coloring of blood.

22. In 1856, no one had carried the experimental question further, and in my course at the Collège de France on toxic and medicinal substances, I again took up the study of poisoning by carbon monoxide which I had begun in 1846. I found myself then in a confused situation, for at this time I already knew that poisoning with carbon monoxide makes the blood scarlet in the whole circulatory system. I had to make hypotheses, and establish a preconceived idea about my first observation, so as to go ahead. Now, reflecting on the fact of scarlet blood, I tried to interpret it by my earlier knowledge as to the cause of the color of blood. Whereupon all the following reflections presented themselves to my mind. The scarlet color, said I, is peculiar to arterial blood and connected with the presence of a large proportion of oxygen, while dark coloring belongs with absence of oxygen and presence of a larger proportion of carbonic acid; so the idea occurred to me that carbon monoxide, by keeping venous blood scarlet, might perhaps have prevented the oxygen from changing into carbonic acid in the capillaries. Yet it seemed hard to understand how that could be the cause of death. But still keeping on with my inner preconceived reasoning, I added: If that is true, blood taken from the veins of animals poisoned with carbon monoxide should be like arterial blood in containing oxygen; we must see if that is the fact.

23. Following this reasoning, based on interpretation of my observation, I tried an experiment to verify my hypothesis as to the persistence of

oxygen in the venous blood. I passed a current of hydrogen through scarlet venous blood taken from an animal poisoned with carbon monoxide, but I could not liberate the oxygen as usual. I tried to do the same with arterial blood; I had no greater success. My preconceived idea was therefore false. But the impossibility of getting oxygen from the blood of a dog poisoned with carbon monoxide was a second observation which suggested a fresh hypothesis. What could have become of the oxygen in the blood? It had not changed into carbonic acid, because I had not set free large quantities of that gas in passing a current of hydrogen through the blood of the poisoned animals. Moreover, that hypothesis was contrary to the color of the blood. I exhausted myself in conjectures about how carbon monoxide could cause the oxygen to disappear from the blood; and as gases displace one another I naturally thought that the carbon monoxide might have displaced the oxygen and driven it out of the blood. To learn this, I decided to vary my experimentation by putting the blood in artificial conditions that would allow me to recover the displaced oxygen. So I studied the action of carbon monoxide on blood experimentally. For this purpose I took a certain amount of arterial blood from a healthy animal; I put this blood on the mercury in an inverted test tube containing carbon monoxide; I then shook the whole thing so as to poison the blood sheltered from contact with the outer air. Then, after an interval, I examined whether the air in the test-tube in contact with the poisoned blood had been changed, and I noted that the air thus in contact with the blood had been remarkably enriched with oxygen, while the proportion of carbon monoxide was lessened. Repeated in the same conditions, these experiments taught me that what had occurred was an exchange, volume by volume, between the carbon monoxide and the oxygen of the blood. But the carbon monoxide, in displacing the oxygen that it had expelled from the blood, remained chemically combined in the blood and could no longer be displaced either by oxygen or by other gases. So that death came through death of the molecules of blood, or in other words by stopping their exercise of a physiological property essential to life.

24. This last example, which I have very briefly described, is complete; it shows from one end to the other, how we proceed with the experimental method and succeeded in learning the immediate cause of phenomena. To begin with I knew literally nothing about the mechanism of the phenomenon of poisoning with carbon monoxide. I undertook an experiment to see, i.e., to observe. I made a preliminary observation of a special change in the coloring of blood. I interpreted this observation, and I made an hypothesis which proved false. But the experiment provided me with a second observation about which I reasoned anew, using it as a starting point for making a new hypothesis as to the mechanism, by which the oxygen in the blood was removed. By building up hypotheses, one by one, about the facts as I observed them, I finally succeeded in showing that carbon mon-

oxide replaces oxygen in a molecule of blood, by combining with the substance of the molecule. Experimental analysis, here, has reached its goal. This is one of the cases, rare in physiology, which I am happy to be able to quote. Here the immediate cause of the phenomenon of poisoning is found and is translated into a theory which accounts for all the facts and at the same time includes all the observations and experiments. Formulated as follows, the theory posits the main facts from which all the rest are deduced: Carbon monoxide combines more intimately than oxygen with the hemoglobin in a molecule of blood. It has quite recently been proved that carbon monoxide forms a definite combination with hemoglobin.[5] So that the molecule of blood, as if petrified by the stability of the combination, loses its vital properties. Hence everything is logically deduced: because of its property of more intimate combination, carbon monoxide drives out of the blood the oxygen essential to life; the molecules of blood become inert, and the animal dies, with symptoms of hemorrhage, from true paralysis of the molecules.

25. But when a theory is sound and indeed shows the real and definite physico-chemical cause of phenomena, it not only includes the observed facts but predicts others and leads to rational applications that are logical consequences of the theory. Here again we meet this criterion. In fact, if carbon monoxide has the property of driving out oxygen by taking its place in combining with a molecule of blood, we should be able to use the gas to analyze the gases in blood, and especially for determining oxygen. From my experiments I deduced this application which has been generally adopted to-day.[6] Applications of this property of carbon monoxide have been made in legal medicine for finding the coloring matter of blood; and from the physiological facts described above we may also already deduce results connected with hygiene, experimental pathology, and notably with the mechanism of certain forms of anemia.

26. As in every other case, all the deductions from the theory doubtless still require experimental verification; and logic does not suffice. But this is because the conditions in which carbon monoxide acts on the blood may present other complex circumstances and any number of details which the theory cannot yet predict. Otherwise, as we have often said, we could reach conclusions by logic alone, without any need of experimental verifications. Because of possible unforeseen and variable new elements in the conditions of a phenomenon, logic alone can in experimental science never suffice. Even when we have a theory that seems sound, it is never more than relatively sound, and it always includes a certain proportion of the unknown.

[5] Hoppe-Seyler, *Handbuch der physiologisch- und pathologisch-chemischen Analyse*. Berlin, 1865.
[6] Claude Bernard, *De l'emploi de l'oxude de carbone pour la détermination de l'oxygène du sang* (*Compt. rend. de l'Acad. des sciences*, Meeting of Sept. 6, 1858, Vol. XLVII).

## WHEN THE STARTING POINT OF EXPERIMENTAL RESEARCH IS AN HYPOTHESIS OR A THEORY

27. We have already said and we shall see further on, that in noting an observation we must never go beyond facts. But in making an experiment, it is different. I wish to show that hypotheses are indispensable, and that they are useful, therefore, precisely because they lead us outside of facts and carry science forward. The object of hypotheses is not only to make us try new experiments; they also often make us discover new facts which we should not have perceived without them. In the preceding examples, we saw that we can start from a particular fact and rise one by one to more general ideas, i.e., to a theory. But as we have just seen, we can also sometimes start with an hypothesis deduced from a theory. Though we are dealing in this case with reasoning logically deduced from a theory, we have an hypothesis that must still be verified by experiment. Indeed, theories are only an assembling of the earlier facts, on which our hypothesis rests, and cannot be used to demonstrate it experimentally. We said that, in this instance, we must not submit to the yoke of theories, and that keeping our mental independence is the best way to discover the truth. This is proved by the following examples.

28. *First example.*—In 1843, in one of my first pieces of work, I undertook to study what becomes of different alimentary substances in nutrition. As I said before, I began with sugar, a definite substance that is easier than any other to recognize and follow in the bodily economy. With this in view, I injected solutions of cane sugar into the blood of animals, and I noted that even when injected in weak doses the sugar passed into the urine. I recognized later that, by changing or transforming sugar, the gastric juice made it capable of assimilation, i.e., of destruction in the blood.[7]

29. Thereupon I wished to learn in what organ the nutritive sugar disappeared, and I conceived the hypothesis that sugar introduced into the blood through nutrition might be destroyed in the lungs or in the general capillaries. The theory, indeed, which then prevailed and which was naturally my proper starting point, assumed that the sugar present in animals came exclusively from foods, and that it was destroyed in animal organisms by the phenomena of combustion, i.e., of respiration. Thus sugar had gained the name of *respiratory nutriment.* But I was immediately led to see that the theory about the origin of sugar in animals, which served me as a starting point, was false. As a result of the experiments which I shall describe further on, I was not indeed led to find an organ for destroying sugar, but, on the contrary, I discovered an organ for making it, and I found that all animal blood contains sugar even when they do not eat it.

[7] Claude Bernard, Thesis for doctorate in medicine, Paris, 1843.

So I noted a new fact, unforeseen in theory, which men had not noticed, doubtless because they were under the influence of contrary theories which they had too confidently accepted. I therefore abandoned my hypothesis on the spot, so as to pursue the unexpected result which has since become the fertile origin of a new path for investigation and a mine of discoveries that is not yet exhausted.

30. In these researches I followed the principles of the experimental method that we have established, i.e., that, in presence of a well-noted, new fact which contradicts a theory, instead of keeping the theory and abandoning the fact, I should keep and study the fact, and I hastened to give up the theory, thus conforming to the precept which we proposed in the second chapter: "When we meet a fact which contradicts a prevailing theory, we must accept the fact and abandon the theory, even when the theory is supported by great names and generally accepted."

31. We must therefore distinguish, as we said, between principles and theories, and never believe absolutely in the latter. We had a theory here which assumed that the vegetable kingdom alone had the power of creating the individual compounds which the animal kingdom is supposed to destroy. According to this theory, established and supported by the most illustrious chemists of our day, animals were incapable of producing sugar in their organisms. If I had believed in this theory absolutely, I should have had to conclude that my experiment was vitiated by some inaccuracy; and less wary experimenters than I might have condemned it at once, and might not have tarried longer at an observation which could be theoretically suspected of including sources of error, since it showed sugar in the blood of animals on a diet that lacked starchy or sugary materials. But instead of being concerned about the theory, I concerned myself only with the fact whose reality I was trying to establish. By new experiments and by means of suitable counterproofs, I was thus led to confirm my first observation and to find that the liver is the organ in which animal sugar is formed in certain given circumstances, to spread later into the whole blood supply and into the tissues and fluids.

32. Animal glycogenesis which I thus discovered, i.e., the power of producing sugar, possessed by animals as well as vegetables, is now an acquired fact for science; but we have not yet fixed on a plausible theory accounting for the phenomenon. The fresh facts which I made known are the source of numerous studies and many varied theories in apparent contradiction with each other and with my own. When entering on new ground we must not be afraid to express even risky ideas so as to stimulate research in all directions. As Priestley put it, we must not remain inactive through false modesty based on fear of being mistaken. So I made more or less hypothetical theories of glycogenesis; after mine came others; my theories, like other men's, will live the allotted life of necessarily very partial and temporary theories at the opening of a new series of investiga-

tions; they will be replaced later by others, embodying a more advanced stage of the question, and so on. Theories are like a stairway; by climbing, science widens its horizon more and more, because theories embody and necessarily include proportionately more facts as they advance. Progress is achieved by exchanging our theories for new ones which go further than the old, until we find one based on a larger number of facts. In the case which now concerns us, the question is not one of condemning the old to the advantage of a more recent theory. What is important is having opened a new road; for well-observed facts, though brought to light by passing theories, will never die; they are the material on which alone the house of science will at last be built, when it has facts enough and has gone sufficiently deep into the analysis of phenomena to know their law or their causation.

33. To sum up, theories are only hypotheses, verified by more or less numerous facts. Those verified by the most facts are the best; but even then they are never final, never to be absolutely believed. We have seen in the preceding examples that if we had had complete confidence in the prevailing theory of the destruction of sugar in animals, and if we had only had its confirmation in view, we should probably not have found the road to the new facts which we met. It is true that an hypothesis based on a theory produced the experiment; but as soon as the results of the experiment appeared, theory and hypothesis had to disappear, for the experimental facts were now just an observation, to be made without any preconceived idea.

34. In sciences as complex and as little developed as physiology, the great principle is therefore to give little heed to hypotheses or theories and always to keep an eye alert to observe everything that appears in every aspect of an experiment. An apparently accidental and inexplicable circumstance may occasion the discovery of an important new fact, as we shall see in the continuation of the example just noted.

35. *Second example* (*Sequel to the Last*).—After finding, as I said above, that there is sugar in the livers of animals in their normal state, and with every sort of nutriment, I wished to learn the proportion of this substance and its variation in certain physiological and pathological states. So I began to estimate the sugar in the livers of animals placed in various physiologically defined circumstances. I always made two determinations of carbohydrate for the same liver tissue. But pressed for time one day, it happened that I could not make my two analyses at the same moment; I quickly made one determination just after the animal's death and postponed the other analysis till next day. But then I found much larger amounts of sugar than those which I got the night before with the same material. I noticed, on the other hand, that the proportion of sugar, which I had found just after the animal's death the night before, was much smaller than I had found in the experiments which I had announced as

giving the normal proportion of liver sugar. I did not know how to account for this singular variation, got with the same liver and the same method of analysis. What was to be done? Should I consider two such discordant determinations as an unsuccessful experiment and take no account of them? Should I take the mean between these experiments? More than one experimenter might have chosen this expedient to get out of an awkward situation. But I disapprove of this kind of action for reasons which I have given elsewhere. I said, indeed, that we must never neglect anything in our observation of fact, and I consider it indispensable, never to admit the existence of an unproved source of error in an experiment and always to try to find a reason for the abnormal circumstances that we observe. Nothing is accidental, and what seems to us accident is only an unknown fact whose explanation may furnish the occasion for a more or less important discovery. So it proved in this case.

36. I wished, in fact, to learn the reason for my having found two such different values in the analysis of my rabbit's liver. After assuring myself that there was no mistake connected with the method of analysis, after noting that all parts of the liver were practically equally rich in sugar, there remained to be studied only the elapsed time between the animal's death and the time of my second determination. Without ascribing much importance to it, up to that time I had made my experiments a few hours after the animal's death; now for the first time I was in the situation of making one determination only a few minutes after death and postponing the other till next day, i.e., twenty-four hours later. In physiology, questions of time are always very important because organic matter passes through numerous and incessant changes. Some chemical change might therefore have taken place in the liver tissue. To make sure, I made a series of new experiments which dispelled every obscurity by showing me that liver tissue becomes more and more rich in sugar for some time after death. Thus we may have a very variable amount of sugar according to the moment when we make our examination. I was therefore led to correct my old determination and to discover the new fact that considerable amounts of sugar are produced in animals' livers after death. For instance, by forcibly injecting a current of cold water through the hepatic vessels and passing it through a liver that was still warm, just after an animal's death, I showed that the tissue was completely freed from the sugar which it contained; but next day or a few hours later, if we keep the washed liver at a mild temperature, we again find its tissue charged with a large amount of sugar produced after it was washed.[8]

37. Once in possession of the first discovery that sugar is formed in animals after death as during life, I wished to carry my study of this singu-

[8] Claude Bernard, *Sur le mécanisme de la formation du sucre dans le foie* (*Comptes rendus par l'Acad. des sciences*, Sept. 24, 1855, and *Comptes rendus de l'Acad. des sciences*, March 23, 1857).

lar phenomenon further; I was then led to find that sugar is produced in the liver with the help of an enzyme reacting on an amylaceous substance which I isolated and which I called *glycogenous matter,* so that I succeeded in proving in the most clear-cut way that sugar is formed in animals by a mechanism in every respect like the mechanism found in vegetables.

38. This second series of facts embodied results, which are also firmly acquired for science, and which have greatly advanced our knowledge of glycogenesis in animals. I have just very briefly told how these facts were discovered, and how they started with an experimental circumstance that was apparently inconsequential. I quote this case so as to prove that we must never neglect anything in experimental research, for every accident has a necessary cause. We must, therefore, never be too much absorbed by the thought we are pursuing, nor deceive ourselves about the value of our ideas or scientific theories; we must always keep our eyes open for every event, the mind doubting and independent, ready to study whatever presents itself and to let nothing go without seeking its reason. In a word, we must be in an intellectual attitude which seems paradoxical but which, in my opinion, expresses the true spirit of an investigator. We must have robust faith and not believe. Let me explain myself by saying that in science we must firmly believe in principles, but must question formulæ; on the one hand, indeed, we are sure that determinism exists, but we are never certain we have attained it. We must be immovable as to the principles of experimental science (determinism), but must not absolutely believe in theories. The aphorism which I just uttered is sustained by what we expounded elsewhere, to wit, that for experimental science principles are in our mind, while formulæ are external things. In practical matters, we are indeed forced to tolerate the belief that truth (at least temporary truth) is embodied in a theory or a formula. But in scientific experimental philosophy those who put their faith in formulæ and theories are wrong. All human science consists in seeking the true formula and true theory. We are always approaching it; but shall we ever find it completely? This is not the place to go into an explanation of philosophic ideas: let us return to our subject and pass on to a fresh experimental example.

39. *Third example.*—About the year 1852, my studies led me to make experiments on the influence of the nervous system on the phenomena of nutrition and temperature regulation. It had been observed in many cases that complex paralyses with their seat in the mixed nerves are followed, now by a rise and again by a fall of temperature in the paralyzed parts. Now this is how I reasoned, in order to explain this fact, basing myself first on known observations and then on prevailing theories of the phenomena of nutrition and temperature regulation. Paralysis of the nerves, said I, should lead to cooling of the parts by slowing down the phenomena of combustion in the blood, since these phenomena are considered as the

cause of animal heat. On the other hand, anatomists long ago noticed that the sympathetic nerves especially follow the arteries. So, thought I inductively, in a lesion of a mixed trunk of nerves, it must be the sympathetic nerves that produce the slowing down of chemical phenomena in capillary vessels, and their paralysis that then leads to cooling the parts. If my hypothesis is true, I went on, it can be verified by severing only the sympathetic, vascular nerves leading to a special part, and sparing the others. I should then find the part cooled by paralysis of the vascular nerves, without loss of either motion or sensation, since the ordinary motor and sensory nerves would still be intact. To carry out my experiment, I therefore sought a suitable experimental method that would allow me to sever only the vascular nerves and to spare the others. Here the choice of animals was important in solving the problem; for in certain animals, such as rabbits and horses, I found that the anatomical arrangement isolating the cervical sympathetic nerve made this solution possible.

*40.* Accordingly, I severed the cervical sympathetic nerve in the neck of a rabbit, to control my hypothesis and see what would happen in the way of change of temperature on the side of the head where this nerve branches out. On the basis of a prevailing theory and of earlier observation, I had been led, as we have just seen, to make the hypothesis that the temperature should be reduced. Now what happened was exactly the reverse. After severing the cervical sympathetic nerve about the middle of the neck, I immediately saw in the whole of the corresponding side of the rabbit's head a striking hyperactivity in the circulation, accompanied by increase of warmth. The result was therefore precisely the reverse of what my hypothesis, deduced from theory, had led me to expect; thereupon I did as I always do, that is to say, I at once abandoned theories and hypothesis, to observe and study the fact itself, so as to define the experimental conditions as precisely as possible. To-day my experiments on the vascular and thermo-regulatory nerves have opened a new path for investigation and are the subject of numerous studies which, I hope, may some day yield really important results in physiology and pathology.[9] This example, like the preceding ones, proves that in experiments we may meet with results different from what theories and hypothesis lead us to expect. But I wish to call more special attention to this third example, because it gives us an important lesson, to wit: without the original guiding hypothesis, the experimental fact which contradicted it would never have been perceived. Indeed, I was not the first experimenter to cut this part of the cervical sympathetic nerve in living animals. Pourfour du Petit performed the experiment at the beginning of the last century and discovered the

[9] Claude Bernard, *Recherches expérimentales sur le grand sympathique, etc.* (*Mémoires de la Société de biologie,* Vol. V, 1853). *Sur les nerfs vasculaires et caloriques du grand sympathique* (*Comptes rendus de l'Acad. des sciences,* 1852, Vol. XXXIV; 1862, Vol. LV).

nerve's action on the pupil, by starting from an anatomical hypothesis according to which this nerve was supposed to carry animal spirits to the eye.[10] Many physiologists have since repeated the same operation, with the purpose of verifying or explaining the changes in the eye which Pourfour du Petit first described. But none of them noticed the local temperature phenomenon, of which I speak, or connected it with the severing of the cervical sympathetic nerve, though this phenomenon must necessarily have occurred under the very eyes of all who, before me, had cut this part of the sympathetic nerve. The hypothesis, as we see, had prepared my mind for seeing things in a certain direction, given by the hypothesis itself; and this is proved by the fact that, like the other experimenters, I myself had often divided the cervical sympathetic nerve to repeat Pourfour du Petit's experiment, without perceiving the fact of heat production which I later discovered when an hypothesis led me to make investigations in this direction. Here, therefore, the influence of the hypothesis could hardly be more evident; we had the fact under our eyes and did not see it because it conveyed nothing to our mind. However, it could hardly be simpler to perceive, and since I described it, every physiologist without exception has noted and verified it with the greatest ease.

*41.* To sum up, even mistaken hypotheses and theories are of use in leading to discoveries. This remark is true in all the sciences. The alchemists founded chemistry by pursuing chimerical problems and theories which are false. In physical science, which is more advanced than biology, we might still cite men of science who make great discoveries by relying on false theories. It seems, indeed, a necessary weakness of our mind to be able to reach truth only across a multitude of errors and obstacles.

*42.* What general conclusions shall physiologists draw from the above examples? They should conclude that in the present state of biological science accepted ideas and theories embody only limited and risky truths which are destined to perish. They should consequently have very little confidence in the ultimate value of theories, but should still make use of them as intellectual tools necessary to the evolution of science and suitable for the discovery of new facts. The art of discovering new phenomena and of noting them accurately should to-day be the special concern of all biologists. We must establish experimental criticism by creating rigorous methods of investigation and experimentation, which will enable us to define our observations unquestionably, and thus get rid of the errors of fact which are the source of errors in theory. A man who to-day attempted a generalization for biology as a whole would prove that he had no accurate feeling for the present state of the science. To-day, the biological problem has hardly begun to be put; and, as stones must first be got to-

---

[10] Pourfour du Petit, *Mémoire dans lequel il est démontré que les nerfs intercostaux fournissent des rameaux qui portent des esprits dans les yeux* (*Histoire de l'Académie pour l'année* 1727).

gether and cut, before we dream of erecting a monument, just so must the facts first be got together and prepared which are destined to create the science of living bodies. This rôle falls to experimentation; its method is fixed, but the phenomena to be analyzed are so complex that, for the moment, the true promoters of science are those who succeed in giving its methods of analysis a few principles of simplification or in introducing improvements in instruments of research. When there are enough quite clearly established facts, generalizations never keep us waiting. I am convinced that, in experimental sciences that are evolving, and especially in those as complex as biology, discovery of a new tool for observation or experiment is much more useful than any number of systematic or philosophic dissertations. Indeed, a new method or a new means of investigation increases our power and makes discoveries and researches possible which would not have been possible without its help. Thus researches as to the formation of sugar in animals could be made only after chemistry gave us reagents for recognizing sugar, which were much more sensitive than those we had before.

## ·16·

*James Thurber*

# SEX EX MACHINA

*1.* With the disappearance of the gas mantle and the advent of the short circuit, man's tranquility began to be threatened by everything he put his hand on. Many people believe that it was a sad day indeed when Benjamin Franklin tied that key to a kite string and flew the kite in a thunderstorm; other people believed that if it hadn't been Franklin, it would have been someone else. As, of course, it was in the case of the harnessing of steam and the invention of the gas engine. At any rate, it has come about that so-called civilized man finds himself today surrounded by the myriad mechanical devices of a technological world. Writers of books on how to control your nerves, how to conquer fear, how to cultivate calm, how to be happy in spite of everything, are of several minds as regards the relation of man and the machine. Some of them are prone to believe that the mind and body, if properly disciplined, can get the upper hand of this mechanized existence. Others merely ignore the

From *The New Yorker* (March 13, 1937). Reprinted by permission; Copyright © 1937 The New Yorker Magazine, Inc.

situation and go on to the profitable writing of more facile chapters of inspiration. Still others attribute the whole menace of the machine to sex, and so confuse the average reader that he cannot always be certain whether he has been knocked down by an automobile or is merely in love.

2. Dr. Bisch, the Be-Glad-You're-Neurotic man, has a remarkable chapter which deals, in part, with man, sex, and the machine. He examines the case of three hypothetical men who start across a street on a red light and get in the way of an oncoming automobile. A dodges successfully; B stands still, "accepting the situation with calm and resignation," thus becoming one of my favorite heroes in modern belles-lettres; and C hesitates, wavers, jumps backward and forward, and finally runs head on into the car. To lead you through Dr. Bisch's complete analysis of what was wrong with B and C would occupy your whole day. He mentions what the McDougallians would say ("Instinct!"), what the Freudians would retort ("Complexes!"), and what the behaviorists would shout ("Conditioned reflexes!"). He also brings in what the physiologists would say—deficient thyroid, hypoadrenal functioning, and so on. The average sedentary man of our time who is at all suggestible must emerge from this chapter believing that his chances of surviving a combination of instinct, complexes, reflexes, glands, sex, and present-day traffic conditions are about equal to those of a one-legged blind man trying to get out of a labyrinth.

3. Let us single out what Dr. Bisch thinks the Freudians would say about poor Mr. C, who ran right into the car. He writes, " 'Sex hunger,' the Freudians would declare. 'Always keyed up and irritable because of it. Undoubtedly suffers from insomnia and when he does sleep his dream life must be productive, distorted, and possibly frightening. Automobile unquestionably has sex significance for him . . . to C the car is both enticing and menacing at one and the same time. . . . A thorough analysis is indicated. . . . It might take months. But then, the man needs an analysis as much as food. He is heading for a complete nervous collapse.' " It is my studied opinion, not to put too fine a point on it, that Mr. C is heading for a good mangling, and that if he gets away with only a nervous collapse, it will be a miracle.

4. I have not always, I am sorry to say, been able to go the whole way with the Freudians, or even a very considerable distance. Even though, as Dr. Bisch says, "One must admit that the Freudians have had the best of it thus far. At least they have received the most publicity." It is in matters like their analysis of men and machines, of Mr. C and the automobile, that the Freudians and I part company. Of course, the analysis above is simply Dr. Bisch's idea of what the Freudians would say, but I think he has got it down pretty well. Dr. Bisch himself leans toward the Freudian analysis of Mr. C, for he says in this same chapter, "An automobile bearing down upon you may be a sex symbol at that, you know, especially if

you dream it." It is my contention, of course, that even if you dream it, it is probably not a sex symbol, but merely an automobile bearing down upon you. And if it bears down upon you in real life, I am sure it is an automobile. I have seen the same behavior that characterized Mr. C displayed by a squirrel (Mr. S) that lives in the grounds of my house in the country. He is a fairly tame squirrel, happily mated and not sex-hungry, if I am any judge, but nevertheless he frequently runs out toward my automobile when I start down the driveway, and then hesitates, wavers, jumps forward and backward, and occasionally would run right into the car except that he is awfully fast on his feet and that I always hurriedly put on the brakes of the 1935 V-8 Sex Symbol that I drive.

5. I have seen this same behavior in the case of rabbits (notoriously uninfluenced by any sex symbols save those of other rabbits), dogs, pigeons, a doe, a young hawk (which flew at my car), a blue heron that I encountered on a country road in Vermont, and once, near Paul Smith's in the Adirondacks, a fox. They all acted exactly like Mr. C. The hawk, unhappily, was killed. All the others escaped with nothing worse, I suppose, than a complete nervous collapse. Although I cannot claim to have been conversant with the private life and the secret compulsions, the psychoneuroses and the glandular activities of all these animals, it is nevertheless my confident and unswervable belief that there was nothing at all the matter with any one of them. Like Mr. C, they suddenly saw a car swiftly bearing down upon them, got excited, and lost their heads. I do not believe, you see, there was anything the matter with Mr. C, either. But I do believe that, after a thorough analysis lasting months, with a lot of harping on the incident of the automobile, something might very well come to be the matter with him. He might even actually get to suffering from the delusion that he believes automobiles are sex symbols.

6. It seems to me worthy of note that Dr. Bisch, in reciting the reactions of three persons in the face of an oncoming car, selected three men. What would have happened had they been Mrs. A, Mrs. B, and Mrs. C? You know as well as I do: all three of them would have hesitated, wavered, jumped forward and backward, and finally run head on into the car if some man hadn't grabbed them. (I used to know a motorist who, every time he approached a woman standing on a curb preparing to cross the street, shouted, "Hold it, stupid!") It is not too much to say that, with a car bearing down upon them, ninety-five women out of a hundred would act like Mr. C—or Mr. S, the squirrel, or Mr. F, the fox. But it is certainly too much to say that ninety-five out of every hundred women look upon an automobile as a sex symbol. For one thing, Dr. Bisch points out that the automobile serves as a sex symbol because of the "mechanical principle involved." But only one woman in a thousand really knows anything about the mechanical principle involved in an automobile. And yet, as I have said, ninety-five out of a hundred would hesitate, waver, and jump,

just as Mr. C did. I think we have the Freudians here. If we haven't proved our case with rabbits and a blue heron, we have certainly proved it with women.

7. To my notion, the effect of the automobile and of other mechanical contrivances on the state of our nerves, minds, and spirits is a problem which the popular psychologists whom I have dealt with know very little about. The sexual explanation of the relationship of man and the machine is not good enough. To arrive at the real explanation, we have to begin very far back, as far back as Franklin and the kite, or at least as far back as a certain man and woman who appear in a book of stories written more than sixty years ago by Max Adeler. One story in this book tells about a housewife who bought a combination ironing board and card table, which some New England genius had thought up in his spare time. The husband, coming home to find the devilish contraption in the parlor, was appalled. "What is that thing?" he demanded. His wife explained that it was a card table, but that if you pressed a button underneath, it would become an ironing board. Whereupon she pushed the button and the table leaped a foot into the air, extended itself, and became an ironing board. The story goes on to tell how the thing finally became so finely sensitized that it would change back and forth if you merely touched it— you didn't have to push the button. The husband stuck it in the attic (after it had leaped up and struck him a couple of times while he was playing euchre), and on windy nights it could be heard flopping and banging around, changing from a card table to an ironing board and back. The story serves as one example of our dread heritage of annoyance, shock, and terror arising out of the nature of mechanical contrivances *per se*. The mechanical principle involved in this damnable invention had, I believe, no relationship to sex whatsoever. There are certain analysts who see sex in anything, even a leaping ironing board, but I think we can ignore these scientists.

8. No man (to go on) who has wrestled with a self-adjusting card table can ever be quite the man he once was. If he arrives at the state where he hesitates, wavers, and jumps at every mechanical device he encounters, it is not, I submit, because he recognizes the enticements of sex in the device, but only because he recognizes the menace of the machine as such. There might very well be, in every descendant of the man we have been discussing, an inherited desire to jump at, and conquer, mechanical devices before they have a chance to turn into something twice as big and twice as menacing. It is not reasonable to expect that his children and their children will have entirely escaped the stigma of such traumata. I myself will never be the man I once was, nor will my descendants probably ever amount to much, because of a certain experience I had with an automobile.

9. I had gone out to the barn of my country place, a barn which was

used both as a garage and a kennel, to quiet some large black poodles. It
was 1 A.M. of a pitch-dark night in winter and the poodles had apparently
been terrified by some kind of a prowler, a tramp, a turtle, or perhaps a
fiend of some sort. Both my poodles and I myself believed, at the time, in
fiends, and still do. Fiends who materialize out of nothing and nowhere,
like winged pigweed or Russian thistle. I had quite a time quieting the
dogs, because their panic spread to me and mine spread back to them
again, in a kind of vicious circle. Finally, a hush as ominous as their uproar fell upon them, but they kept looking over their shoulders, in a kind
of apprehensive way. "There's nothing to be afraid of," I told them as
firmly as I could, and just at that moment the klaxon of my car, which
was just behind me, began to shriek. Everybody has heard a klaxon on a
car suddenly begin to sound; I understand it is a short circuit that causes
it. But very few people have heard one scream behind them while they
were quieting six or eight alarmed poodles in the middle of the night in
an old barn. I jump now whenever I hear a klaxon, even the klaxon on
my own car when I push the button intentionally. The experience has
left its mark. Everybody, from the day of the jumping card table to the
day of the screaming klaxon, has had similar shocks. You can see the
result, entirely unsuperinduced by sex, in the strained faces and mutter-
ing lips of people who pass you on the streets of great, highly mechanized
cities. There goes a man who picked up one of those trick matchboxes that
whir in your hands; there goes a woman who tried to change a fuse without turning off the current; and yonder toddles an ancient who cranked
an old Reo with the spark advanced. Every person carries in his consciousness the old scar, or the fresh wound, of some harrowing misadventure
with a contraption of some sort. I know people who would not deposit a
nickel and a dime in a cigarette-vending machine and push the lever even
if a diamond necklace came out. I know dozens who would not climb
into an airplane even if it didn't move off the ground. In none of these
people have I discerned what I would call a neurosis, an "exaggerated"
fear; I have discerned only a natural caution in a world made up of
gadgets that whir and whine and whiz and shriek and sometimes explode.

10. I should like to end with the case history of a friend of mine in
Ohio named Harvey Lake. When he was only nineteen, the steering bar
of an old electric runabout broke off in his hand, causing the machine to
carry him through a fence and into the grounds of the Columbus School
for Girls. He developed a fear of automobiles, trains, and every other kind
of vehicle that was not pulled by a horse. Now, the psychologists would
call this a complex and represent the fear as abnormal, but I see it as a
purely reasonable apprehension. If Harvey Lake had, because he was
catapulted into the grounds of the Columbus School for Girls, developed
a fear of girls, I would call that a complex; but I don't call his normal
fear of machines a complex. Harvey Lake never in his life got into a plane

(he died in a fall from a porch), but I do not regard that as neurotic, either, but only sensible.

*11.* I have, to be sure, encountered men with complexes. There was, for example, Marvin Belt. He had a complex about airplanes that was quite interesting. He was not afraid of machinery, or of high places, or of crashes. He was simply afraid that the pilot of any plane he got into might lose his mind. "I imagine myself high over Montana," he once said to me, "in a huge, perfectly safe tri-motored plane. Several of the passengers are dozing, others are reading, but I am keeping my eyes glued on the door to the cockpit. Suddenly the pilot steps out of it, a wild light in his eyes, and in a falsetto like that of a little girl he says to me, 'Conductor, will you please let me off at One-Hundred-and-Twenty-fifth Street?'" "But," I said to Belt, "even if the pilot does go crazy, there is still the co-pilot." "No, there isn't," said Belt. "The pilot has hit the co-pilot over the head with something and killed him." Yes, the psychoanalysts can have Marvin Belt. But they can't have Harvey Lake, or Mr. C, or Mr. S, or Mr. F, or, while I have my strength, me.

*Part Two*

STYLE

# Words and Tone

## ∼ V ∼

·17·

*George Orwell*

# POLITICS AND THE ENGLISH
# LANGUAGE

1. Most people who bother with the matter at all would admit that the English language is in a bad way, but it is generally assumed that we cannot by conscious action do anything about it. Our civilization is decadent, and our language—so the argument runs—must inevitably share in the general collapse. It follows that any struggle against the abuse of language is a sentimental archaism, like preferring candles to electric light or hansom cabs to aeroplanes. Underneath this lies the half-conscious belief that language is a natural growth and not an instrument which we shape for our own purposes.

2. Now, it is clear that the decline of a language must ultimately have political and economic causes: it is not due simply to the bad influence of this or that individual writer. But an effect can become a cause, reinforcing the original cause and producing the same effect in an intensified form, and so on indefinitely. A man may take to drink because he feels himself to be a failure, and then fail all the more completely because he drinks. It is rather the same thing that is happening to the English language. It becomes ugly and inaccurate because our thoughts are foolish, but the slovenliness of our language makes it easier for us to have foolish thoughts. The point is that the process is reversible. Modern English, especially written English, is full of bad habits which spread by imitation and which can be avoided if one is willing to take the necessary trouble. If one gets rid of these habits one can think more clearly, and to think clearly is a necessary first step towards political regeneration: so that the

fight against bad English is not frivolous and is not the exclusive concern of professional writers. I will come back to this presently, and I hope that by that time the meaning of what I have said here will have become clearer. Meanwhile, here are five specimens of the English language as it is now habitually written.

3. These five passages have not been picked out because they are especially bad—I could have quoted far worse if I had chosen—but because they illustrate various of the mental vices from which we now suffer. They are a little below the average, but are fairly representative samples. I number them so that I can refer back to them when necessary:

(1) I am not, indeed, sure whether it is not true to say that the Milton who once seemed not unlike a seventeenth-century Shelley had not become, out of an experience ever more bitter in each year, more alien (*sic*) to the founder of that Jesuit sect which nothing could induce him to tolerate.

PROFESSOR HAROLD LASKI (Essay in *Freedom of Expression*)

(2) Above all, we cannot play ducks and drakes with a native battery of idioms which prescribes such egregious collocations of vocables as the Basic *put up with* for *tolerate* or *put at a loss* for *bewilder*.

PROFESSOR LANCELOT HOGBEN (*Interglossa*)

(3) On the one side we have the free personality; by definition it is not neurotic, for it has neither conflict nor dream. Its desires, such as they are, are transparent, for they are just what institutional approval keeps in the forefront of consciousness; another institutional pattern would alter their number and intensity; there is little in them that is natural, irreducible, or culturally dangerous. But *on the other side*, the social bond itself is nothing but the mutual reflection of these self-secure integrities. Recall the definition of love. Is not this the very picture of a small academic? Where is there a place in this hall of mirrors for either personality or fraternity?

ESSAY ON PSYCHOLOGY in *Politics* (New York)

(4) All the "best people" from the gentlemen's clubs, and all the frantic fascist captains, united in common hatred of Socialism and bestial horror of the rising tide of the mass revolutionary movement, have turned to acts of provocation, to foul incendiarism, to medieval legends of poisoned wells, to legalize their own destruction of proletarian organizations, and rouse the agitated petty-bourgeoisie to chauvinistic fervor on behalf of the fight against the revolutionary way out of the crisis.

COMMUNIST PAMPHLET

(5) If a new spirit *is* to be infused into this old country, there is one thorny and contentious reform which must be tackled, and that is the humanization and galvanization of the B.B.C. Timidity here will bespeak canker and atrophy of the soul. The heart of Britain may be sound and of strong beat, for instance, but the British lion's roar at present is like that of Bottom in Shakespeare's *Midsummer Night's Dream*—as gentle as any sucking dove. A virile new Britain

cannot continue indefinitely to be traduced in the eyes, or rather ears, of the world by the effete languors of Langham Place, brazenly masquerading as "standard English." When the Voice of Britain is heard at nine o'clock, better far and infinitely less ludicrous to hear aitches honestly dropped than the present priggish, inflated, inhibited, school-ma'am-ish arch braying of blameless bashful mewing maidens.

LETTER in Tribune

*4.* Each of these passages has faults of its own, but quite apart from avoidable ugliness, two qualities are common to all of them. The first is staleness of imagery; the other is lack of precision. The writer either has a meaning and cannot express it, or he inadvertently says something else, or he is almost indifferent as to whether his words mean anything or not. This mixture of vagueness and sheer incompetence is the most marked characteristic of modern English prose, and especially of any kind of political writing. As soon as certain topics are raised, the concrete melts into the abstract and no one seems able to think of turns of speech that are not hackneyed: prose consists less and less of *words* chosen for the sake of their meaning, and more and more of *phrases* tacked together like the sections of a prefabricated hen-house. I list below, with notes and examples, various of the tricks by means of which the work of prose-construction is habitually dodged:

*Dying metaphors.* A newly-invented metaphor assists thought by evoking a visual image, while on the other hand a metaphor which is technically "dead" (e.g., *iron resolution*) has in effect reverted to being an ordinary word and can generally be used without loss of vividness. But in between these two classes there is a huge dump of worn-out metaphors which have lost all evocative power and are merely used because they save people the trouble of inventing phrases for themselves. Examples are: *Ring the changes on, take up the cudgels for, toe the line, ride roughshod over, stand shoulder to shoulder with, play into the hands of, an axe to grind, grist to the mill, fishing in troubled waters, on the order of the day, Achilles' heel, swan song, hotbed.* Many of these are used without knowledge of their meaning (what is a "rift," for instance?), and incompatible metaphors are frequently mixed, a sure sign that the writer is not interested in what he is saying. Some metaphors now current have been twisted out of their original meaning without those who use them even being aware of the fact. For example, *toe the line* is sometimes written *tow the line.* Another example is *the hammer and the anvil,* now always used with the implication that the anvil gets the worst of it. In real life it is always the anvil that breaks the hammer, never the other way about: a writer who stopped to think what he was saying would be aware of this, and would avoid perverting the original phrase.

*Operators,* or *verbal false limbs.* These save the trouble of picking out appropriate verbs and nouns, and at the same time pad each sentence with extra syllables which give it an appearance of symmetry. Characteristic phrases are: *render inoperative, militate against, prove unacceptable, make contact with, be subjected to, give rise to, give grounds for, having the effect of, play a lead-*

*ing part (role) in, make itself felt, take effect, exhibit a tendency to, serve the purpose of, etc., etc.* The keynote is the elimination of simple verbs. Instead of being a single word, such as *break, stop, spoil, mend, kill,* a verb becomes a phrase, made up of a noun or adjective tacked on to some general-purposes verb as *prove, serve, form, play, render.* In addition, the passive voice is wherever possible used in preference to the active, and noun constructions are used instead of gerunds (*by examination of* instead of *by examining*). The range of verbs is further cut down by means of the *-ize* and *de-* formations, and banal statements are given an appearance of profundity by means of the *not un-* formation. Simple conjunctions and prepositions are replaced by such phrases as *with respect to, having regard to, the fact that, by dint of, in view of, in the interests of, on the hypothesis that;* and the ends of sentences are saved from anti-climax by such resounding commonplaces as *greatly to be desired, cannot be left out of account, a development to be expected in the near future, deserving of serious consideration, brought to a satisfactory conclusion,* and so on and so forth.

*Pretentious diction.* Words like *phenomenon, element, individual* (as noun), *objective, categorical, effective, virtual, basis, primary, promote, constitute, exhibit, exploit, utilize, eliminate, liquidate,* are used to dress up simple statements and give an air of scientific impartiality to biased judgments. Adjectives like *epoch-making, epic, historic, unforgettable, triumphant, age-old, inevitable, inexorable, veritable,* are used to dignify the sordid processes of international politics, while writing that aims at glorifying war usually takes on an archaic color, its characteristic words being: *realm, throne, chariot, mailed fist, trident, sword, shield, buckler, banner, jackboot, clarion.* Foreign words and expressions such as *cul de sac, ancien régime, deus ex machina, mutatis mutandis, status quo, gleichschaltung, weltanschauung,* are used to give an air of culture and elegance. Except for the useful abbreviations *i.e., e.g.,* and *etc.,* there is no real need for any of the hundreds of foreign phrases now current in English. Bad writers, and especially scientific, political and sociological writers, are nearly always haunted by the notion that Latin or Greek words are grander than Saxon ones, and unnecessary words like *expedite, ameliorate, predict, extraneous, deracinated, clandestine, subaqueous* and hundreds of others constantly gain ground from their Anglo-Saxon opposite numbers.[1] The jargon peculiar to Marxist writing (*hyena, hangman, cannibal, petty bourgeois, these gentry, lackey, flunky, mad dog, White Guard, etc.*) consists largely of words and phrases translated from Russian, German or French; but the normal way of coining a new word is to use a Latin or Greek root with the appropriate affix and, where necessary, the *-ize* formation. It is often easier to make up words of this kind (*deregionalize, impermissible, extramarital, non-fragmentary* and so forth) than to think up the English words that will cover one's meaning. The result, in general, is an increase in slovenliness and vagueness.

[1] An interesting illustration of this is the way in which the English flower names which were in use till very recently are being ousted by Greek ones, *snap-dragon* becoming *antirrhinum, forget-me-not* becoming *myosotis,* etc. It is hard to see any practical reason for this change of fashion: it is probably due to an instinctive turning-away from the more homely word and a vague feeling that the Greek word is scientific.

*Meaningless words.* In certain kinds of writing, particularly in art criticism and literary criticism, it is normal to come across long passages which are almost completely lacking in meaning.[2] Words like *romantic, plastic, values, human, dead, sentimental, natural, vitality,* as used in art criticism, are strictly meaningless, in the sense that they not only do not point to any discoverable object, but are hardly even expected to do so by the reader. When one critic writes, "The outstanding feature of Mr. X's work is its living quality," while another writes, "The immediately striking thing about Mr. X's work is its peculiar deadness," the reader accepts this as a simple difference of opinion. If words like *black* and *white* were involved, instead of the jargon words *dead* and *living,* he would see at once that language was being used in an improper way. Many political words are similarly abused. The word *Fascism* has now no meaning except in so far as it signifies "something not desirable." The words *democracy, socialism, freedom, patriotic, realistic, justice,* have each of them several different meanings which cannot be reconciled with one another. In the case of a word like *democracy,* not only is there no agreed definition, but the attempt to make one is resisted from all sides. It is almost universally felt that when we call a country democratic we are praising it: consequently the defenders of every kind of régime claim that it is a democracy, and fear that they might have to stop using the word if it were tied down to any one meaning. Words of this kind are often used in a consciously dishonest way. That is, the person who uses them has his own private definition, but allows his hearer to think he means something quite different. Statements like *Marshal Pétain was a true patriot, The Soviet Press is the freest in the world, The Catholic Church is opposed to persecution,* are almost always made with intent to deceive. Other words used in variable meanings, in most cases more or less dishonestly, are: *class, totalitarian, science, progressive, reactionary, bourgeois, equality.*

5. Now that I have made this catalogue of swindles and perversions, let me give another example of the kind of writing that they lead to. This time it must of its nature be an imaginary one. I am going to translate a passage of good English into modern English of the worst sort. Here is a well-known verse from *Ecclesiastes:*

I returned, and saw under the sun, that the race is not to the swift, nor the battle to the strong, neither yet bread to the wise, nor yet riches to men of understanding, nor yet favor to men of skill; but time and chance happeneth to them all.

Here it is in modern English:

Objective consideration of contemporary phenomena compels the conclusion that success or failure in competitive activities exhibits no tendency to be com-

[2] Example: "Comfort's catholicity of perception and image, strangely Whitmanesque in range, almost the exact opposite in aesthetic compulsion, continues to evoke that trembling atmospheric accumulative hinting at a cruel, an inexorably serene timelessness . . . Wrey Gardiner scores by aiming at simple bullseyes with precision. Only they are not so simple, and through this contented sadness runs more than the surface bittersweet of resignation." (*Poetry Quarterly.*)

mensurate with innate capacity, but that a considerable element of the unpredictable must invariably be taken into account.

6. This is a parody, but not a very gross one. Exhibit (3), above, for
instance, contains several patches of the same kind of English. It will be
seen that I have not made a full translation. The beginning and ending
of the sentence follow the original meaning fairly closely, but in the
middle the concrete illustrations—race, battle, bread—dissolve into the
vague phrase "success or failure in competitive activities." This had to be
so, because no modern writer of the kind I am discussing—no one capable
of using phrases like "objective consideration of contemporary phenomena"—would ever tabulate his thoughts in that precise and detailed
way. The whole tendency of modern prose is away from concreteness.
Now analyze these two sentences a little more closely. The first contains
49 words but only 60 syllables, and all its words are those of everyday
life. The second contains 38 words of 90 syllables: 18 of its words are from
Latin roots, and one from Greek. The first sentence contains six vivid
images, and only one phrase ("time and chance") that could be called
vague. The second contains not a single fresh, arresting phrase, and in
spite of its 90 syllables it gives only a shortened version of the meaning
contained in the first. Yet without a doubt it is the second kind of sentence
that is gaining ground in modern English. I do not want to exaggerate.
This kind of writing is not yet universal, and outcrops of simplicity will
occur here and there in the worst-written page. Still, if you or I were told
to write a few lines on the uncertainty of human fortunes, we should
probably come much nearer to my imaginary sentence than to the one
from *Ecclesiastes*.

7. As I have tried to show, modern writing at its worst does not consist
in picking out words for the sake of their meaning and inventing images
in order to make the meaning clearer. It consists in gumming together
long strips of words which have already been set in order by someone
else, and making the results presentable by sheer humbug. The attraction
of this way of writing is that it is easy. It is easier—even quicker, once you
have the habit—to say *In my opinion it is a not unjustifiable assumption
that* than to say I *think*. If you use ready-made phrases, you not only
don't have to hunt about for words; you also don't have to bother with the
rhythms of your sentences, since these phrases are generally so arranged
as to be more or less euphonious. When you are composing in a hurry—
when you are dictating to a stenographer, for instance, or making a public
speech—it is natural to fall into a pretentious, Latinized style. Tags like *a
consideration which we should do well to bear in mind* or *a conclusion to
which all of us would readily assent* will save many a sentence from coming down with a bump. By using stale metaphors, similes and idioms,
you save much mental effort at the cost of leaving your meaning vague,

not only for your reader but for yourself. This is the significance of mixed metaphors. The sole aim of a metaphor is to call up a visual image. When these images clash—as in *The Fascist octopus has sung its swan song, the jackboot is thrown into the melting pot*—it can be taken as certain that the writer is not seeing a mental image of the objects he is naming; in other words he is not really thinking. Look again at the examples I gave at the beginning of this essay. Professor Laski (1) uses five negatives in 53 words. One of these is superfluous, making nonsense of the whole passage, and in addition there is the slip *alien* for akin, making further nonsense, and several avoidable pieces of clumsiness which increase the general vagueness. Professor Hogben (2) plays ducks and drakes with a battery which is able to write prescriptions, and, while disapproving of the everyday phrase *put up with,* is unwilling to look *egregious* up in the dictionary and see what it means. (3), if one takes an uncharitable attitude towards it, is simply meaningless: probably one could work out its intended meaning by reading the whole of the article in which it occurs. In (4), the writer knows more or less what he wants to say, but an accumulation of stale phrases chokes him like tea leaves blocking a sink. In (5), words and meaning have almost parted company. People who write in this manner usually have a general emotional meaning—they dislike one thing and want to express solidarity with another—but they are not interested in the detail of what they are saying. A scrupulous writer, in every sentence that he writes, will ask himself at least four questions, thus: What am I trying to say? What words will express it? What image or idiom will make it clearer? Is this image fresh enough to have an effect? And he will probably ask himself two more: Could I put it more shortly? Have I said anything that is avoidably ugly? But you are not obliged to go to all this trouble. You can shirk it by simply throwing your mind open and letting the ready-made phrases come crowding in. They will construct your sentences for you—even think your thoughts for you, to a certain extent—and at need they will perform the important service of partially concealing your meaning even from yourself. It is at this point that the special connection between politics and the debasement of language becomes clear.

8. In our time it is broadly true that political writing is bad writing. Where it is not true, it will generally be found that the writer is some kind of rebel, expressing his private opinions and not a "party line." Orthodoxy, of whatever color, seems to demand a lifeless, imitative style. The political dialects to be found in pamphlets, leading articles, manifestoes, White Papers and the speeches of under-secretaries do, of course, vary from party to party, but they are all alike in that one almost never finds in them a fresh, vivid, home-made turn of speech. When one watches some tired hack on the platform mechanically repeating the familiar phrases—*bestial atrocities, iron heel, bloodstained tyranny, free peoples of*

*the world, stand shoulder to shoulder*—one often has a curious feeling that
one is not watching a live human being but some kind of dummy: a feeling which suddenly becomes stronger at moments when the light catches
the speaker's spectacles and turns them into blank discs which seem to
have no eyes behind them. And this is not altogether fanciful. A speaker
who uses that kind of phraseology has gone some distance towards turning himself into a machine. The appropriate noises are coming out of his
larynx, but his brain is not involved as it would be if he were choosing
his words for himself. If the speech he is making is one that he is accustomed to make over and over again, he may be almost unconscious of
what he is saying, as one is when one utters the responses in church. And
this reduced state of consciousness, if not indispensable, is at any rate
favorable to political conformity.

9. In our time, political speech and writing are largely the defense of
the indefensible. Things like the continuance of British rule in India, the
Russian purges and deportations, the dropping of the atom bombs on
Japan, can indeed be defended, but only by arguments which are too
brutal for most people to face, and which do not square with the professed aims of political parties. Thus political language has to consist
largely of euphemism, question-begging and sheer cloudy vagueness.
Defenseless villages are bombarded from the air, the inhabitants driven
out into the countryside, the cattle machine-gunned, the huts set on fire
with incendiary bullets: this is called *pacification*. Millions of peasants are
robbed of their farms and sent trudging along the roads with no more
than they can carry: this is called *transfer of population* or *rectification of
frontiers*. People are imprisoned for years without trial, or shot in the
back of the neck or sent to die of scurvy in Arctic lumber camps: this is
called *elimination of unreliable elements*. Such phraseology is needed if
one wants to name things without calling up mental pictures of them.
Consider for instance some comfortable English professor defending
Russian totalitarianism. He cannot say outright, "I believe in killing off
your opponents when you can get good results by doing so." Probably,
therefore, he will say something like this:

While freely conceding that the Soviet régime exhibits certain features which
the humanitarian may be inclined to deplore, we must, I think, agree that a
certain curtailment of the right to political opposition is an unavoidable concomitant of transitional periods, and that the rigors which the Russian people
have been called upon to undergo have been amply justified in the sphere of
concrete achievement.

10. The inflated style is itself a kind of euphemism. A mass of Latin
words falls upon the facts like soft snow, blurring the outlines and cover-
ing up all the details. The great enemy of clear language is insincerity.
When there is a gap between one's real and one's declared aims, one turns,
as it were instinctively, to long words and exhausted idioms, like a cuttle-

fish squirting out ink. In our age there is no such thing as "keeping out of politics." All issues are political issues, and politics itself is a mass of lies, evasions, folly, hatred and schizophrenia. When the general atmosphere is bad, language must suffer. I should expect to find—this is a guess which I have not sufficient knowledge to verify—that the German, Russian and Italian languages have all deteriorated in the last ten or fifteen years as a result of dictatorship.

*11.* But if thought corrupts language, language can also corrupt thought. A bad usage can spread by tradition and imitation, even among people who should and do know better. The debased language that I have been discussing is in some ways very convenient. Phrases like *a not unjustifiable assumption, leaves much to be desired, would serve no good purpose, a consideration which we should do well to bear in mind,* are a continuous temptation, a packet of aspirins always at one's elbow. Look back through this essay, and for certain you will find that I have again and again committed the very faults I am protesting against. By this morning's post I have received a pamphlet dealing with conditions in Germany. The author tells me that he "felt impelled" to write it. I open it at random, and here is almost the first sentence that I see: "[The Allies] have an opportunity not only of achieving a radical transformation of Germany's social and political structure in such a way as to avoid a nationalistic reaction in Germany itself, but at the same time of laying the foundations of a cooperative and unified Europe." You see, he "feels impelled" to write—feels, presumably, that he has something new to say—and yet his words, like cavalry horses answering the bugle, group themselves automatically into the familiar dreary pattern. This invasion of one's mind by ready-made phrases (*lay the foundations, achieve a radical transformation*) can only be prevented if one is constantly on guard against them, and every such phrase anesthetizes a portion of one's brain.

*12.* I said earlier that the decadence of our language is probably curable. Those who deny this would argue, if they produced an argument at all, that language merely reflects existing social conditions, and that we cannot influence its development by any direct tinkering with words and constructions. So far as the general tone or spirit of a language goes, this may be true, but it is not true in detail. Silly words and expressions have often disappeared, not through any evolutionary process but owing to the conscious action of a minority. Two recent examples were *explore every avenue* and *leave no stone unturned,* which were killed by the jeers of a few journalists. There is a long list of fly-blown metaphors which could similarly be got rid of if enough people would interest themselves in the job; and it should also be possible to laugh the *not un-* formation out of existence,[3] to reduce the amount of Latin and Greek in the average sentence, to drive out foreign phrases and strayed scientific words, and, in

[3] One can cure oneself of the *non un-* formation by memorizing this sentence: *A not unblack dog was chasing a not unsmall rabbit across a not ungreen field.*

general, to make pretentiousness unfashionable. But all these are minor points. The defense of the English language implies more than this, and perhaps it is best to start by saying what it does *not* imply.

*13.* To begin with, it has nothing to do with archaism, with the salvaging of obsolete words and turns of speech, or with the setting-up of a "standard-English" which must never be departed from. On the contrary, it is especially concerned with the scrapping of every word or idiom which has outworn its usefulness. It has nothing to do with correct grammar and syntax, which are of no importance so long as one makes one's meaning clear, or with the avoidance of Americanisms, or with having what is called a "good prose style." On the other hand it is not concerned with fake simplicity and the attempt to make written English colloquial. Nor does it even imply in every case preferring the Saxon word to the Latin one, though it does imply using the fewest and shortest words that will cover one's meaning. What is above all needed is to let the meaning choose the word, and not the other way about. In prose, the worst thing one can do with words is to surrender them. When you think of a concrete object, you think wordlessly, and then, if you want to describe the thing you have been visualizing, you probably hunt about till you find the exact words that seem to fit it. When you think of something abstract you are more inclined to use words from the start, and unless you make a conscious effort to prevent it, the existing dialect will come rushing in and do the job for you, at the expense of blurring or even changing your meaning. Probably it is better to put off using words as long as possible and get one's meaning as clear as one can through pictures or sensations. Afterwards one can choose—not simply *accept*—the phrases that will best cover the meaning, and then switch round and decide what impressions one's words are likely to make on another person. This last effort of the mind cuts out all stale or mixed images, all prefabricated phrases, needless repetitions, and humbug and vagueness generally. But one can often be in doubt about the effect of a word or a phrase, and one needs rules that one can rely on when instinct fails. I think the following rules will cover most cases:

   (i)  Never use a metaphor, simile or other figure of speech which you are used to seeing in print.
  (ii)  Never use a long word where a short one will do.
 (iii)  If it is possible to cut a word out, always cut it out.
 (iv)  Never use the passive where you can use the active.
  (v)  Never use a foreign phrase, a scientific word or a jargon word if you can think of an everyday English equivalent.
 (vi)  Break any of these rules sooner than say anything barbarous.

These rules sound elementary, and so they are, but they demand a deep change of attitude in anyone who has grown used to writing in the style now fashionable. One could keep all of them and still write bad English, but one could not write the kind of stuff that I quoted in these five specimens at the beginning of this article.

*14.* I have not here been considering the literary use of language, but merely language as an instrument for expressing and not for concealing or preventing thought. Stuart Chase and others have come near to claiming that all abstract words are meaningless, and have used this as a pretext for advocating a kind of political quietism. Since you don't know what Fascism is, how can you struggle against Fascism? One need not swallow such absurdities as this, but one ought to recognize that the present political chaos is connected with the decay of language, and that one can probably bring about some improvement by starting at the verbal end. If you simplify your English, you are freed from the worst follies of orthodoxy. You cannot speak any of the necessary dialects, and when you make a stupid remark its stupidity will be obvious, even to yourself. Political language—and with variations this is true of all political parties, from Conservatives to Anarchists—is designed to make lies sound truthful and murder respectable, and to give an appearance of solidity to pure wind. One cannot change this all in a moment, but one can at least change one's own habits, and from time to time one can even, if one jeers loudly enough, send some worn-out and useless phrase—some *jackboot, Achilles' heel, hotbed, melting pot, acid test, veritable inferno* or other lump of verbal refuse—into the dustbin where it belongs.

## ·18·

*Samuel T. Williamson*

# HOW TO WRITE LIKE A SOCIAL SCIENTIST

*1.* During my years as an editor, I have seen probably hundreds of job applicants who were either just out of College or in their senior year. All wanted "to write." Many brought letters from their teachers. But I do not recall one letter announcing that its bearer could write what he wished to say with clarity and directness, with economy of words, and with pleasing variety of sentence structure.

From *The Saturday Review of Literature* (October 4, 1947). Reprinted by permission of *The Saturday Review* and Mrs. Cora Chase Williamson.

2. Most of these young men and women could not write plain English. Apparently their noses had not been rubbed in the drudgery of putting one simple well-chosen word behind the other. If this was true of teachers' pets, what about the rest? What about those going into business and industry? Or those going into professions? What about those who remain at college —first for a Master of Arts degree, then an instructorship combined with work for a Ph.D., then perhaps an assistant professorship, next a full professorship and finally, as an academic crown of laurel, appointment as head of a department or as dean of a faculty?

3. Certainly, faculty members of a front-rank university should be better able to express themselves than those they teach. Assume that those in the English department have this ability. Can the same be said of the social scientists—economists, sociologists, and authorities on government? We need today as we never needed so urgently before all the understanding they can give us of problems of earning a living, caring for our fellows, and governing ourselves. Too many of them, I find, can't write as well as their students.

4. I am still convalescing from overexposure some time ago to products of the academic mind. One of the foundations engaged me to edit manuscripts of a socio-economic research report designed for the thoughtful citizen as well as for the specialist. My expectations were not high—no deathless prose, merely a sturdy, no-nonsense report of explorers into the wilderness of statistics and half-known facts. I knew from experience that economic necessity compels many a professional writer to be a cream-skimmer and a gatherer of easily obtainable material; for unless his publishers will stand the extra cost, he cannot afford the exhaustive investigation which endowed research makes possible. Although I did not expect fine writing from a trained, professional researcher, I did assume that a careful fact-finder would write carefully.

5. And so, anticipating no literary treat, I plunged into the forest of words of my first manuscript. My weapons were a sturdy eraser and several batteries of sharpened pencils. My armor was a thesaurus. And if I should become lost, a near-by public library was a landmark, and the Encyclopedia of Social Sciences on its reference shelves was an ever-ready guide.

6. Instead of big trees, I found underbrush. Cutting through involved, lumbering sentences was bad enough, but the real chore was removal of the burdocks of excess verbiage which clung to the manuscript. Nothing was big or large; in my author's lexicon, it was "substantial." When he meant "much," he wrote "to a substantially high degree." If some event took place in the early 1920's, he put it "in the early part of the decade of the twenties." And instead of "that depends," my author wrote, "any answer to this question must bear in mind certain peculiar characteristics of the industry."

7. So it went for 30,000 words. The pile of verbal burdocks grew—sometimes twelve words from a twenty-word sentence. The shortened version of 20,000 words was perhaps no more thrilling than the original report; but it was terser and crisper. It took less time to read and it could be understood quicker. That was all I could do. As S. S. McClure once said to me, "An editor can improve a manuscript, but he cannot put in what isn't there."

8. I did not know the author I was editing; after what I did to his copy it may be just as well that we have not met. Aside from his cat-chasing-its-own-tail verbosity, he was a competent enough workman. Apparently he is well thought of. He has his doctorate, he is a trained researcher and a pupil of an eminent professor. He has held a number of fellowships and he has performed competently several jobs of economic research. But, after this long academic preparation for what was to be a life work, it is a mystery why so little attention was given to acquiring use of simple English.

9. Later, when I encountered other manuscripts, I found I had been too hard on this promising Ph.D. Tone-deaf as he was to words, his report was a lighthouse of clarity among the chapters turned in by his so-called academic betters. These brethren—and sister'n—who contributed the remainder of the foundation's study were professors and assistant professors in our foremost colleges and universities. The names of one or two are occasionally in newspaper headlines. All of them had, as the professorial term has it, "published."

10. Anyone who edits copy, regardless of whether it is good or bad, discovers in a manuscript certain pet phrases, little quirks of style and other individual traits of its author. But in the series I edited, all twenty reports read alike. Their words would be found in any English dictionary, grammar was beyond criticism, but long passages in these reports demanded not editing but actual translation. For hours at a time, I floundered in brier patches like this: "In eliminating wage changes due to purely transitory conditions, collective bargaining has eliminated one of the important causes of industrial conflict, for changes under such conditions are almost always followed by a reaction when normal conditions appear."

11. I am not picking on my little group of social scientists. They are merely members of a caste; they are so used to taking in each other's literary washing that it has become a habit for them to clothe their thoughts in the same smothering verbal garments. Nor are they any worse than most of their colleagues, for example:

In the long run, developments in transportation, housing, optimum size of plant, etc., might tend to induce an industrial and demographic pattern similar to the one that consciousness of vulnerability would dictate. Such a tendency might be advanced by public persuasion and governmental inducement, and advanced more effectively if the causes of urbanization had been carefully studied.

*12.* Such pedantic Choctaw may be all right as a sort of code language or shorthand of social science to circulate among initiates, but its perpetrators have no right to impose it on others. The tragedy is that its users appear to be under the impression that it is good English usage.

*13.* Father, forgive them; for they know not what they do! There once was a time when everyday folk spoke one language, and learned men wrote another. It was called the Dark Ages. The world is in such a state that we may return to the Dark Ages if we do not acquire wisdom. If social scientists have answers to our problems yet feel under no obligation to make themselves understood, then we laymen must learn their language. This may take some practice, but practice should become perfect by following six simple rules of the guild of social science writers. Examples which I give are sound and well tested; they come from manuscripts I edited.

*14. Rule 1. Never use a short word when you can think of a long one.* Never say "now," but "currently." It is not "soon" but "presently." You did not have "enough" but a "sufficiency." Never do you come to the "end" but to the "termination." This rule is basic.

*15. Rule 2. Never use one word when you can use two or more.* Eschew "probably." Write, "it is improbable," and raise this to "it is not improbable." Then you'll be able to parlay "probably" into "available evidence would tend to indicate that it is not unreasonable to suppose."

*16. Rule 3. Put one-syllable thought into polysyllabic terms.* Instead of observing that a work force might be bigger and better, write, "In addition to quantitative enlargement, it is not improbable that there is need also for qualitative improvement in the personnel of the service." If you have discovered that musicians out of practice can't hold jobs, report that "the fact of rapid deterioration of musical skill when not in use soon converts the employed into the unemployable." Resist the impulse to say that much men's clothing is machine made. Put it thus: "Nearly all operations in the industry lend themselves to performance by machine, and all grades of men's clothing sold in significant quantity involve a very substantial amount of machine work."

*17. Rule 4. Put the obvious in terms of the unintelligible.* When you write that "the product of the activity of janitors is expended in the identical locality in which that activity takes place," your lay reader is in for a time of it. After an hour's puzzlement, he may conclude that janitors' sweepings are thrown on the town dump. See what you can do with this: "Each article sent to the cleaner is handled separately." You become a member of the guild in good standing if you put it like this. "Within the cleaning plant proper the business of the industry involves several well-defined processes, which, from the economic point of view, may be characterized simply by saying that most of them require separate handling of each individual garment or piece of material to be cleaned."

18. *Rule 5. Announce what you are going to say before you say it*. This pitcher's wind-up technique before hurling towards—not at—home plate has two varieties. First is the quick wind-up: "In the following section the policies of the administration will be considered." Then you become strong enough for the contortionist wind-up: "Perhaps more important, therefore, than the question of what standards are in a particular case, there are the questions of the extent of observance of these standards and the methods of their enforcement." Also you can play with reversing Rule 5 and *say what you have said after you have said it*.

19. *Rule 6. Defend your style as "scientific."* Look down on—not up to —clear simple English. Sneer at it as "popular." Scorn it as "journalistic." Explain your failure to put more mental sweat into your writing on the ground that "the social scientists who want to be scientific believe that we can have scientific description of human behavior and trustworthy predictions in the scientific sense only as we build adequate taxonomic systems for observable phenomena and symbolic systems for the manipulation of ideal and abstract entities."

20. For this explanation I am indebted to Lyman Bryson in the *Saturday Review of Literature* article (Oct. 13, 1945) "Writers: Enemies of Social Science." Standing on ground considerably of his own choosing, Mr. Bryson argued against judging social science writing by literary standards.

21. Social scientists are not criticized because they are not literary artists. The trouble with social science does not lie in its special vocabulary. Those words are doubtless chosen with great care. The trouble is that too few social scientists take enough care with words outside their special vocabularies.

22. It is not much to expect that teachers should be more competent in the art of explanation than those they teach. Teachers of social sciences diligently try to acquire knowledge; too few exert themselves enough to impart it intelligently.

23. Too long has this been excused as "the academic mind." It should be called by what it is: intellectual laziness and grubbymindedness.

·19·

*William H. Whyte, Jr.*

# YOU, TOO, CAN WRITE THE
# CASUAL STYLE

*1.* A revolution has taken place in American prose. No longer the short huffs and puffs, the unqualified word, the crude gusto of the declarative sentence. Today the fashion is to write casually.

*2.* The Casual Style is not exactly new. Originated in the early Twenties, it has been refined and improved and refined again by a relatively small band of writers, principally for the *New Yorker,* until now their mannerisms have become standards of sophistication. Everybody is trying to join the club. Newspaper columnists have forsaken the beloved metaphors of the sports page for the Casual Style, and one of the quickest ways for an ad man to snag an award from other ad men is to give his copy the low-key, casual pitch; the copy shouldn't sing these days—it should whisper. Even Dr. Rudolf Flesch, who has been doing so much to teach people how to write like other people, is counseling his followers to use the Casual Style. Everywhere the ideal seems the same: be casual.

*3.* But how? There is very little down-to-earth advice. We hear about the rapier-like handling of the bromide, the keen eye for sham and pretension, the exquisite sense of nuance, the unerring ear for the vulgate. But not much about actual technique. The layman, as a consequence, is apt to look on the Casual Style as a mandarin dialect which he fears he may never master.

*4.* Nonsense. The Casual Style is within everyone's grasp. It has now become so perfected by constant polishing that its devices may readily be identified, and they change so little that their use need be no more difficult for the novice than for the expert. (That's not quite all there is to it, of course. Some apparently casual writers, Thurber and E. B. White, among others, rarely use the devices.)

*5.* The subject matter, in the first place, is not to be ignored. Generally speaking, the more uneventful it is, or the more pallid the writer's reaction

From *Harper's Magazine* (October, 1953). Reprinted by permission of *Harper's Magazine* and William H. Whyte.

to it, the better do form and content marry. Take, for example, the cocktail party at which the writer can show how bored everyone is with everyone else, and how utterly fatuous they all are anyhow. Since a non-casual statement—*e.g.*, "The party was a bore"—would destroy the reason for writing about it at all, the Casual Style here is not only desirable but mandatory.

6. Whatever the subject, however, twelve devices are the rock on which all else is built. I will present them one by one, illustrating them with examples from such leading casual stylists as Wolcott Gibbs, John Crosby, John McCarten, and (on occasion) this magazine's "Mr. Harper." If the reader will digest what follows, he should be able to dash off a paragraph indistinguishable from the best casual writing being done today.

7. (1) *Heightened Understatement*. Where the old-style writer would say, "I don't like it," "It is not good," or something equally banal, the casual writer says it is *"something less than* good." He avoids direct statement and strong words—except, as we will note, where he is setting them up to have something to knock down. In any event, he qualifies. "Somewhat" and "rather," the bread-and-butter words of the casual writer, should become habitual with you; similarly with such phrases as "I suppose," "it seems to me," "I guess," or "I'm afraid." "Elusive" or "elude" are good, too, and if you see the word "charm" in a casual sentence you can be pretty sure that "eludes me," or "I find elusive," will not be far behind.

8. (2) *The Multiple Hedge*. Set up an ostensibly strong statement, and then, with your qualifiers, shoot a series of alternately negative and positive charges into the sentence until finally you neutralize the whole thing. Let's take, for example, the clause, "certain names have a guaranteed nostalgic magic." Challenge enough here; the names not only have magic, they have guaranteed magic. A double hedge reverses the charge. "Names which have, *I suppose* [hedge 1], a guaranteed nostalgic magic, *though there are times that I doubt it* [hedge 2]. . . ."

9. We didn't have to say they were guaranteed in the first place, of course, but without such straw phrases we wouldn't have anything to construct a hedge on and, frequently, nothing to write at all. The virtue of the hedge is that by its very negating effect it makes any sentence infinitely expansible. Even if you have so torn down your original statement with one or two hedges that you seem to have come to the end of the line, you have only to slip in an anti-hedge, a strengthening word (*e.g.*, "definitely," "unqualified," etc.), and begin the process all over again. Witness the following quadruple hedge: "I found Mr. Home entertaining *from time to time* [hedge 1] on the ground, *I guess* [hedge 2], that the singular idiom and unearthly detachment of the British upper classes have *always* [anti-hedge] seemed *reasonably* [hedge 3] droll to me, *at least in moderation* [hedge 4]." The art of plain talk, as has been pointed out, does not entail undue brevity.

*10.* If you've pulled hedge on hedge and the effect still remains too vigorous, simply wipe the slate clean with a cancellation clause at the end. "It was all exactly as foolish as it sounds," says Wolcott Gibbs, winding up some 570 casual words on a subject, "and I wouldn't give it another thought."

*11.* (3) *Narcissizing Your Prose.* The casual style is nothing if not personal; indeed, you will usually find in it as many references to the writer as to what he's supposed to be talking about. For you do not talk about the subject; you talk about its impact on you. With the reader peering over your shoulder, you look into the mirror and observe your own responses as you run the entire range of the casual writer's emotions. You may reveal yourself as, in turn, listless ("the audience seemed not to share my boredom"); insouciant ("I was really quite happy with it"); irritated ("The whole thing left me tired and cross"); comparatively gracious ("Being in a comparatively gracious mood, I won't go into the details I didn't like"); or hesitant ("I wish I could say that I could accept his hypothesis").

*12.* (4) *Preparation for the Witticism.* When the casual writer hits upon a clever turn of phrase or a nice conceit, he uses this device to insure that his conceit will not pass unnoticed. Suppose, for example, you have thought of something to say that is pretty damn good if you say so yourself. The device, in effect, is to say so yourself. If you want to devastate a certain work as "a study of vulgarity in high places," don't say this flat out. Earlier in the sentence prepare the reader for the drollery ahead with something like "what I am tempted to call" or "what could best be described as" or "If it had to be defined in a sentence, it might well be called. . . ."

*13.* Every writer his own claque.

*14.* (5) *Deciphered Notes Device; or Cute-Things-I-Have-Said.* In this one you are your own stooge as well. You feed yourself lines. By means of the slender fiction that you have written something on the back of an envelope or the margin of a program, you catch yourself good-humoredly trying to decipher these shrewd, if cryptic, little jottings. *Viz.:* "Their diagnoses are not clearly as crisp as those I find in my notes"; ". . . sounds like an inadequate description, but it's all I have in my notes, and it may conceivably be a very high compliment."

*15.* (6) *The Kicker.* An echo effect. "My reactions [included] an irritable feeling that eleven o'clock was past Miss Keim's bedtime,"—and now the Kicker—"*not to mention my own.*" This type of thing practically writes itself. "She returns home. She should never have left home in the first place. ____ _____ _____ ___."[1]

*16.* (7) *Wit of Omission.* By calling attention to the fact that you are not going to say it, you suggest that there is something very funny you could say if only you wanted to. "A thought occurred to me at this point,"

---

[1] "And neither should I."

you may say, when otherwise stymied, "but I think we had better not go into *that*."

17. (8) *The Planned Colloquialism*. The casual writer savors colloquialisms. This is not ordinary colloquial talk—nobody is more quickly provoked than the casual writer by ordinary usage. It is, rather, a playful descent into the vulgate. Phrases like "darn," "awfully," "as all getout," "mighty," and other folksy idioms are ideal. The less you would be likely to use the word normally yourself the more pointed the effect. Contrast is what you are after, for it is the facetious interplay of language levels— a blending, as it were, of the East Fifties and the Sticks—that gives the Casual Style its off-hand charm.

18. (9) *Feigned Forgetfulness*. Conversation gropes; it is full of "what I really meant was" and "maybe I should have added," backings and fillings and second thoughts of one kind or another. Writing is different; theoretically, ironing out second thoughts beforehand is one of the things writers are paid to do. In the Casual Style, however, it is exactly this exposure of the writer composing in public that makes it so casual. For the professional touch, then, ramble, rebuke yourself in print ("what I really meant, I guess"), and if you have something you feel you should have said earlier, don't say it earlier, but say later that you guess you should have said it earlier.

19. (10) *The Subject-Apologizer, or Pardon-Me-for-Living*. The Casual Stylist must always allow for the possibility that his subject is just as boring to the reader as it is to him. He may forestall this by seeming to have stumbled on it by accident, or by using phrases like: "If this is as much news to you as it is to me," or "This, in case you've been living in a cave lately, is. . . ."

20. (11) *The Omitted Word*. This all began modestly enough the day a *New Yorker* writer dropped the articles "the" and "a" from the initial sentence of an anecdote (*e.g.*, "Man we know told us"; "Fellow name of Brown"). Now even such resolutely lowbrow writers as Robert Ruark affect it, and they are applying it to any part of speech anywhere in the sentence. You can drop a pronoun ("Says they're shaped like pyramids"); verb ("You been away from soap opera the last couple of weeks?"); or preposition ("Far as glamour goes . . .").

21. (12) *The Right Word*. In the lexicon of the casual writer there are a dozen or so adjectives which in any context have, to borrow a phrase, a guaranteed charm. Attrition is high—"brittle," "febrile," "confected," for example, are at the end of the run. Ten, however, defy obsolescence: *antic, arch, blurred, chaste, chill, crisp, churlish, disheveled, dim, disembodied*.

22. They are good singly, but they are even better when used in tandem; *c.f.*, "In an arch, antic sort of way"; "In an arch, blurred sort of way;" "In an arch, crisp sort of way." And so on.

23. Finally, the most multi-purpose word of them all: "altogether." Frequently it is the companion of "charming" and "delightful," and in this coupling is indispensable to any kind of drama criticism. It can also modify the writer himself (*e.g.*, "Altogether, I think . . ."). Used best, however, it just floats, unbeholden to any other part of the sentence.

24. Once you have mastered these twelve devices, you too should be able to write as casually as all getout. At least it seems to me, though I may be wrong, that they convey an elusive archness which the crisp literary craftsman, in his own dim sort of way, should altogether cultivate these days. Come to think of it, the charm of the Casual Style is something less than clear to me, but we needn't go into *that*. Fellow I know from another magazine says this point of view best described as churlish. Not, of course, that it matters.

## ·20·

## *Jacques Barzun*

# HOW TO WRITE AND BE READ

1. Writing comes before reading, in logic and also in the public mind. No one cares whether you read fast or slow, well or ill, but as soon as you put pen to paper, somebody may be puzzled, angry, bored, or ecstatic; and if the occasion permits, your reader is almost sure to exclaim about the schools not doing their duty. This is the oldest literary tradition, of which here is a modern instance:—

### WHAT KIND OF TEACHING IN THE PRIMARY SCHOOLS?
BY 'DISGUSTED'

Recently a letter came into my office from a boy who described himself as a first-year high school student. He wanted *infirmation* about *Africia,* because for his project in the social studies class he had *chozen Africia.* If we could not help him, *were* could he write? In closing, he was ours *sinceerly.* His handwriting was comparable to that of my 6-year-old nephew.

2. Too bad, but I am not alarmed. This student of 'Africia' may or may not learn to spell: it is not nearly so important as his diction and his sentence structure, which the plaintiff withheld, though they would have

better enabled us to judge what the schools were really doing. What I fear about this boy is that when grown-up and provided with a secretary who can spell, he will write something like this:—

DEAR SIR:—
As you know, security prices have been advancing rapidly in the recent past *in belated recognition of the favorable fundamentals that exist.* [Italics mine]

3. What is decadent about this I shall shortly explain. Meantime, the fact should be faced squarely that good writing is and has always been extremely rare. I do not mean fine writing, but the simple, clear kind that everyone always demands—from others. The truth is that Simple English is no one's mother tongue. It has to be worked for. As an historian, I have plowed through state papers, memoirs, diaries, and letters, and I know that the ability to write has only a remote connection with either intelligence, or greatness, or schooling. Lincoln had no schooling yet became one of the great prose writers of the world. Cromwell went to Cambridge and was hardly ever able to frame an intelligible sentence. Another man of thought and action, Admiral Lord Howe, generally refrained from writing out his plan of battle, so as to save his captains from inevitable misunderstanding. Yet Howe managed to win the famous First of June by tactics that revolutionized the art, and led directly to Nelson's Trafalgar plan— itself a rather muddled piece of prose. Let us then start with no illusion of an imaginary golden age of writing.

4. Which leaves the problem of doing the best with what nature gives us. And here I have some convictions born of long struggle, with myself and with others. First, I pass by all considerations of penmanship and elementary spelling to remark only that I think it a mistake to start children writing on typewriters, and worse yet to let them grow up unable to do anything but print capitals.

5. Above the beginner's level, the important fact is that writing cannot be taught exclusively in a course called English Composition. Writing can only be taught by the united efforts of the entire teaching staff. This holds good of any school, college, or university. Joint effort is needed, not merely to 'enforce the rules'; it is needed to insure accuracy in every subject. How can an answer in physics or a translation from the French or an historical statement be called correct if the phrasing is loose or the key word wrong? Students argue that the reader of the paper knows perfectly well what is meant. Probably so, but a written exercise is designed to be read; it is not supposed to be a challenge to clairvoyance. My Italian-born tailor periodically sends me a postcard which runs: 'Your clothes is ready and should come down for a fitting.' I understand him, but the art I honor him for is cutting cloth, not precision of utterance. Now a student in college must be inspired to achieve in all subjects the utmost accuracy of perception combined with the utmost artistry of expression. The two merge and develop

the sense of good workmanship, of preference for quality and truth, which is the chief mark of the genuinely educated man.

6. This is obviously a collective task, in which every department and every faculty has a common stake. But it is not enough to give notice that these are the faculty's sentiments. Even supposing that all teachers were willing and able to exert vigilance over written work, there would still be many practical problems of detail. And first, what motive for writing well can the student be made to feel? There is only one valid motive: the desire to be read. You will say that most students have no urge either to write or to be read. True, but (a) they know that they have to write and (b) most of them want to be well thought of. They should accordingly be made to see that reading the ordinary student paper can be a nuisance and a bore to the teacher, and that the proper aim of writing should be to make it a pleasure. This is another way of saying that most school writing is bad because student and teacher play at writing and reading instead of taking it seriously. The teacher expects second-rate hokum and the student supplies it. Let the teacher assert his rights just as the students do: in many college classes the men protest—quite rightly—when they are asked to read a dull or ill-organized book. Similarly, the instructor may warn the students that when they turn in filler and padding, jargon and lingo, stuff and nonsense, he will mark them down, not only in his grade book, but in his violated soul.

7. Naturally, this conscious brutality must go with a helping hand; in fact a revision of all usual practices is in order. The embargo on hokum will already work a healthy elimination of bad prose. Then the long Term Paper must be discarded and replaced with the short essay, not more than five typewritten pages in length. Students always ask how long a final paper should be and they are absolutely right in believing that most instructors are impressed by mere bulk. But when one knows how difficult it is to articulate even three measly thoughts around a single point, it is folly to ask eighteen-year-olds to produce thirty- or forty-page monographs that shall be readable. What they produce is an uncarded mattress of quotations, paraphrase, 'however's,' and 'Thus we see's.' Size being aimed at, there is not time for rewriting or reordering the material culled from half a dozen books, and the main effort goes into the irrelevant virtues of neat typing, plentiful footnotes, and the mannerisms of scholarship.

8. The short paper—and I speak from a large pile accumulated over twelve years—aims and arrives at different ends. It answers the reader's eternal question: Just what are you trying to tell me? It is in that spirit that student writing must be read, corrected, and if need be rewritten. When first presented, it must already be a second or third draft. The only reason I can think of for the somewhat higher average of good writing in France is that the *brouillon* is a national institution. The *brouillon* (literally: scrambled mess) is the first draft, and even the concierge writing to the

police about anarchists on the third floor begins with a *brouillon,* later found by his heirs.

9. Of course it is no use telling an American boy or girl that the essay must be written, laid aside, and rewritten at least once before handing in: the innocents do not know what to do after their first painful delivery. So the simplest thing is to ask early in the term for a good five-page essay, which turns out to be pretty bad. This is fully annotated by the reader and turned back before the next one is called for. But the corrections on it are not merely the conventional *sp., ref., punc.,* and *awk.* which the writers have seen in their margins from the seventh grade on. The comments are intensely and painfully personal, being the responses that an alert reader would feel if he were encountering the essay in print. The result is that even the best students feel abashed, if not actually resentful. To which one can only say that they should resent the neglect in which all their previous teachers have left them.

10. This neglect has not damaged their grammar so much as their vocabulary. Since the last thing any writer learns is the uses of words, it is no wonder if untutored youths of ability write like the stockbroker whom I quoted about 'favorable fundamentals that exist'—spineless, vague, and incoherent prose. Indeed, the exact parallel comes this moment under my hand, taken from a very able student's report on Newman's *University Sketches:* 'A University that rests on a firm financial foundation has the greater ability to unleash the minds of its students.' Despite the difference in names, the stockbroker is that boy's putative father. Their failure comes from a like inattention to meaning—their own and that of the words they use.

11. This means that words and tone are the main things to be taught. Spelling, grammar, and punctuation do not precede but follow in the order of importance. They follow also quite naturally in the order of facility. Accordingly, the teacher-critic must slowly and carefully explain to the student what each word conveys in its particular context. I find that in the essay just cited I have written such comments as: 'I can't follow—This repeats in disguise—"avocational fruit" suggests alligator pears: why?—We now have about eight "problems" on hand: Begin!—What! more issues and problems?—Commercial lingo—Who is "we"?—Why "cradle": the metaphor is lost—Who says this?—"Patina" is not "clothing"—Don't scold and then trail off in this way—This is your point at last.' In addition, images are changed, synonyms proposed, and bad sentences recast, sometimes in alternative ways, in order to show precisely how the original misleads and how clarity is to be reached.

12. Tone grows naturally out of diction, but the choice of words betrays feelings of which the young writer is usually unaware. 'Are you pleading, denouncing, coaxing, or laughing? Do you back up this exaggeration? Why suddenly talk down, or turn pedant? If you want to change the mood

inside the piece, you must modulate, otherwise your reader will stumble and you will lose him.' The student who learns to quiz himself in this fashion over his first draft is learning not only something about English, about writing, and about thinking, but about the human heart as well.

*13.* At the risk of tediousness I repeat that what has to be done is to dramatize the relation between writer and reader. The blunt comments are just a device to break the spell of routine, and though they administer an unpleasant shock at first, they are also flattering. 'Somebody cares about what I want to say.' The teacher is no longer a paid detective hunting stray commas.

*14.* To point these lessons up in minute detail to a student of average powers is of course time-consuming—but what else is the teacher there for? Time spent on reading and writing, in any subject, is never a waste, and the reward almost always comes, often astonishingly great. The excitement aroused by the discovery that words live is like finding that you can balance on skates. A new world of motion and of feeling is opened out to the student, a source of some anguish balanced by lifelong delight. George Gissing writes somewhere that he saw an excursion steamer advertised as being 'Replete with Ladies' Lavatories' and he comments on how many people could pass by the sign without a smile. My own favorite recollection is of a guarantee pasted on a modest shop window: 'Hats fitted to the head exclusively'—fun in every ad and at the company's expense.

*15.* The pleasure to be taken in words is as innocent and satisfying as the moral effect is clear: unless words are used deftly to set the imagination on its travels, language, literature, conversation, and friendship are full of snares. Much of our modern anxiety about the tyranny of words and of our desire for foolproof Basic comes from the uneasy suspicion that we have lost the art of diction and with it the control over our own minds. This is more serious than it seems, for there is no doubt that the world outside the school largely checks what present instruction attempts, as we shall see. But having spoken of the imagination, let me first meet a likely objection to the advice here proposed. I can fancy some reader for whom school compositions were torture shaking a skeptical head and saying: 'Most young children have very little to say and school assignments blot out even that little.' I agree and the second great practical problem is, What to ask boys and girls to write about?

*16.* The don'ts are easy. Don't ask them for 'A vacation experience,' or 'My most embarrassing moment,' or 'I am the Mississippi River.' Such topics will only elicit the driest kind of hokum, though to be fair I must say that they are an improvement on the older practice of expecting infant moralizing and 'What the flag means to me.' Although as a child I enjoyed writing—history chiefly—I can remember the blankness of mind that overtook me when we had to do a *dissertation morale*. I still have a school text with some of those themes checked as having been done—for example: '*The Faithful Dog.*—A poor man has resolved to drown his dog. Thrown into the river, the dog tries to scramble up the bank, but his master lunges out to kill him with a stick. In so doing, he slips and falls. The dog saves him. Remorse of the owner.'

*17.* I regret to say that French school life is stuffed with such thorns as these, but I am not sure that the opposite 'progressive' extreme of turning children into researchers on their own is desirable either. The eleven-year-old son of a friend of mine once told me that he was writing a 'project' on Papyrus. Why papyrus? Well, the class had been 'doing' Egypt and each child was assigned one aspect of Egyptian civilization. Where was the information to come from? From encyclopedias, museums, friends, and paper manufacturers—hence such letters to strangers as the one about 'Africria' quoted earlier. As I see it, two things are wrong with this scheme. One is that it gives a false freedom; the other is that it hardly trains in the art of composing. Did this boy care at all about Egypt, let alone about the technicalities of papyrology? A child should select a topic that truly engages his interest. To eliminate pretense he must be helped to do this by means of questions and suggestions. At any age, it is very reassuring to be told that you don't really want to write about the Tariff. After two or three casts a real subject emerges, satisfactory to both parties.

*18.* Next should come into play the single good feature of the French dissertation, namely its furnishing a plan or program. Depending on the child's age a briefer or longer table of contents should be set out for each theme, either in logically organized form, or pell-mell for the student himself to disentangle. After all, what is wanted is prose, not a riot of fancy. In my experience, even examination questions are answered better when they consist of five or six sentences outlining a topic for discussion. This means further that brevity should never be accounted a fault in itself. After thirty, we can all spin tall tales, mostly secondhand,[1] but students, even of college age, have had very little conscious experience of life or books and it is no wonder their minds are bone dry. One should moreover keep in view the possibility that in some of them brevity may come from genius. American schoolmarms who relate the anecdote of Lincoln's 'failure' with the Gettysburg Address are just as likely to say at one glance, 'Jane, this is too short.' How do they know? Perhaps they unwittingly agree with the Gettysburg crowd that Everett's speech, being longer, was better.

*19.* Some secondary schools, particularly the private ones, require the writing of verse as well as of prose. If the students are really shown how to go about versifying and are not expected to be 'poetic,' there is no harm

[1] No course, therefore, should ever be called Creative Writing. Let us have at least a collective modesty and leave to charlatans the advertising of 'How to Write Powerful Plays.'

in it. Verse writing is excellent practice for the prose writer and the striving for correct rhythm and rhyme gives the student of literature a feeling for words that may not otherwise be obtained. What can be done in this way before college by a gifted teacher has been shown by the experience of my friend, the poet Dudley Fitts, formerly at Choate and now at Andover. In collegiate circles, it is now well known that a freshman prepared under him is a literate, sometimes a polished writer, who can be safely allowed to skip into advanced work. No doubt Fitts has had his failures like all of us, but it is the successes we are looking for and that count in leavening the mass.

20. I am not so foolish as to think that carrying out my few suggestions would get rid of illiterate A.B.'s. I am too conscious of my initial point about 'Education,' which is that the school does not work in a vacuum but rather in a vortex of destructive forces. As regards writing, we in the twentieth century must offset not only the constant influence of careless speech and the indifference of parents, but the tremendous output of jargon issuing from the new mechanical means at man's disposal. Worst of all, circumstances have conspired to put the most corrupting force at the very heart of the school system. It is not newspapers, radio scripts, and movies that spoil our tongue so much as textbooks, official documents, commencement speeches, and learned works.[2]

21. The rise, at the turn of the century, of what James called 'the softer pedagogy' is responsible for a debasement of language beyond all bounds of forgiveness. The desire to be kind, to sound new, to foster useful attitudes, to appear 'scientific,' and chiefly also the need to produce rapidly, account for this hitherto unheard-of deliquescence. In the victims, the softness goes to the very roots of the mind and turns it into mush. And among the "new" educators thus afflicted, the Progressive vanguard has naturally outstripped the rest. I shall not multiply examples from catalogues, reports, and speeches, though over the years I have gathered a blush-making collection. I want only to identify the evil because it spreads like the plague.

22. It consists mainly of what our forefathers called 'cant phrases,' strung together without continuity, like wash on a line. At a faculty meeting, a teacher asks the Director of Admissions why there seem to be more music students applying than before. The Director replies, 'Well, I should say that the forces undergirding the process are societal.' Or a committee chairman wants to know what we do next. 'I think,' says the secretary, 'that we should go on to institute actual implementation.'

[2] See Mr. Maury Maverick's excellent denunciation of what he calls Gobbledygook in the *New York Times* for May 21, 1944. The rebuttals attempting to show that round-about expressions spare shocks to the sick are hardly to the point. The healthy ought to be able to stand directness and even mention of 'death and taxes.' 'Loss of life' and 'fiscal levies' cost just as much in the end.

23. Teachers steeped in this medium are bound to ooze it out themselves, particularly if weekly and daily they receive official instructions like these: 'Specify the kinds of change or permanence the student seems to crave, reject, or fear; the reasons given for liking-disliking, giving up-persistence; complaining-boasting . . . It cannot be too strongly emphasized that the observations of characteristics associated with age and background are not being made in the general area of adolescent behavior but under specific and limited conditions—those set by the aims, emphases, and assumptions of one particular faculty.[3] Moreover, the observations of what appear to be the interests of freshmen conceal a possible ambiguity. The term "interests" may refer to fairly superficial interests in the sense of surprise, pleasure, enjoyment, which are comparatively temporary; or "interests" may involve an awakening curiosity which leads to consistent inquiry along the lines of some project.' The reader must imagine not merely a paragraph taken at random, but pages and pages of similar woolly abstractions, mimeographed at the rate of nine and one-half pounds per person per semester. If the words 'specific' and 'objective' were blotted out of the English language, Progressive Education would have to shut up . . . shop.

24. As for students in teachers' colleges, the long climb up the ladder of learning comes to mean the mastering of this ghoulish *Desperanto*, so that with the attainment of the M.A. degree, we get the following utterance:—

In the proposed study I wish to describe and evaluate representative programs in these fields as a means of documenting what seems to me a trend of increasing concern with the role of higher education in the improvement of interpersonal and intergroup relations and of calling attention in this way to outstanding contributions in practice.

25. Some readers might think this quotation very learned and highbrow indeed. But in fact it says nothing definite. It only embodies the disinclination to think. This is a general truth, and nothing is more symptomatic of the whole jargon than the fantastic use and abuse it makes of the phrase 'in terms of.' The fact is worth a moment's attention. 'In terms of' used to refer to things that had terms, like algebra. 'Put the problem in terms of *a* and *b*.' This makes sense. But in educational circles today 'in terms of' means any connection between any two things. 'We should grade students in terms of their effort'—that is, *for* or *according to* their effort. The *New York Public Library Bulletin* prints: 'The first few months of employment would be easier . . . and more efficient in terms of service . . .'—that is, would yield more efficient service. But no one seems to care how or when or why his own two ideas are related. The gap in thought is plugged with 'in terms of.' I have been asked, 'Will you have dinner with me, not tonight

---

[3] I regret to say that 'faculty' here means 'faculty member'—a usage so far confined to the progressive schools.

or tomorrow, but *in terms of* next week?' A modern Caesar would write: 'All Gaul is to be considered in terms of three parts.'[4]

26. From this Educator's patois, easily the worst English now spoken, we ought to pass to the idiom of textbooks, since they are written either by educators or by teachers. Happily, there is a standard set by other books—trade books—and it is not true that all textbooks are as badly written as those on education. On the contrary, it is very encouraging that the leading ones in every field are usually well planned *and* well written. The success of Morison and Commager's *Growth of the American Republic* is only the most recent case in point. Students, nevertheless, are asked to read many ill-written books. There is no excuse for this, though it is by no means the only source of error. We must remember that students do not read only books; they read what every man reads, and this would do no harm—it does no harm—when the mind is trained to resilience by the kind of writing practice I have advocated.

27. Unfortunately, with the vast increase in public schooling since 1870, an entirely new notion of what is good English has come to prevail. Awakened by free schooling, the people have shown worthy intentions. They want to be right and even elegant, and so become at once suspicious of plainness and pedantic. They purchase all sorts of handbooks that make a fetish of spelling, of avoiding split infinitives, of saying 'it is I' (with the common result of 'between you and I')—in short, dwell on trivialities or vulgarisms which do not affect style or thought in the slightest. But with this intolerance towards crude and plain error goes a remarkable insensitivity to inflated nonsense. Most bad journalism is only highbrow verbosity, yet the popular mind continues to believe that the pedantry which it likes is simple and the simplicity which it finds hard is complex. Here is the opening of a serial thriller in a Boston paper:—

Strange things happen in Chinatown. But even that exotic and perverse district seldom presented drama as fantastic as the secret that hid among the silk and jade and porcelain splendors of the famous House of the Mandarin on Mulberry Lane.

28. There is a certain art in this, and I take note of 'porcelain splendors' as the *mot juste* for bathtubs on exhibit. But the passage as a whole contains nothing but arty and highfalutin words, joined by the good will of the reader rather than the mind of the writer. Still, every newspaper reader feels he understands it. Take now a well-known sentence composed of common words, all but two of them single syllables: 'If there are more trees in the world than there are leaves on any one tree, then there must be at least two trees with the same number of leaves.' Read this aloud and

---

[4] The objectionable phrase is now to be found in newspapers, business reports, and private correspondence. It is a menace *in terms of* the whole nation.

almost any listener will respond with 'Huh? Say that again.' For this sentence records a thought, and the Chinatown 'drama' did not.

29. The close logic in the truly 'simple' sentence makes the contrast sharper, but it would be just as sharp between a feeling clearly put and a feeble attempt to thrill. Thus there is a superstition that the novels of Henry James are written in a 'difficult style.' Yet if you examine them, you will find that the words and sentences—in *The Ambassadors,* for example —are in themselves quite usual. But the feelings they convey are unusual and subtle, and require attention. At the same time they also compel it, which is all that an artist takes pains for in writing.

30. Conversely, the only thing that can be asked of a writer is that he should know his own meaning and present it as forcibly as he can. The rule has not changed since Byron affirmed that 'easy writing makes damned hard reading.' Hence there is great value, as I think, in having college graduates recognize good prose when they see it, know that a tolerable paragraph must have gone through six or seven versions, and be ready to follow athletically on the trail of articulate thoughts, rather than look for the soapy incline to muddled meaning.

31. One does not have to go very far for the enjoyment of precise, sinewy writing. The same newspaper that furnishes tripe for the morning meal also brings such rarer tidbits as these: 'They [the robot bombs] are of much the same shape and size as a small fighter plane, with stubby wings. They come over with tails aglow from the propelling rocket force, like little meteors moving at a nightmare pace by dark, and by day like little black planes with tails afire.' This is perfection; and here is poetry: 'Mr. McCaffrey, himself the father of two children, *and therefore schooled in apprehension,* ran across the street . . . shouting a warning.'

32. When the daily reporter, harried by falling bombs or hustled by a city editor, can write like this, it is depressing to return to agencies closer to the school and find verbal laziness encouraged and imbecility taken for granted. One publisher of reference works sends out a circular stressing the fact that his books give the pronunciation of "all difficult—'hard-to-say' —words." Is this where we are after fifty years of quasi-universal literacy? Is the word 'difficult' so difficult that it has to be translated in its own sentence? The question is one for readers, and it is to the subject of readers that I now turn.

# Theme Topics

1. Compare and contrast the rules for good writing (Orwell) and the rules for writing like a social scientist (Williamson).

2. Draw up a list of twenty-five examples, none of which is listed by any of the four writers here, of dying metaphors, operators (or verbal false limbs), pretentious diction, meaningless words. Quote and cite, if possible, a source in which you have found each used.

3. Orwell asserts, "In our time it is broadly true that political writing is bad writing." Choose from the files of *The New York Times* or elsewhere, the text of two or more political speeches delivered by candidates for high political office in a state or national election. Analyze them from the point of view of the categories established by Orwell.

4. Take any issue of the *New Yorker* and analyze the sections entitled "The Talk of the Town" and "The Current Cinema" as well as that issue's short story from the point of view of the twelve devices of casual stylists listed by Whyte.

5. On the basis of inferences from evidence you find only in the four essays themselves, discuss the probable backgrounds of each of the authors, the audiences to which they seem to be speaking and the effectiveness with which each uses evidence and direct quotation to support his criticisms. Which one (or ones), in discussing the prevalence of stale imagery, imprecision and pretentiousness in contemporary writing, is the most vivid, precise, direct? Document your choice.

# The Triumph of Language

## ⁓ VI ⁓

### ·21·

*John Ciardi*

## THE ACT OF LANGUAGE

*1.* At the beginning of *The Divine Comedy*, Dante finds himself in a Dark Wood, lost from the light of God. It was no single, specific evil act that led Dante into that darkness but, rather, the sin of omission. Its name is Acedia, the fourth of the Seven Deadly Sins, and by us generally translated "Sloth."

*2.* In American-English, however, Sloth may seem to imply mere physical laziness and untidiness. The torpor of Acedia, it must be understood, is spiritual rather than physical. It is to know the good, but to be lax in its pursuit.

*3.* Whether one thinks of it as a sin or as a behavioral failure, Acedia is also the one fault for which no artist can be forgiven. Time, as W. H. Auden wrote in his poem titled *In Memory of W. B. Yeats:*

> Worships language and forgives
> Everyone by whom it lives;
> Pardons cowardice, conceit,
> Lays its honors at their feet.

*4.* In place of cowardice and conceit, Auden might have cited any catalogue of pride, envy, wrath, avarice, gluttony or carnality, and he could still have said that time forgives. The poet may cheat anything else and still win honor from time, but he may not cheat the poem and live.

*5.* For a man is finally defined by what he does with his attention. It was Simone Weil who said, "Absolute attention is absolute prayer." I do not, of course, know what an absolute attention is, except as an absolutely unattainable goal. But certainly to seek that increasing purity and concentration of one's attention that will lead to more and more meaningful perception, is not only possible but is the basic human exercise of any art. It must be added, however, that *in art it does not matter what one pays attention to; the quality of the attention is what counts.*

6. I have just made a dangerous statement; one that will probably breed protest, that will be difficult to explain, and that will turn out in the end to be only partly true. It is still necessary to make the statement first, and then to go the long way round to explaining why it is necessary, and in what way it is true.

7. The need to go the long way round brings matters back to another parable of poetry that one may read in Dante's opening situation. The language of parables is always likely to be apt to the discussion of poetry.

8. As soon as Dante realizes that he is in darkness, he looks up and sees the first light of the dawn shawling the shoulders of a little hill. (In Dante, the Sun is always a symbol of God as Divine Illumination.) The allegory should be clear enough: The very realization that one is lost is the beginning of finding oneself.

9. What happens next is the heart of the matter. His goal in sight, Dante tries to race straight up the hill—to reach the light, as it were, by direct assault. Note that common sense would certainly be on Dante's side. There is the light and there is the hill: go to it. Nothing could be simpler. Nor, as Dante discovers, could anything be more false. Almost immediately his way is blocked by three beasts. These beasts—a Leopard, a Lion and a She-wolf—represent all the sins of the world. They represent, therefore, the world's total becloudment of any man's best attention, for all that has ever lured any man away from his own good is contained within them.

10. The three beasts drive Dante back into the darkness. There Dante comes on the soul of Virgil, who symbolizes Human Reason. In that role Virgil explains that a man may reach the light only by going the long way round. Dante must risk the dangerous descent into Hell—to the recognition of sin. And he must make the arduous ascent of Purgatory—to the renunciation of sin. Only then may he enter, bit by bit, the final presence of the light, which is to say, Heaven.

11. The point of the parable is that in art as in theology—as in all things that concern a man in his profoundest being—the long way round is the only way home. Short cuts are useful only in mechanics. The man who seeks mortal understanding must go the long, encompassing way of his deepest involvement.

12. Americans, susceptible as they are to the legend of mechanical knowhow and get-it-done, may especially need to be told that there is no easy digest of understanding and no gift package of insight. May they learn, too, that "common sense," useful as it can be in its own sphere, cannot lead a man as deeply into himself as he must be led if he is to enter a meaningful experience of art or of life. Every man who looks long enough at the stars must come to feel their other-reality engulfing his mortal state,

and nothing from the world's efficiencies and practicalities is specific to that awareness in him.

*13.* Poetry is written of that man under the stars in trouble and in joy, and the truth of poetry cannot be spoken meaningfully in simple common-sense assertions. In poetry, as in all our deepest emotions, many feelings and many thoughts and half-thoughts happen at once. Often these feelings and thoughts are in conflict:

*14.* We love and hate the same thing, desire it and dread it, need it and are destroyed by it. Always, too, there are more thoughts and feelings in a profound experience than we can put a finger on. What has common sense to say to such states of man? Common sense tends always to the easier assumption that only one thing is "really" happening in a man at one time, and that a simple, straightforward course of action will take care of it.

*15.* Such an assumption can only blind one to poetry. To read a poem with no thought in mind but to paraphrase it into a single, simple, and usually high-minded, prose statement is the destruction of poetry. Nor does it make much difference that one can quote poetry, and good poetry, in defense of such destruction. At the end of *Ode on a Grecian Urn,* John Keats wrote:

> "Beauty is truth, truth beauty,"—that is all
> Ye know on earth, and all ye need to know.

*16.* Heaven knows how many enthusiasts have used these lines as evidence that poetry is somehow an act of inspiration not to be measured by any criteria but an undefined devotion to "beauty," "truth" and "inspiring message."

*17.* But if beauty and truth are all that Grecian urns and men need know on earth, Keats makes evident by his own practice that a poet also needs to know a great deal about his trade, and that he must be passionately concerned for its basic elements.

*18.* Those basic elements are not beauty and truth but *rhythm, diction, image* and *form.* Certainly Keats cared about beauty and truth. Any sensitive man must care. No matter that one must forever fumble at the definition of such ideas; they are still matters of ultimate concern. But so was Dante's yearning for the light, and he discovered at once that it can be reached only by the long way round.

*19.* The poet's way round is by way of rhythm, diction, image and form. It is the right, the duty and the joy of his trade to be passionate about these things. To be passionate about them in the minutest and even the most frivolous detail. To be passionate about them. if need be, to the exclusion of what is generally understood by "sincerity" and "meaning." To be more passionate about them than he is about the cold war, the Gunpowder Plot, the next election, abolition, the H-bomb, the Inquisition, juvenile delinquency, the Spanish Armada, or his own survival.

20. The good poets have not generally sneered at the world of affairs. Some have, but many others have functioned well within that world. Yet the need and the right of all poets to detach themselves from the things of the world in order to pursue the things of the poetic trade have always been inseparable from their success as poets.

21. The poet must be passionate about the four elements of his trade for the most fundamental of reasons. He must be so because those passions are both a joy and an addiction within him. Because they are the life of the poem, without which nothing of value can happen either in the poem or to the reader. Because writing a poem is a more sentient way of living than not writing it, because no poem can be written well except as these passions inform it, and because only when the poem is so written can the beauty and truth of that more sentient way of living be brought to mortal consequence.

22. The act of poetry may seem to have very simple surfaces, but it is always compounded of many things at once. As Robert Frost wrote in *Two Tramps in Mud Time:*

> Only where love and need are one,
> And the work is play for mortal stakes,
> Is the deed ever really done
> For Heaven and the future's sakes.

23. The voice of common sense rises immediately in protest. "Mystification!" it cries. "A poem still has to *mean* something. What does it *mean?*" And the poet must answer, "Never what you think. Not when you ask the question in that way."

24. But how shall the question be asked? Let the questioner listen first to a kind of statement he has probably passed over without enough attention. He can find one such in Walter Pater's essay on Winckelman. "Let us understand by poetry," wrote Pater, "all literary production which attains the power of giving pleasure by its form as distinct from its matter."

25. He can find another in a book titled *The Fire and the Fountain* by the English poet and critic John Press. "The essence of the poet," wrote Press, "is to be found less in his opinions than in his idiom." He may even find one in a textbook titled *Reading Poems*, in which Prof. Wright Thomas says, "The *subject* is a very poor indication of what the *poem* is" —to which I should add only that it is no indication whatever.

26. But if the meaning is not in the subject, what then does a poem mean? It means always and above all else the poet's deep involvement in the four basic elements of his trade. It means not the subject but the way the poetic involvement transfigures the subject. It means, that is to say, the very act of language by which it comes into existence. The poem may purport to be about anything from pussy willows to battleships, but the meaning of any good poem is its act of language.

27. Because it is an act of language, a good poem is deeply connected with everything men are and do. For language is certainly one of the most fundamental activities in which human beings engage. Take away a man's language, and you take most of his ability to think and to experience. Enrich his language, and you cannot fail to enrich his experience. Any man who has let great language into his head is the richer for it.

28. He is not made richer by what is being said. It is the language itself that brings his enrichment. Could poetry be meaningful aside from its act of language, it would have no reason for being, and the whole history of poetry could be reduced to a series of simple paraphrases.

29. Consider as simple a passage as the beginning of Herrick's *Upon Julia's Clothes:*

> Whenas in silks my Julia goes,
> Then, then, methinks, how sweetly flows
> The liquefaction of her clothes.

30. Who can read those lines without a thrill of pleasure? But now consider the paraphrase: "I like the rustle of Julia's silks when she walks." The poetry and the paraphrase are certainly about equal in subject matter. The difference is that the poetry is a full and rich act of language, whereas the paraphrase, though faultless, lacks, among other things, measure, pause, stress, rhyme and the pleasure of lingering over the word "liquefaction."

31. "But what is Julia doing there?" cries that voice of common sense, "She must have something to do with the poem or she wouldn't be in it!"

32. The owner of that voice would do well to ponder the relation between a good portrait and its subject. The subject is there, to be sure—at least in most cases. But the instant the painter puts one brush stroke on the canvas and then another, the two brush strokes take on a relation to each other and to the space around them. The two then take on a relation to the third, and it to them. And so forth. The painting immediately beings to exert its own demands upon the painter, its own way of going. Immediately the subject begins to disappear.

33. All too soon, for that matter, the subject will have changed with age or will have died. After a while no living person will have any recollection of what the subject looked like. All that will remain then is a portrait head which must be either self-validating or worthless. Because the subject cannot validate the painting, he or she will have become irrelevant. All that can finally validate the portrait is the way in which the painter engaged the act of painting.

34. And one more thing—the good artist always thinks in long terms. He knows, even at the moment of the painting, that both he and the subject will disappear. Any good painter will be painting for the painting—for the time when the subject will have blown away into time.

35. So with poetry. The one final and enduring meaning of any poem

lies not in what it seems to have set out to say, but in its act of language.

36. The only test of that act of language is the memory of the race. Bad poetry is by nature forgettable; it is, therefore, soon forgotten. But good poetry, like any good act of language, hooks onto human memory and stays there. Write well, and there will always be someone somewhere who carries in his mind what you have written. It will stay in memory because man is the language animal, and because his need of language is from the roots of his consciousness. That need in him is not a need for meaning. Rather, good language in him takes possession of meaning; it fills him with a resonance that the best of men understand only dimly, but without which no man is entirely alive. Poetry is that presence and that resonance. As Archibald MacLeish put it in his much-discussed *Ars Poetica:*

> A poem should not mean
> But be.

37. If the reader truly wishes to engage poetry, let him forget meaning. Let him think rather: "I shall summon great language to mind. I shall summon language so fully, so resonantly and so precisely used that it will bring all my meanings to me." Then let him turn to poetry, and let him listen to the passions of the poet's trade.

38. Listen to great rhythms. Here is the opening stanza of John Donne's *The Anniversarie:*

> All Kings, and all their favorites,
> All glory of honours, beauties, wits,
> The Sun it selfe, which makes times as they passe,
> Is elder by a yeare, now, than it was
> When thou and I first one another saw:
> All other things, to their destruction draw,
> Only our love hath no decay;
> This, no to morrow hath, nor yesterday.
> Running, it never runs from us away,
> But truly keeps his first, last, everlasting day.

39. Worldly things pass away, but true love is constant, says the subject matter. All true enough and tried enough. But listen to the rhythm enforce itself upon the saying, especially in the last four lines. For present purposes, let the voice ignore the lesser accents. Let it stress only those syllables printed in capital letters below, while observing the pauses as indicated by the slash marks. And forget the meaning. Read for the voice emphasis and the voice pauses:

> Only OUR LOVE hath no deCAY //
> THIS // no to MOrrow hath // nor YESterday //
> RUNning // it never runs from us aWAY //
> But truly keeps his FIRST // LAST // EVerlasting DAY

*40.* Not all rhythms are so percussive, so measured out by pauses, and so metrically irregular. Listen to this smoother rhythm from Poe's *Israfel:*

> If I could dwell
> Where Israfel
>   Hath dwelt, and he where I,
> He might not sing so wildly well
>   A mortal melody,
> While a bolder note than his might swell
>   From my lyre within the sky.

*41.* Or the rhythm may be percussive, but without substantial pauses, as in the last line of this passage from the end of Gerard Manley Hopkins' *Felix Randal,* an elegy for a blacksmith:

> How far from then forethought of, all thy more boisterous years,
> When thou at the random grim forge, powerful amidst peers,
> Didst fettle for the great gray drayhorse his bright and battering sandal.

*42.* Listen to the hammerfall of that last line: "Didst FEttle for the GREAT GRAY DRAYhorse his BRIGHT and BAttering SANdal."

*43.* Or listen to the spacing of the "ah" sounds as a rhythmic emphasis in the last line of this final passage from Meredith's *Lucifer in Starlight:*

> Around the ancient track marched, rank on rank,
> The ARmy of unALterable LAW.

*44.* Percussive, smooth, flowing or studded with pauses—there is no end to the variety and delight of great language rhythms. For the poet, his rhythms are forever more than a matter of making a "meaningful" statement; they are a joy in their own right. No poet hates meaning. But the poet's passion is for the triumph of language. No reader can come to real contact with a poem until he comes to it through the joy of that rhythmic act of language.

*45.* As for rhythm, so for diction. The poet goes to language—or it comes to him and he receives it—for his joy in the precision of great word choices. Give him such a line as Whitman's "I witness the corpse with the dabbled hair," and he will register the corpse, to be sure, but it will be "dabbled" he seizes upon with the joy of a botanist coming on a rare specimen. So when Keats speaks of Ruth amid "the alien corn" or when Theodore Roethke speaks of sheep "strewn" on a field, the good reader will certainly care about the dramatic situation of the poem, but he cannot fail to answer with a special joy to "alien" and to "strewn."

*46.* What, after all, is the subject as compared to his joy in such rich precision? Thousands of English poems have described the passing of winter and the coming of spring. Certainly there is little in that subject as a subject to attract him. But listen to the pure flutefall of the word choices I have italicized in the following passage from Stanley Kunitz's *Deciduous Bough,* and note how the self-delight in language makes everything immediate and new again:

> Winter that *coils* in the thicket now
> Will *glide* from the field, the *swinging* rain
> Be *knotted* with flowers, on every bough
> A bird will *meditate* again.

47. "Poetry," said Coleridge, "is the best words in the best order." How can anyone reading the Kunitz passage escape a sense that the language is being ultimately and unimprovably selected? The delight one feels in coming on such language is not only in the experience of perfection but also in the fact that perfection has been made to seem not only effortless but inevitable.

48. And let this much more be added to the idea of poetic meaning: Nothing in a good poem happens by accident; every word, every comma, every variant spelling must enter as an act of the poet's choice. A poem is a machine for making choices. The mark of the good poet is his refusal to make easy or cheap choices. The better the poet, the greater the demands he makes upon himself, and the higher he sets his level of choice. Thus, a good poem is not only an act of mind but an act of devotion to mind. The poet who chooses cheaply or lazily is guilty of aesthetic acedia, and he is lost thereby. The poet who spares himself nothing in his search for the most demanding choices is shaping a human attention that offers itself as a high and joyful example to all men of mind and devotion. Every act of great language, whatever its subject matter, illustrates an idea of order and a resonance of human possibility without which no man's mind can sense its own fullest dimensions.

49. As for rhythm and diction, so for imagery. To be sure, every word is at root an image, and poetic images must be made of words. Yet certainly there is in a well-constructed image an effect that cannot be said to rise from any one word choice, but from the total phrasing.

50. So for the sensory shiver of Keats' "The silver snarling trumpets 'gan to chide." So for the wonderfully woozy effect of John Frederick Nims' "The drunk clambering on his undulant floor." So for the grand hyperbole of Howard Nemerov saying that the way a young girl looks at him "sets his knees to splashing like two waves."

51. We learn both imagination and precision from the poet's eye. And we learn correspondences. Consider the following image from *Aereopagus* by Louis MacNeice, a poem as playful as it is serious, in which MacNeice describes Athens as a cradle of the western mind. Cradles, he makes clear, generally contain children, and all those boy-gods and girl-goddesses had their childish side:

> . . . you still may glimpse
> The child-eyed Fury tossing her shock of snakes,
> Careering over the Parthenon's ruined playpen.

52. It is a bit shocking to have the Parthenon spoken of as a playpen, but once the shock has passed, what a triumph there is in the figure: everything corresponds! Think how much would have been lost had the Parthenon a surviving roof, or had its general proportions or the placement of the pillars—slats—resisted the comparison. The joy of it is that, despite the first shock, nothing resists the comparison; and we find that the surprise turns out to be a true correspondence.

53. One of the poet's happiest—and most mortal—games is in seeking such correspondences. But what flows from them is more than a game. Every discovery of a true correspondence is an act of reason and an instruction to the mind. For intelligence does not consist of masses of factual detail. It consists of seeing essential likenesses and essential differences and of relating them, allowing for differences with the likenesses and for likenesses within the differences. Mentality is born of analogy.

54. Note, too, that the image-idea of "ruined playpen" does not simply happen, but is prepared for in "child-eyed." And note, further, the nice double meaning of "careering" as both "a wild rush" and "to make a career of."

55. A good extended image, that is to say, is made of various elements and is marked by both sequence and structure. Thus we have already touched upon the essence of the fourth element of the poet's trade: form.

56. There are many kinds of poetic form, but since all are based on pattern and sequence, let a tightly patterned poem illustrate. Here is Emily Dickinson's *The Soul Selects*:

> The soul selects her own society,
> Then shuts the door;
> On her divine majority
> Obtrude no more.
>
> Unmoved, she notes the chariot's pausing
> At her low gate;
> Unmoved, an emperor is kneeling
> Upon her mat.
>
> I've known her from an ample nation
> Choose one;
> Then close the valves of her attention
> Like stone.

57. Whatever the hunters of beauty and truth find for their pleasure in such a poem, the poet's joy will be in its form and management. He re-

sponds to the passion of the language for its own sparseness, to the pattern
of rhyme and half-rhyme, to the flavor of the images (connotation), and
to the way those flavors relate to one another. He responds to the interplay
of the four-foot feminine lines (feminine lines end on an unaccented
syllable) and the two-foot masculine lines (which end on an accented
syllable).

58. And he responds, above all, to the way those two-foot lines develop
in the last stanza into two boldly stroked syllables apiece (monosyllabic
feet) so that the emotion held down throughout the poem by the sparseness of the language is hammered into sensation by the beat of those last
two words: "Like stone"—thud! thud!

59. Beauty and truth are no irrelevancies, but they are abstractions that
must remain meaningless to poetry until they are brought to being in the
management of a specific form. It is that management the poet must love:
the joy of sensing the poem fall into inescapable form, and therefore into
inescapable experience. For the poet's trade is not to talk about experience, but to make it happen. His act of making is all he knows of beauty
and truth. It is, in fact, his way of knowing them. His only way of knowing them.

60. As I. A. Richards, poet and scholar of the language, put it in a recent poem titled *The Ruins:*

> Sometimes a word is wiser much than men:
> "Faithful" e.g., "responsible" and "true."
> And words it is, not poets, make up poems.
> Our words, we say, but we are theirs, too,
> For words made men and may unmake again.

61. And now, at last, it is time to repeat the statement from which this
long way round began. "In art," I said, "it does not matter what one pays
attention to; the quality of the attention is what counts." It is time to
amend that necessary false statement.

62. For it does matter where the poet fixes his attention. Attention must
be to *something.* That something, however, is so casually connected with
the subject of the poem that any reader will do well to dismiss the subject
as no more than a point of departure. Any impassioning point of departure
will do. The poet, being a man, must believe something, but what that
something is does not matter so long as he believes it strongly enough to
be passionate about it. What he believes, moreover, may be touched off
by an image, a rhythm, or the quality of a word *in pursuit of which the
subject is invented.*

63. The poem, in any case, is not in its point of departure, but in its
journey to itself. That journey, the act of the poem, is its act of language.
That act is the true final subject and meaning of any poem. It is to that act
of language the poet shapes his most devoted attention—to the fullness of

rhythm, diction, image and form. Only in that devotion can he seize the
world and make it evident.

# Questions

1. What are the four elements of a poet's trade? To which of them, if any, does
   Ciardi seem to devote most of his discussion?

2. In talking about the poet and his acts of language, what word, in various
   forms, does Ciardi use most frequently? How is the meaning of this word
   related on the one hand to the element of a poet's trade and on the other to
   Ciardi's general assertion (later amended) about art?

3. List at least four striking images that Ciardi, who is also a practicing poet,
   uses in his own discussion of the act of language.

4. "Mentality," says Ciardi, "is born of analogy." What extensive analogy from
   a past writer does he cite? Name the point of correspondence Ciardi
   achieves throughout his entire piece between this analogy and his own special analogic use of it.

5. How many quotations—acts of language other than his own—does Ciardi
   use? How many are from poems, how many from prose works? Does he
   quote the same poem or poet twice? Examine the *occasion* for each quotation: that is, does it illustrate a generalization he has just made, formulate
   succinctly a point of view he endorses? Examine the *sequel* to each quotation. In which cases does he (1) explain the quotation's fuller import for
   his discourse, (2) anticipate the reader's reaction and attempt to discount
   it, (3) make no comment at all?

6. What function does "the voice of common sense" play in Ciardi's article?
   What is its relation to your answers to question 2 above?

·22·

## W. H. Auden

# THE UNKNOWN CITIZEN

*(To JS/07/M/378 This Marble Monument Is Erected by the State)*

He was found by the Bureau of Statistics to be
One against whom there was no official complaint,
And all the reports on his conduct agree
That, in the modern sense of an old-fashioned word, he was a saint,
For in everything he did he served the Greater Community.
Except for the War till the day he retired
He worked in a factory and never got fired,
But satisfied his employers, Fudge Motors Inc.
Yet he wasn't a scab or odd in his views,
10 For his Union reports that he paid his dues,
(Our report on his Union shows it was sound)
And our Social Psychology workers found
That he was popular with his mates and liked a drink.
The Press are convinced that he bought a paper every day
And that his reactions to advertisements were normal in every way.
Policies taken out in his name prove that he was full insured,
And his Health-card shows he was once in hospital but left it cured.
Both Producers Research and High-Grade Living declare
He was fully sensible to the advantages of the Installment Plan
20 And had everything necessary to the Modern Man,
A phonograph, a radio, a car and a frigidaire.
Our researchers into Public Opinion are content
That he held the proper opinions for the time of year;
When there was peace, he was for peace; when there was war, he
    went.
He was married and added five children to the population,
Which our Eugenist says was the right number for a parent of his
    generation,
And our teachers report that he never interfered with their education.
Was he free? Was he happy? The question is absurd:
Had anything been wrong, we should certainly have heard.

*William Blake*

# LONDON

I wander thro' each charter'd street,
Near where the charter'd Thames does flow,
And mark in every face I meet
Marks of weakness, marks of woe.

In every cry of every Man,
In every Infant's cry of fear,
In every voice, in every ban,
The mind-forg'd manacles I hear.

How the Chimney-sweeper's cry
Every black'ning Church appalls;        10
And the hapless Soldier's sigh
Runs in blood down Palace walls.

But most thro' midnight streets I hear
How the youthful Harlot's curse
Blasts the new born Infant's tear,
And blights with plagues the Marriage hearse.

## ·24·

*Thomas Hardy*

# DURING WIND AND RAIN

They sing their dearest songs—
He, she, all of them—yea,
Treble and tenor and bass,
   And one to play;
With the candles mooning each face. . . .
   Ah, no; the years O!
How the sick leaves reel down in throngs!

They clear the creeping moss—
Elders and juniors—aye,
Making the pathways neat
   And the garden gay;
And they build a shady seat. . . .
   Ah, no; the years, the years;
See, the white storm-birds wing across!

They are blithely breakfasting all—
Men and maidens—yea,
Under the summer tree,
   With a glimpse of the bay,
While pet fowl come to the knee. . . .
   Ah, no; the years O!
And the rotten rose is ript from the wall.

They change to a high new house,
He, she, all of them—aye,
Clocks and carpets and chairs
   On the lawn all day,
And brightest things that are theirs. . . .
   Ah, no; the years, the years;
Down their carved names the rain-drop ploughs.

·25·

*Robert Huff*

# RAINBOW

After the shot the driven feathers rock
In the air and are by sunlight trapped.
Their moment of descent is eloquent.
It is the rainbow echo of a bird
Whose thunder, stopped, puts in my daughter's eyes
A question mark. She does not see the rainbow,
And the folding bird-fall was for her too quick.
It is about the stillness of the bird
Her eyes asking. She is three years old;
Has cut her fingers; found blood tastes of salt;        10
But she has never witnessed quiet blood,
Nor ever seen before the peace of death.
I say: "The feathers—Look!" but she is torn
And wretched and draws back. And I am glad
That I have wounded her, have winged her heart,
And that she goes beyond my fathering.

·26·

*W. D. Snodgrass*

# TEN DAYS LEAVE

He steps down from the dark train, blinking; stares
At trees like miracles. He will play games
With boys or sit up all night touching chairs.
Talking with friends, he can recall their names.

Noon burns against his eyelids, but he lies
Hunched in his blankets; he is half awake
But still lacks nerve to open up his eyes;
Supposing it were just his old mistake?

10    But no; it seems just like it seemed. His folks
Pursue their lives like toy trains on a track.
He can foresee each of his father's jokes
Like words in some old movie that's come back.

He is like days when you've gone some place new
To deal with certain strangers, though you never
Escape the sense in everything you do,
"We've done this all once. Have I been here, ever?"

But no; he thinks it must recall some old film, lit
By lives you want to touch; as if he's slept
And must have dreamed this setting, peopled it,
20    And wakened out of it. But someone's kept

His dream asleep here like a small homestead
Preserved long past its time in memory
Of some great man who lived here and is dead.
They have restored his landscape faithfully:

The hills, the little houses, the costumes:
How real it seems! But he comes, wide awake,
A tourist whispering through the priceless rooms
Who must not touch things or his hand might break

Their sleep and black them out. He wonders when
30    He'll grow into his sleep so sound again.


· 27 ·


*William Shakespeare*


# SINCE BRASS, NOR STONE . . .

Since brass, nor stone, nor earth, nor boundless sea,
But sad mortality o'er-sways their power,
How with this rage shall beauty hold a plea,
Whose action is no stronger than a flower?

O, how shall summer's honey breath hold out
Against the wrackful siege of battering days,
When rocks impregnable are not so stout,
Nor gates of steel so strong, but Time decays?
O fearful meditation! where, alack,
Shall Time's best jewel from Time's chest lie hid?                10
Or what strong hand can hold his swift foot back?
Or who his spoil of beauty can forbid?
   O, none, unless this miracle have might,
   That in black ink my love may still shine bright.

## ·28·

*Gerard Manley Hopkins*

# SPRING AND FALL: TO A
# YOUNG CHILD

Márgarét, are you gríeving
Over Goldengrove unleaving?
Leáves, like the things of man, you
With your fresh thoughts care for, can you?
Áh! ás the heart grows older
It will come to such sights colder
By and by, nor spare a sigh
Though worlds of wanwood leafmeal lie;
And yet you wíll weep and know why.
Now no matter, child, the name:                                 10
Sórrow's springs áre the same.
Nor mouth had, no nor mind, expressed
What heart heard of, ghost guessed:
It ís the blight man was born for,
It is Margaret you mourn for.

From *The Poems of Gerard Manley Hopkins*, Third ed. 1948. Reprinted by permission of Oxford University Press, Inc.

*Andrew Marvell*

# TO HIS COY MISTRESS

Had we but World enough, and Time,
This coyness Lady were no crime.
We would sit down, and think which way
To walk, and pass our long Loves Day.
Thou by the *Indian Ganges* side
Should'st Rubies find: I by the Tide
Of *Humber* would complain. I would
Love you ten years before the Flood:
And you should if you please refuse
10     Till the Conversion of the *Jews*.
My vegetable Love should grow
Vaster than Empires, and more slow.
An hundred years should go to praise
Thine Eyes, and on thy Forehead Gaze.
Two hundred to adore each Breast:
But thirty thousand to the rest.
An Age at least to every part,
And the last Age should show your Heart.
For Lady you deserve this State;
20     Nor would I love at lower rate.
    But at my back I alwaies hear
Times winged Charriot hurrying near:
And yonder all before us lye
Desarts of vast Eternity.
Thy Beauty shall no more be found;
Nor, in thy marble Vault, shall sound
My ecchoing Song: then Worms shall try
That long preserv'd Virginity:
And your quaint Honour turn to dust;
30     And into ashes all my Lust.
The Grave's a fine and private place,
But none I think do there embrace.
    Now therefore, while the youthful hew

Sits on thy skin like morning lew,[1]
And while thy willing Soul transpires
At every pore with instant Fires,
Now let us sport us while we may;
And now, like am'rous birds of prey,
Rather at once our Time devour,
Than languish in his slow chapt pow'r.                    40
Let us roll all our Strength, and all
Our sweetness, up into one Ball:
And tear our Pleasures with rough strife,
Thorough the Iron gates of Life.
Thus, though we cannot make our Sun
Stand still, yet we will make him run.

[1] warmth

## ·30·

*Eudora Welty*

# DEATH OF A TRAVELLING SALESMAN

R. J. Bowman, who for fourteen years had travelled for a shoe company through Mississippi, drove his Ford along a rutted dirt path. It was a long day! The time did not seem to clear the noon hurdle and settle into soft afternoon. The sun, keeping its strength here even in winter, stayed at the top of the sky, and every time Bowman stuck his head out of the dusty car to stare up the road, it seemed to reach a long arm down and push against the top of his head, right through his hat—like the practical joke of an old drummer, long on the road. It made him feel all the more angry and helpless. He was feverish, and he was not quite sure of the way.

This was his first day back on the road after a long siege of influenza. [10] He had had very high fever, and dreams, and had become weakened and pale, enough to tell the difference in the mirror, and he could not think clearly. . . . All afternoon, in the midst of his anger, and for no reason, he had thought of his dead grandmother. She had been a comfortable soul. Once more Bowman wished he could fall into the big feather bed that had been in her room. . . . Then he forgot her again.

This desolate hill country! And he seemed to be going the wrong way—
it was as if he were going back, far back. There was not a house in sight.
. . . There was no use wishing he were back in bed, though. By paying
the hotel doctor his bill he had proved his recovery. He had not even been
sorry when the pretty trained nurse said good-bye. He did not like illness,
he distrusted it, as he distrusted the road without signposts. It angered
him. He had given the nurse a really expensive bracelet, just because she
was packing up her bag and leaving.

But now—what if in fourteen years on the road he had never been ill
10 before and never had an accident? His record was broken, and he had
even begun almost to question it. . . . He had gradually put up at better
hotels, in the bigger towns, but weren't they all, eternally, stuffy in summer and draughty in winter? Women? He could only remember little
rooms within little rooms, like a nest of Chinese paper boxes, and if he
thought of one woman he saw the worn loneliness that the furniture of
that room seemed built of. And he himself—he was a man who always
wore rather wide-brimmed black hats, and in the wavy hotel mirrors had
looked something like a bull-fighter, as he paused for that inevitable instant on the landing, walking downstairs to supper. . . . He leaned out of
20 the car again, and once more the sun pushed at his head.

Bowman had wanted to reach Beulah by dark, to go to bed and sleep
off his fatigue. As he remembered, Beulah was fifty miles away from the
last town, on a gravelled road. This was only a cow trail. How had he ever
come to such a place? One hand wiped the sweat from his face, and he
drove on.

He had made the Beulah trip before. But he had never seen this hill or
this petering-out path before—or that cloud, he thought shyly, looking up
and then down quickly—any more than he had seen this day before. Why
did he not admit he was simply lost and had been for miles? . . . He was
30 not in the habit of asking the way of strangers, and these people never
knew where the very roads they lived on went to; but then he had not
even been close enough to anyone to call out. People standing in the fields
now and then, or on top of the haystacks, had been too far away, looking
like leaning sticks or weeds, turning a little at the solitary rattle of his car
across their countryside, watching the pale sobered winter dust where it
chunked out behind like big squashes down the road. The stares of these
distant people had followed him solidly like a wall, impenetrable, behind
which they turned back after he had passed.

The cloud floated there to one side like the bolster on his grandmother's
40 bed. It went over a cabin on the edge of a hill, where two bare chinaberry
trees clutched at the sky. He drove through a heap of dead oak leaves, his
wheels stirring their weightless sides to make a silvery melancholy whistle
as the car passed through their bed. No car had been along this way ahead

of him. Then he saw that he was on the edge of a ravine that fell away, a
red erosion, and that this was indeed the road's end.

He pulled the brake. But it did not hold, though he put all his strength
into it. The car, tipped toward the edge, rolled a little. Without doubt, it
was going over the bank.

He got out quietly, as though some mischief had been done him and he
had his dignity to remember. He lifted his bag and sample case out, set
them down, and stood back and watched the car roll over the edge. He
heard something—not the crash he was listening for, but a slow un-up-
roarious crackle. Rather distastefully he went to look over, and he saw
that his car had fallen into a tangle of immense grape vines as thick as
his arm, which caught it and held it, rocked it like a grotesque child in a
dark cradle, and then, as he watched, concerned somehow that he was not
still inside it, released it gently to the ground.

He sighed.

Where am I? he wondered with a shock. Why didn't I do something?
All his anger seemed to have drifted away from him. There was the house,
back on the hill. He took a bag in each hand and with almost childlike
willingness went toward it. But his breathing came with difficulty, and he
had to stop to rest.

It was a shotgun house, two rooms and an open passage between,
perched on the hill. The whole cabin slanted a little under the heavy
heaped-up vine that covered the roof, light and green, as though forgotten
from summer. A woman stood in the passage.

He stopped still. Then all of a sudden his heart began to behave
strangely. Like a rocket set off, it began to leap and expand into uneven
patterns of beats which showered into his brain, and he could not think.
But in scattering and falling it made no noise. It shot up with great power,
almost elation, and fell gently, like acrobats into nets. It began to pound
profoundly, then waited irresponsibly, hitting in some sort of inward
mockery first at his ribs, then against his eyes, then under his shoulder
blades, and against the roof of his mouth when he tried to say, "Good
afternoon, madam." But he could not hear his heart—it was as quiet as
ashes falling. This was rather comforting; still, it was shocking to Bowman
to feel his heart beating at all.

Stockstill in his confusion, he dropped his bags, which seemed to drift
in slow bulks gracefully through the air and to cushion themselves on the
grey prostrate grass near the doorstep.

As for the woman standing there, he saw at once that she was old. Since
she could not possibly hear his heart, he ignored the pounding and now
looked at her carefully, and yet in his distraction dreamily, with his mouth
open.

She had been cleaning the lamp, and held it, half blackened, half clear, in front of her. He saw her with the dark passage behind her. She was a big woman with a weather-beaten but unwrinkled face; her lips were held tightly together, and her eyes looked with a curious dulled brightness into his. He looked at her shoes, which were like bundles. If it were summer she would be barefoot. . . . Bowman, who automatically judged a woman's age on sight, set her age at fifty. She wore a formless garment of some grey coarse material, rough-dried from a washing, from which her arms appeared pink and unexpectedly round. When she never said a
10 word, and sustained her quiet pose of holding the lamp, he was convinced of the strength in her body.

"Good afternoon, madam," he said.

She stared on, whether at him or at the air around him he could not tell, but after a moment she lowered her eyes to show that she would listen to whatever he had to say.

"I wonder if you would be interested—" He tried once more. "An accident—my car . . ."

Her voice emerged low and remote, like a sound across a lake. "Sonny he ain't here."

20    "Sonny?"

"Sonny ain't here now."

Her son—a fellow able to bring my car up, he decided in blurred relief. He pointed down the hill. "My car's in the bottom of the ditch. I'll need help."

"Sonny ain't here, but he'll be here."

She was becoming clearer to him and her voice stronger, and Bowman saw that she was stupid.

He was hardly surprised at the deepening postponement and tedium of his journey. He took a breath, and heard his voice speaking over the silent
30 blows of his heart. "I was sick. I am not strong yet. . . . May I come in?"

He stooped and laid his big black hat over the handle on his bag. It was a humble motion, almost a bow, that instantly struck him as absurd and betraying of all his weakness. He looked up at the woman, the wind blowing his hair. He might have continued for a long time in this unfamiliar attitude; he had never been a patient man, but when he was sick he had learned to sink submissively into the pillows, to wait for his medicine. He waited on the woman.

Then she, looking at him with blue eyes, turned and held open the door, and after a moment Bowman, as if convinced in his action, stood erect
40 and followed her in.

Inside, the darkness of the house touched him like a professional hand, the doctor's. The woman set the half-cleaned lamp on a table in the centre of the room and pointed, also like a professional person, a guide, to a chair with a yellow cowhide seat. She herself crouched on the hearth, drawing her knees up under the shapeless dress.

At first he felt hopefully secure. His heart was quieter. The room was enclosed in the gloom of yellow pine boards. He could see the other room, with the foot of an iron bed showing, across the passage. The bed had been made up with a red-and-yellow pieced quilt that looked like a map or a picture, a little like his grandmother's girlhood painting of Rome burning.

He had ached for coolness, but in this room it was cold. He stared at the hearth with dead coals lying on it and iron pots in the corners. The hearth and smoked chimney were of the stone he had seen ribbing the hills, mostly slate. Why is there no fire? he wondered.

And it was so still. The silence of the fields seemed to enter and move familiarly through the house. The wind used the open hall. He felt that he was in a mysterious, quiet, cool danger. It was necessary to do what? . . . To talk.

"I have a nice line of women's low-priced shoes . . ." he said.

But the woman answered, "Sonny'll be here. He's strong. Sonny'll move your car."

"Where is he now?"

"Farms for Mr. Redmond."

Mr. Redmond. Mr. Redmond. That was someone he would never have to encounter, and he was glad. Somehow the name did not appeal to him. . . . In a flare of touchiness and anxiety, Bowman wished to avoid even mention of unknown men and their unknown farms.

"Do you two live here alone?" He was surprised to hear his old voice, chatty, confidential, inflected for selling shoes, asking a question like that— a thing he did not even want to know.

"Yes. We are alone."

He was surprised at the way she answered. She had taken a long time to say that. She had nodded her head in a deep way too. Had she wished to affect him with some sort of premonition? he wondered unhappily. Or was it only that she would not help him, after all, by talking with him? For he was not strong enough to receive the impact of unfamiliar things without a little talk to break their fall. He had lived a month in which nothing had happened except in his head and his body—an almost inaudible life of heartbeats and dreams that came back, a life of fever and privacy, a delicate life which had left him weak to the point of—what? Of begging. The pulse in his palm leapt like a trout in a brook.

He wondered over and over why the woman did not go ahead with cleaning the lamp. What prompted her to stay there across the room, silently bestowing her presence upon him? He saw that with her it was not a time for doing little tasks. Her face was grave; she was feeling how right she was. Perhaps it was only politeness. In docility he held his eyes stiffly wide; they fixed themselves on the woman's clasped hands as though she held the cord they were strung on.

Then, "Sonny's coming," she said.

He himself had not heard anything, but there came a man passing the window and then plunging in at the door, with two hounds beside him. Sonny was a big enough man, with his belt slung low about his hips. He looked at least thirty. He had a hot, red face that was yet full of silence. He wore muddy blue pants and an old military coat stained and patched. World War? Bowman wondered. Great God, it was a Confederate coat.
10 On the back of his light hair he had a wide filthy black hat which seemed to insult Bowman's own. He pushed down the dogs from his chest. He was strong with dignity and heaviness in his way of moving. . . . There was the resemblance to his mother.

They stood side by side. . . . He must account again for his presence here.

"Sonny, this man, he had his car to run off over the prec'pice an' wants to know if you will git it out for him," the woman said after a few minutes.

Bowman could not even state his case.

Sonny's eyes lay upon him.
20 He knew he should offer explanations and show money—at least appear either penitent or authoritative. But all he could do was to shrug slightly.

Sonny brushed by him going to the window, followed by the eager dogs, and looked out. There was effort even in the way he was looking, as if he could throw his sight out like a rope. Without turning Bowman felt that his own eyes could have seen nothing: it was too far.

"Got me a mule out there an' got me a block an' tackle," said Sonny meaningfully. "I *could* catch me my mule an' git me my ropes, an' before long I'd git your car out the ravine."

He looked completely round the room, as if in meditation, his eyes
30 roving in their own distance. Then he pressed his lips firmly and yet shyly together, and with the dogs ahead of him this time, he lowered his head and strode out. The hard earth sounded, cupping to his powerful way of walking—almost a stagger.

Mischievously, at the suggestion of those sounds, Bowman's heart leapt again. It seemed to walk about inside him.

"Sonny's goin' to do it," the woman said. She said it again, singing it almost, like a song. She was sitting in her place by the hearth.

Without looking out, he heard some shouts and the dogs barking and the pounding of hoofs in short runs on the hill. In a few minutes Sonny
40 passed under the window with a rope, and there was a brown mule with quivering, shining, purple-looking ears. The mule actually looked in the window. Under its eyelashes it turned target-like eyes into his. Bowman averted his head and saw the woman looking serenely back at the mule, with only satisfaction in her face.

She sang a little more, under her breath. It occurred to him, and it seemed quite marvellous, that she was not really talking to him, but rather following the thing that came about with words that were unconscious and part of her looking.

So he said nothing, and this time when he did not reply he felt a curious and strong emotion, not fear, rise up in him.

This time, when his heart leapt, something—his soul—seemed to leap too, like a little colt invited out of a pen. He stared at the woman while the frantic nimbleness of his feeling made his head sway. He could not move; there was nothing he could do, unless perhaps he might embrace this 10 woman who sat there growing old and shapeless before him.

But he wanted to leap up, to say to her, I have been sick and I found out then, only then, how lonely I am. Is it too late? My heart puts up a struggle inside me, and you may have heard it, protesting against emptiness. . . . It should be full, he would rush on to tell her, thinking of his heart now as a deep lake, it should be holding love like other hearts. It should be flooded with love. There would be a warm spring day . . . Come and stand in my heart, whoever you are, and a whole river would cover your feet and rise higher and take your knees in whirlpools, and draw you down to itself, your whole body, your heart too.                    20

But he moved a trembling hand across his eyes, and looked at the placid crouching woman across the room. She was still as a statue. He felt ashamed and exhausted by the thought that he might, in one more moment, have tried by simple words and embraces to communicate some strange thing—something which seemed always to have just escaped him . . .

Sunlight touched the farthest pot on the hearth. It was late afternoon. This time to-morrow he would be somewhere on a good gravelled road, driving his car past things that happened to people, quicker than their happening. Seeing ahead to the next day, he was glad, and knew that this 30 was no time to embrace an old woman. He could feel in his pounding temples the readying of his blood for motion and for hurrying away.

"Sonny's hitched up your car by now," said the woman. "He'll git it out the ravine right shortly."

"Fine!" he cried with his customary enthusiasm.


Yet it seemed a long time that they waited. It began to get dark. Bowman was cramped in his chair. Any man should know enough to get up and walk around while he waited. There was something like guilt in such stillness and silence.

But instead of getting up, he listened. . . . His breathing restrained, 40 his eyes powerless in the growing dark, he listened uneasily for a warning sound, forgetting in wariness what it would be. Before long he heard something—soft, continuous, insinuating.

"What's the noise?" he asked, his voice jumping into the dark. Then wildly he was afraid it would be his heart beating so plainly in the quiet room, and she would tell him so.

"You might hear the stream," she said grudgingly.

Her voice was closer. She was standing by the table. He wondered why she did not light the lamp. She stood there in the dark and did not light it.

Bowman would never speak to her now, for the time was past. I'll sleep in the dark, he thought, in his bewilderment pitying himself.

Heavily she moved on to the window. Her arm, vaguely white, rose
10 straight from her full side and she pointed out into the darkness.

"That white speck's Sonny," she said, talking to herself.

He turned unwillingly and peered over her shoulder; he hesitated to rise and stand beside her. His eyes searched the dusky air. The white speck floated smoothly toward her finger, like a leaf on a river, growing whiter in the dark. It was as if she had shown him something secret, part of her life, but had offered no explanation. He looked away. He was moved almost to tears, feeling for no reason that she had made a silent declaration equivalent to his own. His hand waited upon his chest.

Then a step shook the house, and Sonny was in the room. Bowman felt
20 how the woman left him there and went to the other man's side.

"I done got your car out, mister," said Sonny's voice in the dark. "She's settin' a-waitin' in the road, turned to go back where she come from."

"Fine!" said Bowman, projecting his own voice to loudness. "I'm surely much obliged—I could never have done it myself—I was sick. . . ."

"I could do it easy," said Sonny.

Bowman could feel them both waiting in the dark, and he could hear the dogs panting out in the yard, waiting to bark when he should go. He felt strangely helpless and resentful. Now that he could go, he longed to stay. From what was he being deprived? His chest was rudely shaken by
30 the violence of his heart. These people cherished something here that he could not see, they withheld some ancient promise of food and warmth and light. Between them they had a conspiracy. He thought of the way she had moved away from him and gone to Sonny, she had flowed toward him. He was shaking with cold, he was tired, and it was not fair. Humbly and yet angrily he stuck his hand into his pocket.

"Of course I'm going to pay you for everything—"

"We don't take money for such," said Sonny's voice belligerently.

"I want to pay. But do something more . . . Let me stay—to-night.
. . ." He took another step toward them. If only they could see him, they
40 would know his sincerity, his real need! His voice went on, "I'm not very strong yet, I'm not able to walk far, even back to my car, maybe, I don't know—I don't know exactly where I am—"

He stopped. He felt as if he might burst into tears. What would they think of him!

Sonny came over and put his hands on him. Bowman felt them pass (they were professional too) across his chest, over his hips. He could feel Sonny's eyes upon him in the dark.

"You ain't no revenuer come sneakin' here, mister, ain't got no gun?"

To this end of nowhere! And yet *he* had come. He made a grave answer. "No."

"You can stay."

"Sonny," said the woman, "you'll have to borry some fire."

"I'll go git it from Redmond's," said Sonny.

"What?" Bowman strained to hear their words to each other.          10

"Our fire, it's out, and Sonny's got to borry some, because it's dark an' cold," she said.

"But matches—I have matches—"

"We don't have no need for 'em," she said proudly. "Sonny's goin' after his own fire."

"I'm goin' to Redmond's," said Sonny with an air of importance, and he went out.

After they had waited a while, Bowman looked out the window and saw a light moving over the hill. It spread itself out like a little fan. It zig-zagged along the field, darting and swift, not like Sonny at all. . . . Soon  20 enough, Sonny staggered in, holding a burning stick behind him in tongs, fire flowing in his wake, blazing light into the corners of the room.

"We'll make a fire now," the woman said, taking the brand.

When that was done she lit the lamp. It showed its dark and light. The whole room turned golden-yellow like some sort of flower, and the walls smelled of it and seemed to tremble with the quiet rushing of the fire and the waving of the burning lampwick in its funnel of light.

The woman moved among the iron pots. With the tongs she dropped hot coals on top of the iron lids. They made a set of soft vibrations, like the sound of a bell far away.                                          30

She looked up and over at Bowman, but he could not answer. He was trembling. . . .

"Have a drink, mister?" Sonny asked. He had brought in a chair from the other room and sat astride it with his folded arms across the back. Now we are all visible, to one another, Bowman thought, and cried, "Yes sir, you bet, thanks!"

"Come after me and do just what I do," said Sonny.

It was another excursion into the dark. They went through the hall, out to the back of the house, past a shed and a hooded well. They came to a wilderness of thicket.                                                    40

"Down on your knees," said Sonny.

"What?" Sweat broke out on his forehead.

He understood when Sonny began to crawl through a sort of tunnel
that the bushes made over the ground. He followed, startled in spite of
himself when a twig or a thorn touched him gently without making a
sound, clinging to him and finally letting him go.

Sonny stopped crawling and, crouched on his knees, began to dig with
both his hands into the dirt. Bowman shyly struck matches and made a
light. In a few minutes Sonny pulled up a jug. He poured out some of the
whisky into a bottle from his coat pocket, and buried the jug again. "You
never know who's liable to knock at your door," he said, and laughed.
"Start back," he said, almost formally. "Ain't no need for us to drink out-
doors, like hogs."

At the table by the fire, sitting opposite each other in their chairs, Sonny
and Bowman took drinks out of the bottle, passing it across. The dogs
slept; one of them was having a dream.

"This is good," said Bowman. "That is what I needed." It was just as
though he were drinking the fire off the hearth.

"He makes it," said the woman with quiet pride.

She was pushing the coals off the pots, and the smells of corn bread
and coffee circled the room. She set everything on the table before the
men, with a bone-handled knife stuck into one of the potatoes, splitting
out its golden fibre. Then she stood for a minute looking at them, tall and
full above them where they sat. She leaned a little toward them.

"You-all can eat now," she said, and suddenly smiled.

Bowman had just happened to be looking at her. He set his cup back
on the table in unbelieving protest. A pain pressed at his eyes. He saw
that she was not an old woman. She was young, still young. He could
think of no number of years for her. She was the same age as Sonny, and
she belonged to him. She stood with the deep dark corner of the room
behind her, the shifting yellow light scattering over her head and her grey
formless dress, trembling over her tall body when it bent over them in its
sudden communication. She was young. Her teeth were shining and her
eyes glowed. She turned and walked slowly and heavily out of the room,
and he heard her sit down on the cot and then lie down. The pattern on
the quilt moved.

"She goin' to have a baby," said Sonny, popping a bite into his mouth.

Bowman could not speak. He was shocked with knowing what was
really in this house. A marriage, a fruitful marriage. That simple thing.
Anyone could have had that.

Somehow he felt unable to be indignant or protest, although some sort
of joke had certainly been played upon him. There was nothing remote or
mysterious here—only something private. The only secret was the ancient
communication between two people. But the memory of the woman's
waiting silently by the cold hearth, of the man's stubborn journey a mile
away to get fire, and how they finally brought out their food and drink

and filled the room proudly with all they had to show, was suddenly too
clear and too enormous within him for response. . . .

"You ain't as hungry as you look," said Sonny.

The woman came out of the bedroom as soon as the men had finished,
and ate her supper while her husband stared peacefully into the fire.

Then they put the dogs out, with the food that was left.

"I think I'd better sleep here by the fire, on the floor," said Bowman.

He felt that he had been cheated, and that he could afford now to be
generous. Ill though he was, he was not going to ask them for their bed.
He was through with asking favours in this house, now that he understood 10
what was there.

"Sure, mister."

But he had not known yet how slowly he understood. They had not
meant to give him their bed. After a little interval they both rose and
looking at him gravely went into the other room.

He lay stretched by the fire until it grew low and dying. He watched
every tongue of blaze lick out and vanish. "There will be special reduced
prices on all footwear during the month of January," he found himself repeating quietly, and then he lay with his lips tight shut.

How many noises the night had! He heard the stream running, the fire 20
dying, and he was sure now that he heard his heart beating, too, the sound
it made under his ribs. He heard breathing, round and deep, of the man
and his wife in the room across the passage. And that was all. But emotion
swelled patiently within him, and he wished that the child were his.

He must get back to where he had been before. He stood weakly before the red coals, and put on his overcoat. It felt too heavy on his shoulders. As he started out he looked and saw that the woman had never got
through with cleaning the lamp. On some impulse he put all the money
from his billfold under its fluted glass base, almost ostentatiously.

Ashamed, shrugging a little, and then shivering, he took his bags and 30
went out. The cold of the air seemed to lift him bodily. The moon was in
the sky.

On the slope he began to run, he could not help it. Just as he reached
the road, where his car seemed to sit in the moonlight like a boat, his
heart began to give off tremendous explosions like a rifle, bang bang bang.

He sank in fright on to the road, his bags falling about him. He felt as
if all this had happened before. He covered his heart with both hands to
keep anyone from hearing the noise it made.

But nobody heard it.

# Questions

1. What images in the first four paragraphs seem particularly vivid to you? Which is established more clearly by means of these images and the paragraphs as a whole, Bowman's character or his environment?

2. What additional dimension does Miss Welty use to reveal Bowman that she does not use to reveal Sonny and his wife? How did this difference shape your own psychological responses toward the characters as the story progressed?

3. How does the author, without fatiguing the reader or appearing uncertain herself, gradually convey a sense of fatigue and uncertainty in Bowman which culminates in panic and death?

4. At what points in the story does the author emphasize the difference between the way Bowman feels and thinks and the way he speaks and acts?

5. What are the apparent dignities of Bowman's life and the apparent indignities in the lives of Sonny and his wife? How, by diction, event and tone, are both sets of appearances extinguished and new sets of realities established?

# Theme Topics

1. Write a study of the diction and style of "Death of a Travelling Salesman" as they relate to its meaning.

2. Discuss the salesman of this story as he was conditioned by his environment and as he is representative of conditioning forces in America.

# Some Devices of Style

## ～ VII ～

## PARALLELISM, REPETITION, METAPHOR

### ·31·

*James Baldwin*

## NOTES OF A NATIVE SON

*1.* On the 29th of July, in 1943, my father died. On the same day, a few hours later, his last child was born. Over a month before this, while all our energies were concentrated in waiting for these events, there had been, in Detroit, one of the bloodiest race riots of the century. A few hours after my father's funeral, while he lay in state in the undertaker's chapel, a race riot broke out in Harlem. On the morning of the 3rd of August, we drove my father to the graveyard through a wilderness of smashed plate glass.

*2.* The day of my father's funeral had also been my nineteenth birthday. As we drove him to the graveyard, the spoils of injustice, anarchy, discontent, and hatred were all around us. It seemed to me that God himself had devised, to mark my father's end, the most sustained and brutally dissonant of codas. And it seemed to me, too, that the violence which rose all about us as my father left the world had been devised as a corrective for the pride of his eldest son. I had declined to believe in that apocalypse which had been central to my father's vision; very well, life seemed to be saying, here is something that will certainly pass for an apocalypse until the real thing comes along. I had inclined to be contemptuous of my father for the conditions of his life, for the conditions of our lives. When his life had ended I began to wonder about that life and also, in a new way, to be apprehensive about my own.

3. I had not known my father very well. We had got on badly, partly because we shared, in our different fashions, the vice of stubborn pride. When he was dead I realized that I had hardly ever spoken to him. When he had been dead a long time I began to wish I had. It seems to be typical of life in America, where opportunities, real and fancied, are thicker than anywhere else on the globe, that the second generation has no time to talk to the first. No one, including my father, seems to have known exactly how old he was, but his mother had been born during slavery. He was of the first generation of free men. He, along with thousands of other Negroes, came North after 1919 and I was part of that generation which had never seen the landscape of what Negroes sometimes call the Old Country.

4. He had been born in New Orleans and had been a quite young man there during the time that Louis Armstrong, a boy, was running errands for the dives and honky-tonks of what was always presented to me as one of the most wicked of cities—to this day, whenever I think of New Orleans, I also helplessly think of Sodom and Gomorrah. My father never mentioned Louis Armstrong, except to forbid us to play his records; but there was a picture of him on our wall for a long time. One of my father's strong-willed female relatives had placed it there and forbade my father to take it down. He never did, but he eventually maneuvered her out of the house and when, some years later, she was in trouble and near death, he refused to do anything to help her.

5. He was, I think, very handsome. I gather this from photographs and from my own memories of him, dressed in his Sunday best and on his way to preach a sermon somewhere, when I was little. Handsome, proud, and ingrown, "like a toe-nail," somebody said. But he looked to me, as I grew older, like pictures I had seen of African tribal chieftains: he really should have been naked, with war-paint on and barbaric mementos, standing among spears. He could be chilling in the pulpit and indescribably cruel in his personal life and he was certainly the most bitter man I have ever met; yet it must be said that there was something else in him, buried in him, which let him his tremendous power and, even, a rather crushing charm. It had something to do with his blackness, I think—he was very black—with his blackness and his beauty, and with the fact that he knew that he was black but did not know that he was beautiful. He claimed to be proud of his blackness but it had also been the cause of much humiliation and it had fixed bleak boundaries to his life. He was not a young man when we were growing up and he had already suffered many kinds of ruin; in his outrageously demanding and protective way he loved his children, who were black like him and menaced, like him; and all these things sometimes showed in his face when he tried, never to my knowledge with any success, to establish contact with any of us. When he took

one of his children on his knee to play, the child always became fretful
and began to cry; when he tried to help one of us with our homework the
absolutely unabating tension which emanated from him caused our minds
and our tongues to become paralyzed, so that he, scarcely knowing why,
flew into a rage and the child, not knowing why, was punished. If it ever
entered his head to bring a surprise home for his children, it was, almost
unfailingly, the wrong surprise and even the big watermelons he often
brought home on his back in the summertime led to the most appalling
scenes. I do not remember, in all those years, that one of his children was
ever glad to see him come home. From what I was able to gather of his
early life, it seemed that this inability to establish contact with other people had always marked him and had been one of the things which had
driven him out of New Orleans. There was something in him, therefore,
groping and tentative, which was never expressed and was buried with
him. One saw it most clearly when he was facing new people and hoping
to impress them. But he never did, not for long. We went from church to
smaller and more improbable church, he found himself in less and less demand as a minister, and by the time he died none of his friends had come
to see him for a long time. He had lived and died in an intolerable bitterness of spirit and it frightened me, as we drove him to the graveyard
through those unquiet, ruined streets, to see how powerful and overflow-
ing this bitterness could be and to realize that this bitterness now was
mine.

6. When he died I had been away from home for a little over a year.
In that year I had had time to become aware of the meaning of all my
father's bitter warnings, had discovered the secret of his proudly pursed
lips and rigid carriage: I had discovered the weight of white people in the
world. I saw that this had been for my ancestors and now would be for
me an awful thing to live with and that the bitterness which had helped
to kill my father could also kill me.

7. He had been ill a long time—in the mind, as we now realized, re-
living instances of his fantastic intransigence in the new light of his afflic-
tion and endeavoring to feel a sorrow for him which never, quite, came
true. We had not known that he was being eaten up by paranoia, and the
discovery that his cruelty, to our bodies and our minds, had been one of
the symptoms of his illness was not, then, enough to enable us to forgive
him. The younger children felt, quite simply, relief that he would not be
coming home anymore. My mother's observation that it was he, after all,
who had kept them alive all these years meant nothing because the problems of keeping children alive are not real for children. The older children
felt, with my father gone, that they could invite their friends to the house
without fear that their friends would be insulted or, as had sometimes
happened with me, being told that their friends were in league with the
devil and intended to rob our family of everything we owned. (I didn't

fail to wonder, and it made me hate him, what on earth we owned that anybody else would want.)

8. His illness was beyond all hope of healing before anyone realized that he was ill. He had always been so strange and had lived, like a prophet, in such unimaginably close communion with the Lord that his long silences which were punctuated by moans and hallelujahs and snatches of old songs while he sat at the living-room window never seemed odd to us. It was not until he refused to eat because, he said, his family was trying to poison him that my mother was forced to accept as a fact what had, until then, been only an unwilling suspicion. When he was committed, it was discovered that he had tuberculosis and, as it turned out, the disease of his mind allowed the disease of his body to destroy him. For the doctors could not force him to eat, either, and, though he was fed intravenously, it was clear from the beginning that there was no hope for him.

9. In my mind's eye I could see him, sitting at the window, locked up in his terrors; hating and fearing every living soul including his children who had betrayed him, too, by reaching towards the world which had despised him. There were nine of us. I began to wonder what it could have felt like for such a man to have had nine children whom he could barely feed. He used to make little jokes about our poverty, which never, of course, seemed very funny to us; they could not have seemed very funny to him, either, or else our all too feeble response to them would never have caused such rages. He spent great energy and achieved, to our chagrin, no small amount of success in keeping us away from the people who surrounded us, people who had all-night rent parties to which we listened when we should have been sleeping, people who cursed and drank and flashed razor blades on Lenox Avenue. He could not understand why, if they had so much energy to spare, they could not use it to make their lives better. He treated almost everybody on our block with a most uncharitable asperity and neither they, nor, of course, their children were slow to reciprocate. *shortness of temper*

10. The only white people who came to our house were welfare workers and bill collectors. It was almost always my mother who dealt with them, for my father's temper, which was at the mercy of his pride, was never to be trusted. It was clear that he felt their very presence in his home to be a violation: this was conveyed by his carriage, almost ludicrously stiff, and by his voice, harsh and vindictively polite. When I was around nine or ten I wrote a play which was directed by a young, white schoolteacher, a woman, who then took an interest in me, and gave me books to read and, in order to corroborate my theatrical bent, decided to take me to see what she somewhat tactlessly referred to as "real" plays. Theater-going was forbidden in our house, but, with the really cruel intuitiveness of a child, I suspected that the color of this woman's skin would carry the day for me.

When, at school, she suggested taking me to the theater, I did not, as I might have done if she had been a Negro, find a way of discouraging her, but agreed that she should pick me up at my house one evening. I then, very cleverly, left all the rest to my mother, who suggested to my father, as I knew she would, that it would not be very nice to let such a kind woman make the trip for nothing. Also, since it was a schoolteacher, I imagine that my mother countered the idea of sin with the idea of "education," which word, even with my father, carried a kind of bitter weight.

*11.* Before the teacher came my father took me aside to ask *why* she was coming, what *interest* she could possibly have in our house, in a boy like me. I said I didn't know but I, too, suggested that it had something to do with education. And I understood that my father was waiting for me to say something—I didn't quite know what; perhaps that I wanted his protection against this teacher and her "education." I said none of these things and the teacher came and we went out. It was clear, during the brief interview in our living room, that my father was agreeing very much against his will and that he would have refused permission if he had dared. The fact that he did not dare caused me to despise him: I had no way of knowing that he was facing in that living room a wholly unprece dented and frightening situation.

*12.* Later, when my father had been laid off from his job, this woman became very important to us. She was really a very sweet and generous woman and went to a great deal of trouble to be of help to us, particularly during one awful winter. My mother called her by the highest name she knew: she said she was a "christian." My father could scarcely disagree but during the four or five years of our relatively close association he never trusted her and was always trying to surprise in her open, Midwestern face the genuine, cunningly hidden, and hideous motivation. In later years, particularly when it began to be clear that this "education" of mine was going to lead me to perdition, he became more explicit and warned me that my white friends in high school were not really my friends and that I would see, when I was older, how white people would do anything to keep a Negro down. Some of them could be nice, he admitted, but none of them were to be trusted and most of them were not even nice. The best thing was to have as little to do with them as possible. I did not feel this way and I was certain, in my innocence, that I never would.

*13.* But the year which preceded my father's death had made a great change in my life. I had been living in New Jersey, working in defense plants, working and living among southerners, white and black. I knew about the south, of course, and about how southerners treated Negroes and how they expected them to behave, but it had never entered my mind that anyone would look at me and expect me to behave that way. I learned in New Jersey that to be a Negro meant, precisely, that one was never looked at but was simply at the mercy of the reflexes the color of one's skin caused in other people. I acted in New Jersey as I had always acted, that is as though I thought a great deal of myself—I had to *act* that way—with results that were, simply, unbelievable. I had scarcely arrived before I had earned the enmity, which was extraordinarily ingenious, of all my superiors and nearly all my co-workers. In the beginning, to make matters worse, I simply did not know what was happening. I did not know what I had done, and I shortly began to wonder what *anyone* could possibly do, to bring about such unanimous, active, and unbearably vocal hostility. I knew about jim-crow but I had never experienced it. I went to the same self-service restaurant three times and stood with all the Princeton boys before the counter, waiting for a hamburger and coffee; it was always an extraordinarily long time before anything was set before me; but it was not until the fourth visit that I learned that, in fact, nothing had ever been set before me: I had simply picked something up. Negroes were not served there, I was told, and they had been waiting for me to realize that I was always the only Negro present. Once I was told this, I determined to go there all the time. But now they were ready for me and, though some dreadful scenes were subsequently enacted in that restaurant, I never ate there again.

14. It was the same story all over New Jersey, in bars, bowling alleys, diners, places to live. I was always being forced to leave, silently, or with mutual imprecations. I very shortly became notorious and children giggled behind me when I passed and their elders whispered or shouted—they really believed that I was mad. And it did begin to work on my mind, of course; I began to be afraid to go anywhere and to compensate for this I went places to which I really should not have gone and where, God knows, I had no desire to be. My reputation in town naturally enhanced my reputation at work and my working day became one long series of acrobatics designed to keep me out of trouble. I cannot say that these acrobatics succeeded. It began to seem that the machinery of the organization I worked for was turning over, day and night, with but one aim: to eject me. I was fired once, and contrived, with the aid of a friend from New York, to get back on the payroll; was fired again, and bounced back again. It took a while to fire me for the third time, but the third time took. There were no loopholes anywhere. There was not even any way of getting back inside the gates.

15. That year in New Jersey lives in my mind as though it were the year during which, having an unsuspected predilection for it, I first contracted some dread, chronic disease, the unfailing symptom of which is a kind of blind fever, a pounding in the skull and fire in the bowels. Once this disease is contracted, one can never be really carefree again, for the fever, without an instant's warning, can recur at any moment. It can wreck more important things than race relations. There is not a Negro alive who does not have this rage in his blood—one has the choice, merely, of living with

it consciously or surrendering to it. As for me, this fever has recurred in me, and does, and will until the day I die.

*16.* My last night in New Jersey, a white friend from New York took me to the nearest big town, Trenton, to go to the movies and have a few drinks. As it turned out, he also saved me from, at the very least, a violent whipping. Almost every detail of that night stands out very clearly in my memory. I even remember the name of the movie we saw because its title impressed me as being so patly ironical. It was a movie about the German occupation of France, starring Maureen O'Hara and Charles Laughton and called *This Land Is Mine.* I remember the name of the diner we walked into when the movie ended: it was the "American Diner." When we walked in the counterman asked what we wanted and I remember answering with the casual sharpness which had become my habit: "We want a hamburger and a cup of coffee, what do you think we want?" I do not know why, after a year of such rebuffs, I so completely failed to anticipate his answer, which was, of course, "We don't serve Negroes here." This reply failed to discompose me, at least for the moment. I made some sardonic comment about the name of the diner and we walked out into the streets.

*17.* This was the time of what was called the "brown-out," when the lights in all American cities were very dim. When we re-entered the streets something happened to me which had the force of an optical illusion, or a nightmare. The streets were very crowded and I was facing north. People were moving in every direction but it seemed to me, in that instant, that all of the people I could see, and many more than that, were moving toward me, against me, and that everyone was white. I remember how their faces gleamed. And I felt, like a physical sensation, a *click* at the nape of my neck as though some interior string connecting my head to my body had been cut. I began to walk. I heard my friend call after me, but I ignored him. Heaven only knows what was going on in his mind, but he had the good sense not to touch me—I don't know what would have happened if he had—and to keep me in sight. I don't know what was going on in my mind, either; I certainly had no conscious plan. I wanted to do something to crush these white faces, which were crushing me. I walked for perhaps a block or two until I came to an enormous, glittering, and fashionable restaurant in which I knew not even the intercession of the Virgin would cause me to be served. I pushed through the doors and took the first vacant seat I saw, at a table for two, and waited.

*18.* I do not know how long I waited and I rather wonder, until today, what I could possibly have looked like. Whatever I looked like, I frightened the waitress who shortly appeared, and the moment she appeared all of my fury flowed towards her. I hated her for her white face, and for her great, astounded, frightened eyes. I felt that if she found a black man so frightening I would make her fright worth-while.

*19.* She did not ask me what I wanted, but repeated, as though she had learned it somewhere, "We don't serve Negroes here." She did not say it with the blunt, derisive hostility to which I had grown so accustomed, but, rather, with a note of apology in her voice, and fear. This made me colder and more murderous than ever. I felt I had to do something with my hands. I wanted her to come close enough for me to get her neck between my hands.

*20.* So I pretended not to have understood her, hoping to draw her closer. And she did step a very short step closer, with her pencil poised incongruously over her pad, and repeated the formula: ". . . don't serve Negroes here."

*21.* Somehow, with the repetition of that phrase, which was already ringing in my head like a thousand bells of a nightmare, I realized that she would never come any closer and that I would have to strike from a distance. There was nothing on the table but an ordinary watermug half full of water, and I picked this up and hurled it with all my strength at her. She ducked and it missed her and shattered against the mirror behind the bar. And, with that sound, my frozen blood abruptly thawed, I returned from wherever I had been, I *saw,* for the first time, the restaurant, the people with their mouths open, already, as it seemed to me, rising as one man, and I realized what I had done, and where I was, and I was frightened. I rose and began running for the door. A round, potbellied man grabbed me by the nape of the neck just as I reached the doors and began to beat me about the face. I kicked him and got loose and ran into the streets. My friend whispered, *"Run!"* and I ran.

*22.* My friend stayed outside the restaurant long enough to misdirect my pursuers and the police, who arrived, he told me, at once. I do not know what I said to him when he came to my room that night. I could not have said much. I felt, in the oldest, most awful way, that I had somehow betrayed him. I lived it over and over and over again, the way one relives an automobile accident after it has happened and one finds oneself alone and safe. I could not get over two facts, both equally difficult for the imagination to grasp, and one was that I could have been murdered. But the other was that I had been ready to commit murder. I saw nothing very clearly but I did see this: that my life, my *real* life, was in danger, and not from anything other people might do but from the hatred I carried in my own heart.

## II

*23.* I had returned home around the second week in June—in great haste because it seemed that my father's death and my mother's confinement were both but a matter of hours. In the case of my mother, it soon became clear that she had simply made a miscalculation. This had always been her tendency and I don't believe that a single one of us arrived in the world, or has since arrived anywhere else, on time. But none of us dawdled so intolerably about the business of being born as did my baby sister. We sometimes amused ourselves, during those endless, stifling weeks, by picturing the baby sitting within in the safe, warm dark, bitterly regretting the necessity of becoming a part of our chaos and stubbornly putting it off as long as possible. I understood her perfectly and congratulated her on showing such good sense so soon. Death, however, sat as purposefully at my father's bedside as life stirred within my mother's womb and it was harder to understand why he so lingered in that long shadow. It seemed that he had bent, and for a long time, too, all of his energies towards dying. Now death was ready for him but my father held back.

24. All of Harlem, indeed, seemed to be infected by waiting. I had never before known it to be so violently still. Racial tensions throughout this country were exacerbated during the early years of the war, partly because the labor market brought together hundreds of thousands of ill-prepared people and partly because Negro soldiers, regardless of where they were born, received their military training in the south. What happened in defense plants and army camps had repercussions, naturally, in every Negro ghetto. The situation in Harlem had grown bad enough for clergymen, policemen, educators, politicians, and social workers to assert in one breath that there was no "crime wave" and to offer, in the very next breath, suggestions as to how to combat it. These suggestions always seemed to involve playgrounds, despite the fact that racial skirmishes were occurring in the playgrounds, too. Playground or not, crime wave or not, the Harlem police force had been augmented in March, and the unrest grew—perhaps, in fact, partly as a result of the ghetto's instinctive hatred of policemen. Perhaps the most revealing news item, out of the steady parade of reports of muggings, stabbings, shootings, assaults, gang wars, and accusations of police brutality, is the item concerning six Negro girls who set upon a white girl in the subway because, as they all too accurately put it, she was stepping on their toes. Indeed she was, all over the nation.

25. I had never before been so aware of policemen, on foot, on horseback, on corners, everywhere, always two by two. Nor had I ever been so aware of small knots of people. They were on stoops and on corners and in doorways, and what was striking about them, I think, was that they did not seem to be talking. Never, when I passed these groups, did the usual sound of a curse or a laugh ring out and neither did there seem to be any hum of gossip. There was certainly, on the other hand, occurring between them communication extraordinarily intense. Another thing that was striking was the unexpected diversity of the people who made up these groups. Usually, for example, one would see a group of sharpies standing on the street corner, jiving the passing chicks; or a group of older men, usually, for some reason, in the vicinity of a barber shop, discussing baseball

scores, or the numbers, or making rather chilling observations about
women they had known. Women, in a general way, tended to be seen
less often together—unless they were church women, or very young girls,
or prostitutes met together for an unprofessional instant. But that summer
I saw the strangest combinations: large, respectable, churchly matrons
standing on the stoops or the corners with their hair tied up, together with
a girl in sleazy satin whose face bore the marks of gin and the razor, or
heavy-set, abrupt, no-nonsense older men, in company with the most dis-
reputable and fanatical "race" men, or these same "race" men with the
sharpies, or these sharpies with the churchly women. Seventh Day Ad-
ventists and Methodists and Spiritualists seemed to be hobnobbing with
Holyrollers and they were all, alike, entangled with the most flagrant dis-
believers; something heavy in their stance seemed to indicate that they
had all, incredibly, seen a common vision, and on each face there seemed
to be the same strange, bitter shadow.

26. The churchly women and the matter-of-fact, no-nonsense men had
children in the Army. The sleazy girls they talked to had lovers there, the
sharpies and the "race" men had friends and brothers there. It would have
demanded an unquestioning patriotism, happily as uncommon in this
country as it is undesirable, for these people not to have been disturbed
by the bitter letters they received, by the newspaper stories they read,
not to have been enraged by the posters, then to be found all over New
York, which described the Japanese as "yellow-bellied Japs." It was only
the "race" men, to be sure, who spoke ceaselessly of being revenged—how
this vengeance was to be exacted was not clear—for the indignities and
dangers suffered by Negro boys in uniform; but everybody felt a direction-
less, hopeless bitterness, as well as that panic which can scarcely be suppressed when one knows that a human being one loves is beyond one's
reach, and in danger. This helplessness and this gnawing uneasiness does
something, at length, to even the toughest mind. Perhaps the best way to
sum all this up is to say that the people I knew felt, mainly, a peculiar
kind of relief when they knew that their boys were being shipped out of
the south, to do battle overseas. It was, perhaps, like feeling that the most
dangerous part of a dangerous journey had been passed and that now,
even if death should come, it would come with honor and without the
complicity of their countrymen. Such a death would be, in short, a fact
with which one could hope to live.

27. It was on the 28th of July, which I believe was a Wednesday, that I
visited my father for the first time during his illness and for the last time
in his life. The moment I saw him I knew why I had put off this visit so
long. I had told my mother that I did not want to see him because I hated
him. But this was not true. It was only that I *had* hated him and I wanted
to hold on to this hatred. I did not want to look on him as a ruin: it was
not a ruin I had hated. I imagine that one of the reasons people cling to

their hates so stubbornly is because they sense, once hate is gone, that they will be forced to deal with pain.

28. We traveled out to him, his older sister and myself, to what seemed to be the very end of a very Long Island. It was hot and dusty and we wrangled, my aunt and I, all the way out, over the fact that I had recently begun to smoke and, as she said, to give myself airs. But I knew that she wrangled with me because she could not bear to face the fact of her brother's dying. Neither could I endure the reality of her despair, her unstated bafflement as to what had happened to her brother's life, and her own. So we wrangled and I smoked and from time to time she fell into a heavy reverie. Covertly, I watched her face, which was the face of an old woman; it had fallen in, the eyes were sunken and lightless; soon she would be dying, too.

29. In my childhood—it had not been so long ago—I had thought her beautiful. She had been quick-witted and quick-moving and very generous with all the children and each of her visits had been an event. At one time one of my brothers and myself had thought of running away to live with her. Now she could no longer produce out of her handbag some unexpected and yet familiar delight. She made me feel pity and revulsion and fear. It was awful to realize that she no longer caused me to feel *complaining* affection. The closer we came to the hospital the more [querulous] she became and at the same time, naturally, grew more dependent on me. Between pity and guilt and fear I began to feel that there was another me trapped in my skull like a jack-in-the-box who might escape my control at any moment and fill the air with screaming.

30. She began to cry the moment we entered the room and she saw him lying there, all shriveled and still, like a little black monkey. The great, gleaming apparatus which fed him and would have compelled him to be still even if he had been able to move brought to mind, not beneficence, but torture; the tubes entering his arm made me think of pictures I had seen when a child, of Gulliver, tied down by the pygmies on that island. My aunt wept and wept, there was a whistling sound in my father's throat; nothing was said; he could not speak. I wanted to take his hand, to say something. But I do not know what I could have said, even if he could have heard me. He was not really in that room with us, he had at last really embarked on his journey; and though my aunt told me that he said he was going to meet Jesus, I did not hear anything except that whistling in his throat. The doctor came back and we left, into that unbearable train again, and home. In the morning came the telegram saying that he was dead. Then the house was suddenly full of relatives, friends, hysteria, and confusion and I quickly left my mother and the children to the care of those impressive women, who, in Negro communities at least, automatically appear at times of bereavement armed with lotions, proverbs, and patience, and an ability to cook. I went downtown. By the time

I returned, later the same day, my mother had been carried to the hospital and the baby had been born.

## III

*31.* For my father's funeral I had nothing black to wear and this posed a nagging problem all day long. It was one of those problems, simple, or impossible of solution, to which the mind insanely clings in order to avoid the mind's real trouble. I spent most of that day at the downtown apartment of a girl I knew, celebrating my birthday with whiskey and wondering what to wear that night. When planning a birthday celebration one naturally does not expect that it will be up against competition from a funeral and this girl had anticipated taking me out that night, for a big dinner and a night club afterwards. Sometime during the course of that long day we decided that we would go out anyway, when my father's funeral service was over. I imagine I decided it, since, as the funeral hour approached, it became clearer and clearer to me that I would not know what to do with myself when it was over. The girl, stifling her very lively concern as to the possible effects of the whiskey on one of my father's chief mourners, concentrated on being conciliatory and practically helpful. She found a black shirt for me somewhere and ironed it and, dressed in the darkest pants and jacket I owned, and slightly drunk, I made my way to my father's funeral.

*32.* The chapel was full, but not packed, and very quiet. There were, mainly, my father's relatives, and his children, and here and there I saw faces I had not seen since childhood, the faces of my father's one-time friends. They were very dark and solemn now, seeming somehow to suggest that they had known all along that something like this would happen. Chief among the mourners was my aunt, who had quarreled with my father all his life; by which I do not mean to suggest that her mourning was insincere or that she had not loved him. I suppose that she was one of the few people in the world who had, and their incessant quarreling proved precisely the strength of the tie that bound them. The only other person in the world, as far as I knew, whose relationship to my father rivaled my aunt's in depth was my mother, who was not there.

*33.* It seemed to me, of course, that it was a very long funeral. But it was, if anything, a rather shorter funeral than most, nor, since there were no overwhelming, uncontrollable expressions of grief, could it be called— if I dare to use the word—successful. The minister who preached my father's funeral sermon was one of the few my father had still been seeing as he neared his end. He presented to us in his sermon a man whom none of us had ever seen—a man thoughtful, patient, and forbearing, a Christian inspiration to all who knew him, and a model for his children. And no doubt the children, in their disturbed and guilty state, were almost ready to believe this; he had been remote enough to be anything and, anyway, the shock of the incontrovertible, that it was really our father lying up there in that casket, prepared the mind for anything. His sister moaned and this grief-stricken moaning was taken as corroboration. The other faces held a dark, non-committal thoughtfulness. This was not the man they had known, but they had scarcely expected to be confronted with *him*; this was, in a sense deeper than questions of fact, the man they had not known, and the man they had not known may have been the real one. The real man, whoever he had been, had suffered and now he was dead: this was all that was sure and all that mattered now. Every man in the chapel hoped that when his hour came he, too, would be eulogized, which is to say forgiven, and that all of his lapses, greeds, errors, and strayings from the truth would be invested with coherence and looked upon with charity. This was perhaps the last thing human beings could give each other and it was what they demanded, after all, of the Lord. Only the Lord saw the midnight tears, only He was present when one of His children, moaning and wringing hands, paced up and down the room. When one slapped one's child in anger the recoil in the heart reverberated through heaven and became part of the pain of the universe. And when the children were hungry and sullen and distrustful and one watched them, daily, growing wilder, and further away, and running headlong into danger, it was the Lord who knew what the charged heart endured as the strap was laid to the backside; the Lord alone who knew what one *would* have said if one had had, like the Lord, the gift of the living word. It was the Lord who knew of the impossibility every parent in that room faced: how to prepare the child for the day when the child would be despised and how to *create* in the child—by what means?—a stronger antidote to this poison than one had found for oneself. The avenues, side streets, bars, billiard halls, hospitals, police stations, and even the playgrounds of Harlem—not to mention the houses of correction, the jails, and the morgue—testified to the potency of the poison while remaining silent as to the efficacy of whatever antidote, irresistibly raising the question of whether or not such an antidote existed; raising, which was worse, the question of whether or not an antidote was desirable; perhaps poison should be fought with poison. With these several schisms in the mind and with more terrors in the heart than could be named, it was better not to judge the man who had gone down under an impossible burden. It was better to remember: *Thou knowest this man's fall; but thou knowest not his wrassling.*

34. While the preacher talked and I watched the children—years of changing their diapers, scrubbing them, slapping them, taking them to school, and scolding them had had the perhaps inevitable result of making me love them, though I am not sure I knew this then—my mind was busily breaking out with a rash of disconnected impressions. Snatches of popular songs, indecent jokes, bits of books I had read, movie sequences, faces, voices, political issues—I thought I was going mad; all these impressions

suspended, as it were, in the solution of the faint nausea produced in me by the heat and liquor. For a moment I had the impression that my alcoholic breath, inefficiently disguised with chewing gum, filled the entire chapel. Then someone began singing one of my father's favorite songs and, abruptly, I was with him, sitting on his knee, in the hot, enormous, crowded church which was the first church we attended. It was the Abyssinia Baptist Church on 138th Street. We had not gone there long. With this image, a host of others came. I had forgotten, in the rage of my growing up, how proud my father had been of me when I was little. Apparently, I had had a voice and my father had liked to show me off before the members of the church. I had forgotten what he had looked like when he was pleased but now I remembered that he had always been grinning with pleasure when my solos ended. I even remembered certain expressions on his face when he teased my mother—had he loved her? I would never know. And when had it all begun to change? For now it seemed that he had not always been cruel. I remembered being taken for a haircut and scraping my knee on the footrest of the barber's chair and I remembered my father's face as he soothed my crying and applied the stinging iodine. Then I remembered our fights, fights, which had been of the worst possible kind because my technique had been silence.

35. I remembered the one time in all our life together when we had really spoken to each other.

36. It was on a Sunday and it must have been shortly before I left home. We were walking, just the two of us, in our usual silence, to or from church. I was in high school and had been doing a lot of writing and I was, at about this time, the editor of the high school magazine. But I had also been a Young Minister and had been preaching from the pulpit. Lately, I had been taking fewer engagements and preached as rarely as possible. It was said in the church, quite truthfully, that I was "cooling off."

37. My father asked me abruptly, "You'd rather write than preach, wouldn't you?"

38. I was astonished at his question—because it was a real question. I answered, "Yes."

39. That was all we said. It was awful to remember that that was all we had *ever* said.

40. The casket now was opened and the mourners were being led up the aisle to look for the last time on the deceased. The assumption was that the family was too overcome with grief to be allowed to make this journey alone and I watched while my aunt was led to the casket and, muffled in black, and shaking, led back to her seat. I disapproved of forcing the children to look on their dead father, considering that the shock of his death, or, more truthfully, the shock of death as a reality, was already a little more than a child could bear, but my judgment in this matter

had been overruled and there they were, bewildered and frightened and very small, being led, one by one, to the casket. But there is also something very gallant about children at such moments. It has something to do with their silence and gravity and with the fact that one cannot help them. Their legs, somehow, seem *exposed*, so that it is at once incredible and terribly clear that their legs are all they have to hold them up.

41. I had not wanted to go to the casket myself and I certainly had not wished to be led there, but there was no way of avoiding either of these forms. One of the deacons led me up and I looked on my father's face. I cannot say that it looked like him at all. His blackness had been equivocated by powder and there was no suggestion in that casket of what his power had or could have been. He was simply an old man dead, and it was hard to believe that he had ever given anyone either joy or pain. Yet, his life filled that room. Further up the avenue his wife was holding his newborn child. Life and death so close together, and love and hatred, and right and wrong, said something to me which I did not want to hear concerning man, concerning the life of man.

42. After the funeral, while I was downtown desperately celebrating my birthday, a Negro soldier, in the lobby of the Hotel Braddock, got into a fight with a white policeman over a Negro girl. Negro girls, white policemen, in or out of uniform, and Negro males—in or out of uniform—were part of the furniture of the lobby of the Hotel Braddock and this was certainly not the first time such an incident had occurred. It was destined, however, to receive an unprecedented publicity, for the fight between the policeman and the soldier ended with the shooting of the soldier. Rumor, flowing immediately to the streets outside, stated that the soldier had been shot in the back, an instantaneous and revealing invention, and that the soldier had died protecting a Negro woman. The facts were somewhat different—for example, the soldier had not been shot in the back, and was not dead, and the girl seems to have been as dubious a symbol of womanhood as her white counterpart in Georgia usually is, but no one was interested in the facts. They preferred the invention because this invention expressed and corroborated their hates and fears so perfectly. It is just as well to remember that people are always doing this. Perhaps many of those legends, including Christianity, to which the world clings began their conquest of the world with just some such concerted surrender to distortion. The effect, in Harlem, of this particular legend was like the effect of a lit match in a tin of gasoline. The mob gathered before the doors of the Hotel Braddock simply began to swell and to spread in every direction, and Harlem exploded.

43. The mob did not cross the ghetto lines. It would have been easy, for example, to have gone over Morningside Park on the west side or to have crossed the Grand Central railroad tracks at 125th Street on the east side, to wreak havoc in white neighborhoods. The mob seems to have been

mainly interested in something more potent and real than the white face, that is, in white power, and the principal damage done during the riot of the summer of 1943 was to white business establishments in Harlem. It might have been a far bloodier story, of course, if, at the hour the riot began, these establishments had still been open. From the Hotel Braddock the mob fanned out, east and west along 125th Street, and for the entire length of Lenox, Seventh, and Eighth avenues. Along each of these avenues, and along each major side street—116th, 125th, 138th, and so on—bars, stores, pawnshops, restaurants, even little luncheonettes had been smashed open and entered and looted—looted, it might be added, with more haste than efficiency. The shelves really looked as though a bomb had struck them. Cans of beans and soup and dog food, along with toilet paper, corn flakes, sardines, and milk tumbled every which way, and abandoned cash registers and cases of beer leaned crazily out of the splintered windows and were strewn along the avenues. Sheets, blankets, and clothing of every description formed a kind of path, as though people had dropped them while running. I truly had not realized that Harlem *had* so many stores until I saw them all smashed open; the first time the word *wealth* ever entered my mind in relation to Harlem was when I saw it scattered in the streets. But one's first, incongruous impression of plenty was countered immediately by an impression of waste. None of this was doing anybody any good. It would have been better to have left the plate glass as it had been and the goods lying in the stores.

*44.* It would have been better, but it would also have been intolerable, for Harlem had needed something to smash. To smash something is the ghetto's chronic need. Most of the time it is the members of the ghetto who smash each other, and themselves. But as long as the ghetto walls are standing there will always come a moment when these outlets do not work. That summer, for example, it was not enough to get into a fight on Lenox Avenue, or curse out one's cronies in the barber shops. If ever, indeed, the violence which fills Harlem's churches, pool halls, and bars erupts outward in a more direct fashion, Harlem and its citizens are likely to vanish in an apocalyptic flood. That this is not likely to happen is due to a great many reasons, most hidden and powerful among them the Negro's real relation to the white American. This relation prohibits, simply, anything as uncomplicated and satisfactory as pure hatred. In order really to hate white people, one has to blot so much out of the mind—and the heart—that this hatred itself becomes an exhausting and self-destructive pose. But this does not mean, on the other hand, that love comes easily: the white world is too powerful, too complacent, too ready with gratuitous humiliation, and, above all, too ignorant and too innocent for that. One is absolutely forced to make perpetual qualifications and one's own reactions are always canceling each other out. It is this, really, which has driven so many people mad, both white and black. One is always in the position of having to decide between amputation and gangrene. Amputation is swift but time may prove that the amputation was not necessary—or one may delay the amputation too long. Gangrene is slow, but it is impossible to be sure that one is reading one's symptoms right. The idea of going through life as a cripple is more than one can bear, and equally unbearable is the risk of swelling up slowly, in agony, with poison. And the trouble, finally, is that the risks are real even if the choices do not exist.

45. "But as for me and my house," my father had said, "we will serve the Lord." I wondered, as we drove him to his resting place, what this line had meant for him. I had heard him preach it many times. I had preached it once myself, proudly giving it an interpretation different from my father's. Now the whole thing came back to me, as though my father and I were on our way to Sunday school and I were memorizing the golden text: *And if it seem evil unto you to serve the Lord, choose you this day whom you will serve; whether the gods which your fathers served that were on the other side of the flood, or the gods of the Amorites, in whose land ye dwell: but as for me and my house, we will serve the Lord.* I suspected in these familiar lines a meaning which had never been there for me before. All of my father's texts and songs, which I had decided were meaningless, were arranged before me at his death like empty bottles, waiting to hold the meaning which life would give them for me. This was his legacy: nothing is ever escaped. That bleakly memorable morning I hated the unbelievable streets and the Negroes and whites who had, equally, made them that way. But I knew that it was folly, as my father would have said, this bitterness was folly. It was necessary to hold on to the things that mattered. The dead man mattered, the new life mattered; blackness and whiteness did not matter; to believe that they did was to acquiesce in one's own destruction. Hatred, which could destroy so much, never failed to destroy the man who hated and this was an immutable law.

46. It began to seem that one would have to hold in the mind forever two ideas which seemed to be in opposition. The first idea was acceptance, the acceptance, totally without rancor, of life as it is, and men as they are: in the light of this idea, it goes without saying that injustice is a commonplace. But this did not mean that one could be complacent, for the second idea was of equal power: that one must never, in one's own life, accept these injustices as commonplace but must fight them with all one's strength. This fight begins, however, in the heart and it now had been laid to my charge to keep my own heart free of hatred and despair. This intimation made my heart heavy and, now that my father was irrecoverable, I wished that he had been beside me so that I could have searched his face for the answers which only the future would give me now.

# Questions

1. How do the ideas of paragraph 5 relate to the thesis of the whole selection? What is that thesis? In paragraph 5, find the places where Baldwin has repeated the same sound, and describe the effects achieved by the linking. Find the repetition of grammatical units that builds through parallel structure the sentence rhythms of paragraph 5.

2. What is the function of the incident with the waitress in New Jersey? What part does it illustrate of the whole thesis?

3. Baldwin speaks of his attending a movie entitled *"This Land is Mine"* and of going subsequently to a café labeled "American Diner" as—in view of his feelings and what happened to him—"patly ironical." What less "patly ironical" use can you perceive in Baldwin's emphasis on " 'real' " (paragraph 10) and *"real"* (paragraph 22)?

4. Notice that the opening paragraph suggests a connection between the race riots and the death of the author's father. Later we see this idea developed. What images are used? What is the point of making this connection? What is its relationship to the whole thesis?

5. Study paragraph 36. What devices of transition can you identify? Where is the style most vivid and concrete? Can the associations of the phrase "apocalyptic flood" be justified? Is there any paradox in Baldwin's application of the terms "ignorant and innocent" to the white world? Is there paradox in the last sentence? What does that sentence mean? *a statement that seems absurd or contradictory*

6. In paragraph 36 Baldwin says, "One is always in the position of having to decide between amputation and gangrene." Explain what he means. Is the analogy appropriate?

7. Find the Old Testament allusions in the selection. Find word choices suggesting the patriarchal temper of Baldwin's father. Does Baldwin's outlook as expressed here also show the influence of the Old Testament? If so, where?

8. Is Baldwin in any way speaking here beyond the context of the Negro's unhappy life in America? What evidence can you find for a definitive answer one way or another?

9. How does Baldwin fit the description of "the poet's way round" given by Ciardi in paragraph 19 of his essay?

## ·32·

*John Fitzgerald Kennedy*

# INAUGURAL ADDRESS: 1961

*1.* We observe today not a victory of party but a celebration of freedom —symbolizing an end as well as a beginning—signifying renewal as well as change. For I have sworn before you and Almighty God the same solemn oath our forebears prescribed nearly a century and three-quarters ago.

*2.* The world is very different now. For man holds in his mortal hands the power to abolish all forms of human poverty and all forms of human life. And yet the same revolutionary beliefs for which our forebears fought are still at issue around the globe—the belief that the rights of man come not from the generosity of the state but from the hand of God.

*3.* We dare not forget today that we are the heirs of that first revolution. Let the word go forth from this time and place, to friend and foe alike, that the torch has been passed to a new generation of Americans—born in this century, tempered by war, disciplined by a hard and bitter peace, proud of our ancient heritage—and unwilling to witness or permit the slow undoing of those human rights to which this nation has always been committed, and to which we are committed today at home and around the world.

*4.* Let every nation know, whether it wishes us well or ill, that we shall pay any price, bear any burden, meet any hardship, support any friend, oppose any foe to assure the survival and the success of liberty.

*5.* This much we pledge—and more.

*6.* To those old allies whose cultural and spiritual origins we share, we pledge the loyalty of faithful friends. United, there is little we cannot do in a host of new cooperative ventures. Divided, there is little we can do— for we dare not meet a powerful challenge at odds and split asunder.

*7.* To those new states whom we welcome to the ranks of the free, we pledge our word that one form of colonial control shall not have passed away merely to be replaced by a far more iron tyranny. We shall not always expect to find them supporting our view. But we shall always hope to find them strongly supporting their own freedom—and to remember that, in the past, those who foolishly sought power by riding the back of the tiger ended up inside.

Delivered at the Capitol in Washington, D.C., January 20, 1961.

8. To those peoples in the huts and villages of half the globe struggling to break the bonds of mass misery, we pledge our best efforts to help them help themselves, for whatever period is required—not because the Communists may be doing it, not because we seek their votes, but because it is right. If a free society cannot help the many who are poor, it cannot save the few who are rich.

9. To our sister republics south of our border, we offer a special pledge—to convert our good words into good deeds—in a new alliance for progress—to assist free men and free governments in casting off the chains of poverty. But this peaceful revolution of hope cannot become the prey of hostile powers. Let all our neighbors know that we shall join with them to oppose aggression or subversion anywhere in the Americas. And let every other power know that this hemisphere intends to remain the master of its own house.

10. To that world assembly of sovereign states, the United Nations, our last best hope in an age where the instruments of war have far outpaced the instruments of peace, we renew our pledge of support—to prevent it from becoming merely a forum for invective—to strengthen its shield of the new and the weak—and to enlarge the area in which its writ may run.

11. Finally, to those nations who would make themselves our adversary, we offer not a pledge but a request: that both sides begin anew the quest for peace, before the dark powers of destruction unleashed by science engulf all humanity in planned or accidental self-destruction.

12. We dare not tempt them with weakness. For only when our arms are sufficient beyond doubt can we be certain beyond doubt that they will never be employed.

13. But neither can two great and powerful groups of nations take comfort from our present course—both sides overburdened by the cost of modern weapons, both rightly alarmed by the steady spread of the deadly atom, yet both racing to alter that uncertain balance of terror that stays the hand of mankind's final war.

14. So let us begin anew—remembering on both sides that civility is not a sign of weakness, and sincerity is always subject to proof. Let us never negotiate out of fear. But let us never fear to negotiate.

15. Let both sides explore what problems unite us instead of belaboring those problems which divide us.

16. Let both sides, for the first time, formulate serious and precise proposals for the inspection and control of arms—and bring the absolute power to destroy other nations under the absolute control of all nations.

17. Let both sides seek to invoke the wonders of science instead of its terrors. Together let us explore the stars, conquer the deserts, eradicate disease, tap the ocean depths and encourage the arts and commerce.

18. Let both sides unite to heed in all corners of the earth the command

of Isaiah—to "undo the heavy burdens . . . [and] let the oppressed go free."

19. And if a beachhead of cooperation may push back the jungles of suspicion, let both sides join in creating a new endeavor—not a new balance of power, but a new world of law, where the strong are just and the weak secure and the peace preserved.

20. All this will not be finished in the first 100 days. Nor will it be finished in the first 1,000 days, nor in the life of this Administration, nor even perhaps in our lifetime on this planet. But let us begin.

21. In your hands, my fellow citizens, more than mine, will rest the final success or failure of our course. Since this country was founded, each generation of Americans has been summoned to give testimony to its national loyalty. The graves of young Americans who answered the call to service surround the globe.

22. Now the trumpet summons us again—not as a call to bear arms, though arms we need—not as a call to battle, though embattled we are— but a call to bear the burden of a long twilight struggle year in and year out, "rejoicing in hope, patient in tribulation"—a struggle against the common enemies of man: tyranny, poverty, disease and war itself.

23. Can we forge against these enemies a grand and global alliance, north and south, east and west, that can assure a more fruitful life for all mankind? Will you join in that historic effort?

24. In the long history of the world, only a few generations have been granted the role of defending freedom in its hour of maximum danger. I do not shrink from this responsibility—I welcome it. I do not believe that any of us would exchange places with any other people or any other generation. The energy, the faith, the devotion which we bring to this endeavor will light our country and all who serve it—and the glow from that fire can truly light the world.

25. And so, my fellow Americans: ask not what your country can do for you—ask what you can do for your country.

26. My fellow citizens of the world: ask not what America will do for you, but what together we can do for the freedom of man.

27. Finally, whether you are citizens of America or citizens of the world, ask of us here the same high standards of strength and sacrifice which we ask of you. With a good conscience our only sure reward, with history the final judge of our deeds, let us go forth to lead the land we love, asking His blessing and His help, but knowing that here on earth God's work must truly be our own.

# Questions

1. Comment upon the transition between paragraphs 1 and 2.
2. Why is the first sentence of paragraph 3 both a transitional and a topic sentence?
3. What repetition connects paragraphs 3 through 9?
4. Is paragraph 4 a periodic sentence?
5. What is the stylistic effect of the dash in paragraph 5?
6. In the last sentence of paragraph 6 what two allusions can you identify?
7. What is the meaning of paragraph 7? Describe a situation to which it applies. How is the allusion to riding the tiger appropriate?
8. Describe the sentence structure of paragraph 8. What is the meaning and logic of the last sentence?
9. Comment in paragraphs 8 and 9 upon the parallelism and the repetition of sounds and structure and words.
10. Find the metaphors and other figures of speech in the following paragraphs: 11, 13, 19, 22, 24.
11. Find as many examples of triads as you can throughout the speech.

# Concreteness and Symbol

## ~ VIII ~

### ·33·

*Alexander H. Leighton*

## THAT DAY AT HIROSHIMA

1. We approached Hiroshima a little after daybreak on a winter day, driving in a jeep below a leaden sky and in the face of a cold, wet wind. On either side of the road, black flat fields were turning green under winter wheat. Here and there peasants worked, swinging spades or grubbing in mud and water with blue hands. Some in black split-toed shoes left tracks like cloven hoofs. To the north, looming close over the level land, mountains thrust heavy summits of pine darkly against the overcast. To the south and far away, the bay lay in dull brightness under fitful rain.

2. "Hiroshima," said the driver, a GI from a Kansas farm, who had been through the city many times, "don't look no different from any other bombed town. You soon get used to it. You'll see little old mud walls right in the middle of town that wasn't knocked down. They been exaggerating about that bomb."

3. Within a few miles the fields along the road were replaced by houses and shops that looked worn and dull yet intact. On the road itself people straggled to work, some on bicycles, most of them on foot—tattered and bandy-legged old men, girls with red cheeks and bright eyes, ancient women under towering bundles, middle-aged men looking stiff in Western business suits. In one place there were several Koreans together, the women easily distinguished from the Japanese by their white blouses and the full skirts that swung as they strode. At a bus stop a crowd stood waiting in a line long enough to fill a train. Half a mile farther on we passed the bus, small, battered, and gray, standing half obliterated by the cloud of smoke that came from the charcoal burner at the back while the driver stood working at its machinery.

*4.* Children of all ages waved, laughed, and shouted at us as had the children in other parts of Japan.

*5.* "Haro-goodabye! Haro-goodabye!"

*6.* "Jeepu! Jeeeepu!"

*7.* Like the children of Hamelin to the piper, they came rushing, at the sound of our approach, from doorways and alleyways and from behind houses, to line up by the road and cheer. One little fellow of about six threw himself into the air, his little body twisting and feet kicking in a fit of glee.

*8.* The adults gazed at us with solemn eyes or looked straight ahead. They were more subdued than those I had seen elsewhere in Japan. The children seemed different, possessed by some common animation denied their elders—an animation which impelled them toward the occupation forces, toward the strong and the new.

*9.* Presently a two-story trade school appeared, with boards instead of window glass, and then a factory in the same condition. Soon there were shops and houses all along the way with windows missing. A house came into view with its roof pressed down, tiles scattered, and walls bulging outward. A shop with no front, like an open mouth, showed its contents, public and private, clear to the rear window.

*10.* The road turned to the Ota River, where the tide was running out and boats lay heaved over on the beach. A bridge ended suddenly like a headless neck. Now every house and shop was damaged and lay with only one end or a corner standing.

*11.* Then all the buildings ceased and we came as if from a forest out on a plain, as if from tumult into silence. Imagine a city dump with its smells of wet ashes, mold, and things rotting, but one that runs from your feet almost to the limits of vision. As is often the case with level and desolate places on the earth, the sky seemed close above it. The predominant colors were red and yellow, crumbles of stone, bricks, red earth, and rust. Low walls made rectangles that marked where houses had stood, like sites of prehistoric villages. Here and there in the middle distance, a few large buildings stood about, buttes in the rubble of the plain.

*12.* "You see them?" said the driver, as if it were a triumph for his side. "The bomb didn't knock *them* down."

*13.* Running like ruler lines through the waste were black roads surprisingly dotted with people, some on foot and some in carts of all sizes drawn by man, woman, horse, or cow. Clothing was old and tattered and of every combination from full European to full Japanese. People looked as if they had grabbed what they could from a rummage sale.

*14.* Occasionally, blending like protective coloration with the rubble were shacks built out of fragments of boards and iron. Around them were vegetable gardens, for the most part full of *daikon*, Japanese radish. A few more pretentious sheds were going up, shining bright yellow with new boards.

15. We slowed down to go around a piece of cornice that lay partly across the road like a glacial boulder, and from somewhere in a band of children who cheered and called to us came the gift of a tangerine that landed on the floor of the jeep. Wondering at them, I picked it up and put it in my pocket.

16. When crossing a bridge, we could see down through the swiftly running water to the stones and shells on the bottom. This clearness gave a feeling of odd contrast to the disorder of the land. We passed a number of trees burned black but still holding up some leafless branches as if in perpetual winter.

17. The drive ended at a large building that was still standing, a former bank, now a police headquarters, where I had an appointment with the chief to arrange for office space and guides. The driver said, as he got out, "This is it."

## II

18. One hears it said that, after all, Japanese cities were really a collection of tinderboxes, while American urban centers are made of stronger stuff. In Hiroshima there were many buildings of types common in the United States and some, prepared against earthquakes, far stronger. The engineers of the U.S. Strategic Bombing Survey concluded from their examination that "the overwhelming bulk of buildings in American cities would not stand up against an atomic bomb bursting at a mile or a mile and a half from them." To this must be added the realization that the bomb dropped at Hiroshima will be considered primitive by future standards.

19. The bank building which housed the police headquarters was a well-made structure of stone, three stories high. Through an imposing entrance my interpreter and I went past tall and solid metal doors that were bent inward like cardboard and no longer usable. The lobby was large and high, but dark because it had no window glass and the openings were boarded to keep out the wind. Through poor light there loomed the white face of a clock up on one wall, its hands pointing to 8:10—the time it had stopped on August 6.

20. In the years when that clock had been going, Hiroshima had been a city, at first unknown to Europe and America, then a source of immigrants to the United States, and finally an enemy port. It lay on a delta between the seven mouths of the Ota and was traversed by canals and an ancient highway that connected Kyoto in the east with Shimonoseki in the west. Close around the city stood mountains covered with red pine, while before it stretched the bay, indented with headlands and spread with

islands, in places narrow and steep like a fjord. In shallows near the shore, rows of poles stood as if in a bean patch, set in the sea to anchor oysters and to catch edible seaweed passing in the tide. In deeper water, fishing boats with hawkish prows and planked with red pine were tending nets. A few fishermen used cormorants to make their catch.

*21.* Hiroshima had expanses of park, residences, gardens, orange and persimmon trees. Since there had been much traveling back and forth by relatives of immigrants to California, the influence of the United States was marked. On main streets there were movies and restaurants with façades that would have fitted into shopping districts of Bakersfield or San Diego.

*22.* But Hiroshima was also ancient. Its feudal castle raised a five-story keep that could be seen a long distance over the level land of the delta. There were three large temples and many smaller ones and the tombs of the Asano family and of the wife and son of the leader of the Forty-seven Ronin, Oishi-Yoshio. There were also Christian churches, whose bells mingled with the temple gongs and the honking of auto horns and the rattling of trolleys.

*23.* The people of the city had earned their living by buying and selling farm produce and fish, by making mountain pines into boats for the fishing fleet of the Inland Sea, by meat packing, rubber processing, and oil refining, by making textiles from the cocoons of wild silkworms, by brewing rice and grape wine, by manufacturing paper umbrellas, needles, *tabi* socks, small arms, metal castings, and by working in utilities and services such as electricity, transportation, schools, and hospitals.

*24.* During the war there was an increase of industrialization, and plants grew up, chiefly in the outskirts.

*25.* There was a famous gay district with little streets along which a person walking in the night could hear laughter, the twang of the *shamisen,* and geishas singing.

*26.* The university had been an active cultural center but also stressed athletics, particularly swimming. There were sometimes mass aquatic exercises when hundreds of students would swim for miles, strung out in the bay in a long line with boats attending.

*27.* Although not a fortified town, Hiroshima was a major military command station, supply depot, and staging area because of its protected position and because of Ujina Harbor with access to the Pacific, the Sea of Japan, and the East China Sea. More than a third of the city's land was taken up with military installations, and from the harbor troopships left for Korea, Manchuria, China, and the southern regions. However, toward the end of hostilities, most of the shipping had ceased because of sinkings in the Inland Sea.

*28.* The population of Hiroshima was given as well over 300,000 before the war, but this was reduced by evacuation, before the atomic bomb fell, probably to about 245,000. It is still not certain how many the bomb killed, but the best estimate is from 70,000 to 80,000.

## III

29. About seven o'clock on the morning of August 6 there was an air-raid warning and three planes were reported in the vicinity. No one was much disturbed. For a long time B-29's flying over in small numbers had been a common sight. At some future date, Hiroshima might suffer an incendiary raid from masses of planes such as had devastated other Japanese cities. With this possibility in mind there had been evacuations, and firebreaks were being prepared. But on this particular morning there could be no disaster from just three planes.

30. By 7:30 the "all clear" had sounded and people were thinking again of the day's plans, looking forward to their affairs and engagements of the morning and afternoon. The castle keep stood in the sun. Children bathed in the river. Farmers labored in the fields and fishermen on the water. City stores and factories got under way with their businesses.

31. In the heart of the city near the buildings of the Prefectural Government and at the intersection of the business streets, everybody had stopped and stood in a crowd gazing up at three parachutes floating down through the blue air.

32. The bomb exploded several hundred feet above their heads.

33. The people for miles around Hiroshima, in the fields, in the mountains, and on the bay, saw a light that was brilliant even in the sun, and felt heat. A countrywoman was going out to her farm when suddenly, "I saw a light reflected on the mountain and then a streak just like lightning came."

34. A town official was crossing a bridge on his bicycle about ten miles from the heart of the city when he felt the right side of his face seared, and thinking that he had sunstroke, he jumped to the ground.

35. A woman who was washing dishes noticed that she felt "very warm on the side of my face next the wall. I looked out the window toward the city and saw something like a sun in bright color."

36. At a slower pace, after the flash, came the sound of the explosion, which some people have no recollection of hearing, while others described it as an earth-shaking roar, like thunder or a big wind. A black smoky mass, lit up with color, ascended into the sky and impressed beholders with its beauty. Red, gold, blue, orange, and many other shades mingled with the black.

37. Nearer to the city and at its edges, the explosion made a more direct and individual impact on people. Almost everyone thought that an ordinary bomb had landed very close to him, and only later realized the extent of the damage.

38. A man who was oiling the machinery in a factory saw the lights go

out and thought that something must be wrong with the electricity. "But when the roof started crumbling down, I was in a daze, wondering what was happening. Then I noticed my hands and feet were bleeding. I don't know how I hurt myself."

*39.* Another, who was putting points on needles, was knocked unconscious, and when he came to, found "all my surroundings burned to the ground and flames raging here and there. I ran home for my family without knowing I was burned around my head. When I arrived home, our house was devastated and destroyed by flames. I ran to the neighbors and inquired about my family and learned that they had all been taken to safety across the river."

*40.* An invalid who was drinking tea said, "The tin roof sidings came swirling into my room and everything was black. Rubble and glass and everything you can think of was blasted into my house."

*41.* Said a woman, "I was in the back of the house doing the washing. All of a sudden, the bomb exploded. My clothes were burned off and I received burns on my legs, arms, and back. The skin was just hanging loose. The first thing I did was run in the air-raid shelter and lie there exhausted. Then I thought of my baby in the house and ran back to it. The whole house was knocked down and was burning. My mother and father came crawling out of the debris, their faces and arms just black. I heard the baby crying, and crawled in and dug it out from under the burning embers. It was pretty badly burned. My mother carried it to the shelter."

*42.* In the heart of the city death prevailed and few were left to tell us about it. That part of the picture has to be reconstructed, as in archeology, from the remains.

*43.* The crowd that stood gazing upward at the parachutes went down withered and black, like a burned-out patch of weeds. Flames shot out of the castle keep. Trolleys bulging with passengers stopped, and all died at once, leaving burned figures still standing supporting each other and fingers fused to the straps. The military at their barracks and offices were wiped out. So too were factories full of workers, including students from schools, volunteers from neighboring towns working on the firebreaks, children scavenging for wood, the Mayor's staff, and the units for air-raid precaution, fire, welfare, and relief. The larger war industries, since they were on the fringe of the city, were for the most part not seriously damaged. Most of the personnel in the Prefectural Government offices were killed, though the Governor himself happened to be in Tokyo. In hospitals and clinics, patients, doctors, and nurses all died together, as did the priests and pastors of the temples and the churches. Of 1780 nurses, 1654 were killed, and 90 per cent of the doctors in Hiroshima were casualties.

*44.* People who were in buildings that sheltered them from the instantaneous effects that accompanied the flash were moments later decapitated or cut to ribbons by flying glass. Others were crushed as walls and floors gave way even in buildings that maintained their outer shells erect. In the thousands of houses that fell, people were pinned below the wreckage, not killed in many cases, but held there till the fire that swept the city caught up with them and put an end to their screams.

45. A police chief said that he was in his back yard when the bomb went off. He was knocked down and a concrete wall fell over him, but he was able to dig himself out and go at once toward the police station in the bank. "When I arrived at the office, I found ten policemen, some severely wounded. These were evacuated to a place of safety where they could get aid. We tried to clean up the glass from the windows, but fire was spreading and a hot southerly wind was blowing. We used a hose with water pump water from a well. We carried buckets up from the basement to the from a hydrant and also formed a bucket brigade. At noon the water in the hydrants gave out, but in this building we were lucky because we could pump water from a well. We carried buckets up from the basement to the roof and threw water down over the building. People on the road were fainting from the heat and we threw water on them too and carried them into the one room in the building that had not been affected by the bomb. We applied oil and ointment to those who had burns.

46. "About 1:00 P.M. we began to apply first aid to the people outside, since the fire seemed under control as far as this building was concerned. A doctor came to help. He himself was wounded in one leg. By night this place was covered by a mass of people. One doctor applied all the first aid."

47. A doctor who was at a military hospital outside Hiroshima said that about an hour after the bomb went off, "many, many people came rushing to my clinic. They were rushing in all directions of the compass from the city. Many were stretcher cases. Some had their hair burned off, were injured in the back, had broken legs, arms, and thighs. The majority of the cases were those injured from glass; many had glass imbedded in the body. Next to the glass injuries, the most frequent were those who had their faces and hands burned, and also the chest and back. Most of the people arrived barefooted; many had their clothes burned off. Women were wearing men's clothing and men were wearing women's. They had put on anything they could pick up along the way.

48. "On the first day about 250 came, who were so injured they had to stay in the hospital, and we also attended about 500 others. Of all of these about 100 died."

49. A talkative man in a newspaper office said that the most severely burned people looked like red shrimps. Some had "skin which still burned sagging from the face and body with a reddish-white skin underneath showing."

50. A reporter who was outside the city at the time of the explosion, but came in immediately afterward, noticed among the dead a mother with a baby held tightly in her arms. He saw several women running around

nude, red from burns, and without hair. Many people climbed into water tanks kept for putting out fires and there died. "The most pathetic cases were the small children looking for their parents. There was one child of about eleven with a four-year-old on his back, looking, looking for his mother in vain."

51. Shortly after the bomb fell, there was a high wind, or "fire storm" engendered by the heat, that tore up trees and, whirling over the river, made waterspouts. In some areas rain fell.

52. The severely burned woman who had been washing when the bomb fell said that she went down to the river, where "there were many people just dripping from their burns. Many of them were so badly burned that you could see the meat. By this time it was raining pretty badly. I could not walk or lie down or do anything. Water poured into the shelter and I received water blisters as well as blisters from the burns. It rained a lot right after the bomb."

53. Although the fire burned for days, the major destruction did not take very long. A fisherman out on the bay said, "I saw suddenly a flash of light. I thought something burned my face. I hid in the boat face down. When I looked up later, Hiroshima was completely burned."

IV

54. Hiroshima, of course, never had been prepared for a disaster of the magnitude which overtook it, but in addition the organized sources of aid that did exist were decimated along with everything else. As a result, rescue had to come from surrounding areas, and soon trucks and trains were picking up the wounded, while hospitals, schools, temples, assembly halls, and tents were preparing to receive them. However, the suburbs and surrounding areas were overwhelmed by the rush of immediate survivors out of the bombed region and so, for about a day, help did not penetrate far into the city. This, together with the fact that survivors who were physically uninjured were stunned and bewildered, resulted in great numbers of the wounded dying from lack of aid.

55. The vice-mayor of a neighboring town that began receiving the wounded about 11:30 in the morning said, "Everybody looked alike. The eyes appeared to be a mass of melted flesh. The lips were split up and also looked like a mass of molten flesh. Only the nose appeared the same as before. The death scene was awful. The patient would turn blue and when we touched the body the skin would stick to our hands."

56. Those who ventured into Hiroshima were greeted by sights they were reluctant to describe. A businessman reported: "The bodies of half-dead people lay on the roadside, on the bridges, in the water, in the gardens, and everywhere. It was a sight no one wants to see. Practically all of these people were nude. Their color was brownish blackish and some of their bodies were dripping. There was a fellow whose head was half

burned so that I thought he was wearing a hat." Another man said, "The bodies of the dead were so burned that we could not distinguish men from women."

57. In the public parks great numbers of both wounded and dead were congregated. There were cries for aid and cries for water and there were places where unidentifiable shapes merely stirred.

58. In the late afternoon, aid began to come farther into the city from the outer edges. Rice balls and other food were brought. From their mission up the valley a number of Jesuits came, and one of them, Father Siemes, gave a vivid and careful description of what he had seen, when he was later interviewed by members of the Bombing Survey in Tokyo. He said, "Beneath the wreckage of the houses along the way many had been trapped and they screamed to be rescued from the oncoming flames. They had to be left to their fate."

59. On a bridge, he encountered a procession of soldiers "dragging themselves along with the help of staves or carried by their less severely injured comrades. Abandoned on the bridge there stood with sunken heads a number of horses with large burns on their flanks.

60. "Fukai, the secretary of the mission, was completely out of his mind. He did not want to leave the house when the fires were burning closer, and explained that he did not want to survive the destruction of his fatherland." He had to be carried away by force.

61. After dark, the priests helped pull from the river two children who suffered chills and then died. There was a sand-spit in the river, covered with wounded, who cried for help and who were afraid that the rising tide would drown them. After midnight, "only occasionally did we hear calls for help."

62. Many patients were brought to an open field right behind Hiroshima station, and tents were set up for them. Doctors came in from the neighboring prefectures and from near-by towns such as Yamaguchi, Okayama, and Shimane. The Army also took part in relief measures, and all available military facilities and units were mobilized to that end.

63. A fisherman who came to Hiroshima to see what had happened said, "I cannot describe the situation in words, it was so pitiful. To see so many people dead was a terrible sight. Their clothes were shredded and their bodies puffed up, some with tongues hanging out. They were dead in all shapes."

64. As late as the second day the priests noted that among cadavers there were still many wounded alive. "Frightfully injured forms beckoned to us and then collapsed."

65. They carried some to the hospitals, but "we could not move everybody who lay exposed to the sun." It did not make much difference, anyway, for in the hospitals there was little that could be done. They just lay in the corridors, row on row, and died.

66. A businessman came into Hiroshima on the third day. "I went to my brother's house in the suburbs and found that all were wounded but none killed. They were stunned and could hardly speak. The next day, one of the four children died. She got black and blue in the face, just as if you had mashed your finger, and had died fifteen minutes after that. In another half hour, her sister did the same thing and she died also."

67. The wife of a soldier who had been with the Hiroshima troops said, "My husband was a soldier and so he was to die, but when it actually happened, I wondered why we did not all go with him. They called me and I went to see. I was to find him in the heap, but I decided against looking at the bodies. I want to remember him as he was—big and healthy, not some horribly charred body. If I saw that, it would remain forever in my eyes."

68. A police chief told how the dead were collected and burned. "Many could not be identified. In cases where it was possible, the corpses or the ashes were given to the immediate family. Mostly, the cremation was done by the police or the soldiers, and the identified ashes were given to the family. The ashes of those not identified were turned over to the City Hall. There still are boxes in the City Hall. Occasionally even now one is identified, or is supposed to be identified, and is claimed."

69. The destroyed heart of Hiroshima consisted of 4.7 square miles, and the best estimates indicate that the mortality rate was 15,000 to the square mile. For many days funeral processions moved along the roads and through the towns and villages all around Hiroshima. The winds were pervaded by the smell of death and cremation. At night the skies were lit with the flames of funeral pyres.

V

70. Very few of the people we interviewed at Hiroshima attempted to make a play for sympathy or to make us feel guilty. The general manner was one which might be interpreted as due either to lingering apathy and absence of feeling consequent on shock, or to reserve which masked hate. It was probably a mixture of both, in varying degrees in different people. But on the surface everyone appeared willing to coöperate and oblige.

71. An official of a near-by small town thought that "if America had such a weapon, there was no use to go on. Many high school students in Hiroshima who were wounded in the raid spoke incoherently on their deathbeds, saying, 'Please avenge that raid for us somehow.' However, most of the people felt that since it was war, it was just *shikata ga nai*, could not be helped. But we were unified in the idea that we had to win the war."

72. A newspaper reporter said that after the bomb fell, some felt that this was the end, while others wanted to go on regardless. "Those who

had actually experienced the bomb were the ones who wanted to quit, while those who had not, wanted to go on."

73. The wife of a soldier killed in the blast said, "Though many are resentful against America, I feel no animosity. It was an understood war and the use of weapons was fair. I only wonder why they didn't let the people know about this bomb and give us a chance, before bombing us, to give up."

74. A police chief believed that the general reaction among the people was one of surprise and a feeling that "we have taken the worst beating, we have been the goats." He said, "They felt that America had done a terrible thing and were very bitter, but after the surrender they turned on the Japanese military. They felt they had been fooled, and wondered if the military knew that the bomb was coming and why they did not take steps. The bomb made no difference in the fighting spirit of the people: it drew them together and made them more coöperative. My eldest son was killed, but I felt that it was destiny that ruled. When I see people who got away without any injury, I feel a little pang of envy naturally, but I don't feel bitter toward them."

75. Poking in the ruins one day, I came on the stone figure of a dog, one of that grinning type derived from China which commonly guards the entrances to temples. It was tilted on its pedestal but undamaged, and the grin gleamed out as if it were hailing me. Its rakish air and its look of fiendish satisfaction with all that lay around drew me on to inspect it more closely. It was then apparent that the look was not directed at me, but out somewhere beyond. It was, of course, only a piece of stone, and it displayed no particular artistic merit; yet in looking at it I felt that I was a clod, while it had a higher, sentient wisdom locked up within.

76. The look and the feeling it inspired were familiar and I groped to remember where I had seen it before other than on temple dogs. The eyes were creased in a fashion that did not exactly connotate mirth, and the lips were drawn far back in a smile that seemed to blend bitterness, glee, and compassion. The word "sardonic" came to mind, and this led to recognition and a realization of terrible appropriateness.

77. All who have acquaintance with the dead know the curious smile that may creep over the human face as *rigor mortis* sets in, a smile of special quality called by doctors *risus sardonicus*. The dog had this look, and it seemed to me probable that some ancient Oriental sculptor, in seeking an expression for temple guardians that would drive off evil spirits, had taken this death grin as his model, and thus it had come down through hundreds of years to this beast looking out on Hiroshima.

78. Many a soldier has seen this face looking up at him from the field of battle, before he himself was wearing it, and many a priest and doctor has found himself alone with it in a darkened room. As with the dog, at

first the look seems at you, and then beyond you, as if there lay at last behind it knowledge of the huge joke of life which the rest of us feel vaguely but cannot comprehend. And there is that tinge of compassion that is as dreadful as it is unknowable.

79. As I continued to study this stone face, it began to appear that the grin was not directed at the waste and the destruction around, at the red and yellow and the smells, any more than it was at me. It was not so much a face looking at Hiroshima as it was the face of Hiroshima. The carved eyes gazed beyond the rubble, beyond the gardens of radishes and fields of winter wheat, beyond the toiling adults and the rippling children with their tangerines and shouts of "Haro-goodabye!" surging up with new life like flowers and weeds spreading over devastation, beyond the mountains with red pines in the blue sky, beyond all these, over the whole broad shoulder of the world to where, in cities and towns, watches on wrists and clocks on towers still ticked and moved. The face seemed to be smiling and waiting for the harvest of the wind that had been sown.

80. There was one woman in Hiroshima who said, "If there are such things as ghosts, why don't they haunt the Americans?"

81. Perhaps they do.

# Questions

1. The mind, when overwhelmed in experience with sheer pain, horror or numbers, tends to shut itself off. How does Leighton use the principles of *selectivity* and *contrast* throughout his report in order to keep the horror of that day fresh in the reader's mind as he recounts it?

2. In spite of the factual form of this essay, what indications can you find that Leighton is trying to persuade the reader to a point of view or emotional attitude? List them and describe it.

3. Explain the reasons for the essay's division into five parts. What unity does each part have and how are they related to each other?

4. What function does the driver serve in Part I?

5. Explain why Leighton presents the kind of census and guidebook information he does in Part II. What general justification can be made for its inclusion, for each of the details?

6. Should paragraphs 30 and 31 perhaps have been omitted since Leighton was not there and could not have seen what he reports?

7. In the final section of Part V, the symbol of the smiling stone dog is clearly a means for Leighton to make a statement about his experience. What is that statement? List the elements that paragraph 79 echoes from the first

section of the essay. How does the perspective from which they are now seen differ from that of the first section? Why does he refer to clocks and watches in paragraph 79? What does the dog's sardonic knowledge seem to be?

·34·

*Alfred Kazin*

# FROM THE SUBWAY TO THE SYNAGOGUE

*1.* . . . All my early life lies open to my eye within five city blocks. When I passed the school, I went sick with all my old fear of it. With its standard New York public-school brown brick courtyard shut in on three sides of the square and the pretentious battlements overlooking that cockpit in which I can still smell the fiery sheen of the rubber ball, it looks like a factory over which has been imposed the facade of a castle. It gave me the shivers to stand up in the courtyard again; I felt as if I had been mustered back into the service of those Friday morning "tests" that were the terror of my childhood.

*2.* It was never learning I associated with that school: only the necessity to succeed, to get ahead of the others in the daily struggle to "make a good impression" on our teachers, who grimly, wearily, and often with ill-concealed distaste watched against our relapsing into the natural savagery they expected of Brownsville boys. The white, cool, thinly ruled record book sat over us from their desks all day long, and had remorselessly entered into it each day—in blue ink if we had passed, in red ink if we had not—our attendance, our conduct, our "effort," our merits and demerits; and to the last possible decimal point in calculation, our standing in an unending series of "tests"—surprise tests, daily tests, weekly tests, formal midterm tests, final tests. They never stopped trying to dig out of us whatever small morsel of fact we had managed to get down the night before. We had to prove that we were really alert, ready for anything, always in the race. That white thinly ruled record book figured in my mind as the judgment seat; the very thinness and remote blue lightness of its lines instantly showed its cold authority over me; so much space

had been left on each page, columns and columns in which to note down
everything about us, implacably and forever. As it lay there on a teacher's
desk, I stared at it all day long with such fear and anxious propriety that
I had no trouble believing that God, too, did nothing but keep such record
books, and that on the final day He would face me with an account in
Hebrew letters whose phonetic dots and dashes looked strangely like
decimal points counting up my every sinful thought on earth.

3. All teachers were to be respected like gods, and God Himself was
the greatest of all school superintendents. Long after I had ceased to believe that our teachers could see with the back of their heads, it was still
understood, by me, that they knew everything. They were the delegates
of all visible and invisible power on earth—of the mothers who waited on
the stoops every day after three for us to bring home tales of our daily
triumphs; of the glacially remote Anglo-Saxon principal, whose very name
was King; of the incalculably important Superintendent of Schools who
would someday rubberstamp his name to the bottom of our diplomas in
grim acknowledgment that we had, at last, given satisfaction to him, to
the Board of Superintendents, and to our benefactor the City of New York
—and so up and up, the government of the United States and to the great
Lord Jehovah Himself. My belief in teachers' unlimited wisdom and power
rested not so much on what I saw in them—how impatient most of them
looked, how wary—but on our abysmal humility, at least in those of us
who were "good" boys, who proved by our ready compliance and "manners" that we wanted to get on. The road to a professional future would be
shown us only as we pleased *them. Make a good impression the first day
of the term, and they'll help you out. Make a bad impression, and you
might as well cut your throat.* This was the first article of school folklore,
whispered around the classroom the opening day of each term. You
made the "good impression" by sitting firmly at your wooden desk, hands
clasped; by silence for the greatest part of the live-long day; by standing up obsequiously when it was so expected of you; by sitting down noise-
lessly when you had answered a question; by "speaking nicely," which
meant reproducing their painfully exact enunciation; by "showing manners," or an ecstatic submissiveness in all things; by outrageous flattery;
by bringing little gifts at Christmas, on their birthdays, and at the end
of the term—the well-known significance of these gifts being that they
come not from us, but from our parents, whose eagerness in this matter
showed a high level of social consideration, and thus raised our standing
in turn.

4. It was not just our quickness and memory that were always being
tested. Above all, in that word I could never hear without automatically
seeing it raised before me in gold-plated letters, it was our *character*.
I always felt anxious when I heard the word pronounced. Satisfactory as
my "character" was, on the whole, except when I stayed too long in the

playground reading; outrageously satisfactory, as I can see now, the very sound of the word as our teachers coldly gave it out from the end of their teeth, with a solemn weight on each dark syllable, immediately struck my heart cold with fear—they could not believe I really had it. Character was never something you had; it had to be trained in you, like a technique. I was never very clear about it. On our side *character* meant demonstrative obedience; but teachers already had it—how else could they have become teachers? They had it; the aloof Anglo-Saxon principal whom we remotely saw only on ceremonial occasions in the assembly was positively encased in it; it glittered off his bald head in spokes of triumphant light; the President of the United States had the greatest conceivable amount of it. Character belonged to great adults. Yet we were constantly being driven onto it; it was the great threshold we had to cross. *Alfred Kazin, having shown proficiency in his course of studies and having displayed satisfactory marks of character. . . .* Thus someday the hallowed diploma, passport to my further advancement in high school. But there—I could already feel it in my bones—they would put me through even more doubting tests of character; and after that, if I should be good enough and bright enough, there would be still more. *Character* was a bitter thing, racked with my endless striving to please. The school—from every last stone in the courtyard to the battlements frowning down at me from the walls—was only the stage for a trial. I felt that the very atmosphere of learning that surrounded us was fake—that every lesson, every book, every approving smile was only a pretext for the constant probing and watching of me, that there was not a secret in me that would not be decimally measured into that white record book. All week long I lived for the blessed sound of the dismissal gong at three o'clock on Friday afternoon.

5. I was awed by this system, I believed in it, I respected its force. The alternative was "going bad." The school was notoriously the toughest in our tough neighborhood, and the dangers of "going bad" were constantly impressed upon me at home and in school in dark whispers of the "reform school" and in examples of boys who had been picked up for petty thievery, rape, or flinging a heavy inkwell straight into a teacher's face. Behind any failure in school yawned the great abyss of a criminal career. Every refractory attitude doomed you with the sound "Sing Sing." Anything less than absolute perfection in school always suggested to my mind that I might fall out of the daily race, be kept back in the working class forever, or—dared I think of it?—fall into the criminal class itself.

6. I worked on a hairline between triumph and catastrophe. Why the odds should always have felt so narrow I understood only when I realized how little my parents thought of their own lives. It was not for myself alone that I was expected to shine, but for them—to redeem the constant anxiety of their existence. I was the first American child, their offering to the strange new God; I was to be the monument of their liberation from

the shame of being—what they were. And that there was shame in this was a fact that everyone seemed to believe as a matter of course. It was in the gleeful discounting of themselves—what do we know? with which our parents greeted every fresh victory in our savage competition for "high averages," for prizes, for a few condescending words of official praise from the principal at assembly. It was in the sickening invocation of "Americanism"—the word itself accusing us of everything we apparently were not. Our families and teachers seemed tacitly agreed that we were somehow to be a little ashamed of what we were. Yet it was always hard to say why this should be so. It was certainly not—in Brownsville!— because we were Jews, or simply because we spoke another language at home, or were absent on our holy days. It was rather that a "refined," "correct," "nice" English was required of us at school that we did not naturally speak, and that our teachers could never be quite sure we would keep. This English was peculiarly the ladder of advancement. Every future young lawyer was known by it. Even the Communists and Socialists on Pitkin Avenue spoke it. It was bright and clean and polished. We were expected to show it off like a new pair of shoes. When the teacher sharply called a question out, then your name, you were expected to leap up, face the class, and eject those new words fluently off the tongue.

7. There was my secret ordeal: I could never say anything except in the most roundabout way; I was a stammerer. Although I knew all those new words from my private reading—I read walking in the street, to and from the Children's Library on Stone Avenue; on the fire escape and the roof; at every meal when they would let me; read even when I dressed in the morning, propping my book up against the drawers of the bureau as I pulled on my long black stockings—I could never seem to get the easiest words out with the right dispatch, and would often miserably signal from my desk that I did not know the answer rather than get up to stumble and fall and crash on every word. If, angry at always being put down as lazy or stupid, I did get up to speak, the black wooden floor would roll away under my feet, the teacher would frown at me in amazement, and in unbearable loneliness I would hear behind me the groans and laughter: *tuh-tuh-tuh-tuh.*

8. The word was my agony. The word that for others was so effortless and so neutral, so unburdened, so simple, so exact, I had first to meditate in advance, to see if I could make it, like a plumber fitting together odd lengths and shapes of pipe. I was always preparing words I could speak, storing them away, choosing between them. And often, when the word did come from my mouth in its great and terrible birth, quailing and bleeding as if forced through a thornbush, I would not be able to look the others in the face, and would walk out in the silence, the infinitely echoing silence behind my back, to say it all cleanly back to myself as

I walked in the streets. Only when I was alone in the open air, pacing the roof with pebbles in my mouth, as I had read Demosthenes had done to cure himself of stammering; or in the street, where all words seemed to flow from the length of my stride and the color of the houses as I remembered the perfect tranquillity of a phrase in *Beethoven's Romance in F* I could sing back to myself as I walked—only then was it possible for me to speak without the infinite premeditations and strangled silences I toiled through whenever I got up at school to respond with the expected, the exact answer.

9. It troubled me that I could speak in the fullness of my own voice only when I was alone on the streets, walking about. There was something unnatural about it; unbearably isolated. I was not like the others! At midday, every freshly shocking Monday noon, they sent me away to a speech clinic in a school in East New York, where I sat in a circle of lispers and cleft palates and foreign accents holding a mirror before my lips and rolling difficult sounds over and over. To be sent there in the full light of the opening week, when everyone else was at school or going about his business, made me feel as if I had been expelled from the great normal body of humanity. I would gobble down my lunch on my way to the speech clinic and rush back to the school in time to make up for the classes I had lost. One day, one unforgettable dread day, I stopped to catch my breath on a corner of Sutter Avenue, near the wholesale fruit markets, where an old drugstore rose up over a great flight of steps. In the window were dusty urns of colored water floating off iron chains; cardboard placards advertising hairnets, EX-LAX: a great illustrated medical chart headed THE HUMAN FACTORY, which showed the exact course a mouthful of food follows as it falls from chamber to chamber of the body. I hadn't meant to stop there at all, only to catch my breath; but I so hated the speech clinic that I thought I would delay my arrival for a few minutes by eating my lunch on the steps. When I took the sandwich out of my bag, two bitterly hard pieces of hard salami slipped out of my hand and fell through a grate onto a hill of dust below the steps. I remember how sickeningly vivid an odd thread of hair looked on the salami, as if my lunch were turning stiff with death. The factory whistles called their short, sharp blasts stark through the middle of noon, beating at me where I sat outside the city's magnetic circle. I had never known, I knew instantly I would never in my heart again submit to, such wild passive despair as I felt at that moment, sitting on the steps before THE HUMAN FACTORY, where little robots gathered and shoveled the food from chamber to chamber of the body. They had put me out into the streets, I thought to myself; with their mirrors and their everlasting pulling at me to imitate their effortless bright speech and their stupefaction that a boy could stammer and stumble on every other English word he carried in his head,

they had put me out into the streets, had left me high and dry on the steps of that drugstore staring at the remains of my lunch turning black and grimy in the dust. '

# Questions

1. What images convey "the terror of my childhood" in the first paragraph?
2. What words and phrases in paragraph 2 amplify and make concrete the causes of young Kazin's fear? Explain the symbolism involved in the final sentence of this paragraph.
3. How does the cultural premise "God is terrible but just" explain the young Kazin's outlook and control author Kazin's account of his early schooling? How does the imagery of the final paragraph reflect a basic psychological change in the author as a young boy?
4. What does THE HUMAN FACTORY symbolize in the last paragraph?
5. In paragraph 5, defend the ordering of the details in series in the second and last sentences. Is the first sentence arranged in the order of climax?
6. In the last paragraph what function is served by the sentence, "I remember how sickeningly vivid an odd thread of hair looked on the salami, as if my lunch were turning stiff with death"? Why is the hair vivid? Why does the sentence end in death?
7. Discuss the tone of the last paragraph by considering the following: "I would gobble down my lunch," EX-LAX, "two bitterly hard pieces of hard salami," the "sharp blasts stark through the middle of noon," the paradox of "wild passive despair," the lunch "turning black and grimy in the dust," and the rhythm of the sentence structures.
8. How do Kazin's responses to his early years at school compare and contrast with your own?

# Illustration and Naturalness

## ~ IX ~

·35·

*George Orwell*

# SHOOTING AN ELEPHANT

*1.* In Moulmein, in Lower Burma, I was hated by large numbers of people—the only time in my life that I have been important enough for this to happen to me. I was sub-divisional police officer of the town, and in an aimless, petty kind of way anti-European feeling was very bitter. No one had the guts to raise a riot, but if a European woman went through the bazaars alone somebody would probably spit betel juice over her dress. As a police officer I was an obvious target and was baited whenever it seemed safe to do so. When a nimble Burman tripped me up on the football field and the referee (another Burman) looked the other way, the crowd yelled with hideous laughter. This happened more than once. In the end the sneering yellow faces of young men that met me everywhere, the insults hooted after me when I was at a safe distance, got badly on my nerves. The young Buddhist priests were the worst of all. There were several thousands of them in the town and none of them seemed to have anything to do except stand on street corners and jeer at Europeans.

*2.* All this was perplexing and upsetting. For at that time I had already made up my mind that imperialism was an evil thing and the sooner I chucked up my job and got out of it the better. Theoretically—and secretly, of course—I was all for the Burmese and all against their oppressors, the British. As for the job I was doing, I hated it more bitterly than I can perhaps make clear. In a job like that you see the dirty work of Empire at close quarters. The wretched prisoners huddling in the stinking cages of the lock-ups, the grey, cowed faces of the long-term convicts, the scarred buttocks of the men who had been flogged with bamboos—all these oppressed me with an intolerable sense of guilt. But I could get nothing into perspective. I was young and ill-educated and I had had to think out my problems in the utter silence that is imposed on every Englishman in the East. I did not even know that the British Empire is dying, still less did I know that it is a great deal better than the younger empires that are going to supplant it. All I knew was that I was stuck between my hatred of the empire I served and my rage against the evil-spirited little beasts who tried to make my job impossible. With one part of my mind I thought of the British Raj as an unbreakable tyranny, as something clamped down, in *saecula saeculorum*, upon the will of prostrate peoples; with another part I thought that the greatest joy in the world would be to drive a bayonet into a Buddhist priest's guts. Feelings like these are the normal by-products of imperialism; ask any Anglo-Indian official, if you can catch him off duty.

*3.* One day something happened which in a roundabout way was enlightening. It was a tiny incident in itself, but it gave me a better glimpse than I had had before of the real nature of imperialism—the real motives for which despotic governments act. Early one morning the sub-inspector at a police station the other end of the town rang me up on the 'phone and said that an elephant was ravaging the bazaar. Would I please come and do something about it? I did not know what I could do, but I wanted to see what was happening and I got on to a pony and started out. I took my rifle, an old .44 Winchester and much too small to kill an elephant, but I thought the noise might be useful *in terrorem*. Various Burmans stopped me on the way and told me about the elephant's doings. It was not, of course, a wild elephant, but a tame one which had gone "must." It had been chained up, as tame elephants always are when their attack of "must" is due, but on the previous night it had broken its chain and escaped. Its mahout, the only person who could manage it when it was in that state, had set out in pursuit, but had taken the wrong direction and was now twelve hours' journey away, and in the morning the elephant had suddenly reappeared in the town. The Burmese population had no weapons and were quite helpless against it. It had already destroyed somebody's bamboo hut, killed a cow and raided some fruit-stalls and devoured the stock; also it had met the municipal rubbish van and, when the driver jumped out and took to his heels, had turned the van over and inflicted violences upon it.

*4.* The Burmese sub-inspector and some Indian constables were waiting for me in the quarter where the elephant had been seen. It was a very poor quarter, a labyrinth of squalid bamboo huts, thatched with palm-leaf, winding all over a steep hillside. I remember that it was a cloudy, stuffy morning at the beginning of the rains. We began questioning the people as to where the elephant had gone and, as usual, failed to get any definite information. That is invariably the case in the East; a story always sounds clear enough at a distance, but the nearer you get to the scene of events the vaguer it becomes. Some of the people said that the elephant had gone in one direction, some said that he had gone in another, some professed not even to have heard of any elephant. I had almost made up my mind that the whole story was a pack of lies, when we heard yells a little distance away. There was a loud, scandalized cry of "Go away, child! Go away this instant!" and an old woman with a switch in her hand came round the corner of a hut, violently shooing away a crowd of naked children. Some more women followed, clicking their tongues and exclaiming; evidently there was something that the children ought not to have seen. I rounded the hut and saw a man's dead body sprawling in the mud. He was an Indian, a black Dravidian coolie, almost naked, and he could not have been dead many minutes. The people said that the elephant had come suddenly upon him round the corner of the hut, caught him with its trunk, put its foot on his back and ground him into the earth. This was the rainy season and the ground was soft, and his face had scored a trench a foot deep and a couple of yards long. He was lying on his belly with arms crucified and head sharply twisted to one side. His face was coated with mud, the eyes wide open, the teeth bared and grinning with an expression of unendurable agony. (Never tell me, by the way, that the dead look peaceful. Most of the corpses I have seen looked devilish.) The friction of the great beast's foot had stripped the skin from his back as neatly as one skins a rabbit. As soon as I saw the dead man I sent an orderly to a friend's house nearby to borrow an elephant rifle. I had already sent back the pony, not wanting it to go mad with fright and throw me if it smelt the elephant.

5. The orderly came back in a few minutes with a rifle and five cartridges, and meanwhile some Burmans had arrived and told us that the elephant was in the paddy fields below, only a few hundred yards away. As I started forward practically the whole population of the quarter flocked out of the houses and followed me. They had seen the rifle and were all shouting excitedly that I was going to shoot the elephant. They had not shown much interest in the elephant when he was merely ravaging their homes, but it was different now that he was going to be shot. It was a bit of fun to them, as it would be to an English crowd; besides they wanted the meat. It made me vaguely uneasy. I had no intention of shooting the elephant—I had merely sent for the rifle to defend myself if necessary—and it is always unnerving to have a crowd following you. I marched down the hill, looking and feeling a fool, with the rifle over my shoulder and an ever-growing army of people jostling at my heels. At the bottom, when you got away from the huts, there was a metalled road and beyond that a miry waste of paddy fields a thousand yards across, not yet ploughed but soggy from the first rains and dotted with coarse grass. The elephant was standing eight yards from the road, his left side towards us. He took not the

slightest notice of the crowd's approach. He was tearing up bunches of grass, beating them against his knees to clean them and stuffing them into his mouth.

6. I had halted on the road. As soon as I saw the elephant I knew with perfect certainty that I ought not to shoot him. It is a serious matter to shoot a working elephant—it is comparable to destroying a huge and costly piece of machinery—and obviously one ought not to do it if it can possibly be avoided. And at that distance, peacefully eating, the elephant looked no more dangerous than a cow. I thought then and I think now that his attack of "must" was already passing off; in which case he would merely wander harmlessly about until the mahout came back and caught him. Moreover, I did not in the least want to shoot him. I decided that I would watch him for a little while to make sure that he did not turn savage again, and then go home.

7. But at that moment I glanced round at the crowd that had followed me. It was an immense crowd, two thousand at the least and growing every minute. It blocked the road for a long distance on either side. I looked at the sea of yellow faces above the garish clothes—faces all happy and excited over this bit of fun, all certain that the elephant was going to be shot. They were watching me as they would watch a conjurer about to perform a trick. They did not like me, but with the magical rifle in my hands I was momentarily worth watching. And suddenly I realized that I should have to shoot the elephant after all. The people expected it of me and I had got to do it; I could feel their two thousand wills pressing me forward, irresistibly. And it was at this moment, as I stood there with the rifle in my hands, that I first grasped the hollowness, the futility of the white man's dominion in the East. Here was I, the white man with his gun, standing in front of the unarmed native crowd—seemingly the leading actor of the piece; but in reality I was only an absurd puppet pushed to and fro by the will of those yellow faces behind. I perceived in this moment that when the white man turns tyrant it is his own freedom that he destroys. He becomes a sort of hollow, posing dummy, the conventionalized figure of a sahib. For it is the condition of his rule that he shall spend his life in trying to impress the "natives," and so in every crisis he has got to do what the "natives" expect of him. He wears a mask, and his face grows to fit it. I had got to shoot the elephant. I had committed myself to doing it when I sent for the rifle. A sahib has got to act like a sahib; he has got to appear resolute, to know his own mind and do definite things. To come all that way, rifle in hand, with two thousand people marching at my heels, and then to trail feebly away, having done nothing—no, that was impossible. The crowd would laugh at me. And my whole life, every white man's life in the East, was one long struggle not to be laughed at.

8. But I did not want to shoot the elephant. I watched him beating his

bunch of grass against his knees, with that preoccupied grandmotherly air that elephants have. It seemed to me that it would be murder to shoot him. At that age I was not squeamish about killing animals, but I had never shot an elephant and never wanted to. (Somehow it always seems worse to kill a *large* animal.) Besides, there was the beast's owner to be considered. Alive, the elephant was worth at least a hundred pounds; dead, he would only be worth the value of his tusks, five pounds, possibly. But I had got to act quickly. I turned to some experienced-looking Burmans who had been there when we arrived, and asked them how the elephant had been behaving. They all said the same thing: he took no notice of you if you left him alone, but he might charge if you went too close to him.

9. It was perfectly clear to me what I ought to do. I ought to walk up to within, say, twenty-five yards of the elephant and test his behavior. If he charged, I could shoot; if he took no notice of me, it would be safe to leave him until the mahout came back. But also I knew that I was going to do no such thing. I was a poor shot with a rifle and the ground was soft mud into which one would sink at every step. If the elephant charged and I missed him, I should have about as much chance as a toad under a steam-roller. But even then I was no thinking particularly of my own skin, only of the watchful yellow faces behind. For at that moment, with the crowd watching me, I was not afraid in the ordinary sense, as I would have been if I had been alone. A white man mustn't be frightened in front of "natives"; and so, in general, he isn't frightened. The sole thought in my mind was that if anything went wrong those two thousand Burmans would see me pursued, caught, trampled on and reduced to a grinning corpse like that Indian up the hill. And if that happened it was quite probable that some of them would laugh. That would never do. There was only one alternative. I shoved the cartridges into the magazine and lay down on the road to get a better aim.

10. The crowd grew very still, and a deep, low, happy sigh, as of people who see the theatre curtain go up at last, breathed from innumerable throats. They were going to have their bit of fun after all. The rifle was a beautiful German thing with cross-hair sights. I did not then know that in shooting an elephant one would shoot to cut an imaginary bar running from ear-hole to ear-hole. I ought, therefore, as the elephant was sideways on, to have aimed straight at his ear-hole; actually I aimed several inches in front of this, thinking the brain would be further forward.

11. When I pulled the trigger I did not hear the bang or feel the kick— one never does when a shot goes home—but I heard the devilish roar of glee that went up from the crowd. In that instant, in too short a time, one would have thought, even for the bullet to get there, a mysterious, terrible change had come over the elephant. He neither stirred nor fell, but every line of his body had altered. He looked suddenly stricken,

shrunken, immensely old, as though the frightful impact of the bullet had paralysed him without knocking him down. At last, after what seemed a long time—it might have been five seconds, I dare say—he sagged flabbily to his knees. His mouth slobbered. An enormous senility seemed to have settled upon him. One could have imagined him thousands of years old. I fired again into the same spot. At the second shot he did not collapse but climbed with desperate slowness to his feet and stood weakly upright, with legs sagging and head drooping. I fired a third time. That was the shot that did for him. You could see the agony of it jolt his whole body and knock the last remnant of strength from his legs. But in falling he seemed for a moment to rise, for as his hind legs collapsed beneath him he seemed to tower upward like a huge rock toppling, his trunk reaching skyward like a tree. He trumpeted, for the first and only time. And then down he came, his belly towards me, with a crash that seemed to shake the ground even where I lay.

*12.* I got up. The Burmans were already racing past me across the mud. It was obvious that the elephant would never rise again, but he was not dead. He was breathing very rhythmically with long rattling gasps, his great mound of a side painfully rising and falling. His mouth was wide open—I could see far down into caverns of pale pink throat. I waited a long time for him to die, but his breathing did not weaken. Finally I fired my two remaining shots into the spot where I thought his heart must be. The thick blood welled out of him like red velvet, but still he did not die. His body did not even jerk when the shots hit him, the tortured breathing continued without a pause. He was dying, very slowly and in great agony, but in some world remote from me where not even a bullet could damage him further. I felt that I had got to put an end to that dreadful noise. It seemed dreadful to see the great beast lying there, powerless to move and yet powerless to die, and not even to be able to finish him. I sent back for my small rifle and poured shot after shot into his heart and down his throat. They seemed to make no impression. The tortured gasps continued as steadily as the ticking of a clock.

*13.* In the end I could not stand it any longer and went away. I heard later that it took him half an hour to die. Burmans were bringing dahs and baskets even before I left, and I was told they had stripped his body almost to the bones by the afternoon.

*14.* Afterwards, of course, there were endless discussions about the shooting of the elephant. The owner was furious, but he was only an Indian and could do nothing. Besides, legally I had done the right thing, for a mad elephant has to be killed, like a mad dog, if its owner fails to control it. Among the Europeans opinion was divided. The older men said I was right, the younger men said it was a damn shame to shoot an elephant for killing a coolie, because an elephant was worth more than any damn Coringhee coolie. And afterwards I was very glad that the coolie had been killed; it put me legally in the right and it gave me a sufficient pretext for shooting the elephant. I often wondered whether any of the others grasped that I had done it solely to avoid looking a fool.

## ·36·

### *C. S. Lewis*

# THE LAW OF RIGHT AND WRONG

### I

1. Every one has heard people quarrelling. Sometimes it sounds funny and sometimes it sounds merely unpleasant; but however it sounds, I believe we can learn something very important from listening to the kind of things they say. They say things like this: "That's my seat, I was there first"—"Leave him alone, he isn't doing you any harm"—"Why should you shove in first?"—"Give me a bit of your orange, I gave you a bit of mine"—"How'd you like it if anyone did the same to you?"—"Come on, you promised." People say things like that every day, educated people as well as uneducated, and children as well as grown-ups.

2. Now what interests me about all these remarks is that the man who makes them isn't just saying that the other man's behaviour doesn't happen to please him. He is appealing to some kind of standard of behaviour which he expects the other man to know about. And the other man very seldom replies, "To hell with your standard." Nearly always he tries to make out that what he has been doing doesn't really go against the standard, or that if it does, there is some special excuse. He pretends there is some special reason in this particular case why the person who took the seat first should not keep it, or that things were quite different when he was given the bit of orange, or that something has turned up which lets him off keeping his promise. It looks, in fact, very much as if both parties had in mind some kind of Law or Rule of fair play or decent behaviour or morality or whatever you like to call it, about which they really agreed. And they have. If they hadn't, they might, of course, fight like animals, but they couldn't *quarrel* in the human sense of the word. Quarrelling means trying to show that the other man is in the wrong. And there'd be no sense

in trying to do that unless you and he had some part of agreement as to what Right and Wrong are; just as there'd be no sense in saying that a footballer had committed a foul unless there was some agreement about the rules of football.

3. Now this Law or Rule about Right and Wrong used to be called the Law of Nature. Nowadays, when we talk of the "laws of nature" we usually mean things like gravitation, or heredity, or the laws of chemistry. But when the older thinkers called the Law of Right and Wrong the Law of Nature, they really meant the Law of *Human* Nature. The idea was that, just as falling stones are governed by the law of gravitation and chemicals by chemical laws, so the creature called man also had *his* law—with this great difference, that the stone couldn't choose whether it obeyed the law of gravitation or not, but a man could choose either to obey the Law of Human Nature or to disobey it. They called it Law of Nature because they thought that every one knew it by nature and didn't need to be taught it. They didn't mean, of course, that you mightn't find an odd individual here and there who didn't know it, just as you find a few people who are colour-blind or have no ear for a tune. But taking the race as a whole, they thought that the human idea of Decent Behaviour was obvious to every one. And I believe they were right. If they weren't, then all the things we say about this war are nonsense. What is the sense in saying the enemy are in the wrong unless Right is a real thing which the Germans at bottom know as well as we do and ought to practise? If they had no notion of what we mean by right, then, though we might still have to fight them, we could no more blame them for that than for the colour of their hair.

4. I know that some people say the idea of Law of Nature or decent behaviour known to all men is unsound, because different civilisations and different ages have had quite different moralities. But they haven't. They have only had *slightly* different moralities. Just think what a *quite* different morality would mean. Think of a country where people were *admired* for running away in battle, or where a man felt *proud* for double-crossing all the people who had been kindest to him. You might just as well to try to imagine a country where two and two made five. Men have differed as regards what people you ought to be unselfish to—whether it was only your own family, or your fellow countrymen, or every one. But they have always agreed that you oughtn't to put yourself first. Selfishness has never been admired. Men have differed as to whether you should have one wife or four. But they have always agreed that you mustn't simply have any woman you liked.

5. But the most remarkable thing is this. Whenever you find a man who says he doesn't believe in a real Right and Wrong, you will find the same man going back on this a moment later. He may break his promise to you, but if you try breaking one to him he'll be complaining "It's not

fair" before you can say Jack Robinson. A nation may say treaties don't matter; but then, next minute, they spoil their case by saying that the particular treaty they want to break was an unfair one. But if treaties don't matter, and if there's no such things as Right and Wrong—in other words, if there is no Law of Nature—what is the difference between a fair treaty and an unfair one? Haven't they given away the fact that, whatever they say, they really know the Law of Nature just like anyone else?

6. It seems, then, we are forced to believe in a real Right and Wrong. People may be sometimes mistaken about them, just as people sometimes get their sums wrong; but they are not a matter of mere taste and opinion any more than the multiplication table. Now if we're agreed about that, I go on to my next point, which is this. None of us are really keeping the Law of Nature. If there are any exceptions among you, I apologise to them. They'd better switch on to another station, for nothing I'm going to say concerns them. And now, turning to the ordinary human beings who are left:

7. I hope you won't misunderstand what I'm going to say. I'm not preaching, and Heaven knows I'm not pretending that I'm better than anyone else. I'm only trying to call attention to a fact; the fact that this year, or this month, or, more likely, this very day, we have failed to practise ourselves the kind of behaviour we expect from other people. There may be all sorts of excuses for us. That time you were so unfair to the children was when you were very tired. That slightly shady business about the money—the one you've almost forgotten—came when you were very hard up. And what you promised to do for old So-and-so and have never done—well, you never would have promised if you'd known how frightfully busy you were going to be. And as for your behaviour to your wife (or husband), if I knew how irritating they could be, I wouldn't wonder at it—and who the dickens am I, anyway? I am just the same. That is to say, I don't succeed in keeping the Law of Nature very well, and the moment anyone tells me I'm not keeping it, there starts up in my mind a string of excuses as long as your arm. The question at the moment is not whether they are good excuses. The point is that they are one more proof of how deeply, whether we like it or not, we believe in the Law of Nature. If we didn't believe in decent behaviour, why should we be so anxious to make excuses for not having behaved decently? The truth is, we believe in decency so much—we feel the Rule or Law pressing on us so— that we can't bear to face the fact that we're breaking it, and consequently we try to shift the responsibility. For you notice that it's only for our bad behaviour that we find all these explanations. We put our *bad* temper down to being tired or worried or hungry; we put our good temper down to ourselves.

8. Well, those are the two points I wanted to make tonight. First, that human beings, all over the earth, have this curious idea that they

*ought* to behave in a certain way, and can't really get rid of it. Secondly, that they don't in fact behave in that way. They know the Law of Nature; they break it. These two facts are the foundation of all clear thinking about ourselves and the universe we live in.

## II

9. IF THEY are the foundation, I had better stop to make that foundation firm before I go on. Some of the letters I have had from listeners show that a good many people find it difficult to understand just what this Law of Human Nature, or Moral Law, or Rule of Decent Behaviour is.

10. For example, some people write to me saying, "Isn't what you call the Moral Law simply our herd instinct and hasn't it been developed just like all our other instincts?" Now I don't deny that we may have a herd instinct: but that isn't what I mean by the Moral Law. We all know what it feels like to be prompted by instinct—by mother love, or sexual instinct, or the instinct for food. It means you feel a strong want or desire to act in a certain way. And, of course, we sometimes do feel just that sort of desire to help another person: and no doubt that desire is due to the herd instinct. But feeling a desire to help is quite different from feeling that you ought to help whether you want to or not. Supposing you hear a cry for help from a man in danger. You will probably feel two desires—one a desire to give help (due to your herd instinct), the other a desire to keep out of danger (due to the instinct for self-preservation). But you will find inside you, in addition to these two impulses, a third thing which tells you that you ought to follow the impulse to help, and suppress the impulse to run away. Now this thing that judges between two instincts, that decides which should be encouraged, can't itself be either of them. You might as well say that the sheet of music which tells you, at a given moment, to play one note on the piano and not another, is itself one of the notes on the keyboard. The Moral Law is, so to speak, the tune we've got to play: our instincts are merely the keys.

11. Another way of seeing that the Moral Law is not simply one of our instincts is this. If two instincts are in conflict, and there is nothing in a creature's mind except those two instincts, obviously the stronger of the two must win. But at those moments when we are most conscious of the Moral Law, it usually seems to be telling us to side with the weaker of the two impulses. You probably *want* to be safe much more than you want to help the man who is drowning: but the Moral Law tells you to help him all the same. And doesn't it often tell us to try to make the right impulse stronger than it naturally is? I mean, we often feel it our duty to stimulate the herd instinct, by waking up our imaginations and arousing our pity and so on, so as to get up enough steam for doing the right thing. But surely we are not acting *from* instinct when we set about making an instinct stronger than it is? The thing that says to you, "Your herd instinct

is asleep. Wake it up," can't itself *be* the herd instinct. The thing that tells you which note on the piano needs to be played louder can't itself be that note!

12. Here is a third way of seeing it. If the Moral Law was one of our instincts, we ought to be able to point to some one impulse inside us which was always what we call "good," always in agreement with the rule of right behaviour. But you can't. There is none of our impulses which the Moral Law won't sometimes tell us to suppress, and none which it won't sometimes tell us to encourage. It is a mistake to think that some of our impulses—say, mother love or patriotism—are good, and others, like sex or the fighting instinct, are bad. All we mean is that the occasions on which the fighting instinct or the sexual desire need to be restrained are rather more frequent than those for restraining mother love or patriotism. But there are situations in which it is the duty of a married man to encourage his sexual impulse and of a soldier to encourage the fighting instinct. There are also occasions on which a mother's love for her own children or a man's love for his own country have to be suppressed or they'll lead to unfairness towards other people's children or countries. Strictly speaking, there aren't such things as good and bad impulses. Think once again of a piano. It hasn't got two kinds of notes on it, the "right" notes and the "wrong" ones. Every single note is right at one time and wrong at another. The Moral Law isn't any one instinct or any set of instincts: it is something which makes a kind of tune (the tune we call goodness or right conduct) by directing the instincts.

13. By the way, this point is of great practical consequence. The most dangerous thing you can do is to take any one impulse of your own nature and set it up as the thing you ought to follow at all costs. There's not one of them which won't make us into devils if we set it up as an absolute guide. You might think love of humanity in general was safe, but it isn't. If you leave out justice you'll find yourself breaking agreements and faking evidence in trials "for the sake of humanity," and become in the end a cruel and treacherous man.

14. Other people write to me saying, "Isn't what you call the Moral Law just a social convention, something that is put into us by education?" I think there is a misunderstanding here. The people who ask that question are usually taking it for granted that if we have learned a thing from parents and teachers, then that thing must be merely a human invention. But, of course, that isn't so. We all learned the multiplication table at school. A child who grew up alone on a desert island wouldn't know it. But surely it doesn't follow that the multiplication table is simply a human convention, something human beings have made up for themselves and might have made different if they had liked? *Of course* we learn the Rule of Decent Behaviour from parents and teachers, as we learn everything else. But some of the things we learn are mere convention which might

have been different—we learn to keep to the left of the road, but it might just as well have been the rule to keep to the right—and others of them, like mathematics, are real truths. The question is which class the Law of Human Nature belongs to.

*15.* There are two reasons for saying it belongs to the same class as mathematics. The first is, as I said last time, that though there are differences between the moral ideas of one time or country and those of another, the differences aren't really very big—you can recognise the same Law running through them all: whereas mere conventions—like the rule of the road or the kind of clothes people wear—differ completely. The other reason is this. When you think about these differences between the morality of one people and another, do you think that the morality of one people is ever better or worse than that of another? Have any of the changes been improvements? If not, then of course there could never be any moral progress. Progress means not just changing, but changing for the better. If no set of moral ideas were truer or better than any other there would be no sense in preferring civilised morality to savage morality, or Christian morality to Nazi morality. In fact, of course, we all do believe that some moralities *are* better than others. We do believe that some of the people who tried to change the moral ideas of their own age were what we'd call Reformers or Pioneers—people who understood morality better than their neighbours did. Very well then. The moment you say that one set of moral ideas can be better than another, you are, in fact, measuring them both by a standard, saying that one of them conforms to that standard more nearly than the other. But the standard that measures two things is something different from either. You are, in fact, comparing them both with some Real Morality, admitting that there is *really* such a thing as Right, independent of what people think, and that some people's ideas get nearer to that real Right than others. Or put it this way. If your moral ideas can be truer, and those of the Nazis less true, there must be something—some Real Morality—for them to be true *about*. The reason why your idea of New York can be truer or less true than mine is that New York is a real place, existing quite apart from what either of us thinks. If when each of us said "New York" each meant merely "The town I am imagining in my own head," how could one of us have truer ideas than the other? There'd be no question of truth or falsehood at all. In the same way, if the Rule of Decent Behaviour meant simply, "whatever each nation happens to approve," there'd be no sense in saying that any one nation had ever been more correct in its approval than any other; no sense in saying that the world could ever grow better or worse.

*16.* So you see that though the differences between people's ideas of Decent Behaviour often make you suspect that there is no real natural Law of Behaviour at all, yet the things we are bound to think about these differences really prove just the opposite. But one word before I end. I think that some listeners have been exaggerating the differences, because they have not distinguished between differences of morality and differences of belief about facts. For example, one listener wrote and said, "Three hundred years ago people in England were putting witches to death. Was that what you call the Rule of Human Nature or Right Conduct?" But surely the reason we don't execute witches is that we don't believe there are such things. If we did—if we really thought that there were people going about who had sold themselves to the devil and received supernatural powers from him in return and were using these powers to kill their neighbours or drive them mad or bring bad weather, surely we'd all agree that if anyone deserved the death penalty, then these filthy quislings did? There's no difference of moral principle here: the difference is simply about matter of fact. It may be a great advance in *knowledge* not to believe in witches: there's no moral advance in not executing them when you don't think they are there! You wouldn't call a man humane for ceasing to set mouse-traps if he did so because he believed there were no mice in the house.

# Theme Topics

1. Write a description of an event (an accident, a fire, a lost child) or a place (a mountain or sea in storm, a desert, a city street, an airport, bus or train station) first with the disciplined reporting of concrete details of Leighton's style then employing some of the more elaborate devices and personal response of Baldwin's style.

2. Describe a place or a person, first making the person or place attractive, then, using many of the same details, making it unattractive.

3. Write a description of a street in which you employ details from all five senses and discipline them to create a single dominant impression.

4. Write a subjective description of a place in which you report your emotion (fear, joy, boredom) in the place, making each detail contribute to that emotion.

5. Describe yourself in a situation with another person in which you attempt to make clear the complexity and irony of the situation and the relationship, as Baldwin did with his father and Orwell did in "Shooting An Elephant."

6. Write an analysis of the style, tone, and organization of one of the essays in this section.

*Part Three*

# ARGUMENT

# Language and Correctness

## ~ X ~

# ISSUES, ASSUMPTIONS, AND METHODS OF REFUTATION

### ISSUES

Before one can argue he must make the question clear. The question, called in debate the proposition, must not only be a single question but usually state or imply a judgment. Propositions of fact, which are common in the realm of law, history, and medicine, are rare in everyday student and nonprofessional life. One does not argue about easily verifiable facts, even though whether or not Mr. X was at his home on the night of January 26th may require complex argument in a courtroom. Argument usually focuses on which of two courses of action to take, or on whether a certain action or decision was good or bad. Intelligent people do not argue about how much aid the United States provided to South America last year. A little research uncovers the answer. But whether we should provide more or less aid this year, or whether we provided too little or too much last year, are questions for argument. Of central importance in that argument will be the establishment of criteria for judging what was enough aid, and it is on this question of establishing values that the two sides take their stand.

The article by Wilson Follett and the typical answer to his position made by Bergen Evans are both arguments insofar as they are concerned with establishing values upon which a dictionary can be judged. Both are concerned, as are the essays following, with the proposition that *Webster's Third International Dictionary* is or is not a good dictionary, that it is or is not what a new dictionary should be. Wilson Follett's article, however, is a review and is not formally organized even though the argument, and the assumptions on which it is based, are implied. The dictionary is not what it should be for a reason; and this reason, since it is common to most of the particular cases cited, is crucial. The dictionary is not what it should be, according to Follett, because the lexicographers have abrogated their authority to judge language usage. This, then, is the crucial issue: in selecting words and putting labels on them, must dictionary makers record what usages they find to be prevalent without passing judgment on them?

Other issues are raised in this argument by the opposition, for example, problems of capitalization, the omission of many proper names from literature and mythology, and the failure to include other information that may very well more properly be found in an encyclopedia; but all participants admit these issues to be of distinctly secondary importance.

A secondary issue of this kind should be distinguished from an admitted issue. An issue granted by a writer as a valid objection to his case is referred to as an admitted issue. One might, for example, admit that he disapproves of the politics of a certain nation and yet argue in favor of granting U.S. aid to that nation. Such an admission would not only clarify the argument but also strengthen it; for readers would then not be alienated by inferring that tacit approval of the nation's politics entered the argument to grant aid to that nation.

### ASSUMPTIONS

Notice that the above example operates upon an assumption: that we can afford to provide economic aid to other nations. Wilson Follett in the essay that follows bases his case against *Webster's Third International Dictionary* upon assumptions. Aside from the assumption, implied by the crucial issue, that certain standards of usage should have been indicated either by selection or by labels, Follett bases his case upon others. First, he assumes that there is "a standard, staple, traditional language of general reading." Secondly, he assumes that readers will accept as standard anything included in a dictionary. Such assumptions, whether they are valid, invalid, or partially one or the other, are obviously an important part of an argument: an opponent who is unwilling to accept them can undercut a whole case. Defenders of the dictionary attack these very assumptions on the part of Follett. They say that a standard English does not exist and that readers need not assume a word to be correct for all occasions simply because they find it in a dictionary.

A student should thus clarify his argument in terms of its issues, its values, and its assumptions. What issue is crucial, what is secondary, and what is to be admitted—without loss and with possible gain—to the other side? What am I assuming that the other side may not grant to be the common ground of the discussion?

An argument must be defensive. Not only in answering a case already stated but in presenting your own, you should consider the other side, construct the issues of the case against you, and either admit or refute those issues.

### METHODS OF REFUTATION

Denial is a matter of counter-assertion; one counters an assertion with its opposite. One must then correct the opponent's facts, deny the relevance of his proof, or deny that what he presents as proof, though relevant, is sufficient.

Distinction may involve discrimination in the use of a word or reinterpretation of a motive or an action. In regard to the principles of liberty and equality, for example, one might attempt to distinguish precisely where the rights of an individual end and those of society begin. Here in the opening pieces on *Webster's Third* Follet summarizes his charges by calling the dictionary a "fighting document." Evans, on the other hand, writing under "sound and fury" from Follett and others, attempts to distinguish the principles behind the making of the dictionary by examining the achievements of "the science of descriptive linguistics."

Retort is the twisting of an opponent's statement or his evidence so that it cuts against his own position. The announcement of a price for a public project may be evidence of frugality to one political party, and to the other evidence of wild extravagance.

Identification of a fallacy in an opponent's reasoning may be a fourth method of refutation or a supplement to denial, distinction, and retort. (*See* Robert Gorham Davis, "Logic and Logical Fallacies.")

Challenging an opponent's authority to discuss a subject may, in some instances, be a fair method of refutation. James Sledd, for example, challenges the preparation of some critics of the dictionary. He assumes that a knowledge of language, dictionaries, and current controversy is a prerequisite for good reviewing. We would expect historians to present evidence on historical questions and doctors to give medical evidence. The distinction should be observed, however, between challenging the authority of an opponent to speak on a particular question and challenging his authority on questions where no specific knowledge or experience is required. Obviously open or covert attacks upon the character of an opponent are entirely out of order.

· 37 ·

*Wilson Follett*

# SABOTAGE IN SPRINGFIELD

*1.* Of dictionaries, as of newspapers, it might be said that the bad ones are too bad to exist, the good ones too good not to be better. No dictionary of a living language is perfect or ever can be, if only because the time

From *The Atlantic Monthly* (January, 1962). Reprinted by permission of Mrs. Wilson Follett.

required for compilation, editing, and issuance is so great that shadows of obsolescence are falling on parts of any such work before it ever gets into the hands of a user. Preparation of *Webster's Third New International Dictionary of the English Language* began intensively in the Springfield establishment of G. & C. Merriam Company in 1936, but the century was nine months into its seventh decade before any outsider could have his first look at what had been accomplished. His first look is, of course, incompetent to acquaint him with the merits of the new work; these no one can fully discover without months or years of everyday use. On the other hand, it costs only minutes to find out that what will rank as the great event of American linguistic history in this decade, and perhaps in this quarter century, is in many crucial particulars a very great calamity.

2. Why should the probable and possible superiorities of the Third New International be so difficult to assess, the shortcomings so easy? Because the superiorities are special, departmental, and recondite, the shortcomings general and within the common grasp. The new dictionary comes to us with a claim of 100,000 new words or new definitions. These run almost overwhelmingly to scientific and technological terms or meanings that have come into existence since 1934, and especially to words classified as ISV (belonging to the international scientific vocabulary). No one person can possibly use or even comprehend all of them; the coverage in this domain, certainly impressive to the nonspecialist, may or may not command the admiration of specialists. It is said that historians of the graphic arts and of architecture were displeased with the 1934 Webster, both for its omissions and for some definitions of what it included in their fields. Its 1961 successor may have disarmed their reservations; only they can pronounce.

3. But all of us may without brashness form summary judgments about the treatment of what belongs to all of us—the standard, staple, traditional language of general reading and speaking, the ordinary vocabulary and idioms of novelist, essayist, letter writer, reporter, editorial writer, teacher, student, advertiser; in short, fundamental English. And it is precisely in this province that Webster III has thrust upon us a dismaying assortment of the questionable, the perverse, the unworthy, and the downright outrageous.

4. Furthermore, what was left out is as legitimate a grievance to the ordinary reader as anything that has been put in. Think—if you can—of an unabridged dictionary from which you cannot learn who Mark Twain was (though *mark twain* is entered as a leadsman's cry), or what were the names of the apostles, or that the Virgin was Mary the mother of Jesus of Nazareth, or what and where the District of Columbia is!

5. The disappointment and the shock are intensified, of course, because of the unchallenged position earned by the really unabridged immediate predecessor of this strange work. *Webster's New International Dictionary,*

Second Edition (1934), consummated under the editorship of William
Allan Neilson, at once became the most important reference book in the
world to American writers, editors, teachers, students, and general readers
—everyone to whom American English was a matter of serious interest.
What better could the next revision do than extend the Second Edition in
the direction of itself, bring it up to date, and correct its scattering of over-
sights and errata?

6. The 1934 dictionary had been, heaven knows, no citadel of conservatism, no last bastion of puristical bigotry. But it had made shrewd reports
on the status of individual words; it had taken its clear, beautifully written
definitions from fit uses of an enormous vocabulary by judicious users; it
had provided accurate, impartial accounts of the endless guerrilla war between grammarian and antigrammarian and so given every consultant the
means to work out his own decisions. Who could wish the forthcoming
revision any better fortune than a comparable success in applying the
same standards to whatever new matter the new age imposed?

7. Instead, we have seen a century and a third of illustrious history
largely jettisoned; we have seen a novel dictionary formula improvised,
in great part out of snap judgments and the sort of theoretical improve
ment that in practice impairs; and we have seen the gates propped wide
open in enthusiastic hospitality to miscellaneous confusions and corruptions. In fine, the anxiously awaited work that was to have crowned cisat-
lantic linguistic scholarship with a particular glory turns out to be a scandal
and a disaster. Worse yet, it plumes itself on its faults and parades as
siduously cultivated sins as virtues without precedent.

8. Examination cannot proceed far without revealing that Webster III,
behind its front of passionless objectivity, is in truth a fighting document.
And the enemy it is out to destroy is every obstinate vestige of linguistic
punctilio, every surviving influence that makes for the upholding of standards, every criterion for distinguishing between better usages and worse.
In other words, it has gone over bodily to the school that construes traditions as enslaving, the rudimentary principles of syntax as crippling, and
taste as irrelevant. This revolution leaves it in the anomalous position of
loudly glorifying its own ancestry—which is indeed glorious—while tacitly
sabotaging the principles and ideals that brought the preceding Merriam-
Webster to its unchallengeable pre-eminence. The Third New International is at once a resounding tribute of lip service to the Second and a
wholesale repudiation of it—a sweeping act of apology, contrition, and
reform.

9. The right-about-face is, of course, particularly evident in the vocabulary approved. Within a few days of publication the new dictionary was
inevitably notorious for its unreserved acceptance as standard of *wise up,
get hep* (it uses the second as a definition of the first), *ants in one's pants,
one for the book; hugeous, nixie, passel, hepped up* (with *hepcat* and

*hepster*), *anyplace, someplace,* and so forth. These and a swarm of their kind it admits to full canonical standing by the suppression of such qualifying status labels as *colloquial, slang, cant, facetious,* and *substandard.* The classification *colloquial* it abolishes outright: "it is impossible to know whether a word out of context is colloquial or not." Of *slang* it makes a chary occasional use despite a similar reservation: "No word is invariably slang, and many standard words can be given slang connotations or used so inappropriately as to become slang." *Cornball* is ranked as slang, *corny* is not.

10. The overall effect signifies a large-scale abrogation of one major responsibility of the lexicographer. He renounces it on the curious ground that helpful discriminations are so far beyond his professional competence that he is obliged to leave them to those who, professing no competence at all, have vainly turned to him for guidance. If some George Ade of the future, aspiring to execute a fable in slang, were to test his attempt by the status labels in Webster III, he would quickly discover with chagrin that he had expressed himself almost without exception in officially applauded English. With but slight exaggeration we can say that if an expression can be shown to have been used in print by some jaded reporter, some candidate for office or his speech writer, some potboiling minor novelist, it is well enough credentialed for the full blessing of the new lexicography.

11. This extreme tolerance of crude neologisms and of shabby diction generally, however, is but one comparatively trifling aspect of the campaign against punctilio. We begin to sound its deeper implications when we plunge into the definitions and the copious examples that illustrate and support them. Under the distributive pronoun *each* we find, side by side: "(each of them is to pay his own fine) (each of them are to pay their own fine)." Where could anyone look for a neater, more succinct way to outlaw the dusty dogma that a pronoun should agree in number with its antecedent? Here is the same maneuver again under another distributive, *everybody:* "usu. referred to by the third person singular (everybody is bringing his own lunch) but sometimes by a plural personal pronoun (everybody had made up their minds)." Or try *whom* and *whomever:* "(a . . . recruit whom he hoped would prove to be a crack salesman) (people . . . whom you never thought would sympathize) . . . (I go out to talk to whomever it is) . . . (he attacked whomever disagreed with him)." It is, then, all right to put the subject of a finite verb in the accusative case—"esp. after a preposition or a verb of which it might mistakenly be considered the object."

12. Shall we look into what our dictionary does with a handful of the more common solecisms, such as a publisher might introduce into a cooked-up test for would-be copy editors? Begin with *center around* (or *about*). It seems obvious that expressions derived from Euclidean geometry should make Euclidean sense. A center is a point; it is what things

are around, not what is around them; they center *in* or *on* or *at* the point. The Second Edition defined the Great White Way as "That part of Broadway . . . centering about Times Square"—patently an oversight. Is it the same oversight that produces, in the Third: "*heresy* . . . *3:* a group or school of thought centering around a particular heresy"? We look up *center* itself, and, lo: "(a story to tell, centered around the political development of a great state) . . . (more scholarship than usual was centered around the main problems)," followed by several equivalent specimens.

13. Here is *due to*. First we come on irreproachable definitions, irreproachably illustrated, of *due* noun and *due* adjective, and we think we are out of the woods. Alas, they are followed by the manufacture of a composite preposition, *due to*, got up solely to extenuate such abominations as "the event was canceled due to inclement weather." An adjective can modify a verb, then. And here is a glance at that peculiarly incriminating redundancy of the slipshod writer, *equally as:* "equally opposed to Communism as to Fascism." The intolerable *hardly than* or *scarcely than* construction is in full favor: "hardly had the birds dropped than she jumped into the water and retrieved them." The sequence *different than* has the double approbation of editorial use and a citation: conjunctive *unlike* means "in a manner that is different than," and a passage under *different* reads "vastly different in size than it was twenty-five years ago." Adjectival *unlike* and conjunctive *unlike* both get illustrations that implicitly commend the unanchored and grammarless modifier: "so many fine men were outside the charmed circle that, unlike most colleges, there was no disgrace in not being a club man"; "unlike in the gasoline engine, fuel does not enter the cylinder with air on the intake stroke."

14. This small scattering should not end without some notice of that darling of the advanced libertarians, *like* as a conjunction, first in the meaning of *as*, secondly (and more horribly) in that of *as if.* Now, it is well known to the linguistic historian that *like* was so used for a long time before and after Langland. But it is as well known that the language rather completely sloughed off this usage; that it has long been no more than a regional colloquialism, a rarely seen aberration among competent writers, or an artificially cultivated irritant among defiant ones. The *Saturday Evening Post,* in which *like* for *as* is probably more frequent than in any other painstakingly edited magazine, has seldom if ever printed that construction except in reproducing the speech or tracing the thoughts of characters to whom it might be considered natural. The arguments for *like* have been merely defensive and permissive. Not for centuries has there been any real pressure of authority on a writer to use *like* as a conjunction—until our Third New International Dictionary decided to exert its leverage.

15. How it is exerted will appear in the following: "(impromptu programs where they ask questions much like I do on the air) . . . (looks like they can raise better tobacco) (looks like he will get the job) (wore

his clothes like he was . . . afraid of getting dirt on them) (was like he'd come back from a long trip) (acted like she felt sick) . . . (sounded like the motor had stopped) . . . (the violin now sounds like an old masterpiece should) (did it like he told me to) . . . (wanted a doll like she saw in the store window) . . . (anomalies like just had occurred)."

*16.* By the processes represented in the foregoing and countless others for which there is no room here, the latest Webster whittles away at one after another of the traditionary controls until there is little or nothing left of them. The controls, to be sure, have often enough been overvalued and overdone by pedants and purists, by martinets and bigots; but more often, and much more importantly, they have worked as aids toward dignified, workmanlike, and cogent uses of the wonderful language that is our inheritance. To erode and undermine them is to convert the language into a confusion of unchanneled, incalculable williwaws, a capricious wind blowing whithersoever it listeth. And that, if we are to judge by the total effect of the pages under scrutiny—2720 of them and nearly 8000 columns of vocabulary, all compact in Times roman—is exactly what is wanted by the patient and dedicated saboteurs in Springfield. They, if they keep their ears to the ground, will hear many echoes of the despairing cry already wrung from one editorial assistant on a distinguished magazine that still puts its faith in standards: "Why have a Dictionary at all if anything goes?"

*17.* The definitions are reinforced, it will have been conveyed, with copious citations from printed sources. These citations occupy a great fraction of the total space. They largely account for the reduction in the number of entries (from 600,000 to 450,000) and for the elimination of the Gazetteer, the Biographical Dictionary, and the condensed key to pronunciation and symbols that ran across the bottoms of facing pages—all very material deprivations. Some 14,000 authors, we are told, are represented in the illustrative quotations—"mostly from the mid-twentieth century."

*18.* Can some thousands of authors truly worth space in a dictionary ever be found in any one brief period? Such a concentration can hardly fail to be, for the purposes of a dictionary, egregiously overweighted with the contemporary and the transient. Any very short period, such as a generation, is a period of transition in the history of English, and any great mass of examples drawn primarily from it will be disproportionately focused on transitional and ephemeral elements. To say that recording English *as we find it today* is precisely the purpose of a new dictionary is not much of a retort. For the bulk of the language that we use has come down to us with but minor, glacially slow changes from time out of mind, and a worthy record of it must stand on a much broader base than the fashions of yesterday.

*19.* It is, then, a mercy that among the thousands of scraps from recent authors, many of them still producing, we can also find hundreds from Shakespeare, the English Bible, Fielding, Dickens, Hawthorne, Melville, Henry James, Mark Twain, and so on. But the great preponderance of latter-day prose, little of it worth repeating and a good deal of it hardly worth printing in the first place, is likely to curtail by years the useful life of the Third New International.

20. So much is by the way. When we come to the definitions proper we face something new, startling, and formidable in lexicography. The definitions, all of them conformed to a predetermined rhetorical pattern, may be products of a theory—Gestaltist, perhaps?—of how the receiving mind works. The pattern, in the editor's general preface, is described as follows: "The primary objective of precise, sharp defining has been met through development of a new dictionary style based upon completely analytical one-phrase definitions throughout the book. Since the headword in a definition is intended to be modified only by structural elements restrictive in some degree and essential to each other, the use of commas either to separate or to group has been severely limited, chiefly to elements in apposition or in series. The new defining pattern does not provide for a predication which conveys further expository comment."

21. This doctrine of the strictly unitary definition is of course formulated and applied in the interest of a logical integrity and a simplification never before consistently attained by lexical definitions. What it produces, when applied with the rigor here insisted on, is in the first place some of the oddest prose ever concocted by pundits. A typical specimen, from the definition of the simplest possible term: "*rabbit punch* . . . : a short chopping blow delivered to the back of the neck or the base of the skull with the edge of the hand opposite the thumb that is illegal in boxing." When the idea, being not quite so simple, requires the one-phrase statement of several components, the definition usually turns out to be a great unmanageable and unpunctuated blob of words strung out beyond the retentive powers of most minds that would need the definition at all. Both theory and result will emerge clearly enough from a pair of specimens, the first dealing with a familiar everyday noun, the second with a mildly technical one:

*groan* . . . *1:* a deep usu. inarticulate and involuntary often strangled sound typically abruptly begun and ended and usu. indicative of pain or grief or tension or desire or sometimes disapproval or annoyance.

*kymograph* . . . *1:* a recording device including an electric motor or clockwork that drives a usu. slowly revolving drum which carries a roll of plain or smoked paper and also having an arrangement for tracing on the paper by means of a stylus a graphic record of motion or pressure (as of the organs of speech, blood pressure, or respiration) often in relation to particular intervals of time.

22. About these typical definitions as prose, there is much that any good reader might well say. What must be said is that the grim suppression of commas is a mere crotchet. It takes time to read such definitions anyway; commas in the right places would speed rather than slow the reading and would clarify rather than obscure the sense, so that the unitary effect—largely imaginary at best—would be more helped than hurt. In practice, the one-phase design without further expository predication lacks all the asserted advantages over a competently written definition of the free conventional sort; it is merely more difficult to write, often impossible to write well, and tougher to take in. Compare the corresponding definitions from the Second Edition:

*groan* . . . A low, moaning sound: usually, a deep, mournful sound uttered in pain or great distress; sometimes, an expression of strong disapprobation; as, the remark was received with *groans.*

*kymograph* . . . *a* An automatic apparatus consisting of a motor revolving a drum covered with smoked paper, on which curves of pressure, etc., may be traced.

Everyone professionally concerned with the details of printed English can be grateful to the new Webster for linking the parts of various expressions that have been either hyphenated compounds or separate words—*highlight, highbrow* and *lowbrow, overall, wisecrack, lowercase and uppercase,* and so on. Some of the unions now recognized were long overdue; many editors have already got them written into codes of house usage. But outside this small province the new work is a copy editor's despair, a propounder of endless riddles.

23. What, for example, are we to make of the common abbreviations *i.e.* and *e.g.?* The first is entered in the vocabulary as *ie* (no periods, no space), the second as *e g* (space, no periods). In the preliminary list, "Abbreviations Used in This Dictionary," both are given the customary periods. (Oddly, the list translates its *i.e.* into "that is," but merely expands *e.g.* into "exempli gratia.") Is one to follow the vocabulary or the list? What point has the seeming inconsistency?

24. And what about capitalization? All vocabulary entries are in lowercase except for such abbreviations as ARW (air raid warden), MAB (medical advisory board), and PX (post exchange). Words possibly inviting capitalization are followed by such injunctions as *cap, usu cap, sometimes not cap, usu cap 1st A, usu cap A&B.* (One of the small idiosyncrasies is that "usu.," the most frequent abbreviation, is given a period when roman, denied it when italic.) From *america,* adjective—all proper nouns are excluded—to *american yew* there are over 175 consecutive entries that require such injunctions; would it not have been simpler and more economical to capitalize the entries? A flat *"cap,"* of course, means

"always capitalized." But how often is "usually," and when is "sometimes"? We get dictionaries expressly that they may settle such problems for us. This dictionary seems to make a virtue of leaving them in flux, with the explanation that many matters are subjective and that the individual must decide them for himself—a curious abrogation of authority in a work extolled as "more useful and authoritative than any previous dictionary."

25. The rock-bottom practical truth is that the lexicographer cannot abrogate his authority if he wants to. He may think of himself as a detached scientist reporting the facts of language, declining to recommend use of anything or abstention from anything; but the myriad consultants of his work are not going to see him so. He helps create, not a book of fads and fancies and private opinions, but a Dictionary of the English Language. It comes to every reader under auspices that say, not "Take it or leave it," but rather something like this: "Here in 8000 columns is a definitive report of what a synod of the most trustworthy American experts consider the English language to be in the seventh decade of the twentieth century. This is your language; take it and use it. And if you use it in conformity with the principles and practices here exemplified, your use will be the most accurate attainable by any American of this era." The fact that the compilers disclaim authority and piously refrain from judgments is meaningless: the work itself, by virtue of its inclusions and exclusions, its mere existence, is a whole universe of judgments, received by millions as the Word from on high.

26. And there we have the reason why it is so important for the dictionary maker to keep his discriminations sharp, why it is so damaging if he lets them get out of working order. Suppose he enters a new definition for no better reason than that some careless, lazy, or uninformed scribbler has jumped to an absurd conclusion about what a word means or has been too harassed to run down the word he really wanted. This new definition is going to persuade tens of thousands that, say, *cohort*, a word of multitude, means one associate or crony "(he and three alleged housebreaking cohorts were arraigned on attempted burglary charges)" or that the vogue word *ambivalence*, which denotes simultaneous love and hatred of someone or something, means "continual oscillation between one thing and its opposite (novels . . . vitiated by an ambivalence between satire and sentimentalism)." To what is the definer contributing if not to subversion and decay? To the swallower of the definition it never occurs that he can have drunk corruption from a well that he has every reason to trust as the ultimate in purity. Multiply him by the number of people simultaneously influenced, and the resulting figure by the years through which the influence continued, and a great deal of that product by the influences that will be disseminated through speech and writing and teaching, and you begin to apprehend the scope of the really enormous disaster that can and will be wrought by the lexicographer's abandonment of his responsibility.

# Questions

1. Upon what assumption concerning the public's attitude toward the concept of a dictionary does Follett's argument finally rest?

2. What function do the first two paragraphs serve in relation to the third paragraph and specifically its last sentence?

3. At what points do you find justification, in terms of Follett's word choice and tone, for his title?

4. Does the issue raised in paragraph 4 seem relevant? Why?

5. Do you, as a member of the dictionary-using public, agree with Follett's position in the issue raised in paragraphs 9 and 10? With the examples in paragraphs 11 through 15? How would Follett most probably answer dissent on your part?

6. What admission does Follett make in paragraph 16? What appeals in the same paragraph?

7. In paragraph 18 Follett raises an issue and presents the reply of his opponents. He calls the reply a retort. Is it a retort? How do the assumptions of the two sides differ here?

8. The final two paragraphs restate the crucial issue. How many parts has it? What defensive elements, if any, can you find in its statement?

9. Follett holds the maintenance of "standards" in high regard. What "standards," if any, does he attribute to the makers of *Webster's Third*, and how does he deal with them in his argument?

10. Analyze Follett's use of the principles of parallelism and balance throughout his essay.

### ·38·

*Bergen Evans*

# BUT WHAT'S A DICTIONARY FOR?

*1.* The storm of abuse in the popular press that greeted the appearance of *Webster's Third New International Dictionary* is a curious phenomenon. Never had a scholarly work of this stature been attacked with

From *The Atlantic Monthly* (May, 1962). Reprinted by permission of the author.

such unbridled fury and contempt. An article in the *Atlantic* viewed it as a "disappointment," a "shock," a "calamity," "a scandal and a disaster." The New York *Times,* in a special editorial, felt that the work would "accelerate the deterioration" of the language and sternly accused the editors of betraying a public trust. The *Journal* of the American Bar Association saw the publication as "deplorable," "a flagrant example of lexicographic irresponsibility," "a serious blow to the cause of good English." *Life* called it "a non-word deluge," "monstrous," "abominable," and "a cause for dismay." They doubted that "Lincoln could have modelled his Gettysburg Address" on it—a concept of how things get written that throws very little light on Lincoln but a great deal on *Life.*

2. What underlies all this sound and fury? Is the claim of the G & C. Merriam Company, probably the world's greatest dictionary maker, that the preparation of the work cost $3.5 million, that it required the efforts of three hundred scholars over a period of twenty-seven years, working on the largest collection of citations ever assembled in any language—is all this a fraud, a hoax?

3. So monstrous a discrepancy in evaluation requires us to examine basic principles. Just what's a dictionary for? What does it propose to do? What does the common reader go to a dictionary to find? What has the purchaser of a dictionary a right to expect for his money?

4. Before we look at basic principles, it is necessary to interpose two brief statements. The first of these is that a dictionary is concerned with words. Some dictionaries give various kinds of other useful information. Some have tables of weights and measures on the flyleaves. Some list historical events, and some, home remedies. And there's nothing wrong with their so doing. But the great increase in our vocabulary in the past three decades compels all dictionaries to make more efficient use of their space. And if something must be eliminated, it is sensible to throw out these extraneous things and stick to words.

5. Yet wild wails arose. The *Saturday Review* lamented that one can no longer find the goddess Astarte under a separate heading—though they point out that a genus of mollusks named after the goddess is included! They seemed to feel that out of sheer perversity the editors of the dictionary stooped to mollusks while ignoring goddesses and that, in some way, this typifies modern lexicography. Mr. Wilson Follett, folletizing (his mental processes demand some special designation) in the *Atlantic,* cried out in horror that one is not even able to learn from the Third International "that the Virgin was Mary the mother of Jesus"!

6. The second brief statement is that there has been even more progress in the making of dictionaries in the past thirty years than there has been in the making of automobiles. The difference, for example, between the much-touted Second International (1934) and the much-clouted Third International (1961) is not like the difference between

yearly models but like the difference between the horse and buggy and the automobile. Between the appearance of these two editions a whole new science related to the making of dictionaries, the science of descriptive linguistics, has come into being.

7. Modern linguistics gets its charter from Leonard Bloomfield's *Language* (1933). Bloomfield, for thirteen years professor of Germanic philology at the University of Chicago and for nine years professor of linguistics at Yale, was one of those inseminating scholars who can't be relegated to any department and don't dream of accepting established categories and procedures just because they're established. He was as much an anthropologist as a linguist, and his concepts of language were shaped not by Strunk's *Elements of Style* but by his knowledge of Cree Indian dialects.

8. The broad general findings of the new science are:

1. All languages are systems of human conventions, not systems of natural laws. The first—and essential—step in the study of any language is observing and setting down precisely what happens when native speakers speak it.

2. Each language is unique in its pronunciation, grammar, and vocabulary. It cannot be described in terms of logic or of some theoretical, ideal language. It cannot be described in terms of any other language, or even in terms of its own past.

3. All languages are dynamic rather than static, and hence a "rule" in any language can only be a statement of contemporary practice. Change is constant—and normal.

4. "Correctness" can rest only upon usage, for the simple reason that there is nothing else for it to rest on. And all usage is relative.

9. From these propositions it follows that a dictionary is good only insofar as it is a comprehensive and accurate description of current usage. And to be comprehensive it must include some indication of social and regional associations.

10. New dictionaries are needed because English has changed more in the past two generations than at any other time in its history. It has had to adapt to extraordinary cultural and technological changes, two world wars, unparalleled changes in transportation and communication, and unprecedented movements of populations.

11. More subtly, but pervasively, it has changed under the influence of mass education and the growth of democracy. As written English is used by increasing millions and for more reasons than ever before, the language has become more utilitarian and more informal. Every publication in America today includes pages that would appear, to the purist of forty years ago, unbuttoned gibberish. Not that they are; they simply show that you can't hold the language of one generation up as a model for the next.

*12.* It's not that you mustn't. You *can't.* For example, in the issue in which *Life* stated editorially that it would follow the Second International, there were over forty words, constructions, and meanings which are in the Third International but not in the Second. The issue of the New York *Times* which hailed the Second International as the authority to which it would adhere and the Third International as a scandal and a betrayal which it would reject used one hundred and fifty-three separate words, phrases, and constructions which are listed in the Third International but not in the Second and nineteen others which are condemned in the Second. Many of them are used many times, more than three hundred such uses in all. The Washington *Post,* in an editorial captioned "Keep Your Old Webster's," says, in the first sentence, "don't throw it away," and in the second, "hang on to it." But the old Webster's labels *don't* "colloquial" and doesn't include "hang on to," in this sense, at all.

*13.* In short, all of these publications are written in the language that the Third International describes, even the very editorials which scorn it. And this is no coincidence, because the Third International isn't setting up any new standards at all; it is simply describing what *Life,* the Washington *Post,* and the New York *Times* are doing. Much of the dictionary's material comes from these very publications, the *Times,* in particular, furnishing more of its illustrative quotations than any other newspaper.

*14.* And the papers have no choice. No journal or periodical could sell a single issue today if it restricted itself to the American language of twenty-eight years ago. It couldn't discuss half the things we are interested in, and its style would seem stiff and cumbrous. If the editorials were serious, the public—and the stockholders—have reason to be grateful that the writers on these publications are more literate than the editors.

*15.* And so back to our questions: what's a dictionary for, and how, in 1962, can it best do what it ought to do? The demands are simple. The common reader turns to a dictionary for information about the spelling, pronunciation, meaning, and proper use of words. He wants to know what is current and respectable. But he wants—and has a right to—the truth, the full truth. And the full truth about any language, and especially about American English today, is that there are many areas in which certainty is impossible and simplification is misleading.

*16.* Even in so settled a matter as spelling, a dictionary cannot always be absolute. *Theater* is correct, but so is *theatre.* And so are *traveled* and *travelled, plow* and *plough, catalog* and *catalogue,* and scores of other variants. The reader may want a single certainty. He may have taken an unyielding position in an argument, he may have wagered in support of his conviction and may demand that the dictionary "settle" the matter. But neither his vanity nor his purse is any concern of the dictionary's; it must record the facts. And the fact here is that there are many words in our language which may be spelled, with equal correctness, in either of two ways.

17. So with pronunciation. A citizen listening to his radio might notice that James B. Conant, Bernard Baruch, and Dwight D. Eisenhower pronounce *economics* as ECKuhnomiks, while A. Whitney Griswold, Adlai Stevenson, and Herbert Hoover pronounce it EEKuhnomiks. He turns to the dictionary to see which of the two pronunciations is "right" and finds that they are both acceptable.

18. Has he been betrayed? Has the dictionary abdicated its responsibility? Should it say that one *must* speak like the president of Harvard or like the president of Yale, like the thirty-first President of the United States or like the thirty-fourth? Surely it's none of its business to make a choice. Not because of the distinction of these particular speakers; lexicography, like God, is no respecter of person. But because so widespread and conspicuous a use of two pronunciations among people of this elevation shows that there *are* two pronunciations. Their speaking establishes the fact which the dictionary must record.

19. Among the "enormities" with which *Life* taxes the Third International is its listing of "the common mispronunciation" *heighth*. That it is labeled a "dialectal variant" seems, somehow, to compound the felony. But one hears the word so pronounced, and if one professes to give a full account of American English in the 1960s, one has to take some cognizance of it. All people do not possess *Life's* intuitive perception that the word is so "monstrous" that even to list it as a dialect variation is to merit scorn. Among these, by the way, was John Milton, who, in one of the greatest passages in all literature, besought the Holy Spirit to raise him to the "highth" of his great argument. And even the *Oxford English Dictionary* is so benighted as to list it, in full boldface, right alongside of *Height* as a variant that has been in the language since at least 1290.

20. Now there are still, apparently, millions of Americans who retain, in this as in much else, some of the speech of Milton. This particular pronunciation seems to be receding, but the *American Dialect Dictionary* still records instances of it from almost every state on the Eastern seaboard and notes that it is heard from older people and "occasionally in educated speech," "common with good speakers," "general," "widespread."

21. Under these circumstances, what is a dictionary to do? Since millions speak the word this way, the pronunciation can't be ignored. Since it has been in use as long as we have any record of English and since it has been used by the greatest writers, it can't be described as substandard or slang. But it is heard now only in certain localities. That

makes it a dialectal pronunciation, and an honest dictionary will list it as such. What else can it do? Should it do?

22. The average purchaser of a dictionary uses it most often, probably, to find out what a word "means." As a reader, he wants to know what an author intended to convey. As a speaker or writer, he wants to know what a word will convey to his auditors. And this, too, is complex, subtle, and forever changing.

23. An illustration is furnished by an editorial in the Washington *Post* (January 17, 1962). After a ringing appeal to those who "love truth and accuracy" and the usual bombinations about "abdication of authority" and "barbarism," the editorial charges the Third International with "pretentious and obscure verbosity" and specifically instances its definition of "so simple an object as a door."

24. The definition reads:

a movable piece of firm material or a structure supported usu. along one side and swinging on pivots or hinges, sliding along a groove, rolling up and down, revolving as one of four leaves, or folding like an accordion by means of which an opening may be closed or kept open for passage into or out of a building, room, or other covered enclosure or a car, airplane, elevator, or other vehicle.

Then follows a series of special meanings, each particularly defined and, where necessary, illustrated by a quotation.

25. Since, aside from roaring and admonishing the "gentlemen from Springfield" that "accuracy and brevity are virtues," the *Post's* editorial fails to explain what is wrong with the definition, we can only infer from "so simple" a thing that the writer takes the plain, downright, man-in-the-street attitude that a door is a door and any damn fool knows that.

26. But if so, he has walked into one of lexicography's biggest booby traps: the belief that the obvious is easy to define. Whereas the opposite is true. Anyone can give a fair description of the strange, the new, or the unique. It's the commonplace, the habitual, that challenges definition, for its very commonness compels us to define it in uncommon terms. Dr. Johnson was ridiculed on just this score when his dictionary appeared in 1755. For two hundred years his definition of a network as "any thing reticulated or decussated, at equal distances, with interstices between the intersections" has been good for a laugh. But in the merriment one thing is always overlooked: no one has yet come up with a better definition! Subsequent dictionaries defined it as a mesh and then defined a mesh as a network. That's simple, all right.

27. Anyone who attempts sincerely to state what the word *door* means in the United States of America today can't take refuge in a log cabin. There has been an enormous proliferation of closing and demarking devices and structures in the past twenty years, and anyone who tries to thread his way through the many meanings now included under *door* may

have to sacrifice brevity to accuracy and even have to employ words that a limited vocabulary may find obscure.

*28.* Is the entrance to a tent a door, for instance? And what of the thing that seals the exit of an airplane? Is this a door? Or what of those sheets and jets of air that are now being used, in place of old-fashioned oak and hinges, to screen entrances and exits. Are they doors? And what of those accordion-like things that set off various sections of many modern apartments? The fine print in the lease takes it for granted that they are doors and that spaces demarked by them are rooms—and the rent is computed on the number of rooms.

*29.* Was I gypped by the landlord when he called the folding contraption that shuts off my kitchen a door? I go to the Second International, which the editor of the *Post* urges me to use in preference to the Third International. Here I find that a door is

The movable frame or barrier of boards, or other material, usually turning on hinges or pivots or sliding, by which an entranceway into a house or apartment is closed and opened; also, a similar part of a piece of furniture, as in a cabinet or bookcase.

This is only forty-six words, but though it includes the cellar door, it excludes the barn door and the accordion-like thing.

*30.* So I go on to the Third International. I see at once that the new definition is longer. But I'm looking for accuracy, and if I must sacrifice brevity to get it, then I must. And, sure enough, in the definition which raised the *Post's* blood pressure, I find the words "folding like an accordion." The thing *is* a door, and my landlord is using the word in one of its currently accepted meanings.

*31.* We don't turn to a work of reference merely for confirmation. We all have words in our vocabularies which we have misunderstood, and to come on the true meaning of one of these words is quite a shock. All our complacency and self-esteem rise to oppose the discovery. But eventually we must accept the humiliation and laugh it off as best we can.

*32.* Some, often those who have set themselves up as authorities, stick to their error and charge the dictionary with being in a conspiracy against them. They are sure that their meaning is the only "right" one. And when the dictionary doesn't bear them out they complain about "permissive" attitudes instead of correcting their mistake.

*33.* The New York *Times* and the *Saturday Review* both regarded as contemptibly "permissive" the fact that one meaning of one word was illustrated by a quotation from Polly Adler. But a rudimentary knowledge of the development of any language would have told them that the underworld has been a far more active force in shaping and enriching speech than all the synods that have ever convened. Their attitude is like that of the patriot who canceled his subscription to the *Dictionary of American*

*Biography* when he discovered that the very first volume included Benedict Arnold!

34. The ultimate of "permissiveness," singled out by almost every critic for special scorn, was the inclusion in the Third International of *finalize*. It was this, more than any other one thing, that was given as the reason for sticking to the good old Second International—that "peerless authority on American English," as the *Times* called it. But if it was such an authority, why didn't they look into it? They would have found *finalize* if they had.

35. And why shouldn't it be there? It exists. It's been recorded for two generations. Millions employ it every day. Two Presidents of the United States—men of widely differing cultural backgrounds—have used it in formal statements. And so has the Secretary-General of the United Nations, a man of unusual linguistic attainments. It isn't permitting the word but omitting it that would break faith with the reader. Because it is exactly the sort of word we want information about.

36. To list it as substandard would be to imply that it is used solely by the ignorant and the illiterate. But this would be a misrepresentation: President Kennedy and U Thant are highly educated men, and both are articulate and literate. It isn't even a freak form. On the contrary, it is a classic example of a regular process of development in English, a process which has given us such thoroughly accepted words as *generalize, minimize, formalize*, and *verbalize*. Nor can it be dismissed on logical grounds or on the ground that it is a mere duplication of *complete*. It says something that *complete* doesn't say and says it in a way that is significant in the modern bureaucratic world: one usually *completes* something which he has initiated but *finalizes* the work of others.

37. One is free to dislike the word. I don't like it. But the editor of a dictionary has to examine the evidence for a word's existence and seek it in context to get, as clearly and closely as he can, the exact meaning that it conveys to those who use it. And if it is widely used by well-educated, literate, reputable people, he must list it as a standard word. He is not compiling a volume of his own prejudices.

38. An individual's use of his native tongue is the surest index to his position within his community. And those who turn to a dictionary expect from it some statement of the current status of a word or a grammatical construction. And it is with the failure to assume this function that modern lexicography has been most fiercely charged. The charge is based on a naïve assumption that simple labels can be attached in all instances. But they can't. Some words are standard in some constructions and not in others. There may be as many shades of status as of meaning, and modern lexicography instead of abdicating this function has fulfilled it to a degree utterly unknown to earlier dictionaries.

39. Consider the word *fetch*, meaning to "go get and bring to." Until

recently a standard word of full dignity ("Fetch me, I pray thee, a little water in a vessel"—I Kings 17:10), it has become slightly tainted. Perhaps the command latent in it is resented as undemocratic. Or maybe its use in training dogs to retrieve has made some people feel that it is an undignified word to apply to human beings. But, whatever the reason, there is a growing uncertainty about its status, and hence it is the sort of word that conscientious people look up in a dictionary.

*40.* Will they find it labeled "good" or "bad"? Neither, of course, because either applied indiscriminately would be untrue. The Third International lists nineteen different meanings of the verb *to fetch*. Of these some are labeled "dialectal," some "chiefly dialectal," some "obsolete," one "chiefly Scottish," and two "not in formal use." The primary meaning—"to go after and bring back"—is not labeled and hence can be accepted as standard, accepted with the more assurance because the many shades of labeling show us that the word's status has been carefully considered.

*41.* On grammatical questions the Third International tries to be equally exact and thorough. Sometimes a construction is listed without comment, meaning that in the opinion of the editors it is unquestionably respectable. Sometimes a construction carries the comment "used by speakers and writers on all educational levels though disapproved by some grammarians." Or the comment may be "used in substandard speech and formerly also by reputable writers." Or "less often in standard than in substandard speech." Or simply "dial."

*42.* And this very accurate reporting is based on evidence which is presented for our examination. One may feel that the evidence is inadequate or that the evaluation of it is erroneous. But surely, in the face of classification so much more elaborate and careful than any known heretofore, one cannot fly into a rage and insist that the dictionary is "out to destroy . . . every vestige of linguistic punctilio . . . every criterion for distinguishing between better usages and worse."

*43.* Words, as we have said, are continually shifting their meanings and connotations and hence their status. A word which has dignity, say, in the vocabulary of an older person may go down in other people's estimation. Like *fetch*. The older speaker is not likely to be aware of this and will probably be inclined to ascribe the snickers of the young at his speech to that degeneration of manners which every generation has deplored in its juniors. But a word which is coming up in the scale—like *jazz*, say, or, more recently, *crap*—will strike his ear at once. We are much more aware of offenses given us than of those we give. And if he turns to a dictionary and finds the offending word listed as standard—or even listed, apparently —his response is likely to be an outburst of indignation.

*44.* But the dictionary can neither snicker nor fulminate. It records. It will offend many, no doubt, to find the expression *wise up*, meaning to inform or to become informed, listed in the Third International with no re-

stricting label. To my aging ears it still sounds like slang. But the evidence
—quotations from the *Kiplinger Washington Letter* and the *Wall Street
Journal*—convinces me that it is I who am out of step, lagging behind. If
such publications have taken to using *wise up* in serious contexts, with no
punctuational indication of irregularity, then it is obviously respectable.
And finding it so listed and supported, I can only say that it's nice to be
informed and sigh to realize that I am becoming an old fogy. But, of
course, I don't have to use it (and I'll be damned if I will! "Let them smile,
as I do now, At the old forsaken bough Where I cling").

45. In part, the trouble is due to the fact that there is no standard
for standard. Ideas of what is proper to use in serious, dignified speech
and writing are changing—and with breathtaking rapidity. This is one
of the major facts of contemporary American English. But it is no more
the dictionary's business to oppose this process than to speed it up.

46. Even in our standard speech some words are more dignified and
some more informal than others, and dictionaries have tried to guide us
through these uncertainties by marking certain words and constructions
as "colloquial," meaning "inappropriate in a formal situation." But this distinction, in the opinion of most scholars, has done more harm than good.
It has created the notion that these particular words are inferior, when
actually they might be the best possible words in an informal statement.
And so—to the rage of many reviewers—the Third International has
dropped this label. Not all labels, as angrily charged, but only this one
out of a score. And the doing so may have been an error, but it certainly
didn't constitute "betrayal" or "abandoning of all distinctions." It was intended to end a certain confusion.

47. In all the finer shades of meaning, of which the status of a word
is only one, the user is on his own, whether he likes it or not. Despite
*Life's* artless assumption about the Gettysburg Address, nothing worth
writing is written *from* a dictionary. The dictionary, rather, comes along
afterwards and describes what *has been* written.

48. Words in themselves are not dignified, or silly, or wise, or malicious. But they can be used in dignified, silly, wise, or malicious ways
by dignified, silly, wise, or malicious people. *Egghead,* for example, is
a perfectly legitimate word, as legitimate as *highbrow* or *long-haired.*
But there is something very wrong and very undignified, by civilized
standards, in a belligerent dislike for intelligence and education. *Yak* is
an amusing word for persistent chatter. Anyone could say, "We were just
yakking over a cup of coffee," with no harm to his dignity. But to call
a Supreme Court decision *yakking* is to be vulgarly insulting and so, undignified. Again, there's nothing wrong with *confab* when it's appropriate. But when the work of a great research project, employing hundreds
of distinguished scholars over several decades and involving the honor
of one of the greatest publishing houses in the world, is described as

*confabbing* (as the New York *Times* editorially described the preparation of the Third International), the use of this particular word asserts
that the lexicographers had merely sat around and talked idly. And the
statement becomes undignified—if not, indeed, slanderous.

49. The lack of dignity in such statements is not in the words, nor
in the dictionaries that list them, but in the hostility that deliberately
seeks this tone of expression. And in expressing itself the hostility frequently shows that those who are expressing it don't know how to use
a dictionary. Most of the reviewers seem unable to read the Third International and unwilling to read the Second.

50. The *American Bar Association Journal,* for instance, in a typical
outburst ("a deplorable abdication of responsibility"), picked out for special scorn the inclusion in the Third International of the word *irregardless.* "As far as the new Webster's is concerned," said the *Journal,* "this
meaningless verbal bastard is just as legitimate as any other word in the
dictionary." Thirty seconds spent in examining the book they were so
roundly condemning would have shown them that in it *irregardless* is labeled "nonstand"—which means "nonstandard," which means "not conforming to the usage generally characteristic of educated native speakers of the language." Is that "just as legitimate as any other word in the
dictionary"?

51. The most disturbing fact of all is that the editors of a dozen of
the most influential publications in America today are under the impression that *authoritative* must mean *authoritarian.* Even the "permissive"
Third International doesn't recognize this identification—editors' attitudes
being not yet, fortunately, those of the American people. But the Fourth
International may have to.

52. The new dictionary may have many faults. Nothing that tries to
meet an ever-changing situation over a terrain as vast as contemporary
English can hope to be free of them. And much in it is open to honest,
and informed, disagreement. There can be linguistic objection to the
eradication of proper names. The removal of guides to pronunciation
from the foot of every page may not have been worth the valuable space
it saved. The new method of defining words of many meanings has disadvantages as well as advantages. And of the half million or more defin-
tions, hundreds, possibly thousands, may seem inadequate or imprecise.
To some (of whom I am one) the omission of the label "colloquial" will
seem meritorious; to others it will seem a loss.

53. But one thing is certain: anyone who solemnly announces in the
year 1962 that he will be guided in matters of English usage by a dictionary published in 1934 is talking ignorant and pretentious nonsense.

# Questions

1. Compare and contrast the first three paragraphs of Evans' article with the first three of Follett's from the point of view of method of approach to the subject. Describe the tone achieved by each writer and the expectations he creates in the mind of an attentive reader.

2. What kind of issue is raised in paragraph 4, and how effectively is it dealt with in paragraph 5? What kind of issue is raised in paragraph 6, and how effectively is it dealt with in paragraphs 7 and 8? How does the implied analogy between the passing of time and the making of automobiles and of dictionaries help or hinder Evans' argument?

3. How does Evans apply the fourth finding of modern linguistics in defense of the makers of the *Third?* Can you convict or acquit Evans of the charge of an argument *ad hominem* in this defense? How does he apply it in defense of the *Third* itself?

4. Does Evans anywhere face the following argument:
   The linguistic needs of any native speaker of a Cree Indian dialect for an unabridged dictionary of his language are so different in degree from the linguistic needs of any native speaker of contemporary American English for a comparable dictionary of his language that a difference in kind exists. Therefore, whatever may be the validity of Bloomfield's findings about Cree Indian dialects and the generalizations based on them, they are irrelevant for a maker of an unabridged dictionary of American English for today's native speakers?
   How relevant is this argument against Evans' position?

5. What tactics of argument does Evans use to silence the "sound and fury" by critics of the *Third?* Where, for example, does he demonstrate ignorance on the part of opponents of the *Third?* How persuasive is he in each instance in building his own case?

6. Paragraphs 23 through 30 defend the complex definition of *door* in the *Third.* Which definition, that in the *Second* or that in the *Third,* seems the better to you? Why?

7. Why does Evans confront the usage of one native speaker with that of another in an apparent attempt to discredit distinctions among *standards* of usage? Do his efforts ultimately leave him with any margin for linguistic authority (as distinguished from linguistic authoritarianism) apart from his own conscious or unconscious preferences (see the end of paragraph 44)?

8. In paragraph 45 Evans states "there is no standard for standard," and at the beginning of the next paragraph he says "in our standard speech." Is he contradicting himself? How or how not?

9. Evans derides those who object to Polly Adler's being quoted as a linguistic authority and implies that grounds for this objection are similar to those

of the patriot who cancelled his subscription to *The Dictionary of American Biography* when the initial volume arrived with a listing for Benedict Arnold. Is Evans' analogy a true or false one? Why?

10. Granted that change makes language less precise and that an unabridged dictionary of any language is more a stream or current than it is a rule or measuring stick, do you think resistance to linguistic change is desirable? On the part of whom? To what extent? Should such a dictionary as the *Third* aim to oppose or to speed up change? What probable effects follow—and even for the makers themselves of a massive dictionary—if it does in fact succeed in accelerating lexical changes in a language?

## ·39·

*Mario Pei*

# THE DICTIONARY AS A BATTLE FRONT

*1.* For some years, there have been more and more insistent rumblings from all sorts of quarters concerning the quality of the English imparted in our schools and colleges. Graduates of our educational institutions, the critics have charged, do not know how to spell, punctuate, or capitalize; to divide a thought concept into phrases, sentences, and paragraphs; or to express themselves, either in speech or writing, in the sort of English that is meaningful and acceptable. As a single sample of the many complaints that have been voiced, I may cite a friend who is a high official in WNBC-TV: "Recently we interviewed over a hundred college graduates to fill a post calling for a knowledge of good English. Not one of them made the grade. None of them knew the rules of good writing, and none of them could express himself or herself in clear, simple, forthright English sentences."

*2.* The blame for this state of affairs has consistently been put upon two branches of the educational world: the teachers of English and the progressive educationists. Books such as "Why Johnny Can't Read" are indictments of modern educational practice. A cultured lay writer, J. Donald Adams of the New York *Times Book Review*, said in his column of December 20, 1959:

If more parents who were themselves the recipients of a decent education could be made aware of the asinine statements about the teaching of the English

From *The Saturday Review* (July 21, 1962). Reprinted by permission of the author.

language which are being spewed forth by today's educational theorists, there would be an armed uprising among the Parent-Teacher Associations all over the United States. It would be an uprising armed by common sense and hot indignation, and it would demand and get the scalps of those so-called educators whose indefensible doctrines are rapidly producing a generation of American illiterates . . . The root responsibility for the decline in standards of English rests, I think, with the teachers of English in our primary and secondary schools, and even more so, with the teachers of education who produced them. . . . There is an organization called the National Council of Teachers of English, whose attitudes and activities constitute one of the chief threats to the cultivation of good English in our schools.

3. What critics of present-day methods of teaching English have in the past failed to realize is that the responsibility for the situation lies deeper than the departments of English and the teachers colleges. The practices of both are merely a reflection of the philosophy and theories of a school of linguistics that is in turn linked with a school of cultural anthropology of the equalitarian persuasion whose views color far more than the teaching of languages in general or English in particular.

4. As far back as 1948, in a New York *Herald Tribune* book review, Bernard De Voto came out with a blast at the cultural anthropologists for assuming that methods that seem to work with the Ubangi and the Trobriand Islanders will produce dependable results when applied to the English or Americans. But his was a voice crying in the wilderness. Few people were sufficiently specialized, or interested, to perceive the link between theories presented in scholarly books on anthropology or linguistics and practices that affect the daily lives of all of us.

5. It was only with the appearance of the new third edition of "Webster's Unabridged International Dictionary" late in 1961 that the issues at stake, at least for what concerns language, became clear to the cultured, educated layman of America. For this there was a deep, underlying reason that reaches down to the grass roots of our mores.

6. The English language, as is well known, has no set standard and no accepted authority, in the sense that countries such as France, Italy, and Spain have language academies that undertake to tell the speakers what is and what is not good standard practice. Since the days of Dr. Johnson, who refused to embalm the language and thereby destroy liberty, English speakers have submitted to the Doctrine of Usage rather than to the Voice of Authority. But usage has its own canons. In Britain, something called the King's (or Queen's) English has been enshrined over and above local dialects that range from London's Cockney to super-cultivated Oxford, and from the harsh speech of the North Country to the mellifluous accents of Kent. In America there is no President's American, but there is the Dictionary. From the time of Noah Webster, Amer-

icans have been wont to dip into a dictionary, the more abridged the better, to settle questions of usage and proper practice.

7. It may be stressed at this point that at no time did the compilers of the various editions of the Merriam Webster, the most comprehensive dictionary of America, set themselves up as authorities or arrogate the right to tell the people what was right and what was wrong in the matter of language. All they did was to record prevailing usage among the more educated classes. They listed and described plenty of variant regional pronunciations and words. They recorded, too, speech-forms of the lower classes, carefully labeling them "colloquial," "substandard," "vulgar," or "slang." This was not meant to prescribe or proscribe the use of certain forms, but merely to inform the reader as to the distribution of their occurrence. The attitude of the earlier lexicographers seemed to be: "Go ahead and use this form if you want to; but if you do, don't complain if someone says you are using a slang term."

8. The new 1961 edition of the Merriam-Webster has many features to commend it. Not only does it list the multitude of new terms, technological and otherwise, that have entered the language in recent years; it also has the merit of listing, with full definitions and examples, word combinations that have acquired special connotations not inherent in their component parts. The older Webster's defines both "guilt" and "association"; but the new Webster's also gives you "guilt by association." This means that the new edition is a handier tool than the older.

9. But the new edition makes one startling innovation which has recommended itself to the attention of all reviewers and of the general public as well. It blurs to the point of obliteration the older distinction between standard, substandard, colloquial, vulgar, and slang. "Ain't," it says, is now used by many cultivated speakers; "who" in the accusative function and "me" after a copulative verb are of far more frequent occurrence than "whom" and "I," and, by implication, should be preferred. This viewpoint goes right down the line. It led the editor of the New York *Times* to compose a passage that starts:

> A passel of double-domes at the G. & C. Merriam Company joint in Springfield, Mass., have been confabbing and yakking for twenty-seven years—which is not intended to infer that they have not been doing plenty work—and now they have finalized Webster's Third New International Dictionary, Unabridged, a new edition of that swell and esteemed word book.
>
> Those who regard the foregoing paragraphs as acceptable English prose will find that the new Webster's is just the dictionary for them.

10. There is more: the older Webster's, insofar as it gave citations, used only established authors, recognized masters of the language. The new Webster's cites profusely from people who are in the public eye, but who can hardly be said to qualify as shining examples of fine speaking

or writing. This leads another critic to complain that Churchill, Maritain, Oppenheimer, and Schweitzer are ranged as language sources side by side with Billy Rose, Ethel Merman, James Cagney, and Ted Williams; Shakespeare and Milton with Polly Adler and Mickey Mantle.

*11.* Dr. Gove's defense, fully presented in the pages of the same New York *Times* that had thundered editorially against his product, is both able and forthright: a dictionary's function, he said in substance, is to record the language, not to judge or prescribe it. Language, like practically everything else, is in a state of constant flux. It is not responsible to expect it to remain static, to retain unchanged forms that were current at one period but are no longer current today. We have changed our point of view in many fields; why not in language? His defense is, in a sense, a counterattack against the forces of purism, conservatism, and reaction. Why disguise the true function of a dictionary by turning it into a tool of prescriptivism, a fortress of a language traditionalism that no one today really wants? Language, after all, is what people speak, not what someone, be it even Webster, thinks they ought to speak.

*12.* This both clarifies and restricts the issue. But an issue still remains. Should a dictionary be merely a record of what goes on in language (all language, both high and low), or should it also be not so much a prescriptive tool as a guide for the layman, to not merely what *is* usage, but what is the *best* usage?

*13.* A speaking community that has been accustomed for the better part of two centuries to rely upon the dictionary to settle questions of usage balks at finding all usage now set on an identical plane. The contention of the objectors is that there are different, clearly identifiable levels of usage, which it is the duty of the dictionary to define. Without necessarily using the terms "correct" and "incorrect," they still would like to see a distinction made between what is better and what is worse.

*14.* In opposition to their stand, the new philosophy, linguistic and otherwise, seems to be summed up in this formula: "What is is good, simply because it is." Good and bad, right and wrong, correct and incorrect no longer exist. Any reference to any of these descriptive adjectives is a value judgment, and unworthy of the scientific attitude, which prescribes that we merely observe and catalogue the facts, carefully refraining from expressing either judgment or preference.

*15.* This relativistic philosophy, fully divorced from both ethics and esthetics, is said to be modern, sophisticated, and scientific. Perhaps it is. Some claim that its fruits are to be seen in present-day moral standards, national, international, and personal, as well as in modern so-called art, music, literature, and permissive education.

*16.* But we are concerned here only with its reflections on the language. The appearance of the new Webster's International has had several major effects. It has brought the question of permissiveness in language squarely to the attention of millions of educated laymen, who use the dictionary and refer to it for guidance. Without forcing a renunciation of Anglo-American reliance on usage rather than on the Voice of Authority, it has brought into focus the paramount question: "Whose usage? That of the cultivated speakers, or that of the semiliterates?" Finally, it has for the first time brought forth, into the view of the general public, those who are primarily responsible for the shift in attitude and point of view in matters of language—not the ordinary classroom teachers of English, not the educationists of the teachers colleges, but the followers of the American, anthropological, descriptive, structuralistic school of linguistics, a school which for decades has been preaching that one form of language is as good as another; that there is no such thing as correct or incorrect so far as native speakers of the language are concerned; that at the age of five anyone who is not deaf or idiotic has gained a full mastery of his language; that we must not try to correct or improve language, but must leave it alone; that the only language activity worthy of the name is speech on the colloquial, slangy, even illiterate plane; that writing is a secondary, unimportant activity which cannot be dignified with the name of language; that systems of writing serve only to disguise the true nature of language; and that it would be well if we completely refrained from teaching spelling for a number of years.

*17.* If these pronouncements come as a novelty to some of my readers, it is the readers themselves who are at fault. The proponents of these language theories certainly have made no mystery about them; they have been openly, even vociferously advancing them for years, and this can easily be documented from their voluminous writings.

*18.* The real novelty of the situation lies in the fact that, through the publication of the new Webster's—compiled in accordance with these principles—the principles themselves and their original formulators, rather than their effects upon the younger generations, now come to the attention of the general public. Lay reviewers generally display their complete awareness.

*19.* Dwight MacDonald, reviewing the new Webster extensively in the March 10, 1962 *New Yorker*, after claiming that the "scientific" revolution in linguistics has meshed gears with a trend toward permissiveness, in the name of democracy, that is debasing our language by rendering it less precise and thus less effective as communication, goes on to say:

> Dr. Gove and the other makers of 3 are sympathetic to the school of language study that has become dominant since 1934. It is sometimes called Structural Linguistics and sometimes, rather magnificently, just Modern Linguistic Science. . . . Dr. Gove and his editors are part of the dominant movement in the professional study of language—one that has in the last few years established strong beachheads in the National Council of Teachers of English

and the College English Association. . . . As a scientific discipline, Structural Linguistics can have no truck with values or standards. Its job is to deal only with The Facts.

20. Max S. Marshall, Professor of Microbiology at the University of California, writing in *Science*, March 2, 1962, says in part:

Opposed to [believers in a standard of quality in English] with several ringleaders at the head, is a group which goes back some thirty years, but has been actively proselytizing only in relatively recent years. These are the advocates of 'observing precisely what happens when native speakers speak.' These are the self-styled structural linguists, presenting language in a way so foreign that it might be imposed before users of the language discover its existence. . . . Gove declares himself flatly on the side of the structural linguists, calmly assuming, as do their ringleaders, that they are about to take over.

21. The principles of the American school of linguistics described above may come as a shock to some, but there is no need to be shocked. They are based upon definitely observable historical facts. Language invariably changes. Within our own personal experience we have noticed certain forms and expressions once considered slangy turning into regularly accepted parts of the standard language.

22. All that the American school of linguistics advocates is that we accept the process of change in language and submit gracefully to its inevitability. If we persist in hanging on to language forms and concepts that are antiquated and superceded, then we are merely subscribing to what they call "the superstitions of the past." We should be forward-looking, and progressive-minded. We renounce imperialism and colonialism in international relations, and admit nations like Ghana and the Congo to full equality with the established countries of Europe; by the same token, we should view the languages of the Arapahoes and the Zulus as being of equal importance with Latin and French. We believe in democracy and majority rule in political elections. Then, if a majority of the speakers of American English use "ain't," "knowed," "I'll learn you," "I laid on the bed," "who did you see," "between you and I," "like a cigarette should," these forms are by definition standard usage, and the corresponding minority forms, though sanctioned by traditional grammars, are, if not incorrect, at least obsolescent.

23. It may be argued, as does our Professor of Microbiology in *Science*, that "weighing the speech of casual speakers with no pretense of expertness on the same IBM card as usages of topnotch writers of past and present is an example of what the modern linguist calls 'science.' Tabulation is not science. Public opinion polls do not settle questions of science, or even of right and wrong. . . . If the guttersnipes of language do more talking than professors of English they get proportionally more votes."

24. But the structuralistic linguists can easily reply that language is a

matter of habit and convention, not of dogma or esthetics, and that if the
basic purpose of semantic communication is achieved, it matters little
what linguistic form is used. In engineering, calculations as to stresses and
structures must be precise and correct, under penalty of seeing the bridge
collapse. In medicine, correct dosage is essential, under penalty of seeing
your patient die. But in language, the use of a substandard for a standard
form seldom leads to irreparable consequences; at the most, as pictur-
esquely stated by a leader of the school, you may not be invited to tea
again.

25. On the other hand, members of the American school of linguistics
are not always consistent in the application of their democratic and equalitarian principles. In reply to his critics, Dr. Gove remarked that while
comments in lay newspapers and magazines had generally been unfavorable, the learned journals had not yet reviewed the new edition. The implication seemed to be that favorable reviews from a few members of his
own clique, read and approved by a small circle of professional structuralistic linguists, would more than offset the generally unfavorable reaction of newspapers like the New York *Times* and magazines like the *New
Yorker*, which appeal to large audiences of cultivated laymen. This not
only puts the process of democracy into reverse; it comes close to setting
up a hierarchy of professional linguists acting as the Voice of Authority for
a recalcitrant majority of educated people.

26. There is no doubt in my mind that widespread localisms, slang, vulgarisms, colloquialisms, even obscenities and improprieties, should be duly
noted in a comprehensive dictionary, whose first duty is to record what
goes on in the field of language. Should such forms be labeled and described for what they are, not in a spirit of condemnation, but merely for
the guidance of the reader? That, too, seems reasonable. If this procedure
helps to slow up the inevitable process of language change by encouraging
the speakers to use what the older dictionaries call standard forms, and
discouraging them from using substandard forms, this impresses me as a
distinct advantage. Too rapid and too widespread language change is a
hindrance to communications. It lends itself to confusion and misunderstanding. The use of a more or less uniform standard by all members of
the speaking community is desirable in the interests of efficiency rather
than of esthetics. There is no question that within the next 500 years the
English language, along with all other languages spoken today, will be so
changed as to be practically unrecognizable. This will happen whether
we like it or not. But need we deliberately hasten and amplify the process?
Between sudden revolution and stolid reaction there is a middle ground
of sound conservatism and orderly change.

27. Also, without being puristic to the point of ejecting "ain't" and kin-
dred forms from a dictionary of recorded usage, it might be worth while
to recognize the existence of a standard language, neither literary nor

slangy, which has acceptance and is understood practically everywhere in the country, even if everybody does not use it. Such phrases as "Them dogs is us'uns" and "I'll call you up without I can't," which an American structural linguist claims are good, meaningful language to him, merely because they are uttered by some native American speakers, definitely do not form part of that standard language. By all means let us record them for our own information and amusement, but let us not try to palm them off on the public on the general ground that the native speaker can do no wrong, and that "correct" and "incorrect" are terms that can be legitimately applied only to the speech of foreigners attempting to use English.

28. Language is something more than a heritage of sentimental value. It is an indispensable tool of communication and exchange of ideas. The more standardized and universal it is, the more effective it is. The more it is allowed to degenerate into local and class forms, the less effective it becomes. It may be perfectly true that in the past language has been allowed to run its own sweet, unbridled course, with the chips falling where they might. We are now in an age where we no longer believe in letting diseases and epidemics run their natural course, but take active, artificial means to control them. In fact, we endeavor to control natural, physical, and sociological phenomena of all descriptions, from floods to business cycles, from weather to diet, from the monetary system to racial relations. Is it unreasonable for us, far from leaving our language alone, as advocated by the American school of linguistics, to wish to channel it in the directions where it will prove of maximum efficiency for its avowed function, which is that of semantic transfer?

29. For the concern of that other burning question, standards of writing, as apart from standards of speech, ought we not to recognize that until such a time as tapes, recordings, dictaphones and spoken films altogether replace our system of written communications, the latter should be viewed and treated with respect? Again, we need not let ourselves be led too far afield by purely literary or esthetic considerations. The written language, in a modern civilization, is practically on a par with speech as a communications tool. It is incongruous to see our American structuralistic linguists devote so much painstaking attention to phonetic phenomena like pitch, stress, intonation, and juncture, to the fine distinctions between "a light housekeeper" and "a lighthouse keeper," "an iceman" and "a nice man," and yet shrug their shoulders at correct spelling, punctuation, and capitalization. More misunderstandings have occurred over misplaced commas than over misplaced junctures and, a wrong spelling can be just as fatal as a wrong intonation.

30. Perhaps the time has come, in language as in other fields, for the return of reason, and its ascendancy over dogma, whether the latter be of the puristic or of the structuralistic variety.

*31.* Above all, there is need for sound, scientific consideration of *all* the facts of language, not merely that portion which happens to suit the tastes and inclinations of a small group. Language is more than a set of phonemes, morphemes, junctures, and stresses. It also happens to be our most important instrument of semantic transfer, and the common possession of all of us. If democracy means anything, we, the speakers, have the right to have our say as to how it shall be viewed and used, and not to be forced to subscribe to the prescriptive excesses of what the European professor of linguistics describes as "the God's Truth School."

# Questions

1. How does Pei enlarge the context of the argument over the *Third* in his opening paragraphs? To what extent does this enlargement enable him to establish values for judging the dictionary not touched upon by Follett and by Evans?

2. What assumption made by Evans about previous editions of the Merriam Webster is refuted in paragraph 7?

3. What admission is made in paragraph 8? What devices does he use to indicate that the point is merely an admission?

4. What is accomplished by paragraphs 9 and 10? Why does paragraph 11 seem appropriately placed?

5. How is Pei in his statement of the critical issue in paragraph 12 less restrictive than we might expect a critic to be? How is Pei's case strengthened thereby?

6. Paragraphs 14 and 15 state the defender's case. Does Pei's statement of that case seem fair? Is his inclusion of relativism in ethics, art, and philosophy relevant?

7. Paragraph 16 presents Pei's summary of the views of the American structuralist school of linguistics. Compare this summary with that made by Bergen Evans. To what extent is the difference a matter of language and tone?

8. To what extent does Evans focus on stating the principles of the American school of linguistics while Pei discusses the implications and the results of the practice of these principles? What answer does Evans provide to the charges implied by Mario Pei in paragraph 16?

9. What function do paragraphs 18 through 20 serve?

10. Is Pei's charge in paragraph 22 that the structural linguists would have us view the languages of the Arapahoes and the Zulus as being of equal importance with French and Latin relevant? (See Evans, paragraph 7)

11. Are the analogies in paragraphs 24 and 28 valid?

## ·40·

*James Sledd*

# THE LEXICOGRAPHER'S UNEASY CHAIR

> *. . . this latest dictionary to bear the Merriam-Webster label is an intellectual achievement of the very highest order.*
>
> —Sumner Ives in *Word Study*

> *. . . the anxiously awaited work that was to have crowned cisatlantic linguistic scholarship with a particular glory turns out to be a scandal and a disaster.*
>
> —Wilson Follett in the *Atlantic*

> *Somebody had goofed.*
>
> —Ethel Merman in *Webster's Third New International Dictionary*

1. But who? Is the goof trademarked, a Merriam-Webster, or is scholarship in Springfield trans-*Atlantic?* The experts will have to answer that question, and thoughtful laymen after using the new dictionary for a long time. This review has more modest aims. Mainly it examines a few issues which less inhibited critics have already raised, suggests some possible limitations of their criticisms, and urges that the serious work of serious scholars must be seriously judged.

2. Everyone knows that the *Third International* is an entirely new dictionary for use today. In this eighth member of a series which began in 1828, the Merriam Company has invested over $3,500,000, almost three times the cost of the 1934 *New International,* so that the statements in *Webster's Third* are backed by over a century of experience, by the evidence of more than 10,000,000 citations, and by the knowledge and skill of a large permanent staff and more than 200 special consultants. To a reviewer, those facts should be rather sobering.

3. Some editors, however, and some reviewers have not been restrained from prompt attacks. They have criticized the *Third International* for its failure to include expected encyclopedic matter, for its technique of definition, and especially for its treatment of what is called usage; and they have charged Dr. Gove and his associates with unwise

From *College English* (May, 1962). Reprinted with the permission of the National Council of Teachers of English and James Sledd.

innovations motivated by the desire to destroy all standards of better
and worse in the use of English. While insisting upon the responsibility
of lexicographers, some of the attackers have not been equally alert to
the responsibility of critics.

4. The question of motives can be dismissed at once. The lexicographers at the Merriam Company, it may safely be assumed, have just one
motive: to make the best possible dictionaries. They may have failed,
in one respect or another; but such innovations as they actually have
made have not been made without the most serious and responsible consideration.

5. The charge of unwise innovation has two parts: first, that an innovation has been made; and second, that it is unwise. Some of the critics
have assumed that the editors of the *Third International* have departed
from established lexicographical custom by assuming the role of historians, not lawgivers. One reviewer, indeed, to prove his accusation that
the lexicographers had abandoned authority for permissiveness, quoted a
part of their statement that "the standard of English pronunciation . . .
is the usage that now prevails among the educated and cultured people
to whom the language is vernacular." He had not bothered to read precisely the same statement in the 1934 *New International*.

6. More generally, too many of the unfavorable critics have ignored
the whole history of English lexicography since Samuel Johnson: they
have hurried to denounce an innovation as unwise before establishing
the fact of innovation. Already in the eighteenth century, the ideal of
the standard and standardizing dictionary had been sharply questioned.
The encyclopedist Ephraim Chambers declared his view that "the Dic-
tionary-Writer is not supposed to have any hand in the things he relates;
he is no more concerned to make the improvements, or establish the
significations, than the historian" to fight the battles he describes. Even
Johnson said of himself that he did not "form, but register the language,"
that he did not "teach men how they should think, but relate how they
have hitherto expressed their thoughts"; and when Englishmen a century later set out to make the great *Oxford Dictionary*, they assumed
from the beginning that the lexicographer is "an historian" of the language, "not a critic." It may be that professional lexicographers have
been on the wrong track for two centuries and that in two hours an
amateur can set them straight; but in that event the amateur and not
the lexicographer would be the innovator. He would do well, before attempting to put his lawgiving theory into practice, to face Johnson's
doubts in that magnificent "Preface" and to ask himself the unanswerable
question how rational choice among the resources of a language is possible for the man who does not know what those resources are.

7. The relation between a dictionary and an encyclopedia is another
problem whose history should have been better known to some review-

ers. Few lexicographers are likely to solve it either to their own full
satisfaction or to the satisfaction of all their readers. From the *Third
International*, the objectors miss the gazetteer and the biographical dictionary of the 1934 volume, and they dislike the new decision to restrict
the world-list "to generic words . . . as distinguished from proper names
that are not generic." Other readers might just as well make opposite
complaints. The hairy-nosed wombat and the hickory shuckworm do not
greatly interest the average American, who has equally little need to
know the incubation period of the ostrich or the gestation period of the
elephant, to contemplate the drawing of a milestone marked "Boston 20
miles," or to examine a colorplate of fishes which is a slander to the cat-
fish and the brook trout; and the occasional philologist might hope for
a dictionary which explains words and leaves to the encyclopedia, as
Murray said, the description of things. But who can say that he knows
infallibly how such decisions should be made? Murray did not claim
infallibility but admitted inconsistency in his omission of *African* and
inclusion of *American*. Since man and the universe cannot be put between two covers, some things must be omitted; "selection is guided by
usefulness"; and usefulness can be guessed at but not measured. Readers
who can get the use of a Webster's unabridged will have access to an
encyclopedia. They should consult it when they need to know about
people and places. Meanwhile they may be grateful that the *Third International* has made space for as many quotations as it now includes.
A dictionary without quotations is like a table of contents without a book.

8. There remain, of the critics' favorite subjects, the technique of definition and the matter of usage. The technique of definition is briefly explained in the editor's preface:

The primary objective of precise, sharp defining has been met through development of a new dictionary style based upon completely analytical one-phrase
definitions throughout the book. Since the headword in the definition is intended to be modified only by structial elements restrictive in some degree
and essential to each other, the use of commas either to separate or to group
has been severely limited, chiefly to units in apposition or in series. The new
defining pattern does not provide for a predication which conveys further expository comment. . . . Defining by synonym is carefully avoided by putting
all unqualified or undifferentiated terms in small capital letters. Such a term in
small capitals should not be considered a definition but a cross-reference to
a definition of equivalent meaning that can be substituted for the small capitals.

A large number of verbal illustrations mostly from the mid-twentieth century has been woven into the defining pattern with a view of contributing
considerably to the user's interest and understanding by showing a word used
in context.

9. If it is not naively optimistic to expect most critics of a dictionary
to agree on anything, general approval may be expected for careful syn-

onymies and for the distinction between a synonym and a definition; and the value of illustrative quotations has been demonstrated by centuries of English lexicography. The objection that not many mid-century authors deserve quotation has already been answered, for it is only another form of the notion that the lexicographer should be a lawgiver and not a historian. It would, moreover, be rash to suggest either that many of the quotations are not particularly informative or that identification by the mere names of the authors makes it impossible to check the quotations or to examine them in their contexts: with 10,000,000 quotations to choose from, the editors must know the possibilities of choice more fully than any critic, and precise references would take up much valuable space.

*10.* The definitions themselves are another matter. Without advancing any claim to special competence, an ordinary reader may fairly report that he finds some of the definitions extraordinarily clumsy and hard to follow and that as an English teacher he would not encourage his students to follow the new Merriam-Webster model. The one-phrase definitions of nouns in particular may become confusing because in English it is hard to keep track of the relations among a long series of prepositional phrases, participial phrases, and relative clauses; the reader may simply forget what goes with what, if indeed he ever can find out. A less serious criticism is that the new typeface and the long entries unbroken by indentation are bad for middle-aged eyes. Real mistakes, of course, are extremely rare, but a fisherman may be pardoned an objection to the fourth numbered definition of the noun *keeper* as "a fish large enough to be legally caught." The crime is not catching but keeping an undersized or oversized fish.

*11.* Perhaps such a quibble is itself no keeper, and some criticism of the dictionary's treatment of usage has been equally frivolous. An excellent bad example appeared in *Life,* whose editors compressed a remarkable amount of confusion into a single sentence when they attacked "Editor Gove" for "saying that if a word is misused often enough, it becomes acceptable." Though one can argue how much use and by what speakers is enough, consistency would force *Life's* editors into silence. Their sacred kye are scrawnier than Pharaoh's seven kine, and it is shocking that the influence of such a magazine should force learning to debate with ignorance.

*12.* Yet so loud a stridulation of critics cannot simply be ignored. There is a real question whether the *Third International,* though justly called "the most comprehensive guide to usage currently available," has recorded usage as precisely as it might have done. Were the editors right to abandon "the status label *colloquial*"? Have they adequately reported not only what people say and write but also those opinions concerning speech and writing which properly enter into their own definitions of *standard* and of *Standard English?* Those are legitimate questions to ask of a dictionary "prepared with a constant regard for the needs of the high school and college student" and of the general reader. However diffidently and respectfully, a reviewer must give the best answers that he can.

*13.* Several reasons have been offered, by various authorities, for the abandonment of the label *colloquial.* Those reasons are not all alike. It is one thing to say that we cannot know "whether a word out of context is colloquial or not" (Gove), that lexicographers cannot distinguish the "many different degrees of standard usage" by status labels but can only suggest them by quotations (Gove), or that "the bases for discrimination are often too subtle for exact and understandable verbal statement" (Ives); it is quite another thing to argue against marking words *colloquial* because many readers have wrongly concluded that a word so marked is somehow bad (Ives). In a matter to which the editors must have given their best thought, the variety itself of these justifications and the failure to order them in any coherent and inclusive statement is somewhat puzzling; and the impertinent might be tempted to inquire how 200,000 quotations will enable the inexpert reader to do what 10,000,000 quotations did not make possible for the expert lexicographer or how a dictionary can be made at all if nothing can go into it which the ignorant might misinterpret. One reason for the widespread misinterpretation of the policy adopted is surely that the underlying theory has not been clearly explained.

*14.* And that is not all. The very defenses of the new policy appear sometimes to refute the contention that finer discriminations are not possible than those in *Webster's Third.* When the newspapers attack the dictionary for listing words like *double-dome* and *finalize* as standard, defenders reply by citing other slangy or colloquial or much reprobated terms from the columns of those same newspapers. What is the force of the attack or the defense unless the intelligent layman can draw precisely that distinction between "the formal and informal speech and writing of the educated" which the *Third International* refuses to draw for him? If he lacked that ability, both attackers and defenders would be wasting their citations.

*15.* Much can be said, of course, about the confusion of styles in modern writing. Perhaps distinctions among styles are now indeed less clear and stable than they were in a less troubled age; perhaps the clumsier writers do ignore the existing distinctions while the sophisticated use them to play sophisticated tunes; perhaps the scrupulously objective lexicographer cannot establish those distinctions from his quotation slips alone. For all that, distinctions do exist. They exist in good writing, and they exist in the linguistic consciousness of the educated. Dr. Gove's definers prove they exist when they give *egghead* as a synonym for *double-*

*dome* but then define *egghead* in impeccably formal terms as "one with intellectual interests or pretensions" or as "a highly educated person." Such opposition between theory and practice strikes even a timid and generally admiring reviewer as rather odd, as though some notion of scientific objectivity should require the scientist to deny that he knows what he knows because he may not know how he knows it.

*16.* In the absence, then, of convincing argument to the contrary, a simple reader is left with the uneasy feeling that the abandonment of *"Colloq."* was a mistake which the introduction of more quotations does not quite rectify and that as a teacher he must now provide foreigners and inexperienced students both with some general principles of linguistic choice and with specific instruction in instances where the new dictionary does not discriminate finely enough among stylistic variants. The dictionary leaves unlabeled many expressions which this teacher would not allow a beginning writer to use in serious exposition or argument except for clearly intended and rather special effects: (*to be caught*) *with one's pants down, dollarwise, stylewise* (*s.v. -wise*), (*to give one*) *the bird, dog* "something inferior of its kind," *to enthuse, to level* "deal frankly," *schmaltz, chintzy, the catbird seat, to roll* "rob," *to send* "delight," *shindig, shook-up, square* "an unsophisticated person," *squirrelly, to goof,* and the like. Enforcing such modest niceties will now be more difficult; for classroom lawyers and irate parents will be able to cite the dictionary which the teacher has taught Johnny how to read but which has collapsed the distinction between formal and informal Standard English. Similar difficulties could occur with various mild obscenities, such as *pissed off* and *pisspoor,* which should be marked not only as slang but with some one of the warning labels that the dictionary attaches to the almost quite adequately recorded four-letter words; and the label *slang* itself might well be more freely used with the various synonyms for *drunk—stewed, stinko, stoned, tight, tanked, sozzled, potted, pie-eyed, feeling no pain, blind, looped, squiffed, boiled, fried, high,* etc. Odzooks!

*17.* The convenience of a classroom teacher, however, is a rather petty criterion by which to judge a great dictionary, and the tiny handful of evidence here alleged must not be taken as justifying the shrill lament that *Webster's Third* is "a scandal and a disaster." The wake has been distinctly premature. Both the dictionary and the language it records are likely to survive the keening critics, whose exaggerations are something of a stumbing block themselves. The mere extent of the information in a dictionary unabridged should fix in a reviewer's mind the salutary knowledge that as no one man can make such a book, so no one man can judge it; but the popular reviews of the *Third International* have merely skimmed its surface and have said little of its technical fea-

tures or substantial accomplishments. The present discussion will conclude with a few slight remarks on some such matters and with the
renewed insistence that longer use and more expert study will be necessary before the dictionary can be definitely judged.

*18.* Teachers of elementary composition may be especially interested
in the dictionary's three well-filled pages on English punctuation. As several recent grammarians have done, the editors attempt to establish definite relations between pointing and intonation, and they pursue that
end with some care and vigor: the theory that punctuation may in
part be taught by relating it to pitch-contours and to pauses here receives
a better-than-average statement.

*19.* Yet the composition teacher may still be sceptical. For one thing,
no account of English intonation has deserved or won universal acceptance. The editors themselves thus seem to postulate more than the three
"pauses" allowed in the Trager-Smith phonology, which their description directly or indirectly follows. What is worse is the failure of the
proposed relationships between speech and pointing as one moves from
dialect to dialect: rules that may hold in one region do not hold in
another. For much Southern American speech and for much Southern
British, it is simply not the case that "the rising pause . . . is usually
indicated in writing by a comma"; for many speakers and writers in
many areas, an exclamation point may correspond to a *low*-pitched "ter-
minal stress" as well as to a high one; and a colon may be used in writing
not just for "a fading or sustained pause in speech" but for a "rising
pause" or for no pause at all. The editors have weakened their case by
stating it too simply and too strongly.

*20.* For the linguistically inclined, Mr. Edwin Artin's extensive "Guide
to Pronunciation" will have a particular attraction. The "Guide" is just
that—a guide; "not a treatise on phonetics" or a structural dialectologist's
systematic account of American pronunciation, but an explanation of the
way the editors have used their new alphabet in their transcriptions.
Though the forgetful will regret that the key is no longer before them
at each opening, and though a stern phonemicist might call the whole
system sloppy, the new alphabet is an arguable solution to an extremely
complex theoretical and practical problem and a definite improvement
over the more complicated yet less accurate and more misleading diacriti-
cal key in the *Webster's* of 1934. The objective in devising the alphabet
"was a set of symbols which would represent each speech sound which
distinguishes one word from another and each difference in sound which
is associated with some large region of the country" (Ives), so that the
editors might record both the formal and the informal pronunciations
actually heard in cultivated conversation from speakers of the standard
dialects in the various regions. The *Third International* can thus do fuller

justice than its predecessor did to regional variation and to modes of speech less artificial than the "formal platform speech" of the earlier work.

21. Like every competent writer on American pronunciation, Mr. Artin will be criticized as well as praised. He writes, indeed, at a particularly difficult time, when phonological theory is so unsettled that rival groups among the linguists can scarcely communicate with one another. Since pleasing one group of theorists means displeasing its opponents, since it is easily possible to please neither or none, and since Mr. Artin does not include in his "Guide" the sort of general and historical information which could be found in the corresponding section of the 1934 dictionary, perhaps he will not have so large an audience as Kenyon reached. His readers will be the kind who will argue the results of equating the medial consonants of *tidal* and *title* because in some dialects they are phonetically identical or of distinguishing them because the preceding diphthongs may be of different lengths and because the consonants of *tide* and *titular* clearly differ. Other readers, if they find the "Guide" hard going, will not risk too much confusion by limiting their study to the table of symbols and to the short section on pronunciation in the "Explanatory Notes."

22. Within the dictionary proper, the word-list first invites examination. Like the addenda to the later editions of the *Second*, the vexing miscellaneous entries at the bottoms of the pages are now gone from *Webster's Third*, either dropped or worked into the main alphabet; numerous obsolete words have disappeared, since the cut-off date has been advanced from 1500 to 1755; and further space for additions has been found by rejecting many no longer useful terms from the rapidly changing and never generally current technical vocabulary with which both the *Second* and the *Third International* are stuffed. This plethora of scientific and technical terms, carefully gathered in an elaborate reading program, is of course no plethora at all but only a comfortable supply for the scientist and technologist, who seem pleased with the dictionary's coverage of their fields; and a general dictionary must make room as well for some regionalisms, for a certain amount of recent slang, and for the new words in general use which so eloquently damn our culture. When all this has been done, it would be unfair to complain that perhaps not enough attention has been paid to the distinctive vocabularies of English-speaking nations other than Britain and the United States.

23. Beyond the word-list, neither space nor the reviewer's competence will allow him to go. He has few complaints about spelling, the only loud one being against *alright;* as far as a layman's knowledge goes, the etymologies are accurate, and beyond that point they remain clear and comprehensible; the discrimination and the arrangement of senses impose silence on the reader who has not studied them with the same care that went into their making; and the synonymies have already proved their

practical value. A sweeping conclusion will not be expected of a review whose thesis is that the prematurity of sweeping conclusions has already been sufficiently exemplified, but a moderately serious examination has made a few things perfectly plain about the *Third International*. As a completely new, independent, responsibly edited, unabridged dictionary, no other work can rival it on precisely its own ground. Its merits are infinitely greater than those of the reviews which have lightly questioned them. Time and the experts will ultimately decide its just rank in the world of English lexicography, whether above, below, or alongside its predecessor; but meanwhile it can usefully fill a place in the libraries of a generation.

# Questions

1. What issues in the argument over the *Third* does Sledd set aside as secondary and for what reasons?
2. What issues does he single out as primary or crucial? How do they compare and contrast with those distinguished by the previous writers in this section?
3. Although Sledd admits some of the definitions are faulty and the omission of labels of usage is unwise and confusing to the layman, how does he temper the force of his admissions?
4. Granted that Sledd is partially serious when he casually asserts "the convenience of the classroom teacher, however, is a rather petty criterion by which to judge a great dictionary," what criterion is in Sledd's view major and significant in judging a work such as the *Third?*
5. Show at what points Sledd's discussion is the least emotional and the most heavily qualified of these four discussions of *Webster's Third International.* Is a tempered, balanced view always (or ever) the truest view of any controversy or subject?
6. How does Sledd make the theory upon which the *Third* is based clearer than does Follett, Evans, or Pei? Where does he find gaps or weaknesses in the theory?
7. How does Sledd by means of word choice and tone establish a friendly but tentative attitude toward the *Third* and its makers and a reproving but explanatory attitude toward their detractors?
8. Paragraph 6 enlists Samuel Johnson on the side of the defenders. After studying the following section from Johnson's *Preface* to his own dictionary, point out how Sledd has reported Johnson's views correctly or incorrectly.

## · 41 ·

*Samuel Johnson*

# Preface to A DICTIONARY OF THE ENGLISH LANGUAGE

1. It is the fate of those who toil at the lower employments of life, to be rather driven by the fear of evil, than attracted by the prospect of good; to be exposed to censure, without hope of praise; to be disgraced by miscarriage, or punished for neglect, where success would have been without applause, and diligence without reward.

2. Among these unhappy mortals is the writer of dictionaries; whom mankind have considered, not as the pupil, but the slave of science, the pionier of literature, doomed only to remove rubbish and clear obstructions from the paths through which Learning and Genius press forward to conquest and glory, without bestowing a smile on the humble drudge that facilitates their progress. Every other authour may aspire to praise; the lexicographer can only hope to escape reproach, and even this negative recompense has been yet granted to very few.

3. I have, notwithstanding this discouragement, attempted a dictionary of the *English* language, which, while it was employed in the cultivation of every species of literature, has itself been hitherto neglected; suffered to spread, under the direction of chance, into wild exuberance; resigned to the tyranny of time and fashion; and exposed to the corruptions of ignorance, and caprices of innovation.

4. When I took the first survey of my undertaking, I found our speech copious without order, and energetick without rules: wherever I turned my view, there was perplexity to be disentangled, and confusion to be regulated; choice was to be made out of boundless variety, without any established principle of selection; adulterations were to be detected, without a settled test of purity; and modes of expression to be rejected or received, without the suffrages of any writers of classical reputation or acknowledged authority.

5. Having therefore no assistance but from general grammar, I applied myself to the perusal of our writers; and noting whatever might be of use to ascertain or illustrate any word or phrase, accumulated in time the materials of a dictionary, which, by degrees, I reduced to method, establish-

ing to myself, in the progress of the work, such rules as experience and analogy suggested to me; experience, which practice and observation were continually increasing; and analogy, which, though in some words obscure, was evident in others.

6. In adjusting the ORTHOGRAPHY, which has been to this time unsettled and fortuitous, I found it necessary to distinguish those irregularities that are inherent in our tongue, and perhaps coeval with it, from others which the ignorance or negligence of later writers has produced. Every language has its anomalies, which, though inconvenient, and in themselves once unnecessary, must be tolerated among the imperfections of human things, and which require only to be registered, that they may not be increased, and ascertained, that they may not be confounded: but every language has likewise its improprieties and absurdities, which it is the duty of the lexicographer to correct or proscribe.

7. As language was at its beginning merely oral, all words of necessary or common use were spoken before they were written; and while they were unfixed by any visible signs, must have been spoken with great diversity, as we now observe those who cannot read catch sounds imperfectly, and utter them negligently. When this wild and barbarous jargon was first reduced to an alphabet, every penman endeavoured to express, as he could, the sounds which he was accustomed to pronounce or to receive, and vitiated in writing such words as were already vitiated in speech. The powers of the letters, when they were applied to a new language, must have been vague and unsettled, and therefore different hands would exhibit the same sound by different combinations. . . .

8. In this part of the work, where caprice has long wantoned without controul, and vanity sought praise by petty reformation, I have endeavoured to proceed with a scholar's reverence for antiquity, and a grammarian's regard to the genius of our tongue. I have attempted few alterations, and among those few, perhaps the greater part is from the modern to the ancient practice; and I hope I may be allowed to recommend to those, whose thoughts have been perhaps employed too anxiously on verbal singularities, not to disturb, upon narrow views, or for minute propriety, the orthography of their fathers. It has been asserted, that for the law to be *known*, is of more importance than to be *right*. Change, says *Hooker*, is not made without inconvenience, even from worse to better. There is in constancy and stability a general and lasting advantage, which will always overbalance the slow improvements of gradual correction. Much less ought our written language to comply with the corruptions of oral utterance, or copy that which every variation of time or place makes different from itself, and imitate those changes, which will again be changed, while imitation is employed in observing them.

9. This recommendation of steadiness and uniformity does not proceed from an opinion, that particular combinations of letters have much influ-

ence on human happiness; or that truth may not be successfully taught by modes of spelling fanciful and erroneous: I am not yet so lost in lexicography, as to forget that *words are the daughters of earth, and that things are the sons of heaven.* Language is only the instrument of science, and words are but the signs of ideas: I wish, however, that the instrument might be less apt to decay, and that signs might be permanent, like the things which they denote. . . .

*10.* That part of my work on which I expect malignity most frequently to fasten, is the *Explanation;* in which I cannot hope to satisfy those, who are perhaps not inclined to be pleased, since I have not always been able to satisfy myself. To interpret a language by itself is very difficult; many words cannot be explained by synonimes, because the idea signified by them has not more than one appellation; nor by paraphrase, because simple ideas cannot be described. When the nature of things is unknown, or the notion unsettled and indefinite, and various in various minds, the words by which such notions are conveyed, or such things denoted, will be ambiguous and perplexed. And such is the fate of hapless lexicography, that not only darkness, but light, impedes and distresses it; things may be not only too little, but too much known, to be happily illustrated. To explain, requires the use of terms less abstruse than that which is to be explained, and such terms cannot always be found; for as nothing can be proved but by supposing something intuitively known, and evident without proof, so nothing can be defined but by the use of words too plain to admit a definition. . . .

*11.* In every word of extensive use, it was requisite to mark the progress of its meaning, and show by what gradations of intermediate sense it has passed from its primitive to its remote and accidental signification; so that every foregoing explanation should tend to that which follows, and the series be regularly concatenated from the first notion to the last. . . .

*12.* When first I collected these authorities, I was desirous that every quotation should be useful to some other end than the illustration of a word; I therefore extracted from philosophers principles of science; from historians remarkable facts; from chymists complete processes; from divines striking exhortations; and from poets beautiful descriptions. Such is design, while it is yet at a distance from execution. When the time called upon me to range this accumulation of elegance and wisdom into an alphabetical series, I soon discovered that the bulk of my volumes would fright away the student, and was forced to depart from my scheme of including all that was pleasing or useful in *English* literature, and reduce my transcripts very often to clusters of words, in which scarcely any meaning is retained; thus to the weariness of copying, I was condemned to add the vexation of expunging. Some passages I have yet spared, which may relieve the labour of verbal searches, and intersperse with verdure and flowers the dusty desarts of barren philology. . . .

*13.* My purpose was to admit no testimony of living authours, that I might not be misled by partiality, and that none of my cotemporaries might have reason to complain; nor have I departed from this resolution, but when some performance of uncommon excellence excited my veneration, when my memory supplied me, from late books, with an example that was wanting, or when my heart, in the tenderness of friendship, solicited admission for a favourite name.

*14.* So far have I been from any care to grace my pages with modern decorations, that I have studiously endeavoured to collect examples and authorities from the writers before the restoration, whose works I regard as *the wells of English undefiled,* as the pure sources of genuine diction. Our language, for almost a century, has, by the concurrence of many causes, been gradually departing from its original *Teutonick* character, and deviating towards a *Gallick* structure and phraseology, from which it ought to be our endeavour to recal it, by making our ancient volumes the ground-work of stile, admitting among the additions of later times, only such as may supply real deficiencies, such as are readily adopted by the genius of our tongue, and incorporate easily with our native idioms.

*15.* But as every language has a time of rudeness antecedent to perfection, as well as of false refinement and declension, I have been cautious lest my zeal for antiquity might drive me into times too remote, and croud my book with words now no longer understood. I have fixed *Sidney's* work for the boundary, beyond which I make few excusions. From the authours which rose in the time of *Elizabeth*, a speech might be formed adequate to all the purposes of use and elegance. If the language of theology were extracted from *Hooker* and the translation of the Bible; the terms of natural knowledge from *Bacon;* the phrases of policy, war, and navigation from *Raleigh;* the dialect of poetry and fiction from *Spenser* and *Sidney;* and the diction of common life from *Shakespeare*, few ideas would be lost to mankind, for want of *English* words, in which they might be expressed. . . .

*16.* Thus have I laboured by settling the orthography, displaying the analogy, regulating the structures, and ascertaining the signification of *English* words, to perform all the parts of a faithful lexicographer: but I have not always executed my own scheme, or satisfied my own expectations. The work, whatever proofs of diligence and attention it may exhibit, is yet capable of many improvements: the orthography which I recommend is still controvertible, the etymology which I adopt is uncertain, and perhaps frequently erroneous; the explanations are sometimes too much contracted, and sometimes too much diffused, the significations are distinguished rather with subtilty than skill, and the attention is harassed with unnecessary minuteness. . . .

*17.* Yet these failures, however frequent, may admit extenuation and apology. To have attempted much is always laudable, even when the enterprize is above the strength that undertakes it: To rest below his own aim is incident to every one whose fancy is active, and whose views are comprehensive; nor is any man satisfied with himself because he has done much, but because he can conceive little. When first I engaged in this work, I resolved to leave neither words nor things unexamined, and pleased myself with a prospect of the hours which I should revel away in feasts of literature, with the obscure recesses of northern learning, which I should enter and ransack; the treasures with which I expected every search into those neglected mines to reward my labour, and the triumph with which I should display my acquisitions to mankind. When I had thus enquired into the original of words, I resolved to show likewise my attention to things; to pierce deep into every science, to enquire the nature of every substance of which I inserted the name, to limit every idea by a definition strictly logical, and exhibit every production of art or nature in an accurate description, that my book might be in place of all other dictionaries whether appellative or technical. But these were the dreams of a poet doomed at last to wake a lexicographer. I soon found that it is too late to look for instruments, when the work calls for execution, and that whatever abilities I had brought to my task, with those I must finally perform it. To deliberate whenever I doubted, to enquire whenever I was ignorant, would have protracted the undertaking without end, and, perhaps, without much improvement; for I did not find by my first experiments, that what I had not of my own was easily to be obtained: I saw that one enquiry only gave occasion to another, that book referred to book, that to search was not always to find, and to find was not always to be informed; and that thus to persue perfection, was, like the first inhabitants of Arcadia, to chace the sun, which, when they had reached the hill where he seemed to rest, was still beheld at the same distance from them.

*18.* I then contracted my design, determining to confide in myself, and no longer to solicit auxiliaries, which produced more incumbrance than assistance: by this I obtained at least one advantage, that I set limits to my work, which would in time be ended, though not completed. . . .

*19.* Of the event of this work, for which, having laboured it with so much application, I cannot but have some degree of parental fondness, it is natural to form conjectures. Those who have been persuaded to think well of my design, will require that it should fix our language, and put a stop to those alterations which time and chance have hitherto been suffered to make in it without opposition. With this consequence I will confess that I flattered myself for a while; but now begin to fear that I have indulged expectation which neither reason nor experience can justify. When we see men grow old and die at a certain time one after another, from century to century, we laugh at the elixir that promises to prolong life to a thousand years; and with equal justice may the lexicographer be derided, who being able to produce no example of a nation that has preserved their words and phrases from mutability, shall imagine that his dictionary can embalm his language, and secure it from corruption and decay, that it is in his power to change sublunary nature, and clear the world at once from folly, vanity, and affectation.

20. With this hope, however, academies have been instituted, to guard the avenues of their languages, to retain fugitives, and repulse intruders; but their vigilance and activity have hitherto been vain; sounds are too volatile and subtile for legal restraints; to enchain syllables, and to lash the wind, are equally the undertakings of pride, unwilling to measure its desires by its strength. The *French* language has visibly changed under the inspection of the academy; the stile of *Amelot's* translation of Father *Paul* is observed by *Le Courayer* to be *un peu passé;* and no *Italian* will maintain that the diction of any modern writer is not perceptibly different from that of *Boccace, Machiavel,* or *Caro.*

21. Total and sudden transformations of a language seldom happen; conquests and migrations are now very rare: but there are other causes of change, which, though slow in their operation, and invisible in their progress, are perhaps as much superiour to human resistance, as the revolutions of the sky, or intumescence of the tide. Commerce, however necessary, however lucrative, as it depraves the manners, corrupts the language; they that have frequent intercourse with strangers, to whom they endeavour to accommodate themselves, must in time learn a mingled dialect, like the jargon which serves the traffickers on the *Mediterranean* and *Indian* coasts. This will not always be confined to the exchange, the warehouse, or the port, but will be communicated by degrees to other ranks of the people, and be at last incorporated with the current speech.

22. There are likewise internal causes equally forcible. The language most likely to continue long without alteration, would be that of a nation raised a little, and but a little above barbarity, secluded from strangers, and totally employed in procuring the conveniences of life; either without books, or, like some of the *Mahometan* countries, with very few: men thus busied and unlearned, having only such words as common use requires, would perhaps long continue to express the same notions by the same signs. But no such constancy can be expected in a people polished by arts, and classed by subordination, where one part of the community is sustained and accommodated by the labour of the other. Those who have much leisure to think, will always be enlarging the stock of ideas, and every increase of knowledge, whether real or fancied, will produce new words, or combinations of words. When the mind is unchained from necessity, it will range after convenience; when it is left at large in the fields of speculation, it will shift opinions; as any custom is disused, the words that expressed it must perish with it; as any opinion grows popular, it will innovate speech in the same proportion as it alters practice.

23. As by the cultivation of various sciences, a language is amplified, it

will be more furnished with words deflected from original sense; the geometrician will talk of a courtier's zenith, or the excentrick virtue of a wild hero, and the physician of sanguine expectations and phlegmatick delays. Copiousness of speech will give opportunities to capricious choice, by which some words will be preferred, and others degraded; vicissitudes of fashion will enforce the use of new, or extend the signification of known terms. The tropes of poetry will make hourly encroachments, and the metaphorical will become the current sense: pronunciation will be varied by levity or ignorance, and the pen must at length comply with the tongue; illiterate writers will at one time or other, by publick infatuation, rise into renown, who, not knowing the original import of words, will use them with colloquial licentiousness, confound distinction, and forget propriety. As politeness increases, some expressions will be considered as too gross and vulgar for the delicate, others as too formal and ceremonious for the gay and airy; new phrases are therefore adopted, which must, for the same reasons, be in time dismissed. *Swift*, in his petty treatise on the *English* language, allows that new words must sometimes be introduced, but proposes that none should be suffered to become obsolete. But what makes a word obsolete, more than general agreement to forbear it? and how shall it be continued, when it conveys an offensive idea, or recalled again into the mouths of mankind, when it has once become unfamiliar by disuse, and unpleasing by unfamiliarity?

24. There is another cause of alteration more prevalent than any other, which yet in the present state of the world cannot be obviated. A mixture of two languages will produce a third distinct from both, and they will always be mixed, where the chief part of education, and the most conspicuous accomplishment, is skill in ancient or in foreign tongues. He that has long cultivated another language, will find its words and combinations croud upon his memory; and haste and negligence, refinement and affectation, will obtrude borrowed terms and exotick expressions.

25. The great pest of speech is frequency of translation. No book was ever turned from one language into another, without imparting something of its native idiom; this is the most mischievous and comprehensive innovation; single words may enter by thousands, and the fabrick of the tongue continue the same, but new phraseology changes much at once; it alters not the single stones of the building, but the order of the columns. If an academy should be established for the cultivation of our stile, which I, who can never wish to see dependance multiplied, hope the spirit of *English* liberty will hinder or destroy, let them, instead of compiling grammars and dictionaries, endeavour, with all their influence, to stop the licence of translatours, whose idleness and ignorance, if it be suffered to proceed, will reduce us to babble a dialect of *France*.

26. If the changes that we fear be thus irresistible, what remains but to acquiesce with silence, as in the other insurmountable distresses of hu-

manity? It remains that we retard what we cannot repel, that we palliate what we cannot cure. Life may be lengthened by care, though death cannot be ultimately defeated: tongues, like governments, have a natural tendency to degeneration; we have long preserved our constitution, let us make some struggles for our language.

27. In hope of giving longevity to that which its own nature forbids to be immortal, I have devoted this book, the labour of years, to the honour of my country, that we may no longer yield the palm of philology, without a contest, to the nations of the continent. The chief glory of every people arises from its authours: whether I shall add any thing by my own writings to the reputation of *English* literature, must be left to time: much of my life has been lost under the pressures of disease; much has been trifled away; and much has always been spent in provision for the day that was passing over me; but I shall not think my employment useless or ignoble, if by my assistance foreign nations, and distant ages, gain access to the propagators of knowledge, and understand the teachers of truth; if my labours afford light to the repositories of science, and add celebrity to *Bacon,* to *Hooker,* to *Milton,* and to *Boyle.*

28. When I am animated by this wish, I look with pleasure on my book, however defective, and deliver it to the world with the spirit of a man that has endeavoured well. That it will immediately become popular I have not promised to myself: a few wild blunders, and risible absurdities, from which no work of such multiplicity was ever free, may for a time furnish folly with laughter, and harden ignorance in contempt; but useful diligence will at last prevail, and there never can be wanting some who distinguish desert; who will consider that no dictionary of a living tongue ever can be perfect, since while it is hastening to publication, some words are budding, and some falling away; that a whole life cannot be spent upon syntax and etymology, and that even a whole life would not be sufficient; that he, whose design includes whatever language can express, must often speak of what he does not understand; that a writer will sometimes be hurried by eagerness to the end, and sometimes faint with weariness under a task, which *Scaliger* compares to the labours of the anvil and the mine, that what is obvious is not always known, and what is known is not always present; that sudden fits of inadvertency will surprize vigilance, slight avocations will seduce attention, and casual eclipses of the mind will darken learning; and that the writer shall often in vain trace his memory at the moment of need, for that which yesterday he knew with intuitive readiness, and which will come uncalled into his thoughts tomorrow.

29. In this work, when it shall be found that much is omitted, let it not be forgotten that much likewise is performed; and though no book was ever spared out of tenderness to the authour, and the world is little

solicitous to know whence proceeded the faults of that which it condemns; yet it may gratify curiosity to inform it, that the *English Dictionary* was written with little assistance of the learned, and without any patronage of the great; not in the soft obscurities of retirement, or under the shelter of academick bowers, but amidst inconvenience and distraction, in sickness and in sorrow. It may repress the triumph of malignant criticism to observe, that if our language is not here fully displayed, I have only failed in an attempt which no human powers have hitherto completed. If the lexicons of ancient tongues, now immutably fixed, and comprised in a few volumes, be yet, after the toil of successive ages, inadequate and delusive; if the aggregated knowledge, and co-operating diligence of the *Italian* academicians, did not secure them from the censure of *Beni;* if the embodied criticks of *France,* when fifty years had been spent upon their work, were obliged to change its oeconomy, and give their second edition another form, I may surely be contented without the praise of perfection, which, if I could obtain, in this gloom of solitude, what would it avail me? I have protracted my work till most of those whom I wished to please have sunk into the grave, and success and miscarriage are empty sounds: I therefore dismiss it with frigid tranquillity, having little to fear or hope from censure or from praise.

# Questions

1. What irony is there in paragraph 1?
2. What stylistic devices can you identify in paragraph 3?
3. Name some of the irregularities inherent in our tongue that Johnson discusses in paragraph 6.
4. Does the spelling and capitalization of Marvell's "To His Coy Mistress" give any insight into what Johnson discusses in paragraphs 6 through 9?
5. In paragraph 8, is Johnson's general approach that of the permissive scholar or the prescriptive? Explain. Would he agree with Evans? Follett? Pei? Sledd?
6. How does the phrase in paragraph 9 "words are the daughters of earth, and that things are the sons of heaven" explain Johnson's position? Does he temper his statement?
7. Why did Johnson not use living authors as sources?
8. What period did Johnson set for his earliest limit and why?
9. Would the editors of the *Third* be able to use paragraphs 19 and 20 as testimony in their defense?
10. Would Evans agree with paragraph 26?

11. Why does Johnson conclude the preface to his monumental dictionary with these words: "I therefore dismiss it with frigid tranquillity, having little to fear or hope from censure or from praise"?

12. In paragraph 28, when Johnson is considering his final attitude toward the dictionary, there is an extremely long sentence which begins: "That it will immediately become popular. . . ." The sentence continues to the end of the paragraph. What stylistic devices does Johnson employ to hold the sentence together, to keep it from becoming unwieldy?

13. In paragraph 29, Johnson contrasts his working conditions with those of others who have written. Name some of the balanced contrasts he presents and comment on their effectiveness.

# Theme Topics

1. Write an essay in which you refute the position taken by one of the critics of Webster's *Third* by using evidence from the others.

2. Isolate a single issue of the controversy over Webster's *Third* and argue your position.

3. Write a statement of the entire controversy over Webster's *Third* to be read by the general reader who knows nothing of either the controversy or the dictionary.

4. Write a *slanted* statement of the entire controversy which pretends to be a simple report of the situation but which actually attempts to sway your innocent reader's response.

5. Write a short satire of either the dictionary, the entire controversy or the critics of the dictionary. You might, for example, write a letter to the editors from a confused man looking for an answer, from an English teacher of the dogmatic school, or from a misguided champion of liberty congratulating the editors. You might write a dialogue in which one person tries to explain the controversy to another. You might write a piece of prose for some specific occasion using the new permissiveness—a speech introducing a guest speaker, a letter to an editor, etc.

# The American Scene

## ~ XI ~

## VALUES, ABSOLUTES, AND FOCUS FOR ARGUMENT

ARGUMENTS ARE ESSENTIALLY of two kinds: those for or against a certain course of action and those for or against a certain judgment. What one favors as a course of future action as well as what one approves of the past are both decided on the basis of one's values. The question of values would itself be a simple one if our culture passed on to us a set of absolutes, standards by which we might make judgments. Such, unfortunately, is not the case, as the essays of C. S. Lewis and Philip Wheelwright in this volume illustrate. As C. S. Lewis demonstrates, however, we do believe in right and wrong. For example, in a certain instance we might advocate mercy killing and long before we encountered someone who directed our attention to the absolute "Thou shalt not kill," we would have encountered it in our own sense of guilt. We are then in the grips of an ethical dilemma. On the one hand we feel that in this instance the value above all others is to relieve another of pain in a situation where his agony is acute and his imminent death certain. We argue that "Thou shalt not kill" is no absolute anyway since war and self-defense have already made its application relative to circumstances. On the other hand, we know that the standards by which ordinary men in Western society live, backed by their church, do not admit this to be a circumstance where an exception can be made. There may be exceptions to the absolute of "Thou shalt not kill," but they do not reduce the force of the absolute in this instance. In this argument, then, it is possible to take an absolute position since a fairly clear ethical absolute is relevant. Another instance where it is possible to take an absolute stand, as most college professors do, is in questions of changing college grades. A student gets the grade he earned even though that grade may not represent his superior ability or may prevent a senior from graduating. But most questions are more complex than a simple choice between whether to take the absolute position or make an exception in a particular instance.

There are really four positions possible in certain arguments. These are possible when there are absolute positions both for and against the

344

proposition as well as relative or practical positions on both sides. Arguments of policy are really questions of whether to leave things as they are (maintain the *status quo*) or change them, and sometimes absolutes can be discerned for both positions. One might favor lowering the legal age for drinking on the basis that any restrictions of individual freedom (drinking being an activity that affects the individual alone) are wrong; and one might oppose the change, arguing to keep the present law, on the basis that drinking is wrong and any restrictions on it, therefore, are right. But other positions are also possible and they are not absolute positions. We might argue that nineteen-year-olds drink anyway; and, while admitting that they should not, we might advocate lowering the legal age for the practical, amoral reason that the law should harmonize with practice that cannot be altered without enormous social cost and stress. Notice that this position does not treat the ethical absolute as a crucial issue but as an admitted or secondary one. On the other side, one might argue that lowering the legal age for drinking will increase the amount of drinking and that the change in the law is therefore wrong. This issue might be countered with the position that it is not the amount of drinking but the amount of *bad* drinking that matters and that lowering the legal age would greatly reduce not just illegal drinking but drinking in cars and secret places. Legalizing drinking would reduce the challenge alcohol presents not just to the worst elements of American teen-age society but to all. The last two positions represent relative or practical positions, one for and one against, the proposition that the legal drinking age should be lowered.

The point of the above example is to illustrate that arguments must be given some focus. Decisions must be made about what issue or issues you will treat as crucial and what answer you will give to the positions of all possible opponents. It is possible to focus on either of the absolute positions on drinking and the law, to admit both and focus elsewhere, or to deny either or both of them. It is also possible to focus on a practical issue and use an absolute as a supporting or secondary issue, to argue that the reductions of *bad* drinking is the crucial point and add that individual morality cannot be legislated anyway. It cannot, as the amount of illegal drinking proves; and it should not since it is an infringement of personal rights.

*Plato*

# CRITO

SOCRATES. Why have you come at this hour, Crito? It must be quite early?
CRITO. Yes, certainly.
SOCRATES. What is the exact time?
CRITO. The dawn is breaking.
SOCRATES. I wonder that the keeper of the prison would let you in.
CRITO. He knows me, because I often come, Socrates; moreover I have done him a kindness.
SOCRATES. And are you only just come?
CRITO. No, I came some time ago.
SOCRATES. Then why did you sit and say nothing, instead of awakening me at once?
CRITO. Why, indeed, Socrates, I myself would rather not have all this sleeplessness and sorrow. But I have been wondering at your peaceful slumbers, and that was the reason why I did not awaken you, because I wanted you to be out of pain. I have always thought you happy in the calmness of your temperament; but never did I see the like of the easy, cheerful way in which you bear this calamity.
SOCRATES. Why, Crito, when a man has reached my age he ought not to be repining at the prospect of death.
CRITO. And yet other old men find themselves in similar misfortunes, and age does not prevent them from repining.
SOCRATES. That may be. But you have not told me why you come at this early hour.
CRITO. I come to bring you a message which is sad and painful; not, as I believe, to yourself, but to all of us who are your friends, and saddest of all to me.

From *The Works of Plato*, translated by Benjamin Jowett. Published by The Clarendon Press, Oxford.
Socrates, in Plato's *Apology*, states the charge against him: "Socrates is an evildoer, and a curious person, who searches into things under the earth and in heaven, and he makes the worse appear the better cause; and he teaches the aforesaid doctrines to others." The word *evildoer* in the above quotation is defined by the remainder of the quotation. There is no other action than that of free inquiry of which Socrates was guilty.

SOCRATES. What! I suppose that the ship has come from Delos, on the arrival of which I am to die?

CRITO. No, the ship has not actually arrived, but she will probably be here to-day, as persons who have come from Sunium tell me that they left her there; and therefore to-morrow, Socrates, will be the last day of your life.

SOCRATES. Very well, Crito; such is the will of God, I am willing; but my belief is that there will be a delay of a day.

CRITO. Why do you say this?

SOCRATES. I will tell you. I am to die on the day after the arrival of the ship?

CRITO. Yes; that is what the authorities say.

SOCRATES. But I do not think that the ship will be here until to-morrow; this I gather from a vision which I had last night, or rather only just now, when you fortunately allowed me to sleep.

CRITO. And what was the nature of the vision?

SOCRATES. There came to me the likeness of a woman, fair and comely, clothed in white raiment, who called to me and said: "O Socrates, the third day hence to Phthia shalt thou go."

CRITO. What a singular dream, Socrates!

SOCRATES. There can be no doubt about the meaning, Crito, I think.

CRITO. Yes; the meaning is only too clear. But, Oh! my beloved Socrates, let me entreat you once more to take my advice and escape. For if you die I shall not only lose a friend who can never be replaced, but there is another evil: people who do not know you and me will believe that I might have saved you if I had been willing to give money, but that I did not care. Now, can there be a worse disgrace than this—that I should be thought to value money more than the life of a friend? For the many will not be persuaded that I wanted you to escape, and that you refused.

SOCRATES. But why, my dear Crito, should we care about the opinion of the many? Good men, and they are the only persons who are worth considering, will think of these things truly as they happened.

CRITO. But do you see, Socrates, that the opinion of the many must be regarded, as is evident in your own case, because they can do the very greatest evil to any one who has lost their good opinion.

SOCRATES. I only wish, Crito, that they could; for then they could also do the greatest good, and that would be well. But the truth is, that they can do neither good nor evil: they can not make a man wise or make him foolish; and whatever they do is the result of chance.

CRITO. Well, I will not dispute about that; but please to tell me, Socrates, whether you are not acting out of regard to me and your other friends: are you not afraid that if you escape hence we may get into trouble with the informers for having stolen you away, and lose either the whole or a great part of our property; or that even a worse evil may happen to us? Now, if this is your fear, be at ease; for in order to save you we ought surely to run this, or even a greater risk; be persuaded, then, and do as I say.

SOCRATES. Yes. Crito, that is one fear which you mention, but by no means the only one.

CRITO. Fear not. There are persons who at no great cost are willing to save you and bring you out of prison; and as for the informers, you may observe that they are far from being exorbitant in their demands; a little money will satisfy them. My means, which, as I am sure, are ample, are at your service, and if you have a scruple about spending all mine, here are strangers who will give you the use of theirs; and one of them, Simmias the Theban, has brought a sum of money for this very purpose; and Cebes and many others are willing to spend their money too. I say therefore, do not on that account hesitate about making your escape, and do not say, as you did in the court, that you will have a difficulty in knowing what to do with yourself if you escape. For men will love you in other places to which you may go, and not in Athens only; there are friends of mine in Thessaly, if you like to go to them, who will value and protect you, and no Thessalian will give you any trouble. Nor can I think that you are justified, Socrates, in betraying your own life when you might be saved; this is playing into the hands of your enemies and destroyers; and moreover I should say that you were betraying your children; for you might bring them up and educate them; instead of which you go away and leave them, and they will have to take their chance; and if they do not meet with the usual fate of orphans, there will be small thanks to you. No man should bring children into the world who is unwilling to persevere to the end in their nurture and education. But you are choosing the easier part, as I think, not the better and manlier, which would rather have become one who professes virtue in all his actions, like yourself. And indeed, I am ashamed not only of you, but of us who are your friends, when I reflect that this entire business of yours will be attributed to our want of courage. The trial need never have come on, or might have been brought to another issue; and the end of all, which is the crowning absurdity, will seem to have been permitted by us, through cowardice and baseness, who might have saved you, as you might have saved yourself, if we had been good for anything (for there was no difficulty in escaping); and we did not see how disgraceful, Socrates, and also miserable all this will be to us as well as to you. Make your mind up then, or rather have your mind already made up, for the time of deliberation is over, and there is only one thing to be done, which must be done, if at all, this very night, and which any delay will render all but impossible; I beseech you therefore, Socrates, to be persuaded by me, and to do as I say.

SOCRATES. Dear Crito, your zeal is invaluable, if a right one; but if wrong, the greater the zeal the greater the evil; and therefore we ought to consider whether these things shall be done or not. For I am and always have been one of those natures who must be guided by reason, whatever the reason may be which upon reflection appears to me to be the best; and now that this fortune has come upon me, I can not put away the reasons which I have before given: the principles which I have hitherto honored and revered I still honor, and unless we can find other and better principles on the instant, I am certain not to agree with you; no, not even if the power of the multitude could inflict many more imprisonments, confiscations, deaths, frightening us like children with hobgoblin terrors. But what will be the fairest way of considering the question? Shall I return to your old argument about the opinions of men? some of which are to be regarded, and others, as we were saying, are not to be regarded. Now were we right in maintaining this before I was condemned? And has the argument which was once good now proved to be talk for the sake of talking;—in fact an amusement only, and altogether vanity? That is what I want to consider with your help, Crito:—whether, under my present circumstances, the argument appears to be in any way different or not; and is to be allowed by me or disallowed. That argument, which, as I believe, is maintained by many who assume to be authorities, was to the effect, as I was saying, that the opinions of some men are to be regarded, and of other men not to be regarded. Now you, Crito, are a disinterested person who are not going to die to-morrow—at least, there is no human probability of this, and you are therefore not liable to be deceived by the circumstances in which you are placed. Tell me then, whether I am right in saying that some opinions, and the opinions of some men only, are to be valued, and other opinions, and the opinions of other men, are not to be valued. I ask you whether I was right in maintaining this?

CRITO. Certainly.

SOCRATES. The good are to be regarded, and not the bad?

CRITO. Yes.

SOCRATES. And the opinions of the wise are good, and the opinions of the unwise are evil?

CRITO. Certainly.

SOCRATES. And what was said about another matter? Was the disciple in gymnastics supposed to attend to the praise and blame and opinion of every man, or of one man only—his physician or trainer, whoever that was?

CRITO. Of one man only.

SOCRATES. And he ought to fear the censure and welcome the praise of that one only, and not of the many?

CRITO. That is clear.

SOCRATES. And he ought to live and train, and eat and drink in the way which seems good to his single master who has understanding, rather than according to the opinion of all other men put together?

CRITO. True.

SOCRATES. And if he disobeys and disregards the opinion and approval of the one, and regards the opinion of the many who have no understanding, will he not suffer evil?

CRITO. Certainly he will.

SOCRATES. And what will the evil be, whither tending and what affecting, in the disobedient person?

CRITO. Clearly, affecting the body; that is what is destroyed by the evil.

SOCRATES. Very good; and is not this true, Crito, of other things which we need not separately enumerate? In the matter of just and unjust, fair and foul, good and evil, which are the subjects of our present consultation, ought we to follow the opinion of the many and to fear them; or the opinion of the one man who has understanding, and whom we ought to fear and reverence more than all the rest of the world: and whom deserting we shall destroy and injure that principle in us which may be assumed to be improved by justice and deteriorated by injustice;—is there not such a principle?

CRITO. Certainly there is, Socrates.

SOCRATES. Take a parallel instance:—if, acting under the advice of men who have no understanding, we destroy that which is improvable by health and deteriorated by disease—when that has been destroyed, I say, would life be worth having? And that is—the body?

CRITO. Yes.

SOCRATES. Could we live, having an evil and corrupted body?

CRITO. Certainly not.

SOCRATES. And will life be worth having, if that higher part of man be depraved, which is improved by justice and deteriorated by injustice? Do we suppose that principle, whatever it may be in man, which has to do with justice and injustice, to be inferior to the body?

CRITO. Certainly not.

SOCRATES. More honored, then?

CRITO. Far more honored.

SOCRATES. Then, my friend, we must not regard what the many say of us: but what he, the one man who has understanding of just and unjust, will say, and what the truth will say. And therefore you begin in error when you suggest that we should regard the opinion of the many about just and unjust, good and evil, honorable and dishonorable.—Well, some one will say, "but the many can kill us."

CRITO. Yes, Socrates; that will clearly be the answer.

SOCRATES. That is true: but still I find with surprise that the old argument is, as I conceive, unshaken as ever. And I should like to know whether

I may say the same of another proposition—that not life, but a good life, is to be chiefly valued?

CRITO. Yes, that also remains.

SOCRATES. And a good life is equivalent to a just and honorable one—that holds also?

CRITO. Yes, that holds.

SOCRATES. From these premises I proceed to argue the question whether I ought or ought not to try and escape without the consent of the Athenians: and if I am clearly right in escaping, then I will make the attempt; but if not, I will abstain. The other considerations which you mention, of money and loss of character and the duty of educating children, are, as I fear, only the doctrines of the multitude, who would be as ready to call people to life, if they were able, as they are to put them to death—and with as little reason. But now, since the argument has thus far prevailed, the only question which remains to be considered is, whether we shall do rightly either in escaping or in suffering others to aid in our escape and paying them in money and thanks, or whether we shall not do rightly; and if the latter, then death or any other calamity which may ensue on my remaining here must not be allowed to enter into the calculation.

CRITO. I think that you are right, Socrates; how then shall we proceed?

SOCRATES. Let us consider the matter together, and do you either refute me if you can, and I will be convinced, or else cease, my dear friend, from repeating to me that I ought to escape against the wishes of the Athenians: for I am extremely desirous to be persuaded by you, but not against my own better judgment. And now please to consider my first position, and do your best to answer me.

CRITO. I will do my best.

SOCRATES. Are we to say that we are never intentionally to do wrong, or that in one way we ought and in another way we ought not to do wrong, or is doing wrong always evil and dishonorable, as I was just now saying, and as has been already acknowledged by us? Are all our former admissions which were made within a few days to be thrown away? And have we, at our age, been earnestly discoursing with one another all our life long only to discover that we are no better than children? Or are we to rest assured, in spite of the opinion of the many, and in spite of consequences whether better or worse, of the truth of what was then said, that injustice is always an evil and dishonor to him who acts unjustly? Shall we affirm that?

CRITO. Yes.

SOCRATES. Then we must do no wrong?

CRITO. Certainly not.

SOCRATES. Nor when injured injure in return, as the many imagine; for we must injure no one at all?

CRITO. Clearly not.

SOCRATES. Again, Crito, may we do evil?

CRITO. Surely not, Socrates.

SOCRATES. And what of doing evil in return for evil, which is the morality of the many—is that just or not?

CRITO. Not just.

SOCRATES. For doing evil to another is the same as injuring him?

CRITO. Very true.

SOCRATES. Then we ought not to retaliate or render evil for evil to anyone, whatever evil we may have suffered from him. But I would have you consider, Crito, whether you really mean what you are saying. For this opinion has never been held, and never will be held, by any considerable number of persons; and those who are agreed and those who are not agreed upon this point have no common ground, and can only despise one another when they see how widely they differ. Tell me, then, whether you agree with and assent to my first principle, that neither injury nor retaliation nor warding off evil by evil is ever right. And shall that be the premise of our argument? Or do you decline and dissent from this? For this has been of old and is still my opinion; but, if you are of another opinion, let me hear what you have to say. If, however, you remain of the same mind as formerly, I will proceed to the next step.

CRITO. You may proceed, for I have not changed my mind.

SOCRATES. Then I will proceed to the next step, which may be put in the form of a question:—Ought a man to do what he admits to be right, or ought he to betray the right?

CRITO. He ought to do what he thinks right.

SOCRATES. But if this is true, what is the application? In leaving the prison against the will of the Athenians, do I wrong any? or rather do I not wrong those whom I ought least to wrong? Do I not desert the principles which were acknowledged by us to be just? What do you say?

CRITO. I can not tell, Socrates; for I do not know.

SOCRATES. Then consider the matter in this way:—Imagine that I am about to play truant (you may call the proceeding by any name which you like), and the laws and the government come and interrogate me: "Tell us, Socrates," they say; "what are you about? are you going by an act of yours to overturn us—the laws and the whole state, as far as in you lies? Do you imagine that a state can subsist and not be overthrown, in which the decisions of law have no power, but are set aside and overthrown by individuals?" What will be our answer, Crito, to these and the like words? Anyone, and especially a clever rhetorician, will have a good deal to urge about the evil of setting aside the law which requires a sentence to be carried out; and we might reply, "Yes; but the state has injured us and given an unjust sentence." Suppose I say that?

CRITO. Very good, Socrates.

SOCRATES. "And was that our agreement with you?" the law would say; "or were you to abide by the sentence of the state?" And if I were to express astonishment at their saying this, the law would probably add: "Answer, Socrates, instead of opening your eyes: you are in the habit of asking and answering questions. Tell us what complaint you have to make against us which justifies you in attempting to destroy us and the state? In the first place did we not bring you into existence? Your father married your mother by our aid and begat you. Say whether you have any objection to urge against those of us who regulate marriage?" None, I should reply. "Or against those of us who regulate the system of nurture and education of children in which you were trained? Were not the laws, who have the charge of this, right in commanding your father to train you in music and gymnastic?" Right, I should reply. "Well then, since you were brought into the world and nurtured and educated by us, can you deny in the first place that you are our child and slave, as your fathers were before you? And if this is true you are not on equal terms with us; nor can you think that you have a right to do to us what we are doing to you. Would you have any right to strike or revile or do any other evil to a father or to your master, if you had one, when you have been struck or reviled by him, or received some other evil at his hands? —you would not say this? And because we think right to destroy you, do you think that you have any right to destroy us in return, and your country as far as in you lies? And will you, O professor of true virtue, say that you are justified in this? Has a philosopher like you failed to discover that our country is more to be valued and higher and holier far than mother or father or any ancestor, and more to be regarded in the eyes of the gods and of men of understanding? also to be soothed, and gently and reverently entreated when angry, even more than a father, and if not persuaded, obeyed? And when we are punished by her, whether with imprisonment or stripes, the punishment is to be endured in silence; and if she lead us to wounds or death in battle, thither we follow as is right; neither may any one yield or retreat or leave his rank, but whether in battle or in a court of law, or in any other place, he must do what his city and his country order him; or he must change their view of what is just: and if he may do no violence to his father or mother, much less may he do violence to his country." What answer shall we make to this, Crito? Do the laws speak truly, or do they not?

CRITO. I think that they do.

SOCRATES. Then the laws will say: "Consider, Socrates, if this is true, that in your present attempt you are going to do us wrong. For, after having brought you into the world, and nurtured and educated you, and given you and every other citizen a share in every good that we had to give, we further proclaim and give the right to every Athenian, that if he does not like us when he has come of age and has seen the ways of the city, and made our acquaintance, he may go where he pleases and take his goods with him; and none of us laws will forbid him or interfere with him. Any of you who does not like us and the city, and who wants to go to a colony or to any other city, may go where he likes, and take his goods with him. But he who has experience of the manner in which we order justice and administer the state, and still remains, has entered into an implied contract that he will do as we command him. And he who disobeys us is, as we maintain, thrice wrong; first, because in disobeying us he is disobeying his parents; secondly, because we are the authors of his education; thirdly, because he has made an agreement with us that he will duly obey our commands; and he neither obeys them nor convinces us that our commands are wrong; and we do not rudely impose them, but give them the alternative of obeying or convincing us;—that is what we offer, and he does neither. These are the sort of accusations to which, as we were saying, you, Socrates, will be exposed if you accomplish your intentions; you, above all other Athenians." Suppose I ask, why is this? they will justly retort upon me that I above all other men have acknowledged the agreement. "There is clear proof," they will say, "Socrates, that we and the city were not displeasing to you. Of all Athenians you have been the most constant resident in the city, which, as you never leave, you may be supposed to love. For you never went out of the city either to see the games, except once when you went to the Isthmus, or to any other place unless when you were on military service; nor did you travel as other men do. Nor had you any curiosity to know other states or their laws: your affections did not go beyond us and our state; we were your special favorites, and you acquiesced in our government of you; and this is the state in which you begat your children, which is proof of your satisfaction. Moreover, you might, if you had liked, have fixed the penalty at banishment in the course of the trial—the state which refuses to let you go now would have let you go then. But you pretended that you preferred death to exile, and that you were not grieved at death. And now you have forgotten these fine sentiments, and pay no respect to us the laws, of whom you are the destroyer; and are doing what only a miserable slave would do, running away and turning your back upon the compacts and agreements which you made as a citizen. And first of all answer this very question: Are we right in saying that you agreed to be governed according to us in deed, and not in word only? Is that true or not?" How shall we answer that, Crito? Must we not agree?

CRITO. There is no help, Socrates.

SOCRATES. Then will they not say: "You, Socrates, are breaking the covenants and agreements which you made with us at your leisure, not in any haste or under any compulsion or deception, but having had seventy years to think of them, during which time you were at liberty to leave the city, if we were not to your mind, or if our covenants appeared to you to be unfair. You had your choice, and might have gone either to Lacedaemon or Crete, which you often praise for their good government, or to some other Hellenic or foreign state. Whereas you, above all other Athenians, seemed to be so fond of the state, or, in other words, of us her laws (for who would like a state that has no laws), that you never stirred out of her; the halt, the blind, the maimed were not more stationary in her than you were. And now you run away and forsake your agreements. Not so, Socrates, if you will take our advice; do not make yourself ridiculous by escaping out of the city.

"For just consider, if you transgress and err in this sort of way, what good will you do either to yourself or to your friends? That your friends will be driven into exile and deprived of citizenship, or will lose their property, is tolerably certain; and you yourself, if you fly to one of the neighboring cities, as, for example, Thebes or Megara, both of which are well-governed cities, will come to them as an enemy, Socrates, and their government will be against you, and all patriotic citizens will cast an evil eye upon you as a subverter of the laws, and you will confirm in the minds of the judges the justice of their own condemnation of you. For he who is a corrupter of the laws is more than likely to be corrupter of the young and foolish portion of mankind. Will you then flee from well-ordered cities and virtuous men? and is existence worth having on these terms? Or will you go to them without shame, and talk to them, Socrates? And what will you say to them? What you say here about virtue and justice and institutions and laws being the best things among men. Would that be decent of you? Surely not. But if you go away from well-governed states to Crito's friends in Thessaly, where there is a great disorder and license, they will be charmed to have the tale of your escape from prison, set off with ludicrous particulars of the manner in which you were wrapped in a goatskin or some other disguise, and metamorphosed as the fashion of runaways is—that is very likely; but will there be no one to remind you that in your old age you violated the most sacred laws from a miserable desire of a little more life. Perhaps not, if you keep them in a good temper; but if they are out of temper you will hear many degrading things; *you will live, but how?* —as the flatterer of all men, and the servant of all men; and doing what?—eating and drinking in Thessaly, having gone abroad in order that you may get a dinner. And where will be your fine sentiments about justice and virtue then? Say that you wish to live for the sake of your *children*, that you may bring them up and educate them—will you take them into Thessaly and deprive them of Athenian citizenship? Is that the benefit which you would confer upon them? Or are you under the impression that they will be better cared for and educated here if you are still alive, although absent from them; or that your

friends will take care of them? Do you fancy that if you are an inhabitant of Thessaly they will take care of them, and if you are an inhabitant
of the other world they will not take care of them? Nay; but if they
who call themselves friends are truly friends, they surely will.

"Listen, then, Socrates, to us who have brought you up. Think not of
life and children first, and of justice afterwards, but of justice first, that
you may be justified before the princes of the world below. For neither
will you nor any that belong to you be happier or holier or juster in this
life, or happier in another, if you do as Crito bids. Now you depart in
innocence, a sufferer and not a doer of evil; a victim, not of the laws,
but of men. But if you go forth, returning evil for evil, and injury for
injury, breaking the covenants and agreements which you have made
with us, and wronging those whom you ought least to wrong, that is to
say, yourself, your friends, your country, and us, we shall be angry with
you while you live, and our breathren, the laws in the world below, will
receive you as an enemy; for they will know that you have done your
best to destroy us. Listen, then, to us and not to Crito."

This is the voice which I seem to hear murmuring in my ears, like the
sound of the flute in the ears of the mystic; that voice, I say, is humming
in my ears, and prevents me from hearing any other. And I know that
anything more which you may say will be vain. Yet speak, if you have
anything to say.

CRITO. I have nothing to say, Socrates.

SOCRATES. Then let me follow the intimations of the will of God.

# Questions

1. When Socrates says that the many can make a man neither wise nor foolish
   and that what they do is the result of chance, what does he mean?
2. If the opinion of the many can result in the death of Socrates, why does he
   rebuke Crito for saying that the many can do the greatest evil to one who
   has lost their good opinion?
3. Show how Socrates' position in the argument with Crito—and presumably
   his entire life and thought—is based on the following premise (or absolute):
   "Not life, but a good life is to be chiefly valued."
4. What for Socrates is the good life and what is its relation to his distinction
   between "the one and the many"? If the one is to be valued over the many,
   why, as Socrates presumably reports on the voices humming in his ear, are
   the many (i.e. the laws) so decisive in the argument?
5. How will Socrates harm the state by escaping?
6. What absolute (or premise) underlies Crito's arguments for urging Socra-

tes to escape? How could you argue more persuasively from this same absolute?

7. What relationship exists between Socrates' absolute and the last line of the dialogue: "Then let me follow the intimations of the will of God"?

8. If the opinion of the good—who are few in number—should be regarded only, how shall we recognize them when they speak?

9. How is the basic relation between the state and its citizens in the United States today different from or similar to that of the state and its citizens in ancient Athens?

# Theme Topics

1. Write a summary of Socrates' reasoning and his decision.

2. Write an essay showing the contemporary importance of Socrates' view of the opinion of the many.

3. Write a dialogue, as realistic as possible, to illustrate the irrationality of most people's thinking in certain areas; one party should attempt either to persuade the other to or dissuade him from a certain decision and course of action.

## · 43 ·

*Phyllis McGinley*

## SUBURBIA: OF THEE I SING

*1.* Twenty miles east of New York City as the New Haven Railroad flies sits a village I shall call Spruce Manor. The Boston Post Road, thoro, for the length of two blocks, becomes Main Street, and on one side of that thundering thoroughfare are the grocery stores and the drug stores and the Village Spa where teen-agers gather of an afternoon to drink their cokes and speak their curious confidences. There one finds the shoe repairers and the dry cleaners and the second-hand stores which sell "antiques" and the stationery stores which dispense comic books to ten-year-olds and greeting cards and lending library masterpieces to their mothers.

From *A Short Walk to the Station* by Phyllis McGinley. Copyright 1949 by Phyllis McGinley. Reprinted by permission of the Viking Press, Inc.

On the opposite side stand the bank, the fire house, the public library. The rest of this town of perhaps four or five thousand people lies to the south and is bounded largely by Long Island Sound, curving protectively on three borders. The movie theater (dedicated to the showing of second-run, single-feature pictures) and the grade schools lie north, beyond the Post Road, and that is a source of worry to Spruce Manorites. They are always a little uneasy about the children, crossing, perhaps, before the lights are safely green. However, two excellent policemen—Mr. Crowley and Mr. Lang—station themselves at the intersections four times a day, and so far there have been no accidents.

2. Spruce Manor in the spring and summer and fall is a pretty town, full of gardens and old elms. (There are few spruces, but the village Council is considering planting a few on the station plaza, out of sheer patriotism.) In the winter, the houses reveal themselves as comfortable, well-kept, architecturally insignificant. Then one can see the town for what it is and has been since it left off being farm and woodland some sixty years ago—the epitome of Suburbia, not the country and certainly not the city. It is a commuter's town, the living center of a web which unrolls each morning as the men swing aboard the locals, and contracts again in the evening when they return. By day, with even the children pent in schools, it is a village of women. They trundle mobile baskets at the A&P, they sit under driers at the hairdressers, they sweep their porches and set out bulbs and stitch up slip covers. Only on weekends does it become hetero-geneous and lively, the parking places difficult to find.

3. Spruce Manor has no country club of its own, though devoted golfers have their choice of two or three not far away. It does have a small yacht club and a beach which can be used by anyone who rents or owns a house here. The village supports a little park with playground equipment and a counselor, where children, unattended by parents, can spend summer days if they have no more pressing engagements.

4. It is a town not wholly without traditions. Residents will point out the two-hundred-year-old manor house, now a minor museum; and in the autumn they line the streets on a scheduled evening to watch the Volunteer Firemen parade. That is a fine occasion, with so many heads of households marching in their red blouses and white gloves, some with flaming helmets, some swinging lanterns, most of them genially out of step. There is a bigger parade on Memorial Day with more marchers than watchers and with the Catholic priest, the rabbi, and the Protestant ministers each delivering a short prayer when the paraders gather near the War Memorial. On the whole, however, outside of contributing generously to the Community Chest, Manorites are not addicted to municipal get-togethers.

5. No one is very poor here and not many families rich enough to be awesome. In fact, there is not much to distinguish Spruce Manor from any other of a thousand suburbs outside of New York City or San Fran-

cisco or Detroit or Chicago or even Stockholm, for that matter. Except for one thing. For some reason, Spruce Manor has become a sort of symbol to writers and reporters familiar only with its name or trivial aspects. It has become a symbol of all that is middle-class in the worst sense, of settled-downness or rootlessness, according to what the writer is trying to prove; of smug and prosperous mediocrity—or even, in more lurid novels, of lechery at the country club and Sunday morning hangovers.

6. To condemn Suburbia has long been a literary cliché, anyhow. I have yet to read a book in which the suburban life was pictured as the good life or the commuter as a sympathetic figure. He is nearly as much a stock character as the old stage Irishman: the man who "spends his life riding to and from his wife," the eternal Babbitt who knows all about Buicks and nothing about Picasso, whose sanctuary is the club locker room, whose ideas spring ready-made from the illiberal newspapers. His wife plays politics at the P.T.A. and keeps up with the Joneses. Or—if the scene is more gilded and less respectable—the commuter is the high-powered advertising executive with a station wagon and an eye for the ladies, his wife a restless baggage given to too many cocktails in the afternoon.

7. These clichés I challenge. I have lived in the country, I have lived in the city. I have lived in an average Middle Western small town. But for the best eleven years of my life I have lived in Suburbia and I like it.

8. "Compromise!" cried our friends when we came here from an expensive, inconvenient, moderately fashionable tenement in Manhattan. It was the period in our lives when everyone was moving somewhere. Farther uptown, farther downtown, across town to Sutton Place, to a half-dozen rural acres in Connecticut or New Jersey or even Vermont. But no one in our rather rarefied little group was thinking of moving to the suburbs except us. They were aghast that we could find anything appealing in the thought of a middle-class house on a middle-class street in a middle-class village full of middle-class people. That we were tired of town and hoped for children, that we couldn't afford both a city apartment and a farm, they put down as feeble excuses. To this day they cannot understand us. You see, they read the books. They even write them.

9. Compromise? Of course we compromise. But compromise, if not the spice of life, is its solidity. It is what makes nations great and marriages happy and Spruce Manor the pleasant place it is. As for its being middle-class, what is wrong with acknowledging one's roots? And how free we are! Free of the city's noise, of its ubiquitous doormen, of the soot on the windowsill and the radio in the next apartment. We have released ourselves from the seasonal hegira to the mountains or the seashore. We have only one address, one house to keep supplied with paring knives and blankets. We are free from the snows that block the countryman's roads in winter and his electricity which always goes off in a thunderstorm. I do not insist that we are typical. There is nothing really typical about any

of our friends and neighbors here, and therein lies my point. The true suburbanite needs to conform less than anyone else; much less than the gentleman farmer with his remodeled salt-box or than the determined cliff dweller with his necessity for living at the right address. In Spruce Manor all addresses are right. And since we are fairly numerous here, we need not fall back on the people nearest us for total companionship. There is not here, as in a small city away from truly urban centers, some particular family whose codes must be ours. And we could not keep up with the Joneses even if we wanted to, for we know many Joneses and they are all quite different people leading the most various lives.

*10.* The Albert Joneses spend their weekends sailing, the Bertram Joneses cultivate their delphinium, the Clarence Joneses—Clarence being a handy man with a cello—are enthusiastic about amateur chamber music. The David Joneses dote on bridge, but neither of the Ernest Joneses understands it, and they prefer staying home of an evening so that Ernest Jones can carve his witty caricatures out of pieces of old fruit wood. We admire each other's gardens, applaud each other's sailing records; we are too busy to compete. So long as our clapboards are painted and our hedges decently trimmed, we have fulfilled our community obligations. We can live as anonymously as in a city or we can call half the village by their first names.

*11.* On our half-acre or three-quarters, we can raise enough tomatoes for our salads and assassinate enough bettles to satisfy the gardening urge. Or we can buy our vegetables at the store and put the whole place to lawn without feeling that we are neglecting our property. We can have privacy and shade and the changing of the seasons and also the Joneses next door from whom to borrow a cup of sugar or a stepladder. Despite the novelists, the shadow of the country club rests lightly on us. Half of us wouldn't be found dead with a golf stick in our hands, and loathe Saturday dances. Few of us expect to be deliriously wealthy or world-famous or divorced. What we do expect is to pay off the mortgage and send our healthy children to good colleges.

*12.* For when I refer to life here, I think, of course, of living with children. Spruce Manor without children would be a paradox. The summer waters are full of them, gamboling like dolphins. The lanes are alive with them, the yards overflow with them, they possess the tennis courts and the skating pond and the vacant lots. Their roller skates wear down the asphalt, and their bicycles make necessary the twenty-five-mile speed limit. They converse interminably on the telephones and make rich the dentist and the pediatrician. Who claims that a child and a half is the American middle-class average? A nice medium Spruce Manor family runs to four or five, and we count proudly, but not with amazement, the many solid households running to six, seven, eight, nine, even up to twelve. Our houses here are big and not new, most of them, and there is a temptation to fill them up, let the décor fall where it may.

*13.* Besides, Spruce Manor seems designed by providence and town planning for the happiness of children. Better designed than the city; better, I say defiantly, than the country. Country mothers must be constantly arranging and contriving for their children's leisure time. There is no neighbor child next door for playmate, no school within walking distance. The ponds are dangerous to young swimmers, the woods full of poison ivy, the romantic dirt roads unsuitable for bicycles. An extra acre or two gives a fine sense of possession to an adult; it does not compensate children for the give-and-take of our village, where there is always a contemporary to help swing the skipping rope or put on the catcher's mitt. Where in the country is the Friday evening dancing class or the Saturday morning movie (approved by the P.T.A.)? It is the greatest fallacy of all time that children love the country as a year-around plan. Children would take a dusty corner of Washington Square or a city sidewalk, even, in preference to the lonely sermons in stones and books in running brooks which their contemporaries cannot share.

*14.* As for the horrors of bringing up progeny in the city, for all its museums and other cultural advantages (so perfectly within reach of suburban families if they feel strongly about it), they were summed up for me one day last winter. The harried mother of one, speaking to me on the telephone just after Christmas, sighed and said, "It's been a really wonderful time for me, as vacations go. Barbara has had an engagement with a child in our apartment house every afternoon this week. I have had to take her almost nowhere." Barbara is eleven. For six of those eleven years, I realized, her mother must have dreaded Christmas vacation, not to mention spring, as a time when Barbara had to be entertained. I thought thankfully of my own daughters whom I had scarcely seen since school closed, out with their skis and their sleds and their friends, sliding down the roped-off hill half a block away, coming in hungrily for lunch and disappearing again, hearty, amused, and safe—at least as safe as any sled-borne child can be.

*15.* Spruce Manor is not Eden, of course. Our taxes are higher than we like, and there is always that eight-eleven in the morning to be caught, and we sometimes resent the necessity of rushing from a theater to a train on a weekday evening. But the taxes pay for our really excellent schools and for our garbage collections (so that the pails of orange peels need not stand in the halls overnight as ours did in the city) and for our water supply which does not give out every dry summer as it frequently does in the country. As for the theaters—they are twenty miles away and we don't get to them more than twice a month. But neither, I think, do many of our friends in town. The eight-eleven is rather a pleasant train, too, say the husbands; it gets them to work in thirty-four minutes and they read the papers restfully on the way.

*16.* "But the suburban mind!" cry our die-hard friends in Manhattan and Connecticut. "The suburban conversation! The monotony!" They imply that they and I must scintillate or we perish. Let me anatomize Spruce Manor, for them and for the others who envision Suburbia as a congregation of mindless housewives and amoral go-getters.

*17.* From my window, now, on a June morning, I have a view. It contains neither solitary hills or dramatic skyscrapers. But I can see my roses in bloom, and my foxglove, and an arch of trees over the lane. I think comfortably of my friends whose houses line this and other streets rather like it. Not one of them is, so far as I know, doing any of the things that suburban ladies are popularly supposed to be doing. One of them, I happen to know, has gone bowling for her health and figure, but she has already tidied up her house and arranged to be home before the boys return from school. Some, undoubtedly, are ferociously busy in the garden. One lady is on her way to Ellis Island, bearing comfort and gifts to a Polish boy—a seventeen-year-old stowaway who did slave labor in Germany and was liberated by a cousin of hers during the war—who is being held for attempting to attain the land of which her cousin told him. The boy has been on the Island for three months. Twice a week she takes this tedious journey, meanwhile besieging courts and immigration authorities on his behalf. This lady has a large house, a part-time maid, and five children.

*18.* My friend around the corner is finishing her third novel. She writes daily from nine-thirty until two. After that her son comes back from school and she plunges into maternity; at six, she combs her pretty hair, refreshes her lipstick, and is charming to her doctor husband. The village dancing school is run by another neighbor, as it has been for twenty years. She has sent a number of ballerinas on to the theatrical world as well as having shepherded for many a successful season the white-gloved little boys and full-skirted little girls through their first social tasks.

*19.* Some of the ladies are no doubt painting their kitchens or a nursery; one of them is painting the portrait, on assignment, of a very distinguished personage. Some of them are nurses' aides and Red Cross workers and supporters of good causes. But all find time to be friends with their families and to meet the 5:32 five nights a week. They read something besides the newest historical novel, Braque is not unidentifiable to most of them, and their conversation is for the most part as agreeable as the tables they set. The tireless bridge players, the gossips, the women bored by their husbands live perhaps in our suburb, too. Let them. Our orbits need not cross.

*20.* And what of the husbands, industriously selling bonds or practicing law or editing magazines or looking through microscopes or managing

offices in the city? Do they spend their evenings and their weekends in
the gaudy bars of Fifty-second Street? Or are they the perennial house-
holders, their lives a dreary round of taking down screens and mending
drains? Well, screens they have always with them, and a man who is
good around the house can spend happy hours with the plumbing even
on a South Sea island. Some of them cut their own lawns and some of
them try to break par and some of them sail their little boats all summer
with their families for crew. Some of them are village trustees for nothing
a year and some listen to symphonies and some think Milton Berle ought
to be President. There is a scientist who plays wonderful bebop, and an
insurance salesman who has bought a big old house nearby and with his
own hands is gradually tearing it apart and reshaping it nearer to his
heart's desire. Some of them are passionate hedge-clippers and some read
Plutarch for fun. But I do not know many—though there may be such—who
either kiss their neighbor's wives behind doors or whose idea of sprightly
talk is to tell you the plot of an old movie.

21. It is June, now, as I have said. This afternoon my daughters will
come home from school with a crowd of their peers at their heels. They
will eat up the cookies and drink up the ginger ale and go down for a swim
at the beach if the water is warm enough, that beach which is only three
blocks away and open to all Spruce Manor. They will go unattended by
me, since they have been swimming since they were four, and besides
there are lifeguards and no big waves. (Even our piece of ocean is a compromise.) Presently it will be time for us to climb into our very old
Studebaker—we are not car-proud in Spruce Manor—and meet the 5:32.
That evening expedition is not vitally necessary, for a bus runs straight
down our principal avenue from the station to the shore, and it meets all
trains. But it is an event we enjoy. There is something delightfully ritual-
istic about the moment when the train pulls in and the men swing off,
with the less sophisticated children running squealing to meet them. The
women move over from the driver's seat, surrender the keys, and receive
an absentminded kiss. It is the sort of picture that wakes John Marquand
screaming from his sleep. But, deluded people that we are, we do not
realize how mediocre it all seems. We will eat our undistinguished meal,
probably without even a cocktail to enliven it. We will drink our coffee at
the table, not carry it into the living room; if a husband changes for dinner here it is into old and spotty trousers and more comfortable shoes.
The children will then go through the regular childhood routine—complain about their homework, grumble about going to bed, and finally accomplish both ordeals. Perhaps later the Gerald Joneses will drop in. We
will talk a great deal of unimportant chatter and compare notes on food
prices; we will also discuss the headlines and disagree. (Some of us in the
Manor are Republicans, some are Democrats, a few lean plainly leftward.
There are probably anti-Semites and anti-Catholics and even anti-Ameri-

cans. Most of us are merely anti-antis.) We will all have one highball, and the Joneses will leave early. Tomorrow and tomorrow and tomorrow the pattern will be repeated. This is Suburbia.

22. But I think that some day people will look back on our little interval here, on our Spruce Manor way of life, as we now look back on the Currier and Ives kind of living, with nostalgia and respect. In a world of terrible extremes, it will stand out as the safe, important medium.

23. Suburbia, of thee I sing!

# Questions

1. In singing the praises of life in suburbia, Miss McGinley is careful to raise and refute point by point the case stated by others against it. What issues does she raise on behalf of her opponents and then discount?

2. What methods of refutation does she employ against her opponents and how successfully does she use them?

3. Are there any issues that she ignores, that is, fails to raise and answer? If so, what are they?

4. What aspects of suburban life does she personally seem to prize most highly?

5. What is the function of the following word choices in the first two paragraphs: thundering thoroughfare, curious confidences, lending library masterpieces, curving protectively, trundle mobile baskets? Why has she chosen these and other details for the opening paragraphs? Name choices from her essay that would, if listed initially, destroy the dominant impression she creates there.

6. Compromise is the charge she says her friends make against her. She retorts that compromise is life's solidity. "It is what makes nations great and marriages happy." How true or false is this analogy when applied to suburban life?

7. In paragraph 9 she says that the true suburbanite needs to conform less than anyone else. What evidence does she give and how persuasive is it?

# Theme Topics

1. Write a description of some suburban community which makes the opposite impression of that made by Phyllis McGinley's opening paragraphs.

2. Write the argument against suburbia that Phyllis McGinley has refuted in her essay.

3. Write an argument against Phyllis McGinley's in which you refute her refutation.

## ·44·

*Alexis de Tocqueville*

# SOCIAL CONDITION OF THE ANGLO-AMERICANS

*1.* Social condition is commonly the result of circumstances, sometimes of laws, oftener still of these two causes united; but when once established, it may justly be considered as itself the source of almost all the laws, the usages, and the ideas which regulate the conduct of nations: whatever it does not produce, it modifies.

*2.* If we would become acquainted with the legislation and the manners of a nation, therefore, we must begin by the study of its social condition.

### THE STRIKING CHARACTERISTICS OF THE SOCIAL CONDITION OF THE ANGLO-AMERICANS IS ITS ESSENTIAL DEMOCRACY

*3.* Many important observations suggest themselves upon the social condition of the Anglo-Americans; but there is one which takes precedence of all the rest. The social condition of the Americans is eminently democratic; this was its character at the foundation of the colonies, and it is still more strongly marked at the present day.

*4.* I have stated in the preceding chapter that great equality existed among the emigrants who settled on the shores of New England. Even the germs of aristocracy were never planted in that part of the Union. The only influence which obtained there was that of intellect; the people were used to reverence certain names as the emblems of knowledge and virtue. Some of their fellow-citizens acquired a power over the others which might truly have been called aristocratic, if it had been capable of transmission from father to son.

*5.* This was the state of things to the east of the Hudson: to the southwest of that river, and as far as the Floridas, the case was different. In most of the States situated to the southwest of the Hudson some great

From *Democracy in America* by Alexis de Tocqueville, translated by Henry Reeve, edited and revised by Francis Bowen (New York, The Century Company, 1898).

English proprietors had settled, who had imported with them aristocratic principles and the English law of inheritance. I have explained the reasons why it was impossible ever to establish a powerful aristocracy in America; these reasons existed with less force to the southwest of the Hudson. In the South, one man, aided by slaves, could cultivate a great extent of country; it was therefore common to see rich landed proprietors. But their influence was not altogether aristocratic, as that term is understood in Europe, since they possessed no privileges; and the cultivation of their estates being carried on by slaves, they had no tenants depending on them, and consequently no patronage. Still, the great proprietors south of the Hudson constituted a superior class, having ideas and tastes of its own, and forming the centre of political action. This kind of aristocracy sympathized with the body of the people, whose passions and interests it easily embraced; but it was too weak and too short-lived to excite either love or hatred. This was the class which headed the insurrection in the South, and furnished the best leaders of the American Revolution.

6. At this period, society was shaken to its centre. The people, in whose name the struggle had taken place, conceived the desire of exercising the authority which it had acquired; its democratic tendencies were awakened; and having thrown off the yoke of the mother country, it aspired to independence of every kind. The influence of individuals gradually ceased to be felt, and custom and law united to produce the same result.

7. But the law of inheritance was the last step to equality. I am surprised that ancient and modern jurists have not attributed to this law a greater influence on human affairs.[1] It is true that these laws belong to civil affairs; but they ought, nevertheless, to be placed at the head of all political institutions; for they exercise an incredible influence upon the social state of a people, whilst political laws only show what this state already is. They have, moreover, a sure and uniform manner of operating upon society, affecting, as it were, generations yet unborn. Through their means, man acquires a kind of preternatural power over the future lot of his fellow-creatures. When the legislator has once regulated the law of inheritance, he may rest from his labor. The machine once put in motion will go on for ages, and advance, as if self-guided, towards a point indicated beforehand. When framed in a particular manner, this law unites, draws together, and vests property and power in a few hands; it causes an aristocracy, so to speak, to spring out of the

---

[1] I understand by the law of inheritance all those laws whose principal object it is to regulate the distribution of property after the death of its owner. The law of entail is of this number: it certainly prevents the owner from disposing of his possessions before his death; but this is solely with the view of preserving them entire for the heir. The principal object, therefore, of the law of entail, is to regulate the descent of property after the death of its owner: its other provisions are merely means to this end.

ground. If formed on opposite principles, its action is still more rapid; it divides, distributes, and disperses both property and power. Alarmed by the rapidity of its progress, those who despair of arresting its motion endeavor, at least, to obstruct it by difficulties and impediments. They vainly seek to counteract its effect by contrary efforts; but it shatters and reduces to powder every obstacle, until we can no longer see anything but a moving and impalpable cloud of dust, which signals the coming of the Democracy. When the law of inheritance permits, still more when it decrees, the equal division of a father's property amongst all his children, its effects are of two kinds: it is important to distinguish them from each other, although they tend to the same end.

8. In virtue of the law of partible inheritance, the death of every proprietor brings about a kind of revolution in the property; not only do his possessions change hands, but their very nature is altered, since they are parcelled into shares, which become smaller and smaller at each division. This is the direct, and as it were the physical, effect of the law. It follows, then, that, in countries where equality of inheritance is established by law, property, and especially landed property, must constantly tend to division into smaller and smaller parts. The effects, however, of such legislation would only be perceptible after a lapse of time, if the law were abandoned to its own working; for, supposing the family to consists of only two children, (and, in a country peopled as France is, the average number is not above three,) these children, sharing amongst them the fortune of both parents, would not be poorer than their father or mother.

9. But the law of equal division exercises its influence not merely upon the property itself, but it affects the minds of the heirs, and brings their passions into play. These indirect consequences tend powerfully to the destruction of large fortunes, and especially of large domains.

10. Among nations whose law of descent is founded upon the right of primogeniture, landed estates often pass from generation to generation without undergoing division,—the consequence of which is, that family feeling is to a certain degree incorporated with the estate. The family represents the estate, the estate the family,—whose name, together with its origin, its glory, its power, and its virtues, is thus perpetuated in an imperishable memorial of the past and a sure pledge of the future.

11. When the equal partition of property is established by law, the intimate connection is destroyed between family feeling and the preservation of the paternal estate; the property ceases to represent the family; for, as it must inevitably be divided after one or two generations, it has evidently a constant tendency to diminish, and must in the end be completely dispersed. The sons of the great landed proprietor, if they are few in number, or if fortune befriends them, may indeed entertain the hope of being as wealthy as their father, but not of possessing the same

property that he did; their riches must be composed of other elements than his. Now, as soon as you divest the land-owner of that interest in the preservation of his estate which he derives from association, from tradition, and from family pride, you may be certain that, sooner or later, he will dispose of it; for there is a strong pecuniary interest in favor of selling, as floating capital produces higher interest than real property, and is more readily available to gratify the passions of the moment.

*12.* Great landed estates which have once been divided never come together again; for the small proprietor draws from his land a better revenue, in proportion, than the large owner does from his; and of course, he sells it at a higher rate.[2] The calculations of gain, therefore, which decide the rich man to sell his domain, will still more powerfully influence him against buying small estates to unite them into a large one.

*13.* What is called family pride is often founded upon an illusion of self-love. A man wishes to perpetuate and immortalize himself, as it were, in his great-grandchildren. Where family pride ceases to act, individual selfishness comes into play. When the idea of family becomes vague, indeterminate, and uncertain, a man thinks of his present convenience; he provides for the establishment of his next succeeding generation, and no more. Either a man gives up the idea of perpetuating his family, or at any rate, he seeks to accomplish it by other means than by a landed estate.

*14.* Thus, not only does the law of partible inheritance render it difficult for families to preserve their ancestral domains entire, but it deprives them of the inclination to attempt it, and compels them in some measure to co-operate with the law in their own extinction. The law of equal distribution proceeds by two methods: by acting upon things, it acts upon persons; by influencing persons, it affects things. By both these means, the law succeeds in striking at the root of landed property, and dispersing rapidly both families and fortunes.[3]

*15.* Most certainly it is not for us, Frenchmen of the nineteenth cen-

---

[2] I do not mean to say that the small proprietor cultivates his land better, but he cultivates it with more ardor and care: so that he makes up by his labor for his want of skill.

[3] Land being the most stable kind of property, we find, from to time, rich individuals who are disposed to make great sacrifices in order to obtain it, and who willingly forfeit a considerable part of their income to make sure of the rest. But these are accidental cases. The preference for landed property is no longer found habitually in any class but among the poor. The small land-owner, who has less information, less imagination, and fewer passions than the great one, is generally occupied with the desire of increasing his estate: and it often happens that by inheritance, by marriage, or by the chances of trade, he is gradually furnished with the means. Thus, to balance the tendency which leads men to divide their estates, there exists another, which incites them to add to them. This tendency, which is sufficient to prevent estates from being divided *ad infinitum,* is not strong enough to create great territorial possessions, certainly not to keep them up in the same family.

tury, who daily witness the political and social changes which the law of partition is bringing to pass, to question its influence. It is perpetually conspicuous in our country, overthrowing the walls of our dwellings, and removing the landmarks of our fields. But although it has produced great effects in France, much still remains for it to do. Our recollections, opinions, and habits present powerful obstacles to its progress.

*16.* In the United States, it has nearly completed its work of destruction, and there we can best study its results. The English laws concerning the transmission of property were abolished in almost all the States at the time of the Revolution. The law of entail was so modified as not materially to interrupt the free circulation of property. The first generation having passed away, estates began to be parcelled out; and the change became more and more rapid with the progress of time. And now, after a lapse of a little more than sixty years, the aspect of society is totally altered; the families of the great landed proprietors are almost all commingled with the general mass. In the State of New York, which formerly contained many of these, there are but two who still keep their heads above the stream; and they must shortly disappear. The sons of these opulent citizens have become merchants, lawyers, or physicians. Most of them have lapsed into obscurity. The last trace of hereditary ranks and distinctions is destroyed,—the law of partition has reduced all to one level.

*17.* I do not mean that there is any lack of wealthy individuals in the United States; I know of no country, indeed, where the love of money has taken stronger hold on the affections of men, and where a profounder contempt is expressed for the theory of the permanent equality of property. But wealth circulates with inconceivable rapidity, and experience shows that it is rare to find two succeeding generations in the full enjoyment of it.

*18.* This picture, which may, perhaps, be thought to be overcharged, still gives a very imperfect idea of what is taking place in the new States of the West and Southwest. At the end of the last century, a few bold adventurers began to penetrate into the valley of the Mississippi; and the mass of the population very soon began to move in that direction: communities unheard of till then suddenly appeared in the desert. States whose names were not in existence a few years before, claimed their place in the American Union; and in the Western settlements we may behold democracy arrived at its utmost limits. In these States, founded off-hand, and as it were by chance, the inhabitants are but of yesterday. Scarcely known to one another, the nearest neighbors are ignorant of each other's history. In this part of the American continent, therefore, the population has escaped the influence not only of great names and great wealth, but even of the natural aristocracy of knowledge and virtue. None are there able to wield that respectable power which men willingly grant to the remembrance of a life spent in doing good before their eyes. The new States of the West are already inhabited; but society has no existence among them.

*19.* It is not only the fortunes of men which are equal in America; even their acquirements partake in some degree of the same uniformity. I do not believe that there is a country in the world where, in proportion to the population, there are so few ignorant, and at the same time so few learned, individuals. Primary instruction is within the reach of everybody; superior instruction is scarcely to be obtained by any.[4] This is not surprising; it is, in fact, the necessary consequence of what we have advanced above. Almost all the Americans are in easy circumstances, and can, therefore, obtain the first elements of human knowledge.

*20.* In America, there are but few wealthy persons; nearly all Americans have to take a profession. Now, every profession requires an apprenticeship. The Americans can devote to general education only the early years of life. At fifteen, they enter upon their calling, and thus their education generally ends at the age when ours begins.[5] Whatever is done afterwards is with a view to some special and lucrative object; a science is taken up as a matter of business, and the only branch of it which is attended to is such as admits of an immediate practical application.

*21.* In America, most of the rich men were formerly poor; most of those who now enjoy leisure were absorbed in business during their youth; the consequence of which is, that, when they might have had a taste for study, they had no time for it, and when the time is at their disposal, they have no longer the inclination.

*22.* There is no class, then, in America, in which the taste for intellectual pleasures is transmitted with hereditary fortune and leisure, and by which the labors of the intellect are held in honor. Accordingly, there is an equal want of the desire and the power of application to these objects.

*23.* A middling standard is fixed in America for human knowledge. All approach as near to it as they can; some as they rise, others as they

---

[4] This was an exaggerated statement even when De Tocqueville wrote, thirty years ago. But now, in the Atlantic States, through the influence of the Universities and of scientific and literary associations, there are probably, in proportion to the population, as many scholars, men of science, and highly educated men, as in any country of Europe.—Am. Ed.

[5] Members of what are called the learned professions—law, physic, and divinity—do not usually begin practice in America before they are twenty-two or twenty-three years old. The average age of the graduates of American Colleges is over twenty years, and two or three years after graduation must be devoted to professional studies. Boys become apprentices to the mechanic trades, it is true, at fourteen years; but this is the usuage age for the beginning of apprenticeship in England and on the continent of Europe. As a general rule, children of the poorest parents are not compelled to begin hard labor at so early an age in the United States as in Great Britain. De Tocqueville's statement is confused, because he does not sufficiently indicate which "professions" or "callings" he is speaking of.—Am. Ed.

descend. Of course, a multitude of persons are to be found who entertain the same number of ideas on religion, history, science, political economy, legislation, and government. The gifts of intellect proceed directly from God, and man cannot prevent their unequal distribution. But it is at least a consequence of what we have just said, that although the capacities of men are different, as the Creator intended they should be, Americans find the means of putting them to use are equal.

24. In America, the aristocratic element has always been feeble from its birth; and if at the present day it is not actually destroyed, it is at any rate so completely disabled, that we can scarcely assign to it any degree of influence on the course of affairs.

25. The democratic principle, on the contrary, has gained so much strength by time, by events, and by legislation, as to have become not only predominant, but all-powerful. There is no family or corporate authority, and it is rare to find even the influence of individual character enjoy any durability.

26. America, then, exhibits in her social state an extraordinary phenomenon. Men are there seen on a greater equality in point of fortune and intellect, or, in other words, more equal in their strength, than in any other country in the world, or in any age of which history has preserved the remembrance.

## POLITICAL CONSEQUENCES OF THE SOCIAL CONDITION OF THE ANGLO-AMERICANS

27. The political consequences of such a social condition as this are easily deducible.

28. It is impossible to believe that equality will not eventually find its way into the political world, as it does everywhere else. To conceive of men remaining forever unequal upon a single point, yet equal on all others, is impossible; they must come in the end to be equal upon all.

29. Now I know of only two methods of establishing equality in the political world; every citizen must be put in possession of his rights, or rights must be granted to no one. For nations which are arrived at the same stage of social existence as the Anglo-Americans, it is, therefore, very difficult to discover a medium between the sovereignty of all and the absolute power of one man: and it would be vain to deny that the social condition which I have been describing is just as liable to one of these consequences as to the other.

30. There is, in fact, a manly and lawful passion for equality which incites men to wish all to be powerful and honored. This passion tends to elevate the humble to the rank of the great; but there exists also in the human heart a depraved taste for equality, which impels the weak to attempt to lower the powerful to their own level, and reduces men

to prefer equality in slavery to inequality with freedom. Not that those nations whose social condition is democratic natually despise liberty; on the contrary, they have an instinctive love of it. But liberty is not the chief and constant object of their desires; equality is their idol: they make rapid and sudden efforts to obtain liberty, and, if they miss their aim, resign themselves to their disappointment; but nothing can satisfy them without equality, and they would rather perish than lose it.

*31.* On the other hand, in a state where the citizens are all nearly on an equality, it becomes difficult for them to preserve their independence against the aggressions of power. No one among them being strong enough to engage in the struggle alone with advantage, nothing but a general combination can protect their liberty. Now, such a union is not always possible.

*32.* From the same social position, then, nations may derive one or the other of two great political results; these results are extremely different from each other, but they both proceed from the same cause.

*33.* The Anglo-Americans are the first nation who, having been exposed to this formidable alternative, have been happy enough to escape the dominion of absolute power. They have been allowed by their circumstances, their origin, their intelligence, and especially by their morals, to establish and maintain the sovereignty of the people.

# Questions

1. What reciprocity between cause and effect does Tocqueville point to in his opening paragraphs?
2. What causes, according to Tocqueville, formed the "social condition" of democracy he observed in mid-nineteenth-century America?
3. What is the full scope of operation of the "law of equal distribution of inheritance"? Does Tocqueville see it as a necessary or a sufficient cause?
4. Sustained enjoyment of wealth by a family is a necessary condition for what effect, in Tocqueville's view?
5. Have we today left behind the social aspects of the "democratic principle" described by Tocqueville? What evidence can you cite from your knowledge of present-day America to confirm or challenge Tocqueville's causal analysis?
6. What alternative social consequences does Tocqueville see between the application of the principle of liberty and that of equality? What evidence do you see today to confirm or deny his prediction of the result of this contest between liberty and equality in the United States?

# Theme Topics

1. Explain what you see as the contemporary relevance of Tocqueville's remarks on the absence of an aristocratic tradition in America.
2. Write an essay explaining your understanding of Tocqueville as he related cause and effect in the America he knew.
3. Discuss, both in reference to the United States of today and Bettelheim's essay "Adjustment for Survival," the validity of Tocqueville's assertion: "To conceive of men remaining forever unequal upon a single point, yet equal on all others is impossible; they must come in the end to be equal upon all."

·45·

*D. W. Brogan*

# THE CHARACTER OF AMERICAN CULTURE

*1.* "Culture" is a highly ambiguous term. However I may limit my definition of it, "culture" remains a wide term demanding for its full definition and illustration a range of knowledge that I do not possess.

2. Culture can have two meanings. There is the meaning given to the word by the anthropologist, in which all social habits, techniques, religious practices, marriage customs, in fact everything—including the kitchen sink—is examined to throw light on how a particular society lives and moves, or just exists. Then there is "culture" in a narrower sense, in which we are concerned not with material techniques, not with the social organization that holds society together, but with the ideas, the aesthetic experiences and achievements, and the philosophical or religious ideas that affect and are affected by the aesthetic experiences and achievements of a given society. A special variant of the last sense of "culture" is the narrow identification of the word with the fine arts and the implicit relegation of the fine arts to the margin of life, to what is done in leisure or for leisure.

From *America in the Modern World* by D. W. Brogan. Copyright 1960, by Rutgers University Press and reprinted by permission of the publisher.

3. None of these usages of the word is strictly separable from the others. The first usage obviously includes all the possible variations on the meaning and even the most restricted implies the wider meaning as a background. I shall not try, therefore, to attain a rigorous standard of definition or eschew all overlapping of one definition of culture and another. I shall try to deal with the problem of the level and the tone of American culture in its second sense, but I shall not try to define that second sense narrowly or regard myself as debarred from using illustrations from American life that a culture snob would think showed a confusion of ideas or a lowering of standards. In my view culture that is merely a set of aesthetic practices, merely exemplified in private or even in public taste, is a theme of importance—to be treated by somebody else. What I am concerned with is the problem of cultural standards and achievements in an advanced democratic society, specifically the United States. And that cultural achievement cannot be separated from religion, education, the character of the state, the general aims and ambitions of American society.

4. To fall back on one of my devices already used, what is the cultural "mark" of American society? It is the absence of a strong, received aristocratic tradition, on the one side, and, on the other, the presence of a number of what can loosely, in a social if not a purely political sense, be called "democratic" biases and practices. The fine arts, literature, music, the content of the higher education have from the beginning been affected by the general egalitarian, progressive, optimistic, factual, future-discounting tone of American life. As I shall have occasion to note later, this bias of American life has often produced a powerful reaction and some of the classics of American literature are in the nature of minority protests against just those marks of American society that I have stressed. Nevertheless, American culture, in its widest sense, has these marks and American culture in its narrower sense has them too, even if to many the marks appear as scars.

5. What in the beginning marked off the nascent American culture from that of Europe? One thing I would suggest was poverty, poverty in a society already more egalitarian than that of Europe. People came to America to get rich (among other reasons); they did not arrive rich. Establishing their culture beachheads on the eastern coast, they had not the resources of time or of energy for the reproduction on the American shore of the elaborate cultural life that some of them had shared and all of them had heard of in Europe. There was no demand for a Vandyke, an Inigo Jones, a Milton in seventeenth-century America; no means of producing or sustaining such artists.

6. The contrast with Spanish America is striking in at least one field, that of architecture. The Spanish colonists had two resources that the English colonists lacked: a docile and utilizable Indian population and

"treasure," gold and silver. There was from the first in Spanish America a surplus for the fine arts. There was more. There was a government and a church that both aimed at splendor and had the political resources to use the surplus to produce it. It was not only that in English America there were no easily exploitable human and material resources to permit the creation of a materially splendid society. There were no institutions to insist that such splendor should be provided. The royal government, the churches could not, even if they had wished, force the colonists to produce art works on the scale of the Cathedral of Mexico.

7. Dwelling houses, churches and public buildings were necessarily simple, utilitarian. They could be and sometimes were aesthetically satisfactory as well, but the aim was not splendor. It was utility. Simplicity often is a form of beauty and elegance, but I think that some harm is done to the modern American sense of the beautiful by too much insistence on the triumphs of a simplicity that was imposed by need rather than by choice. From the beginning beauty was associated in American experience with functional fitness. It is an admirable association and, if one has to choose, it is better to have functional fitness than irrelevant ornament, but a certain Puritanical indifference or hostility to mere beauty, mere ornament is or was part of the American inheritance.

8. "Puritanical." I am aware that the word is ambiguous and I have no intention of using it as a term of abuse. But it did matter that the predominant religious tradition of early English America was one that left little place for the "luxe pour Dieu" that produced the great cathedrals and abbeys of Europe. I am aware that English (and American) Puritans had a high and competent sense of the place of music in divine worship. Nevertheless, the new environment was not that provided by Rome for Palestrina or by Leipzig for Bach. Milton was a musically minded Puritan poet, but he would not have found much to gratify his tastes had he emigrated to New England or to Virginia.

9. And if the material and ideological obstacles to the transfer of the more lavish, extravagant and nonutilitarian forms of the arts to America did not work so effectually in the case of literature, the transfer had some special difficulties all the same. One was material; there was, again, no means of accumulating an economic surplus to support the career of letters. It was possible to export the old classical learning and equally important the old and new biblical learning and, what was more important, the Bible itself. And no people that had the Bible made available and treasured by the established order was cut off from the highest literary excellence. Yet again the colonies—with no theaters, no court, no court patronage, as yet no equivalent of the new academies like the Royal Society of London, with the new life constantly calling for new effort, with no leisure class—could not be expected to and did not produce a variegated, nonutilitarian, original culture in the arts or, indeed, in the sciences, in what

was then called natural philosophy. It would be absurd to make this a
matter of reproach. It was part of the price paid for the establishment of
the peculiar and successful Anglo-American society out of which the
United States and its present culture have come. All I should like to suggest is that there was a necessary price; it was paid.

*10.* I am now coming to a more controversial part of my subject, the
character of this necessarily democratic culture. That the American culture, on its aesthetic and intellectual side, is democratic I shall try to show
later. What I want to do at the moment is to stress its early nonaristocratic
character. The European culture from which it stemmed had its democratic elements: its folk ballads dealing with the woes and happiness of
the "lower orders," the "short and simple annals of the poor." It had in its
material works of art plenty of scenes from vulgar life, on the porches of
great cathedrals, or the illuminations of the *Hours* of the Duc de Berry.
But the more splendid forms of artistic achievement in the Middle Ages,
as in the Renaissance, were aristocratic. The great popular legends were
of kings and queens, of princes and princesses, of knights, of crusades and
battles, feuds in castles, not of their less interesting equivalents in cot-
tages. No doubt there are signs of a protest against this concentration on
the great. The Robin Hood legend is an example. But most people accepted
the distinction. Poor French peasants passed on, with faith and admiration, the legend of the Four Sons of Aymon and even now it is
legends of the higher feudalism that Sicilian peasants paint on their carts.
They would have agreed with Calpurnia:

> When beggars die, there are no comets seen;
> The heavens themselves blaze forth the death of princes.

*11.* Now, the settlers brought out from Europe, more specifically from
the British Isles, this aristocratic culture. (The Bible, after all, is full of
kings and nobles; sinners most of them, but interesting sinners. The metaphorical language of the Bible is royal, not democratic.) But in the American environment the aristocratic culture, accepted and admired by the
people, began to wither. The old ballads were brought over but were
transformed, given an American, frontier-bred, forest-bred character. The
legends of kings and princes became legends of men of the people winning the endless war against the wilderness and the Indian. Robin Hood
was a hero that could be transported to the frontier; Richard Coeur de
Lion was not.

*12.* I attach great importance to the creation of this frontier folk epic,
not only because it tells us of the formation of the modern American culture but because it is the greatest American cultural export. It should be
remembered that it is English America that has produced the only universally accepted new epic theme. The "matter of America" is in the true
succession from the "matter of France" (Roland and the Paladins) and

the "matter of Britain" (King Arthur and the Knights of the Round Table).

*13.* It is a matter not of kings and great nobles but of the self-made men of the forest and later of the prairie; it is a democratic epic theme. As far as there is a genuine American national tradition of legend, this is it. I am not altogether convinced that scholars, as well as hard-pressed men of letters, have not invented some of the prestige of the frontier heroes. I know how the Buffalo Bill legend was created; I have suspicions about Paul Bunyan and Mike Fink; but even if the legend has undergone the shaping hand of the poet or the poetaster or the scholar, that is how great legends are given their final and effective traditional form. And the legend of the West is still living in America—and still exportable to Europe. The conquest of the TV screen by the West is conclusive proof of the power of the legend that for a time represented a fact and for longer met a need of the new American social culture, a need for heroes and heroic deeds in an American and egalitarian context. I should not assert that as an art form the way in which this legend has been given to the American public is one of the greatest human achievements. I doubt if even Fenimore Cooper as a writer is in the class of his model, Scott. But the legend he launched on the world was unlike the legend Scott exported to Europe and America, a modern living legend with a future. It was a legend of heroes chosen not by birth but by themselves.

*14.* As far as American literary culture has been the embodiment of this heroic legend it has been one of the makers and the marks of the American national ethic. And I, for one, am not disposed to look this gift horse too closely in the mouth or to assess this national asset in a purely literary crucible. If (as I think is true) the American national hero who is most effectively cast in the epic mold and most excites the national curiosity, as well as admiration, is Lincoln, the lesson is reinforced, for here is the folk hero, coming from the folk, embodying in the highest power their possibilities of promotion and achievement. That is one way in which American culture is democratic.

*15.* There is another, one that is perhaps less edifying, less a pure acquisition. In a famous passage in his book on Hawthorne, Henry James stresses and laments the poverty of resources available to the American man of letters. Compared to his European brother, how little he has to use, how simple the social structure in which he is to set the characters! There is something comic in this long list of things that America has not got. It is, oddly enough, the converse of what Goethe had to say: he congratulated America on its escape from the feudal past that James coveted. And obviously James exemplified in his own work the possibilities of the new American theme contrasted with the old, traditional European themes. But there was something in the Jamesian lament, if not quite what James thought it was. For in the more sophisticated forms of literary art, the egalitarian bias of American life worked against the reception of the more subtle forms of art by the great American public—and there was no substitute for the great American public. There was no center of patronage, of support, of protection for the artist.

16. It is not necessary to swallow all the criticisms of American society fashionable with writers for over a hundred years—criticisms of the aridity of American culture, of the dry, inhospitable air in which the artist found it difficult to breathe—to recognize that, for some types of artist at any rate, nineteenth-century America—busy building itself up, completing the conquest of the frontier, assimilating the vast immigrant floods—could not be, or at any rate was not, very hospitable to the arts.

17. It was perhaps not accidental that the "golden day" of New England marked not the first efflorescence of a culture but the sunset of the old, learned, theocratic New England way of life, the marriage of the old Puritan conscience with the optimism of the Enlightenment. Emerson, Hawthorne, and the lesser men, Holmes, Lowell and the rest, were fruits of a society declining and which owed its charm and some of its force to its nearly twilight character. There is something paradoxical in this situation and it is a paradox that many Americans refuse to face, but there it is. The New England culture, the best integrated, the most internally harmonious regional culture that America has known, knew its golden day only when its decline was imminent. "Minerva's owl flies only in the dusk," said Hegel, and this deep saying applies to Boston, Concord, Salem. And—a banality that I am almost ashamed to utter—the great figures of American literary culture have been on the whole hostile to or at any rate highly critical of American life. Emerson had his repeated bursts of optimism but the world in which he spent the second half of his life was a world that listened not at all to his deepest message. It is hardly necessary to stress the pessimism of Hawthorne or the ostentatious disillusionment of Henry Adams.

18. And it was not only the New Englanders who were disillusioned, cut off. Whitman alone kept his spirits up and it is to be doubted if his best poetry is really to be found in those paeans to the spirit of democracy, those laudations of "Pioneers, O Pioneers." For Mark Twain the human situation was incurably tragic and for Melville the human illusion inevitably led to a dead end. "Round the world! There is much in that sound to inspire proud feelings, but whereto does all that circumnavigation conduct? Only through numberless perils to the very point whence we started, whence those we left behind secure, were all the time before us." Could there be a more un-American attitude than Melville's (and there are other lessons to the same effect)?

19. Classical American literature is not notably "useful" in the narrow nationalist sense. It is useful in a deeper sense, as is any penetrating, truthful, moving insight into the human situation. But the average American —optimistic, energetic, convinced, despite Melville, that circumnaviga-

tion does conduct us somewhere and somewhere worth arriving at—was and is naturally put off by the insistence on the darker side of the American situation. He has too often despised and distrusted the artist who has reciprocated the attitude. Exiled even if he did not leave the territorial bounds of the United States, the artist, the philosopher, the pure scientist were both cut off and cut themselves off from the main, cheerful stream of national tradition.

20. Of course, the alienation of the artist was not purely an American problem. War on the bourgeoisie, on bourgeois ideals and practices, was one of the common slogans of European life, especially in France. But Dickens and Hugo, social critics as they were, were not cut off from the life of their age as were their American opposite numbers and they were and have remained effective national heroes as no American author, not even as Mark Twain, has been.

21. The consequence has been a separation of what I am prepared to call the higher culture and the less original, more perishable, more optimistic, more American (in the patriotic sense) culture that has unfortunate results even today—or especially today.

22. Here it is necessary to say something of the picture of the American cultural past that American academics have been presenting not so much to the public as to the captive audiences of the colleges. Nothing could be more admirable from a moral as well as an intellectual point of view than the industry and the acuteness and probity with which American scholars have examined all the American past, the works of the great, the near great, and the merely "interesting." But here I take my life in my hands and, as a foreigner, I should like to suggest that in their desire to assess accurately the American cultural past they have tended to stress its utility for the American student to an excessive degree. The ordinary, intelligent, interested but not totally fascinated young man or woman who is introduced to the idea of literature as more than a mere diversion, as an illumination of life and not as a mere distraction from it, may find the great American classics depressing and the lesser lights, so laboriously resurrected or at any rate exhumed, both mediocre and boring. American literary culture is not varied enough (is especially not rich enough in first-class poetry) to provide adequate nutriment for the young.

23. In a legitimate attempt to prove the original value of the American contribution American critics and scholars, it seems to me, have tended to put blinkers round their charges, who might otherwise look out at the great world and discover there much that is profound, illuminating, and nourishing, even for Americans, but which has the handicap of having been written not by Americans nor for Americans but by human beings for human beings. It was the advantage of the old classical curriculum on which the New England masters were brought up that it enforced knowledge of nonnational, of remote types of human achievement, that

it insinuated the idea of a common human experience that Homer and Vergil threw light on. Today only the Bible (as far as it is still read apart from being bought) performs that function.

24. Something of the same limitation arises in the study of other aspects of American culture. It was a misfortune that the great expansion of the United States, in area, in wealth, in ambition, came at a time when in all countries of the new machine world taste was at its lowest, most timid, least connected with the forces of real creation. It is not only in the United States that money was squandered in atrocious imitations of the "Gothic," in inappropriate revivals of the classical, in ingenious and learned but not very relevant exercises in the Romanesque. To repeat, the United States was not the only sufferer. Is there any worse piece of church building erected regardless of cost anywhere in the United States than the Sacré-Coeur in Montmartre? Germany, France, and England are full of railway stations, government buildings, town halls that cannot be exceeded for unbeautiful ingenuity in any American city. (And I have some peculiarly unlucky America cities in mind.) Yet in the European cities, as a rule, the past has left achievements that ought to have put the modern architects and patrons to shame.

25. In many American cities there was nothing to offset the extravagantly outrageous taste of the gilded age—or later. Of course, there were pioneers like Louis Sullivan and many American cities have buildings of the late nineteenth and the early twentieth century that architects from Europe go on pilgrimage to. But visually the United States boomed at a bad time. And we have here, I think, another cause of alienation between the American and the higher culture of his country and age.

26. What of it? Is his situation any worse than that of the representative Englishman or Frenchman? Do they admire and use the products of the highest culture in their age and country? Of course not. But the American is in a special position. He is in Henry James's America, where the background to the arts has to be created and assimilated, where democratic judgment is part of the national ethos, where reverence is a quality reserved for a few sacred political slogans and institutions, where the not totally harmful snob values of an aristocratic culture are absent. The American is left to himself, not only because he does not accept leaders but because many leaders will not lead. For that reason, and possibly for others, the American cultural scene is peculiarly divided, the national unity, so remarkable at other levels, is here almost totally missing.

27. On the one hand, the American willingness to try anything once aids the arts, aids the preacher of new aesthetic or social doctrine. Just as American law tolerates, to a degree that surprises the European visitor, unorthodox systems of medicine, just as every known form of religious belief gets a welcome, so every new form of the arts, every new theory, every new form of practice finds buyers, in both a financial and a psycho-

logical sense. If from one point of view America suffers by having no accepted standards of excellence, she gains in another by not being hidebound by accepted standards of excellence. The very absence of what I may call "normative" institutions is a blessing. At any rate, it may seem so when the role of the French Academy in one field and the English Royal Academy in another is contemplated.

28. Probably at no time in history has the seller of cultural gods had it so good, in the sense that buyers will not be choked off by a mere inability to understand what it is all about. In face of the claims of the new art forms, in literature, in music, in painting, in sculpture, even in architecture, millions of Americans act like so many Texans afraid not to buy a potential oil well. What is offered may be unintelligible and unattractive, but it may conceal a gusher all the same. (I hasten to say that I am not describing buyers who are looking for a cash capital gain, but buyers in the widest sense of the term, who do not want to miss what may be the great cultural revelation of the age.)

29. This hospitality applies not only to the arts but to other aspects of culture, and notably to religion and what may be called philosophy. The American who seeks deliverance in analysis or in some new psychological school, who wants to master Zen Buddhism in ten easy lessons is a direct descendant of the seekers after knowledge whom Emerson made fun of more than a century ago—but who provided Emerson with a great part of his audiences and readers. It is not the searching after new things that is new, it is the evaporation, in the century since the decline of the Transcendentalists, of the old orthodoxy against which Emerson and his brethren reacted.

30. Here, again, the American situation is not unique. All over the Western world the seekers are as numerous as in St. Paul's Athens and the doctrines offered are much more varied. I am reduced to uttering a platitude when I stress the speed and diversity of change in our contemporary world. Our picture of it is changing so fast that it is vain to look for a central core of doctrine round which we can arrange our cultural life. If the modern world has such a core, a central and triumphant discipline, it is in physics, and who that is not quite a respectable mathematician can even begin to grasp what the physicists are doing? We can grasp in general what their allies and pupils, the engineers, are doing. Each new satellite, each new threat of more murderous rocketry, keeps them in our mind and we know that they can provide the means for destroying us. We are all in the Western world in the same cultural boat, in a world we never made where old patterns are dissolving and changing too fast for us to adjust easily or comfortably or even to decide what we should adjust to.

31. But what is different in the American situation is first of all the democratic tradition of culture which I have briefly described. The old

traditional order of a "higher" culture handed down from above—representing overtly aristocratic values or, at any rate, being based on the premise that some forms of culture are superior to others and that superiority is not simply an aspect of their popularity—is probably dying in Europe. But it is not yet dead. It visibly survives in the curriculum of the schools, in the prestige still attached to traditional hierarchical values, and (this is a matter where nothing but intuition can be relied on) in a genuine humility before the claims of the traditional culture that produces a willingness to learn that in turn results, in a good many cases, in a genuine conversion to the standards of a higher culture and a genuine appreciation of its products.

32. It is true that this acceptance of the traditional culture, this docile readiness to be initiated into it as far as natural talents and acquired knowledge make it possible, is not quite that immersion in the highest things that the preachers of culture, Matthew Arnold and T. S. Eliot, have meant. Nevertheless, the attitude preserves the older culture long enough for it to be possible to hope that a new culture, fusing the best of old and new, may arrive before general barbarism does.

33. The 800,000 copies of a translation of the *Odyssey* sold in England may not represent a genuine readiness to put oneself in the way of understanding of a remote way of life or a willingness to see and feel the human situation in another form from that to which we are habituated. But they do represent something that, faced with the products of the lower culture, with rock 'n' roll and the comics, we may be inclined to forget does exist.

34. If (as I think is the case) much of the pessimism of the "intellectuals" in America, in Britain, in Europe, arises from the collapse of the hopes based on the democratization of society, the end of the belief that the only things needed to win the masses to the higher culture were leisure, abundance, more "education," cheap books as well as the novel possibilities of radio and TV, then it is worth while to remind ourselves that not all those hopes were vain.

35. It is even more dangerous to blind ourselves to the facts of our situation (here I include both Britain and the United States in a common dilemma). We can do this in a new way as well as in the old way that asserted that we all must needs love the better when we see it. We can persuade ourselves that the new popular art forms are the natural successors of the old art forms, that they represent an inevitable adjustment to a new form of society. Thus rock 'n' roll is a necessary reflection of contemporary malaise; Li'l Abner, the equivalent of the great popular authors of the past, of Mark Twain and Dickens. If the boys and girls who pour out from high schools don't want to read, in a sense can't read, the reflection is on the absurd prestige we attach to reading or on the

absurd and irrelevant reading matter issued to the aspiring young and their turning to other art forms than literature.

36. There is some plausibility in all these defenses of abdication in favor of popular adolescent taste. I think it likely that the literary arts may be giving way in prestige, perhaps in cultural utility, to other arts, to the plastic arts and, above all, to music. Music, I think, has become the refuge of the intelligent man and woman today and that not because hi-fi has enabled him to gratify his tastes but because those tastes have produced the market for hi-fi. I think that a timid reverence for "classics" may mean that school reading programs have a diseducative effect, since serious reading becomes associated with boredom. And in any group of intelligent boys and girls there are sure to be young men and young women of whom some have no more an eye for reading than others have an ear for music, or others the ability to do simple sums.

37. But the present cultural crisis is not concerned with these cases. It is right to discriminate among comics, to point out the superiority of "Li'l Abner" over records of violence, empty of ideas, for example. It is right to insist on the technical superiority of a great jazz performer like Louis Armstrong over the current wailers and moaners. These last may enable a great many of the young to express themselves vicariously, but it is a dangerous extension of democratic prejudice to assert that all forms of self-expression are commendable or equally admirable and promising. It is wrong and a "treason of the learned" to exalt the art forms that are most popular today simply because they are popular in merely numerical terms. "Dare to be a Daniel" was the message of a popular hymn. "Dare to be a square" is a motto I should like to see adopted by more academics and other ex officio molders of the public mind.

38. The reasons why this motto is not adopted are various. One is the division, at any rate in the literary field, between the temper of the greatest American artists and the national temper. The national temper is optimistic, still deeply impressed by the belief in progress and still prone to believe that somewhere a solution can be found, if we try hard enough, for the temporarily distressing human condition. Yet this was not and is not the temper of the most critically esteemed American writers and to be a devoted admirer of Mr. Faulkner, for example, is to be in that degree unAmerican.

39. Then there is a division between the more sophisticated artists and the aspiring public that I believe to be greater than in any historical period known to me. Again, this division is not confined to the United States; it is a chasm in all the Western countries. Literature, the visual arts, music, philosophy are all practiced at a high degree of sophistication by highly trained specialists. They are also studied and appreciated by highly sophisticated devotees. But much of the production of the mod-

ern artist (using the term in its widest connotation) makes small or no appeal to the average man, not even to the intelligent average man who is conscious that his life would be fuller and better if the arts spoke more loudly to him than they do.

*40.* I have said that this division is new. I do not believe that in the thirteenth and fourteenth centuries all the good Catholic worshipers appreciated the scholastic philosophers or fully understood the achievement of Chartres. *The Divine Comedy* and the *Summa* were not popular works or within the reach of everybody. Nor do I believe that all Athenians knew by what divine skill the Parthenon got its proportions or appreciated all that Sophocles meant or were fit to be admitted to the Academy. I could multiply the examples.

*41.* But I think the modern situation is different. What a very modern musician means by music or a very modern nonrepresentational artist means by painting or many modern writers mean by literature has only a remote and often invisible connection with what the average sensual man means by these arts. I am aware that public taste has to be educated, that there were people who thought Mozart hard to follow and definitely discordant, that there were people who thought the Impressionists were simply incompetent. Maybe it is going to be like that for all the arts now in such confusion, now cut off, as so often they are, from what used to be their normal audience.

*42.* Even if we are all going to make the grade we haven't made it yet, and the average man is tempted, not unreasonably, to throw his hand in. He may exalt the claims of various jazz schools to be art forms as rich as classical music and its heirs or he may deny that classical music has any legitimate heirs. He may see or profess to see in fine camera work the true succession to the great painters, in the engineers the fit heirs of the architects. He may abandon pure literature altogether as a means of spiritual refreshment and turn to history, geography, travel, "know-how" books for more information. If he does so he will be in grave danger of reinforcing in himself the innate American belief that George Santayana commented on, the confidence in quantity, the preference for things that can be measured, the emphasis on more rather than on better, the identification of more *with* better. In our world emphasis on number, on measurable magnitudes, is one of the necessities of life, a necessity that presses ever more hardly on us.

*43.* But a life based on a belief that all that should be valued can be measured is like a life based on the belief that all that has to be learned can be taught. It is doomed to emotional sterility and to a sense of deception. Life is not like that and it is painful to find this out too late. What is missing in that life is what I have already alluded to in my remarks on education—the sense of excellence.

*44.* The danger to the notion of excellence does not lie only in the

irrelevant emphasis on measurable quantity. It can and often does lie in
the attribution to mediocrity of the power and prestige of excellence.
Here, again at the risk of uttering platitudes, I have to join in the attack
on the mass media. For it is possible to argue that they do less harm in
their exaltation of the palpably trivial and transitory than in the excessive seriousness with which minor triumphs in the lively arts are greeted.
That these lively arts can be diverting I do not deny. So can detective
stories, so can much light and some low literature. I do not shudder at
a *Saturday Evening Post* cover or wince when I hear of the prices paid
for tickets to a fashionable musical.

45. But a lot of harm is done when a great popular success like *South
Pacific* or *My Fair Lady* is puffed up until the distinction between talent
and genius is lost sight of, between the work to which one may give the
adjective "immortal" with no pedantic scruple and commercial productions of high amusement value that are extremely unlikely to survive the
generation that welcomed them. It is not a question of commercial motive. Shakespeare and Molière were both highly commercial men of the
theater. It is a question of not giving the rank of a masterpiece to what
is simply agreeable, for if you do that you cannot savor the real masterpieces—which is a great loss to the individual and in the aggregate to
the national culture. *My Fair Lady* is not *The Marriage of Figaro; By
Love Possessed* is not *War and Peace* or *The Ambassadors.*

46. What I am pleading for is the presentation to the young of the
concept that there is such a thing as excellence, that the unexamined
life, the emotionally banal life, the life animated by a religion of mere
good works and with no philosophy behind it, is inferior to the fuller
life of the artist, the philosopher, the saint. And since most of us cannot
be any of these things, the next best thing for us is the humble, industrious, and informed admiration for these great achievements of the human spirit.

47. This is, above all, the function of the universities. To them come a
high proportion of the young people who are capable of this initiation.
It is against these young people that so much in the modern world—not
only in the American modern world but especially in the American modern world—conspires. They need fortification; they need knowledge imparted without pedantry but also without any easy submission to the taste
of the hour or the natural laziness of the human mind. The United States
has probably never known a period in which its cultural prestige was
greater, in literature, in painting, in music, but the achievements that
win the respectful interest of the outside world are not those that the
mass of the American people (including congressmen in that mass) understand or are likely to understand.

48. A society that in addition to its immense economic and technical
prestige has the prestige of being hospitable to the new, the original, the

fruitful in the arts, that welcomes new ideas as well as new gimmicks, has an immense advantage in the contest for men's minds. It is not the novelty of the offerings so much as the possibility of novelty that wins the doubtful faced as an alternative with dogmatism, irrelevant domination of the arts by politics, the regular search for a safe common denominator. There is no such common denominator that is compatible with excellence. The notion of excellence is in this sense undemocratic, but it is not unAmerican. It was certainly an idea dear to Jefferson and to Lincoln. It will suffice if American public opinion and its official organs remember that "every man hath business and desire such as it is."

49. American life will be richer and more seductive if it permits and encourages the really exceptional, the really original man to pursue his bent, of course allowing for the fact that there will be phonies and flops at least as often as men of genius or even of remarkable talent. But this waste is one of the luxuries that the United States can now afford. And it must afford it if its way of life is to compete at all levels with that of its rival. It can compete on the technical level (if the United States goes all out). It can compete hands down at the level of popular diversion for, as we know, the iron curtain can hardly keep out American popular music and I suspect that the comics would please millions behind the curtain. But it is not merely as an instrument in the cold war that I urge a bold and possibly offensive insistence on excellence. It is because the great success story of the American people deserves excellence in every human activity. It would be unworthy of the people who have wrought the American miracle in so many fields to settle for less.

50. A great triumph of the American spirit would be the fostering of a literary and artistic culture that freely took in all the contributions of its ancestral cultures, confident that to be American is to be not exclusive but welcoming and that Shakespeare and the Bible play a greater part in the making of American culture than Melville, than even Mark Twain. It will be most American when it is most universal.

# Questions

1. At what points in his essay does Brogan call attention to a subject only to divide it into two portions and then balance one against the other?
2. Examine again Whyte's essay on the casual style. What devices that he enumerates there does Brogan use? Would you call Brogan a "casual stylist"? Why?
3. Compare and contrast Tocqueville's discussion of the United States and its absence of a strong aristocratic tradition with Brogan's.

4. Distinguish the various senses in which Brogan uses the word "culture."

5. What conditions does Brogan see as unique in American cultural history? What conditions are shared in common with other cultures?

6. Has Brogan himself "dared to be a square" in discussing America and its culture? Has he elicited your consent to most of his hopes and prescriptions for the present and future of American cultural life? Why?

7. What does Brogan mean at the end, after having stressed the uniqueness of American culture, when he says America will be "most American when it is most universal"?

# Theme Topics

1. Write a definition of American culture using elements from your own observation and others from Brogan, Trilling, Tocqueville, and McGinley.

2. Write a defense of American culture which answers Brogan's charges. Make certain that you admit some issues and provide concrete evidence from your own observation for your refutation.

3. Write a defense of American culture that focuses upon Brogan's charge that America lacks the higher culture of Europe with which to counter forces of the Atomic Age.

·46·

*Lionel Trilling*

# A NOTE ON DAVID RIESMAN: INNER-DIRECTION AND OTHER-DIRECTION

1. David Riesman's *The Lonely Crowd* seems to me one of the most important books about America to have been published in recent times. And quite apart from the particularity of its subject, it is one of the most interesting books I have ever read.

2. This is very large praise, and as I write it I find myself wondering

From "Two Notes on David Riesman," from *A Gathering of Fugitives* by Lionel Trilling. Reprinted by permission of the Beacon Press, copyright © 1956 by Lionel Trilling. Reprinted by permission also of Martin Secker & Warburg Limited.

whether I may not be overstating the case for this sociological study in order to counteract the antagonisms to the social sciences which I know to be pretty common among people who like literature very much. But I do not think I am saying more than I mean. My opinion was formed before I ever thought of writing about Mr. Riesman's book and I have tested it by more than one reading.

3. Yet since I have raised the question of the literary suspiciousness of the social sciences, especially sociology, it might be well to take it specifically into account in connection with *The Lonely Crowd.*

4. One reason for this suspiciousness is that sociology tends to use a kind of language which must arouse antagonism in people who are at all sensitive to language. This is not because the language of sociology is scientific but because it is often pseudoscientific and jargonistic and has the effect of giving a false value to ideas that are simple and platitudinous. To any such charge *The Lonely Crowd* is certainly not liable. Mr. Riesman uses two terms that some might boggle at—he speaks of people as being "inner-directed" and "other-directed." But I do not know how else he could denominate the two categories of character that are essential to his thought. In general the book is precisely a work of literature in the old comprehensive sense of the word according to which Hume's essays are literature, or Gibbon's history, or Tocqueville's *Democracy in America.*

5. Another objection is that sociology is likely to be tendentious without admitting it is, and that it proceeds on unexamined assumptions while insisting that it is wholly objective. But we can count on Mr. Riesman's objectivity because he admits his subjectivity and the hypothetical nature of his enterprise. He is under no illusion of scientific neutrality. He admires certain human qualities and makes no bones about wanting them to be influential in our national life.

6. Then it is said, and with justice, that sociology often gives the appearance of denying personal autonomy. What is more, much sociological investigation has for its avowed aim the discovery of how to manipulate human behavior in clandestine ways. But Mr. Riesman's book is as far as it can be from denying the possibility of autonomy without denying the inescapable limits of civilized society. Its whole effort, indeed, is directed toward the affirmation of the possibility of autonomy.

7. People of literary inclinations, I believe, have a natural jealousy of sociology because it seems to be in process of taking over from literature one of literature's most characteristic functions, the investigation and criticism of morals and manners. Yet it is but fair to remark that sociology has pre-empted only what literature has voluntarily surrendered. Twenty years ago, when the Lynds produced their famous study, *Middletown,* it was possible to say that with all their staff and paraphernalia they had not really told us more about American life than we had learned

from a solitary insightful observer, which is what some sociologists call a novelist—they had done no more than confirm *Babbitt* by statistics. Since that time, however, few novelists have added anything genuinely new to our knowledge of American life. But the sociologists have, and Mr. Riesman, writing with a sense of social actuality which Scott Fitzgerald might have envied, does literature a service by suggesting to the novelists that there are new and wonderfully arable social fields for them to till.

8. The research from which *The Lonely Crowd* developed began as an investigation of the social causes of political attitudes, specifically that of apathy to politics. The book does not consist of conclusions drawn from this research but was written in the course of the still continuing enterprise as the hypothesis on which the research might proceed. In its simplest form this hypothesis consists of the statement that there has been a change in the character of the American people, that where once men whose character was "inner-directed" were dominant in our culture, the tendency is now toward the dominance of men of "other-directed" character. Inner-directed persons are those who internalize adult authority, most notably the ideals and demands of their parents. Other-directed persons are those whose character is formed chiefly by their contemporaries and peers, the formation beginning as soon as they enter social life in play or at school.

9. Something of the nature of the inner-directed man may be understood from the phrase which, in the nineteenth century, he so often made his motto—"*Ad astra per aspera*," through difficulties to the seemingly unattainable heights. The old tag might also be translated, "To the heights by means of asperity," for a kind of asperity marks the dealings of the inner-directed man with the world, his fellow-men, and himself. The man of business as well as the scientific or artistic genius, or the religious leader, or the philosopher, were all at one in their submission to inner-direction. The belief that energy, self-control, and self-reverence would achieve miracles was held not only by the dullest spirits of the age but also by the noblest. We must think of the Alger books as being the expression not merely of a strenuous philistinism but of a general culture in which strenuousness was valued in all walks of life. There was a connection between the passions of a Bounderby and a Beethoven.

10. In America, even as far back as Tocqueville's visit, there was always a tendency for inner-direction to be modified by what Tocqueville regarded as an extravagant awareness of the opinion of others. Emerson believed that this tendency constituted a prime threat to the American spirit and he never wearied of warning his countrymen that Self Reliance—his name for inner-direction—was sadly on the wane. Yet in nineteenth century America the "hardness of the material" still called for a large measure of inner-direction—there were still frontiers to be conquered, social forms to be imposed or broken, technology to be estab-

lished. It was still useful to idealize "faith," the belief that one's personal vision was right no matter how the world mocked it. School children were assiduously taught in their readers that the heroic man was one who followed his gleam, and that society as a whole was likely to be stupid, retrograde, and cowardly, as witness its treatment of Columbus. And in the poem that every child learned, it was right of Columbus, and not arrogant or undemocratic of him, to say, "Sail on! Sail on!" when his men begged him to turn back. To be "misunderstood," to be alone with one's rightness and virtue, was the stuff of the dreams of youth.

*11.* But in the early years of the twentieth century—around 1920, Mr. Riesman believes—the inner-directed character began to lose its ascendancy. The hard, resistant materiality of the world no longer supplied the goal and validated the hard, strenuous will of inner-directed people. Children were less impelled to establish the old parental authority within themselves—parents were less certain of how to establish it in their children and of whether it ought to be established at all. It was by no means clear that the old standards applied to the new kind of work. For in the degree that work had less to do with *things,* it had more to do with *people.* In Mr. Riesman's phrase, the interest shifted from the hardness of the material to the softness of the personnel, and the arts of personality, by which one could manipulate one's fellows or win valuable approval from them, became more important to more people than the direct force of the will exerted upon material difficulties. And children increasingly formed their characters according to the demands of their playmates and schoolmates, equipping themselves with a quick, unconscious sensitivity to the judgment of others—they became increasingly other-directed.

*12.* The evidence of this new means of character-formation is manifest in every discussion of juvenile or adolescent social behavior, in which it is always taken for granted that parents are virtually helpless before the power of the child-society. And indeed this power is supported and rationalized by the family and the school, which, on theories of normality and adjustment, second the anxious antagonism which the child-society directs upon any show of difference. For the group life of contemporary children achieves its particular kind of democracy by suppressing special interests and abilities (except in athletics) and by prohibiting the display of vanity or ambition. Even before the child is ready for sociability, his life in literature has prepared him for social adjustment and conformity. *Scuffy the Tugboat* instructs him in the dangers of the Columbus principle, while *Tootle the Engine* leads him to believe that he must not fail to be like all the other little engines and never leave the track to stray into green fields, like a horse.

*13.* The ideal of behavior which is indigenous to the social life of the modern child is the model and perhaps the mold of the ideal of adults, at least of the middle class. We are coming to be a civilization in which overt ambition, aggression, and competition are a discount. Not, of course, that the sources of natural aggression are drying up or that people no longer seek prestige. But self-aggrandizement takes new forms as the ideals of other-direction become increasingly compelling. Overt ambition gives way to what Mr. Riesman calls antagonistic co-operation, which implies affability, blandness, a lively sensitivity to the opinion of the group, the suppression of asperity. Social differences must be minimized as far as possible. Wealth must depreciate itself, and must seek to express itself not in symbols of power but in fineness of taste. Food is ordered less for the old-fashioned virtues of substantiality and abundance, than for the new charms of elegance and artistry—but in this limited space it is impossible to follow Mr. Riesman in the fascinating detail of his description of the cultural changes which other-direction is instituting.

*14.* The general opinion is not likely to be in accord with Mr. Riesman —the general opinion is that our culture is marked by an especially fierce and open competitiveness, an unmasked aggressiveness, a crude assertiveness. This is the received idea of a great deal of our literature and of our progressive social thought. It is the pious certainty of Europe, constituting, one sometimes feels, the larger part of the European social and political thought of the moment. And Mr. Riesman's students at the University of Chicago tell him that American life resembles the grim, paranoid Dobu culture or the competitive conspicuously-consuming Kwakiutl culture— none ever finds any resemblance to the peaceable, co-operative Pueblo Indians, although *all* of them wish they could.

*15.* I am sure that it is Mr. Riesman who is in the right of the matter. My own experience in teaching confirms his, one incident in particular. For some time I had been increasingly aware that my students had no very great admiration for Stendhal's *The Red and the Black*, gave it nothing like the response that it had had from my college generation. Then one day a whole class, almost all its members gifted men, agreed in saying that they were bored by Julien Sorel and didn't like him. Bored by Julien Sorel! But didn't he, I asked, represent their own desires for preeminence, their own natural young ambition? They snubbed me with their answer and fixed between themselves and me the great gulf of the generations: they did not, they said, understand ambition of Julien's self-referring kind; what they wanted was a decent, socially useful co-operative work to do. I felt like an aging Machiavelli among the massed secretariat of the U.N.

*16.* Young men of this kind certainly do not represent anything like the full development of the other-directed character which Mr. Riesman describes. It is even possible that their rejection of the extreme inner-direction of Julien Sorel is not so much in favor of other-direction as of the "autonomous" character which Mr. Riesman proposes as the possible optimum of our culture. More likely, however, they represent a compromise between inner-direction and other-direction. As such they make a spectacle which in many ways is very attractive.

*17.* But the tendency of other-direction does not stop with the character of these young men. And the consequences of its fuller development are disquieting. Mr. Riesman remarks that he has found it almost impossible to make a comparison of the two forms of character-direction without making inner-direction seem the more attractive of the two. I don't agree with Mr. Riesman that the preference is a mere prejudice which we must guard against. Granting all that is to be said against the tendency of inner-direction to cut itself off from what is warm and personal, granting too all that may be said for what other-direction does to refine leisure and consumption, it is still inner-direction that must seem the more fully human, even in its excess. Mr. Riesman himself seems to be saying something of this sort when, in speaking of the autonomous character, he remarks that the inner-directed character more closely resembles it than does the other-directed, and that, indeed, it is easier for inner-directed people to approach actual autonomy.

*18.* It is in any case true, on Mr. Riesman's showing, that the political life is far more likely to be healthy in a culture in which inner-direction is dominant. The exacerbated sense of others, of oneself in relation to others, does not, it seems, make for the sense of the polity. On the contrary—other-direction is concomitant with a sense of powerlessness in political matters, and this impotence masks itself in many ways, often as hatred of or contempt for politics. This in turn is easily rationalized into a desire for a meta-politics, for a perfect and absolute form of government which shall make impossible the conflict of wills of actual politics.

*19.* And the apathy which marks our political life lies as a threat beneath all the life of other-direction. Social approval and the desire for it are not love, nor even friendship, nor even community. The life of leisure, of fun, of narcissism, of right choice among the articles of consumption, of sex as the "last frontier" of adventure, of bland adjustment—this life is at every moment susceptible to the cankering boredom which lies beneath its surface.

*20.* This is not, I must make clear, the note on which Mr. Riesman ends. It is one of his decisive intellectual virtues that he has no love for the opiate of pessimism. He is not charmed by apocalyptic visions. It is not the end of a culture that he has undertaken to describe but a moment in its history.

# Questions

1. Trilling, although he was reviewing *The Lonely Crowd,* has actually written an essay with a clear thesis. What is that thesis?
2. What prejudices on the part of his readers does Trilling anticipate and how does he attempt to allay them?
3. Define: asperity, autonomy, inner-direction, other-direction, meta-politics.
4. Why does Trilling prefer inner-direction?
5. What connection can you see between Riesman's distinction of these types of social character and the last paragraph of the essay by Tocqueville? Which type of character would be more likely to abandon apathetically his liberty to maintain his equality?
6. Paragraphs 15 and 16 employ the method of example. Is the example effective as Trilling has used it? Does it convince you?
7. What connection do you see between Brogan's discussion of man's need for heroes even in an egalitarian context and Trilling's discussion in paragraphs 10 and 11 of America's present failure to create them? Do the two men make the same point?
8. Do you agree with the opinion expressed in paragraphs 18 and 19? How is the life described there the antithesis of the good life Socrates described?

# Theme Topics

1. Write an essay relating the passion for equality that Tocqueville discusses, the conformity discussed by Fromm, and Trilling's attitude toward other-direction.
2. Develop an essay on the following remark by Trilling: "Social approval and the desire for it are not love, nor even friendship, nor even community."

# Education in America

## ~ XII ~

### ·47·

*Clifton Fadiman*

## WHO IS TO BLAME FOR THE CURRENT MESS IN EDUCATION?

*1.* At the Madison High School in Rochester, New York, twelve-year-old boys are forced to take a course in coeducational "homemaking," including diapering. In another, in California, scholastic credit is given to students for working as carry-out boys in supermarkets. There is another California school in which teen-age lads attend a class called "Bachelor Living." A Maryland high school proudly announces that it offers the only course in dry cleaning in the county system. A high school in Schenectady, New York, boasts five gymnasiums, plus other educational paraphernalia, including a retail store and a classroom devoted to something called, simply, "Living"; its faculty socializes with the children in a "faculty-student lounge"; and the nonacademic part of the school (comprising 80 per cent of the available space) is air-conditioned, whereas the academic classes are not, presumably on the theory that any child so vicious as actually to prefer education to cosmetology should be penalized for this aberration. In San Francisco's City College a course labeled "Humanities" guarantees that "emphasis is also given to art in everyday life—for example, the appropriate selection of neckties and socks by the men of the class, and of dresses and costume jewelry by the women." Somebody named Ken Miller, according to the Champaign-Urbana *Courier*, expects shortly to receive his master's degree for a thesis on football punting.

*2.* I shall cut short our *catalogue déraisonné* [1] with a statement by a college dean, quoted in John Keats' recent *Schools Without Scholars*. He

From *Holiday* (August, 1958). Reprinted by special permission from *Holiday*, copyright 1958, by the Curtis Publishing Co. and by Fadiman Associates Ltd.
[1] Many of these horrors I first encountered in the *Bulletin of the Council for Basic Education*, a non-profit organization of scholars who devote themselves to telling the bitter truth about American schooling.

was asked whether a man, well adjusted and helpful in his community but unable to count his fingers or write his name, could be considered educated.

3. The dean replied, "Yes."

4. Horrified? Or, perhaps, merely moved to derisive laughter? If so, you—and that includes the writer—are horrified at yourself, or laughing at yourself. For these enormities are precisely what we ordered. Each time, during the last twenty-five years, that we voted for a school bond issue to provide our children with a swimming pool instead of an acquaintance with the multiplication table; each time that we taxed ourselves to guarantee hot lunches for the kiddies and a continuance of starvation salaries for the teachers; each time that we failed to cry bloody murder when a report-card system was abolished, or compulsory promotion introduced: at each of these moments we were making dead sure that our children would turn out to be—what they are. We knew what we wanted: the garroting of the mind. And we got it.

5. And now it turns out that we don't like it after all.

6. How, if I may borrow from the eloquence of our President, did we get into this mess?

7. The Great Debate on education, now raging all over the land, may turn out to be as important as the Lincoln-Douglas debates, or even those that preceded the adoption of the Constitution. No matter how it is decided, it is apparent that our school system is going to be improved. It is crystal-clear that from now on almost as much attention will be paid to the encouragement of a genius as we devote at present to the wet-nursing of the retarded. But the issue is not the improvement of the school system. The issue is the improvement of our minds. And our minds cannot improve unless we first rid ourselves of a few comforting delusions.

8. I have touched on the first. It is the delusion that at the bottom of the trouble is a Villain; and that if we can only find this Villain and chastise him, all will be rosy. *Life* has of late been doing a superb job of pointing out the flaws in our school system. But, the livelier journalism of our time having become a branch of the dramatic art, *Life* had to uncover something and someone for us to hiss: a desperate doctrine called Progressive Education and a Desperate Desmond called John Dewey.

9. Now, if you are looking for an indignation vent, these will do; but if you are looking for something duller, namely the truth, they will not. For, as with all large movements of degeneration (for example, the decline of the Roman Empire), the guilt cannot be assigned to a specific doctrine or a specific individual. In the case of the movement of degeneration known as modern American education, the guilt must be assigned to a widely held theory of human life, a theory championed, in varying degrees of intensity, by all of us. There *is* a villain; seek him in your mirror.

10. The theory of human life which has become the unconscious philos-

ophy of most Americans is simply a perversion of the Constitutional phrase guaranteeing our right to pursue happiness. By happiness the Founding Fathers, who were well educated, meant more or less what Aristotle did. Happiness for them was a state of mind ensuing when one was sufficiently wise to make the right moral choices. It was associated with wisdom and morality.

*11.* In our time it has become equivalent, to use a peculiarly American phrase, to "having a good time." If you doubt this, ask the average teenager (and we have seen to it, of course, that as many of them as possible will *be* average) what he wants out of life. It will boil down to two things: "a good time" and "security." And the average grownup will agree.

*12.* A citizen recently removed some reservation tickets on chairs at the hotel sun deck at the annual Atlantic City beauty pageant, so that he could get a better view of the girls. Taken into custody, he rested his case on the Constitution of the United States, maintaining that the hotel had no right to deprive a man of his pursuit of happiness. His plea was disallowed; but it must have been a near thing, and I would suggest that the judge who disallowed it might very well merit a little observation by the FBI.

*13.* A few months ago I noted an advertisement for a public country club. Its slogan was: "The Family That Plays Together Stays Together." I am sure that few readers of this obscenity felt anything strange in the notion that the maintenance of a property family life is bound up with the communal enjoyment of shuffle-board and wienie roasts.

*14.* In education this idolization of the Good Time is translated into the child-centered school; into an elective system gone insane, to the point where a high-school graduate will choose a college because it offers sailing; into the religious enshrinement of athletics; and so forth. Once we accept, as we obviously do, the Good Time Theory of happiness it is inevitable that our children, instead of being taught how to read, write, speak and reason, will be taught how to train dogs, use the telephone, play in the school band, wield drum-majorette batons and select socks.

*15.* I repeat then that there is a Villain. But he is not named John Dewey. He is called Frivolity. The worship of Frivolity is, as it were, our non-Sunday religion. When we recognize that, we will no longer be surprised when our schools turn out millions of happy, healthy illiterates; or saddened by the circumstance, as recently reported in the New York *Times*, that the Army finds one third of the draftees unteachable and untrainable for anything but menial labor. We will at least have the satisfaction of being honest with ourselves. Then we can proceed to a legal expression of our self-knowledge, amending the Constitution so that it reads "Life, Security and the Pursuit of a Good Time."

*16.* But some of us, reactionary old fogies, may feel that happiness—real happiness, the kind of happiness the Founding Fathers were talking about—is too precious to be wasted on children. We sour-visaged Puritans may argue that happiness should be reserved for old folks; that it is not a packageable commodity to be given away to the kiddies at those gigantic supermarkets masquerading as educational institutions. We crusty Tories may even believe that country blessed where the young men have furrowed brows and the old men laughing eyes.

17. The second delusion that must be dissipated before the Great Debate can produce its finest fruits is the curious notion that the debate has just started. Forty-three years ago John Erskine published a book called *The Moral Obligation to be Intelligent*. We did not recognize the obligation. Twenty-five years ago a group of educators, among them Robert M. Hutchins, Mortimer Adler and Mark Van Doren, were urging a return to the liberal traditions in education and warning us that the enshrinement of athletics and vocational courses could lead only to the intellectual impoverishment of the nation. They were ignored or howled down. And, three years before the arrival of Sputnik, Arthur Bestor had surveyed our educational system, told us what was wrong, and been discounted as an extremist. The truth has been before us for at least a generation; we closed our eyes to it.

18. What opened them? Insight? Remorse? Reflection? Not any of these. Our eyes were opened by a flying box containing a dying dog. We are going to reform American education not because we are eager to produce finer American citizens but because we are scared stiff. Whatever changes we make in our schooling will consequently be changes spurred on by a respect for the Russians rather than a respect for the intelligence. Let us see the Great Debate in perspective and admit that what the reformers have been urging for the last fifty years is only loosely connected with what is today being urged by the newer reformers.

19. This brings us to the third delusion. That is the notion that our basic weakness is in something vaguely called "the sciences"; if we can only improve our mathematics and physics courses and attract to them a greater proportion of able students, all may yet be well. This delusion is the most dangerous because it seems to be connected with concrete things, such as space satellites, intercontinental ballistic missiles, and improved bombs, of all degrees of sanitariness. And as for at least twenty-five years our schools have been pooh-poohing abstract thought and cheering for concrete objects, it is probable that the physics-and-arithmetic reforms will go through, and that nothing else will.

20. Perhaps the only important matter *is* the production of hundreds of thousands of trained technicians who, outside of their specialized talents, will have not the remotest idea of what it means to be a good citizen or lead a good life. But let us be aware of what we are doing. We are not, in that case, engaging in an educational task, but in a paramilitary one. Once we know this, we will not be disillusioned with the results. We will be happy when we can send a thousand dying dogs into

the air. We will be happier still when, using taxpayers' money, we can dispatch Doctor Teller to the moon so that he may satisfy his curiosity as to what lies on its thither side.

*21.* Now let us suppose that we have divested ourselves of these three delusions. We are now at least in a position to do some deciding. We may decide, as many educators in the secret, sad depths of their hearts have already decided, that the cultural jig is up; that the pressures of the modern world, the crushing competition of the entertainment trade and the athletics business, our present tendency to spawn on the level of the lower animals—that all these make impossible a return to traditional liberal education, guided by first-rate teachers. If that is our decision—and there is much evidence to sustain it—we should at once organize our degeneracy with the efficiency peculiar to us as a people. More swimming pools, more bowling alleys, more courses in dog training, more schools devoted to making children happy, more colleges functioning as a combination of health resort, country club and mating seminary; with perhaps special inducements held out to future technologists who may be useful for the defense of the country.

*22.* The school then becomes purely a custodial institution and its staff an army of baby sitters. If we go ahead on these lines we should be honest enough to drop from our vocabulary such traditional terminology as school, scholar, student, teacher, education, college, bachelor of arts, and so forth. We can then proceed energetically to create a new barbarism of well-adjusted citizens untouched by the irritation of thought.

*23.* But suppose we should decide the other way. Suppose we conclude that the Founding Fathers had a good idea after all, that a republic of free men (which means men with liberated minds) is worth striving for, even in the face of apparently insuperable obstacles. What do we do then?

*24.* The answer is so simple as to seem impossible. We change our minds. I mean we actually change them by a conscious act of will, almost as Paul changed his on the road to Damascus.

*25.* The change involves so radical an alteration of our folkways and mindways that the chances are a thousand to one against its succeeding. But unless we at least try it, on a national scale, we may as well abandon our schools to the vocationalists, the life-adjusters, the Happiness Boys and the dean who believes a man can be educated without knowing how to count his fingers or spell his name.

*26.* Changing our minds basically involves agreeing with Aristotle, who tells us that all men by nature desire to know. *All* men—not some. By *nature*—not as a consequence of conditioning. *Desire to know*—not passive acceptance of instruction. If we do not accept this—then back to the gymnasiums and the classes in baton twirling.

27. Another of Aristotle's dicta is "Education is accompanied by pain." This, too, we must accept. T. S. Eliot tells us "No one can become really educated without having pursued some study in which he took no interest—for it is a part of education to learn to interest ourselves in subjects for which we have no aptitude." If this be true, it makes hay of our elective system in which the student selects courses as if he were choosing penny candy in a candy store.

28. In brief, our change of mind involves a radical rearrangement of our hierarchy of admirations. It means that the man of thought, the statesman of creative intelligence, the businessman trained to understand his business as part of a larger historical process, the abstract scientist who furnishes the single great idea that all the little technologists and salesmen later exploit, the artist and writer who makes life meaningful, the teacher who helps to form all these—they are the heroes who must displace the mere manipulator of other men's ideas, the adroit politician, the businessman who claims that "pure research is when you don't know what you're doing," the laboratory gadgeteer, the Hollywood star, the football hero, and the man in the gray flannel suit.

29. If by some miracle the creative intelligence could be made as glamorous as Pat Boone, it would not be long, for example, before we ceased appointing ambassadors who know nothing of the language or the history of the country to which they are accredited. We might even go so far as to modify our idea of representative government and insist that our more important public servants be well-educated men. We might teach our children that all the material miracles that surround them are only incidentally the consequence of our extraordinary system of production and distribution, and that we wear such fine stockings only because Wallace H. Carothers, of the DuPont Company, happened to come across Nylon while he was making a purely scientific investigation of the molecular structure of certain chemical compounds.

30. The prestige symbols must be changed. Somehow or other the child will have to be taught the stark, chilly truth—that the intellectual is and always has been the most valuable man in the world, the one on whom we all live, the one whose ideas and discoveries and inventions afford us the opportunity for a livelihood and show us how interesting life can be. It is only when he is convinced that this is so, and that Mickey Mantle and Elvis Presley and Rock Hudson, while doubtless estimable creatures, are mere specks of thin icing on a very large and solid cake— it is only when he deeply feels the truth of this that his natural desire to know will express itself freely, and he will learn what it is now difficult to teach him—how to read, write, calculate, speak, listen, and think.

# Questions

1. How would you characterize the tone of this essay? List as many expressions as you can from it to support your conclusion.
2. Indicate the points at which Fadiman uses exaggeration to persuade his reader of "the stark, chilly truth." How might apologists answer Fadiman's charges by using the principle of exaggeration against his position?
3. What admissions does Fadiman make? What admissions does he fail to make? How could these additional admissions strengthen his case?
4. Fadiman spends more time here than most writers on this subject in depicting the nature of the society that has produced our high schools. What details does he include, however, to depict our schools rather than our society?
5. List the three delusions that he says are at the bottom of the confusion in the debate on education. What others might you add?
6. If we should decide in favor of change, what does Fadiman say the change would involve?
7. In paragraph 21 Fadiman suggests that we may decide that it is too late to change our society and our schools. He claims there is much evidence to sustain the decision. What evidence is there?
8. As a part of his discussion of the first delusion he derides the worship of frivolity and thus brings the discussion back to the nature of society that produced the schools. In what sense is it true that American citizens have produced American schools? What public influences shape our schools and thus determine their nature?
9. Can it be said that since our schools reflect our society that we have the kind of schools we deserve, that their weaknesses reflect a fundamental degeneracy in American life? What strengths are reflected in our schools?

# Theme Topics

1. Write a paper disagreeing with Fadiman.
2. Write a paper agreeing with the essentials of Fadiman's case but modifying it, admitting more than he does, and perhaps refuting one of his contentions.
3. Write a paper suggesting how Fadiman's recommendations could be put into practice. Show specifically how they could, step by step, be made effective.

## ·48·

*Robert M. Hutchins*

# SOME IDEALS FOR AMERICAN EDUCATION

*1.* If American education continues on its present lines, it seems likely that it will ultimately be regarded as a place of accommodation.[1] A combination of forces has made the community, most parents, and most young people agree that the rising generation should not go to work until the age of eighteen or even twenty-two. The American educational system seems to be taking shape in response to the demand for occupation for the young from the time they are able to be absent from home until the time it is thought right for them to go to work.

*2.* What these children and adolescents do while they are in educational institutions is not the most important concern to them, their parents, or the community. It is agreed that young people should not be exposed to bad influences. They should have opportunities for exercise and what is called social life. Either in or out of the curriculum they should have some experience of art, music, and drama. Their health should be attended to. But the main thing is that they should be accommodated.[2]

*3.* They should all be accommodated. And they should be accommodated as long as they wish to be. In general the length of their accommodation is determined by the capacity of their parents to support them while they are not gainfully employed.

*4.* The standards applied to this place of accommodation are not un-

[1] The article on Psychology in the *Encyclopaedia Britannica* says, 'The educational system has contributions to make to crime prevention. For one thing it keeps the youngsters out of mischief while they are in school.'

[2] Or as Professor H. H. Wilson of Princeton University put it in a recent speech: 'Parents in general do not want their offspring educated; they want them *housebroken.*' Professor Wilson went on to say: 'Students in general do not want to start on the disturbing road to education—they want to acquire saleable skills and/or degrees. Teachers in general and in the climate of today do not want to arouse anxiety on the part of either students or parents—they want to survive!'

*— youngest University President ever U of Chicago*

*innovator of Education*

like those invoked in the appraisal of any other such place. One asks at a hotel, what is the price? Are the rooms neat and clean? Is the service prompt? Is the food good? Will I meet nice people? What are the opportunities for recreation? What is the view? As might be expected, these are the questions that the catalogues and brochures of American colleges and universities set out first of all to answer.

5. The United States has not set great store by intellectual achievements. In fact a general suspicion of intellectuals and intellectualism pervades the country. In some quarters there is a tendency to equate intellectualism with radicalism, or even more dangerous proclivities. Apprised that the Massachusetts legislature might investigate Communist activities at Westfield State Teachers College, its President defended it by saying, 'I know of no Reds or Communist-minded persons either among the faculty or the students here. . . . The type of students who go here are not of the highly intellectual type among which such tendencies exist. . . .'[3]

6. It cannot be said with confidence that the American, if confronted by the choice between having his child learn and having the child become 'well adjusted' or 'successful' would cast his vote for learning. Learning is not necessary for adjustment or success, and may, if carried too far, interfere with both. In some other countries intellectual achievements have been valued for their own sake; in some countries, as in Imperial China, they may have been valued too highly. In some countries, as in Imperial China, intellectual achievements, interpreted in the best way in which the country knew how to interpret them, have been the road to social advancement and political power. By this I do not mean that they have been the only road, or in all cases the shortest or surest road. But we have only to remember the advantages once enjoyed by graduates of Oxford and Cambridge in competition for positions in the Civil Service to recognize the importance attributed in Britain to having the best educated citizens recruited for these posts. No such advantages have ever been attached to graduation from Harvard and Yale.

7. Even if the graduates of Harvard and Yale had an inside track into the public service, it is doubtful whether their number or their quality would be much affected. The ideal American is not the secure, respectable influential civil servant.[4] Far from it. The ideal American is the successful man.[5] Mary McCarthy, the American writer, has noted the ef-

---

[3] 'Years ago, it was demonstrated that the states which boast the largest *per capita* expenditures on education are the states in which the percentage of Communists is greatest. The states with the lowest *per capita* expenditures on education have the smallest per cent of Communists.' *American Mercury* (July 1955).

[4] 'It is nevertheless today still true that it is better to be born and die a man than to be born a man and die an official.' R. C. Unmack in *The Fortnightly Review* (1953), p. 351.

[5] A bitter attack on this ideal and its educational consequences is found in *Business be Damned*, by Elijah Jordan (New York, 1952), ch. 6.

fect of this ideal on the character and aims of teachers. 'The young man who goes into college teaching today is geared to action, not to renunciation; he has taken a vow of success.' [6] But we are not entirely clear what we mean by success.

8. Education has been said to be the deliberate attempt to form men in terms of an ideal. This is one of those statements more easily made than understood. Yet I think it possible to identify the kind of man that the Greeks, Romans, and medieval Europeans were seeking to produce through formal education, and it is possible to see the connection between what they did in education and the result they hoped to achieve. A British or French educator today would not have quite as much difficulty as an American in saying what sort of person the educational system of his country aimed to form.[7] Again, the British and French educational systems seem to bear some direct relationship to the ideal of the educated man that the British and French propose to themselves.

9. The originality and courage of the resolution taken by eighteenth-century Americans toward education should not be forgotten. The novelty of their conception may be appreciated by comparing their statements with the notable absence of references to popular education by their British and Continental contemporaries. I find none, for example, in all the writings of Edmund Burke. Not until the passage of the Reform Bills did British politicians take popular education seriously, and universal, free, compulsory education did not become law in England until more than 200 years after it was well established in America.

10. Sixty years ago Lord Bryce said of the United States, 'That the education of the masses is nevertheless a superficial education goes without saying. It is sufficient to enable them to think they know something about the great problems of politics: insufficient to show them how little they know. The public elementary school gives everybody the key to knowledge in making reading and writing familiar but it has not time to teach him how to use the key, whose use is in fact, by the pressure of daily work, almost confined to the newspaper and the magazine. So we may say that if the political education of the average American voter be compared with that of the average voter in Europe, it stands high; but if it be compared with the functions which the theory of the American government lays on him, which its spirit implies, which the methods of its party organization assume, its inadequacy is manifest.'[8]

[6] *The Listener* (24 July 1952), p. 137.

[7] The French ideal has been entertainingly described by Robert Guillain, *The Listener* (22 May, 1952). M. Guillain seems to make the mistake, all too common in Europe, of identifying general culture with the possession of useless information. He says that his fourteen-year-old niece has *culture générale*, offering as evidence that she knows the names of the three sons of Bach, and then goes on to complain of the inadequacy of *culture générale*.

[8] *The American Commonwealth*, vol. ii, pp. 284-5.

*11.* Today the notion that education is designed primarily to prepare the voter to exercise the suffrage wisely has receded into the background. On ceremonial occasions much praise is lavished on education: it is the foundation of our liberties and the salvation of the Republic. But what goes on in the educational system, whether it does actually produce the literate citizen able to cope with public affairs—these questions are less often mentioned.

*12.* We thus confront a paradox. The America people are nominally devoted to education, for they have memorized the slogans that were realities to their ancestors. They seem actually indifferent to education, for they do not care to think about what education is. Or as Irving Babbitt once put it, 'The firmness of the American's faith in the blessings of education is equalled only by the vagueness of his ideas as to the kind of education to which these blessings are annexed.'[9]

*13.* This situation must result in part from the nature of the ideal that the American parent holds before himself as he thinks of the future of his children. If this ideal is the successful man, then the difficulties of the educational system become apparent, for the qualities that go into the making of the successful man are by no means obvious, and it is hard to see how those which seem to be required can be inculcated in the educational system.

*14.* Because an interest in ideas, or the mastery of even such rudimentary techniques as reading and writing is not indispensable, and may not even be helpful, to success, students and their parents think that courses preparing, or seeming to prepare, for a specific career in business will help the student to fulfil the whole duty of man, or at least his first duty, which is to be successful. Since there is an infinite number of specific careers open to the young American, the schools, colleges, and universities, partly because they agree with the students and their parents, and partly because they want to attract students, offer an infinite number of courses alleged to lead on to success in specific vocations.[10]

[9] The following quotation from *Educator's Washington Dispatch,* 16 July 1953, reflects a general view: '*Traditional, progressive or just modern?* Child-centred, subject-centred, or society-centred? Academic, vocational, or general? Which should the schools be, and to what extent? These are philosophical questions that can stir up considerable emotion. . . . Superintendent H. I. Willett of Richmond, Virginia recognized this problem when he assumed his duties in 1946. But he and his associates approached it with a device which proved to be as successful as it is simple: By-pass the troublesome questions of philosophy; concentrate on this question—what do our children need in their schools?' The *Dispatch* does not suggest how we can tell what our children need without resort to philosophy.

[10] This notion of the necessity of adjusting education to the future occupations of the student has led to particular difficulties in the education of women. Since women are obviously different from men, since their occupations may be in certain respects different, for only a woman can become a mother and a housewife, the doctrine of adjustment to immediate needs and future occupations has tended to promote the development of all kinds of special courses, such as those in Home Economics or Domes-

15. Of course, it is possible to get an education in American colleges and universities today. There are dedicated professors; there are commodious, well stocked libraries and laboratories; there are young men and young women interested in learning how to use their minds. In spite of the general attitude of the community, which is that intellectual pursuits are not of much importance, and in spite of the frustrating maze of courses and requirements that make up the curriculum, many American students, often by contact with a great teacher, do emerge from the educational system more enlightened than they went in.

16. The President of Columbia University has said,[11]

I think that far too many of our institutions contribute unconsciously to popular confusion by trying much too zealously to be all things to all men. They are too prone to yield to external pressures, too willing to accept offers of funds which have embarrassing strings attached to them, too eager to have a bewildering profusion of course offerings which make their catalogues resemble in variety the offerings of a mail-order house. An impressive array of courses is no substitute for intellectual leadership, but the saving factor in the situation is that there is virtually no known curricular device by which an earnest and intelligent young man can be prevented from getting some kind of an education.

It does seem, however, that the tremendous consumption of materal and human resources by the educational institutions of the United States leads to results disproportionately small. *The science of teaching*

17. The pedagogical problem is not solved even if one's ideal is clear or even if it is an ideal that may be achieved with the help of the educational system. The pedagogical problem is how to use the educational system to form the kind of man that the country wants to produce. But in the absence of a clear ideal, and one that is attainable through education, the pedagogical problem is insoluble: it cannot even be stated. The loss of an intelligible and attainable ideal lies at the root of the troubles of American education.

# Questions

1. What proof does Hutchins offer in his article for his major contention that the "United States has not set great store by intellectual achievement"? *p. 402*

---

tic Science, in disregard of the fact that, though women are different from men, they are also citizens and human beings with the same political and human powers and duties. Contrast the views of President Harold Taylor of Sarah Lawrence College: 'I reject the idea that there is a special role in society to be played by men or women for which the colleges should train either sex. Liberal education is not an instrument for training women or men.'

11 The *New York Times*, 12 January 1954.

2. What function does the term "ideal" serve in Hutchins' discourse?

3. Notice that Hutchins, like Fadiman, isolates the failure of our values and ideals as the source of the difficulty with our schools. What observations about American values does Hutchins add to Fadiman's?

4. How would you characterize the difference in tone between the essays by Fadiman and Hutchins? Substantiate your conclusions as best you can from the language of each essay.

5. Hutchins argues that we would have far more difficulty than the ancient Greeks or the modern Europeans in formulating an ideal of the kind of person we hope to achieve by our educational system and, further, that there is a closer relationship between the actual system and its ideal in Europe than here. What discrepancy does he note between our ideals and our practice?

6. By their references to persons of the past and the history of education both Fadiman and Hutchins argue for a continuity with the higher ideal of an earlier time. To what extent does the argument for such continuity seem valid and to what extent does it seem valid to argue that the different conditions of our time make a different educational policy necessary?

7. Hutchins says elsewhere that "American education is founded on the belief that democracy is served if its schools, colleges and universities charge low fees, or none; and if, at the same time, there is no discrimination among students in terms of their intellectual ability." To what extent is this allegation true? Argue for or against discrimination among students in high schools according to marks of intellectual ability.

# Theme Topics

1. How can high schools encourage better students to enter and to remain in college? Distinguish between what high schools presently do toward this end, but do poorly, and what they do not now do but ought to do.

2. Discuss how revisions of our educational ideals will (will not) improve education in America.

## ·49·

*Sloan Wilson*

# IT'S TIME TO CLOSE OUR CARNIVAL

1. The facts of the school crisis are all out in plain sight—and pretty dreadful to look at. First of all, it has been shown that a surprisingly small percentage of high school students is studying what used to be considered basic subjects. Only 12½% are taking any mathematics more advanced than algebra, and only 25% are studying physics. A foreign language is studied by fewer than 15% of the students. Ten million Russians are studying English, but only 8,000 Americans are studying Russian.

2. People are complaining that the diploma has been devaluated in this nation to the point of meaninglessness. Bernard Leibson, principal of a junior high in New York City, recently admitted that while signing diplomas he suffers "great pangs of pedagogical conscience. Although Johnny cannot read above the fifth-grade level and Mary has barely mastered the fourth-grade arithmetic fundamentals, I have with the connivance of the duly constituted authorities helped to perpetuate the fiction that John and Mary have completed the course of study with a satisfactory record.' . . ."

3. Almost every conceivable reason has been offered for this state of affairs. Marion B. Folsom, who as Secretary of Health, Education and Welfare is a top man in U.S. public education, has demanded fewer "so-called popular or easy courses" and "less chrome, less country-clubbing." Admiral Hyman Rickover, father of the atomic submarine, concurs, citing specifically such courses as love and marriage: "You can learn how to make love outside of school in the good old-fashioned ways."

4. The teachers are to blame, say some critics. Lester Vander Werf, dean of Northeastern University's College of Education, recently accused teachers of not being intelligent enough for the functions they perform.

5. The students are lazy, says another group. Surveys by Margaret Mead and by a group of Purdue scientists have shown that most youngsters consciously avoid taking science subjects because they do not think a scientific career is worth all the effort. A junior high school teacher recently wrote that students nowadays "are being smothered with anxious

concern, softened with lack of exercise, seduced with luxuries, then flung into the morass of excessive sex interest. . . . They are overfed and under-worked. They have too much leisure and too little discipline."

6. It is all the parents' fault, says a third group of critics, Dean Harry D. Bonham of the University of Alabama recently said, "I believe there is altogether too much parental laxity in requiring that the youngsters de-velop the habit of studying and doing their homework." Dean Thomas Clark Pollock of New York University's Washington Square branch blames the communities. Good high schools, he says, try to get rid of frills, "but too often their communities fail to understand or support them prop-erly."

7. And finally the whole nation has been accused. A Dartmouth pro-fessor of chemistry wrote recently: "I am concerned about the easy living in this country. In the past, classes relieved from physical labor—the leisure class—always had some demanding ideal, bravery in war, social grace, or the responsible wielding of power. The only corresponding ideal in U.S. society that I can make out is being a good guy."

8. This is only a small sampling of the criticism of the schools that has been heard lately. The attack may seem unwarranted to many parents in conscientious communities whose good high schools regularly send graduates to the best colleges, but in the rest of the U.S. it is amply justi-fied. And its cumulative effect has been devastating.

9. Obviously it is impossible to make sweeping pronouncements on the industry or intelligence of some 34 million schoolchildren and more than a million teachers. Some of the criticism is the inevitable blowing off of steam which always accompanies a democracy's efforts toward self-im-provement. Still, the statistics cannot be disputed and it would be diffi-cult to deny that few diplomas stand for a fixed level of accomplishment, or that great numbers of students fail to pursue their studies with vigor. Studies show that brilliant children in this country are nowhere near as advanced in the sciences as their opposite numbers in Europe or Russia. Why?

10. To find an answer it may be useful to go back in history and recall the way the U.S. school system developed. As recently as 50 years ago our high schools were almost carbon copies of their European counter-parts. They offered a narrow selection of strictly academic subjects. The question of whether a youngster attended them depended at least as much on his social and economic station in life as on his intelligence. The age-old custom still held: education beyond grammar school was the privilege of the well-to-do.

11. Modern America changed that. This was the land of equality where no class distinctions were tolerated. If a rich man's son could go to high school, so could a poor man's son, and his daughter too. The schools began

taking not only those who once would have fallen by the wayside for social or economic reasons, but also those who would formerly have been excluded for lack of aptitude or desire for academic work. It was pointed out that even the least intelligent youngster can learn something. A new dream was born in America, and as a dream it was neither cynical nor naive.

12. Instead of trying to find students to fit a rigid curriculum, the schools decided to try to hand-tailor a course of instruction for each child. If poor Johnny could not learn chemistry or mathematics, the schools would not throw him onto the street. They would teach him woodworking, they would adjust him to life, they would make him a better citizen. And after he served his four years in high school, they would give him a diploma as fancily lettered as everyone else's.

13. There was a basic humanity in these changes and common sense too. It is true that even the dullest can learn something. Johnny undoubtedly was a better person and a more useful citizen after his four years of high school, even if he did not learn much in academic terms. And the destruction of social and economic barriers to education profited the nation enormously. The schools released a flood of energy and talent such as the world had never seen.

14. To run the new schools a whole new breed of educator appeared. They were men such as John Dewey and his disciples, who invented some of the silliest language ever heard (the "total personality" of a child was to be developed through "group psychological engineering"). The development—their apologists say the distortion—of their aims was disastrous in many cases. But these educators also emphasized some things that good teachers had known for centuries—briefly, that children learn quicker when they are led to understand and to enjoy their studies rather than simply being made to learn by rote, and that teachers should take the child's entire environment and nature into account in deciding how to teach him.

15. What went wrong?

16. In the first place, nobody foresaw how enormously expensive such a school system would be. We were already spending more on education than any other nation, but we were hardly able to provide the money needed for so much individual attention to so many. Educators as a result were forced to design programs for "the average student." Special courses were provided for those experiencing unusual difficulty, but the gifted students were largely ignored.

17. The lack of funds was only the beginning of the trouble. One by one the traditional spurs to effort were removed. With students no longer being held to a rigid level of accomplishment, report cards, as well as diplomas, became almost meaningless. Laws were passed requiring even the dullest students to remain in school until their middle or late teens,

and the educators found they could expel almost no one. Soon they discovered that it was less damaging to all concerned to. let dullards progress through the grades with their contemporaries than to hold them back and let them disrupt classes of younger children. Automatic promotion, automatic graduation and report cards on which rarely was heard a discouraging word became the rule, and it was not one which inspired every student to do his best.

*18.* The fountainhead of the "new education" became Columbia University's Teachers College, which exaggerated the bad aspects of "progressive education" at least as much as it emphasized the good. This led in due course to the greater glory of the professional educationist and the increasing disillusion of many parents and teachers.

*19.* Unless a youngster arrived at school with a genuine desire for knowledge, there was very little incentive for him to study hard. And as we were to discover, precious few youngsters came equipped with anything like a real drive to learn.

*20.* In Russia and in Western Europe children had more reason to study. In the Soviet Union, especially, scientists and technicians were the new aristocrats, and the only way to join their ranks was through academic accomplishment. Today if a Russian boy fails in school he may face the bleak prospect of being a day laborer or serving in some other lowly capacity. No one in Russia can entertain the dream of leaving school early and making a million rubles as a salesman.

*21.* In Europe the possession of a diploma has continued to be a social distinction, and the educated man there is respected even if he is poor. And in both Russia and the other European countries the bright student, because he is very likely to become an important man, is widely admired by his contemporaries.

*22.* The American youngster who miraculously does arrive in school with an honest drive to learn finds himself having to play the role of "queer duck"—a difficult role indeed for most adolescents. Most of the public schools are simply not geared for him. True, he can usually find a chemistry or trigonometry course, and if he is lucky he may find a knowledgeable teacher who will greet him with open arms. But he must also contend with hordes of youngsters drifting through school in search of easy roads to high pay and with the bland disregard of intellectual values which has affected many school administrators and teachers, along with most other Americans.

*23.* Upon arriving at high school today an American youngster is faced with a bewildering choice of literally scores of subjects, many combinations of which can lead to a diploma, and many of which are far easier than physics, mathematics or a foreign language. He can study marriage, chorus or "advertising arts." In some schools he must give time to the study of safe driving and the evils of alcohol. Courses in typewriting and dancing vie for his time.

24. With the accident rate and the divorce rate as high as they are, a good case can be made for instruction in both driving and marriage, and there is no real reason why a youngster should not be taught dancing if the school has the extra money and the pupil has the extra time for it. But all too often the school provides courses in safe driving when it doesn't have the money for adequate courses in chemistry. The schools are becoming increasingly vulnerable to the charge that in trying to do everything for everyone, they are succeeding in doing almost nothing well.

25. The upshot is that many a brilliant youngster finds that his school has assumed the aspects of a carnival. In one room pretty girls practice twirling batons. The sound of cheers is heard from the football field. The safe-driving class circles the block in new automobiles lent by an enterprising dealer. Upstairs funny Mr. Smith sits wearily on a stool in the chemistry lab trying to explain to a few boys that science can be fun, but who pays any attention to him?

26. It is hard to deny that America's schools, which were supposed to reflect one of history's noblest dreams and to cultivate the nation's youthful minds, have degenerated into a system for coddling and entertaining the mediocre. It is one thing to establish courses of varying purpose and of varying degrees of difficulty to fit the talents of various individuals, but it is quite another to run schools in which *most* of the students avoid the tough courses—and get away with it.

27. There is no point in trying to return to the 19th Century to find a cure for these ills. No one could seriously suggest nowadays that high schools should be restricted to the brilliant few, or to a small social or economic group. No, what we have to do is to recapture the enthusiasm for the great dream we once had, and to pursue it with a better sense of values. We must quit perverting it as we have in the past.

28. In the midst of the blare of commercial success we must recapture an honest respect for learning and for learned people. Abandoning that basic virtue in the first place was never meant to be a part of modern education and is part of no theory. It is one thing for us to glory in the tradition of the frontiersman in his buckskins who shouted "I'm as good as you are" to the whole world of bewigged and beribboned aristocracy, but it is quite another to allow a callow adolescent to slouch in his jeans and motorcycle jacket in smirking disrespect for a good and earnest physics teacher.

29. Democracy was never supposed to substitute license for discipline. Instead, it was meant to substitute self-discipline for oppression. But not even the most doctrinaire psychologists say that children can be expected

to survive with self-discipline alone. Often they have to be told by both parents and teachers what to study and how to behave.

*30.* If we are going to start insisting upon honest respect for learning, hard work and good conduct, most of us will have to get tough with ourselves as well as with our children and the schools. A child who hears "eggheads" derided at home, and who sees his parents caring for little more than economic success and entertainment, can hardly be expected to excel as a scholar. And those who administer the schools cannot be expected to provide an education suited to each child's ambitions and needs if the money for small classes and good teachers is not forthcoming.

*31.* The sort of effort that is required is one which can only be expected in time of emergency. Such a time is, however, at hand. In past decades we could pride ourselves on the multitude of untutored geniuses who could and did devise the reaper, the electric light bulb, the airplane and countless other mechanisms which are now part of civilization. But times have changed. Space ships and intercontinental missiles are not invented by self-educated men in home workshops. They are developed by teams of highly trained scientists, most of whom must begin (and get much of) their education in the public schools.

*32.* It goes without saying nowadays that the outcome of the arms race will depend eventually on our schools and those of the Russians. It is just as obvious, if less often pointed out, that the kind of understanding between peoples which some day may perhaps make arms races unnecessary also depends in large part upon education.

*33.* The United States was the first nation in the world to provide schools for all children, and that is one reason we have prospered. If our schools fail, it will not be because we care too much for our ideals but because we care too little. We should not need the threat of Russia to be convinced that it is time to close the carnival and go to work.

# Questions

1. What is the function of the first two paragraphs?
2. Comment on the devices of coherence which hold together paragraphs 3 to 8.
3. What is the argumentative function of paragraphs 9 and 24?
4. What linking devices connect paragraphs 9 and 10, 10 and 11, 11 and 12, 12 and 13, 13 and 14, 14 and 15, 15 and 16, 16 and 17, 17 and 18, 18 and 19?
5. Find in the paragraphs listed above topic sentences that are also linking sentences.

6. What is the logical connection between paragraphs 13 and 15? How else is it evident that the admission—"Johnny undoubtedly was a better person and a more useful citizen"—is not to be taken seriously?
7. How do paragraphs 20 to 22 relate to Fadiman's general thesis?
8. What are Wilson's recommendations?
9. Harold C. Hand in the essay that follows attacks not only Wilson's statistics but also his failure to recognize that only the top third of the intelligence distribution is likely to profit from the study of physics and only the top half is likely to profit from the study of foreign languages. Why would you agree or disagree with Hand?

# Theme Topics

1. Write a paper on Wilson's statement: "Democracy was never supposed to substitute license for discipline. Instead it was meant to substitute self-discipline for oppression."
2. Read the answer to Wilson by Harold C. Hand in the article that follows and write a paper modifying both positions, granting some point to both sides.

## ·50·

*Harold C. Hand*

### *LIFE*'S FICTIONS

1. The first in *Life* magazine's widely advertised series on American education (March 24, 1958, issue) is entitled "It's Time to Close Our Carnival." It was written by Mr. Sloan Wilson, who *Life* says is "best known as a novelist."

2. This is not impossible to believe when one attempts to verify the high school enrollment statistics set forth in Mr. Wilson's opening paragraph—statistics underlying certain facts which he says are "all out in plain sight—and pretty dreadful to look at." For when one checks Mr. Wilson's high school enrollment data, it is found that two of the three figures given are fictional.

Life's Fictions, Pamphlet (1958), reprinted by permission of the author.

3. Here are the "dreadful" statistics given by Mr. Wilson: "Only 12½ per cent [of American high school students] are taking any mathematics more advanced than algebra, and only 25 per cent are studying physics. A foreign language is studied by fewer than 15 per cent of the students."

4. Nowhere in his article did Mr. Wilson seem to recognize that only the students in the upper third of the intelligence distribution are likely to do well in or to profit very much from taking physics or advanced mathematics, or that only those in the top half are likely to perform capably in or to benefit very much from enrolling in foreign language classes.

5. It should also be noted that only the more capable students in the U.S.S.R. and other foreign countries are enrolled in the last three or four years of their selective secondary schools. In America, about 90 per cent of our total youth population 14-17 years of age are in our secondary schools. It seems unfair to compare the academic achievements of a highly selected group of youths in one country with those of the generality of the youths of another country.

6. Now let us turn to our analysis of the enrollment data which Mr. Wilson says are "dreadful to look at." We shall begin with the datum for physics.

7. This figure of 25 per cent is the approximate fraction of the students in grade twelve, the school level at which this subject is usually taught, who are enrolled in physics.[1] By the time they complete high school, then, this fraction of today's high school student body has taken physics. This figure is equal to about three-fourths of the number of seniors in the upper third of the intelligence distribution, hence the presumption is that about three-fourths of those who could do well in physics are now enrolled in this subject. To say that this is "pretty dreadful" seems unwarranted—unless one assumes that all or nearly all of the more able students should be channeled into physics—or, worse yet, that students should take this subject regardless of their capacity to succeed in it.

8. Next, let us consider Mr. Wilson's assertion that "a foreign language is studied by fewer than 15 per cent of the [high school] students." A recent NEA *Research Bulletin* reports that 6.9 per cent of the public high school pupils were enrolled in Latin and 13.7 per cent in modern foreign languages in 1955.[2] This totals approximately 21 per cent, a figure more than a third larger than that asserted by Mr. Wilson.

9. But this figure of 21 per cent is quite misleading, however, if one assumes that it tells us that some 79 per cent of our youths take no work in foreign language during their high school careers—for it definitely does

[1] U. S. Office of Education, Federal Security Agency, *Offerings and Enrollments in Science and Mathematics,* 1956, p. 12.

[2] National Education Association, "Ten Criticisms of Public Education," *Research Bulletin,* Vol. 35, No. 4, December, 1957, p. 157.

not. This 21 per cent datum is for but *one* of the *four* years that a pupil spends in high school. By a process too complicated to reproduce in the space available here, it can be demonstrated that 37 per cent of our high school students take one or more years of foreign language during one or more of their four high school years. If by "foreign language" Mr. Wilson meant to exclude enrollments in Latin, this figure is 25 per cent instead of 37 per cent but still of a magnitude two-thirds larger than the "fewer than 15 per cent" figure that he asserts. The presumption, then, is that about three-fourths of the youths in the upper half of the I.Q. range are enrolled in a foreign language course of some kind. This is scarcely a spectacle "dreadful to look at."

*10.* Finally, let us consider Mr. Wilson's assertion that "only 12½ per cent are taking any mathematics more advanced than algebra," presumably ninth-grade algebra. The U. S. Office of Education reports[3] that 42 per cent of all tenth-grade pupils were enrolled in plane geometry in 1956-57, so we know that no less than this fraction of today's high school graduates have this course entered on their records. Intermediate algebra is an eleventh-grade subject, and solid geometry and trigonometry are taught in the twelfth grade. The U. S. Office of Education reports for 1956-57 that 32 per cent of the high school juniors were enrolled in intermediate algebra, and that the enrollments in solid geometry and trigonometry were equivalent to about 13 per cent and 16 per cent, respectively, of the senior class. All told, the enrollments in the mathematics courses which are more advanced than ninth-grade algebra totaled 1,632,000 students in 1956-57. This would approximate 23 per cent, and not 12½ per cent, of the total high school enrollment. But this is the figure for but *one* of the *four* years that students spend in high school and does *not* tell what proportion takes or does not take mathematics during their high school careers; this proportion can be no smaller than 42 per cent, the figure for plane geometry. We see, then, that Mr. Wilson's 12½ per cent figure is grossly in error.

*11.* The U. S. Office of Education enrollment data reported above make it appear that either all or virtually all of the more fortunately endowed students are enrolled in plane geometry and in intermediate algebra, and that from well over a third to nearly half of the top one third of the senior students are taking solid geometry and trigonometry. On the advice of mathematicians, solid geometry is being absorbed into plane geometry, so the gradual disappearance of this subject from the high school curriculum seems desirable. Only in respect to trigonometry, then, can the enrollment data in mathematics be said to be disturbing. But here the public high schools are well on their way, as a comparison of 1928-29 with 1956-57 data makes clear. Since 1928-29, the total number of youths of

[3] U. S. Office of Education, Federal Security Agency, *op. cit.*, pp. 32, 44.

twelfth-grade age in this country has increased by but 2.1 per cent and the number of seniors has not quite doubled (96 per cent). During these years, however, the enrollment in trigonometry has increased by 440.5 per cent.[4]

*12.* To cavil a bit, it would seem that *Life* might well have entrusted the task of securing and interpreting enrollment data to someone with enough first-hand experience in public secondary schools to do so competently—someone with enough feel for the data to keep him from committing the grossly misleading "bloopers" of which Novelist Wilson is guilty in his opening, and tone-setting, paragraph. However innocently these mistakes and misinterpretations may have been made, they led Mr. Wilson to set up a straw man at the very outset of the series of *Life* articles. Obviously, a straw man has no place in what purports to be a serious and dependable analysis of our public school situation. Novelist Wilson distorts and misrepresents the actual activities in our secondary schools in parts of the remainder of this article, thereby subjecting *Life* to the charge of irresponsible reporting of the true conditions in our schools.

[4] Harold C. Hand, "A Scholar's Devil Theory," *High School Journal,* Spring 1958.

## ·51·

*Bureau of the Census*

# EDUCATIONAL ATTAINMENT:
# March, 1962

[Quite apart from any controversy regarding *what* students are or are not studying in U.S. schools are data from the Bureau of the Census in regard to *how many* years of schooling American "civilians" have actually completed. The following statistics reveal that as of March 1962, 53.7% of the total population 25 years of age and over had not completed requirements for a high school diploma, and 36.1% in the same age group failed to complete so much as a single year of high school. Further study of the percentages and figures given below will permit you to test various claims and counterclaims concerning formal education in the United States.]

### DEFINITIONS AND EXPLANATIONS

*Population coverage.*—The figures in this report for March 1962 are sample survey data and relate to the civilian population of the 50 States and the District of Columbia. Inmates of institutions are included in the sample. Members of the Armed Forces living off post or with their families on post are included, but all other members of the Armed Forces are excluded. For convenience, this population is referred to as "the civilian population."

*Age.*—The age classification is based on the age of the person at his last birthday.

*Years of school completed.*—Data on years of school completed in this report were derived from the combination of answers to two questions:

From *Current Population Reports: Population Characteristics*, Series P-20, No. 121 (Washington, D. C., U. S. Department of Commerce, 1963), pp. 3-4, 7.

(a) "What is the highest grade of school he has ever attended?" and (b) "Did he finish this grade?"

The questions on educational attainment apply only to progress in "regular" schools. Such schools include graded public, private, and parochial elementary and high schools (both junior and senior high), colleges, universities, and professional schools, whether day schools or night schools. Thus, regular schooling is that which may advance a person toward an elementary school certificate or high school diploma, or a college, university, or professional school degree. Schooling in other than regular schools was counted only if the credits obtained were regarded as transferable to a school in the regular school system.

The median years of school completed is defined as the value which divides the population group into two equal parts—one-half having completed more schooling and one-half having completed less schooling than the median. This median was computed after the statistics on years of school completed had been converted to a continuous series of numbers (e.g., completion of the first year of high school was treated as completion of the 9th year and the completion of the first year of college as completion of the 13th year). The persons completing a given school year were assumed to be distributed evenly within the interval from .0 to .9 of the year (for example, persons completing the 12th year were assumed to be distributed evenly between 12.0 and 12.9). In fact, at the time of the March survey, most of the enrolled persons had completed about three-fourths of a school year beyond the highest grade completed, whereas a large majority of persons who were not enrolled had not attended any part of a grade beyond the highest one completed. The effect of the assumption is to place the median for younger persons slightly below, and for older persons slightly above, the true median. Because of the inexact assumption as to the distribution within an interval, this median is more appropriately used for comparing groups and the same group at different dates than as an absolute measure of educational attainment.

*Assignment of educational attainment for those not reporting.*—When information on either the highest grade attended or completion of the grade was not reported in the 1962 survey, entries for the items were assigned using an edit in the computer. The general procedure was to assign an entry for a person that was consistent with entries for other persons with similar characteristics. The specific technique used in the March 1962 survey was as follows:

1. The computer stored reported data on highest grade attended by color and age, and on completion of the grade by age and highest grade attended, for persons 14 years old and over in the population.

2. Each stored value was retained in the computer only until a succeeding person having the same characteristics (e.g., same color and age, in the case of assignments for highest grade attended) and having the item reported was processed through the computer. Then, the reported data for the succeeding person were stored in place of the one previously stored.

3. When one or both of the education items for a person 14 years old and over was not reported, the entry assigned to this person was that stored for the last person who had the same characteristics.

*Rounding of estimates.*—The individual figures in this report are rounded to the nearest thousand and adjusted to group totals.

## Table 1.—Years of School Completed by Persons 14 Years Old and Over, by Age and Sex, for the United States: Civilian Population, March 1962

(Numbers in thousands. The "civilian" population for March 1962 includes 978,000 members of the Armed Forces living off post or on post with their families but excludes all other members of the Armed Forces)

| Age and sex | Total population | Years of school completed | | | | | | | | | Median school years completed |
| --- | --- | --- | --- | --- | --- | --- | --- | --- | --- | --- | --- |
| | | None | Elementary school | | | High school | | College | | | |
| | | | 1 to 4 years | 5 to 7 years | 8 years | 1 to 3 years | 4 years | 1 to 3 years | 4 years | 5 years or more | |
| Total, 14 years and over.......... | 129,295 | 2,232 | 5,947 | 14,421 | 20,957 | 28,349 | 35,676 | 11,998 | 6,482 | 3,233 | 11.2 |
| 14 to 17 years................ | 12,465 | 57 | 85 | 2,101 | 3,424 | 6,667 | 110 | 21 | ... | ... | 9.3 |
| 18 and 19 years............... | 5,201 | 20 | 26 | 177 | 170 | 1,669 | 2,504 | 628 | 7 | ... | 12.2 |
| 20 to 24 years................ | 10,965 | 44 | 121 | 407 | 661 | 2,262 | 4,585 | 2,179 | 565 | 141 | 12.4 |
| 25 years and over............. | 100,664 | 2,111 | 5,715 | 11,736 | 16,702 | 17,751 | 28,477 | 9,170 | 5,910 | 3,092 | 12.4 |
| 25 to 29 years................ | 10,646 | 69 | 191 | 544 | 698 | 2,125 | 4,317 | 1,310 | 1,018 | 374 | 12.4 |
| 30 to 34 years................ | 11,484 | 89 | 248 | 708 | 986 | 2,246 | 4,498 | 1,242 | 922 | 545 | 12.3 |
| 35 to 44 years................ | 24,241 | 211 | 772 | 1,860 | 2,698 | 4,815 | 8,835 | 2,498 | 1,633 | 919 | 12.2 |
| 45 to 54 years................ | 21,046 | 255 | 943 | 2,614 | 3,623 | 4,123 | 5,833 | 1,934 | 1,064 | 637 | 11.2 |
| 55 to 64 years................ | 16,017 | 386 | 1,248 | 2,659 | 3,944 | 2,625 | 2,826 | 1,188 | 754 | 387 | 8.9 |
| 65 years and over............. | 17,230 | 1,101 | 2,313 | 3,351 | 4,753 | 1,817 | 2,168 | 978 | 519 | 230 | 8.4 |
| Male, 14 years and over........... | 62,129 | 1,140 | 3,290 | 7,384 | 10,191 | 13,462 | 14,946 | 5,844 | 3,502 | 2,370 | 11.0 |
| 14 to 17 years................ | 6,308 | 37 | 59 | 1,188 | 1,735 | 3,229 | 49 | 11 | ... | ... | 9.1 |
| 18 and 19 years............... | 2,442 | 13 | 13 | 108 | 94 | 833 | 1,057 | 321 | 3 | ... | 12.2 |
| 20 to 24 years................ | 5,096 | 21 | 74 | 210 | 313 | 1,001 | 1,908 | 1,197 | 266 | 106 | 12.5 |
| 25 years and over............. | 48,283 | 1,069 | 3,144 | 5,878 | 8,049 | 8,399 | 11,932 | 4,315 | 3,233 | 2,264 | 11.1 |
| 25 to 29 years................ | 5,162 | 32 | 127 | 279 | 347 | 982 | 1,805 | 700 | 590 | 300 | 12.5 |
| 30 to 34 years................ | 5,600 | 34 | 141 | 401 | 542 | 1,026 | 1,895 | 609 | 526 | 426 | 12.3 |
| 35 to 44 years................ | 11,764 | 140 | 436 | 1,006 | 1,355 | 2,345 | 3,647 | 1,185 | 947 | 703 | 12.2 |
| 45 to 54 years................ | 10,317 | 129 | 530 | 1,356 | 1,828 | 2,014 | 2,555 | 977 | 521 | 427 | 11.0 |
| 55 to 64 years................ | 7,730 | 185 | 671 | 1,344 | 1,915 | 1,274 | 1,211 | 471 | 401 | 258 | 8.9 |
| 65 years and over............. | 7,710 | 549 | 1,239 | 1,492 | 2,062 | 758 | 819 | 393 | 248 | 150 | 8.0 |
| Female, 14 years and over......... | 67,166 | 1,092 | 2,657 | 7,037 | 10,766 | 14,887 | 20,730 | 6,154 | 2,980 | 863 | 11.4 |
| 14 to 17 years................ | 6,157 | 20 | 26 | 913 | 1,689 | 3,438 | 61 | 10 | ... | ... | 9.4 |
| 18 and 19 years............... | 2,759 | 7 | 13 | 69 | 76 | 836 | 1,447 | 307 | 4 | ... | 12.3 |
| 20 to 24 years................ | 5,869 | 23 | 47 | 197 | 348 | 1,261 | 2,677 | 982 | 299 | 35 | 12.4 |
| 25 years and over............. | 52,381 | 1,042 | 2,571 | 5,858 | 8,653 | 9,352 | 16,545 | 4,855 | 2,677 | 828 | 11.6 |
| 25 to 29 years................ | 5,484 | 37 | 64 | 265 | 351 | 1,143 | 2,512 | 610 | 428 | 74 | 12.4 |
| 30 to 34 years................ | 5,884 | 55 | 107 | 307 | 444 | 1,220 | 2,603 | 633 | 396 | 119 | 12.3 |
| 35 to 44 years................ | 12,477 | 71 | 336 | 854 | 1,343 | 2,470 | 5,188 | 1,313 | 686 | 216 | 11.2 |
| 45 to 54 years................ | 10,729 | 126 | 413 | 1,258 | 1,795 | 2,109 | 3,278 | 997 | 543 | 210 | 11.5 |
| 55 to 64 years................ | 8,287 | 201 | 577 | 1,315 | 2,029 | 1,351 | 1,615 | 717 | 353 | 129 | 9.0 |
| 65 years and over............. | 9,520 | 552 | 1,074 | 1,859 | 2,691 | 1,059 | 1,349 | 585 | 271 | 80 | 8.5 |

| | 100.0 | 1.7 | 4.6 | 11.2 | 16.2 | 21.9 | 27.6 | 9.3 | 5.0 | 2.5 | ... |
|---|---|---|---|---|---|---|---|---|---|---|---|
| Total, 14 years and over...... | 100.0 | 1.7 | 4.6 | 11.2 | 16.2 | 21.9 | 27.6 | 9.3 | 5.0 | 2.5 | ... |
| 14 to 17 years................ | 100.0 | 0.5 | 0.7 | 16.9 | 27.5 | 53.5 | 0.9 | 0.2 | ... | ... | ... |
| 18 and 19 years............... | 100.0 | 0.4 | 0.5 | 3.4 | 3.2 | 32.1 | 48.1 | 12.1 | 0.1 | ... | ... |
| 20 to 24 years................ | 100.0 | 0.4 | 1.1 | 3.7 | 6.0 | 20.6 | 41.8 | 19.9 | 5.2 | 1.3 | ... |
| 25 years and over............. | 100.0 | 2.1 | 5.7 | 11.7 | 16.6 | 17.6 | 28.3 | 9.1 | 5.9 | 3.1 | ... |
| 25 to 29 years................ | 100.0 | 0.6 | 1.8 | 5.1 | 6.6 | 20.0 | 40.6 | 12.3 | 9.6 | 3.5 | ... |
| 30 to 34 years................ | 100.0 | 0.8 | 2.2 | 6.2 | 8.6 | 19.6 | 39.2 | 10.8 | 8.0 | 4.7 | ... |
| 35 to 44 years................ | 100.0 | 0.9 | 3.2 | 7.7 | 11.1 | 19.9 | 36.4 | 10.3 | 6.7 | 3.8 | ... |
| 45 to 54 years................ | 100.0 | 1.2 | 4.5 | 12.4 | 17.2 | 19.6 | 27.7 | 9.3 | 5.1 | 3.0 | ... |
| 55 to 64 years................ | 100.0 | 2.4 | 7.8 | 16.6 | 24.6 | 16.4 | 17.6 | 7.4 | 4.7 | 2.4 | ... |
| 65 years and over............. | 100.0 | 6.4 | 13.4 | 19.4 | 27.6 | 10.5 | 12.6 | 5.7 | 3.0 | 1.3 | ... |
| Male, 14 years and over........ | 100.0 | 1.8 | 5.3 | 11.9 | 16.4 | 21.7 | 24.1 | 9.4 | 5.6 | 3.8 | ... |
| 14 to 17 years................ | 100.0 | 0.6 | 0.9 | 13.8 | 27.5 | 51.2 | 0.8 | 0.2 | ... | ... | ... |
| 18 and 19 years............... | 100.0 | 0.5 | 0.5 | 4.4 | 3.9 | 34.1 | 43.3 | 13.1 | 0.1 | ... | ... |
| 20 to 24 years................ | 100.0 | 0.4 | 1.5 | 4.1 | 6.1 | 19.6 | 37.4 | 23.5 | 5.2 | 2.1 | ... |
| 25 years and over............. | 100.0 | 2.2 | 6.5 | 12.2 | 16.7 | 17.4 | 24.7 | 8.9 | 6.7 | 4.7 | ... |
| 25 to 29 years................ | 100.0 | 0.6 | 2.5 | 5.4 | 9.7 | 19.0 | 35.0 | 13.6 | 11.4 | 5.8 | ... |
| 30 to 34 years................ | 100.0 | 0.6 | 2.5 | 7.2 | 9.7 | 18.3 | 33.8 | 10.9 | 9.4 | 7.6 | ... |
| 35 to 44 years................ | 100.0 | 1.2 | 3.7 | 8.6 | 11.5 | 19.9 | 31.0 | 10.1 | 8.0 | 6.0 | ... |
| 45 to 54 years................ | 100.0 | 1.3 | 5.1 | 13.1 | 17.7 | 19.5 | 24.8 | 9.3 | 5.0 | 4.1 | ... |
| 55 to 64 years................ | 100.0 | 2.4 | 8.7 | 17.4 | 24.8 | 16.5 | 15.7 | 6.1 | 5.2 | 3.3 | ... |
| 65 years and over............. | 100.0 | 7.1 | 16.1 | 19.4 | 26.7 | 9.8 | 10.6 | 5.1 | 3.2 | 1.9 | ... |
| Female, 14 years and over...... | 100.0 | 1.6 | 4.0 | 10.5 | 16.0 | 22.2 | 30.9 | 9.2 | 4.4 | 1.3 | ... |
| 14 to 17 years................ | 100.0 | 0.3 | 0.4 | 14.8 | 27.4 | 55.8 | 1.0 | 0.2 | ... | ... | ... |
| 18 and 19 years............... | 100.0 | 0.3 | 0.5 | 2.5 | 2.8 | 30.3 | 52.4 | 11.1 | 0.1 | ... | ... |
| 20 to 24 years................ | 100.0 | 0.4 | 0.8 | 3.4 | 5.9 | 21.5 | 45.6 | 16.7 | 5.1 | 0.6 | ... |
| 25 years and over............. | 100.0 | 2.0 | 4.9 | 11.2 | 16.5 | 17.9 | 31.6 | 9.3 | 5.1 | 1.6 | ... |
| 25 to 29 years................ | 100.0 | 0.7 | 1.2 | 4.8 | 6.4 | 20.8 | 45.8 | 11.1 | 7.8 | 1.3 | ... |
| 30 to 34 years................ | 100.0 | 1.0 | 1.8 | 5.2 | 7.5 | 20.7 | 44.2 | 10.8 | 6.7 | 2.0 | ... |
| 35 to 44 years................ | 100.0 | 0.6 | 2.7 | 6.8 | 10.8 | 19.8 | 41.6 | 10.5 | 5.5 | 1.7 | ... |
| 45 to 54 years................ | 100.0 | 1.2 | 3.8 | 11.7 | 16.7 | 19.7 | 30.6 | 9.3 | 5.1 | 2.0 | ... |
| 55 to 64 years................ | 100.0 | 2.4 | 7.0 | 15.9 | 24.5 | 16.3 | 19.5 | 8.7 | 4.3 | 1.6 | ... |
| 65 years and over............. | 100.0 | 5.3 | 11.3 | 19.5 | 28.3 | 11.1 | 14.2 | 6.1 | 2.8 | 0.8 | ... |

# Questions

1. What significant discrepancies do you find between the statistics in this table and those in the preceding article by Harold Hand and in the following speech by Arthur Bestor?
2. These figures from the Bureau of the Census suggest many questions, which you may wish to answer (or qualify before answering) by reflecting on your own schooling and community. Granted that low intelligence may account for about 20 percent of the figure, why does more than 44 percent of the population 25 years and over never complete requirements for a high school diploma, assuming the situation has not changed radically in the years since this study? Should dropouts be provided primarily with various kinds of vocational training under the auspices of the public school system? Or should they also be educated as "responsible citizens of a democracy"? Discuss the difficulties for the community you know best in attempting to follow either one or both of these educational policies.


## ·52·

*Arthur Bestor*


# A CRISIS OF PURPOSE

*1.* The present crisis in the American public-school system is, at bottom, a crisis of purpose. Low achievement is the consequence of low aims. Confusion about the purposes of the high school has produced the shortcomings so appallingly evident today. In an article published in 1952 I spoke of the problem as "Aimlessness in Education." May I repeat what I said then, five years before Sputnik: "If we really believe that education is vital to our safety, then we need to know exactly what kind of schooling constitutes genuine education, and what kind of schooling constitutes genuine education, and what kind is merely a gaudy show." [1]

*2.* For twenty-five years, at least, the purposes of our high schools

From *Vital Speeches,* 24 (September 15, 1958). Reprinted by permission of the author.

(Speech delivered at the Western Washington College of Education, Bellingham, Washington, August 7, 1958.)

[1] *Scientific Monthly,* vol. 75, pp. 109-116 (August 1952).

have been determined by a narrow group of educational theorists who like to describe themselves as "professional" educators—thereby implying that a college professor in the liberal arts or sciences (who may devote a lifetime to teaching) is somehow an amateur in education. Contemptuously rejecting the views of the scholarly and scientific world, these professional educationalists have redefined the purposes of both elementary and secondary schools in terms that are almost completely non-intellectual, and that are often belligerently anti-intellectual. Year by year, the high-school curriculum has come to have less and less connection with the real world of mature intellectual activity. As a consequence, the American high school now prepares its students for a grotesque dream world, where science and mathematics do not count (though in the real world they underlie our whole technology), where foreign languages are unnecessary (though in the real world our responsibilities as a world power make them indispensable), where history can be overlooked (though the real world is a changing world, which history alone can interpret).

3. The educational theory that dominates our public-school system today is an attempt to escape from reality, not an effort to grapple with the actual intellectual problems of the contemporary world. To conceal this fact, professional educationists insist that the school should not be judged in terms of the intellectual achievement of its students. The school is to be looked upon as a welfare agency performing a variety of social services, of which intellectual training is merely one and a relatively minor one. Let us examine this argument in its own terms.

4. The public schools enroll virtually all the young people of the nation. These young people are facing all sorts of personal problems. They must all eventually make a living, hence the question of a well-paid future job is much on their minds. They are all growing up—a disconcerting, even painful, experience—and they can well be "mixed up" without being "crazy." A substantial number of these young people have a most unsatisfactory home life. Poverty, the divorce of their parents, discriminations practised against them as members of a minority group create in them deep-seated emotional and psychological disturbances. Problems like these are much more real to vast numbers of the young people than are the problems presented by Macbeth, by algebra, by grammar, by the American constitution, or by the reaction of hydrochloric acid with zinc.

5. Taking these facts as their starting point, professional educationists insist that the public school must try to solve all the resulting problems. "It is the job of the school," according to a pronouncement of one of the most influential bodies of American professional educators, "to meet the common and the specific individual needs of youth." [2] Because a young man's need for a job is so evident, the school should make every effort

[2] National Association of Secondary-School Principals, *Planning for American Youth* (Washington, 1944), p. 10.

to help him "develop salable skills." For a young woman, cooking and sewing and homemaking should be a central feature of the program. If a child comes from a broken home, then the school must devote its main effort to giving him a sense of security. When young people reach adolescence, and begin to feel excited and disturbed about the opposite sex, the school must move in on the problem with courses in sex education. If accidents are increasing, the school must teach youngsters to drive. Since personal appearance counts for so much, the school ought to show girls how to dress attractively and how to use make-up, and boys how to be well-groomed.

6. Educationists who look upon the school's responsibility in this way believe that every school activity must be placed on a par with every other. If a pupil is getting some kind of practical training that he needs, then he is being "educated," regardless of any intellectual content in what he is doing. To say that one activity is any more "educational" than another—to treat one kind of study as intrinsically more worthwhile and important than another—would be undemocratic. The Educational Policies Commission (set up by the National Education Association and one of its departments) undertook a few years ago to describe an ideal school program in an imaginary community, which it called Farmville. The Commission stated the principle thus: "There is no aristocracy of 'subjects' in the Farmville curriculum. Mathematics and mechanics, art and agriculture, history and homemaking are all peers." [3]

7. Intellectual training gets short shrift in such a conception of education. Educationists who view the school program in this way are apt to think of intellectual training as simply a special form of vocational training, rather than as an exciting venture in ideas, important in its own right and vital to intelligent citizenship. Science and mathematics, these educationists assume, are appropriate only for the few who are going to be scientists or engineers or doctors. History and English, they believe, are for the minority who plan to be writers or historians or lawyers. Pupils destined for other jobs, the educationists insist, can get along without these forms of knowledge, or with minimum dosages.

8. Another aspect of this philosophy must be noted. Many of the social and psychological problems of young people can be handled more effectively through extra-curricular activities—editing the school paper, planning class parties, running student government, managing athletic teams, and the like—than in a formal classroom. Because the handling of these personal problems is so important, educationists wish to erase the traditional line between the curriculum (the course of study) and the other activities connected with the school, thus permitting youngsters to devote all or most of their time to activities rather than studies.

[3] Educational Policies Commission, *Education for All American Youth* (Washington, 1944), p. 142.

9. This shift of emphasis from intellectual to non-intellectual activities in the school leads to some extremely odd statements about the things with which the school should concern itself. One such document from Illinois is worth citing. Under the auspices of the state, a certain professor of education undertook to list the "real-life problems" of young people, which the school should attempt to deal with by a "reorientation" of its curriculum. Among the fifty-five items on the list there was no mention whatever of any branch of science or mathematics, though "camping" and "doing parlor stunts" rated specific attention. Here are some of the problems, put forward in all seriousness as proper concerns of the school: "The problem of developing one or more 'making things,' 'making it go,' or 'tinkering' hobbies," "The problem of improving one's personal appearance," "the problem of developing and maintaining wholesome boy-girl relationships," and "the problem of selecting a 'family dentist' and acquiring the habit of visiting him systematically." [4]

10. I have no doubt that some thoughtless adolescents consider these "problems" significant enough for them to spend precious school time—*their* time, paid for by their parents and by the rest of us—in learning the answers. Did the American people, however, create a nationwide public-school system to deal with problems like these? They did not. Neither parents nor citizens at large originated these proposals. They were devised by doctrinaire educational theorists. Whatever public acceptance they have won is the result of irresponsible, high-pressure salesmanship on the part of professional educationists.

11. The argument, briefly put, is that because a social need exists the school must therefore attempt to satisfy it. This is a complete *non sequitur*. The school is only one of the agencies that exist to satisfy the needs of society. Each agency has its own area of responsibility, because each possesses a particular sort of competence. The particular competence of a school is in providing intellectual training. It was created for this purpose and its facilities and techniques—classrooms, laboratories, libraries; assignments, recitations, lectures, examinations—are adapted to this particular end. To subordinate this end to something else (no matter how worthy) is to deprive society of a vital service that no other agency can provide.

12. When a school takes over a function that it is less competent to perform than some existing social agency, the net effect is to impair the welfare of society, not to improve it. Family life is said to have deteriorated in the United States. The public schools have made a great fuss over courses in "home and family living." Nothing in the present situation suggests that such courses have succeeded in reducing the divorce rate or accomplishing any of the other results so glowingly promised. On the other hand, there is good reason to believe that the influence of the home

[4] Harold C. Hand, "Problems of High School Youth," in Illinois Secondary School Curriculum Program, Bulletin No. 11, pp. 30-32 (August 1950).

upon young people has been seriously undermined by the very effort of
the school to take over functions properly belonging to the family. The
promise that the school will effectively perform these functions is a promise that cannot possibly be kept. Nevertheless the irresponsible utterances
of educationists about taking over responsibilities that the home has neglected contribute to the very breakdown they are talking about. Their
words are an encouragement to weak-minded parents to dump their problems on the school instead of dealing with them as they should

*13.* There is, of course, one kind of school that can and does assume
responsibility for the entire life of the young person in its charge. This is
the full-time residential or boarding school. Such a school stands *in loco
parentis*, exercising the authority and assuming the responsibility of the
home. It provides medical services. It enforces discipline twenty-four
hours a day. It furnishes recreation. It usually sponsors religious services,
making itself the channel through which the church performs its functions. Under these circumstances the influence of every social agency except the school is suspended, and the school not only can but must take
over their duties.

*14.* A strong argument can be made (as, indeed, Admiral Rickover has
done) for creating in the United States a large number of full-time residential schools, in which public funds would provide both subsistence and
tuition for the students enrolled. Such schools would be capable of assuming the responsibilities that American educationists are talking about. But
educationists are not urging the creation of such schools. They are asking
that the public schools, as they now exist, assume these wide-ranging responsibilities. They close their eyes to the basic fact that the American
public school is a *day school*, which has charge of the student for no more
than half (and usually much less than half) of each waking day, for only
five days out of each week's seven. During the greater part of his conscious life, a student is under the influence of—within the sphere of control of—other institutions of society, upon which responsibility also rests.
There must be a distribution of function among the various agencies of
society, the school included, because there is a distribution of time among
them. The school has responsibility for part, but only part, of his time.
*Which* part of the child's upbringing, given this distribution of function,
is the peculiar and inescapable responsibility of the school?

*15.* The experience, practice, and policy of a residential school is peculiarly relevant in this connection. Though such a school must assume responsibility for the entire life of its students, it never permits a blurring
of the line that separates the curriculum from the rest of its activities.
Formal classroom periods are devoted to basic intellectual disciplines and
uninterrupted study periods are set aside. All other functions are performed outside the curriculum. Now, the time available to the day school
is roughly the equivalent of the time devoted in a residential school to

the curriculum proper. A student can expect to receive an education of equal depth and value in a public day school, only if the same number of classroom periods are devoted to serious intellectual training as would be the case in a residential school, and only if the public school insists upon homework equal in amount to the work done in the study periods that a residential school sets aside in the evenings and on weekends and holidays. If a public day school purports to offer a genuine education—rather than a watered-down imitation—then it must prevent any and every encroachment upon the time that students devote to study of the fundamental intellectual disciplines. School administrators must draw a sharp line between the curriculum and extracurricular activities. In the time available to the school for the latter—for activities over and above the basic curriculum—it can accomplish many desirable vocational and social ends. Athletics, shop-work, cooking, and driver-training are perfectly legitimate *extra-curricular* activities, recognized as valuable in the most traditional schools. "The battle of Waterloo," Wellington is supposed to have said, "was won in the playing fields of Eton." [5] Every good school accomplishes much besides intellectual training. Only by distinguishing clearly between the classroom and the playing field, however, can serious and honest results be achieved by either.

*16.* The school must plan its program in terms of the time that has been made available to it. Most of the time made available in America to the public school is *curricular* time, within which the school is under solemn obligation to plan a continuous, cumulative, uninterrupted program of intellectual training. A small balance of time is also available for extra-curricular activities under supervision of the school. The school, if honest and responsible, must promise, in the way of vocational training and social conditioning, no more than it can perform within the limits of this *extra-curricular* segment of time. Before embarking on vast programs purporting to advance social, psychological, and vocational purposes, the school must demand and receive from society whatever additional allotments of student time (as well as whatever additional allotments of money) may be necessary to carry out such programs. If, for example, the school is really to take over the responsibilities of the home, it must take time away from the home life of the student and must be vested with the disciplinary authority of the home. Barring such a grant of time, authority, and money (a grant most unlikely to be forthcoming), the school has no business promising—or even consenting—to assume responsibility for tasks that are outside its province. Indeed, until the school has proved itself willing to carry out honestly, thoroughly, and unremittingly its assigned task of intellectual training, there is no reason in the world for society to say to it, "Well done, thou good and faithful servant: thou hast been faithful over a few things, I will make thee ruler over many things."

[5] *Oxford Dictionary of Quotations* (2nd ed., London, 1953), p. 564.

*17.* The contention that American public schools can carry on the miscellany of activities that professional educationists advocate, can introduce these activities into the curriculum itself, and can at the same time provide basic intellectual training of undiminished quality is a preposterous contention on its very face. The hard, unyielding statistics, moreover, show that American public schools, taken as a whole, have failed—calamitously failed—to provide the mass of our young people with intellectual training of the quality and thoroughness required in the modern world. The frantic efforts of professional educationists to manipulate and, as a last resort, to suppress the figures have not succeeded and will not succeed in concealing the facts of the present situation from a deeply alarmed citizenry.

*18.* Suppression is a harsh word, but what other term is applicable to the letter sent out on 25 March 1958 by the National Association of Secondary-School Principals (a department of the National Education Association) over the signature of its executive secretary, Dr. Paul E. Elicker? In a series of articles entitled "Crisis in Education," the magazine *Life* had expressed views which the directorate of this Association disliked. Promptly Dr. Elicker wrote officially to the 19,000 school administrators—public officials, mind you—enrolled in his organizations, using the following words:

"The only way to be effective in combatting a continuance of this type of irresponsible reporting is to write a letter of protest *NOW* to Mr. Roy Larsen, President, LIFE . . . . We know from experience with another magazine a few years ago that your most effective weapon will be to question the continuation of subscriptions to the LIFE and TIME publications in your school as long as they have an attitude and policy inimical to education.

Also, we suggest that you urge teachers, parents, and citizens to write similar letters to Mr. Larsen. Of course, the force of your letter will be discounted if you indicate that you have been advised to write such a letter.

*19.* I agree with the editorial in the Detroit (Michigan) *Free Press,* which commented that this clandestine effort to suppress free discussion "exhibits motives no less base than those of a frightened but ruthless dictator." With a stroke of his pen, Dr. Elicker has done more damage to public confidence in our schools than any man in our history. The secondary-school principals of the country—whose integrity and whose belief in democracy Dr. Elicker has gravely compromised in hundreds if not thousands of communities—should demand his resignation.

*20.* Certain aspects of this sorry story have not received the attention they ought. Dr. Elicker based his undercover boycott on an allegation that certain statistical statements presented by *Life* were "mistakes and misinterpretations," and he circulated a memorandum by Professor Harold C. Hand to support the accusation. Many newspapers and individuals who condemned the boycott, nevertheless assumed that *Life* had probably misrepresented the statistics, as charged. In fact, the magazine had done no such thing. Those who attacked *Life* were the ones who manipulated the figures. Let us look briefly at Professor Hand's memorandum. He first takes issue with the following statement in *Life*: ". . . only 25% [of high school students in the United States] are studying physics." This is the figure given by the United States Office of Education in its study of *Offerings and Enrollments in Science and Mathematics in Public High Schools, 1956.* The enrollment in physics was 24.3 percent of the total enrollment in the twelfth grade in that year.[6]

21. What does Professor Hand do to this straightforward, official statistic? Here are his words:

We shall begin with the datum for physics. This figure of 25% is the approximate fraction of the students in grade twelve, the school level at which this subject is usually taught, who are enrolled in physics. By the time they complete high school, then, this fraction of today's high-school student body has taken physics. This is about three-fourths of those in the upper third of the intelligence distribution, hence about three-fourths of those who presumably could do well in physics if they were to enroll in it.

22. What does this rigamarole come to? Professor Hand takes the unquestioned percentage and deliberately alters it, justifying his manipulation by the completely undocumented assertion that only the top third of the population is capable of studying physics. By this sleight-of-Hand, 25 percent miraculously becomes 75 percent. But even granting the right of Professor Hand to manipulate the statistics in this way, the final figure he gives is false. There are 2,300,000 seventeen-year-olds in the population.[7] The upper third would come to 767,000. Only 310,000 seventeen-year-olds are enrolled in physics.[8] This is not 75 percent of the upper third of the relevant population. *It is only 40.4 percent.* Professor Hand, moreover, conveniently forgets to mention that in the Soviet Union today, *100 percent* of those in the "upper third of the intelligence distribution are studying physics, not for one year (as with us) but for five. Moreover, 100 percent *of the entire population* are studying it for two years—in the seven-year school, attendance at which is compulsory for all.[9]

23. Of all the statistics that are now available on Soviet education, the ones that reveal most strikingly the failure of our own school system are

[6] Pamphlet No. 120, compiled by Kenneth E. Brown (Washington, 1957), p. 12. Actually, if *Life's* statement were taken literally the figure it should have given would have been 4.4 percent not 24.3 percent, because the smaller percentage is the enrollment in physics expressed as a percentage of *all* high-school students. *Life* took the base *most favorable* to the public-school record.

[7] Ibid., p. 44.

[8] Ibid.

[9] Alexander G. Korol, *Soviet Education for Science and Technology* (New York, 1957), pp. 3, 17, 26, 55, 57. These agree with the findings of the U. S. Office of Education, *Education in the USSR* (Bulletin, 1957, No. 14).

those that pertain to the curriculum of the first seven years. During these years, schooling has become universal in Russia as here. Our system has attained universality for a longer span of time, it is true—ten years instead of seven. But with three more years, we have failed to bring our students in mass up to the level, so far as fundamental fields are concerned, that is attained for the whole mass of Soviet students and attained at an earlier age.

24. Let me summarize the record, reminding you that I am comparing not a selected student body with an unselected one, but the student bodies of the two countries *for the period during which schooling is compulsory and universal for both.*

25. In the Soviet Union every young person reaches maturity with some knowledge of algebra and geometry, because two years of this are required in the grades where universal schooling is in effect. In the United States only 60 percent of our young people reach maturity with some knowledge of algebra and geometry.

26. In the Soviet Union every young person reaches maturity with some systematically taught knowledge of biology, chemistry, and physics, derived from one to four years of course work in these specific fields in the first seven years of the Soviet schools. In the United States only three out of five of our young people reach maturity having had a course in biology, less than one quarter having had a course in chemistry, and little more than one-eighth having had a course in physics.

27. In the Soviet Union every child has studied a foreign language for at least three years before drop-outs begin. In the United States, fewer than one young person in twenty reaches the age of eighteen having had three years of a foreign language.[10]

28. If we go on to the last years of the secondary school (the ten-year school in the U. S. S. R. and the high school in the U. S.), the comparisons are even more devastating. In what follows, be it observed, I am not offering unfair comparisons between selected and unselected Student Bodies. I am comparing *the proportion of total population* which reaches a given level of intellectual attainment in the Soviet Union, with the proportion of the total population which reaches the same level "or a lower one" in the United States.

29. In the Soviet Union the top third of all young people reach maturity with a knowledge of mathematics at least through trigonometry, normally the highest branch taught in secondary schools. In the United States only the top one-twelfth of all young people are reaching maturity with a command of mathematics at this level.

[10] Figures based on the studies previously cited. They are analyzed in greater detail in the author's article "The Choice Before Us in American Education." National University Extension Association, *Thirty-Second Discussion and Debate Manual,* 1958-59 ed. by *American Education;* Bower Aly, Vol. 1, pp. 65-86.

*30.* In the Soviet Union the top third of all young people reach maturity having studied physics for *five* years. In the United States only the top one-eighth reach maturity having studied physics for *one* year. Not a single American, in all probability, has studied the subject systematically for five years in an American high school.

*31.* In the Soviet Union the top third of all young people reach maturity having studied a foreign language for six years. In the United States, less than one percent of the population get as far as the fourth year of a foreign language in high school.

*32.* Let me remind you of the point of these comparisons. No one in his senses would suggest that the United States should take over the Soviet educational system. There are far sounder and far better balanced school programs in the democratic countries of Western Europe. The question in any case is not whether we should have an American educational system or a European one. The question is whether the American educational system should be a good one or a poor one. The most important thing we can learn from European experience is to raise, immediately and by a substantial amount, our judgments about the intellectual ability of young people. Our expectations must go up, and our standards with them. We must repudiate the view that only a minority of American young people can be taught the basic subjects. Noting that Soviet educators harbor no such contemptuous opinion of the intellectual capacity of their own young people, we must deliver a stinging rebuke to those professional educationists who have persistently slandered the children of the American people as uneducable, and have used this malicious judgment as an excuse for selling them down the river.

*33.* With the restoration of faith in our young people will come a restoration to the school system of a clear sense of purpose. To replace the educational aimlessness of recent years, we need only return to the principles and aims that inspired the American public-school system at its creation. A simple definition of education, and a simple democratic corollary thereof, will suffice:

*34.* It is the job of a school to teach young men and women to think. It is the job of a *democratic* school to teach *all* young men and women to think.

*35.* If this is, in fact, the central purpose of education, the school must recognize, at the very outset, that certain studies are vastly more effective than others in developing the capacity to think clearly, seriously, and sustainedly. The school must, accordingly, select its subjects of instruction with infinite care. Typewriting, for example, is a very useful practical skill. It is a training of the fingers, however, rather than of the mind. History, by contrast, is a most unpromising pathway to lucrative employment. (I am an historian, and I speak from experience.) But history is a study that involves the careful weighing of evidence and the continuous exercise of critical judgment. Properly taught, it develops the kind of intellectual power that a democratic nation requires of all its responsible citizens. No matter how skillfully taught, typewriting cannot possibly lay claim to equal educational significance.

36. A school can do only a few things well, consequently the things it does must be the things of very greatest worth. Moreover, the school must organize its work carefully in order to do these things in the most effective way possible. How can one determine the things that it is most important for the school to do, and the ways of doing them that will be most effective? The answers to both questions can be found in the accumulated experience of three thousand years of intellectual and educational history.

37. Let us begin by examining the second question—the question of the most effective way of organizing school instruction. Many persons imagine that there is something arbitrary about the various fields of learning as they exist today. The phenomena of nature are all inter-related, they point out. Why isolate one aspect from another and make separate fields out of chemistry, physics, geology, botany, and zoology? Why not deal with the whole at once? The same argument is applied to society. Why study its various aspects separately under the labels of history, economics, political science, and jurisprudence? Again, why not tackle at once the living whole?

38. The best answer is that the experience of thousands of years has shown that the human mind is best able to grapple with complicated problems by breaking them down into their component parts. Once experience has been *analyzed,* it becomes possible to develop specialized intellectual skills for dealing with the different aspects of experience. These skills can be organized systematically, can be taught, and can be applied with enormous effectiveness to new problems. These organized skills constitute the various scientific and scholarly disciplines. (The latter is the scholar's word; the popular term "subjects" much used by educationists, is inaccurate and misleading, because it suggests that the disciplines are mere collections of facts, rather than methods of investigation and of thought.) Mathematics, history, economics, geology, chemistry, and psychology are examples of such disciplines. The reason for planning an educational curriculum in terms of them is that mankind has discovered that effective, creative, critical thinking can best be done by employing these systematic, organized tools of thought.

39. The scientific and scholarly disciplines, well-defined and efficiently organized, constitute the foundations of mature intellectual effort. These foundations must be laid in the elementary and high schools. Such, in brief, is the educational theory of scientists and scholars. Which disciplines, then, are basic to the *high-school* curriculum? The question is not really as difficult to answer as some people suppose.

*40.* In every age and every country, a person deemed educated must be able to use his own language correctly and fluently, and must be widely read in its literature. Accordingly, English is basic in an American school curriculum. This is obviously a scientific age, hence mathematics, physics, chemistry, and biology are obviously basic. We live in a rapidly changing world, hence history (whose subject is change) belongs among the basic secondary-school disciplines. International contacts are rapidly multiplying, hence foreign languages must be considered essential. Emphasis on the disciplines I have mentioned is simply a matter of common sense, dictated by the obvious facts about the intellectual life in the contemporary world.

*41.* Contrary to popular belief, scientists and scholars, both here and abroad, agree pretty well on the desirable basic curriculum of the secondary school. I know no reputable scholar who is anxious merely to advance his own subject. Scientists are as convinced of the importance of English and foreign languages as I (an historian) am convinced of the importance of science and mathematics. With very few dissenting voices, the scholarly world agrees that the high school should focus the efforts of all students upon five principal fields: the student's native language and its literature; at least one foreign language; mathematics; the natural sciences (specifically biology, chemistry, and physics), and history. The fine arts and music should have a recognized place, though perhaps on the basis of individual instruction. The various social sciences (economics, political science, sociology) might be introduced alongside, but not in replacement of, history, because their full elaboration usually takes place at the college level.

*42.* What we are after, of course, is not a mere list of "subjects," but a training in the basic disciplines of thought. The desirable curriculum can be described in terms of the intellectual skills that the high school should impart. It must, first of all, furnish its students with a store of knowledge, so that they will not be obliged to make bricks without straw. Secondly, it must require them to practice unceasingly the use of the recognized tools of language and thought: reading, mathematics, grammar, logic, and the rest. Beyond this, the school must give its students, at first hand through laboratory work, a grasp of the method of scientific investigation. It must teach them to weigh evidence as an historian does, and to construct therefrom a framework of chronology and historical explanation adequate to organize their accumulating knowledge about the development of their own country and the world. It must make them acquainted with the great ideas embodied in literature, and with the varied forms (poetry, fiction, drama, philosophic discourse) in which great ideas are expressed.

*43.* The school, moreover, must go at these tasks systematically. To think means to apply the mind continuously, often over long periods of time, to the problem at hand. The student must use his mind in this way in school. If he is expected to pick up "snippets" of information from one "project" after another—if his program skips about from topic to unrelated topic—then he will not go forth with a disciplined mind. He will have been trained as a mere intellectual grasshopper. Certain contrived "experiences" may be needed to arouse the first interest of young children, but once serious work has begun, the directing force of further study should be intellectual curiosity, and its organization should represent the logical unfolding of the subject itself. Once a serious subject is taken up there must be continuity, usually over a period of years. Four years of a foreign language, for example, are not twice as valuable as two, but ten or twenty times as valuable, thanks to the cumulative character of learning.

*44.* Progression, as well as continuity, is essential. The school must push its students steadily forward from simple intellectual tasks to increasingly complex and abstract ones. Mere "enrichment"—the multiplying of tasks at the same level of abstraction—does not mean intellectual growth; it may mean intellectual stagnation. Above all, the school must require its students to write, write, write—themes, examinations, original productions in prose and verse; each one to be corrected and criticized, for form as well as content—until young men and women are able, almost instinctively, to set down their own ideas, whatever the subject may be, with clarity, accuracy, cogency, and fluency.

*45.* An education of this kind is not one among several equally valuable kinds of education. It is the one kind that deliberately sets out to produce men and women capable of serious and sustained thinking. If we really believe in democracy, this is the kind of education we ought to bestow upon every single one of our future citizens. If we offer a portion of our children an education different in kind and hence inferior—narrow job-training or shoddy "life-adjustment"—then we are treating them as second-class citizens. We are not providing equality of educational opportunity, we are withholding it.

*46.* A high-school curriculum based squarely upon the basic intellectual disciplines is neither designed nor intended to produce an aloof, self-conscious intellectual *elite.* Quite the reverse. It is designed to give *every* citizen in a democracy a share in the intellectual life of the Republic, by providing him with the kind of education that was once reserved for a small aristocratic class.

*47.* The central problem of education in a democracy is to make intellectual training available to all. This is a difficult task, like all the other tasks of making democracy work. It presents a problem to be solved, however, not one to be avoided. Vocational training and "life adjustment" education are not solutions, they are attempts to dodge the problem, to run away from it yet to conceal the retreat behind high-sounding words.

Programs for the slow learner are required, but programs in *the basic intellectual disciplines*. Both the student himself and the nation are betrayed by school programs that substitute something else for intellectual training. Only when we possess the kind of public school system in which able students can push ahead as fast and as far as their minds can carry them, and in which every other student can tread the same path, at the best pace which he is capable of maintaining, will we have a truly sound and democratic educational structure, worthy of the American Republic.

# Questions

1. Find throughout the essay as many sentences as you can in which Bestor uses the principles of balance and parallelism, including the use of triads.

2. Following the first nine paragraphs, which describe the philosophy and shift in emphasis he will argue against, Bestor asks whether the American people established their public schools to handle the "problems" now widely dealt with by them. Granted that the present *functions* of an institution may differ, either by design or by chance, from what they were originally, what logical relevance does the fact of this difference hold for Bestor?

3. What principle does Bestor cite in paragraph 11 which might be used against him? How could it be so used?

4. What irony does Bestor see (paragraph 12) in the point of view of professional educationists and in the tasks he alleges they have inflicted on our schools? Where, if at all, does he offer proofs of his vision?

5. What partial admission do paragraphs 13 through 15 make?

6. Paragraph 16 attempts to argue from the analogy to residential schools and to define public-school time as curricular time. How valid is this analogy? Can you find any points at which Bestor has protected himself, either by admission or refutation, against objections to his analogy?

7. How does Bestor's paragraph 32 protect him from certain kinds of refutation that might be directed at his analogy of Russian and American schools? How can the statistics he cites be used in any valid way to challenge his analogy between schools in the U.S. and the Soviet Union?

8. Find the slanted diction in the last sentence of paragraph 32.

9. The word *democratic* is common as an approbatory term in educational discussions. What misguided interpretation of the term does Bestor attribute to his opponents, and what correct interpretation does he assume for himself?

10. Explain in detail how the high school you attended was close to the model Bestor abhors or the model he advocates.

# Theme Topics

1. The ultimate conflict between Harold Hand and Arthur Bestor is identified by Bestor as being in their different attitudes toward students' abilities. Bestor admits that programs for the slow learner are required but says they should be in the basic intellectual disciplines, to which every student should have exposure. Do you agree? What evidence, statistics, or what kind of experimentation or research could throw light upon the controversy? Write a paper, with or without citation of published studies in education, to present your own stand on student abilities and how you think a *democratic* school system should deal with these abilities.

2. Write a paper attacking one or more of Bestor's assumptions. In paragraph 34, for instance, the assumption is made that no such thing exists as an uneducable portion of our school-age population; in paragraph 43, the statement "the directing force of further study should be intellectual curiosity" assumes intellectual curiosity to be common to all.

3. Write a summary paper explaining the basic issues in the argument carried on by Wilson, the answer by Hand, and the answer to Hand by Bestor.

## ·53·

*James B. Conant*

## DIVERSIFIED STUDIES FOR DIVERSIFIED STUDENTS

*1.* Some time ago I decided that, when my tour of duty as Ambassador to Germany was over, I would do something to help support and improve public high school education. I wanted to be of assistance to citizens, particularly in helping them understand some of the problems of their schools. But having been away for four years, my information was out of date. So I arranged a year ago for my study of the American public high school and, thanks to a grant from the Carnegie Corporation, I have been visiting comprehensive public high schools in twenty of the more populous

From *The PTA Magazine* (*National Parent-Teacher*), 53 (October, 1958), 4-6. Reprinted by permission of the author.

states. (Comprehensive high schools are those that seek to serve the educational needs of all high school youth in the community.)

2. Beyond doubt my enterprise has been timely. I was not prepared for the torrent of criticism of our schools that started when the Russians hurled their rocket into space. Nor was I prepared for the consequent confusion in which the "man on the street" might find himself. Therefore it seemed doubly important to present to the public a constructive discussion of the actual situation in our high schools. Obviously that meant I must visit high schools, as I have done.

3. A serious obstacle to a good high school education that I saw immediately was the huge number of pitifully small high schools that exist throughout our country—schools so small that they cannot possibly provide the diversified curriculum our diversified high school population requires. Studies by competent experts on American rural life and related educational problems indicate that unless a high school has a graduating class of at least one hundred, it is too small to offer a curriculum adequate to the abilities and interests of its students and to the needs of our nation.

4. This situation is serious, and it demands the attention of our citizens. We have approximately 23,000 high schools, and more than half of them are too small to meet the minimum criterion of a graduating class of one hundred! In fact, 30 per cent of our high school students are in schools too small to do an adequate job. Here, then, is a situation that we need to face resolutely. When we say that geography will not allow us to consolidate high schools let us be sure we do not mean that human nature is the prohibiting agent.

5. Having thus removed from further discussion in this article the needs of students in high schools that are too small, I shall violate the rule of suspense and state immediately what is one of the fundamental conclusions of my study. This conclusion arises from actual observation of schools; from conferences with members of boards of education, school administrators, teachers, and students; from careful study of the specific subject programs of individual students; and from tests given to a sampling of students in subjects usually adjudged difficult in high schools.

6. The conclusion I refer to is this: *I disagree with those who demand radical changes in our high schools.* I am certain that in comprehensive high schools, if they are large enough, it would be possible to have our boys and girls studying effectively and rewardingly the subjects they ought to be studying. (In this conclusion I include our academically talented youth, large numbers of whom I found to be taking the tough programs that some of the insistent critics of high schools accuse them of avoiding.)

7. I do not mean that such a desirable condition will come about automatically. But I am convinced that, without requiring radical changes,

the good practices I have seen in the high schools I visited can become the good practices generally of high schools of sufficient size. Here, I should add, is a situation in which the interest of citizens will be helpful.

8. The question I wanted to answer was this: In the comprehensive high school is it possible to give a good education to those who want to acquire a marketable skill by graduation time; to those whose uncommitted interest is simply in a general education; and to the academically talented who want a good foundation in the academic subjects? My answer, after a year of study of public high schools, is "Yes."

9. I know that it can be done because of what I have seen. However, it does require a first-rate guidance system, well staffed with skillful counselors who can help students and their parents make wise choices from the extensive offerings of the comprehensive high school. Also, it is a matter of what kind of high school education a community really wants.

10. The program of studies in a comprehensive high school is made up of general subjects, required of all, and of electives. The general subjects usually are, and I think they should be (including the ninth grade), four years of English; three or four years of the social studies; one year of science; and one year of mathematics, usually either general mathematics or algebra. In those general classes, enrolling all students, there will be a wide diversity of ability, a diversity so wide as to make it impossible for a teacher to adapt his teaching to the whole range in the class. Therefore students should be grouped in separate classes by ability, but the grouping should be subject by subject. Thus a student might be in a top-level class in English but in an average one in mathematics. Three levels of grouping are probably enough—one for the more able in the subject, another for the middle group, and a third for the slow readers, who need teachers especially qualified to teach them. However, grouping is not recommended in the twelfth-grade course dealing with problems in American democracy. Here great value can accrue from the discussion of problems by students of all levels of ability and of diverse interests and backgrounds.

11. Because of a specific problem in English, I want to say a word about that subject. In English about half the time should be devoted to composition and half to literature. There should be one theme a week, and the themes should be corrected and discussed with students. Yet in many schools I visited too little time was devoted to composition and too few themes written. Why? Because the teachers were responsible for 150 or sometimes as many as 180 students. They simply could not find time to read the themes that ought to be required. Since learning to express oneself with precision and style is very important, the school board ought to engage good English teachers and see that each teacher has responsibility

for not more than 100 students. This policy will cost money, but it will be worth it.

*12.* It is in the electives that the comprehensive high school adapts itself particularly to the individual abilities and interests of its students. In fact, a well-conceived and well-taught program of electives and an excellent corps of guidance counselors are essential characteristics of a good comprehensive high school.

*13.* There are critics who claim that the electives for all students should consist solely of academic subjects, but I find myself completely out of sympathy with them. I am *certain* that in our high schools it is impossible to have *all* the students studying advanced mathematics, chemistry, physics, and foreign languages. And by study, I mean to the point of reasonable mastery. To prescribe advanced academic subjects for all students can result only in watered down courses or a situation in which weaker students are allowed just to sit the courses out.

*14.* Other critics would offer their intellectual bill of fare only to a small proportion of the high school population and in separate schools, even federal regional high schools. These are arguments from the practices of other nations, and they leave me cold. As an amateur student of comparative education, I have looked into schools in several foreign countries. It seems meaningless to compare portions of the educational systems of two countries. The only thing that can really be used for comparison is the entire social and political structure, of which the schools are a part. For instance, the Soviet system is totalitarian. Its inhabitants are under a compulsion that a free society cannot understand.

*15.* In most comprehensive high schools the electives in addition to the five academic areas (English, social studies, mathematics, science, and foreign languages) are home economics, industrial arts, vocational and commercial subjects, art, and music. I should like to give extended attention to each of them, but if I am to keep this article within reasonable limits, I cannot do so. However, I recognize the value of all of them in the curriculum of a comprehensive high school conducted in the best interests of all of its students.

*16.* Because the courses offered academically talented students are today under attack by critics of our high schools, I want to devote the rest of my space to these students.

*17.* In the era in which we live—and for the good of our citizens, our freedom, and our industrialized society—we need men and women with highly specialized professional skills. The road of education leading to such skills is long and arduous, and only those with certain kinds of ability can complete the necessary academic labors. Those who can, I call the academically talented—about 15 per cent of our high school population.

In high school they ought to study four years of English, three or four years of history and social studies, four of mathematics, three of science, and at least three of one foreign language. This program means five subjects a day, with at least fifteen hours of homework a week. Lest there be disagreement with my prescription, let me add that I encountered many students who were taking this array of courses and thriving under it. Furthermore, they were active in the life of the school.

18. As a check on how well the high schools we visited were serving their academically talented youth, we devised what we call the "academic inventory," which I commend to all schools. The academic inventory is an instrument for analyzing the subjects studied by the top 15 to 20 per cent of the students (top in *ability*, not necessarily achievement). Of course names are omitted. The four-year programs of these top students were carefully analyzed. This procedure gave us a clear picture of how well the academically talented students had chosen their high school subjects— and that picture was partial evidence of how well guidance had functioned in particular schools. By the way, this inventory can be adapted for the study of other areas of the school program.

19. Strangely enough, the academic inventory showed the situation to be quite good for academically talented boys in mathematics and science, the very fields that pessimistic critics have been most disturbed about. It was far from favorable in this area for girls, however—which leads us to think that our nation is losing good science and mathematics teachers because many able girls are not studying those subjects.

20. We were dismayed by what the academic inventory showed about foreign language study. School after school *offered* only two years of a language, which is like drilling for oil and stopping just before the oil is reached. It was sad to hear students say that they wanted to take the third and fourth years of a language but could not because the class would be too small to meet the minimum figure set by the board of education for any course. Surely at a time when foreign language study should be zealously nurtured and promoted, boards of education ought to offer advanced courses, no matter how few students enroll for them. How else can the individual's good and the nation's interest be served? The same policy should apply to any subject.

21. All of what I have seen leads me to conclude that communities tend to get the kind of schools they want. The schools are, I am convinced, a composite of the community's views about education. Here is a matter that demands the intelligent, informed interest of citizens in their schools —a purpose that the parent-teacher organization has long served.

# Questions

1. What does Conant mean by the last sentence in paragraph 4? How do you think the costs involved in his proposal for consolidating small high schools would compare with those involved in putting into effect the proposals of Arthur Bestor?

2. What are the advantages as an argumentative tactic of Conant's paragraphs 3 through 5?

3. Conant argues that the comprehensive high school (above a certain size) does give a good education to all three kinds of students. What evidence does he provide for his conclusion? Conant spends much of the latter parts of his essay in qualifying this conclusion so far as one of the three kinds of students is concerned. How significantly do these qualifications weaken his general conclusion?

4. Bestor contends that "the hard, unyielding statistics . . . show that American public schools have failed . . . to provide the mass of our young with the intellectual training of the quality and thoroughness required in the modern world." Bestor thus recommends the same education for all. How do Conant and Bestor differ in principle?

5. Why does Conant exclude the twelfth-grade course in problems in American democracy from the plan to group students according to their ability?

6. Conant defines the academically talented as about 15 percent of the high school population. What reasons are there for educating these people in a special way? Why do you agree or disagree with the way Conant recommends?

7. Are special classes for the academically talented democratic? What harm and what benefits come from separating them as Conant suggests?

8. Conant concludes by saying that communities get the kind of education they want. To what extent can the faults of a given school be attributed to the community? Should the community have this kind of control?

# Theme Topics

1. Should students who are academically untalented, say those in the lowest quartile of an academic inventory based on tests of ability and achievement, ever be allowed to vote in local, state, and national elections? Should those who never enter high school be allowed to vote? Write a paper in which you either defend or attack the right to vote of some group which you limit on the basis of years and kind of schooling completed.

2. Write a paper in which you defend Conant's proposal of the comprehensive high school as the solution to the problems raised by Fadiman and Sloan Wilson and as a solution preferable to the one presented by Bestor.

3. Write a paper in which you make a specific proposal for the improvement of your high school in one of the areas suggested by Fadiman, Wilson, Hutchins, or Bestor. Begin your paper with a clear statement of the situation your proposal aims to improve.

4. Write a paper in which you attack or defend Conant's proposal for separate education of the academically talented. A possible line of attack: to distinguish is to separate; to separate is to alienate; and alienation is morally indefensible. A possible line of defense: to distinguish is to know; to know is to communicate; and communication is morally defensible.

## ·54·

### David Riesman

# THOUGHTS ON TEACHERS
# AND SCHOOLS

*1.* Progressive education in its initial American formulation (between about 1900 and 1925) was the product of highly intellectual teachers. These were men and women of marked individuality, talent, and enthusiasm, who became aware of the emotional shallowness and the rote learning of the traditional schools, and sought to found new schools which would not only encourage the arts, the education of the emotions, and group cooperativeness, but which would do an even better intellectual job because more individualized and more closely geared to the child's developing pattern of motivations. These pioneers (being in this like other reformers whose plans have to some degree miscarried) could take for granted their own cultivation and belief in learning, as well as their own zeal, and they could go on from that foundation to try to give the children in their care—as most of us want to give our own children—the things they had missed in their own schooling. I have myself interviewed children and observed classes at several progressive private schools, and I can testify that at their best they turn out interesting and interested children,

From *The Anchor Review*, No. 1 (Garden City, N. Y.: Doubleday & Company, 1955), pp. 40-60. Reprinted by permission of the author.

some of whom their parents and later teachers may find glib and unruly, but not stuffy or deceitful. For many children from narrow or emotionally frozen families, such a school provides an opportunity to thaw out in a milieu at once therapeutic and stimulating.

2. The doctrinal tenets of such schools have filtered into many public schools with very mixed results. The filtering has not only been "downward" from the superior institutions (such as Teachers College at Columbia) to the junior colleges which have called themselves "teachers colleges" in the hinterland. There has also been a movement "upwards" from the nursery school model, where miracles appear to be accomplished by teachers unable to fall back on the drill of reading or writing in dealing with these preliterate tribes of fours, fives, and sixes: this demonstration of a happy school group, devoted to not much else than its being "happy" and being a "group," has influenced many primary and even high school teachers. It would not have done so to the same degree if the diffusion of progressive (and nursery model) education had not coincided with the growing emphasis on social skills in the community at large—an emphasis itself in part the product of the same social developments which freed millions to attend school and other millions to teach, transport, and feed them. As our society becomes more play-oriented and less work-oriented, more willing to admit personal sensitivity and warmth to the roster of prime virtues, more concerned with the mood of the group and perhaps less with the achievements of the individual, those goals which the original progressive educators wanted to add to traditional purposes tend in many public (and indeed some private) schools to become the only goals —goals, indeed, no longer so essential for the schools to aim at, since parents and the mass media, among many other social forces, are already active in securing them.

3. Listen, for instance, to a Massachusetts bread salesman describing to an interviewer what he hopes for in the high school education of one of his sons (and explaining incidentally why he is not sending the young man to college, though he is intelligent enough and the family could afford it):

I tried to tell him where he isn't going to be a doctor or lawyer or anything like that, I told him he should learn English and learn to meet people. Then he could go out and sell something worthwhile where a sale would amount to something for him. . . . I took typing, shorthand, bookkeeping and we had Latin, French, geometry. We had everything. But anything I would know then I've forgotten now. . . . I don't think a high school diploma is important. I mean only in so far as you might apply for a job and if you can say, "I have a diploma," it might help get the job . . .

Or listen (as recorded by William Whyte, Jr.) to a parent in Park Forest, a suburb of Chicago:

Janet is studying marketing and she's only in the sixth grade. She's studying ads and discounts, things I didn't get until college. The children are certainly getting a broad view of things.

Implicit in the attitude of both these parents is the belief that the school should prepare children for adult life by imitating that life; indeed, the same "child-centered" schools that would fear maladjustment through advancing an intellectually precocious child beyond his social age-mates often do their best to anticipate in the schoolroom the adult "here and now" of buying and selling, of parliamentary procedure and civic responsibility.

4. In this situation, some of our teachers are fighting a losing battle in defense of the traditional intellectual values and the classical curriculum. But others (including many school superintendents) have turned necessity into virtue and favor the sort of programs that the parents I have just quoted would themselves like to see installed. Thus, Eric Baber, the high school superintendent in Park Forest, tells his teachers and parents that American education is still "far too much concentrated on the intellectual aspect of education." As he said in a teachers workshop:

The so-called "bright student" is often one of the dumbest or least apt when he gets away from his textbooks and memory work. This is evidenced by the fact that many $20,000 to $100,000-a-year jobs in business, sales, sports, radio . . . are held by persons with I.Q.'s of less than ninety.

Baber is very proud of the "communication laboratory" his modern school plant includes; as he says, "ours is an age of group action," and one in which the children "must have actual experiences in solving problems that have meaning for *them*." No less explicit is the principal of a junior high school in Urbana, Illinois, speaking to a meeting of the National Association of Secondary-School Principals:

Through the years we've built a sort of halo around reading, writing and arithmetic. . . . The Three R's for All Children and All Children for the Three R's! That was it. We've made some progress in getting rid of that slogan. But every now and then some mother with a Phi Beta Kappa award or some employer who has hired a girl who can't spell stirs up a fuss about the schools . . . and the ground is lost. . . . When we come to the realization that not every child has to read, figure, write, and spell . . . that many of them either cannot or will not master these chores . . . then we shall be on the road to improving the junior high curriculum. Between this day and that a lot of selling must take place. But it's coming. We shall some day accept the thought that it is just as illogical to assume that every boy must be able to read as it is that each one must be able to perform on a violin, that it is no more reasonable to require that each girl shall spell well than it is that each one shall bake a good cherry pie. . . .

When adults finally realize that fact, everyone will be happier . . . and schools will be nicer places in which to live. . . .

5. This official may well be convinced that he is heretical and ahead of his time for, after all, he does come from the same university town as does Arthur Bestor (Professor of History at the University of Illinois) whose *Educational Wastelands* quotes this gem. This book is one of the least intemperate of a number of recent slashing attacks on just these self-styled "progressive" tendencies in secondary school teaching, some of which blame all attenuation of standards on John Dewey. We professors and intellectuals are generally inclined to trace tendencies we do not like to the ideas of other intellectuals, and this may in the long run be legitimate, but I do feel that Bestor exaggerates the autonomous role of the schools, and hence of their mentors, in fostering a mindless pragmatism and vocationalism which they often simply absorb from their constituencies.

6. Indeed, so strong are these constituencies that teachers and school officials are today frequently harassed beyond endurance by outsiders who have more prestige or power than they and who therefore feel free to intervene. The result is that it is hard for many in the school system to distinguish between a Barzun or a Bestor (or a Riesman) who has made some effort to understand their problems from within, and that horde of uninformed and usually reactionary "taxpayer" critics of "new fangled" notions in the schools. The latter are apt to urge that what was good enough for grandpappy is good enough for his descendants. Since the grandchildren will face stiffer competition in terms of formal educational credentials, this penny-pinching view (sometimes abetted by local commerce and industry) simply kicks away a ladder to mobility which the new generation needs if it is to keep step with the rising educational and living standards of the country as a whole. In contrast, my own view is that grandpappy's education was not good enough for him in a day when artistic and emphatic skills were seldom transmitted, but it does have certain redeeming virtues which only become evident when the rest of the society has caught up with an outlook that was rare at the turn of the century. In other words, I feel that schools can perform something of a *counter-cyclical* (or "governor") function, within the limits of their weakness, they can fall back on older traditions with very contemporary purposes in mind.

7. When faced with such a plea coming from a university campus, the school teacher—beleaguered, as I have said, with a multiplicity of special pleading—is apt to appear to turn a deaf ear and to use a diplomatic tongue. She knows that males are apt to be abstract, idealistic, and impractical—and patronizing. There is also the awareness that university professors, like other people, often have vested interests of their own, in discipline and in their "disciplines," to protect. Yet the very democratizing tendencies we have been discussing, which have had such unanticipated regressive consequences, compel teachers and school personnel generally to be accessible. It is hard for them to be other than defensive toward

criticism, or, like all professionals faced with troublesome clients, dupli-
citous in finding the semantics by which all comers can be fended off.

8. Still, would these teachers be so vulnerable to the many competing
demands now made upon them if these demands did not awaken echoes
within them of unsolved problems in their own lives?

9. In interviews with Kansas City high school teachers, the poignant
note comes up again and again of a self-confessed adolescent shyness.
They feel this was bad, that they should have been "more outgoing"
(perhaps they would have found a husband); some indicated that in becoming teachers they had conquered their shyness. In their relations
with other teachers, they have established a coterie that they missed in
school (and one that protects them to some extent from the unflattering
public image of the unmarried school teacher). More important, they
want very much to appear vivacious, warm, and outgoing in class. (One
could make an interesting comparison here with current models of appropriate behavior in social workers and clergymen.) They want very much
to be liked by the children, as well as by their colleagues, and they are
perhaps more aware than before whether or not they are liked, especially
as the children, good little communicators that they are, include among
their social skills the ability to exploit the teachers' need for approval.

10. Is it true, then, that the cultivated and intellectual teacher has lost
her role as a model for other teachers? Not completely. Not a few, whatever their superintendents might sometimes prefer, do not wish to be
merely "outgoing." There is the case of one high school drama teacher,
the daughter of a very cosmopolitan newspaper editor; after a divorce she
returned to the city of her birth and started teaching school there ("political pull," of the sort now waning, helped her get a certificate). This teacher,
well-traveled and sophisticated, has a remarkable gift for exciting her
pupils' interest in the theatre; she is proud of "graduates on Broadway and
in Hollywood." But her fellow-teachers have grave misgivings about her.
They complain that she cares "too much about the drama" and "too little
about the children." They complain that her productions demand too much
time and effort, that the children who get so enthusiastic about putting on
plays have little time for other subjects and for sociability, and they feel
that the plays should involve a greater number of the children in their
production, even at the cost of making the performances less professional.
It would be more democratic, they say, to "give everybody a chance,"
and the drama, like other activities, is seen as one more way to encourage
group participation rather than as a way to encourage vocations in the
theatre. (The new school principal, a younger man who believes that the
duty of the school is to "cultivate the total personality" of the child, has
made life difficult for the drama teacher. What he wants is a good work-
ing-team of teachers, not stars on the Broadway firmament . . . nor ex-

cessive demands on the school auditorium.) I suspect, however, that these teachers would be less critical of their colleague, less articulate about her allegedly disproportionate preoccupation with the theatre, if they did not themselves in some degree aspire to cosmopolitan ways. In taking on responsibility for the child's social and emotional development, they have not wholly relinquished the older responsibility for "culture"; and it is their very ambivalence about partially contending models of school teaching that makes them so angry with those teachers, holdovers from an earlier day, who represent not only unequivocally high and secure social status but also the not entirely downgraded status of intellectual discipline and urbanity.

*11.* And it is equally true that a great many, if not all, of the "old-fashioned" teachers have been influenced and even upset by the newer pressures for a more democratic school system—democratic in its attention to the less scholarly (i.e. the non-college-preparatory) group, and to the standards set by the children and their parents. Here is an elderly English teacher at a high school which once was proud of its high academic demands (it had been modeled on the "Latin schools" of New England):

Mr. ―― believed so thoroughly in education as I really believe in it, yet I realize that it can't go on. I mean you can't go on pounding classical education into everybody's head as long as you are going to have everybody going to the same school. . . . Mr. ――, I am sure, felt that there were a lot of people who couldn't learn. . . . But he never relaxed what he thought were necessary standards . . . and if they couldn't make it they couldn't make it and that was all. . . . The older teachers who grew up with that were hard put—they like Mr. ―― [the new principal], it's hard for anyone not to like him, but they just think everything is going to pot. . . . I think what he is trying to do is win over the student body to the idea that school administrators and school teachers aren't off there in another world. And then once he has their co-operation to let them make some of the rules and regulations they will be willing to abide by. . . . There have been so many educators and educators that have the theory that reading and writing and arithmetic are sort of overrated; that you must teach people how to be people. . . .

It is plain from such interviews that few teachers are so case-hardened as not to feel some ambivalence concerning the "battle of the books."

*12.* This conflict also emerges clearly in a series of group discussions with public school teachers in Chicago and Milwaukee which my colleague, Hedda Bolgar, a clinical psychologist, has been conducting. She finds that once the initial defensiveness of teachers against inquisitiveness is overcome, teachers are very eager to talk to an understanding outsider about their inner aims and external conflicts. Underneath a protective coating of cynicism and careerism these teachers frequently harbor a most grandiose and self-defeating expectation of omnicompetence in the classroom. They expect themselves to respond sympathetically to individual problem-children, even psychotic ones that would baffle an experienced psychologist. Partly aware of current mental-health emphases, they can no longer simply reject a child as "a troublemaker," or if they do they will feel guilty about it. In other words, the teachers have been exposed enough to psychiatric currents of thought to learn that children's aggressive behavior has to be explained and cannot be simply reacted to with counteraggression, but they do not often have sufficient knowledge to accept their own aggression.

13. Overtly, they may resist the expectation that there is no child they cannot handle, no child to whose needs they cannot minister while preventing it from dominating the group; they may say to one another, "Who does the School Board think we are, parking such little bastards with us?" Overtly, they may think they have done their job if they "keep the kids out of a messy home five hours a day," and they may, as we know, punish a teacher who does too much for the children, who is too enthusiastic— who is a scab or rate-buster in setting too high standards of performance. But underneath they seem to be demanding of themselves that they achieve therapeutic or motherly relations with all the children. Just because they no longer think of themselves as teachers of a subject but rather as teachers of an age-grade, they are at once tempted and betrayed by an ideal of omnicompetence. Though they are in fact in the position of the Old Woman Who Lived in a Shoe, they somehow accept the inner responsibility for making up in their own persons for all the deficiencies in the community. They feel badly if "their" children break windows or go to jail or drop out, no matter what the objective situation—much as many mothers feel.

14. I suggest that the cynicism with which many teachers talk among themselves is thus in part a defense against a still unextinguished (if often unconscious) ideal image of themselves as unruffled magnanimous individuals, at once motherly and wholly competent. If it were not for this, the teachers as a close-knit collegial group could cope somewhat better than they do with well-meant interferences by social workers, psychiatrists, superintendents, and educators, who directly and indirectly reinforce this extravagant image of what the teacher should be, pushing it always further from the traditional conception of the teacher as a subject-matter specialist, which is to say, a person of limited competence.

15. When it is pointed out to them that they are not, after all, psychiatrists and cannot expect themselves to cure problem-children, but only at best not to harm them, they react first with anger at the threat to their ideal of omnicompetence, but eventually with relief. And there is some evidence that they become better, less harassed teachers when they can fully realize that their function is limited—primarily, to teach a subject— and that they cannot as individuals compensate for all the ways in which our social organization now puts children in school because it doesn't

want them in the labor force, or on the street corner, or because it has no other place for the disturbed child at the moment.

*16.* This relinquishment of claims, however, is easier said than done. What is a teacher to do when, as happened the other day in a Chicago elementary school, a lonely Negro girl comes to her to complain of the fact that she has "no friends in school," and that her mother will not allow her to make friends by inviting any children to her home? Is the teacher to send this twelve-year-old child back to her hopeless English lesson? What is the teacher to do as she watches a twelve-year-old boy, son of Jewish immigrant parents, develop an increasing contempt for children who have not raced through as many encyclopedias as he has in amassing an armory of unrelated facts with which, in quiz-kid style, he goes into battle? Is she to wait until the school, which needs a new building (though in general our school buildings are the cathedrals of our time) and more teachers, gets around to appointing a school psychologist? She would have to be more unequivocally devoted to learning for its own sake than are most of my university colleagues in order to be able to resist the appeal to her motherly, or clinical, sympathies. The result is that she pays less attention to the balanced and potentially gifted child who, she rationalizes, can look after himself.

*17.* In this situation, where the schools and the teachers cannot possibly meet all the demands they put on themselves, I think it would be helpful to develop a systematic theory of education as *counter-cyclical.* Just as Keynesian economics would have the government and the banks save in a time of inflation and spend in a time of depression, so teachers, in selecting among the expectations held out to them, have some modest opportunities to oppose "life" in its momentary excesses. A generation or so ago teachers were farsighted in being preoccupied with social skills, and in those many too many areas where underprivileged children still lack access to those skills, it remains important to emphasize them. In fact, to return to our theme at the beginning of the article, where the community continues to be production-minded, the schools can afford to emphasize the gentler arts of social and personal understanding; even today, the country is undoubtedly overplentifully supplied with sadistic teachers who employ their subject-matter superiorities to torment children in the Victorian manner. Increasingly, however, such settings would appear to be waning in frequency and impact; as the community becomes more consumption-minded, and as the out-of-school context helps cultivate the children's social skills, humaneness as such in the schools may on occasion be given a slightly lower priority and an emphasis on the teacher's own production-mindedness—whether with respect to French, football, or mathematics—is likely to be more beneficial and less traumatic. For in the middle class homes of today children are listened to—they are no longer seen and not heard. The home is itself a "communication labora-tory," at least in the middle class. Children can and do use the movies, TV, comics, and magazines like *Seventeen,* as well as each other's exam-ple, to learn proper social behavior, especially since they no longer have to do many chores around the house. No one should sneer at the children's social proficiencies: if one compares American young people with their counterparts a generation ago (or in Europe today) one is struck by their poise, their understanding of themselves, each other, and adults; they can often handle touchy questions with a tact and facility our diplomats might well envy. As in the comic strip *Penny,* it is often the adults, not the adolescents, who are the awkward ones. But this very discrepancy, as I have observed, leads both parents and teachers, often conscious of their own childhood inadequacies and gaucheries, to give many children what amounts to postgraduate education in sociability when what they need, for the most part, is something very different. What they need, I suggest, is protection for those long-term intellectual and humanistic in-terests that are momentarily under severe pressure from so many sides.

*18.* From this perspective, progressive education was undoubtedly a counter-cyclical force a generation ago (as it still is in many "backward" areas and for many individual children). It put pressure on conservative and conventional parents, and on their children. It involved the family in a dialectic which, if at times confusing, was frequently productive for all members—for the parents who strove to "keep up," and for the children who strove to understand and even sympathize with parents. Today, in many more prosperous suburbs, it is these children who presently are parents, and whose children are in turn attending schools that are no longer bucking the tide, are no longer experimental. No strong disagree-ments within the family, no tensions between family and school now require creative resolution. Yet the relaxed adjustment achieved in this way, while in some respects an undeniable advance over earlier miseries, means in terms of the life cycle less variety and less challenge.

*19.* This implies that, in many schools, where warm and outgoing teach-ers are present in sufficient number, effort should be directed to seeing that the children have contact with at least one teacher who cares pro-foundly about a subject matter like Latin or music which is at first sight remote from the concerns of everday life. To be sure, such a teacher need not be indifferent to children. She may well come to be particularly at-tached to those pupils who are attached to her subject (as in Mary Mc-Carthy's recent personal memoir). Such a person can do something to set up a competing model to the mediocrity that results from turning a school entirely over to teachers who have been shy and want to be personable and who hence care too much whether the children respond pleasantly to them and to each other; these are the teachers who have entered the profession to escape the farm or the working class and who come to be captivated by the paraphernalia of professionalism, such as "teacher talk" about classroom skills and audio-visual aids. If schools were to eliminate the difficult or eccentric teachers who present alternative models of good teaching, they would indeed become like life in 1955, only more so.

20. For truly high aims, whether they be occupational, personal, or intellectual, tend to contradict life as it is lived in any given place and time. Schools in the past, more by accident and even ignorance than design, have opened vistas to such aims (for at least a minority) by their very *un-lifelike* character. A student who, through a devoted teacher, could learn to live with Cicero or Mercutio, Joan of Arc or Jane Austen, might well succeed in discovering forms of existence transcending the observable in home or playground: transcending both the bread salesman and the idea salesman.

21. If children, tough and adaptable creatures that they are, can stand being confronted with a wider gamut of personal models than most public schools now make available, all I have said so far would imply that teachers—a group who reach a plateau of grown-upness early and stay on it long—are much less hardy and cannot be asked to face the personal consequences of counter-cyclical behavior. Indeed, in writing as I do I have the ironical misgiving that I, too, may only be adding to expectations for omnicompetence which, as I have contended, are already unrealistic. Just as I would not expect a banker who believed a depression was coming, and who had read Keynes, to invest his personal fortune as a way of increasing purchasing power, so I do not expect individual teachers to carry the whole system on their backs while beginning a counter-cyclical revolution. Still, I want to encourage some of them to give up trying to be psychiatrists, mothers, and moralists, to give up making citizens, democrats, and tolerant children. Could they not be persuaded to concentrate more than many now feel justified in doing on their roles as teachers of specific subjects? This is, after all, a job no one else is assigned or trained to do.

22. I am not arguing that the entire responsibility for counter-cyclical cultural activity must be borne by the secondary schools. The universities, the media, and the other makers of taste and opinion have a similar responsibility. Nor am I contending for a simple "middle way" between extremes, which can be discovered by a metaphorical thermostat or servo-mechanism. We lack at present the most elementary indices for telling, let us say, that the coming generation will possess "enough" social skills but not enough musical or mathematical ones. I am arguing that, for the foreseeable future, no agency with any leeway should make it its business to imitate "life" or to be "realistic" in the Philistine sense of that term, but rather that it should make a good guess as to where "life" is leading, and then proceed to criticize and correct it. Since in most quarters the dangers of intellectual arrogance are fast passing, school officials

might make it a matter of professional pride to be as unpopular (short of dismissal) with the community as they can. It would help educate parents as well as children if a few principals and superintendents supported their teachers against any pressures for lowering of standards and insisted on high competence in subject matter in as many appointees as possible. This will occasionally involve them in defending and befriending someone like our drama teacher; eccentric as such teachers are apt to be in their devotion to a subject, they may not be quite the best "team players" in the teacher-colleague group.

23. Paradoxically, it is in a non-academic area that this is already standard practice. I refer to the sports coach, who is ordinarily expected to get his pupils to do their best (even, sometimes, at shocking cost to body and soul). In this field, "democracy" means a free way for talent and not, save in a few schools which are hostile to competition as such, that everyone must proceed at a medium pace, or be elected rather than selected for the team. Many of us—forgetting that before the days of organized sports our schools and colleges were locales of barely controlled roistering—tend to look down on the coach, though he may today be a better teacher than many of his colleagues by virtue of his more unequivocal aims: the excellence of his pupils is the answer to his prayers. Even while we moderate his zeal, we might use it as a model for teachers of painting and poetry, some of whom should unquestionably concern themselves with children's self-expression, but others with giving even the less gifted children the valuable sense that there are cultural continuities and standards of excellence.

24. Is there any chance for such a program? The same social developments which have put brakes on old-fashioned competition have made it possible to recruit a new sort of teacher and school official—a person whose eye is set not on money or social success but on leading a useful life of service. Perhaps the majority of these end up in private schools; and this will go on as long as, in a great many states, public school teachers most easily win a certificate by attending the teachers colleges or those university stepchildren, the education departments of state universities. These colleges and departments are not exactly centers of intellectual excitement or cultivation. Inasmuch as well-established private schools can withstand community prsssures far better than most public schools they are therefore better prepared to experiment with counter-cyclical measures. Yet some teachers manage to shuttle between public and private schools, and it makes sense to encourage as many as possible to spend some time in a model school, even if not permanently retained there. A similar hope guided the Whitney Foundation to invite a group of public high school teachers from different states to spend a year at Columbia or Yale with no assignment to study education but simply to expand their personal as well as broad academic horizons. (When I met with the Columbia group

I was reminded of how many enthusiastic and devoted teachers the public school system can still boast.) Not all of today's young people who (as they often put it) want to "work with children" are devoid of interest in a topic which is to be introduced to children. I am told that the Fellows who have already gone back to their former schools have in many instances taken the leadership in moves to strengthen the humanistic and intellectually challenging elements of the high school program.

25. A last word on one other important counter-cyclical possibility. Chicago research has indicated there are a few schools in slum districts from which teachers do not attempt to flee, even when entitled to by length of service. These turn out to be schools where the principal is of such caliber as to win the devotion of his teachers; as his reputation grows, he can even attract them. The principal therefore can, if he has talent and character, reverse the usual situation in which the most deprived children are taught either by the most inexperienced or by the most hardened and indifferent teachers. He can, in fact, reverse the vicious circle of mediocrity.

26. However, such principals are naturally scarce, and great changes in salaries and systems of recruitment are not in prospect. Indeed, I sometimes feel that even well-intended criticism of the schools serves, in the present climate of budget and opinion, only to make school officials and teachers still more nervous and fearful of community pressure than they already are, with inevitably baneful effects on them and on pupils. Must we then look for counter-cyclical measures outside the education industry entirely? Counter-cyclical strategy in general must be flexible. And I am inclined to ask, for instance, whether educational television may not provide a new opportunity for reaching children with challenging ideas and cultivated goals, either directly or by tie-ins with other community facilities such as libraries and museums. It is at least arguable that TV is at present open and experimental in a way that the public schools cannot possibly be—even though, like the schools, it is subject to enormous pressures to be pious and please everybody.

27. Even now, however, one finds children for whom the mass media have opened windows, and not only children whose addiction to a monotone of programming has simply made the schools' task appear more hopeless than heretofore. Keynesian theory leads one always to look for the "multiplier" effect—the relatively small increase in the rate of capital investment that can set off momentous economic dynamisms. In Williamsburg, a New York City slum of a generation ago, the public library served (as Alfred Kazin has poignantly recalled) as a storehouse of excitement for children bored to distraction at the run-down neighborhood school. If one looks at the little blue lights of TV that serve as compensation for an underprivileged existence in Harlem, or Chicago's Bronzeville, one cannot help but wonder what chances there are of a child's catching fire

from a play, or a poem read aloud, or a concert. But could it be that, just as some TV dramas have followed the movies in making school teachers out to be "good guys" or "pin-ups," the public school teacher who now sees TV as one more enemy may conceivably find her roles clarified and her purposes supported by new images quite beyond the sabotage of the supervisor and the censorship of the school board?

# Questions

1. Why does Riesman object to public schools trying to represent or to imitate "life" for their students?
2. What are the essential differences, so far as Riesman sees them, between old-fashioned and new-fashioned high school teachers?
3. In what sense is the relationship, both historically and presently, between American society and its public schools reciprocal?
4. What does Riesman mean by "counter-cyclical cultural activity" on the part of the schools? What are the bases for his argument for such an activity?
5. In Riesman's view what factors have been most significant in shaping the character of our public school system? How do they compare with those emphasized by other writers in this section?
6. What rhetorical effects does Riesman achieve with the five extensive quotations he uses?
7. How can you explain the difference in the tone of Riesman's article on the basis of the difference in his purpose as compared with that of each previous writer in this section?

# Theme Topics

1. Write a paper classifying the "troublemakers" among the students in your high school and telling how they were handled by the teachers, the principal, or other authorities.
2. Write a paper showing how your high school was "counter-cyclical" (or "pro-cyclical") in its curriculum and in the nature of its extracurricular activities.

# Society and the Individual

## ～ XIII ～

### ·55·

*Aristotle*

## Book First, I, II, THE POLITICS

### I

*1.* Every state is a community of some kind, and every community is established with a view to some good; for mankind always act in order to obtain that which they think good. But, if all communities aim at some good, the state or political community, which is the highest of all, and which embraces all the rest, aims at good in a greater degree than any other, and at the highest good.

*2.* Some people think that the qualifications of a statesman, king, householder, and master are the same, and that they differ, not in kind, but only in the number of their subjects. For example, the ruler over a few is called a master; over more, the manager of a household; over a still larger number, a statesman or king, as if there were no difference between a great household and a small state. The distinction which is made between the king and the statesman is as follows: When the government is personal, the ruler is a king; when, according to the rules of the political science, the citizens rule and are ruled in turn, then he is called a statesman.

*3.* But all this is a mistake; for governments differ in kind, as will be evident to any one who considers the matter according to the method which has hitherto guided us. As in other departments of science, so in politics, the compound should always be resolved into the simple elements or least parts of the whole. We must therefore look at the elements of which the state is composed, in order that we may see in what the different kinds of rule differ from one another, and whether any scientific result can be attained about each one of them.

### II

*4.* He who thus considers things in their first growth and origin, whether a state or anything else, will obtain the clearest view of them. In the first

From Aristotle, *The Politics,* translated by W. D. Ross. Reprinted by permission of the Clarendon Press, Oxford.

place there must be a union of those who cannot exist without each other; namely, of male and female, that the race may continue (and this is a union which is formed, not of deliberate purpose, but because, in common with other animals and with plants, mankind have a natural desire to leave behind them an image of themselves), and of natural ruler and subject, that both may be preserved. For that which can foresee by the exercise of mind is by nature intended to be lord and master, and that which can with its body give effect to such foresight is a subject, and by nature a slave; hence master and slave have the same interest. Now nature has distinguished between the female and the slave. For she is not niggardly, like the smith who fashions the Delphian knife for many uses; she makes each thing for a single use, and every instrument is best made when intended for one and not for many uses. But among barbarians no distinction is made between women and slaves, because there is no natural ruler among them: they are a community of slaves, male and female. Wherefore the poets say—

It is meet that Hellenes should rule over barbarians;

as if they thought that the barbarian and the slave were by nature one.

5. Out of these two relationships between man and woman, master and slave, the first thing to arise is the family, and Hesiod is right when he says—

First house and wife and an ox for the plough,

for the ox is the poor man's slave. The family is the association established by nature for the supply of men's everyday wants, and the members of it are called by Charondas "companions of the cupboard," and by Epimenides the Cretan, "companions of the manger." But when several families are united, and the association aims at something more than the supply of daily needs, the first society to be formed is the village. And the most natural form of the village appears to be that of a colony from the family, composed of the children and grandchildren, who are said to be suckled "with the same milk." And this is the reason why Hellenic states were originally governed by kings; because the Hellenes were under royal rule before they came together, as the barbarians still are. Every family is ruled by the eldest, and therefore in the colonies of the family the kingly form of government prevailed because they were of the same blood. As Homer says:

Each one gives law to his children and to his wives.

For they lived dispersedly, as was the manner in ancient times. Wherefore men say that the Gods have a king, because they themselves either are or were in ancient times under the rule of a king. For they imagine, not only the forms of the Gods, but their ways of life to be like their own.

6. When several villages are united in a single complete community, large enough to be nearly or quite self-sufficing, the state comes into existence, originating in the bare needs of life, and continuing in existence for the sake of a good life. And therefore, if the earlier forms of society are natural, so is the state, for it is the end of them, and the nature of a thing is its end. For what each thing is when fully developed, we call its nature, whether we are speaking of man, a horse, or a family. Besides, the final cause and end of a thing is the best, and to be self-sufficing is the end and the best.

7. Hence it is evident that the state is a creation of nature, and that man is by nature a political animal. And he who by nature and not by mere accident is without a state, is either a bad man or above humanity; he is like the

> Tribeless, lawless, hearthless one,

whom Homer denounces—the natural outcast is forthwith a lover of war; he may be compared to an isolated piece at draughts.

8. Now, that man is more of a political animal than bees or any other gregarious animals is evident. Nature, as we often say, makes nothing in vain, and man is the only animal whom she has endowed with the gift of speech. And whereas mere voice is but an indication of pleasure or pain, and is therefore found in other animals (for their nature attains to the perception of pleasure and pain and the intimation of them to one another, and no further), the power of speech is intended to set forth the expedient and inexpedient, and therefore likewise the just and the unjust. And it is a characteristic of man that he alone has any sense of good and evil, of just and unjust, and the like, and the association of living beings who have this sense makes a family and a state.

9. Further, the state is by nature clearly prior to the family and to the individual, since the whole is of necessity prior to the part; for example, if the whole body be destroyed, there will be no foot or hand, except in an equivocal sense, as we might speak of a stone hand; for when destroyed the hand will be no better than that. But things are defined by their working and power; and we ought not to say that they are the same when they no longer have their proper quality, but only that they have the same name. The proof that the state is a creation of nature and prior to the individual is that the individual, when isolated, is not self-sufficing; and therefore he is like a part in relation to the whole. But he who is unable to live in society, or who has no need because he is sufficient for himself, must be either a beast or a god: he is no part of a state. A social instinct is implanted in all men by nature, and yet he who first founded the state was the greatest of benefactors. For man, when perfected, is the best of animals, but, when separated from law and justice, he is the worst of all; since armed injustice is the more dangerous, and he is equipped at

birth with arms, meant to be used by intelligence and virtue, which he may use for the worst ends. Wherefore, if he have not virtue, he is the most unholy and the most savage of animals, and the most full of lust and gluttony. But justice is the bond of men in states, for the administration of justice, which is the determination of what is just, is the principle of order in political society.

# Questions

1. Aristotle uses a number of explicit first principles, that is, assumptions he states but does not examine, to shape his argument about the nature of the political community. At least four of these principles are concerned with the way we know what we know and not with man and the political community. Show in detail how the following principles function in Book I of the *Politics:*

   resolve every whole into its simplest elements;
   see things in their first growth and origin;
   things are defined by their working and power;
   the nature of a thing is its end (i.e. what it is when fully developed).

2. What other principles, related specifically to his subject matter (man in communities), does he use to build his argument? What is he arguing against and what is he arguing for?

3. What does Aristotle conclude, by use of all the principles invoked in Book I, about the nature of the political community?

## ·56·

*Baruch Spinoza*

# OF THE FOUNDATIONS OF A STATE: OF THE NATURAL AND CIVIL RIGHTS OF INDIVIDUALS: AND OF THE RIGHTS OF THE SOVEREIGN POWER

1. Hitherto our care has been to separate philosophy from theology, and to show the freedom of thought which such separation insures to both. It is now time to determine the limits to which such freedom of thought and discussion may extend itself in the ideal state (*Respublica*). For the due consideration of this question we must examine the foundations of a state, first turning our attention to the natural rights of individuals, and afterwards to religion and the state as a whole.

2. By the right and ordinance of nature, I merely mean those natural laws of every individual wherewith we conceive every individual to be conditioned by nature, so as to live and act in a given way. For instance, fishes are naturally conditioned for swimming, and the greater for devouring the less; therefore fishes enjoy the water, and the greater devour the less by sovereign natural right. For it is certain that nature, considered absolutely, has sovereign right to do anything she can; in other words, her right is co-extensive with her power. The power of nature is the power of God, which has sovereign right over all things; and, inasmuch as the universal power of nature is simply the aggregate of the powers of all her individual components, it follows that every individual has sovereign right to do all that he can; in other words, the rights of an individual extend to the utmost limits of his power as it has been conditioned. Now it is the sovereign law and right of nature that each individual should endeavour to preserve itself as it is, without regard to anything but itself; therefore this sovereign law and right belongs to every individual, namely, to exist and act according to its natural conditions. We do not here acknowledge any difference between mankind and other individual natural

From *Tractatus theologico-politicus* by Baruch Spinoza (The Hague, 1670). Translated into English by R. H. M. Elwes (London, Bohn, 1883).

entities, nor between men endowed with reason and those to whom reason is unknown; nor between fools, madmen, and sane men. Whatsoever an individual does by the laws of its nature it has a sovereign right to do, inasmuch as it acts as it was conditioned by nature, and cannot act otherwise. Wherefore among men, so long as they are considered as living under the sway of nature, he who does not yet know reason, or who has not yet acquired the habit of virtue, acts solely according to the laws of his desire with as sovereign a right as he who orders his life entirely by the laws of reason.

3. That is, as the wise man has sovereign right to do all that reason dictates, or to live according to the laws of reason, so also the ignorant and foolish man has sovereign right to do all that desire dictates, or to live according to the laws of desire. This is identical with the teaching of Paul, who acknowledges that previous to the law—that is, so long as men are considered of as living under the sway of nature,—there is no sin.

4. The natural right of the individual man is thus determined, not by sound reason, but by desire and power. All are not naturally conditioned so as to act according to the laws and rules of reason; nay, on the contrary, all men are born ignorant, and before they can learn the right way of life and acquire the habit of virtue, the greater part of their life, even if they have been well brought up, has passed away. Nevertheless, they are in the meanwhile bound to live and preserve themselves as far as they can by the unaided impulses of desire. Nature has given them no other guide, and has denied them the present power of living according to sound reason; so that they are no more bound to live by the dictates of an enlightened mind, than a cat is bound to live by the laws of the nature of a lion.

5. Whatsoever, therefore, an individual (considered as under the sway [imperium] of nature) thinks useful for himself, whether led by sound reason or impelled by the passions, that he has a sovereign right to seek and to take for himself as he best can, whether by force, cunning, entreaty, or any other means; consequently he may regard as an enemy anyone who hinders the accomplishment of his purpose.

6. It follows from what we have said that the right and ordinance of nature, under which all men are born, and under which they mostly live, only prohibits such things as no one desires, and no one can attain: it does not forbid strife, nor hatred, nor anger, nor deceit, nor, indeed, any of the means suggested by desire.

7. This we need not wonder at, for nature is not bounded by the laws of human reason, which aims only at man's true benefit and preservation; her limits are infinitely wider, and have reference to the eternal order of nature, wherein man is but a speck; it is by the necessity of this alone that all individuals are conditioned for living and acting in a particular way.

If anything, therefore, in nature seems to us ridiculous, absurd, or evil, it is because we only know in part, and are almost entirely ignorant of the order and interdependence of nature as a whole, and also because we want everything to be arranged acording to the dictates of our human reason; in reality that which reason considers evil, is not evil in respect to the order and laws of nature as a whole, but only in respect to the laws of our reason.

8. Nevertheless, no one can doubt that it is much better for us to live according to the laws and assured dictates of reason, for, as we said, they have men's true good for their object. Moreover, everyone wishes to live as far as possible securely beyond the reach of fear, and this would be quite impossible so long as everyone did everything he liked, and reason's claim was lowered to a par with those of hatred and anger; there is no one who is not ill at ease in the midst of enmity, hatred, anger, and deceit, and who does not seek to avoid them as much as he can. When we reflect that men without mutual help, or the aid of reason, must needs live most miserably, we shall plainly see that men must necessarily come to an agreement to live together as securely and well as possible if they are to enjoy as a whole the rights which naturally belong to them as individuals, and their life should be no more conditioned by the force and desire of individuals, but by the power and will of the whole body. This end they will be unable to attain if desire be their only guide (for by the laws of desire each man is drawn in a different direction); they must, therefore, most firmly decree and establish that they will be guided in everything by reason (which nobody will dare openly to repudiate lest he should be taken for a madman), and will restrain any desire which is injurious to a man's fellows, that they will do to all as they would be done by, and that they will defend their neighbour's rights as their own.

9. How such a compact as this should be entered into, how ratified and established, we will now inquire.

10. Now it is a universal law of human nature that no one ever neglects anything which he judges to be good, except with the hope of gaining a greater good, or from the fear of a greater evil; nor does anyone endure an evil except for the sake of avoiding a greater evil, or gaining a greater good. That is, everyone will, of two goods, choose that which he thinks the greater; and, of two evils, that which he thinks the lesser. I say advisedly that which he thinks the greater or the lesser, for it does not necessarily follow that he judges right. This law is so deeply implanted in the human mind that it ought to be counted among eternal truths and axioms.

11. As a necessary consequence of the principle just enunciated, no one can honestly promise to forego the right which he has over all things, and in general no one will abide by his promises, unless under the fear of a greater evil, or the hope of a greater good. An example will make the

matter clearer. Suppose that a robber forces me to promise that I will give him my goods at his will and pleasure. It is plain (inasmuch as my natural right is, as I have shown, co-extensive with my power) that if I can free myself from this robber by stratagem, by assenting to his demands, I have the natural right to do so, and to pretend to accept his conditions. Or again, suppose I have genuinely promised someone that for the space of twenty days I will not taste food or any nourishment; and suppose I afterwards find that my promise was foolish, and cannot be kept without very great injury to myself; as I am bound by natural law and right to choose the lesser of two evils, I have complete right to break my compact, and act as if my promise had never been uttered. I say that I should have perfect natural right to do so, whether I was actuated by true and evident reason, or whether I was actuated by mere opinion in thinking I had promised rashly; whether my reasons were true or false, I should be in fear of a greater evil, which, by the ordinance of nature, I should strive to avoid by every means in my power.

*12.* We may, therefore, conclude that a compact is only made valid by its utility, without which it becomes null and void. It is, therefore, foolish to ask a man to keep his faith with us for ever, unless we also endeavour that the violation of the compact we enter into shall involve for the violator more harm than good. This consideration should have very great weight in forming a state. However, if all men could be easily led by reason alone, and could recognize what is best and most useful for a state, there would be no one who would not forswear deceit, for everyone would keep most religiously to their compact in their desire for the chief good, namely, the preservation of the state, and would cherish good faith above all things as the shield and buckler of the commonwealth. However, it is far from being the case that all men can always be easily led by reason alone; everyone is drawn away by his pleasure, while avarice, ambition, envy, hatred, and the like so engross the mind that reason has no place therein. Hence, though men make promises with all the appearances of good faith, and agree that they will keep to their engagement, no one can absolutely rely on another man's promise unless there is something behind it. Everyone has by nature a right to act deceitfully, and to break his compacts, unless he be restrained by the hope of some greater good, or the fear of some greater evil.

*13.* However, as we have shown that the natural right of the individual is only limited by his power, it is clear that by transferring, either willingly or under compulsion, this power into the hands of another, he in so doing necessarily cedes also a part of his right; and further, that the sovereign right over all men belongs to him who has sovereign power, wherewith he can compel men by force, or restrain them by threats of the universally feared punishment of death; such sovereign right he will retain only so long as he can maintain his power of enforcing his will; otherwise he will totter on his throne, and no one who is stronger than he will be bound unwillingly to obey him.

*14.* In this manner a society (*Societas*) can be formed without any violation of natural right, and the covenant can always be strictly kept—that is, if each individual hands over the whole of his power to the body politic (*Societas*), the latter will then possess sovereign natural right over all things; that is, it will have sole and unquestioned dominion, and everyone will be bound to obey, under pain of the severest punishment. A body politic of this kind is called a Democracy, which may be defined as a society which wields all its power as a whole. The sovereign power is not restrained by any laws, but everyone is bound to obey it in all things; such is the state of things implied when men either tacitly or expressly handed over to it all their power of self-defence, or in other words, all their right. For if they had wished to retain any right for themselves, they ought to have taken precautions for its defence and preservation; as they have not done so, and indeed could not have done so without dividing and consequently ruining the state, they placed themselves absolutely at the mercy of the sovereign power; and, therefore, having acted (as we have shown) as reason and necessity demanded, they are obliged to fulfil the commands of the sovereign power, however absurd these may be, else they will be public enemies, and will act against reason, which urges the preservation of the state as a primary duty. For reason bids us choose the lesser of two evils.

*15.* Furthermore, this danger of submitting absolutely to the dominion and will of another, is one which may be incurred with a light heart: for we have shown that sovereigns only possess this right of imposing their will, so long as they have the full power to enforce it: if such power be lost their right to command is lost also, or lapses to those who have assumed it and can keep it. Thus it is very rare for sovereigns to impose thoroughly irrational commands, for they are bound to consult their own interests, and retain their power by consulting the public good and acting according to the dictates of reason, as Seneca says, "*violenta imperia nemo continuit diu.*" No one can long retain a tyrant's sway.

*16.* In a democracy, irrational commands are still less to be feared: for it is almost impossible that the majority of a people, especially if it be a large one, should agree in an irrational design: and, moreover, the basis and aim of a democracy is to avoid the desires as irrational, and to bring men as far as possible under the control of reason, so that they may live in peace and harmony: if this basis be removed the whole fabric falls to ruin.

*17.* Such being the ends in view for the sovereign power, the duty of subjects is, as I have said, to obey its commands, and to recognize no right save that which it sanctions.

*18.* It will, perhaps, be thought that we are turning subjects into slaves:

for slaves obey commands and free men live as they like; but this idea is based on a misconception, for the true slave is he who is led away by his pleasures and can neither see what is good for him nor act accordingly: he alone is free who lives with free consent under the entire guidance of reason.

*19.* Action in obedience to orders does take away freedom in a certain sense, but it does not, therefore, make a man a slave, all depends on the object of the action. If the object of the action be the good of the state, and not the good of the agent, the latter is a slave and does himself no good: but in a Commonwealth and Dominion (*in Republica et Imperio*) where the weal of the whole people, and not that of the ruler, is the supreme law, obedience to the sovereign power does not make a man a slave, of no use to himself, but a subject. Therefore, that state is the freest whose laws are founded on sound reason, so that every member of it may, if he will, be free; that is, live with full consent under the entire guidance of reason.

*20.* Children, though they are bound to obey all the commands of their parents, are yet not slaves: for the commands of parents look generally to the children's benefit.

*21.* We must, therefore, acknowledge a great difference between a slave, a son, and a subject; their positions may be thus defined. A slave is one who is bound to obey his master's orders, though they are given solely in the master's interest: a son is one who obeys his father's orders, given in his own interest; a subject obeys the orders of the sovereign power, given for the common interest, wherein he is included.

*22.* I think I have now shown sufficiently clearly the basis of a democracy: I have especially desired to do so, for I believe it to be of all forms of government the most natural, and the most consonant with individual liberty. In it no one transfers his natural right so absolutely that he has no further voice in affairs, he only hands it over to the majority of a society, whereof he is a unit. Thus all men remain, as they were in the state of nature, equals.

*23.* This is the only form of government which I have treated of at length, for it is the one most akin to my purpose of showing the benefits of freedom in a state.

*24.* I may pass over the fundamental principles of other forms of government, for we may gather from what has been said whence their right arises without going into its origin. The possessor of sovereign power, whether he be one, or many, or the whole body politic, has the sovereign right of imposing any commands he pleases: and he who has either voluntarily, or under compulsion, transferred the right to defend him to another, has, in so doing, renounced his natural right and is therefore bound to obey, in all things, the commands of the sovereign power; and will be bound so to do so long as the king, or nobles, or the people preserve the sovereign power which formed the basis of the original transfer. I need add no more.

25. The bases and rights of dominion being thus displayed, we shall readily be able to define private civil right, wrong, justice, and injustice, with their relations to the state; and also to determine what constitutes an ally, or an enemy, or the crime of treason.

26. By private civil right we can only mean the liberty every man possesses to preserve his existence, a liberty limited by the edicts of the sovereign power, and preserved only by its authority: for when a man has transferred to another his right of living as he likes, which was only limited by his power, that is, has transferred his liberty and power of self-defence, he is bound to live as that other dictates, and to trust him entirely for his defence. Wrong takes place when a citizen, or subject, is forced by another to undergo some loss or pain in contradiction to the authority of the law, or the edict of the sovereign power.

27. Wrong is conceivable only in an organized community (*in statu civili*) nor can it ever accrue to subjects from any act of the sovereign, from whom all right is derived. It can only arise, therefore, between private persons, who are bound by law and right not to injure one another. Justice consists in the habitual rendering to every man his lawful due; injustice consists in depriving a man, under the pretence of legality, of what the laws, rightly interpreted, would allow him. These last are also called equity and iniquity, because those who administer the laws are bound to show no respect of persons, but to account all men equal, and to defend every man's right equally, neither envying the rich nor despising the poor.

28. The men of two states become allies, when for the sake of avoiding war, or for some other advantage, they covenant to do each other no hurt, but on the contrary, to assist each other if necessity arises, each retaining his independence. Such a covenant is valid so long as its basis of danger or advantage is in force: no one enters into an engagement, or is bound to stand by his compacts unless there be a hope of some accruing good, or the fear of some evil: if this basis be removed the compact thereby becomes void: this has been abundantly shown by experience. For although different states make treaties not to harm one another, they always take every possible precaution against such treaties being broken by the stronger party, and do not rely on the compact, unless there is a sufficiently obvious object and advantage to both parties in observing it. Otherwise they would fear a breach of faith, nor would there be any wrong done thereby: for who in his proper senses, and aware of the right of the sovereign power, would trust in the promises of one who has the will and the power to do what he likes, and who aims solely at the safety and advantage of his dominion? Moreover, if we consult loyalty and religion, we shall see that no one in possession of power ought to abide by his promises to

the injury of his dominion; for he cannot keep such promises without breaking the engagement he made with his subjects, by which both he and they are most solemnly bound.

29. An enemy is one who lives apart from the state, and does not recognize its authority either as a subject or as an ally. It is not hatred which makes a man an enemy, but the rights of the state. The rights of the state are the same in regard to him who does not recognize by any compact the state authority, as they are against him who has done the state an injury: it has the right to force him as best it can, either to submit, or to contract an alliance.

30. Lastly, treason can only be committed by subjects, who by compact, either tacit or expressed, have transferred all their rights to the state: a subject is said to have committed this crime when he has attempted, for whatever reason, to seize the sovereign power, or to place it in different hands. I say, *has attempted,* for if punishment were not to overtake him till he had succeeded, it would often come too late, the sovereign rights would have been acquired or transferred already.

31. I also say, *has attempted, for whatever reason, to seize the sovereign power,* and I recognize no difference whether such an attempt should be followed by public loss or public gain. Whatever be his reason for acting, the crime is treason, and he is rightly condemned: in war, everyone would admit the justice of his sentence. If a man does not keep to his post, but approaches the enemy without the knowledge of his commander, whatever may be his motive, so long as he acts on his own motion, even if he advances with the design of defeating the enemy, he is rightly put to death, because he has violated his oath, and infringed the rights of his commander. That all citizens are equally bound by these rights in time of peace, is not so generally recognized, but the reasons for obedience are, in both cases, identical. The state must be preserved and directed by the sole authority of the sovereign, and such authority and right have been accorded by universal consent to him alone: if, therefore, anyone else attempts, without his consent, to execute any public enterprise, even though the state might (as we said) reap benefit therefrom, such person has none the less infringed the sovereign's right, and would be rightly punished for treason.

# IT IS SHOWN THAT NO ONE CAN, OR NEED, TRANSFER ALL HIS RIGHTS TO THE SOVEREIGN POWER.

32. The theory put forward in the last chapter, of the universal rights of the sovereign power, and of the natural rights of the individual trans-

ferred thereto, though it corresponds in many respects with actual practice, and though practice may be so arranged as to conform to it more
and more, must nevertheless always remain in many respects purely
ideal. No one can ever so utterly transfer to another his power and, consequently, his rights, as to cease to be a man; nor can there ever be a
power so sovereign that it can carry out every possible wish. It will always
be vain to order a subject to hate what he believes brings him advantage,
or to love what brings him loss, or not to be offended at insults, or not to
wish to be free from fear, or a hundred other things of the sort, which
necessarily follow from the laws of human nature. So much, I think, is
abundantly shown by experience: for men have never so far ceded their
power as to cease to be an object of fear to the rulers who received such
power and right; and dominions have always been in as much danger
from their own subjects as from external enemies. If it were really the
case that men could be deprived of their natural rights so utterly as never
to have any further influence on affairs, except with the permission of
the holders of sovereign right, it would then be possible to maintain with
impunity the most violent tyranny, which, I suppose, no one would for
an instant admit.

33. We must, therefore, grant that every man retains some part of his
right, in dependence on his own decision, and no one else's.

34. However, in order to correctly understand the extent of the sovereign's right and power, we must take notice that it does not cover only
those actions to which it can compel men by fear, but absolutely every
action which it can induce men to perform: for it is the fact of obedience,
not the motive for obedience, which makes a man a subject.

35. Whatever be the cause which leads a man to obey the commands
of the sovereign, whether it be fear or hope, or love of his country, or
any other emotion—the fact remains that the man takes counsel with
himself, and nevertheless acts as his sovereign orders. We must not, therefore, assert that all actions resulting from a man's deliberation with himself are done in obedience to the rights of the individual rather than the
sovereign: as a matter of fact, all actions spring from a man's deliberation
with himself, whether the determining motive be love or fear of punishment; therefore, either dominion does not exist, and has no rights over
its subjects, or else it extends over every instance in which it can prevail
on men to decide to obey it. Consequently, every action which a subject
performs in accordance with the commands of the sovereign, whether
such action springs from love, or fear, or (as is more frequently the case)
from hope and fear together, or from reverence compounded of fear
and admiration, or, indeed, any motive whatever, is performed in virtue
of his submission to the sovereign, and not in virtue of his own authority.

36. This point is made still more clear by the fact that obedience does
not consist so much in the outward act as in the mental state of the per-

son obeying; so that he is most under the dominion of another who with his whole heart determines to obey another's commands; and consequently the firmest dominion belongs to the sovereign who has most influence over the minds of his subjects; if those who are most feared possessed the firmest dominion, the firmest dominion would belong to the subjects of a tyrant, for they are always greatly feared by their ruler. Furthermore, though it is impossible to govern the mind as completely as the tongue, nevertheless minds are, to a certain extent, under the control of the sovereign, for he can in many ways bring about that the greatest part of his subjects should follow his wishes in their beliefs, their loves, and their hates. Though such emotions do not arise at the express command of the sovereign they often result (as experience shows) from the authority of his power, and from his direction; in other words, in virtue of his right; we may, therefore, without doing violence to our understanding, conceive men who follow the instigation of their sovereign in their beliefs, their loves, their hates, their contempt, and all other emotions whatsoever.

37. Though the powers of government, as thus conceived, are sufficiently ample, they can never become large enough to execute every possible wish of their possessors. This, I think, I have already shown clearly enough. . . .

38. That the preservation of a state chiefly depends on the subjects' fidelity and constancy in carrying out the orders they receive, is most clearly taught both by reason and experience; how subjects ought to be guided so as best to preserve their fidelity and virtue is not so obvious. All, both rulers and ruled, are men, and prone to follow after their lusts. The fickle disposition of the multitude almost reduces those who have experience of it to despair, for it is governed solely by emotions, not by reason: it rushes headlong into every enterprise, and is easily corrupted either by avarice or luxury: everyone thinks himself omniscient and wishes to fashion all things to his liking, judging a thing to be just or unjust, lawful or unlawful, according as he thinks it will bring him profit or loss: vanity leads him to despise his equals, and refuse their guidance: envy of superior fame or fortune (for such gifts are never equally distributed) leads him to desire and rejoice in his neighbour's downfall. I need not go through the whole list, everyone knows already how much crime results from disgust at the present—desire for change, headlong anger, and contempt for poverty—and how men's minds are engrossed and kept in turmoil thereby.

39. To guard against all these evils, and form a dominion where no room is left for deceit; to frame our institutions so that every man, whatever his disposition, may prefer public right to private advantage, this is the task and this the toil. Necessity is often the mother of invention, but she has never yet succeeded in framing a dominion that was in less danger from its own citizens than from open enemies, or whose rulers

did not fear the latter less than the former. Witness the state of Rome, invincible by her enemies, but many times conquered and sorely oppressed by her own citizens, especially in the war between Vespasian and Vitellius.

# Questions

1. What is "the right and ordinance of nature" and how is it related to "the natural right of the individual man"?
2. How are the laws of nature and the laws of human reason related under "the sway of nature," in a civil state? What is meant by "sovereign power" prior to the social compact? After the social compact?
3. What causes men to renounce the natural sovereignty each holds under the sway of nature in favor of a sovereign power in a civil state?
4. To what unwritten clause are all human agreements, including the social compact or contract, subject?
5. What ambiguity or contradiction can you find in Spinoza's description of the dominion of the sovereign power in a civil state?
6. In what sense are sovereign states, according to Spinoza, under the sway of nature in regard to each other? Show to what extent Spinoza's description in paragraphs 11 and 12, when applied to states rather than individuals, has retained or lost its validity in the world today.

# Theme Topics

1. Write an essay in which you compare and contrast Socrates' point of view toward the laws of Athens (see Plato's *Crito*) and Spinoza's description of the exercise of sovereign power.
2. Write an essay in which you compare and contrast the respective descriptions of Aristotle and Spinoza on the origin of the civil state. Be sure to discuss as fully as you can the principles from which they start and the conclusions which they reach.
3. Write an essay in which you cite as much evidence as you can from events of the last two or three decades to prove or to disprove the description of the causes of social unrest which Spinoza gives in paragraph 38.

*John Stuart Mill*

# OF THE LIMITS TO THE AUTHORITY OF SOCIETY OVER THE INDIVIDUAL

*1.* What, then, is the rightful limit to the sovereignty of the individual over himself? Where does the authority of society begin? How much of human life should be assigned to individuality, and how much to society?

*2.* Each will receive its proper share, if each has that which more particularly concerns it. To individuality should belong the part of life in which it is chiefly the individual that is interested; to society, the part which chiefly interests society.

*3.* Though society is not founded on a contract, and though no good purpose is answered by inventing a contract in order to deduce social obligations from it, every one who receives the protection of society owes a return for the benefit, and the fact of living in society renders it indispensable that each should be bound to observe a certain line of conduct towards the rest. This conduct consists, first, in not injuring the interests of one another; or rather certain interests, which, either by express legal provision or by tacit understanding, ought to be considered as rights; and secondly, in each person's bearing his share (to be fixed on some equitable principle) of the labors and sacrifices incurred for defending the society or its members from injury and molestation. These conditions society is justified in enforcing at all costs to those who endeavor to withhold fulfilment. Nor is this all that society may do. The acts of an individual may be hurtful to others, or wanting in due consideration for their welfare, without going the length of violating any of their constituted rights. The offender may then be justly punished by opinion, though not by law. As soon as any part of a person's conduct affects prejudicially the interests of others, society has jurisdiction over it, and the question whether the general welfare will or will not be promoted by interfering with it, becomes open to discussion. But there is no room for entertaining any such question when a person's conduct affects the interests of no persons besides himself, or needs not affect them unless they like (all the persons

From *Essay on Liberty* by John Stuart Mill (London, 1859).

concerned being of full age, and the ordinary amount of understanding).
In all such cases there should be perfect freedom, legal and social, to do
the action and stand the consequences.

4. It would be a great misunderstanding of this doctrine to suppose
that it is one of selfish indifference, which pretends that human beings
have no business with each other's conduct in life, and that they should
not concern themselves about the well-doing or well-being of one another, unless their own interest is involved. Instead of any diminution,
there is need of a great increase of disinterested exertion to promote the
good of others. But disinterested benevolence can find other instruments
to persuade people to their good, than whips and scourges, either of the
literal or the metaphorical sort. I am the last person to undervalue the self-
regarding virtues; they are only second in importance, if even second, to
the social. It is equally the business of education to cultivate both. But
even education works by conviction and persuasion as well as by compulsion, and it is by the former only that, when the period of education is
past, the self-regarding virtues should be inculcated. Human beings owe
to each other help to distinguish the better from the worse, and encouragement to choose the former and avoid the latter. They should be for ever
stimulating each other to increased exercise of their higher faculties,
and increased direction of their feelings and aims towards wise instead of
foolish, elevating instead of degrading, objects and contemplations. But
neither one person, nor any number of persons, is warranted in saying to
another human creature of ripe years, that he shall not do with his life
for his own benefit what he chooses to do with it. He is the person most
interested in his own well-being: the interest which any other person,
except in cases of strong personal attachment, can have in it, is trifling,
compared with that which he himself has; the interest which society has
in him individually (except as to his conduct to others) is fractional, and
altogether indirect: while, with respect to his own feelings and circumstances, the most ordinary man or woman has means of knowledge im-
measurably surpassing those that can be possessed by any one else. The
interference of society to overrule his judgment and purposes in what
only regards himself, must be grounded on general presumptions; which
may be altogether wrong, and even if right, are as likely as not to be misapplied to individual cases, by persons no better acquainted with the
circumstances of such cases than those are who look at them merely from
without. In this department, therefore, of human affairs, Individuality has
its proper field of action. In the conduct of human beings towards one another, it is necessary that general rules should for the most part be observed, in order that people may know what they have to expect; but in
each person's own concerns, his individual spontaneity is entitled to
free exercise. Considerations to aid his judgment, exhortations to strengthen
his will, may be offered to him, even obtruded on him, by others; but

he himself is the final judge. All errors which he is likely to commit against advice and warning, are far outweighed by the evil of allowing others to constrain him to what they deem his good.

5. I do not mean that the feelings with which a person is regarded by others, ought not to be in any way affected by his self-regarding qualities or deficiencies. This is neither possible nor desirable. If he is eminent in any of the qualities which conduce to his own good, he is, so far, a proper object of admiration. He is so much the nearer to the ideal perfection of human nature. If he is grossly deficient in those qualities, a sentiment the opposite of admiration will follow. There is a degree of folly, and a degree of what may be called (though the phrase is not unobjectionable) lowness or depravation of taste, which, though it cannot justify doing harm to the person who manifests it, renders him necessarily and properly a subject of distaste, or, in extreme cases, even of contempt: a person could not have the opposite qualities in due strength without entertaining these feelings. Though doing no wrong to any one, a person may so act as to compel us to judge him, and feel to him, as a fool, or as a being of an inferior order: and since this judgment and feeling are a fact which he would prefer to avoid, it is doing him a service to warn him of it beforehand, as of any other disagreeable consequence to which he exposes himself. It would be well, indeed, if this good office were much more freely rendered than the common notions of politeness at present permit, and if one person could honestly point out to another that he thinks him in fault, without being considered unmannerly or presuming. We have a right, also, in various ways, to act upon our unfavorable opinion of any one, not to the oppression of his individuality, but in the exercise of ours. We are not bound, for example, to seek his society; we have a right to avoid it (though not to parade the avoidance), for we have a right to choose the society most acceptable to us. We have a right, and it may be our duty, to caution others against him, if we think his example or conversation likely to have a pernicious effect on those with whom he associates. We may give others a preference over him in optional good offices, except those which tend to his improvement. In these various modes a person may suffer very severe penalties at the hands of others, for faults which directly concern only himself; but he suffers these penalties only in so far as they are the natural, and, as it were, the spontaneous consequences of the faults themselves, not because they are purposely inflicted on him for the sake of punishment. A person who shows rashness, obstinacy, self-conceit—who cannot live within moderate means—who cannot restrain himself from hurtful indulgences—who pursues animal pleasures at the expense of those of feeling and intellect— must expect to be lowered in the opinion of others, and to have a less share of their favorable sentiments; but of this he has no right to complain, unless he has merited their favor by special excellence in his

social relations, and has thus established a title to their good offices, which is not affected by his demerits towards himself.

6. What I contend for is, that the inconveniences which are strictly inseparable from the unfavorable judgment of others, are the only ones to which a person should ever be subjected for that portion of his conduct and character which concerns his own good, but which does not affect the interests of others in their relations with him. Acts injurious to others require a totally different treatment. Encroachment on their rights; infliction on them of any loss or damage not justified by his own rights; falsehood or duplicity in dealing with them; unfair or ungenerous use of advantages over them; even selfish abstinence from defending them against injury—these are fit objects of moral reprobation, and, in grave cases, of moral retribution and punishment. And not only these acts, but the dispositions which lead to them, are properly immoral, and fit subjects of disapprobation which may rise to abhorrence. Cruelty of disposition; malice and ill nature; that most antisocial and odious of all passions, envy; dissimulation and insincerity; irascibility on insufficient cause, and resentment disproportioned to the provocation; the love of domineering over others; the desire to engross more than one's share of advantages (the πλεονεξια of the Greeks); the pride which derives gratification from the abasement of others; the egotism which thinks self and its concerns more important than everything else, and decides all doubtful questions in its own favor; —these are moral vices, and constitute a bad and odious moral character: unlike the self-regarding faults previously mentioned, which are not properly immoralities, and to whatever pitch they may be carried, do not constitute wickedness. They may be proofs of any amount of folly, or want of personal dignity and self-respect; but they are only a subject of moral reprobation when they involve a breach of duty to others, for whose sake the individual is bound to have care for himself. What are called duties to ourselves are not socially obligatory, unless circumstances render them at the same time duties to others. The term duty to oneself, when it means anything more than prudence, means self-respect or self-development; and for none of these is any one accountable to his fellow creatures, because for none of them is it for the good of mankind that he be held accountable to them.

7. The distinction between the loss of consideration which a person may rightly incur by defect of prudence or of personal dignity, and the reprobation which is due to him for an offense against the rights of others, is not a merely nominal distinction. It makes a vast difference both in our feelings and in our conduct towards him, whether he displeases us in things in which we think we have a right to control him, or in things in which we know that we have not. If he displeases us, we may express our distaste, and we may stand aloof from a person as well as from a thing that displeases us; but we shall not therefore feel called on to make

his life uncomfortable. We shall reflect that he already bears, or will bear, the whole penalty of his error; if he spoils his life by mismanagement, we shall not, for that reason, desire to spoil it still further: instead of wishing to punish him, we shall rather endeavor to alleviate his punishment, by showing him how he may avoid or cure the evils his conduct tends to bring upon him. He may be to us an object of pity, perhaps of dislike, but not of anger or resentment; we shall not treat him like an enemy of society: the worst we shall think ourselves justified in doing is leaving him to himself, if we do not interfere benevolently by showing interest or concern for him. It is far otherwise if he has infringed the rules necessary for the protection of his fellow creatures, individually or collectively. The evil consequences of his acts do not then fall on himself, but on others; and society, as the protector of all its members, must retaliate on him; must inflict pain on him for the express purpose of punishment, and must take care that it be sufficiently severe. In the one case, he is an offender at our bar, and we are called on not only to sit in judgment on him, but, in one shape or another, to execute our own sentence; in the other case, it is not our part to inflict any suffering on him, except what may incidentally follow from our using the same liberty in the regulation of our own affairs, which we allow to him in his.

8. The distinction here pointed out between the part of a person's life which concerns only himself, and that which concerns others, many persons will refuse to admit. How (it may be asked) can any part of the conduct of a member of society be a matter of indifference to the other members? No person is an entirely isolated being; it is impossible for a person to do anything seriously or permanently hurtful to himself, without mischief reaching at least to his near connections, and often far beyond them. If he injures his property, he does harm to those who directly or indirectly derived support from it, and usually diminishes, by a greater or less amount, the general resources of the community. If he deteriorates his bodily or mental faculties, he not only brings evil upon all who depended on him for any portion of their happiness, but disqualifies himself for rendering the services which he owes to his fellow creatures generally; perhaps becomes a burthen on their affection or benevolence; and if such conduct were very frequent, hardly any offense that is committed would detract more from the general sum of good. Finally, if by his vices or follies a person does no direct harm to others, he is nevertheless (it may be said) injurious by his example; and ought to be compelled to control himself, for the sake of those whom the sight or knowledge of his conduct might corrupt or mislead.

9. And even (it will be added) if the consequences of misconduct could be confined to the vicious or thoughtless individual, ought society to abandon to their own guidance those who are manifestly unfit for it? If protection against themselves is confessedly due to children and per-

sons under age, is not society equally bound to afford it to persons of mature years who are equally incapable of self-government? If gambling, or drunkenness, or incontinence, or idleness, or uncleanliness, are as injurious to happiness, and as great a hindrance to improvement, as many or most of the acts prohibited by law, why (it may be asked) should not law, so far as is consistent with practicability and social convenience, endeavor to repress these also? And as a supplement to the unavoidable imperfections of law, ought not opinion at least to organize a powerful police against these vices, and visit rigidly with social penalties those who are known to practice them? There is no question here (it may be said) about restricting individuality, or impeding the trial of new and original experiments in living. The only things it is sought to prevent are things which have been tried and condemned from the beginning of the world until now; things which experience has shown not to be useful or suitable to any person's individuality. There must be some length of time and amount of experience, after which a moral or prudential truth may be regarded as established: and it is merely desired to prevent generation after generation from falling over the same precipice which has been fatal to their predecessors.

10. I fully admit that the mischief which a person does to himself may seriously affect, both through their sympathies and their interests, those nearly connected with him, and in a minor degree, society at large. When, by conduct of this sort, a person is led to violate a distinct and assignable obligation to any other person or persons, the case is taken out of the self-regarding class, and becomes amenable to moral disapproval in the proper sense of the term. If, for example, a man, through intemperance or extravagance, becomes unable to pay his debts, or, having undertaken the moral responsibility of a family, becomes from the same cause incapable of supporting or educating them, he is deservedly reprobated, and might be justly punished; but it is for the breach of duty to his family or creditors, not for the extravagance. If the resources which ought to have been devoted to them, had been diverted from them for the most prudent investment, the moral culpability would have been the same. George Barnwell murdered his uncle to get money for his mistress, but if he had done it to set himself up in business, he would equally have been hanged. Again, in the frequent case of a man who causes grief to his family by addiction to bad habits, he deserves reproach for his unkindness or ingratitude; but so he may for cultivating habits not in themselves vicious, if they are painful to those with whom he passes his life, or who from personal ties are dependent on him for their comfort. Whoever fails in the consideration generally due to the interests and feelings of others, not being compelled by some more imperative duty, or justified by allowable self-preference, is a subject of moral disapprobation for that failure, but not for the cause of it, nor for the errors, merely

personal to himself, which may have remotely led to it. In like manner, when a person disables himself, by conduct purely self-regarding, from the performance of some definite duty incumbent on him to the public, he is guilty of a social offense. No person ought to be punished simply for being drunk; but a soldier or a policeman should be punished for being drunk on duty. Whenever, in short, there is a definite damage, or a definite risk of damage, either to an individual or to the public, the case is taken out of the province of liberty, and placed in that of morality or law.

*11.* But with regard to the merely contingent, or, as it may be called, constructive injury which a person causes to society, by conduct which neither violates any specific duty to the public, nor occasions perceptible hurt to any assignable individual except himself; the inconvenience is one which society can afford to bear, for the sake of the greater good of human freedom. If grown persons are to be punished for not taking proper care of themselves, I would rather it were for their own sake, than under pretense of preventing them from impairing their capacity of rendering to society benefits which society does not pretend it has a right to exact. But I cannot consent to argue the point as if society had no means of bringing its weaker members up to its ordinary standard of rational conduct, except waiting till they do something irrational, and then punishing them, legally or morally, for it. Society has had absolute power over them during all the early portion of their existence: it has had the whole period of childhood and nonage in which to try whether it could make them capable of rational conduct in life. The existing generation is master both of the training and the entire circumstances of the generation to come; it cannot indeed make them perfectly wise and good, because it is itself so lamentably deficient in goodness and wisdom; and its best efforts are not always, in individual cases, its most successful ones; but it is perfectly well able to make the rising generation, as a whole, as good as, and a little better than, itself. If society lets any considerable number of its members grow up mere children, incapable of being acted on by rational consideration of distant motives, society has itself to blame for the consequences. Armed not only with all the powers of education, but with the ascendancy which the authority of a received opinion always exercises over the minds who are least fitted to judge for themselves; and aided by the *natural* penalties which cannot be prevented from falling on those who incur the distaste or the contempt of those who know them; let not society pretend that it needs, besides all this, the power to issue commands and enforce obedience in the personal concerns of individuals, in which, on all principles of justice and policy, the decision ought to rest with those who are to abide the consequences. Nor is there anything which tends more to discredit and frustrate the better means of influencing conduct, than a resort to the worse. If there be among those whom it is attempted to coerce into prudence or temperance, any of the material of which vigorous and independent characters are made, they will infallibly rebel against the yoke. No such person will ever feel that others have a right to control him in his concerns, such as they have to prevent him from injuring them in theirs; and it easily comes to be considered a mark of spirit and courage to fly in the face of such usurped authority, and do with ostentation the exact opposite of what it enjoins; as in the fashion of grossness which succeeded, in the time of Charles II, to the fanatical moral intolerance of the Puritans. With respect to what is said of the necessity of protecting society from the bad example set to others by the vicious or the self-indulgent; it is true that bad example may have a pernicious effect, especially the example of doing wrong to others with impunity to the wrong-doer. But we are now speaking of conduct which, while it does no wrong to others, is supposed to do great harm to the agent himself: and I do not see how those who believe this, can think otherwise than that the example, on the whole, must be more salutary than hurtful, since, if it displays the misconduct, it displays also the painful or degrading consequences which, if the conduct is justly censured, must be supposed to be in all or most cases attendant on it.

12. But the strongest of all the arguments against the interference of the public with purely personal conduct, is that when it does interfere, the odds are that it interferes wrongly, and in the wrong place. On questions of social morality, of duty to others, the opinion of the public, that is, of an overruling majority, though often wrong, is likely to be still oftener right; because on such questions they are only required to judge of their own interests; of the manner in which some mode of conduct, if allowed to be practiced, would affect themselves. But the opinion of a similar majority, imposed as a law on the minority, on questions of self-regarding conduct, is quite as likely to be wrong as right; for in these cases public opinion means, at the best, some people's opinion of what is good or bad for other people; while very often it does not even mean that; the public, with the most perfect indifference, passing over the pleasure or convenience of those whose conduct they censure, and considering only their own preference. There are many who consider as an injury to themselves any conduct which they have a distaste for, and resent it as an outrage to their feelings; as a religious bigot, when charged with disregarding the religious feelings of others, has been known to retort that they disregard his feelings, by persisting in their abominable worship or creed. But there is no parity between the feeling of a person for his own opinion, and the feeling of another who is offended at his holding it; no more than between the desire of a thief to take a purse, and the desire of the right owner to keep it. And a person's taste is as much his own peculiar concern as his opinion or his purse. It is easy for any one to imagine an ideal public, which leaves the freedom and choice of individuals in all uncertain matters undisturbed, and only requires them to abstain from modes

of conduct which universal experience has condemned. But where has there been seen a public which set any such limit to its censorship? or when does the public trouble itself about universal experience? In its interferences with personal conduct it is seldom thinking of anything but the enormity of acting or feeling differently from itself; and this standard of judgment, thinly disguised, is held up to mankind as the dictate of religion and philosophy, by nine-tenths of all moralists and speculative writers. These teach that things are right because they are right; because we feel them to be so. They tell us to search in our own minds and hearts for laws of conduct binding on ourselves and on all others. What can the poor public do but apply these instructions, and make their own personal feelings of good and evil, if they are tolerably unanimous in them, obligatory on all the world?

*13.* The evil here pointed out is not one which exists only in theory; and it may perhaps be expected that I should specify the instances in which the public of this age and country improperly invests its own preferences with the character of moral laws. I am not writing an essay on the aberrations of existing moral feeling. That is too weighty a subject to be discussed parenthetically, and by way of illustration. Yet examples are necessary, to show that the principle I maintain is of serious and practical moment, and that I am not endeavoring to erect a barrier against imaginary evils. And it is not difficult to show, by abundant instances, that to extend the bounds of what may be called moral police, until it encroaches on the most unquestionably legitimate liberty of the individual, is one of the most universal of all human propensities.

*14.* As a first instance, consider the antipathies which men cherish on no better grounds than that persons whose religious opinions are different from theirs do not practice their religious observances, especially their religious abstinences. To cite a rather trivial example, nothing in the creed or practice of Christians does more to envenom the hatred of Mohammedans against them, than the fact of their eating pork. There are few acts which Christians and Europeans regard with more unaffected disgust, than Mussulmans regard this particular mode of satisfying hunger. It is, in the first place, an offense against their religion; but this circumstance by no means explains either the degree or the kind of their repugnance; for wine also is forbidden by their religion, and to partake of it is by all Mussulmans accounted wrong, but not disgusting. Their aversion to the flesh of the "unclean beast" is, on the contrary, of that peculiar character, resembling an instinctive antipathy, which the idea of uncleanness, when once it thoroughly sinks into the feelings, seems always to excite even in those whose personal habits are anything but scrupulously cleanly, and of which the sentiment of religious impurity, so intense in the Hindoos, is a remarkable example. Suppose now that in a people, of whom the majority were Mussulmans, the majority should insist upon not permitting pork to be eaten within the limits of the country. This would be nothing new in Mohammedan countries.[1] Would it be a legitimate exercise of the moral authority of public opinion? and if not, why not? The practice is really revolting to such a public. They also sincerely think that it is forbidden and abhorred by the Deity. Neither could the prohibition be censured as religious persecution. It might be religious in its origin, but it would not be persecution for religion, since nobody's religion makes it a duty to eat pork. The only tenable ground of condemnation would be, that with the personal tastes and self-regarding concerns of individuals the public has no business to interfere.

15. To come somewhat nearer home: the majority of Spaniards consider it a gross impiety, offensive in the highest degree to the Supreme Being, to worship him in any other manner than the Roman Catholic; and no other public worship is lawful on Spanish soil. The people of all Southern Europe look upon a married clergy as not only irreligious, but unchaste, indecent, gross, disgusting. What do Protestants think of these perfectly sincere feelings, and of the attempt to enforce them against non-Catholics? Yet, if mankind are justified in interfering with each other's liberty in things which do not concern the interests of others, on what principle is it possible consistently to exclude these cases? or who can blame people for desiring to suppress what they regard as a scandal in the sight of God and man? No stronger case can be shown for prohibiting anything which is regarded as a personal immorality, than is made out for suppressing these practices in the eyes of those who regard them as impieties; and unless we are willing to adopt the logic of persecutors, and to say that we may persecute others because we are right, and that they must not persecute us because they are wrong, we must beware of admitting a principle of which we should resent as a gross injustice the application to ourselves.

16. The preceding instances may be objected to, although unreasonably, as drawn from contingencies impossible among us: opinion, in this country, not being likely to enforce abstinence from meats, or to interfere with people for worshiping, and for either marrying or not marrying, according to their creed or inclination. The next example, however, shall be taken from an interference with liberty which we have by no means passed all danger of. Wherever the Puritans have been sufficiently powerful, as in New England, and in Great Britain at the time of the Com-

---

[1] The case of the Bombay Parsees is a curious instance in point. When this industrious and enterprising tribe, the descendants of the Persian fire-worshipers, flying from their native country before the Caliphs, arrived in Western India, they were admitted to toleration by the Hindoo sovereigns, on condition of not eating beef. When those regions afterwards fell under the dominion of Mohammedan conquerors, the Parsees obtained from them a continuance of indulgence, on condition of refraining from pork. What was at first obedience to authority became a second nature, and the Parsees to this day abstain both from beef and pork. Though not required by their religion, the double abstinence has had time to grow into a custom of their tribe; and custom, in the East, is a religion.

monwealth, they have endeavored, with considerable success, to put down all public, and nearly all private, amusements: especially music, dancing, public games, or other assemblages for purposes of diversion, and the theater. There are still in this country large bodies of persons by whose notions of morality and religion these recreations are condemned; and those persons belonging chiefly to the middle class, who are the ascendant power in the present social and political condition of the kingdom, it is by no means impossible that persons of these sentiments may at some time or other command a majority in Parliament. How will the remaining portion of the community like to have the amusements that shall be permitted to them regulated by the religious and moral sentiments of the stricter Calvinists and Methodists? Would they not, with considerable peremptoriness, desire these intrusively pious members of society to mind their own business? This is precisely what should be said to every government and every public, who have the pretension that no person shall enjoy any pleasure which they think wrong. But if the principle of the pretension be admitted, no one can reasonably object to its being acted on in the sense of the majority, or other preponderating power in the country; and all persons must be ready to conform to the idea of a Christian commonwealth, as understood by the early settlers in New England, if a religious profession similar to theirs should ever succeed in regaining its lost ground, as religions supposed to be declining have so often been known to do.

*17.* To imagine another contingency, perhaps more likely to be realized than the one last mentioned. There is confessedly a strong tendency in the modern world towards a democratic constitution of society, accompanied or not by popular political institutions. It is affirmed that in the country where this tendency is most completely realized—where both society and the government are most democratic—the United States—the feeling of the majority, to whom any appearance of a more showy or costly style of living than they can hope to rival is disagreeable, operates as a tolerably effectual sumptuary law, and that in many parts of the Union it is really difficult for a person possessing a very large income, to find any mode of spending it, which will not incur popular disapprobation. Though such statements as these are doubtless much exaggerated as a representation of existing facts, the state of things they describe is not only a conceivable and possible, but a probable result of democratic feeling, combined with the notion that the public has a right to a veto on the manner in which individuals shall spend their incomes. We have only further to suppose a considerable diffusion of Socialist opinions, and it may become infamous in the eyes of the majority to possess more property than some very small amount, or any income not earned by manual labor. Opinions similar in principle to these, already prevail widely among the artisan class, and weigh oppressively on those who are amenable to the opinion chiefly of that class, namely, its own members. It is known that the bad workmen who form the majority of the operatives in many branches of industry, are decidedly of opinion that bad workmen ought to receive the same wages as good, and that no one ought to be allowed, through piecework or otherwise, to earn by superior skill or industry more than others can without it. And they employ a moral police, which occasionally becomes a physical one, to deter skillful workmen from receiving, and employers from giving, a larger remuneration for a more useful service. If the public have any jurisdiction over private concerns, I cannot see that these people are in fault, or that any individual's particular public can be blamed for asserting the same authority over his individual conduct, which the general public asserts over people in general.

*18.* But, without dwelling upon supposititious cases, there are, in our own day, gross usurpations upon the liberty of private life actually practiced, and still greater ones threatened with some expectation of success, and opinions propounded which assert an unlimited right in the public not only to prohibit by law everything which it thinks wrong, but in order to get at what it thinks wrong, to prohibit any number of things which it admits to be innocent.

*19.* Under the name of preventing intemperance, the people of one English colony, and of nearly half the United States, have been interdicted by law from making any use whatever of fermented drinks, except for medical purposes: for prohibition of their sale is in fact, as it is intended to be, prohibition of their use. And though the impracticability of executing the law has caused its repeal in several of the States which had adopted it, including the one from which it derives its name, an attempt has notwithstanding been commenced, and is prosecuted with considerable zeal by many of the professed philanthropists, to agitate for a similar law in this country. The association, or "Alliance" as it terms itself, which has been formed for this purpose, has acquired some notoriety through the publicity given to a correspondence between its Secretary and one of the very few English public men who hold that a politician's opinions ought to be founded on principles. Lord Stanley's share in this correspondence is calculated to strengthen the hopes already built on him, by those who know how rare such qualities as are manifested in some of his public appearances, unhappily are among those who figure in political life. The organ of the Alliance, who would "deeply deplore the recognition of any principle which could be wrested to justify bigotry and persecution," undertakes to point out the "broad and impassable barrier" which divides such principles from those of the association. "All matters relating to thought, opinion, conscience, appear to me," he says, "to be without the sphere of legislation; all pertaining to social act, habit, relation, subject only to a discretionary power vested in the State itself, and not in the individual, to be within it." No mention is made of a third class, different from either of these, viz. acts and habits which are not social, but individual; although it is to this class, surely, that the act of drinking fermented liquors belongs. Selling fermented liquors, however, is trading, and trading is a social act. But the infringement complained of is not on the liberty of the seller, but on that of the buyer and consumer; since the State might just as well forbid him to drink wine, as purposely make it impossible for him to obtain it. The Secretary, however, says, "I claim, as a citizen, a right to legislate whenever my social rights are invaded by the social act of another." And now for the definition of these "social rights." "If anything invades my social rights, certainly the traffic in strong drink does. It destroys my primary right of security, by constantly creating and stimulating social disorder. It invades my right of equality, by deriving a profit from the creation of a misery I am taxed to support. It impedes my right to free moral and intellectual development, by surrounding my path with dangers, and by weakening and demoralizing society, from which I have a right to claim mutual aid and intercourse." A theory of "social rights," the like of which probably never before found its way into distinct language: being nothing short of this—that it is the absolute social right of every individual, that every other individual shall act in every respect exactly as he ought; that whosoever fails thereof in the smallest particular, violates my social right, and entitles me to demand from the legislature the removal of the grievance. So monstrous a principle is far more dangerous than any single interference with liberty; there is no violation of liberty which it would not justify; it acknowledges no right to any freedom whatever, except perhaps to that of holding opinions in secret, without ever disclosing them: for, the moment an opinion which I consider noxious passes any one's lips, it invades all the "social rights" attributed to me by the Alliance. The doctrine ascribes to all mankind a vested interest in each other's moral, intellectual, and even physical perfection, to be defined by each claimant according to his own standard.

20. Another important example of illegitimate interference with the rightful liberty of the individual, not simply threatened, but long since carried into triumphant effect, is Sabbatarian legislation. Without doubt, abstinence on one day in the week, so far as the exigencies of life permit, from the usual daily occupation, though in no respect religiously binding on any except Jews, is a highly beneficial custom. And inasmuch as this custom cannot be observed without a general consent to that effect among the industrious classes, therefore, in so far as some persons by working may impose the same necessity on others, it may be allowable and right that the law should guarantee to each the observance by others of the custom, by suspending the greater operations of industry on a particular day. But this justification, grounded on the direct interest which others have in each individual's observance of the practice, does not apply to the self-chosen occupations in which a person may think fit to employ

his leisure; nor does it hold good, in the smallest degree, for legal restrictions on amusements. It is true that the amusement of some is the day's work of others; but the pleasure, not to say the useful recreation, of many, is worth the labor of a few, provided the occupation is freely chosen, and can be freely resigned. The operatives are perfectly right in thinking that if all worked on Sunday, seven days' work would have to be given for six days' wages: but so long as the great mass of employments are suspended, the small number who for the enjoyment of others must still work, obtain a proportional increase of earnings; and they are not obliged to follow those occupations, if they prefer leisure to emolument. If a further remedy is sought, it might be found in the establishment by custom of a holiday on some other day of the week for those particular classes of persons. The only ground, therefore, on which restrictions on Sunday amusements can be defended, must be that they are religiously wrong; a motive of legislation which never can be too earnestly protested against. "Deorum injuriae Diis curae." It remains to be proved that society or any of its officers holds a commission from on high to avenge any supposed offense to Omnipotence, which is not also a wrong to our fellow creatures. The notion that it is one man's duty that another should be religious, was the foundation of all the religious persecutions ever perpetrated, and if admitted, would fully justify them. Though the feeling which breaks out in the repeated attempts to stop railway traveling on Sunday, in the resistance to the opening of Museums, and the like, has not the cruelty of the old persecutors, the state of mind indicated by it is fundamentally the same. It is a determination not to tolerate others in doing what is permitted by their religion, because it is not permitted by the persecutor's religion. It is a belief that God not only abominates the act of the misbeliever, but will not hold us guiltless if we leave him unmolested.

21. I cannot refrain from adding to these examples of the little account commonly made of human liberty, the language of downright persecution which breaks out from the press of this country, whenever it feels called on to notice the remarkable phenomenon of Mormonism. Much might be said on the unexpected and instructive fact, that an alleged new revelation, and a religion founded on it, the product of palpable imposture, not even supported by the *prestige* of extraordinary qualities in its founder, is believed by hundreds of thousands, and has been made the foundation of a society, in the age of newspapers, railways, and the electric telegraph. What here concerns us is, that this religion, like other and better religions, has its martyrs; that its prophet and founder was, for his teaching, put to death by a mob; that others of its adherents lost their lives by the same lawless violence; that they were forcibly expelled, in a body, from the country in which they first grew up; while, now that they have been chased into a solitary recess in the midst of a desert, many in this country openly declare that it would be right (only that it is not con-

venient) to send an expedition against them, and compel them by force
to conform to the opinions of other people. The article of the Mormonite
doctrine which is the chief provocative to the antipathy which thus breaks
through the ordinary restraints of religious tolerance, is its sanction of
polygamy; which, though permitted to Mohammedans, and Hindoos, and
Chinese, seems to excite unquenchable animosity when practiced by persons who speak English, and profess to be a kind of Christians. No one
has a deeper disapprobation than I have of this Mormon institution; both
for other reasons, and because, far from being in any way countenanced
by the principle of liberty, it is a direct infraction of that principle, being
a mere riveting of the chains of one-half of the community, and an emancipation of the other from reciprocity of obligation towards them. Still, it
must be remembered that this relation is as much voluntary on the part
of the women concerned in it, and who may be deemed the sufferers by
it, as is the case with any other form of the marriage institution; and
however surprising this fact may appear, it has its explanation in the common ideas and customs of the world, which teaching women to think marriage the one thing needful, make it intelligible that many a woman
should prefer being one of several wives, to not being a wife at all. Other
countries are not asked to recognize such unions, or release any portion
of their inhabitants from their own laws on the score of Mormonite opinions. But when the dissentients have conceded to the hostile sentiments
of others, far more than could justly be demanded; when they have left
the countries to which their doctrines were unacceptable, and established
themselves in a remote corner of the earth, which they have been the
first to render habitable to human beings; it is difficult to see on what
principles but those of tyranny they can be prevented from living there
under what laws they please, provided they commit no aggression on
other nations, and allow perfect freedom of departure to those who are
dissatisfied with their ways. A recent writer, in some respects of considerable merit, proposes (to use his own words) not a crusade, but a *civiliz-
ade,* against this polygamous community, to put an end to what seems to
him a retrograde step in civilization. It also appears so to me, but I am
not aware that any community has a right to force another to be civilized.
So long as the sufferers by the bad law do not invoke assistance from other
communities, I cannot admit that persons entirely unconnected with
them ought to step in and require that a condition of things with which
all who are directly interested appear to be satisfied, should be put an
end to because it is a scandal to persons some thousands of miles distant,
who have no part or concern in it. Let them send missionaries, if they
please, to preach against it; and let them, by any fair means (of which
silencing the teachers is not one), oppose the progress of similar doctrines
among their own people. If civilization has got the better of barbarism
when barbarism had the world to itself, it is too much to profess to be

afraid lest barbarism, after having been fairly got under, should revive and conquer civilization. A civilization that can thus succumb to its vanquished enemy, must first have become so degenerate, that neither its appointed priests and teachers, nor anybody else, has the capacity, or will take the trouble, to stand up for it. If this be so, the sooner such a civilization receives notice to quit, the better. It can only go on from bad to worse, until destroyed and regenerated (like the Western Empire) by energetic barbarians.

# Questions

1. What may a society justifiably force its members to do at all costs?
2. What should the precise and ideal boundary be, as you determine it from Mill's general statements and the particular cases he examines, between sanctions imposed by morality (the opinions of others) and those imposed by law (judgments rendered by authority of the state)?
3. Compare and contrast Mill's principal concern and that of Spinoza in describing rightful limits to sovereignty of the individual and to that of society (*societas*).
4. What should society's responsibility be, according to Mill, to restrain a person from acts that will (1) bring him moral disapprobation; (2) cause grave injury to himself only; (3) impair his ability to fulfill a distinct and assignable obligation to another person; (4) impair his ability to fulfill duties to society?
5. Mill cites a number of examples to illustrate his general point of view. Which of the cases referred to by Mill concern the right or wrong use of (1) expressions of moral reprobation; (2) moral retribution and punishment; (3) legal sanctions?
6. Distinguish the propositions made by Mill in paragraph 3 and then show how each is analyzed, expanded, or qualified in paragraphs 4 through 21. At the end of paragraph 13 how does Mill shift the entire focus of his discourse?

# Theme Topics

1. Write an essay describing why you would or would not like to live in a society that embodied the principles advocated by Mill. Compare and contrast this society with the one in which you now find yourself living.
2. Write an essay in which you define "liberal" and "conservative" and then classify Aristotle, Spinoza, and Mill as either one or the other on the basis of evidence you cite and valid inferences you draw from the selections by each of these three writers.

# ·58·

*Walter Lippmann*

# THE DEFENSE OF CIVILITY

### THE LANGUAGE OF ACCOMMODATION

*1.* Men have been laboring with the problem of how to make concrete and real what is abstract and immaterial ever since the Greek philosophers began to feel the need to accommodate the popular Homeric religion to the advance of science. The theologians, says Aristotle, are like the philosophers in that they promulgate certain doctrines; but they are unlike them in that they do so in mythical form.[1]

*2.* The method of accommodation employed by the philosophers has been to treat the materialization in the myth as allegory: as translation of the same knowledge into another language.[2] To converse with the devil, for example, could then mean what literally it says—to talk face to face with the devil, a concrete materialized personage. But it could mean, also, the imitation of a wicked nature without—as the Cambridge Platonist John Smith wrote, "a mutual local presence,"[3] that is to say without meeting a devil in person. This was an accommodation to those who, believing in the wickedness of evil, could not believe in the personified devil. The devil could mean either "some apostate spirit as one particular being," and also "the spirit of apostasie which is lodged in all men's natures." This is the method of plural interpretation; it uses "the language of accommodation." It is justified and legitimate, said John Smith in his discourse entitled "A Christian's Conflicts and Conquests," because "truth is content, when it comes into the world, to wear our mantles, to learn our language, to conform itself as it were to our dress and fashions . . . it speaks with the most idiotical sort of men in the most idiotical way, and becomes all things to all men, as every sonne of truth should do for their good."[4]

[1] Werner Jaeger, *The Theology of the Early Greek Philosophers* (The Gifford Lectures, 1936), p. 10. Cf. Aristotle, *Metaphysics*, Bk. III, Ch. 4, 1000a 4-18.
[2] Cf. Basil Willey, *The Seventeenth Century Background* (1952), Ch. IV.
[3] *Ibid.*, p. 138 *et seq.*
[4] *Ibid.*, p. 146.

### THE LIMITS OF ACCOMMODATION

3. But there are limits beyond which we cannot carry the time-honored method of accommodating the diversity of beliefs. As we know from the variety and sharpness of schisms and sects in our time, we have gone beyond the limits of accommodation. We know, too, that as the divisions grow wider and more irreconcilable, there arise issues of loyalty with which the general principle of toleration is unable to cope.

4. For the toleration of differences is possible only on the assumption that there is no vital threat to the community. Toleration is not, therefore, a sufficient principle for dealing with the diversity of opinions and beliefs. It is itself dependent upon the positive principle of accommodation. The principle calls for the effort to find agreement beneath the differences.

5. In studying how accommodation is achieved, we may begin by observing that it is the philosophers, using Aristotle's broad terminology, who work out and promote the plural interpretation. They propose the terms for accommodating their immaterial belief to the concrete and materialized imagery of the fundamentalists. Thus it was the Cambridge Platonist, John Smith, who took the initiative about the devil. John Smith was not addressing the fundamentalists who believed in the personified devil; in fact what he said about the whole matter was not meant to trouble the fundamentalists at all. He was addressing men who were unable to believe in the personified devil and yet were still in essential communion with the fundamentalists. For they did believe in the spirit of the devil which, as everyone knows, is in all of us. In this accommodation the Christian Platonists gave up trying to believe what they could not believe. They went on believing that which in its essence their fundamentalist neighbors believed. Thus they could continue to live in the same community with them.

6. There is an impressive historical example of how by accommodation it is possible to communicate these difficult truths to a large heterogeneous society. In mediaeval Christendom a great subject of accommodation was the origin and sanction of the public philosophy itself, of the natural laws of the rational order. Otto von Gierke says that despite the innumerable learned controversies of the lawyers, the theologians and the philosophers, "all were agreed that there was natural law, which, on the one hand, radiated from a principle transcending earthly power, and on the other hand was true and perfectly binding law . . . the highest power on earth was subject to the rules of natural law. They stood above the Pope and above the Kaiser, above the ruler and above the sovereign people, nay, above the whole community of mortals. Neither statute nor act of government, neither resolution of the people nor custom, could break the

bounds that thus were set. Whatever contradicted the eternal and immutable principles of natural law was utterly void and would bind no one." [5]

7. But though there was agreement on this, there was deep controversy over whether the natural laws were the commands of God or whether they were the dictates of an eternal reason, grounded on the being of God, and unalterable even by God himself. How were men to imagine, to materialize and make concrete the natural law which is above the Pope and the Kaiser and all mortals? As decrees of an omniscient and omnipotent heavenly king? Or as the principles of the nature of things? There were some who could not conceive of binding laws which had to be obeyed unless there was a lawgiver made in the image of the human lawgivers they had seen or heard about. There were others to whose capacity it was not necessary to condescend with quite that much materialization.

8. The crucial point, however, is not where the naturalists and supernaturalists disagreed. It is that they did agree that there was a valid law which, whether it was the commandment of God or the reason of things, was transcendent. They did agree that it was not something decided upon by certain men and then proclaimed by them. It was not someone's fancy, someone's prejudice, someone's wish or rationalization, a psychological experience and no more. It is there objectively, not subjectively. It can be discovered. It has to be obeyed.

## THE DEATH OF GOD

9. As long, then, as both the philosopher and the theologian believe in the objective order, there can be accommodation about the degree and kind of materialization. The range and variety of men's capacity to understand is very great. So, too, must be the range and variety of the images which condescend to their varying capacities. We can, therefore, avoid much misunderstanding if we do not confound the materialization—which is the mode of communicating belief—with the subject of the belief. For not until we go down under the comparatively superficial question of belief or unbelief, in any particular materialization, do we find the radical problems of belief and unbelief.

10. When Martin Buber speaks of "the great images of God fashioned by mankind." [6] he recognizes that there can be many images, or indeed that there can be no image which has concreteness to our sense perceptions.

[5] Otto von Gierke, *Political Theories of the Middle Age*, translated with an Introduction by Frederick William Maitland (Cambridge University Press, 1927). Cf. pp. 73-87 and more especially Note 256.

[6] Martin Buber, *Eclipse of God* (1952), p. 22.

*11.* The critical question does not turn on whether men do or do not believe in an imagery. It turns on whether they believe that a man is able "to experience a reality absolutely independent of himself." When Sartre, following Nietzsche, says that "God is dead," the critical point is not that he refuses to believe in the existence, however attenuated, of an anthropomorphic God. There can be, indeed there is, great faith and deep religion without any concrete image of God. The radical unbelief lies underneath the metaphor of God's death. It is in Sartre's saying that "if I have done away with God the Father, someone is needed to invent values . . . life has no meaning *a priori* . . . it is up to you to give it a meaning, and value is nothing but the meaning that you choose." [7]

*12.* With this, Sartre has done away not only with God the Father but with the recognition that beyond our private worlds there is a public world to which we belong. If what is good, what is right, what is true, is only what the individual "chooses" to "invent," then we are outside the traditions of civility. We are back in the war of all men against all men. There is left no ground for accommodation among the varieties of men; nor is there in this proclamation of anarchy a will to find an accommodation.

*13.* And why, we may ask, is there among such modern philosophers as these no concern like that of their great predecessors, to find an accommodation? It is not only because they themselves have ceased to believe in the metaphors—in the sacred images. They have ceased to believe that behind the metaphors and the sacred images there is any kind of independent reality that can be known and must be recognized.

*14.* Thus they reject "the concept of 'truth' as something dependent upon facts largely outside human control," which, as Bertrand Russell says, "has been one of the ways in which philosophy hitherto has inculcated the necessary element of humility. When this check upon pride is removed, a further step is taken on the road towards a certain kind of madness—the intoxication of power which invaded philosophy with Fichte . . . and to which modern men, whether philosophers or not, are prone. I am persuaded that this intoxication is the greatest danger of our time, and that any philosophy which, however unintentionally, contributes to it is increasing the danger of vast social disaster." [8]

## THE MANDATE OF HEAVEN

*15.* At the end, then, the questions are how we conceive of ourselves and the public world beyond our private selves. Much depends upon the philosophers. For though they are not kings, they are, we may say, the

---

[7] Jean Paul Sartre, *Existentialism,* translated by Bernard Frechtman (1947), p. 58. See also Martin Buber, *op. cit.,* p. 93.

[8] Bertrand Russell, *History of Western Philosophy* (1945), p. 828.

teachers of the teachers. "In the history of Western governments," says Francis G. Wilson,[9] "the transitions of society can be marked by the changing character of the intellectuals," who have served the government as lawyers, advisers, administrators, who have been teachers in the schools, who have been members of professions like medicine and theology. It is through them that doctrines are made to operate in practical affairs. And their doctrine, which they, themselves, have learned in the schools and universities, will have the shape and the reference and the direction which the prevailing philosophy gives it.

*16.* That is how and why philosophy and theology are the ultimate and decisive studies in which we engage. In them are defined the main characteristics of the images of man which will be acted upon in the arts and science of the epoch. The role of philosophers is rarely, no doubt, creative. But it is critical, in that they have a deciding influence in determining what may be believed, how it can be believed, and what cannot be believed. The philosophers, one might say, stand at the crossroads. While they may not cause the traffic to move, they can stop it and start it, they can direct it one way or the other.

*17.* I do not contend, though I hope, that the decline of Western society will be arrested if the teachers in our schools and universities come back to the great tradition of the public philosophy. But I do contend that the decline, which is already far advanced, cannot be arrested if the prevailing philosophers oppose this restoration and revival, if they impugn rather than support the validity of an order which is superior to the values that Sartre tells each man "to invent."

*18.* What the prevailing philosophers say about religion is not itself, in Tillich's terms, religion as an ultimate concern of worship and of love. But if the philosophers teach that religious experience is a purely psychological phenomenon, related to nothing beyond each man's psychic condition, then they will give educated men a bad intellectual conscience if they have religious experiences. The philosopher cannot give them religion. But they can keep them away from it.

*19.* Philosophers play the same role in relation to the principles of the good society. These require, as we have seen, the mastery of human nature in the raw by an acquired rational second nature. In the literal sense, the principles of the good society must be unpopular until they have prevailed sufficiently to alter the popular impulses. For the popular impulses are opposed to public principles. These principles cannot be made to prevail if they are discredited, if they are dismissed as superstition, as obscurantism, as meaningless metaphysics, as reactionary, as self-seeking rationalizations.

*20.* The public philosophy is in a large measure intellectually discred-

[9] Francis G. Wilson, "Public Opinion and the Intellectuals," in *American Political Science Review* (June 1954).

ited among contemporary men. Because of that, what we may call the terms of discourse in public controversy are highly unfavorable to anyone who adheres to the public philosophy. The signs and seals of legitimacy, of rightness and of truth, have been taken over by men who reject, even when they are not the avowed adversaries of, the doctrine of constitutional democracy.

21. If the decline of the West under the misrule of the people is to be halted, it will be necessary to alter these terms of discourse. They are now set overwhelmingly against the credibility and against the rightness of the principles of the constitutional state; they are set in favor of the Jacobin conception of the emancipated and sovereign people.

22. I have been arguing, hopefully and wishfully, that it may be possible to alter the terms of discourse if a convincing demonstration can be made that the principles of the good society are not, in Sartre's phrase, invented and chosen—that the conditions which must be met if there is to be a good society are there, outside our wishes, where they can be discovered by rational inquiry, and developed and adapted and refined by rational discussion.

23. If eventually this were demonstrated successfully, it would, I believe, rearm all those who are concerned with the anomy of our society, with its progressive barbarization, and with its descent into violence and tyranny. Amidst the quagmire of moral impressionism they would stand again on hard intellectual ground where there are significant objects that are given and are not merely projected, that are compelling and are not merely wished. Their hope would be re-established that there is a public world, sovereign above the infinite number of contradictory and competing private worlds. Without this certainty, their struggle must be unavailing.

24. As the defenders of civility, they cannot do without the signs and seals of legitimacy, of rightness and of truth. For it is a practical rule, well known to experienced men, that the relation is very close between our capacity to act at all and our conviction that the action we are taking is right. This does not mean, of course, that the action is necessarily right. What is necessary to continuous action is that it shall be *believed* to be right. Without that belief, most men will not have the energy and will to persevere in the action. Thus satanism, which prefers evil as such, is present in some men and perhaps potential in many. Yet, except in a condition of the profoundest hysteria, as in a lynching, satanism cannot be preached to multitudes. Even Hitler, who was enormously satanic and delighted in monstrous evil, did nevertheless need, it would seem, to be reassured that he was not only a great man but, in a mysterious way, a righteous one.

25. William Jennings Bryan once said that to be clad in the armor of righteousness will make the humblest citizen of all the land stronger than

all the hosts of error.[10] That is not quite true. But the reason the humblest
citizen is not stronger than the hosts of error is that the latter also are
clad in an armor which they at least believe is the armor of righteousness.
Had they not been issued the armor of righteousness, they would not, as
a matter of fact, be a host at all. For political ideas acquire operative
force in human affairs when, as we have seen, they acquire legitimacy,
when they have the title of being right which binds men's consciences.
Then they possess, as the Confucian doctrine has it, "the mandate of
heaven."

26. In the crisis within the Western society, there is at issue now the
mandate of heaven.

# Questions

1. What meanings does Lippmann give to the following terms and how does
   he relate them to each other: "method of accommodation," "accommodation," "plural interpretation," "materialization."
2. According to Lippmann, what is the role of the philosopher, and the intellectual in general, in the history of the world?
3. What is the meaning of "anomy" (paragraph 23)? (Consult Webster's
   *Third.*) What relationship does it bear to "the death of God"? In what
   sense is "the mandate of heaven" an answer to anomy? What is "satanism"
   (paragraph 24)? Gather what outstanding examples you can from recent
   history of anomic or satanic events.
4. What basic assumption is Lippmann making about the causes of human
   history?
5. In Lippmann's view is "the public philosophy" accommodatable, in the last
   analysis, with the point of view that man can never "experience a reality
   absolutely independent of himself"? In your view? Why? Do you see any
   possible contradiction in the phrase "to experience a reality absolutely
   independent of himself"?

# Theme Topics

1. Write a theme in which you relate the two essays by C. S. Lewis in this
   book with Lippmann's views on natural law and a public philosophy. Show
   how each perceives the need for and the existence of an objective order
   independent of human experience.

[10] Speech at Democratic National Convention (Chicago, 1896).

2. Write an essay that develops the thesis implicit in either of the following titles:

> Lippmann: Basic Strategies for Social Order
> Lippmann: Confessions of a Timid Intellectual

In composing your essay, make as much use as you can of relevant points of view expressed by Aristotle, Spinoza, and Mill.

# ·59·

## *Arthur M. Schlesinger, Jr.*

# WALTER LIPPMANN:
# THE INTELLECTUAL V. POLITICS

*1.* Lippmann began writing *The Public Philosophy* in 1938; it was finally published sixteen years later. Its argument was in curious counterpoint with that of *The Phantom Public,* taking off from a major conclusion of the earlier work but using that conclusion to justify a diametrically opposite philosophical result. In *The Phantom Public,* it is to be recalled, Lippmann's note of hope against the irreducible pluralism of the world was "the maintenance of a regime of rule, contract and custom." In 1925, this was for Lippmann a procedural conception. But in the years thereafter, what began as a functional necessity was somehow hypostatized into a transcendental faith—and then employed to abolish the very pluralism which had originally produced it. The invocation of due process grew into "a universal order on which all reasonable men were agreed," "a common conception of law and order which possesses a universal validity," natural law, the public philosophy. By this he meant the realm of essences ("I am using the ambiguous but irreplaceable word 'essence' as meaning the true and undistorted nature of things"), a world of "immaterial entities . . . not to be perceived by our senses," but nonetheless more real than anything else.

It was not someone's fancy, someone's prejudice, someone's wish or rationalization, a psychological experience and no more. It is there objectively, not subjectively. It can be discovered. It has to be obeyed.

From "Walter Lippmann: the Intellectual vs. Politics" by Arthur M. Schlesinger, Jr. in *Walter Lippmann and His Times,* © 1959 by Marquis Childs and James Reston and reprinted by permission of Harcourt, Brace & World, Inc. and Brandt & Brandt.

2. In the name of the public philosophy, Lippmann spurned his pluralism of the twenties. A "large plural society," he argued, could not be
governed "without recognizing that, transcending its plural interests,
there is a rational order with a superior common law." This was so because it *had* to be so:

As the diversity of belief, opinion and interest became greater, the need for a
common criterion and for common laws became more acute. . . . In this
pluralized and fragmenting society a public philosophy with common and binding principles was more necessary than it had ever been.

And it was the responsibility of intellectuals to propagate the public philosophy. Even if they did, it might not be enough to save the West, Lippmann somberly wrote; but, "if the prevailing philosophers oppose this
restoration and revival," the inexorable decline could not be arrested. In
an unwontedly fierce statement from so normally courteous a man, Lippmann even suggested:

There is no reason to think that this condition of mind can be changed until it
can be proved to the modern skeptic that there are certain principles which,
when they have been demonstrated, only the willfully irrational can deny, that
there are certain obligations binding on all men who are committed to a free
society, and that only the willfully subversive can reject them.[1]

3. No one likes to nominate himself as willfully irrational or willfully
subversive. Yet for those brought up in the tradition of James, Lippmann's
conception of natural law, for all its nobility, cannot help seem an artificial
construct. Was he not succumbing to the very danger he warned against
so eloquently a quarter of a century before—the "attempts to escape from
particular purpose into some universal purpose, from personality into
something impersonal"? Was this not, after all, the "flight from the human
problem," the search for "an adjustment, as perfect as possible, as un-
troubled as it was before we were born"? One wonders indeed whether
so acute and honest a mind as Lippmann's can rest long in this solution.
Are there perhaps signs that he is swinging back to a more vivid appreciation of the reality of pluralism? Certainly he was unsparing in his criticism when John Foster Dulles, almost as if in response to Lippmann's
summons to the philosophers, sought to preach something sounding sus-
piciously like the public philosophy to our erring brothers overseas. In his
most recent book, Lippmann appears to recede sharply from the notion
that a single standard can comprehend the multifarious values and activities of the contemporary world. He condemns

the fallacy of assuming that this is one world and that the social order to which
one belongs must either perish or become the universal order of mankind.

[1] Walter Lippmann, *The Public Philosophy* (Boston, Little, Brown, 1955), pp. 110,
104, 142.

"The truth, as I see it," Lippmann now concludes, "is that there has never been one world, that there has never been a universal state or a universal religion." [2] One is tempted to ask: Has there ever been a public philosophy?

4. One can hardly criticize Walter Lippmann for having failed to clear up the problem of the One and the Many. Doubtless a few more years will go by before the great computers will end civilization's long suspense and break the problem down into its definitive mathematical solution. While the discussion lasts, one must be grateful for the urbanity and intelligence with which Lippmann through the years has pursued in his own mind the long dialogue set off by James and Santayana at Harvard half a century ago.

5. As Lippmann has followed out his explorations, he has envisaged a number of roles for the intellectual, though most often as the disinterested voice of some unifying vision, from socialism through science to the public philosophy. For a season in the twenties, the unifying vision disappeared from view; but the urgencies of a collapsing world brought it back. For Lippmann, the intellectual has been most characteristically engaged in ideas, disengaged from movements; he is something different from the man who makes decisions and does things; his responsibility remains always somehow to influence the actor and permeate the culture. One cannot be sure, though, whether he speaks for the public philosophy or for himself.

6. If Lippmann has not really solved the role of the intellectual in free society, it must be said that he has magnificently exemplified it. In *Public Opinion*, he recounts the scene in Book V of *The Republic* when Socrates stalks out after warning Adeimanthis to attribute the uselessness of philosophers "to the fault of those who will not use them, and not to themselves." Lippmann comments: "Thus, in the first great encounter between reason and politics, the strategy of reason was to retire in anger." [3] As the veteran of many such encounters, Lippmann has rarely taken the easy course of withdrawal into irresponsibility. "We are challenged, every one of us," he wrote as a young man, "to think our way out of the terrors amidst which we live." [4] He has not flinched from that challenge. His manner of meeting it has been a credit to himself and often a salvation to his contemporaries.

7. He once spoke of the Compensated Economy; he is himself a wonderful example of the Compensated Mind, seeking through continuous intervention to restore our society to the paths of decency and ration-

[2] Walter Lippmann, *The Communist World and Ours* (Boston, Little, Brown, 1959), pp. 50-1.

[3] Walter Lippmann, *Public Opinion*, p. 311.

[4] Walter Lippmann, *The Stakes of Diplomacy* (New York, Henry Holt, 1915), p. 10.

ality. When the crowd has boasted a common faith, as in the twenties, Lippmann has stressed pluralism; when the crowd appears to have no faith at all, as in the fifties, he stresses monism (except as against the too insistent faith of Mr. Dulles, when he again turns to pluralism); when the crowd is overcommitted to drift, he stresses mastery; when the crowd is overcommitted to mastery, he stresses drift. The classic clarity of his language, studded, it would seem, with lapidary absolutes, has obscured the almost tactile sensitivity of his mind. His commentary has probed the problems of society and the problems of philosophy with unfailing reason and grace. He has preserved a fine magnanimity of temper in rancorous times and against bitterly unfair innuendoes and attack. His spirit has been both independent and compassionate.

8. Above all, Lippmann has insisted in the heat and clamors of the present on the indispensability of the long view. He once wrote,

This is not the last crisis in human affairs. The world will go on somehow, and more crises will follow. It will go on best, however, if among us there are men who have stood apart, who refused to be anxious or too much concerned, who were cool and inquiring and had their eyes on a longer past and a longer future.

By their example they can remind us that the passing moment is only a moment; by their loyalty they will have cherished those things which only the disinterested mind can use.[5]

9. If this is the intellectual's responsibility, then Walter Lippmann has discharged it superbly; and his age stands deeply in his debt.

# Questions

1. What function do the first three paragraphs perform in exposing the first term of Schlesinger's subtitle?
2. What shift do you perceive in the basis of Schlesinger's argument in the next three paragraphs?
3. In paragraph 7 how does Schlesinger adapt one of Lippmann's own concepts to soften the irony he discerns (sentence 5, paragraph 1) in Lippmann's intellectual history?
4. In what sense is the distinction between theory and practice the basic principle in Schlesinger's appraisal of Lippmann?
5. To what extent has Schlesinger proved or failed to prove his conclusions concerning Lippman?

[5] Walter Lippmann, "The Scholar in a Troubled World."

## ·60·

*Carl L. Becker*

# FREEDOM OF SPEECH AND PRESS

*Congress shall make no law . . . abridging the freedom of speech, or of the press; or the right of the people peacefully to assemble, and to petition the government for a redress of grievances.*

FIRST AMENDMENT TO THE CONSTITUTION

1. The tenth amendment to the Constitution states that "the powers not delegated by the Constitution to the United States, nor prohibited by it to the States, are reserved to the States respectively, *or to the people.*" For our purpose the qualifying phrase "to the people" is more important than the rest of the statement, because it discloses the fundamental principle on which all of our governments, state and Federal, are grounded—the principle that in the last analysis all powers are reserved to the people. We might then, without changing our system of government in any way, add another amendment to all of our constitutions: "The powers not delegated to the governments by the people, nor prohibited by them to the individual, are reserved to the individual." This is only another way of saying that our Government purports to be a government of free men, and that restraints on the individual's freedom to act and to speak for himself are self-imposed because defined in laws made by the will of the people.

2. But the will of the people is an intangible thing. "The people" comprises many people—many individuals with diverse and conflicting desires and wills. How can this conflict of wills be reconciled? The practical way in a republic is by majority vote. If the majority wills to prohibit, for example, the sale and manufacture of spirituous liquors, then the minority has to renounce that right; but how then can we say that the minority is not bound against its will or subject to restraints not self-imposed? Rousseau had a solution for this difficulty. He maintained that all members of society have agreed, by an original social compact, to submit their individual wills in particular measures to the general will.

When, therefore, you and I cast our votes for or against a proposed measure, we are not really voting for or against the measure; we are merely voting to determine what the general will is in respect to that measure. If we vote against it, and it turns out that the majority voted for it, we are not defeated, but only enlightened; and since we now know that the majority is for the measure we are for it too, because we have, by the original social compact, already agreed to submit our individual wills to the general will as soon as we know what that will is.

3. Does all this sound like hocus-pocus—a dialectical run-around? It does, a little. But, after all, does it not describe well enough, although with a good deal of verbal gymnastics, what we actually do and think when we vote for or against this or that measure, or for or against this or that party? When we have an election, more especially a presidential election, the Democrats make a tremendous hullabaloo about the country's going to ruin if the Republicans win, and the Republicans make an equally alarming hullabaloo about the country's going to ruin if "that man" is elected again. But when the shouting is over and the votes are counted, what do we do then? All of us, defeated and despondent minority no less than triumphant and elated majority, take the count, accept the decision, and go about our business. And no one really thinks that the country is going to ruin, or that anyone is going to be deprived of his natural rights because the laws will be made for some time by a party he did not will to place in power. And why do we act and think in this way if it be not that all of us have agreed, not in the explicit terms of an original compact perhaps, but in terms of an implicit understanding consciously or unconsciously subscribed to, that the general will of the nation is to be determined by majority vote, and that all our rights and liberties can best be secured by submitting voluntarily to the will of the majority?

4. However that may be, and whatever fine-spun theories we may devise to resolve or obscure the difficulty, there is no use blinking the fact that the will of the majority is not the same thing as the will of all. Majority rule works well only so long as the minority is willing to accept the will of the majority as the will of the nation and let it go at that. Generally speaking, the minority will be willing to let it go at that so long as it feels that its essential interests and rights are not fundamentally different from those of the current majority, and so long as it can, in any case, look forward with confidence to mustering enough votes within four or sixteen years to become itself the majority and so redress the balance. But if it comes to pass that a large minority feels that it has no such chance, that it is a fixed and permanent minority and that another group or class with rights and interests fundamentally hostile to its own is in permanent control, then government by majority vote ceases in any sense to be government by the will of the people for the

good of all, and becomes government by the will of some of the people for their own interests at the expense of the others.

5. The founders of the republic were fully aware of this danger. Jefferson accepted the device of majority vote because it was the only practicable method of registering the will of the people; but he was not so blind as to think that the majority was always right, or that it would never abuse its power. "I believe," he said, "that there exists a right that is independent of force; . . . that justice is the fundamental law of society; that the majority, oppressing an individual, is guilty of a crime, abuses its strength, and by acting on the principle of the strongest breaks up the foundations of society." Jefferson and his contemporaries had faith in republican government because they believed that it provided the best security for the natural rights of men against the tyranny of kings and aristocrats. But they were fully aware that even in a republic the natural rights of men need to be safeguarded against another sort of tyranny—the tyranny of the majority. Against the tyranny of the majority, or at all events against hasty and ill-considered action by the majority, the founding fathers endeavored, therefore, to erect adequate safeguards.

6. One of these safeguards is to be found in the organization of government and the distribution of powers within it—an organization based on the grand negative principle of checks and balances. But there were certain rights of the individual that the founding fathers regarded as sacred and imprescriptible—rights that no government, even one founded on the will of the people, could ever justly deny. This idea, that natural right is superior to prescriptive law, is indeed fundamental in the political philosophy formulated in the eighteenth century to justify the liberal-democratic revolution of modern times. It was clearly set forth in the French Declaration of the Rights of Man and the Citizen. Jefferson expressed it in the Declaration of Independence by saying that governments are instituted among men to secure the natural and inalienable rights of man, and that when any government becomes destructive of these rights it is the right of the people to alter or to abolish it. This central idea, with much of the phraseology in which Jefferson expressed it, appears in all our constitutions. To this day, therefore, the natural rights philosophy is implicit in our system of government. It still stands, as one may say, in the entrance ways of all our constitutions, safeguarding the imprescriptible rights of man.

7. The most important of these rights, the one that is essential to all the rest and the foundation of democratic government as we understand it, is freedom of the mind—the right of every person, as the Connecticut Constitution puts it, to "speak, write, and publish his sentiments on all subjects, being responsible for the abuse of that liberty."

8. A good many years ago, when Mussolini was much admired for

clearing the streets of beggars and making the trains run on time, a good lady said to me that she couldn't understand all this palaver about freedom of speech and of the press. Isn't everyone, she asked, always free to say what he thinks? Of course, she added, one must be prepared to take the consequences. I was unable on the spur of the moment to find an answer to that one. But it has since occurred to me that the good lady was more profoundly right than she realized. Democratic government rests on the assumption that the people are capable of governing themselves better than any one or any few can do it for them; but this in turn rests on the further assumption that if the people are free to think, speak, and publish their sentiments on any subject, the consequences will be good. Well, sometimes they are and sometimes not. If we have faith in democracy, we get over this inconvenient fact by saying that by and large and in the long run the consequences will be good. But the point is that if we accept democracy we must accord to everyone the right to think, speak, and publish his sentiments on any subject; and in that case we must indeed be prepared to take the consequences, whatever they may turn out to be.

9. It will be well, therefore, to examine this fundamental right with some care, in order to see, first, why Jefferson and his contemporaries were so profoundly convinced that the consequences would always and everywhere be good; and, secondly, whether we are still justified, in the light of a longer practical experience, in supposing that by and large and in the long run the consequences will at least be good enough to go on with.

2

10. The preoccupation of eighteenth-century philosophers with intellectual freedom was nowhere so great perhaps as in France, and it was in France that the natural rights philosophy which provided a theoretical justification for it was the most elaborately and clearly formulated. The reasons for this are easily understood. It is not so much because Frenchmen, as has sometimes been maintained, are more liberty-loving or more logically minded than other people, but rather because there was in France a great number of extraordinarily gifted writers of all sorts who had themselves suffered oppression from church and state for their opinions, and who were, partly for that reason, passionately concerned with the manifest inequities of the existing social system.

11. The best-known and the most valiant defender of the freedom of the mind was Voltaire. It is difficult to think of the mind of Voltaire, whose published works run to ninety volumes, as ever having been much restrained, and it is alarming to think how many volumes his works might have run to if it had been entirely unhampered. But all the same it is a fact that in order to avoid the penalties imposed by church and state for sedi-

tious writing, Voltaire took the trouble to publish many of his works in Holland or England, thought it safer to publish some of them under a false name, and found it more convenient to live much of his life close to the French frontier, where he could at a moment's notice slip across the border into Switzerland.

12. If, then, Voltaire became a passionate defender of the freedom of the mind, it was partly because he himself had been much harassed for the lack of it. Partly; but not entirely, or chiefly. He had always present in his mind the fates of Giordano Bruno, of Galileo, and of many obscure persons, such as Calas in his own time, who had suffered unspeakable torture and death for their religious faith. He had always in mind the illuminating fact that in England everyone, as he said, was permitted to go to Heaven in his own way, and no one the worse for it, and that the incomparable Isaac Newton, who had discovered the invariable laws of nature, instead of suffering the fate of Galileo was proclaimed and honored by church and state as a benefactor of mankind. He had always and especially in mind the essential teaching of history as he conceived it—that the progress of knowledge and the arts and the happiness of mankind had been the greatest in those periods, those "four happy ages," when men were the most free to speak the truth, whereas ignorance and superstition and oppression were universal in Europe during the long Dark Age of ecclesiastical domination.

13. This may have been, and in many respects was, a false reading of history. But for Voltaire, and for most of his contemporaries, it was the correct reading; and if he and his contemporaries regarded freedom of the mind as the essential freedom, on which all other freedoms rested, it was because they were convinced by the history of mankind that the denial of this freedom had always retarded, and would always retard, the advancement of civilization. They accepted the biblical injunction that the truth shall make you free. They agreed with Abélard that "by doubting we are led to questioning, and by questioning we arrive at the truth." They were profoundly convinced, therefore, that if men were free to inquire about all things, to doubt and discuss all things, to form opinions on the basis of knowledge and evidence, and to utter their opinions freely, the competition of knowledge and opinion in the market of rational discourse would ultimately banish ignorance and superstition and enable men to shape their conduct and their institutions in conformity with the fundamental and invariable laws of nature and the will of God.

14. The freedom of the individual mind from the compulsion of church and state was thus a right that Voltaire and Jefferson and their contemporaries derived in the first instance from political experience and the teaching of history. But for them it had a higher validity than that. It was a fundamental article of faith in their religious or philosophical conception of God and nature and of the relation of man to both. For most eighteenth-

century philosophers the laws of nature and the will of God were the same thing, or rather the laws of nature were an intended and adequate expression of the will of God. Natural law, said the French philosopher Volney, is "the constant and regular order of facts by which God rules the universe; the order which his wisdom presents to the sense and reason of men, to serve them as an equal and common rule of conduct, and to guide them, without distinction of race or sect, towards perfection and happiness." In the eighteenth century God the Father had become attenuated into God the First Cause or Creator. Having at the beginning of things constructed the universe on a rational plan as a convenient habitation for mankind, the Creator had withdrawn from the immediate and arbitrary control of human affairs, leaving men to work out their own salvation as best they could. But this they could do very well, because the beneficent intentions of God were revealed, not in sacred scriptures, but in the great open book of nature, which all men endowed with the light of reason could read and interpret. The mysterious ways in which God moved to perform his wonders, so far from being known through official and dogmatic pronouncements of church and state, were to be progressively discovered by the free play of human reason upon accumulated and verifiable knowledge. The free play of human reason, given time enough, could therefore discover the invariable laws of nature and nature's God and, by bringing the ideas and the institutions of men into conformity with them, find the way, as Volney said, to perfection and happiness.

15. This conception of God and nature and of the relation of man to both provided the eighteenth-century philosophers with their faith in the worth and dignity of the individual man and the efficacy of human reason. The eighteenth century was the moment in history when men experienced the first flush and freshness of the idea that man is master of his own fate; the moment in history, also, when this emancipating idea, not yet brought to the harsh test of experience, could be accepted with unclouded optimism. Never had the universe seemed less mysterious, more simply constructed, more open and visible and eager to yield its secrets to common-sense questions. Never had the nature of man seemed less perverse, or the intelligence and will of men more pliable to rational persuasion. Never had social and political evils seemed so wholly the result of ignorance and superstition, or so easily corrected by the spread of knowledge and the construction of social institutions on a rational plan. The first task of political science was to discover the natural rights of man, the second to devise the form of government best suited to secure them. And for accomplishing this high task, for creating and maintaining a society founded on justice and equality, the essential freedom was freedom of the mind.

16. The extraordinary faith of the early prophets of democracy in the efficacy of the human reason and in the native disposition of men to be guided by it is well brought out by John Stuart Mill in reference to his

father, a hard-headed man if there ever was one. "So complete," says Mill, "was my father's reliance on the influence of reason over the minds of mankind, whenever it was allowed to reach them, that he felt that all would be gained if the whole population were taught to read, if all sorts of opinions were allowed to be addressed to them by word and writing, and if by means of the suffrage they could nominate a legislature to give effect to the opinions they adopted." It was as simple as that.

*17.* In practice we find it somewhat less simple, no doubt; but to this day our faith in democracy, if we have any, has the same ideological basis as that of James Mill. Since primitive times virtually all religious or social systems have attempted to maintain themselves by forbidding free criticism and analysis either of existing institutions or of the doctrine that sustains them; of democracy alone is it the cardinal principle that free criticism and analysis by all and sundry is the highest virtue. In its inception modern democracy was, therefore, a stupendous gamble for the highest stakes. It offered long odds on the capacity and integrity of the human mind. It wagered all it had that the freest exercise of the human reason would never disprove the proposition that only by the freest exercise of the human reason can a tolerably just and rational society ever be created.

18. The play is still on, and we are still betting on freedom of the mind, but the outcome seems now somewhat more dubious than it did in Jefferson's time, because a century and a half of experience makes it clear that men do not in fact always use their freedom of speech and of the press in quite the rational and disinterested way they are supposed to. An examination of freedom of the mind in practice should enable us, therefore, to estimate the odds for and against the theory somewhat more accurately than Jefferson and his contemporaries were able to do.

# Questions

1. Why do "Jefferson and his contemporaries" dominate the first half of the essay? What other sources are quoted and for what purposes?

2. Why do "Voltaire and his contemporaries" dominate the second half of the essay? What other sources are quoted and for what purposes? Why does Becker shift from one set of eighteenth-century figures to another? What does he achieve by this shift?

3. How does Becker use questions as devices of transition in the first part of his essay? From the point of view of exposition, what use does the epigraph serve?

4. How does Becker, an eminent historian, achieve a tone of importance and immediacy in the historical exposition he presents under the title "Freedom of Speech and Press"?

5. What is democracy's "stupendous gamble"? Becker admits that the "stakes" in this wager will be won or lost in the realm of practice, not in that of theory. What practical events can you cite from the recent past to confirm or to challenge seriously the theory outlined here by Becker?

# Theme Topics

1. Write a paper in which you compare and contrast the terms "natural law," "reason," "natural rights," and "social contract" as you find one or more concepts used in the selections from Spinoza, Mill, Lippmann, and Becker.
2. Write a paper in which you expand and reorganize carefully your answer to question 5 above. Try especially to achieve logical transitions and to integrate direct quotations smoothly.

·61·

*Richard E. Sullivan*

## THE END OF THE "LONG RUN"

I

*1.* If, a thousand years from now, there still remains a civilized society interested in its past, the historians of that distant era will undoubtedly seek some explanation of the role and significance of the 20th century in the total stream of human history. Their evaluations of this troubled era will probably be numerous. Already the analysts of human behavior have begun to diverge in their generalizations concerning the fundamental nature of the 20th century. They speak in terms of the ethic of the "organization man," of the victory of "the rebel," of the plight of "the lonely crowd," and of "the revolt of the masses." Their estimates of the trends of this century suggest strongly that there is emerging a radical change in human outlook, capable of causing those looking back from the vantage point of a thousand years hence to conclude that the 20th century was the point of departure for a fundamental adjustment of human values.

From *The Centennial Review of Arts & Sciences,* 4, No. 3 (Summer, 1960), pp. 391-408. Reprinted by permission of the author and the publisher.

2.   However, after all manner of historians of the year 3000 A.D. have picked over the bones of the 20th century and pronounced their judgment of its place in the historical continuum, the consummate historian and artist—the Toynbee of the 31st century—will have his say. I suspect that he will disregard most of the trends that seem so world-shaking to us in the 1960's in favor of a very simple characterization of our century. He will say that this was the first century in world history when man ceased believing that time was working in favor of his deliverance. He will point out that during the 20th century all men were faced with the possibility that one twist of fate, one gesture, one ill-chosen word, one ill-conceived act could result in the annihilation of civilization and humanity. Once that fact had sunk into the mass consciousness, our 31st century Toynbee will say, then man could no longer explain his disposition to suffer evils on the ground that developments "in the long run" would remove them. Humanity could no longer depend on its ancient and respectable rationale for delaying the solution of problems, for condoning wickedness, for suffering tyranny, and for fending off danger—dependence on "the long run" developments which would remove the present source of discomfort.

3. Perhaps as an historian I am too sensitive about the phrase "the long run." I have heard my fellow historians use it to explain nearly everything across the whole spectrum of history. I have read repeatedly the works of scholars who went to the utmost pains to describe a problem that bedeviled a past generation and who then proceeded to say that "in the long run" this difficulty resolved itself because of the emergence of new factors and forces. One cannot be subjected to this experience hundreds of times without being seduced into the assumption that "the long run" is some kind of fourth dimensional force which intervenes in human affairs to resolve all problems automatically and painlessly, irrespective of how wisely or foolishly men may act at any given moment. Probably one could best define the historian as a disciple of the gospel of "the long run," meaning that his function is and has always been to assure people that time works in favor of the welfare of men. However, if the historian is the high priest of this cult, around him are legions of worshippers whose acts prove that they are true believers. They go penniless to buy a car or a house with complete trust that in the long run they will find the wherewithal to pay for it. They sire children with genuine faith that the long run course of development will provide happiness for their offspring. They pour their best energies into the creation of some seemingly fantastic machine or organization that promises in the long run to benefit someone. With charming innocence they console the heartbroken with the advice that time has a way of solving everything. They even sacrifice their lives for a cause on the completely unprovable assumption that their immolation will benefit the

future. Faith in the magic of "the long run" is seemingly as much a part of the human make-up as the brain or the liver.

4. So it has been since the beginning of human endeavor. A history of the world could be written around the theme of human reliance on the long run solution. It would leave little unaccounted for. Men have always been more content to wait for things to develop than to grapple with issues actively and immediately. They have been satisfied to suffer unspeakable indignities in the simple faith that eventually, "in the long run," their situation would be alleviated. The revolutionist, intent on acting *immediately* to relieve human misery, is actually a rare figure in human history, although in the past he sometimes has been presented as the prime mover in the historical process. He attracts so much attention, I believe, simply because he represents such a unique specimen in the totality of mankind, such an unusual departure from the norm. The real moving force in human history has been the trusting, essentially lazy, somewhat frightened, yet always optimistic man who was sure that, if he waited, cosmic justice would be done in his favor. So numerous has been his breed that "waiting for the long run developments" has always been a decisive factor in shaping human affairs.

## II

5. Skimming back across the ages will supply numerous examples to demonstrate the antiquity of the "long run" interpretation of the working of destiny. Although he left posterity poorly informed about his mental processes, the most primitive Old Stone Age hunter probably found his greatest consolation during the lean season in the conviction that by waiting he would take his game; indeed the very method of his hunting emphasized the wisdom of waiting for nature to thrust her fruits on him in the form of an unsuspecting animal that wandered across his path by accident. Certainly by the time the great civilizations of the ancient Near East had emerged, men had surrendered to the long run point of view. Both Egyptian and Babylonian religious literature is replete with the spirit of calm resignation to the fact that the divinely ordained and controlled universe contained a safe refuge for puny man. No matter how the raging gods might shake the universal fundaments, still the outcome would be happy. The Nile might not flood for years, bringing desperate famine to Egypt, but the evil days would pass and those who waited would be rewarded. Here is the Egyptian way of expressing this conviction of the inevitable beneficence of the universe, as contained in a hymn to the god of the Nile: "If he is sluggish, then nostrils are stopped up, and everybody is *poor*. If there be a cutting down in the food-offerings of the gods, then a million men perish among mortals, covetousness is practised, the entire land is in fury, and great and small are on the execution block. But people are different when

he approaches. . . . When he rises then the land is in jubilation, then every belly is in joy, every backbone takes on laughter, and every tooth is exposed." Or, as related in Babylonian mythology, a devastating flood loosed by a vengeful god might destroy all things; yet, some other god was always considerate enough to provide for the protection of man, assuring that he would again flourish. In the long run the Egyptians and the Babylonians, plus the many later Near Eastern people who adopted their basic outlooks, felt that they had nothing to fear. The universal order assured them a place and a portion of happiness. What could be fitter symbols of the faith that time worked for man than the pyramids, dedicated to the preservation of a dead body until such time as its immortality was provided for, even if that process required ages?

6. Much more explicit were the Hebrew exponents of the idea that "in the fulness of time"—i.e., in the long run—all things would evolve toward perfection. The idea saturates the prophetic writings of the Old Testament. These writings were produced at a period in Hebrew history when, judged by the expectation of the chosen children of Yahweh, the future looked hopeless. The Hebrews had suffered division of their hard-won national kingdom, conquest at the hands of the vicious Assyrians and sinful Chaldeans, and mass deportation from their native soil and sacred temple to whorish Babylon. These tragedies were accompanied by a paralyzing religious confusion which took the form of extensive apostasy from Yahweh-worship. Yet listen to what the prophets cried in the midst of misery: "Come, my people, enter thou into thy chambers, and shut thy doors about thee: hide thyself as it were for a little moment, until the indignation is overpast." (Isaiah 26:20). How must the "little moment" be spent? "And the people shall be oppressed, everyone by another, and everyone by his neighbor: the child shall behave himself proudly against the ancient, and the base against the honourable." (Isaiah 3:5). "And they shall look unto the earth; and behold trouble and darkness, dimness of anguish; and they shall be driven to darkness." (Isaiah 8:22). But all that would pass. "Behold, the Lord God will come with strong hand. . . . He shall feed his flock like a shepherd." (Isaiah 40:10-11). "The ransomed of the Lord shall return, and come to Zion with songs and everlasting joy upon their heads: they shall obtain joy and gladness, and sorrow and sighing shall flee away." (Isaiah 35:10). How long Zion must wait and suffer the prophets never say. Yet waiting is the solution to the problem. In the fulness of time today's ills will be resolved by a cosmic force beyond man's control, yet working for his ultimate deliverance.

7. Greek thought reflected a similar easy confidence that things would unfold themselves for the good, no matter how dreadful the present might be. Who can forget the patiently waiting Penelope engaged in her senseless spinning amidst her greedy, too anxious suitors? Why did she not

act to resolve her quandary? Because the operation of the universal order would bring back Ulysses. Homer the artist would have outraged man's moral sense by requiring so good a woman to bustle about trying to solve her own problems; time would resolve the issue. Greek drama in general breathes the wisdom of accepting the present with the assurance that the future will remove the evil and the pain at hand. Inexorably, without overt human action, the house of Agamemnon is brought to justice for its transgressions, and the world is set aright. In the *Oresteia,* Aeschylus provides the theme of most Greek tragedies when he has Clytemnestra greet the returning Agamemnon with these words: "Maidservants, why do you delay? Straightway spread the purple tapestry, that Justice may guide his steps to a home he little hoped to see." Orestes sums up what wisdom lay at the other end of that carpet when in the *Eumenides* he says: "Time, that smooths all things, hath smoothed the front of my offence." In the long run all is made right with gods and men; that is a law of the universe. Let none think that in Greece this philosophy was confined to the unenlightened believers in hoary myths. In his *Republic,* the rationalistic Plato reflects a comparable trust that the passage of time would resolve even the greatest difficulties. After wrestling with a definition of the philosopher king and repeatedly demonstrating how remote the perfect political order is from the existent world, Socrates and his companions conclude that no philosopher king or perfect state ever existed. Yet this is no cause for despair. They agree that in the course of ages a philosopher king *might* be born and that his virtue *might* be recognized so that "he might bring into existence the ideal polity about which the world is so incredulous." (*Republic,* VI, 502). Socrates concludes on what is almost a triumphant note: "But we have sufficiently shown, in what has preceded, that all this, if only possible, is assuredly for the best." (*Republic,* VI, 502).

8. Christian thinkers caught up these many threads out of the ancient past to reassert a philosophy of history that assured all believers of the inevitable working out of things for the salvation of humanity. Their confident affirmations, made amid the disheartening spectacle of the collapse of the Roman Empire, the degeneration of Graeco-Roman moral values, and the onslaught of the barbarians, were unquestionably of major significance in unloosing the energy needed to establish a Christian civilization over much of Europe, western Asia, and northern Africa. St. Paul catalogued enough evidence of human iniquity to force a man with any sense of justice to the conclusion that humanity was damned. Yet he did not reach that conclusion. "For I reckon that the sufferings of this present time are not worthy to be compared to the glory which shall be revealed in us." (Romans 8:18). "For we know that the whole creation groaneth and travaileth in pain together until now. . . . We are saved by hope: but hope that is seen is not hope; for what a man seeth, why doth he yet hope for?"

(Romans 8:23-24). "Therefore, my beloved brethren, be ye stedfast, un-
moveable, always abounding in the work of the Lord, forasmuch as ye
know that your labour is not in vain in the Lord." (I Corinthians 15:58).
In the "fulness of time" (Ephesians 1:10) all would be made right; every
Christian could build his life around that precept. St. Augustine made it
unnecessary for the Christian to trust in hope unseen by constructing a
compelling philosophy of history embracing the past in its entirety to
prove that God's will would be done. By his reckoning, abundant evidence
existed outside Scripture to prove that there was a purpose in history and
that that purpose operated to exalt the good over the evil, to alleviate the
tainted past and present by providing a perfect city of God in the future,
to exalt Jerusalem over Babylon. The Christian, according to Augustine,
need not despair, for God "orders all events in His providence until the
beauty of the completed course of time, of which the component parts are
the dispensations adapted to each successive age, shall be finished, like
the grand melody of some ineffably wise master of song." Dante's *Divine
Comedy* supplied the most adroit artistic expression of the Christian conviction that a beneficial order assures human well-being. The poet's long
trek from earth to the bottom of hell and thence into the presence of God
serves as a symbolical representation of humanity's passage through time
to ultimate fulfillment. Few pieces of art surpass the *Divine Comedy* as a
statement of hope in ultimate perfection of mankind.

## III

9. The passage of centuries and the flow of intellectual pursuits into new
channels gradually eroded the basis of the old faith that in the long run
all things work out for the best. Most of the hope of the ancients rested in
their conviction that superhuman powers had ordained the ultimate perfection of man and the world. This premise eventually came under attack.
The humanists of the Renaissance period doubted that man needed to
depend on divinity for anything. Rationalists concluded to their own satisfaction that man possessed in his intellect a tool capable of elevating him
to divine heights. Scientists discovered a method by which rational powers
could be harnessed to the performance of feats surpassing the deeds of the
gods. Slowly the proponents of these new schools of thought hacked to
pieces the foundations of the old cosmic optimism upon which men found
assurance that an almighty power would save everything if one would wait
for that power to unfold its plans through time.

10. However, the revolt against God which, during the last four or five
centuries, has rocked the foundations of the value system of western society has hardly disturbed the superstructure, man's happy confidence that
things will work out for the best. If anything, faith in "the long run" grew
as faith in the Almighty declined. New reasons have been discovered to
assure men that *time* would advance all things toward perfection and re-

solve all the evils that press in upon humanity. God can now be neutral or even non-existent. For the rationalists of the Enlightenment, the key to perfection was education, that is, the process of unshackling man's innate rational powers. Education was a process requiring time, a leading out that occurred step by step. John Locke and his disciples assured the world that the ideal polity could be created by reasonable men entering a compact for that purpose; they need only discover the right moment "in the course of human events" to end forever the tyranny that had plagued unenlightened men. It remained for the scientists of the 19th century with their theory of evolution to formulate a surer guarantee of ultimate perfection than did all the powers of Osiris, Yahweh, or Zeus. Evolutionism was the doctrine of "the long run" *par excellence*. It applied not only to flowers, bugs, planets, and man the physical being; evolutionism became the basic premise for a whole new science: social science. Herbert Spencer defined the new creed in these words: "Whether it be in the development of the Earth, in the development of Life upon its surface, in the development of Society, of Government, of Manufactures, of Commerce, of Language, Literature, Science, Art, this same evolution of the simple into the complex, through successive differentiations, holds throughout. . . . Progress is not an accident but a necessity. What we call evil and immorality must disappear. It is certain that man must become perfect." The prophets of ancient Israel could not have done better in assuring all that the millenium would arrive in spite of anything. Even the most radical revolutionary movements of the last century were in a sense softened by the universal faith in the inevitability of progress. Marx could thunder in one breath that the workers of the world must arise violently to put off their chains; yet in the next he assured his audience that the downfall of the existing order and the coming of Utopia were inevitable. Thus the smashing of the old icons that has made the centuries since the Renaissance so lively has not in the least threatened one of man's greatest refuges, namely, the idea that in "the long run" nothing but good can befall man. Even with God banished, men found powerful reasons to live with "every tooth exposed," sure that all would be well with them.

*11.* These scraps of evidence selected from out of man's past estimates of ultimate lot offer only vague hints of the powerful grip of what has unquestionably been an eternal mooring for human life. Through the ages, in a multitude of ways, individuals and societies have lived and died happy in the thought that ultimately things would be perfect. Again and again the realities staring men in the face have been distorted to fit that frame of reference. Again and again action has been delayed because of a conviction that the passage of time would resolve what was currently evil and inhuman. It has become second nature for men to smile in the face of adversity, to bear all indignities with good cheer, and to move slowly but assuredly toward a happy future.

*12.* And why should not man in the past have felt this trust in "the long run?" His own abilities and his environment have always, at least on the surface, combined to demonstrate empirically that such a faith was infinitely wise. Nature has always seemed an unassailable bastion assuring men that nothing cataclysmic will happen. The processes of reproduction evidenced in nature seemed to bespeak eternity. For all his demonstrated genius for evil, man seemed powerless to effect any fundamental change in nature. He could do no more than scratch the surface of the earth, clear away isolated patches of foliage, block up a few of the myriad streams that ribboned the continents, or kill a handful of his fellows. Who could think that such puny efforts had a chance to alter the fundamental process of nature—storm, earthquake, flood, and reproduction of the species? Neither had man's past efforts to affect changes in his own society been spectacular. Lacking instruments of mass communication and rapid transportation, his evil schemes and good intentions came to fruition slowly and imperfectly in any society and in any age. His days on earth were pitifully limited, making it almost a certainty that he would die, a martyr as it were, before his cause bore fruit. Well might he echo the reproof of Ozymandias: "Look on my works, Ye Mighty, and despair!" It was senseless to joust violently with destiny. The good things came slowly, as many wise men discerned in looking back across the past. Vergil reflected this sense of the necessity of growth in time when he argued in the *Aeneid* that all the centuries between Aeneas' flight from Troy and Augustus' victory at Actium were necessary to bring forth Roman greatness. Medieval chroniclers demonstrated the same concept when they began their histories of local monasteries by starting with Adam. The slowness of change was not, however, cause for despair. Things did improve—in the long run. Herodotus knew of the great antiquity of the Egyptians, but he did not doubt the superiority of the Greeks. Thus, like two great beacons, nature's order and man's own demonstrated capabilities have always taught to past generations a single piece of wisdom: man should live with an eye toward the long run, doing nothing rash to relieve the troubles of the present but continuing down existent paths with assurance that all would be well.

IV

*13.* Now, at mid-20th century, we are face to face with an awesome fact. We no longer have the least assurance that the passage of time will resolve our difficulties, that either the plans of benign gods or the inexorable processes of nature or the wisdom of man are working for the perfection of the unwise and the imperfect. Anyone viewing the present objectively must conclude that man's ancient consoling faith in "the long run" is only an opiate, suspending its users in a fantastic world. Already some have put aside the pipe and, after the initial shock of abstinence, are beginning to discern the realities of the moment. The dimensions of the real situation are indeed monstrous and terrifying. For it is clear that nothing assures that civilization or even life itself will exist a millennium or a year or a minute hence. No one can live as if some force beyond human control assures a happy future unless he is willing to live in a dream world. All must eliminate any considerations of "the long run" from their calculations. For the first time in history, men must face the implications of living within a framework in which the future is a dubious quantity.

*14.* It requires no great wisdom to discern why "the long run" can no longer figure very seriously in human calculations. Man has succeeded in wrecking the pillars upon which he had previously constructed his faith that the cosmic order moved toward perfection. The gods, of course, have long since been made to yield their control of destiny. Nature's processes have been made to surrender to human intervention, so that man has acquired extensive powers of manipulation over nature. So successful has been his assault on nature that it is now conceivable that the course of nature could be changed radically at any moment. The neutralization of gravity, the explosion of planets, the leveling of mountains, the manipulation of the weather, the creation of new forms of life, the transmutation of existent species—these are but a few of the feats that man now has it within his power to perform. Such power signifies that the future order of nature will be what man chooses it to be. Certainly no one can believe any longer that nature is an impersonal force nudging humanity toward a golden age and preventing man from destroying himself. Yet within the memory of living men that assumption was made without question.

*15.* With the gods and nature deposed as protective forces, can man still rely on his own power to save himself and to assure his own inevitable progress? Alas, even man's self-deification has been destroyed by his advancing self-knowledge. His vaunted reason has been demonstrated to be but a thin veneer hiding elemental forces of irrationality, his mind a shapeless lump capable of being twisted into a myriad of transitory forms. His body might well become the plaything of some demon who would choose to endow him with two heads or an aluminum heart or might suffer grotesque mutations resulting from irradiated genes. For human flesh itself is part of the natural order over which man has seized power. Man's senses can be tricked and his cognitive powers blurred by a variety of psychological devices, many of which are already in use to convince him that he needs hundreds of things to make his life more comfortable, happier, safer, and less demanding. Indeed, it is no feat at all at present to empty a man's head of one set of values and pump in another; the job requires not much more effort than changing a tire, or at most, rewiring an electronic computer. On the basis of present knowledge, only the hopelessly naive would place much trust in man's innate trustworthiness to work out—in the long, short, or any length of run—sensible solutions to human problems.

## V

*16.* With God, nature, and man all dethroned as positive forces assuring the ultimate salvation of the universe, it is indeed a strange new world we face. Never in the history of man has life seemed so meaningless, as a legion of modern poets, artists, and philosophers have attested, sometimes too vehemently to suit those who still live in the comfortable old world where one could trust "the long run" to remove all that was unpleasant, ugly, and evil.

*17.* What are the implications of this new world? What is in store for anyone facing reality?

*18.* It is possible that the startling discovery that the world has no built-in mechanism guaranteeing its ultimate perfection will be the most salutary revelation in human history. Man may finally cease squatting on his intellectual and spiritual haunches awaiting the inevitable alleviation of his current misery in "the long run." He might stay his hand at some contemplated evil out of the realization that his power to manipulate nature and other men is so great that an ill-considered act could unloose a cosmic hecatomb. This alone would mark a spectacular improvement in human conduct. More important, man might be spurred to creativity by the realization that only positive, constructive action could affect any improvement in human affairs.

*19.* However, to hold up such a rosy prospect of the new world is to prophesy against all the omens. The end of "the long run" seems rather to presage a troubled future spun out by several truly lost generations. Already men are demonstrating that something precious has been removed from their midst and that they are panic-stricken by the prospect of a future that could bring their destruction as easily as their perfection. Probably no one knows yet how severe will be the trauma caused by the breaking of the idol of "the long run," but at least some portents have emerged to indicate that mankind may be entering an age of fantastic disturbances, all springing from his lost hope that everything will be well in the fulness of time. Disturbing as it may be, let us list a few of these signs, admitting that the list might be lengthened considerably.

*20.* First, men in ever increasing numbers will abandon all interest in the past. Ever since the cave dwellers sat around their fires trying to remember what custom said about the problem of the moment, men have always looked to the past to discern a pattern that would supply them wisdom to meet the present. They did so on the assumption that vast movements developing in time characterized the drama of life and that man must ride along with these movements. This is an almost impossible belief now, since nature and men can be manipulated quickly to achieve prodigious alterations of the course of affairs. The past suddenly becomes irrelevant. Why look back for wisdom when the wisdom gained may be negated by a madman with a hydrogen bomb? Thus a generation with no roots in the past is coming into existence; this is a kind of rootlessness with which the world has not previously had to deal. An historian shudders at the implications.

21. Deprived of hope for the future and trust in the past, men will snatch ever more greedily for the security of the present moment. It will not take them long to decide that the only security of the present lies in pleasure. Only those things and those actions which bring contentment and comfort at this instant offer an intelligent safeguard against believing in false gods in this insecure world where universal destruction is as likely as salvation. Universal Epicureanism may be bearable, but let no one forget Burn's thought: "Pleasures are like poppies spread, /You seize the flower, its bloom is shed."

22. It seems clear that men will become increasingly reluctant to work for the rewards of a tenuous future. Not to sacrifice one's mite of time and pleasure in order to labor for a future that may not emerge is logical to the thoughtful, soothing to the slothful. Yet a world lacking men who are. willing to work or even reluctant to work will be an impossible world. Work in some form is a *sine qua non* for a civilization; its absence in any society threatens the vitality of that society.

23. Most men, doubtful of the future, will hardly find it sensible to serve a cause. For causes are goals that their adherents trust and believe will be fulfilled in "the long run." No historian can evade the conclusions that through the past ages human striving to hasten the inevitable has been a decisive force in shaping human destiny. To serve a cause demands that one assume that there will be a future in which the cause can come true. Put the future in doubt or admit that its shape may be inconceivably different from the present and a great cause makes little sense. The ordinary mortal will be compelled to decide that nothing can be gained from sincere devotion to a cause whose achievement is extremely dubious. He might better live unencumbered by commitments to the future. Needless to say, it will be a strange world when one can find no crusaders; yet that world is being born and may soon be heavily populated.

24. All signs clearly suggest that we are approaching an age that will be marked by a frenzied, hysterical approach to its own current problems. This is to be expected in a world where mere indecision may unloose forces capable of destroying everything. Take away the old assurance that whatever the decision, it cannot be fatal because time operates to solve all things, and individuals and societies can no longer approach the issue with calm and deliberation. Decisions must now be leaped at lest delay spell catastrophe. Petty problems create major dilemmas because of the immense power that man can now unloose with little

effort; thus we must expect to live constantly in a state of hysteria-breeding fear. Under the impact of repeated, soul-wringing crises, men's thresholds of response may rise, necessitating the application of ever stronger stimuli to evoke reaction. This situation, calling into play all the tricks of mass communication, must necessarily increase the cacophony assaulting human sanity. This can hardly be the old world, where the burden of decision could occasionally be put aside for a few moments of rest and blessed silence, a retreat made possible by the conviction that in the long run all would be well, whatever the decision of the moment might be.

25. Finally, and most terrifying of all, is the possibility that we stand at the beginning of an age of complete amorality. For is not any code of morals fundamentally a set of rules for behavior built on the predication that there is a certain unalterable order in the universe? Remove the unalterable and you negate the morality. At the moment it seems obvious that necessity of all kinds has been abolished. God, nature, and humanity are either discredited or malleable, depending on what man chooses to do with his knowledge and skill. It is inconceivable that any code of morals could have sanction or relevance in this situation. Man is finally free to do what he pleases, which is the exact opposite of living in a moral situation.

26. Has the picture been painted too darkly? Is what has been said nothing but an historian's naive lament over the passing of a bygone age? Perhaps. The picture is far from clear at the moment. However, there is every indication that a revolutionary change in our system of values is under way as a consequence of the advances made in human knowledge and skill over the last few decades. What has happened is nothing less than the establishment of man's control over his own destiny. In essence, man has finally become free, no longer restricted by jealous gods, plodding nature, or halting humanity. His knowledge has brought him the power to bend the course of events out of what previously seemed a predetermined trajectory. However, this freedom has required the giving of an earnest which most men are surrendering reluctantly and with grave reservations. Once having gained the power and the freedom to make the world and mankind what he wants, then man can no longer rest assured that impersonal forces, beyond human control, work to improve and eventually perfect humanity. There is no "long run" in which trust can be placed while men indulge in irrationality, meanness, or whatever foible strikes their fancy. A cynic might protest that in reality there never was a "long run" in which men could trust; those things in which men in the past trusted—God, nature, human intelligence—were as much chimeras a thousand years ago as now. This protestation, however true it may be, really is not very impressive. The real significance of the moment, the fundamental condition that will

make the historians of the year 3000 A.D.—if such there be—look back
on the 20th century as a turning point in human history, lies in the fact
that recent developments have demonstrated dramatically, obviously, and
beyond doubt that man is on his own and cannot trust in "the long
run." Never has humanity had to face this fact; therefore, there has never
been a moment comparable to the present.

# Questions

1. Identify the analysts of the twentieth century from the phrases Sullivan
   quotes in paragraph 1. What argumentative value does he extract from the
   Toynbee analogy in paragraph 2? How does he anticipate and discount in
   advance any reservation in the reader's mind that he, as an historian, is discussing events that are remote and esoteric from the point of view of the
   experience of the average man today?
2. Sullivan divides his essay into five numbered parts. What does each contribute to his overall argument? What devices of transition does he use to
   link them together (paragraphs 4 and 5, 8 and 9, 12 and 13, 15 and 16)?
3. How does Sullivan use questions to organize his material? Examine his use
   of quotations. Does he ever make a major generalization without employing
   a direct quotation to illustrate his point? If so, in which cases might direct
   quotation strengthen his overall argument?
4. Sullivan cites evidence to prove God, nature, and man have failed in the
   consciousness of contemporary man as "long-run" hopes for the universe's
   salvation. Does he prove his case to your satisfaction? How would you challenge his "skimming back across the ages"? What corroborative items, which
   he has failed to cite, would you add to his "scraps of evidence"?
5. What in the past has deterred the "long-run" harmful effects of irrationality
   and deliberate evil? Why or why not is all hope of deterrence now gone in
   Sullivan's view? Granted the validity of his thesis, what probable consequences does he foresee? What other probable consequences, if any, would
   you predict from the same evidence, and how would they contradict or
   corroborate Sullivan's?

# Theme Topics

1. Write a paper in which you examine the concepts of "freedom" and "rationality" in the context of points of view expressed or assumed in Becker's and
   Sullivan's essays. Choose your illustrations from sources other than these
   two pieces.

2. Write an essay in which your thesis is either "mankind controls events" or, conversely, "events control mankind." Use points of view and illustrations, quoted directly or indirectly, from essays throughout this section and from any other pertinent selection in this anthology or elsewhere. Strive to achieve logical transitions between paragraphs and to integrate illustrative material smoothly with general statements.